Spanish Vocabulary

David Brodsky

SPANISH
Vocabulary

An Etymological Approach

University of Texas Press Austin

Requests for permission to reproduce material from this work should be sent to:
Permissions, University of Texas Press, P.O. Box 7819, Austin, TX 78713-7819
www.utexas.edu/utpress/about/bpermission.html

∞ The paper used in this book meets the minimum requirements of
ANSI/NISO Z39.48-1992 (R1997) (Permanence of Paper).

Library of Congress Cataloging-in-Publication Data

Brodsky, David.
  Spanish vocabulary : an etymological approach / by David Brodsky. — 1st ed.
    p.   cm.
  Includes bibliographical references.
  ISBN 978-0-292-71668-1

  1. Spanish language—Vocabulary.   2. Spanish language—Textbooks for
foreign speakers—English.   3. Spanish language—Etymology.   I. Title.
  PC4445.B76   2007
  468.2'421—dc22

                                                                2007033997

Contents

Preface

This book is intended for students at all levels who seek to enhance their Spanish vocabulary, as well as for those who wish simply to explore the wide-ranging connections between Spanish and English vocabulary. The approach differs markedly from that of "traditional" Spanish vocabulary books that present lists of words with English definitions, grouped by subject areas. While such lists can be useful for reviewing and maintaining vocabulary, they often are of far less value to students seeking to acquire new vocabulary, or at least to those not blessed with photographic memories.

Spanish Vocabulary: An Etymological Approach offers elements rarely found in a work addressed to a nonspecialist audience, including:

1. etymological connections between Spanish and English vocabulary
2. historical and linguistic information on the origin and evolution of Spanish
3. comparative references to developments in other Romance languages (and English)

A multifaceted approach is employed, ranging from presenting words in a historical context to developing an understanding of the "shape" or "feel" of Spanish. While extensive use of lists is also made, there is a crucial difference: in the large majority of cases, Spanish words are associated explicitly with related English words, an association that can greatly facilitate learning and retaining these words. As an example, the correspondence *amable* (Spanish)—*amiable* (English) can be used as the basis for learning a number of other Spanish words:

Spanish	Definition	[Other Cognate]
amable	*amiable*, kind	
—amabilidad	—*amiability*, kindness	
—amistad	—friendship, *amity*	
—amistoso	—friendly, *amicable*	
—amor	—love	[par*amour*]
—amoroso	—*amorous*, loving	
—amar	—(to) love	
—amante	—loving, lover	
—enamorar	—(to) *enamor*	

—enamorado,	—in love, *enamored,* lover, *inamorato,*
enamorada	*inamorata*

The presentation is divided into four parts, plus four annexes. The book can be studied sequentially or "à la carte" (Spanish *a la carta*). It is in fact recommended that one move back and forth between the sections to provide a greater element of variety.

Part I provides general background material on the origins of Spanish and begins the process of presenting Spanish vocabulary. **Part II** presents "classical" Spanish vocabulary, that is, words whose form (in both Spanish and English) is nearly unchanged from Latin and Greek. **Part III** deals with "popular" Spanish vocabulary, or words that during the evolution from Latin to Spanish underwent significant change in form (and often in meaning as well). A number of "patterns" are set out that can help one to recognize and remember new vocabulary. **Part IV** treats in a more discursive manner various themes, including Germanic and Arabic words, numbers, time, food and animals, the family, the body, and politics.

The annexes present additional words in list form:

Annex A: Principal Exceptions to the "Simplified Gender Rule"
Annex B: 700 Not-So-Easy Words (whose relations, if any, to English words are not immediately obvious)
Annex C: Verbs Ending in -*cer* and Related Words
Annex D: 4,500 Relatively Easy Words (with English correspondences)

Abbreviations and Symbols

acc.	accusative
adj.	adjective
adv.	adverb
AHCD	*American Heritage College Dictionary*
Amer.	American Spanish (not necessarily all countries); or indigenous language
Arab.	Arabic
arch.	architecture
astron.	astronomy
biol.	biology/zoology
bot.	botany
cap.	capitalized
Cat.	Catalan
cf.	compare (from Latin CONFER)
chem.	chemistry
CL	Classical Latin
conj.	conjunction
def.	definition
dim.	diminutive
DRAE	*Diccionario de la lengua española* of the Real Academia Española
eccl.	ecclesiastical
elec.	electricity
Eng.	English
esp.	especially
fam.	familiar, colloquial
f.	feminine
fig.	figuratively; figurative
Fr.	French
freq.	frequently
gen.	generally
genit.	genitive (possessive case)
geog.	geography
geol.	geology
geom.	geometry
Germ.	Germanic

gram.	grammar
Gk.	Greek
incl.	including
inf.	infinitive
It.	Italian
Lat.	Latin
lit.	literally
m.	masculine
m./f.	masculine/feminine
math.	mathematics
med.	medicine
mil.	military
Mod.Fr.	Modern French
Mod.Sp.	Modern Spanish
n.	noun
neg.	negative
n.f.	feminine noun
n.m.	masculine noun
n.m./f.	noun both masculine and feminine
nom.	nominative
obs.	obsolete or archaic
OED	*Oxford English Dictionary*
OldEng.	Old English
OldFr.	Old French
OldSp.	Old Spanish
onom.	onomatopoeia
orig.	originally
part.	participle
pert.	pertaining
pl.	plural
Port.	Portuguese
p.p.	past participle[1]
prep.	preposition
pres.	present
RAE	Real Academia Española (see also *DRAE*)
sing.	singular
s.o.	someone
Sp.	Spanish

---

[1] Used generally in cases where the definition corresponding to the past participle is not presented among the accompanying list of definitions.

UK	United Kingdom
vb.	verb
VL	Vulgar Latin
w/out	without

~	is similar in meaning to (always refers to two Spanish words)
<	is derived from (e.g., *soprano* < It., *sport* < *disport*)
=	is equal to
≠	is not equal to
†	indicates that an English word used as a cognate is "obsolete" or "archaic"[2]

---

[2] In general, this applies to words that either: (a) are listed as "obsolete" or "archaic" in *Webster's Third New International Dictionary, Unabridged* or (b) are not found there but appear in the *Oxford English Dictionary*. The term *rare* is used to mark other cognates that, while perhaps not technically obsolete or archaic, are not normally found in "smaller" dictionaries (e.g., *American Heritage College Dictionary*).

Simplified Gender Rule

Both to streamline the presentation and to serve as a learning tool, the text will employ the following "Simplified Gender Rule" that "predicts" the correct gender for more than 96 percent of all Spanish nouns.

1. Nouns having one of the following endings are assumed to be feminine:

    a) *-a*
    b) *-ión*
    c) *-d*
    d) *-umbre*
    e) *-ie*
    f) *-ez*
    g) *-triz*
    h) *-sis / -tis* (Greek words)

2. Nouns ending in *-ista* are assumed to be *both* masculine and feminine.

3. All other nouns are assumed to be masculine.
ONLY NOUNS WHOSE GENDER IS "UNPREDICTABLE" WILL BE EXPLICITLY MARKED.
Thus:

rosa	rose
tema (m.)	theme
libro	book
mano (f.)	hand
nación	nation
avión (m.)	airplane
corazón	heart
razón (f.)	reason
periodista	journalist
evangelista (m.)	Evangelist (author of one of the four NT gospels)

    Annex A examines in more detail the accuracy of this "rule" and lists some of the principal exceptions.

In general, Spanish is quite flexible in forming feminine nouns from masculine ones by:

(a) changing the final -*o* to -*a*
(b) adding -*a* to a noun or adjective ending in -*or, -án, -ín, -ón*
(c) adding -*a* to a national or regional identifier ending in a consonant
    For (b) and (c), the final-syllable written accent, if any, disappears in the feminine.

	Masculine	Feminine	English
(a)	gato	ga**ta**	cat
	chico	chi**ca**	boy, girl
(b)	director	director**a**	director
	holgazán	holgazan**a**	lazy, loafer
	bailarín	bailarin**a**	dancing, dancer
	ladrón	ladron**a**	thieving, thief
(c)	español	español**a**	Spanish, Spaniard
	francés	frances**a**	French, Frenchman /Frenchwoman

To simplify the presentation, masculine forms *only* will generally be shown for nouns and adjectives that follow these patterns, except in cases where there is a change in written accent, or where English has a distinct female form. Examples:

ladrón (-ona)	thieving, thief or *larcenist*
ciervo, cierva	deer, stag, doe

For "people" nouns not having one of the above endings, the masculine and feminine forms are generally identical. This will frequently be highlighted by using the abbreviation *m./f.* Thus:

atleta (m./f.)	athlete
cómplice (m./f.)	accomplis
estudiante (m./f.)	student

Finally, there are a very small number of "object" nouns that can be either masculine or feminine, with no change in meaning. These will also be marked with *m./f.* For example:

maratón (m./f.)	marathon
tizne (m./f.)	soot

Spanish Vocabulary

Introduction

An English speaker learning Spanish starts with one huge, though generally underutilized, advantage: he or she is already speaking a *Romance* language, and with a little bit of help, can easily recognize and learn to use a very large number of Spanish words. The "romance" of English may come as a surprise to those who have been taught that English is a Germanic language. Nonetheless, in terms of its vocabulary, English is overwhelmingly *Latinate;* in the *Shorter Oxford Dictionary,* for example, there are more than twice as many Latin-Romance words as Germanic ones.[1]

Of course, one does not *learn* words in a foreign language simply by noting their similarities with English words; rather, the basic familiarity that exists (or that with a little practice can be seen to exist) can help one to *remember* new words and to *recognize* them the next time they are encountered and, after a while, to be able to begin using them naturally (in both speaking and writing).

Consider the following seven words:

Spanish	English
hecho	fact
dicho	saying, proverb
pecho	chest
estrecho	narrow
derecho	right, straight
techo	roof
leche	milk

If you haven't studied much Spanish already, chances are that the Spanish words are not instantly recognizable. What you would normally do is look them up in the dictionary and, probably, not remember their definitions (certainly not all of them) the next time you see them. This is the list (or "telephone book") approach to learning vocabulary.

---

[1] In terms of *frequency* of usage, Germanic words dominate; in terms of simple word *numbers,* Latin and Romance ones do. The issue of English as a "Germanic" versus "Romance" language will be revisited in Section 4.10.

There is an alternative approach:

Spanish	Latin	Similar English Word
hecho	FACTUM	fact
dicho	DICTUM	dictum, edict
pecho	PECTUS	pectoral
estrecho	STRICTUS	strict
derecho	DIRECTUS	direct, rectum
techo	TECTUM	(pro)tect
leche	LACTEM	lactose

where the middle column represents the common Latin origin of the corresponding Spanish and English words. Several points can immediately be noted:

(a) in each case, Spanish has changed Latin *ct* to *ch;*
(b) in several cases, the vowel has changed;
(c) the final Latin *um* or *us* has become Spanish *o,* while the final *em* in LACTEM has become *e;*
(d) an initial *e* has been added to *estrecho;*
(e) the *f* in FACTUM has been converted into a silent *h* in Spanish.

Each of these characteristics is in fact a very frequent occurrence in Spanish, as we will see in Part III.

We note also that the English equivalents of the Latin roots do not always have the *identical* meaning of the corresponding Spanish word, but in all cases they are at least *suggestive* and, more importantly, easy to remember. We may not know too much about *lactose,* but most of us know that it is in milk and that some people have problems digesting it (hence *lactose-free* milk in the supermarkets).[2] Similarly, "narrow" and "strict" are not perfect synonyms, but they do have overlapping meanings, since a "strict interpretation" is a "narrow" one.

And how about *derecho,* and what is its possible connection with *rectum?* Latin DIRECTUS meant "in a straight line", hence "*direct*", and is the origin of Spanish *derecho* meaning "right", both in terms of direction ("*directly* ahead", "the right-hand one") and "law". RECTUS, "straight", leads to RECTUM INTESTINUM, the "straight intestine", shortened in English and Spanish to *rectum* and *recto,* respectively.

Finally, *techo* is easily remembered because it *(pro)tects* us from the elements.

---

[2] The same *lac(t)*- appears in *galactic* and *galaxy* (from Greek), the inspiration for the *Milky Way* (a translation of Latin VIA LACTEA).

Apart from being an effective learning tool, this alternative to the "telephone book" approach can help convert vocabulary learning from an essentially painful process with no immediate reward to an enjoyable one with both immediate and longer-term benefits:

(a) It provides valuable insights into the history of both the Spanish language and the Spanish-speaking peoples.

(b) It provides an opportunity to deepen one's understanding of English (e.g., how many people are aware that the English word *check* comes—via Persian, Arabic, Spanish, and French—from the *Shah* of Iran?).

(c) It enables one to enlarge one's *English* vocabulary. For example, all of the following words (some rather obscure) found in the *American Heritage College Dictionary* are closely related—and, in a number of cases, identical in form—to reasonably common Spanish words:

acequia	frijol
acicula	grisaille
alcalde	horologe
bodega	lanose
burnoose	paries, parietal
cespitose	manus
cicatrix	matutinal
comestible	muliebrity
consuetudinary	non obstante
cuirass	playa
estival	seta
finca	stupefacient
fovea	supervene

(d) It will make learning a *second* Romance language (French, Italian, Portuguese, Catalan[3]) far easier; conversely, any preexisting knowledge of one of these languages can immediately be applied to the learning of Spanish.

Returning to our example above, let us consider in more detail

STRICTUS   →   estrecho

---

[3] Or Romanian, Rhaeto-Romance (one of Switzerland's four national languages), Occitan (also known as Provençal), Galician (northwest Spain), or Sardinian.

to illustrate how, with a little effort, learning one word can be the key to learning a large number of others. STRICTUS is the past participle of the Latin verb STRINGERE ("to bind tightly", "to tighten"), which gave rise (via Old French) to English *strain, restrain, constrain,* as well as to the more "classical" forms *strict, restrict, constrict, restriction,* etc.

A similar process occurred in Spanish, giving these correspondences:

Spanish	English
restringir	(to) restrict, (to) restrain
restricción	restriction
restrictivo	restrictive
constreñir	(to) constrain, (to) constrict
constricción	constriction
constreñimiento	constraint, constriction
constrictivo	constrictive
constrictor	constrictor (e.g., boa)
astringir	(to) astringe
astringente	astringent
estricto	strict
estrictamente	strictly
estrechez	straitness (narrowness), (dire) straits
estrechar	(to) straiten (make narrow)

This last word is used most commonly in the expression *estrechar la mano* ("to shake hands"). *Estrecho* is also used as a noun in the sense of the "narrow" part of a river, i.e., English *strait,* with which it shares a common origin:

el *estrecho* de Gibraltar   the *Strait* of Gibraltar

It is often the case that one can trace a Spanish word through French to find one or more relatives in English. Thus, *strait* arrived in English via Old French *estreit,* which meant "narrow", while Old French for "strait" was *destreit.* In later French this became *détroit,* which of course explains the origin of the name of the "Motor City".

In the fifteenth century, Latin DISTRICTUS (DIS + STRICTUS) gave rise to French *district,* initially the exercise of justice ("restraint") in a certain area, then the territory itself, which was marked off for a special administrative purpose. It subsequently entered Spanish (sixteenth century) and English (seventeenth century) with this latter definition. Thus, distrito   district

DISTRICTIA, a "popular" Latin word derived from DISTRICTUS, had earlier given rise via Old French *destrece* to English *distress:* "the sore pressure or *strain* of adversity" (*OED*). A newspaper headline like

DETROIT DISTRICT IN DISTRESS!!!

can therefore be seen, etymologically at least, as being (multiply) redundant.

Old French *estrece* (from popular Latin STRICTIA) was the source of English *stress* (fourteenth century), and six centuries later this was reexported to Spanish:

estrés   stress

Finally, the Spanish verb that corresponds directly to Latin STRINGERE is *estreñir,* cognate with English *strain.* It applies to a particular type of "strain" or "constriction", that which takes place in the intestines:

estreñir   (to) constipate
estreñimiento   constipation
estreñido   constipated

This, of course, raises the question of what *constipado* means in Spanish. Like English *constipated,* it comes from the Latin verb STIPARE ("to crowd together", "to compress"). However, in Spanish the compression generally refers to an altogether different part of the body:

constipar   (to) catch cold
constipado   suffering from a cold, a cold

so that a Spanish speaker suffering from a cold is likely to receive an altogether different remedy from an English-speaking pharmacist than from a Spanish-speaking one.[4]

Thus, without a great deal of effort, we have extended our initial equivalence *estrecho* = "strict" to a score of additional Spanish words, and have at the same time cast new light on several *English* words.

We can see from the above examples that words that share a common Latin origin often evolve along different paths, in both form and meaning. This is in fact one of the principal ways that languages "evolve" and eventually break up

---

[4] English *constipation* was not always restricted to the intestinal variety: until the eighteenth century, *constipate* could also mean "to make firm and compact by pressing together", "to condense or thicken liquids", "to close the pores". Many Spanish speakers, particularly in the Americas, use *resfrío* or *resfriado* for "cold".

into different languages. Taking English as an example, we know that nearly every word has a minimum of two definitions, and in many cases substantially more. Suppose that when we meet, I use only odd-numbered definitions and you use only even-numbered ones. Will we understand each other? Probably not, or if so, only with great difficulty. Suppose now that I alter the form of my words in reasonably systematic ways, say replacing *ct* with *ch, cul* by *j, t* by *d* whenever it occurs between vowels, etc., and you make a series of similar but different changes. We will now have created languages as far apart as Spanish and Italian—in fact, all of the changes mentioned above occurred during the evolution of Latin to Spanish.

False Friends

Nearly every student of a foreign language has been warned about the perils of "false friends" (*falsos amigos, faux amis, falsi amici, falsche Freunde,* etc.), which *seem* to bear a relation to a word in English but actually do not. Lesson of the story: never assume that you can figure out the meaning of an unfamiliar word from its form alone. In Spanish, for example, the following appear in nearly every such list of "false friends":

Spanish	Meaning	False English Friend
actual	"present, current"	actual
arena	"sand"	arena
largo	"long"	large

Much as the "exception proves the rule", false friends often turn out to be great aids in learning new vocabulary. In the majority of cases, they have an important story to tell, which is generally that one language has chosen to focus on, let us say, the even-numbered definitions, and the other, on the odd-numbered ones.

First, consider Spanish *arena*. Everyone knows that an *arena* is a sports stadium, so where in the world did the Spanish come up with *arena* for "sand"?[5] The explanation is very simple: the original Latin meaning of ARENA was *not* "stadium" but "sand". Sand was frequently used to cover the ground in coliseums and other sporting venues, the better to absorb the blood of gladiators. ARENA ("the sand") then became a shorthand term for the stadium in which gladiators performed. SABULUM, which originally meant "sand of a somewhat

---

[5] Spanish *arena* can also mean "arena", either as a classical site for gladiator combat or in the more "modern" sense of a site for bullfighting.

coarser variety", then came to replace ARENA in the generic sense of "sand". SABULUM evolved into French (*sable*) and Italian (*sabbia*) for "sand", while Spanish maintained the older term *arena* in its original sense, limiting *sábulo* to the meaning "coarse sand".[6] This is by no means a rare occurrence: due to the early colonization of the Iberian Peninsula (before France and much of northern Italy) and its relative isolation, Spanish and Portuguese have in many cases maintained meanings of Latin words and expressions that were subsequently dropped in regions closer to Rome.

How is it that Spanish *actual* has a meaning in terms of time ("now"), while in English it means "existing and not merely potential or possible"? If one *actually* looks in the dictionary, one will see that there is another definition of English *actual:*

Being, existing, or acting at the present moment; current (*AHCD*).

Similarly, in Spanish there is also a second definition:

Real, por oposición a "potencial" (Moliner). "Real, as opposed to 'potential.'"

So both Spanish and English *actual* do share common *meanings*, but English has chosen to emphasize one, Spanish another.

From this (not-so-) false friend, one can immediately establish a number of very real correspondences derived from the Latin verb AGERE ("to drive", "to do") and its past participle ACTUS, all of which (actually) *do* correspond in meaning:

Spanish	English	Spanish	English
acto	act	activar	(to) activate
actor	actor	actuario	actuary
actriz	actress	agenda	agenda
acción	action	agente	agent
—acciones	—shares/stocks	agencia	agency
actividad	activity	reacción	reaction
activista	activist	reaccionar	(to) react
activo	active	reaccionario	reactionary
—activos	—assets	reactor	reactor

---

[6] The original sense of Latin ARENA survives in the English adjective *arenaceous* ("resembling, derived from, or containing sand").

Finally, Spanish *largo* means "long" rather than "large". For those who know French, the potential for confusion is even greater, since French *large* means "wide". In fact, all of these definitions are geometric applications of the common theme expressed by Latin LARGUS—"abundant, copious, bountiful, profuse"—and preserved in English *largesse*.[7] Spanish has focused on *length,* French on *width,* and English on overall *size.*

Spanish *largo* and related words also maintain some of the elements of the original definition, as is the case in English.

una *larga* cosecha	an abundant (*large*) harvest
largueza	generosity, *largesse* (or *largess*)
largamente	at length, *largely,* generously
alargar	(to) lengthen, (to) increase (make *larger*)

Etymological Correspondences with English Words

Throughout the book, the large majority of Spanish words—or word families—are associated with corresponding English words, which can be used as an aid in learning, and remembering, the Spanish. Frequently, the corresponding English word is part of the definition of the Spanish, e.g.,

abrupto	steep, craggy, *abrupt*
creíble	*credible*

Where the English cognate does not form part of the definition, it is shown in brackets:

agua	water	[*aquatic*]
pecado	sin	[*peccadillo*]

In the vast majority of cases, the English cognate can be found in the medium-sized *American Heritage College Dictionary.*

In some sections, the English correspondences are systematically highlighted in italics; in other sections, particularly where the large majority of words correspond to English words (e.g., Sections 3.1 and 3.2 and Annex D), italics are used only when the correspondence is not obvious (especially when the word in question is *not* the *first* element of the definition) or to highlight the etymological relationship.

---

[7] "Liberality in bestowing gifts . . . Money or gifts bestowed . . . Generosity."

Latin Roots

In a number of cases, the Latin root of the Spanish word is given, e.g.,

CAPRA	cabra	goat	[*Capricorn*]
TERRA	tierra	earth, land, soil	
	terraza	*terrace*	

The reason for this is not to teach Latin, but rather that the Latin root can help illustrate the connection between the Spanish word and a related English one; in many cases the root itself is easily recognizable.

Each Latin noun (or adjective) had up to six different *singular* forms, depending on the manner in which it was used in the sentence (subject, direct object, etc.).[8] We have generally shown the nominative (subject) form—the one found in dictionaries—but have not hesitated to use another form when it is more suitable for our purposes.[9] In a number of cases, the form shown comes from Medieval Latin or Vulgar Latin (rather than Classical Latin), when it is from one of these two sources that the corresponding Spanish word derives.

Definitions

The brief definitions presented in the text are meant to be suggestive only and are in no manner a substitute for more complete definitions to be found in a suitable dictionary. The definitions are at least theoretically "standard", in the sense that the large majority should be familiar to most native speakers of Spanish. But one should bear in mind that regional differences in Spanish vocabulary are substantially greater than those that exist in the English-speaking world, and a word (or definition) used in one country (or region) is often unknown in another. Even more troublesome, a word that is perfectly "normal" and acceptable in some countries may not be appropriate for public use in others.[10]

---

[8] The adjectives actually had eighteen potentially different singular forms—six each for the masculine, feminine, and neuter.

[9] Specifically, for the so-called *third* declension, the accusative form is frequently shown for words having two different "stems" (e.g., FRONS—FRONTEM, "front"). For the large group of nouns whose nominatives end in -o with accusatives ending in -ONEM (e.g., NATIO—NATIONEM), a "mixed" form is shown: NATIO(N).

[10] Two examples of this are *coger* ("to take", "to catch") and *concha* ("shell"), which in Spain and a number of other countries are perfectly normal words, but in others represent the height of sexual vulgarity.

A very large number of words can be used as both adjectives and nouns, e.g.,

plano	level (adj.), flat (adj.), smooth (adj.), plane (adj.), plane (n.), map or plan (n.)
cuadrado	square (adj.), square (n.)

To simplify the presentation, the parts of speech will generally not be explicitly noted. Adjective definitions (if any) will precede noun ones, and the reader can be guided by the corresponding use of the words in English. Thus:

plano (adj. & n.)	level, flat, smooth, plane, map or plan
cuadrado (adj. & n.)	square
precedente	preceding, precedent

Spanish adjectives are very frequently used as "person" nouns . In some cases, both adjective and noun meanings will be provided, but often only the adjective sense will be shown. Thus,

ciego	blind

rather than

ciego (adj. & n.)	blind, blind man, blind woman

In a number of cases, a specific definition applies only when the word is used as a plural, e.g., *las economías* ("savings"). This is indicated as follows:

economía	economy, economics, savings (pl.)

In other cases, a noun is used only in the plural, e.g., *las finanzas* ("the finances"):

finanzas (pl.)	finances, finance

Sometimes there are two (or more) common spellings of a word, but one is "preferred" by the RAE. This is generally shown in the following manner

chovinismo / chauvinismo	chauvinism

where the first spelling is the preferred one. When different spellings seem to be equally acceptable, they are separated by a comma:

vídeo, video	video, VCR

On occasions, synonyms are explicitly indicated by the symbol ~ :

confort	comfort (~ *comodidad*)

Confort and *comodidad* are thus synonyms.

The symbol $<$ is used to indicate the provenance of a word, particularly when its form (or meaning) appears "un-Spanish". Thus for *bate,*

bate ($<$ Eng.)	baseball *bat*

Many verbs can be used *pronominally* (or *reflexively*), often with a somewhat different meaning than when used "normally":

"normal"	*Levanto* la mano.	I *raise* my hand.
pronominal	**Me** *levanto* a las seis.	I *get up* at six (from the bed).

The definitions presented do not explicitly distinguish between pronominal and regular uses. Thus:

levantar (to) raise, (to) lift, (to) get up (from bed, etc.)

The pronominal form of the infinitive is given when, in common use,[11] the verb is used *only* in a pronominal sense, e.g.,

arrepentir(se)   (to) repent

Expressions

For a relatively small number of words, one or more common expressions are also provided, e.g.,

estrechar	(to) narrow, (to) tighten
estrechar la mano	(to) shake hands

Dictionaries and Alphabets

In deciding on a suitable dictionary, it is useful to keep in mind the very important differences between pre- and post-1994 Spanish dictionaries. Post-1994 dictionaries use virtually the same alphabetical ordering as English dictionaries—the only difference being the inclusion of an additional letter, ñ. For pre-1994 dictionaries, the situation is altogether different. The reasons for this are related to the following not-so-trivial question:

How many letters are there in the Spanish alphabet?

There is in fact considerable confusion both about the total number of letters (generally cited as either twenty-eight or twenty-nine) and which specific ones

---

[11] In general, the *smaller* a dictionary is, the more likely that all of the definitions for a given verb will involve pronominal uses, and hence the more likely it is that the verb will be shown in its pronominal form. For example, most dictionaries show *abstener* ("to abstain") and *atener* ("to keep to") in their pronominal forms (*abstenerse* and *atenerse*), whereas the more complete dictionaries of the RAE and Moliner show them in their "normal" forms.

are to be included. In particular, many dictionaries and grammar books define *rr* as a separate letter and exclude *w* and/or *k*, on the grounds that they are used only in words of foreign origin. Others state that *ch* and *ll*, previously treated as separate letters, no longer qualify for such special treatment.

The actual situation, at least according to the Real Academia Española (RAE),[12] is as follows: there are twenty-nine letters in the Spanish alphabet (*el alfabeto* or *el abecedario*), made up of the twenty-six "English" letters (including both *k* and *w*), plus: *ch, ll*, and *ñ*. The combination *rr* is *not* considered to be a separate letter.

Prior to 1994, Spanish words were alphabetized treating *ch, ll*, and *ñ* as the fully independent letters that they were. In all dictionaries published before that date (and unfortunately in many later ones, particularly "new" editions of older dictionaries), not only are words beginning with *ch, ll*, and *ñ* grouped separately, but within entries for *other* letters this same process takes place. In 1994, under pressure from the various American academies of Spanish, the Tenth Congress of the Asociación de Academias de la Lengua Española adopted the Solomonic compromise that while continuing to exercise all other rights as free and independent letters, *for the purposes of alphabetization only*, *ch* and *ll* would be treated as a normal combination of letters. The letter *ñ* continues to be treated separately for alphabetization, thus representing a further victory in its campaign for survival.[13]

The situation can be illustrated by means of the following example:

Pre-1994 Word Order	Post-1994 Word Order
cantina	cantina
ca**ñ**ón	ca**ñ**ón
cuyo	**ch**icha
chico	**ch**ico
chicha	cuyo
luz	**ll**uvia
lluvia	luz
nunca	nunca
ñato	**ñ**ato

The principal reason for considering *ch* and *ll* to be single letters is that their pronunciation is always that of a single sound (rather than two separate ones).

---

[12] The RAE performs an oversight role for Spanish similar to that exercised by the Académie française for French.

[13] In the interests of "standardization" of printing, the European Union had tried to convince Spain in the early 1990s to eliminate *ñ* (replacing it with *gn* or another such combination), thus inciting a near revolt among the Spaniards.

The same also holds for the letter combination *rr,* which is presumably why many sources classify it as a separate letter.

Shifting from an "English" alphabetization to a pre-1994 "Spanish" one, particularly when using a bilingual dictionary, can be quite a challenge and one that most prefer to avoid whenever possible.

Word Origins and Trivial Pursuits

Many times a word presents difficulties because it seems to embody concepts that are completely unrelated. For example, if one looks up the Spanish word *moral* in the dictionary, one is likely to find the following definitions:

moral	*adj.* moral; *f.* ethics, morals; morale; *m.* black mulberry tree

How is a black mulberry tree *moral?* Perhaps a *moral* person is one who eats black mulberries? In this case, as in many others, the explanation lies in the fact that two (or more) separate words have become *homonyms,* each having its own English correspondent. The presentation in the text seeks to shed light on such potential conundrums. Thus:

mora (1)	*mulberry* (fruit), blackberry	
—moral (1)	—black *mulberry* (tree)	
—morado	—violet or *mulberry* (color)	
—mora (2)	—delay (esp. in payment, *mora* (poetry)	(unrelated)
—moral (2) (adj. & n.f.)	—moral (adj.), ethics, morals, morale	(unrelated)
—moraleja	—moral (of a story)	
—moralidad	—morality	

Throughout the text, information on word origins is frequently provided in order to facilitate the association of a Spanish word with a particular English one. Much of this material is provided in the footnotes, particularly in those sections where a "list" approach is followed. Apart from their pedagogical value, some (if not all) readers may find them of interest in their own right. In particular, the diligent student will discover the answers to the following questions, among others:

1. What is the difference between a *slave* and a *Slav?* [3.1]
2. Why is *colonel* pronounced with an *r?* [3.5]
3. How did Joan of Arc refer to the English? [4.1]
4. What is the difference between *scarlet, crimson, carmine,* and *vermilion?* [4.2]
5. How is an *apricot* precocious? [4.2]

6. What did *algebraists* do before they began to solve equations? [4.2]
7. What is the meaning of the expression below the pyramid on the back of the U.S. one-dollar bill? [4.4]
8. Today is Monday the tenth. My cousin is arriving in *ocho días.* She is left-handed. On what *day* of the week will my cousin arrive? [4.4]
9. How many days are there in a Spanish *fortnight?* [4.4]
10. How do you say "royal peacock" in Spanish? [4.6]
11. What do you call a "turkey" in Turkey? [4.6]
12. In what respect can it be said that *despondency* is an inherent element of a Spanish marriage? [4.8]
13. What is the role of a *ship's husband?* [4.8]
14. What is a Spanish *flea killer* called? [4.9]
15. What was the official title of Charles II's *royal diver?* [4.9]
16. Should *pencils* and *vanilla* ice cream be X-rated? [4.9]
17. What is the inherent relationship between *baldness* and *chauvinism?* [4.9]
18. What is the meaning of the expression above the mysterious eye on the back of the U.S. one-dollar bill? [Annex B]
19. What is the connection between *starboard* and the *stars?* [Annex B]
20. Why do doctors call a kidney stone a *calculus?* [Annex D]
21. What is the relation between an American *hoosegow* and a Spanish *judge?* [Annex D]
22. What was the *modus operandi* of a Roman *plagiarist?* [Annex D]

The section of the text in which the answer can be found is shown in brackets.

PART I

BACKGROUND

Spanish as a Romance Language

If Cicero (or Caesar) were to come back to life and try to speak Spanish (or any other Romance language), he would very quickly come to the conclusion that the barbarians had taken over and "pidginized" his language. In terms of grammar, the structure of the language would have changed almost beyond recognition.[1] Only about half of the vocabulary—what we easily recognize to be "classical" Latin and Greek[2] words in English—would be familiar, and the pronunciation would often seem very strange, his own name in particular (which he pronounced as if it were spelled KIKERO).[3] The other half would strike him as either "gutter" Latin spoken by the uneducated or words of totally unfamiliar origin.

John and Jane Doe, native English speakers of the twenty-first century, should find it far easier to learn Spanish. The differences between Spanish and English grammar are relatively minor—certainly in comparison with the vast difference between the grammar of either one and Latin.[4] And, with a bit of effort, they will recognize that around 90 percent of Spanish words are related to English ones, and that this common origin can be used as the basis for enriching their Spanish vocabulary.

The principal origins of Spanish vocabulary can be broken down as follows:

Source	Example	Definition	
1. Latin			
A. *Classical*	dedicación	*dedication*	
B. *Vulgar*	oveja	sheep	[*ovine*]
2. Classical Greek	dinastía	*dynasty*	

---

[1] In particular, the language would have moved from what linguists call a *synthetic* language to a predominantly *analytic* one. In a synthetic language, relations between nouns and adjectives are expressed by *case* endings of individual words, while in an analytic language such relations are expressed using prepositions. Definite and indefinite articles ("the", "a") would likewise be novelties for Cicero and Caesar, as they did not exist in Classical Latin. Old English was likewise a (largely) synthetic language with neither definite nor indefinite articles.

[2] Like all educated Romans, Cicero and Caesar were fluent in Greek; Caesar's final words "Et tu, Brute?" (from Shakespeare's *Julius Caesar*) were in fact reported to have been uttered in Greek rather than Latin.

[3] German *Kaiser* ("emperor") continues the original Latin pronunciation of CAESAR, from which it was derived.

[4] Or, for that matter, between Modern and Old English.

3. **Germanic**	ropa	clothes	[*robe*]
4. **Arabic**	algodón	*cotton*	
5. **Other Romance languages**			
A. *Latin* origin	jefe	*chief*	(< French)
B. *Germanic* origin	balcón	*balcony*	(< Italian)
6. **Native American**	patata	*potato*	

Vulgar Latin refers to the spoken Latin of the "plebs", or common people, as compared to the more rarefied *Classical* version spoken (and written) by Cicero and those of his ilk. It was this more popular spoken Latin that, following the decline of the (western) Roman Empire, evolved into what is generally called "Proto-Romance" and subsequently into the various individual Romance languages.

It is important to keep in mind that in this context *vulgar* means simply "of the people" (Latin VULGUS, also the basis for *divulge*); initially the word had no "vulgar" connotation.[5] The *Vulgate* (from Latin EDITIO VULGATA) is still the name of the official Latin version of the Bible used by the Roman Catholic Church, based primarily on the translation by St. Jerome in the late fourth to early fifth century AD.

vulgo	common people, ordinary people, the masses
vulgar	vulgar (associated with the "masses": common, ordinary, unrefined)
vulgaridad	commonplace (n.), platitude, *vulgarity*
vulgarismo	vulgarism (word or manner of expression used chiefly by uneducated people)
vulgarizar	(to) vulgarize (popularize, disseminate widely, debase)
Vulgata	Vulgate
divulgar	(to) divulge, (to) popularize

Romanization of Spain

Roman colonization of the Iberian Peninsula (present-day Spain and Portugal) began in the latter third century BC, at about the same time as that of north-

---

[5] In its early history in English, *vulgar* was applied in a non-negative fashion to a wide array of activities with the meaning of "in common or general use" or "familiar", e.g., *vulgar* (common or customary) language and *vulgar* (common) fractions. Its first negative use in terms of "having a common and offensively mean character" is not recorded by the *Oxford English Dictionary* until the mid-seventeenth century, and the first negative reference to "vulgar language" (meaning "rude"), only in 1716.

ern Italy and nearly a full century before that of Gaul (France). This may seem somewhat surprising, given its greater distance from Rome, but the strategic importance of Hispania (as it came to be called) during the Second Punic War (218–201 BC) against Hannibal and the Carthaginians led to the sending of the first Roman troops in 218 BC.

Prior to the arrival of the Romans, the Iberian Peninsula had been occupied by Iberians in the east and south, Celts—also called Celtiberians to distinguish them from their Gallic cousins in what is now France, and to reflect their presumed mixing with the Iberians—in the north, Lusitanians in the west, Carthaginian colonies in the south, and by several small Greek settlements along the northeast Mediterranean coast. The exact origin of the Basques, and their connection, if any, to these other groups, remains a mystery.

The major part of Hispania remained under Roman control for more than six centuries, until the collapse of Roman power in the West and the invasion of Spain by Germanic tribes in the early fifth century AD. Spain's relatively early colonization and geographic remoteness had important implications for the development of Romance languages in the Iberian Peninsula. The Latin that arrived in the Iberian Peninsula was in many cases an "older" Latin than that used in areas added subsequently to the Roman Empire. This effect was magnified by the relative isolation of the Iberian Peninsula, which meant that innovations from Rome often took much longer to arrive or in many cases never did.

Thus, in a number of cases, "early" Latin words (in some cases pre-Classical) form the base of Spanish and Portuguese vocabulary, while later ones are used in other Romance languages. In many of these cases, the word subsequently used by French and Italian represents a more "colorful" or "expressive" (Cicero would have said "vulgar" or "rustic") term.

Early Latin (I)	Later Latin (II)	Spanish	Portuguese	French	Italian
1. COMEDERE	MANDUCARE	comer	comer	manger	mangiare
2. MENSA	TABULA	mesa	mesa	table	tavola
3. FORMOSUS	BELLUS	hermoso	formoso	beau	bello
4. CAPUT	TESTA	cabeza	cabeça	tête	testa
5. HUMERUS	SPATULA	hombro	ombro	épaule	spalla
6. ARENA	SABULUM	arena	areia	sable	sabbia
7. FERVERE	BULLIRE	hervir	ferver	bouillir	bollire
8. FABULARI	PARABOLARE	hablar	falar	parler	parlare
9. CASEUS	[CASEUS] FORMATICUS	queso	queijo	fromage	formaggio

English translations

Latin I	Latin II (Original Meaning)
1. (to) eat[6]	(to) chew
2. table	plank
3. beautiful, handsome	pretty
4. head	shard or earthen pot
5. shoulder, humerus (bone)	small sword, branch
6. sand	coarse sand, gravel
7. (to) boil	(to) bubble
8. (to) speak in *fables*[7]	(to) speak in *parables*
9. cheese	formed (cheese)

As noted in the introduction, ARENA in the sense of "stadium" derived from the fact that the central part of a stadium was covered with sand to soak up contestants' blood (human and animal). *Stadium* (*estadio* in Spanish) comes from STADIUM, the Latin version of the Greek word for racecourse (initially a unit of measure of approximately 600 feet).

---

[6] COMEDERE was in fact a very early "popular" replacement for the basic verb EDERE (cognate with English *eat*), first recorded more than one hundred years *before* the beginning of Classical Latin.

[7] FABULARI was an early popular verb for "to speak"—the initial meaning of FABULA was simply "conversation". In early Christian times, a new popular form arose: PARABOLARE. At no time does it appear that the Classical verb LOQUI (as in *loquacious*) was popular among the plebs.

"Learned" versus "Popular" Words

Words of Latin origin in Spanish have arrived via four essentially different means. They can originate from

a) Classical Latin words that were "borrowed" directly into Spanish (often at a relatively late stage), and that have therefore experienced only relatively minor changes—usually to their endings—to make them look (and sound) more "Spanish": e.g., *audiencia* from AUDIENTIA, and *estricto* from STRICTUS.

b) Classical Latin words also used by the plebs—and hence forming part of the "vulgar" Latin vocabulary—that have undergone a long process of evolution in pronunciation and spelling (and often meaning as well) over the centuries: e.g., *estrecho,* also from STRICTUS.

c) non-Classical Latin words used *only* by the plebs that have undergone the same process of evolution as in b): e.g., *olvidar* ("to forget") from Vulgar Latin OBLITARE, compared to Classical Latin OBLIVISCI.

d) later borrowings by Spanish from other Romance languages—Portuguese, Catalan, Occitan (southern France), French, Italian, *and English*—of words that may have had either a Classical or a non-Classical origin and that underwent the corresponding "popular" evolution in that language: e.g., *reloj* ("clock", "watch") from (old) Catalan *relotge,* from Classical Latin HOROLOGIUM.

Words that have followed the first route are frequently called *learned* words ("lear•ned" in the sense of "erudite", Spanish *culto*), while those following the other routes are called *popular* words. Some also use a third, intermediate category of "semi-learned" words that have undergone substantial linguistic evolution but have nevertheless avoided the full "popular" treatment. For example, *auto* from Latin ACTUS, as in *auto de fe* ("judicial act or sentence of the Inquisition", i.e., an *act of faith,* an *auto-da-fé*[8]), would have become *echo* if it had undergone the "full" popular treatment. The distinction between "popular" and "learned" could perhaps better be expressed as "evolved" versus "marginally changed", without any reference to cultural status: the connection with learn-

---

[8] The English form comes from an older Portuguese version, where *da* means "of the"; the modern Portuguese is *auto-de-fé.*

22

edness is often not obvious, nor is it easy to explain why a "learned" word in one language not infrequently turns out to be a "popular" one in another.

In many cases, Latin words have entered Spanish twice, through both the "popular" and the "learned" routes. Examples of such doublets, with the English definition italicized if it is a cognate, are:

| | Spanish | | English Definition | |
| | "Learned" | "Popular" | | |
Latin	(1)	(2)	(1)	(2)
ANIMAL	animal	alimaña	*animal*	vermin
ARTICULUS	artículo	artejo	*article*	knuckle
AUSCULTARE	auscultar	escuchar	*auscultate*	(to) listen
BLASPHEMIA	blasfemia	lástima	*blasphemy*	pity
CATHEDRA	cátedra	cadera	professorship[9]	hip
COLLOCARE	colocar	colgar	(to) place	(to) hang
COMPUTARE	computar	contar	(to) *compute*	(to) *count*
FABRICARE	fabricar	forjar, fraguar	(to) *fabricate*	(to) *forge*
HOSPITALIS	hospital	hostal, hotel	*hospital*	*hostel, hotel*
INTEGER	íntegro	entero	*entire*	*entire, integer*
LAICUS	laico	lego	*laic*	*lay*
LEGALIS	legal	leal	*legal*	*loyal*
LUCRUM	lucro	logro	profit, *lucre*	accomplishment
MULTITUDO	multitud	muchedumbre	*multitude*	crowd, swarm
PARABOLA	parábola	palabra (de honor)	*parabola*	*parole*
PENSARE	pensar	pesar	(to) think	(to) weigh
RECITARE	recitar	rezar	(to) *recite*	(to) pray
SAECULARIS	secular	seglar	*secular*	*secular*
SECUNDUS	segundo	según	*second*	according to
SEXTUS/SEXTA	sexto	siesta	sixth	*siesta*
SPECIES	especie	especia	*species*	*spice*
SPECULUM	espéculo	espejo	*speculum*	mirror
STRICTUS	estricto	estrecho	*strict*	narrow
TESTIFICARI	testificar	atestiguar	(to) *testify*	(to) *attest*

---

[9] That is, a university *chair*. Spanish *cátedra* also maintains various ecclesiastical senses, as does English *cathedra*.

TITULUS	título	tilde (f.)	*title*	*tilde*
TRADITIO(N)	tradición	traición	*tradition*	*treason*
VERIFICARE	verificar	averiguar	(to) *verify*	(to) ascertain
VOTUM (pl. VOTA)	voto	boda	*vow, vote*	wedding

For students of Spanish, "learned" words are the easier ones, as in most cases they immediately call to mind a similar English word having the same Latin origin. The majority of the "popular" words are not so instantly recognizable, and it is for this reason that they will be the central focus of Part III.

From the above table, one can see that such doublets also occur in English, e.g., *compute—count* and *fabricate—forge.* Given the hybrid nature of English, this actually occurs with extraordinary frequency, and triplets (*hospital—hostel—hotel*) are not uncommon. Additional English examples are provided below, with corresponding Spanish cognates having at least roughly similar definitions—if they exist—shown on the right.[10] Note that QUIETUS has given rise to *four* English words.

Latin	English 1	English 2	Spanish 1	Spanish 2
BLASPHEMIA	blasphemy	blame	blasfemia	—
CALUMNIA	calumny	challenge	calumnia	—
CAMARA/CAMERA	chamber	camera	cámara	cámara
CAPITALIS	capital	chattel	capital	caudal
CAPTARE	chase	catch	cazar	—
CAPUT	chief	chef	jefe	chef
CARRICARE	charge	carry	cargar	acarrear
CURSUS	course	coarse	curso	—
FACTIO(N)	faction	fashion	facción	—
FACTUM	fact	feat	hecho	—
FLOS	flower	flour	flor (f.)	—
FRAGILIS	fragile	frail	frágil	frágil
MAJOR	major	mayor	mayor	—
MANU OPERARI	maneuver	manure	maniobrar	—
NAUSEA	nausea	noise	náusea	—
ORDINARIUS	ordinary	ornery	ordinario	—
PAR	pair	peer, par	par, pareja	par
PAUSARE	pause	pose	pausar	posar

---

[10] Spanish 1 corresponds to English 1, Spanish 2 to English 2.

PRIVATUS	private	privy	privado	privado[11]
PROPRIETAS	propriety	property	propiedad	propiedad
QUIETUS	quiet	quite, quit, coy	quedo, quieto[12]	—
RABIES	rabies	rage	rabia	rabia
RADIUS	radius	radio, ray	radio	radio (f.), rayo
REGALIS	regal	royal	real[13]	real
ROTUNDUS	rotund	round	rotundo	redondo
SECURUS	secure	sure	seguro	seguro
SENIOR	senior	sir, sire	—	señor
THESAURUS	thesaurus	treasure	tesoro	tesoro
UNCIA[14]	ounce	inch	onza	—
UNIO(N)	union	onion	unión	—

The Origin of Spices and the "Soviet *Onion*" certainly have a somewhat different allure in comparison with their more well-known etymological siblings.

---

[11] *El privado del rey* was a confidant of the king; cf. English *privy councilor*. In the sense of *privy* ("toilet"), *privada* exists but is not common.

[12] *Quedo* and *quieto* can both be translated as "quiet", although they generally have different nuances: *quedo* in the sense of "in a hushed voice", *quieto* in the sense of "still", "calm".

[13] Spanish *real* also means "real", a meaning derived independently from Latin REALIS, source of English *real*.

[14] Latin UNCIA meant "twelfth part".

SECTION 1.3

Latin: A Few Useful Tools

There are three easily learned phonetic features of Latin that can be of considerable assistance in augmenting one's Spanish (and English) vocabulary.

(1) DT and TT → s (or ss)

At some point in the path from Indo-European to Latin, a "parasite" *s* intruded into the combinations *dt* and *tt* and eventually took over the whole sound.[15] This was particularly important for the large number of Latin verbs whose *root* ended in *D* or *T*, as the past participle was often formed by adding -TUS directly to the root. Thus,

DEFEND-TUS → DEFEND**S**TUS → DEFEN**S**US

Latin constructed numerous nouns and adjectives using the past participle as a base, which explains why in both English and Spanish there are so many "s" adjectives and nouns associated with verbs whose root ends in *d* or *t*. For the verb *defend,* for example:

English	Spanish
(to) defend	defender
defense	defensa
defenseless	indefenso
defensive	defensivo
(defensor)	defensor

English *defensor* is now largely obsolete, having been replaced by *defender.* Other common verbs showing this pattern include:[16]

---

[15] A similar transformation occurred in the Germanic languages: cf. *wit* versus *wise*.

[16] Note that in two cases the original Latin *D* has disappeared in Spanish (*concluir* and *excluir,* compared to *conclude* and *exclude*). We will see in Section 3.4 that this is not an infrequent occurrence.

| | English | | Spanish |
Verb	Noun or Adjective	Verb	Noun or Adjective
applaud	applause	aplaudir	aplauso
—	plausible	—	plausible[17]
ascend	ascension	ascender	ascensión
collide	collision	—	colisión
collude	collusion	coludir	colusión
comprehend	comprehension	comprender	comprensión
—	incomprehension	—	incomprensión
concede	concession	conceder	concesión
conclude	conclusion	concluir	conclusión
confound	confusion	confundir	confusión
consent	consensus	consentir	consenso
convert	conversion	convertir	conversión
decide	decision	decidir	decisión
dissent	dissension	disentir	disensión
divide	division	dividir	división
evade	evasion	evadir	evasión
exclude	exclusion, exclusive	excluir	exclusión, exclusivo
expand	expansion	expandir	expansión
explode	explosion	explotar[18]	explosión
extend	extension, extensive	extender	extensión, extensivo
intercede	intercession	interceder	intercesión
invade	invasion	invadir	invasión
invader	—	—	invasor
offend	offense	ofender	ofensa
persuade	persuasion	persuadir	persuasión
pretend	pretension	pretender[19]	pretensión
respond	responsible	responder	responsable
ridiculous	risible, derisory	ridículo	risible, irrisorio
submit	submission	someter	sumisión
suspend	suspension	suspender	suspensión
utilize	use	utilizar	usar (vb.), uso (n.)

---

[17] Apart from being "plausible" (i.e., "appearing worthy of belief"), Spanish *plausible* can mean "praiseworthy", "laudable".

[18] *Explotar* ("to explode") was a "back formation" from the noun *explosión,* with a -*t* rather than a -*d* due to its confusion with the unrelated verb *explotar* ("to exploit").

[19] Although English *pretend* and Spanish *pretender* share essentially common meanings, *pretend* has come to specialize almost entirely in the sense of "to feign", "to claim or allege insincerely or falsely", while *pretender* generally means "to try to", "to aspire to". Accordingly, the two words figure on many lists of *falsos amigos.*

(2) *s* → *R* between Vowels

This change is known as *rhotacism* (after the Greek letter for *r*).[20] Evidence of Latin rhotacism is visible in cases where a word with intervocalic *s* had a related form with either *s* + consonant or word-final *s*, which was therefore not subject to this change.[21]

English		Spanish	
adhesive	adhere	adhesivo	adherir
August	augury	agosto	augurio, agüero
cohesion	coherent	cohesión	coherente
genus	general	[género]	general
honest	honor	honesto[22]	honor
ingestion	[ingest]	ingestión	ingerir
inquest	inquire	encuesta	inquirir
just	jury	justo	jurado
modest	moderate	modesto	moderado, moderar (vb.)
onus	onerous	—	oneroso
opus	opera	opus	ópera
plus	plural	plus	plural
pus	purulent	pus	purulento
rustic	rural	rústico	rural
Venus	venereal	Venus	venéreo

(3) Weakening of (Short) Vowels in Interior Syllables

At some stage in its early history, Latin passed through a period with a strong *stress* accent on the *initial* syllable (similar to that of the Germanic languages,

---

[20] It also has a partial parallel in the Germanic languages, the difference being that in Germanic, the change of *s* to *r* was dependent on its location relative to that of the stressed syllable, whereas in Latin it was essentially universal. The relatively few traces of *Germanic* rhotacism remaining in Modern English include the couplets: *was—were, lost—forlorn, raise—rear.*

[21] Most apparent exceptions to this rule (a) entered Latin *after* the mid-fourth century BC, when the phonetic change had been completed (e.g., *rose, asinine, genesis*); (b) arose from DT/TT → *s* (above); or (c) initially had a "hard" *ss* not subject to the rule, which was subsequently shortened to *s* (e.g., CAUSSA → CAUSA → English *cause*, Spanish *causa*).

[22] As noted in Annex D, the more common meaning of *honesto* is "upright", "decent".

including English). As a result, most *short* vowels[23] in interior syllables were weakened. Specifically:

(a) in *open*[24] syllables in the interior of a word, short vowels generally became *I*, less frequently *U*; [25]

(b) in interior *closed* syllables, *A* generally became *E* (but *U* before *L*+ consonant).

These changes left their most visible traces in compound words, where an initial syllable was transformed into an interior one and hence became subject to vowel weakening.

AMICUS → IN-IMICUS	amigo → enemigo	friend → *enemy*
TENAX → PER-TINAX	tenaz → pertinaz	*tenacious → pertinacious*
ANNUALIS → BI-ENNALIS	anual → bienal	*annual → biennial*
ALTERARE → AD-ULTERARE	alterar → adulterar	*alter → adulter*

In the first example, direct English cognates are *amicable → inimical*.

In the following table, words are grouped according to common roots; for example, *cadence* and *accident* are both derived from the verb CADERE ("to fall"), root CAD-. Spanish and English cognates—generally with very similar meanings—occupy corresponding positions.

	English		Spanish	
Root	Initial Syllable	Weakened	Initial Syllable	Weakened
AP-	apt	inept	apto	inepto
CAD-	cadence	accident	cadencia	accidente
	cadaver	occident	cadáver	occidente
	—	recidivist	—	reincidente
CAN-	candle	incendiary	candela	incendiario
CAP-	capture	reception	captura	recepción
	chase	recuperate	cazar	recuperación
	capital	principle	capital	principio

---

[23] In Latin there were five vowels—*A, E, I, O, U*—each of which had a "short" and a "long" variant.

[24] A syllable is called *open* if it ends with a vowel, *closed* if it ends with a consonant. Thus *a* in *bacon* is in an open syllable (ba•con), whereas in *bat* and *banker* (bank•er) it is in a closed syllable.

[25] When *R* followed immediately, the result was generally *E*. The diphthong *AU* became *UU* (→long *U*), and *AE* became *II* (→ long *I*).

	—	principal	—	principal
	—	precipitate	—	precipitar
CAS-	chaste	incest	casto	incesto
CAU-	cause	accuse	causa	acusar
	—	excuse	—	excusar
DAM-	damn	condemn	dañar (vb.)	condenar
	damage	indemnify	daño (n.)	indemnizar
FAC-	face	superficial	faz (f.)	superficial
	faction	confection	facción	confección
	—	office	—	oficina, oficio
	facile	difficult	fácil	difícil
	facility	difficulty	facilidad	dificultad
GRA-	gradual	progress	gradual	progreso
LAES-	lesion	collision	lesión	colisión
PAT-	paternal	perpetrator	paternal	perpetrador
	—	Jupiter	—	Júpiter
SAP-	savor	insipid	sabor	insípido
SED-	sedentary	residence	sedentario	residencia
	Holy See	assiduous	Santa Sede	asiduo
	—	insidious	—	insidioso
TAC-	tacit	reticent, reticence	tácito	reticente, reticencia
TANG-	tangent	contingent[26]	tangente	contingente

---

[26] In Latin, the combination ENG became ING, regardless of its position in the word; hence CON + TANG- first became CONTENG-, then CONTING-. This second change (ENG → ING) occurred also in English around the time of Chaucer—*hinge* and *string* used to be *henge* and *streng*—and is the reason why *England* is pronounced as if it were spelled "Ingland" (cf. Spanish *Inglaterra*).

PART II

CLASSICAL VOCABULARY

SECTION 2.1
"Learned" Latin Words

We have seen in Section 1.2 that Spanish words of Latin origin can be divided into two general categories—"learned" or "popular"—according to the degree of restructuring they have undergone. For the native English speaker, the "learned" words should provide little difficulty, since they are, in the vast majority of cases, similar in both form and meaning to English counterparts.

"Learned" Latin *nouns* most frequently represent *abstract* concepts (e.g., *nation, division, liberty, virtue*). This should come as no surprise: *concrete* objects (e.g., *finger, knife, bird*) are by their very nature far more susceptible to popular "deformations".

In this section we will focus on nouns having the following endings:

(1) *-ción*
(2) *-sión*
(3) *-tad / -dad*
(4) *-tud*

All of these are *feminine* nouns. For the first two groups, we will also introduce related words that have the same base: nouns, adjectives, and verbs.

Numerous other "learned" Latin words will be found in Parts III and IV of the text, as well as in the annexes.

1. Words Ending in *-ción*

These correspond to English words ending in *-tion*. In the large majority of cases, there is an associated verb ending in either *-ar* or *-ir,* and very often other associated nouns, adjectives, and verbs having similar (sometimes identical) English counterparts. Thus, to *centralización* correspond:

centralización	centralization
—centralizar	—(to) centralize
—central (adj. & n.f.)	—central, headquarters, electric power station
—centro	—center, middle
—centrar	—(to) center
—centrífugo	—centrifugal
—centrípeto	—centripetal

while for *abolición:*

abolición	abolition, abolishment
—abolicionista	—abolitionist
—abolir	—(to) abolish

English *-mption* corresponds to Spanish *-nción:*

asunción	assumption	[*Asunción,* Paraguay]
consunción	consumption (illness)	
exención	exemption	
presunción	presumption	
redención	redemption	

There are more than two thousand *-ción* nouns. A sample follows:

abdicación	abdication
—abdicar	—(to) abdicate
abnegación	abnegation, self-denial, altruism
abreviación	abbreviation, shortening, *abridgement*
—abreviar	—(to) *abridge,* (to) abbreviate, (to) shorten
—abreviatura	—abbreviation (of a word)
absolución	absolution, pardon, acquittal
—absolver	—(to) absolve, (to) acquit
abstención	abstention
—abstener(se)	—(to) abstain
—abstinencia	—abstinence
—abstinente	—abstinent
abstracción	abstraction (incl. "preoccupation or absentmindedness")
—abstracto	—abstract
—abstraer	—(to) abstract, (to) become absorbed or lost in thought
aclamación	acclamation, acclaim
—aclamar	—(to) acclaim
acumulación	accumulation
—acumular	—(to) accumulate

—acumulador	—accumulator (esp. UK def. "storage battery")
adaptación	adaptation
—adaptar	—(to) adapt, (to) accommodate
—adaptable	—adaptable
adicción	addiction
—adicto (adj. & n.)	—addicted, addict, follower or supporter
—adicto al trabajo	—workaholic
adjudicación	adjudication, awarding or settling by decree
—adjudicar	—(to) adjudicate, (to) award
administración	administration, manager's office
—administrar	—(to) administer
—administrativo	—administrative
—administrador	—administrator
admiración	admiration (including "wonder")
—signo de admiración	—exclamation point (¡ . . . !)
—admirar	—(to) admire
—admirador	—admirer
—mirador	—mirador, lookout, watchtower
—mirar	—(to) look upon, (to) view
—mirada	—glance, look
—mirón	—spectator, onlooker (gen. pejorative, i.e., "nosy")
adopción	adoption
—adoptar	—(to) adopt
—adoptivo	—adoptive
adoración	adoration
—adorable	—adorable
—adorar	—(to) adore
adulación	adulation
—adular	—(to) adulate, (to) flatter
alienación	alienation (emotional, or of property)
—alienar	—(to) alienate, to dispossess (~ *enajenar*)
alteración	alteration, change

—alterar	—(to) alter, (to) disturb, (to) upset
ambición	ambition
—ambicioso	—ambitious
amplificación	amplification
—amplificar	—(to) amplify
—amplificador (adj. & n.)	—amplifying, amplifier
amputación	amputation
—amputar	—(to) amputate
anotación	annotation, note
—anotar	—(to) annotate, (to) note, (to) score (~ *marcar*)
aplicación	application (in most senses except "request", "form")
—aplicar	—(to) apply (in most senses except "to request")
—aplicado	—applied, hardworking
asimilación	assimilation
—asimilar	—(to) assimilate, (to) be similar to
asociación	association
—asociar	—(to) associate, (to) join
—asociado (adj. & n.)	—associated, associate, member (~ *socio*)
asunción	assumption, Assumption (cap.)
—asumir	—(to) assume
—asunto	—matter, subject, affair, business
—asuntos exteriores	—foreign affairs
calificación	qualification, grade (mark), rating
—cualificación	—professional qualifications (for a specific job)
—calidad	—*quality,* condition, rank
—cualidad[1]	—*quality,* property, characteristic
—calificar ~ cualificar	—(to) qualify (characterize, rate, etc.)

---

[1] *Cualidad* and *calidad* are, broadly speaking, equivalent. The former applies more to *quality* in the sense of property or intrinsic nature, the latter more to *quality* in the sense of good or bad. Thus one says: *No me gusta la **calidad** de esta tela; tiene la **cualidad** de ser muy esponjosa* ("I don't like the *quality* of this fabric; it has the *quality* of being like a sponge").

—calificado ~ cualificado	—qualified (experienced, authoritative)
—calificativo	—qualifying, expression [2]
—cualitativo	—qualitative
celebración	celebration
—celebrar	—(to) celebrate
—célebre	—celebrated, famous
—celebridad	—celebrity, fame
certificación	certification, certificate
—certificar	—(to) certify
—certificado	—certified or registered (mail), certificate
circulación	circulation, traffic
—círculo	—circle
—circular	—circular (adj.), circular (n.f.), (to) circulate
—circulatorio	—circulatory (blood), traffic (adj.)
—circuito	—circuit, excursion (returning to initial point)
—[tortuoso, indirecto]	—circuitous
clasificación	classification
—clase (f.)	—class, category
—clásico (adj. & n.)	—classical, classic
—clasificar	—(to) classify, (to) arrange
colaboración	collaboration
—colaborar	—(to) collaborate
—colaborador (adj. & n.)	—collaborating, collaborator (positive sense)
—colaboracionista	—collaborationist, collaborator (with enemy)
colección	collection
—coleccionar	—(to) collect (stamps, coins, etc.)
—coleccionista	—collector
—colecta	—collection (of money, food, etc.)
—colectividad	—collectivity, community

[2] For example: *No pudo encontrar* **calificativos** *para expresar su enfado* ("He was unable to find *the words* to express his annoyance").

—colectivo	—collective, association, bus (Amer.)
—recolección	—collection (information, money, etc.), harvest
colonización	colonization
—colonizar	—(to) colonize
—colonial	—colonial
—colono	—colonist, settler, tenant farmer
—colonia	—(eau de) cologne,[3] colony
—colonialismo	—colonialism
—colonialista	—colonialist
combinación	combination, mix, lady's slip, cocktail, compound (chem.)
—combinar	—(to) combine, (to) mix
compensación	compensation
—compensar	—(to) compensate, (to) offset
complicación	complication
—complicar	—(to) complicate
—complicado	—complicated
concentración	concentration
—concentrar	—(to) concentrate
—concéntrico	—concentric
concepción	conception (idea, fertilization)
—concepto	—concept, opinion
—concebir	—(to) *conceive* (idea, offspring)
condensación	condensation
—condensar	—(to) condense
—condensador	—condenser
—denso	—dense
—densidad	—density
confederación	confederation, confederacy
—confederar	—(to) confederate
configuración	configuration
—configurar	—(to) configure, (to) shape, (to) form
confirmación	confirmation

---

[3] The perfume *cologne* owes its name to the French form of the German city *Köln,* which in turn comes from the name of the original Latin settlement on the Rhine, *Colonia Agrippina* ("Colony of Agrippina", Agrippina being the mother of the Roman emperor Nero).

—confirmar	—(to) confirm
confiscación	confiscation
—confiscar	—(to) confiscate
—fiscal (adj. & n.)	—fiscal, public prosecutor, district attorney
—fisco	—fisc (treasury of a kingdom or state)
congregación	congregation
—congregar	—(to) congregate, (to) assemble
conjugación	conjugation
—conjugar	—(to) conjugate
—conyugal	—conjugal
—cónyuge (m./f.)	—spouse (~ *esposo, consorte*)
connotación	connotation
conservación	conservation, preservation
—conservar	—(to) conserve, (to) maintain, (to) keep
—conservante	—preservative
—conserva	—preserved (canned) food, *conserve*
—conservatorio	—conservatory
—conservador	—conservative (adj. & n.), curator (museum)
—conservadurismo	—conservatism
consideración	consideration
—considerar	—(to) consider
—considerado (p.p.)	—considerate, held in high regard
—considerable	—considerable
consolidación	consolidation
—consolidar	—(to) consolidate
construcción	construction, building
—construir	—(to) construct
—constructivo	—constructive
—constructor	—construction (adj.), builder, constructor
contaminación	contamination, pollution
—contaminar	—(to) contaminate, (to) pollute
—contaminante (adj. & n.)	—contaminating, polluting, contaminant, pollutant

contemplación	contemplation, complaisance or pampering (pl.)
—sin contemplaciones	—harshly, discourteously
—contemplar	—(to) contemplate, (to) pamper
contrarrevolución	counterrevolution
—contrarrevolucionario	—counterrevolutionary (adj. & n.)
contravención	contravention
—contravenir	—(to) contravene
conversación	conversation
—conversar	—(to) converse, (to) chat
cooperación	cooperation
—cooperar	—(to) cooperate
—cooperativo (adj.)	—cooperative
—cooperativa (n.)	—cooperative, co-op
coordinación	coordination
—coordinar	—(to) coordinate
—coordinado	—coordinated, coordinate (gram.)
—coordenadas	—coordinate (math., geog.)
corroboración	corroboration
—corroborar	—(to) corroborate
declaración	declaration, statement, testimony
—declarar	—(to) declare, (to) state, (to) testify
declinación	declination (falling off; astronomical), *declension*
—declinar	—(to) decline (diminish; refuse politely; grammar)
dedicación	dedication, inscription
—dedicar	—(to) dedicate
definición	definition
—definir	—(to) define
—definido (p.p.)	—definite
—indefinido	—indefinite
—definitivo	—definitive, conclusive
deformación	deformation
—deformar	—(to) deform, (to) distort
—deforme	—deformed, misshapen

degradación	degradation
—degradar	—(to) degrade, (to) moderate in intensity (e.g., light)
—degradante	—degrading
delegación	delegation
—delegar	—(to) delegate
—delegado (p.p.)	—delegate
desolación	desolation, ruin
—desolar	—(to) desolate, (to) devastate
—desolador	—devastating, distressing
detección	detection
—detective (< Eng.)	—detective
—detectar	—(to) detect
—detector	—detector
determinación	determination (act of deciding, firmness of purpose)
—determinar	—(to) determine, (to) decide
devoción	devotion
—devoto (adj. & n.)	—*devout,* pious, devoted, devout person
dicción	diction, enunciation, pronunciation
—diccionario	—dictionary
difamación	defamation
—difamar	—(to) defame
—difamatorio	—defamatory
discriminación	discrimination
—discriminar	—(to) discriminate
disipación	dissipation
—disipar	—(to) dissipate
distribución	distribution, layout (house or building)
—distribuir	—(to) distribute
—distribuidor	—distributing, distributor (person [m./f.], car [m.])
—distribuidora	—distributor (commercial, e.g., movies)
documentación	documentation
—documentar	—(to) document
—documento	—document
—documental (adj. & n.)	—documentary

donación	donation (act)
—donar	—(to) donate, (to) bestow
—donativo	—donation (what is given), donative
—don	—gift, talent
ebullición	ebullition, boiling
—bullir	—(to) *boil,* (to) bubble
edificación	building (act), edifice, edification
—edificar	—(to) build (building or company), (to) *edify* (moral)
—edificante	—edifying (serving as a good example)
—edificio	—building, edifice
educación	education, training, breeding (manners)
—educar	—(to) educate, (to) train
—educativo	—educational, educative
elevación	elevation
—elevar	—(to) raise, (to) elevate
—elevador	elevator (~ *ascensor*), hoist, lift
eliminación	elimination
—eliminar	—(to) eliminate
—eliminatorio	—qualifying or preliminary (e.g., sports competition)
emigración	emigration
—emigrar	—(to) emigrate
—emigrante (adj. & n.)	—emigrant
erudición	erudition
—erudito (adj. & n.)	—erudite, learned person
evacuación	evacuation
—evacuar	—(to) evacuate (incl. "to defecate")
evaporación	evaporation
—evaporar	—(to) evaporate (incl. "to vanish")
—vapor	—vapor, steam, steamboat
—al vapor	—steamed (vegetables, etc.)
—vaporizar	—(to) vaporize, (to) evaporate
evocación	evocation
—evocar	—(to) evoke, (to) recall

—evocador	—evocative
evolución	evolution
—evolucionar	—(to) evolve
—evolutivo	—evolutionary
exasperación	exasperation
—exasperar	—(to) exasperate
excepción	exception
—excepcional	—exceptional
—excepto	—except, excepting
—exceptuar	—(to) except
exclamación	exclamation
—exclamar	—(to) exclaim
exención	exemption
—exento	—exempt, isolated (building, pillar) (old p.p.) [4]
—eximir	—(to) *exempt* († *eximious*)
exhibición	exhibition
—exhibir	—(to) exhibit
—exhibicionista	—exhibitionist
exhortación	exhortation
—exhortar	—(to) exhort
exhumación	exhumation, disinterment
—exhumar	—(to) exhume, (to) disinter
expectación	expectation (act of expecting, eager anticipation)
—expectativa	—expectation, hope
explicación	explication, explanation
—explicar	—(to) explicate, (to) explain
—explícito	—explicit
—inexplicable	—inexplicable, unexplainable
exploración	exploration
—explorar	—(to) explore
—explorador (adj. & n.)	—exploring, explorer
—exploratorio	—exploratory
exportación	exportation, export
—exportar	—(to) export
—exportador (adj. & n.)	—exporting, exporter
exterminación	extermination (~ *exterminio*)

[4] A number of "irregular" Spanish past participles have been replaced by "regular" ones, with the "old" form remaining as a separate adjective. See Brodsky (2005, 112–113).

—exterminar	—(to) exterminate
—exterminio	—extermination
extradición	extradition
—extraditar	—(to) extradite
federación	federation
—federar	—(to) federate
—federal	—federal
felicitación	felicitation, congratulation, congratulations (pl.)
—felicitar	—(to) congratulate, (to) felicitate
fermentación	fermentation
—fermentar	—(to) ferment
—fermento	—ferment
ficción	fiction
—ficticio	—fictitious
fluctuación	fluctuation
—fluctuar	—(to) fluctuate
formación	formation, education, training
—formar	—(to) form, (to) educate, (to) train
—forma	—form (shape, manner, method, etc.)
fortificación	fortification
—fortificar	—(to) fortify
frustración	frustration, disappointment
—frustrar	—(to) frustrate, (to) disappoint
función	function, performance (cinema, circus, etc.)
—funcionar	—(to) function
—funcional	—functional
—funcionario	—functionary, public official, civil servant
generación	generation
—generar	—(to) generate
—generador (adj. & n.)	—generating, (electric) generator
germinación	germination
—germinar	—(to) germinate
—germen	—germ
—germen de trigo	—wheat germ
humillación	humiliation

—humillante	—humiliating, *humbling*
—humilde	—*humble,* modest
—humildad	—humility
—humillar	—(to) *humiliate,* (to) *humble*
identificación	identification
—identificar	—(to) identify
—identidad	—identity
—idéntico	—identical
—ídem	—idem, the same, ditto
ignición	ignition
iluminación	illumination
—iluminar	—(to) illuminate, (to) enlighten
imaginación	imagination
—imagen (f.)	—image
—imaginar	—(to) imagine
—imaginable	—imaginable
—inimaginable	—unimaginable
—imaginario	—imaginary
—imaginativo	—imaginative
imperfección	imperfection
—imperfecto	—imperfect
implicación	implication
—implicar	—(to) *imply,* (to) involve, (to) *implicate*
—implícito	—implicit, implied
importación	importation, import
—importar (1)	—(to) import (merchandise)
—importar (2)	—important (be important), (to) be worth (an amount)
—no (me) importa	—it doesn't matter (to me)
—importador (adj. & n.)	—importing, importer
—importe	—cost, price, value
improvisación	improvisation (musical or otherwise)
—improvisar	—(to) improvise
—de improviso	—unexpectedly, suddenly
imputación	imputation, accusation
—imputar	—(to) impute (charge with fault)

incitación	incitation, incitement
—incitar	—(to) incite
inclinación	inclination, bow, curtsy
—inclinar	—(to) incline (incl. "to influence")
incubación	incubation
—incubar	—(to) incubate
—incubadora	—incubator
indignación	indignation
—indignar	—(to) make indignant, (to) anger
—indigno	—unworthy [† *indign*]
industrialización	industrialization
—industrializar	—(to) industrialize
—industrial	—industrial
—industria	—industry
infección	infection
—infectar	—(to) infect
—infeccioso	—infectious
infestación	infestation
—infestar	—(to) infest, (to) overrun
inflación	inflation
—inflar	—(to) inflate
—inflacionario	—inflationary (~ *inflacionista*)
—deflación (< Eng.)	—deflation (economic)
—desinflar	—(to) deflate
inhibición	inhibition
—inhibir	—(to) inhibit, (to) abstain from
iniciación	initiation, start
—iniciar	—(to) initiate, (to) begin
—inicial	—initial
—iniciativa	—initiative
—inicio	—beginning, start
—iniciático	—initiating (pert. to *initiation* ceremony or ritual)
inspección	inspection
—inspeccionar	—(to) inspect
—inspector	—inspector
instalación	installation
—instalar	—(to) install

instigación	instigation, incitement
—instigar	—(to) instigate, (to) incite
—instigador	—instigator
instrucción	instruction, education
—instruir	—(to) instruct, (to) educate
—instructivo	—instructive
—instructor	—instructor
insurrección	insurrection
—insurrecto (adj. & n.)	—*insurgent,* rebel
—insurgente (adj. & n.)	—insurgent
integración	integration
—integrar	—(to) integrate
—integral (adj. & n.f.)	—integral
—íntegro	—whole, *entire,* upright
interpretación	interpretation
—interpretar	—(to) interpret
—intérprete (m./f.)	—interpreter (languages, actor, musician)
interrogación	interrogation (one question), question mark (~ *interrogante*)
—interrogar	—(to) interrogate, (to) question
—interrogante	—questioning, unresolved issue (m./f.), question mark (m.)
—interrogatorio	—interrogation (series of questions)
interrupción	interruption
—interrumpir	—(to) interrupt
—interruptor	—electric switch, light switch, circuit breaker
intervención	intervention, surgical operation
—intervenir	—(to) intervene (in), (to) operate on (medical)
—interventor	—auditor, controller, monitor (elections)
intimidación	intimidation
—intimidar	—(to) intimidate
introducción	introduction
—introducir	—(to) introduce
—introductorio	—introductory
intuición	intuition
—intuitivo	—intuitive

—intuir	—(to) grasp intuitively, (to) intuit
inundación	inundation, flood, flooding
—inundar	—(to) inundate, (to) flood
investigación	investigation, inquiry, research
—investigar	—(to) investigate, (to) inquire into, (to) research
—investigador (adj. & n.)	—investigating, investigative, investigator
—vestigio	—vestige, trace, sign
invitación	invitation
—invitar	—(to) invite
—invitado (adj. & n.)	—invited (person), guest
invocación	invocation
—invocar	—(to) invoke
irritación	irritation
—irritar	—(to) irritate
—irritable	—irritable
—irritante	—irritant
lamentación	lamentation
—lamentar	—(to) lament
—lamentable	—lamentable
—lamento	—lament
liquidación	liquidation, clearance sale, settlement (debt, account)
—liquidar	—(to) liquidate (debt, business, person)
—liquidador	—liquidator
—líquido (adj. & n.)	—liquid, liquid cash or (commercial) balance
—liquidez	—liquidity (generally financial), liquidness
—licuar	—(to) liquefy, (to) liquate (metals)
—licor	—liquor, liqueur
loción	lotion
medicación	medication, treatment
—médico	—doctor, physician
—medicamento	—medicament, medicine, drug
—medicina	—medicine (medication, branch of science)

—medicinal	—medicinal
meditación	meditation
—meditar	—(to) meditate, (to) ponder
memorización	memorization
—memorizar	—(to) memorize
—memoria	—memory, report
—memorias (pl.)	—memoirs
—memorable	—memorable
—memorial	—memorial (incl. "petition"), memorandum book
—memorándum	—memorandum, memo
migración	migration
—migrar	—(to) migrate
—migratorio	—migratory
mitigación	mitigation, alleviation, soothing
—mitigar	—(to) mitigate, (to) alleviate, (to) soothe
moción	motion (supporting a nomination, of censure, etc.)
—[movimiento]	—motion (physical), movement
modernización	modernization
—modernizar	—(to) modernize
—moderno	—modern
—modernidad	—modernity
—modernismo	—modernism
modificación	modification
—modificar	—(to) modify
munición	munition, ammunition (freq. pl.)
nación	nation
—nacional	—national
—internacional	—international
—nacionalismo	—nationalism
—nacionalista	—nationalist
—nacionalizar	—(to) nationalize, (to) naturalize (grant citizenship)
narración	narration, narrative
—narrar	—(to) narrate
—narrador	—narrator
—narrativo (adj.)	—narrative

—narrativa (n.)	—narrative (literary genre incl. novel and short story)
noción	notion, idea
nominación	nomination, naming (to a position)
—nominar	—(to) nominate (gen. for a prize or honor)
—nominal	—nominal
normalización	normalization
—normalizar	—(to) normalize, (to) become normal
—normal	—normal
—norma	—norm, rule
nutrición	nutrition
—nutrir	—(to) *nourish,* (to) *nurture*
—nutritivo	—nutritive, nutritious, nourishing
observación	observation
—observar	—(to) observe
—observador (adj. & n.)	—observant, observer
—observatorio	—observatory
obstinación	obstinacy
—obstinar(se)	—(to) be obstinate or persist (in)
—obstinado (p.p.)	—obstinate
obstrucción	obstruction
—obstruir	—(to) obstruct
opción	option
—opcional	—optional
—optar	—(to) opt, (to) choose, (to) aspire to (a position)
palpitación	palpitation, throbbing
—palpitar	—(to) palpitate, (to) throb
—palpitante	—palpitating, throbbing, burning (e.g., question)
—palpar	—(to) touch, (to) feel, (to) *palpate*
—palpable	—palpable, evident
participación	participation
—participar	—(to) participate, (to) partake (in or of), (to) notify

—participante (adj. & n.)	—participating, participant
—partícipe	—participant (~ *participante*)
—participio	—participle
penetración	penetration
—penetrar	—(to) penetrate
—penetrante	—penetrating
—impenetrable	—impenetrable
percepción	perception, receiving (of money, rent, etc.)
—percibir	—(to) *perceive*, (to) receive (salary, pension, etc.)
—perceptible	—perceptible
—imperceptible	—imperceptible
perfección	perfection
—perfecto	—perfect
—perfeccionar	—(to) perfect
—perfeccionista	—perfectionist
perforación	perforation, drilling, boring
—perforar	—(to) drill, (to) bore, (to) perforate
perpetuación	perpetuation
—perpetuo	—perpetual
—perpetuar	—(to) perpetuate
—perpetuidad	—perpetuity
perturbación	perturbation, disturbance
—perturbar	—(to) perturb, (to) disturb
—perturbado (adj. & n.)	—perturbed, disturbed (~ *loco*)
petición	petition, (formal) request
poción	potion
predilección	predilection, preference
—predilecto	—favorite, preferred
preparación	preparation (making ready)
—preparativo (adj. & n.)	—preparatory, preparation (something prepared— gen. pl.)
—preparar	—(to) prepare, (to) make ready
preservación	preservation
—preservar	—(to) preserve (protect)
—preservativo	—preservative (adj.), condom
prestidigitación	prestidigitation (sleight of hand, magic)

presunción	presumption
—presumir	—(to) presume or surmise, (to) be vain or conceited
—presumido (p.p.)	—conceited, vain
—presunto (old p.p.)	—presumed, presumptive
—presuntuoso	—presumptuous, pretentious
privación	privation, deprivation
—privar	—(to) *deprive*
—privado (p.p.)	—private, favorite of the king (m.)
proclamación	proclamation
—proclamar	—(to) proclaim
—proclama	—proclamation, public notice (e.g., marriage banns)
producción	production
—producir	—(to) produce
—producto	—product (also mathematical), result
—productor (adj. & n.)	—producing, producer
—productivo	—productive
—productividad	—productivity
—contraproducente	—counterproductive
prohibición	prohibition
—prohibir	—(to) prohibit
—prohibitivo	—prohibitive
prolongación	prolongation, extension
—prolongar	—(to) extend, (to) prolong
promulgación	promulgation (official publication of law or decree)
—promulgar	—(to) promulgate
propagación	propagation
—propagar	—(to) propagate, (to) spread
—propaganda	—advertising, propaganda
proscripción	proscription, exile
—proscribir	—(to) proscribe, (to) banish, (to) exile
—proscrito	—exile, outlaw, proscribed person (old p.p.)
provocación	provocation
—provocar	—(to) provoke, (to) incite

—provocador (adj. & n.)	—provoking, provocative, provoker
—agente provocador	—(agent) provocateur
—provocativo	—provocative
recepción	reception (delivery, hotel lobby, ceremony with guests)
—recepcionista	—receptionist
—receptivo	—receptive
—receptor (adj. & n.)	—receiving, receiver, recipient (transplant, message)
—recibir	—(to) *receive*
—recibo	—*receipt*
—recipiente	—container, *recept*acle [*recipient*]
recitación	recitation, public reading (poetry)
—recital	—recital
—recitar	—(to) recite
reconstrucción	reconstruction
—reconstruir	—(to) reconstruct
rectificación	rectification (correction, conversion of AC to DC)
—rectificar	—(to) rectify (correct, convert AC to DC)
rede**nc**ión	rede**mpt**ion
—redimir	—(to) *redeem* (self, property), (to) *ransom*
—redentor (adj. & n.)	—redeeming, redeemer, Savior (cap.)
reducción	reduction
—reducir	—(to) reduce
refutación	refutation
—refutar	—(to) refute
reiteración	reiteration
—reiterar	—(to) reiterate
—iteración	—iteracion
—iterativo	—iterative
remuneración	remuneration
—remunerar	—(to) remunerate
reparación	repair, reparation
—reparar	—(to) repair, (to) notice

—reparo	—repair, objection, qualm
repetición	repetition
—repetir	—(to) repeat, (to) reiterate
—repetitivo	—repetitive
reproducción	reproduction, imitation or copy
—reproducir	—(to) reproduce
reputación	reputation
—reputar	—(to) esteem, (to) repute
revocación	revocation, annulation
—revocar	—(to) revoke, (to) plaster or paint (exterior wall)
satisfacción	satisfaction
—satisfacer	—(to) *satisfy*
—satisfecho	—satisfied
—satisfactorio	—satisfactory
saturación	saturation
—saturar	—(to) saturate, (to) fill up
sección	section, cross-section
—sector	—sector, area
—intersección	—intersection
—segmento	—segment
sedición	sedition
segregación	segregation, secretion
—segregar	—(to) segregate, (to) separate, (to) secrete
selección	selection
—seleccionar	—(to) select
—selectivo	—selective
—selectividad	—selectivity
—selecto	—select, exclusive (old p.p.)
sensación	sensation
—sensacional	—sensational
separación	separation
—separar	—(to) separate, (to) move apart, (to) *sever*[5]

---

[5] The confusion in the spelling of *separate* (versus *seperate*) goes back to Classical Latin days. The plebs preferred *seperate*, and it was this form that gave rise to French *sevrer* and thence to English *sever*. *Separate* is a "learned" English word formed directly from the original ("correct") Latin past participle. Similarly, *separable* and *several* are etymologically the same word.

—separado	—separate, separated
—separable	—separable
—inseparable	—inseparable
simulación	simulation
—simular	—(to) simulate
sublimación	sublimation, exaltation
—sublimar	—(to) sublimate, (to) exalt
—sublime	—sublime
—subliminal	—subliminal
tradición	tradition
—tradicional	—traditional
transcripción	transcription
—transcribir	—(to) transcribe
transformación[6]	transformation
—transformar	—(to) transform
—transformador	—transforming, (electrical) transformer (m.)
transición	transition
—tránsito	—transit, traffic, stopover
—transitorio	—transitory
—transitar	—(to) walk (along public streets), (to) transit
—transitivo	—transitive
—intransitivo	—intransitive
unificación	unification
—unificar	—(to) unify
—unión	—union
—unir	—(to) unite, (to) join
—desunión	—disunion, discord
usurpación	usurpation
—usurpar	—(to) usurp
utilización	utilization, use
—utilizar	—(to) utilize, (to) use
—utilitario (adj. & n.)	—practical, small (economy class) car
—utilidad	—utility, usefulness, profit
—útil (adj. & n.)	—*useful, utile,* tool

---

[6] These words (and those in the succeeding group) can also be spelled with an initial *tras-*, although the *trans-* forms (preferred by the RAE) are by far the more common.

vacilación	vacillation, hesitation, unsteadiness
—vacilar	—(to) vacillate
vegetación	vegetation, (enlargement of) adenoids (pl.)
—vegetal (adj. & n.)	—vegetal, vegetable (adj.), plant
—vegetar	—(to) vegetate
—vegetariano (adj. & n.)	—vegetarian
veneración	veneration
—venerar	—(to) venerate
—venerable	—venerable
vibración	vibration
—vibrar	—(to) vibrate, (to) quiver
—vibrador (adj. & n.)	—vibrating, vibrator
vocación	vocation
—vocacional	—vocational
votación	voting, balloting
—votar	—(to) vote
—voto	—vote, *vow*

Two subgroups bear special mention—those corresponding to English -*jection* and to (other words ending in) -*ction*.

(a) For English words ending in -*jection,* there are three possible endings in Spanish: -*jección, -jeción,* or -*yección*

interjección	interjection
objeción	objection
sujeción	subjection

abyección	abjection, abjectness	
deyección	droppings (excrement), defecation	[*dejection*[7]]
eyección	ejection	
inyección	injection	
proyección	projection	

Related words—verbs, nouns, and adjectives—maintain the -*j* or -*y* and follow a very specific pattern with regard to the interior consonant combination: for

[7] One of the definitions of English *dejection* is "Evacuation of the intestinal tract; defecation".

those ending in -*cción,* it is -*ct,* while for those having "reduced" endings in -*ción,* it is simply -*t:*

interjectivo (rare)	interjectional (pertaining to interjections)

objetar	(to) object	
—objeto	—object	
—objetivo	—objective	
—objetividad	—objectivity	
sujetar	(to) subject, (to) grasp, (to) hold	
—sujeto	—(securely) attached, subject (adj. & n.)	(old p.p.)
—sujetador	—brassiere (~ *sostén*)	
—subjetivo	—subjective	
—subjetividad	—subjectivity	

abyecto	abject
eyectar	(to) eject
—eyector	—ejector (firearm; pump using jet of water, air, or steam)
inyectar	(to) inject
—inyector	—injector
—inyectable	—injectable
proyectar	(to) project, (to) cast, (to) plan
—proyecto	—project, plan
—proyector	—projector, spotlight
—proyectil	—projectile

Also:

trayecto	course, route, distance, journey
—trayectoria	—trajectory

(b) Other English words ending in -*ction* correspond to Spanish words ending in -*cción:*

acción	action, share (stock market)
confección	confection, dressmaking, tailoring
constricción	constriction
corrección	correction, correctness
destrucción	destruction
elección	election, choice
fricción	friction, rubbing
inducción	induction, inducement
predicción	prediction

protección	protection
succión	suction
transacción	transaction, compromise

2. Words Ending in *-sión*

These correspond to English words ending in *-sion* or *-ssion*. In the large majority of cases, there is an associated verb—generally ending in *-ar* or *-ir*—and often additional related "classical" forms having similar (sometimes identical) English counterparts. Thus, to English *depression* correspond:

depresión	depression (physical, mental, economic)
—depresivo	—depressive
—deprimir[8]	—(to) *depress*
—deprimente	—depressing

In a number of cases, as noted in Section 1.3, the corresponding verb has a stem consonant of *-d* or *-t* rather than *-s;* for example,

transgresión	transgression
—transgre**d**ir	—(to) transgress
—transgresor	—transgressor
dimi**s**ión	demission, resignation
	(of an office)
—dimitir	—(to) resign, (to) *demit*

There are approximately 250 Spanish *-sión* nouns, including:

adhesión	adhesion
—adhesivo	—adhesive
—adherir	—(to) adhere (to a surface or a belief)
—adherente (adj.)	—adherent (sticking or holding fast)
—adherencia	—adhesiveness, adherence
admisión	admission, acceptance
—admitir	—(to) admit, (to) accept (entry)

---

[8] Spanish *-primir* corresponds to English *-press* (*deprimir* comes from Latin DEPRIMERE, whose past participle DEPRESSUS gave rise, via French, to English *depress*).

—admisible	—admissible
—inadmisible	—inadmissible
circuncisión	circumcision
—circuncidar	—(to) circumcise
cohesión	cohesion
—coherencia	—coherence, consistency
—coherente	—coherent (orderly, logical), consistent
—incoherente	—incoherent (lacking cohesion), inconsistent
comisión	commission (act of doing, fee, committee)
—comisionar	—(to) commission, (to) delegate
—comisario	—commissioner (e.g., of police), commissary (deputy)
—comisaría	—police station, commissioner's office
compasión	compassion
—compasivo	—compassionate
compresión	compression
—comprimir	—(to) *compress*
compulsión	compulsion
—compulsivo	—compulsive
—compulsa	—certified copy (legal)
—compulsar	—(to) certify a copy of a document
—compeler	—(to) *compel,* (to) force
concesión	concession, grant
—conceder	—(to) concede, (to) grant
concusión	concussion
confesión	confession
—confesar	—(to) confess
—confeso	—confessed, self-confessed, (old p.p.) converted (Jew)
—confesor	—confessor (priest who hears confession)
—confesionario, confesonario	—confessional box
contusión	contusion, bruise
conversión	conversion, transformation

—convertir	—(to) convert, (to) transform	
—converso	—converted (to Christianity, esp. Jew or Muslim), convert	
convulsión	convulsion	
—convulsivo	—convulsive	
difusión	diffusion, transmission	
—difundir	—(to) diffuse, (to) spread, (to) broadcast	
—difuso	—diffuse, vague	(old p.p.)
digresión	digression	
discusión	discussion, argument	
—discutir	—(to) discuss, (to) argue	
—discutible	—debatable, arguable	
dispersión	dispersion, scattering	
—dispersar	—(to) disperse, (to) scatter, (to) rout (mil.)	
—disperso	—dispersed, scattered	(old p.p.)
disuasión	dissuasion	
—disuadir	—(to) dissuade	
—disuasivo	—dissuasive	
diversión	diversion, amusement	
—divertir	—(to) divert, (to) amuse	
—divertido (p.p.)	—diverting, amusing, fun	
—ser divertido	—(to) be funny	
—estar divertido	—(to) be amused	
—diverso	—diverse, different, various	(old p.p.)
—diversidad	—diversity	
—diversificación	—diversification	
—diversificar	—(to) diversify	
efusión	effusion (outpouring of liquid or feeling)	
—efusivo	—effusive	
emisión	emission, broadcast	
—emitir	—(to) emit, (to) broadcast	
erosión	erosion	
—erosionar	—(to) erode	
exclusión	exclusion	
—excluir	—(to) exclude	
—exclusivo (adj.)	—exclusive	
—exclusiva (n.)	—exclusive (news story, right)	

—exclusive (adv.)	—not including, exclusive of
—hasta el capítulo doce exclusive	—up to but not including chapter 12
excursión	excursion, trip, tour
expansión	expansion, relaxation
—expandir	—(to) expand, (to) extend
—expansivo	—expansive
explosión	explosion
—explosionar	—(to) explode
—explosivo	—explosive (adj. & n.m.), (ex)plosive (*n.f.*)
—explotar (1)	—(to) explode
—explotar (2) [9]	—(to) *exploit*
—explotación	—*exploitation* (of a mine, of a person)
expresión	expression
—expresar	—(to) express
—expresivo	—expressive
—inexpresivo	—inexpressive
—expreso (adj. & n.)	—expressed, express, special, express (train) (old p.p.)
—exprimir	—(to) squeeze, (to) wring out, (to) *express* (juice)
expulsión	expulsion
—expulsar	—(to) *expel,* (to) eject
extensión	extension, expanse, spreading (e.g., fire)
—extender	—(to) extend, (to) write out or draw up (check, deed, etc.)
—extenso	—extensive, vast (old p.p.)
—extensible	—extensible, extendible
fisión	fission
—fisura	—fissure
fusión	fusion, melting, merger
—fusionar	—(to) fuse, (to) merge
impresión	impression, printing
—impresionante	—impressive
—impresionar	—(to) impress

[9] *Explotar* (2) comes from French *exploiter* (source of English *exploit*) and has nothing to do with *explosión.*

—impresionismo	—impressionism	
—impresionista	—impressionist	
—imprimir	—(to) *print,* (to) *imprint*	
—impreso (adj. & n.)	—printed, booklet, printed matter	(old p.p.)
—impresor	—printer (person)	
—impresora	—printer (machine)	
—imprénta	—printing, print shop	[*imprint*]
—pren**sa**	—*press* (vise, hydraulic, printing); "the press"	
—pren**sar**	—(to) *compress,* (to) squeeze	
impulsión	impulsion, impulse, drive	
—impulso	—impulse, impetus, momentum	
—impulsar	—(to) *impel,* (to) drive, (to) prompt	
—impulsivo	—impulsive	
incisión	incision	
—incisivo (adj. & n.)	—incisive, sharp, incisor (tooth)	
inclusión	inclusion	
—incluir	—(to) include	
—incluso	—including, even	(old p.p.)
—incluso los franceses	—even the French	
—inclusa	—foundling home	
—inclusivo (adj.)	—inclusive	
—inclusive (adv.)	—inclusive, including	
—hasta el 7 de marzo inclusive	—up to and including the seventh of March	
incursión	incursion	
—incurrir	—(to) *incur,* (to) commit (fault, crime)	
infusión	infusion	
—infundir	—(to) infuse	
intrusión	intrusion	
—intruso (adj. & n.)	—intrusive, intruder, unauthorized practitioner	(old p.p.)
inversión	inversion, investment	
—invertir	—(to) invert, (to) invest	
—inverso	—inverse, inverted, opposite	(old p.p.)

—inversionista ~ inversor	—investor
mansión	mansion
omisión	omission
—omitir	—(to) omit
—omiso	—careless, re*miss*
opresión	oppression
—opresivo	—oppressive
—opresor (adj. & n.)	—oppressing, oppressor
—oprimir	—(to) *oppress,* (to) press (button), (to) pinch (clothes)
pasión	passion
—pasional	—passionate (e.g., crime), passional
—apasionar	—(to) impassion, (to) appeal deeply to
—apasionado	—impassioned, passionate
—apasionante	—captivating, gripping, exciting
pensión	pension (payment, boarding-house, room and board)
—pensionista	—boarder, pensioner (recipient of pension)
—**pie**nso	—feed (*pensión* for livestock)
persuasión	persuasion
—persuadir	—(to) persuade
—persuasivo	—persuasive
perversión	perversion
—pervertir	—(to) pervert
—perversidad	—perversity
—perverso	—perverse, wicked, perverted
precisión	precision, necessity
—preciso	—precise, necessary
—imprecisión	—imprecision
—impreciso	—imprecise
—precisar	—(to) express precisely, (to) require
presión	pressure
—presionar	—(to) press, (to) exert pressure on
profesión	profession
—profesional	—professional

—profesar	—(to) profess (incl. "practice a profession", "teach")
—profesor	—professor, teacher
progresión	progression
—progresar	—(to) progress
—progreso	—progress
—progresivo	—progressive (that which progresses)
—progresista (adj. & n.)	—progressive (point of view, e.g., political party)
propulsión	propulsion
—propulsar	—(to) *propel,* (to) *push* forward
provisión	provision, supply
—provisional	—provisional
repercusión	repercussion, impact
—repercutir	—(to) affect, (to) reverberate
represión	repression
—represivo	—repressive
—reprimir	—(to) *repress,* (to) restrain
—reprim**e**nda	—reprimand
repulsión	repulsion, repugnance
—repulsa	—repulse (rejection, refusal)
—repulsivo	—repulsive, *repellent*
—repeler	—(to) repel, (to) *repulse*
—repelente	—repellent (adj. & n.), repulsive
subversión	subversion
—subvertir	—(to) subvert
—subversivo	—subversive
supresión	suppression
—suprimir	—(to) *suppress,* (to) abolish, (to) leave out
suspensión	suspension
—suspender	—(to) suspend, (to) hang, (to) fail (an exam)
—suspenso (adj. & n.)	—suspended, perplexed, failing mark (old p.p.)
—en suspenso	—in suspense, pending
—suspense (< Eng.)	—suspense
tensión	tension (incl. electric), stress, blood pressure

—tensar	—(to) tense, (to) tighten
—tenso	—tense, tight, taut
transfusión	transfusion
—transfu**nd**ir	—(to) transfuse
transmisión	transmission
—transmitir	—(to) transmit
—transmisible	—transmissible
—transmisor	—transmitting, transmitter (radio, TV—*m.*)
versión	version (incl. "translation")

English *-tortion* corresponds to Spanish *-torsión,* as in:

contorsión	contortion
—contorsionista	—contortionist
—contorsionar(se)	—(to) contort
distorsión	distortion
—distorsionar	—(to) distort
extorsión	extortion
—extorsionar	—(to) extort
torsión	torsion, twisting

3. Words Ending in -dad and -tad

These generally correspond to English nouns ending in *-ty.* The overwhelming majority—more than one thousand—end in *-dad,* and fewer than twenty end in *-tad.* Apart from *mitad,* the *-tad* ending *always* follows a consonant, while the *-dad* ending can follow either a consonant or a vowel:

consonant + -*tad*	libertad	liberty
vowel + -*dad*	fraternidad	fraternity
consonant + -*dad*	crueldad	cruelty

(a) Words Ending in -tad

This is the list of *all* of the *-tad* words in common use:

amistad	*amity,* friendship
deslealtad	*disloyalty*
dificultad	*difficulty*
enemistad	*enmity,* hostility

facultad	*faculty* (capacity, division of a university)	
lealtad	*loyalty*	
libertad	*liberty*	
majestad	*majesty*	
mitad	half, middle, *moiety*[10]	
potestad	*power,* jurisdiction	[rare *potestas*]
pubertad	*puberty*	
tempestad	*tempest,* storm	
voluntad	will, disposition	[† *volunty*]

(b) Words Ending in -dad

The following is a sampling of words ending in -*dad:*

actividad	activity	
adversidad	adversity	
agilidad	agility	
amabilidad	amiability, kindness, niceness	
ancianidad	old age	[*ancient,* † *ancienty*]
animosidad	animosity	
anormalidad	abnormality	
ansiedad	anxiety	
antigüedad	antiquity, seniority, antique (gen. pl.)	
autenticidad	authenticity	
banalidad	banality	
bondad	goodness, kindness	
brevedad	brevity	
brutalidad	brutality	
calamidad	calamity	
capacidad	capacity, ability	
caridad	charity	
cavidad	cavity (non-dental)	
celebridad	celebrity, fame	
complicidad	complicity	
constitucionalidad	constitutionality	

---

[10] Now rare in the primary meaning of "a half", "a part", "a portion", English *moiety* has found renewed life in anthropology as "Either of two kinship groups based on unilateral descent that together make up a tribe or society".

credibilidad	credibility
crueldad	cruelty
debilidad	debility, weakness
dignidad	dignity, rank
discontinuidad	discontinuity
disparidad	disparity
divinidad	divinity
electricidad	electricity
entidad	entity
extremidad	extremity, limb
fraternidad	fraternity
generalidad	generality (incl. "the majority")
generosidad	generosity
hostilidad	hostility
humanidad	humanity, mankind, humaneness, humanities (pl.)
humedad	humidity, moisture, dampness
imposibilidad	impossibility
inferioridad	inferiority
infinidad	infinity
ingenuidad	ingenuousness, naiveté
integridad	integrity
legalidad	legality
maldad	wickedness, *maliciousness*
maternidad	maternity, motherhood
mediocridad	mediocrity
monstruosidad	monstrosity
moralidad	morality
nacionalidad	nationality
necesidad	necessity
oscuridad /obs-	darkness, obscurity
parcialidad	partiality
paridad	parity
paternidad	paternity, fatherhood
personalidad	personality
pluralidad	plurality, diversity
popularidad	popularity
posibilidad	possibility
posteridad	posterity
prioridad	priority

probabilidad	probability
profundidad	depth, profundity
publicidad	publicity, advertising
puntualidad	punctuality
radiactividad	radioactivity
realidad	reality
regularidad	regularity
relatividad	relativity
religiosidad	religiosity, religiousness
responsabilidad	responsibility
senilidad	senility
serenidad	serenity
sexualidad	sexuality
simplicidad	simplicity
sociedad	society
solemnidad	solemnity
solidaridad	solidarity
superioridad	superiority
tonalidad	tonality
tranquilidad	tranquillity
trinidad	trinity
trivialidad	triviality
unidad	unity
uniformidad	uniformity
universalidad	universality
universidad	university
vaguedad	vagueness, imprecision
vanidad	vanity, conceit
verdad	truth, *verity*
viabilidad	viability, feasibility
visibilidad	visibility
volatilidad	volatility

4. Words Ending in *-tud*

These frequently correspond to English words ending in *-tude*. The most commonly used words are probably:

acritud	acridity, acrimony	[† *acritude*]
actitud	attitude, posture	

amplitud	amplitude, breadth, spaciousness	
aptitud	aptitude	
beatitud	beatitude, blessedness	
decrepitud	decrepitude	
disimilitud	dissimilitude, dissimilarity	
exactitud	exactitude, precision, accuracy	
gratitud	gratitude	
inexactitud	inexactitude, inexactness, inaccuracy	
ingratitud	ingratitude, ungratefulness	
inquietud	inquietude, worry, restlessness	
juventud	youth	[*juvenile*]
lasitud	lassitude, weariness	
latitud	latitude	
laxitud	laxity, laxness	
lentitud	slowness	[*lento*[11]]
longitud	length, longitude	
magnitud	magnitude	
multitud	multitude	
plenitud	plenitude, fullness	
pulcritud	neatness, tidiness, cleanliness	[*pulchritude*]
quietud	quietude, stillness, tranquillity	
rectitud	rectitude, honesty, straightness	
senectud	senectitude (old age)	
similitud	similitude, similarity (~ *semejanza*)	
solicitud	request, application (form), *solicitude*	
vicisitud	vicissitude	
virtud	virtue, quality, capacity	

A relatively small number of Spanish words that "should" end in -*tud* instead end in -*dumbre,* e.g., *certidumbre,* corresponding to English *certitude* (see Section 3.5, no. 12).

---

[11] *Lento* means "slow" in *both* Spanish and English, though in English it is restricted to a musical sense (cf. also English *lentamente* and *lentissimo*).

SECTION 2.2
"Learned" Greek Words

Classical Latin had a large repertoire of words taken from Greek. This base was added to substantially in the early Christian era and again during the Renaissance. Some Greek words passed to Spanish directly, most via Latin. Almost without exception, if an English word is recognizably "Greek", it has an equally recognizable counterpart in Spanish with identical (or at least very similar) meaning.

The passage from Greek to Spanish was anything but *chaotic* (*caótico*). The principal non*catastrophic orthographical metamorphoses,* at least *metaphorically* (*metafóricamente*), of the *Hellenic lexicon* (*léxico helénico*) were:

(a) Y became Spanish *i*
(b) PH, CH, RH, TH became Spanish *f, c, r, t*
(c) MPH became Spanish *nf*
(d) S + consonant became Spanish *es* + consonant (see Section 3.1)

Y → *i*[1]

ABYSS(M)US	abismo	abysm, abyss
	abismal	abysmal (unfathomable, enormous)
CRYSTALLUS	cristal	crystal, glass, windowpane
	cristalizar	(to) crystallize
	cristalización	crystallization
	cristalino	crystalline, transparent
CYCLUS	ciclo	cycle
	cíclico	cyclical
	ciclismo	cycling
	ciclista	cyclist

---

[1] Latin Y corresponds to Greek *u*, whose pronunciation over time changed from [u] to [y]—essentially a "rounded" *i*, as in French *u* or German *ü*—to [i]. It is with this last value that "classical" Greek words are generally pronounced in Spanish and the other Romance languages and in English, while German has preserved the [y] pronunciation. Some Spanish words have maintained the "original" *u* (e.g., *tufo* vs. *tifus* in Annex D); also English *cumin* and *cube* (Spanish *comino* and *cubo*).

	ciclón	cyclone
	reciclar	(to) recycle, (to) retrain
	reciclaje	recycling, retraining
CYLINDRUS	cilindro	cylinder
	cilíndrico	cylindrical
CYNICUS	cínico (adj. & n.)	cynical, cynic
	cinismo	cynicism
DYNASTIA	dinastía	dynasty
ETYMOLOGIA	etimología	etymology
GYRARE	girar	(to) gyrate, (to) turn, (to) spin
	gira	excursion, tour (e.g., musicians)
	giro	gyration, change in direction, money order
	girasol	girasol, sunflower
HYAENA	hiena	hyena
HYBRIDA	híbrido	hybrid
HYGIEINA	higiene (f.)	hygiene
	higiénico	hygienic, sanitary
HYPERBOLA	hipérbola	hyperbola (geometric figure)
HYPERBOLE	hipérbole (f.)	hyperbole (exaggerated statement)
HYPOTHESIS	hipótesis	hypothesis
	hipotético	hypothetical
	hipotecar	(to) hypothecate, (to) mortgage
	hipoteca	mortgage
HYSTERA ("womb")	histeria	hysteria (~ *histerismo*)
	histérico	hysterical, hysteric (m./f.)
IDYLLIUM	idilio	idyll, romance, love affair
	idílico	idyllic
LYRA	lira	lyre
	lírica	lyric poetry
	lírico	lyrical, lyric
MYOPIA	miopía	myopia, nearsightedness
	miope	myopic, myope (nearsighted person—*m./f.*)
MYSTERIUM	misterio	mystery
	misterioso	mysterious
MYTHOLOGIA	mitología	mythology
	mitológico	mythological
	mito	myth
ODYSSEA	odisea	odyssey
OLYMPICUS	olímpico	Olympic

	olimpiada, -íada	Olympiad, Olympics (pl.)
PARALYSIS	parálisis	paralysis
	paralizar	(to) paralyze
PYRAMIDEM	pirámide (f.)	pyramid
SYLLABA	sílaba	syllable
SYLLABUS	sílabo	syllabus
SYMBIOSIS	simbiosis	symbiosis
SYMBOLUM	símbolo	symbol
	simbólico	symbolic
	simbolismo	symbolism
	simbolizar	(to) symbolize
SYMMETRIA	simetría	symmetry
	simétrico	symmetric, symmetrical
	asimetría	asymmetry
	asimétrico	asymmetric, asymmetrical
SYMPATHIA	simpatía	sympathy, congeniality
	simpático	likable, congenial, sympathetic (music, physiology)
SYMPTOMA	síntoma (m.)	symptom
	sintomático	symptomatic
SYNCOPE	síncope	syncope (med.), fainting spell, blackout
SYNDICATUS	sindicato	syndicate (association), labor union
SYNDROME	síndrome	syndrome
SYNONYMUS	sinónimo (adj. & n.)	synonymous, synonym
SYNTHESIS	síntesis	synthesis
SYNTHETICUS	sintético	synthetic
SYSTEMA	sistema (m.)	system
TYPHON	tifón	typhoon
TYRANNUS	tirano	tyrant (also tyrannical)
	tiranía	tyranny
	tiránico	tyrannical

PH → f

APOSTROPHE	apóstrofe (m./f.)	apostrophe (rhetorical)
APOSTROPHUS	apóstrofo	apostrophe (punctuation)
ASPHALTUS	asfalto	asphalt
	asfaltar	(to) pave with asphalt

ASPHYXIA	asfixia	asphyxia, suffocation
ATMOSPHAERA	atmósfera	atmosphere
	atmosférico	atmospheric
ATROPHIA	atrofia	atrophy
BLASPHEMARE	blasfemar	(to) blaspheme, (to) curse
CATASTROPHE	catástrofe (f.)	catastrophe
	catastrófico	catastrophic
DIAPHANUS	diáfano	diaphanous, clear, transparent
DIAPHRAGMA	diafragma (m.)	diaphragm
ELEPHANTEM	elefante	elephant
EPHEMEROS	efímero	ephemeral
EPITAPHIUM	epitafio	epitaph
EUPHEMISMOS	eufemismo	euphemism
EUPHORIA	euforia	euphoria
GEOGRAPHIA	geografía	geography
HEMISPHAERIUM	hemisferio	hemisphere
METAMORPHOSIS	metamorfosis	metamorphosis
METAPHORA	metáfora	metaphor
NYMPHA	ninfa	nymph
PARAPHRASIS	paráfrasis	paraphrase
	parafrasear	(to) paraphrase
PERIPHERIA	periferia	periphery
	periférico	peripheral
PHAENOMENON	fenómeno	phenomenon
	fenomenal	phenomenal
PHANTASIA	fantasía	fantasy
	fantástico	fantastic
PHANTASMA	fantasma (m.)	phantasm, *phantom* (fantom), ghost
PHARMACIA	farmacia	pharmacy
PHAROS	faro	pharos (lighthouse), headlight
	farol	lantern, streetlamp
	farola	large streetlamp (e.g., highway)
PHARYNX	faringe (f.)	pharynx
PHASIS	fase (f.)	phase
PHILANTHROPIA	filantropía	philanthropy
PHIL + ATELEIA	filatelia	philately (stamp collecting)
PHILOLOGIA	filología	philology
PHILOSOPHIA	filosofía	philosophy
	filosófico	philosophical
	filósofo	philosopher
PHOBIA	fobia	phobia

	xenofobia	xenophobia
PHOENIX	fénix	phoenix
PHOSPHORUS	fósforo	phosphorus, match (for igniting)
	fosforescente	phosphorescent
PHRASIS	frase (f.)	phrase, sentence
PHRENESIS	frenesí	frenzy
PHRENETICUS	frenético	frenetic, *frantic, frenzied*
PHYSICA	física	physics
	físico	physical, physique (m.), physicist (m./f.)
	metafísica	metaphysics
PHYSIOGNOMIA	fisonomía	physiognomy, features, face
PHYSIOLOGIA	fisiología	physiology
PROPHETA	profeta (m.)	prophet
	profecía	prophecy
	profético	prophetic
	profetizar	(to) prophesy
SEMA + PHOROS	semáforo	semaphore, traffic light (stoplight)
SPHAERA	esfera	sphere, dial or face (e.g., watch)
SPHINX (acc. SPHINGEM)	esfinge (f.)	sphinx
TELE + PHONE	teléfono	telephone
	telefónico	telephonic, telephone (adj.)
	guía telefónica	telephone book
	telefonista	telephone operator
	telefonear	(to) telephone (~ *llamar por teléfono*)
TROPHAEUM	trofeo	trophy

CH → c (or qu²), RH → r, TH → t

AESTHETICUS	estético	aesthetic / esthetic
	estética	aesthetics / esthetics
AMPHITHEATRUM	anfiteatro	amphitheater, dress circle
ANAESTHESIA	anestesia	anesthesia
	anestésico	anesthetic
ANTHOLOGIA	antología	anthology
ANTIPATHIA	antipatía	antipathy, dislike

---

² The *c* changes to *qu* when followed by *e* or *i* (see Section 3.5, no. 14), as in **quimera, quirúrgico,** *monarquía, oligarquía, psique*. *Cirugía* and *cirujano* (like English *surgery* and *surgeon*) represent a more "popular" evolution.

	antipático	unpleasant, disagreeable, antipathetic	
ARCHAICUS	arcaico	archaic	
ATHLETA	atleta (m./f.)	athlete	
	atlético	athletic	
	atletismo	track and field, athletics (UK)	
AUTOCHTHON	autóctono (adj. & n.)	autochthonous (indigenous), autochthon	
BIBLIOTHECA	biblioteca	library, bookcase	[*bible*]
CATHOLICUS	católico	Catholic, catholic (universal)	
CHAOS	caos	chaos	
CHARACTER	carácter	character (pl. *caracteres*[3])	
CHARISMA	carisma (m.)	charisma	
CHIMAERA	quimera	illusion, pipe dream, *chimera*	
	quimérico	*chimeric(al)*	
CHIRURGIA	cirugía	*surgery*	
	cirujano	surgeon	
	quirúrgico	surgical	
	quirófano[4]	operating room, surgical amphitheater	
CHORUS	coro	chorus, *choir*	
	coral (1)	choral, chorale (f.)	
	coral[5] (2)	coral	
CHRISTUS	Cristo	Christ	
CHRONICUS	crónico	chronic, long-standing	
	crónica	chronicle, article (newspaper)	
	cronista	chronicler, reporter	
	cronología	chronology	
	cronológico	chronological	
	anacronismo	anachronism	
	anacrónico	anachronistic	
DIARRHEA	diarrea	diarrhea	
DICHOTOMIA	dicotomía	dichotomy	

---

[3] *Carácter* is one of only three words in Spanish in which the stressed syllable of the plural is *not* the same as in the singular: ca•**rác**•ter versus ca•rac•**te**•res. (The others are es•**pé**•ci•men [pl. es•pe•**cí**•me•nes] and **ré**•gi•men [pl. re•**gí**•me•nes].)

[4] This arose as a cross between *quirúrgico* and *diáfano* ("diaphanous"), referring to the fact that the transparent windows of the surgical amphitheater permitted others to observe the operation from outside.

[5] This word has a different origin from the musical forms, coming from Greek *korallion* (Latin CORALLIUM).

DIPHTHONGUS	dip**t**ongo	diphthong
ECHO	eco	echo
ENTHUSIASMUS	entusiasmo	enthusiasm
	entusiasta	enthusiastic, enthusiast or fan (m./f.)
	entusiasmar	(to) provoke enthusiasm, (to) captivate
	entusiasmado (p.p.)	enthused, enthusiastic
EPOCHA	época	epoch, era, time
ETHNICUS	étnico	ethnic
	etnia	ethnic group
EUTHANASIA	eutanasia	euthanasia
LABYRINTHUS	laberinto	labyrinth, maze
MARATHON	maratón (m./f.)	marathon
MATHEMATICA	matemática	mathematics (gen. pl.)
	matemático	mathematical, mathematician (m./f.)
MECHANICUS	mecánico	mechanical, mechanic (m./f.)
	mecánica	mechanics (science)
	mecanismo	mechanism
	mecanizar	(to) mechanize
	mecanización	mechanization
MELANCHOLIA	melancolía	melancholy (n.), melancholia
	melancólico	melancholic, melancholy (adj.)
METHODUS	método	method
	metódico	methodical
MONARCHA	monarca (m.)	monarch
	monar**qu**ía	monarchy
	monár**qu**ico	monarchist, royalist
OLIGARCHIA	oligar**qu**ía	oligarchy
	oligár**qu**ico	oligarchic, oligarchical
	oligarca (m.)	oligarch
ORNITHOLOGIA	ornitología	ornithology
ORTHOGRAPHIA	ortografía	spelling, orthography
ORTHO + PAIDEIA	ortopedia	orthopedics
	ortopédico	orthopedic
PANTHEON	panteón	pantheon, Pantheon, (family) tomb, mausoleum
PARENTHESIS	paréntesis (m.)	parenthesis
PSYCHE	psi**qu**e (f.)	psyche

	psiquiatra (m./f.)	psychiatrist
	psiquiatría	psychiatry
RHAPSODIA	rapsodia	rhapsody
RHETORICA	retórica	rhetoric
	retórico	rhetorical, rhetorician (m./f.)
RHEUMATICUS	reumático	rheumatic
	reuma, reúma (m./f.)	rheumatism (~ *reumatismo*)
RHINOCEROS (-ONTEM)	rinoceronte	rhinoceros
RHODODENDRON	rododendro	rhododendron
RHYTHMUS	ritmo	rhythm
	rítmico	rhythmic, rhythmical
	rima[6]	rhyme, short poem (pl.)
	rimar	(to) rhyme, (to) versify
TECHNOLOGIA	tecnología	technology
	técnica	technique, technics
	técnico	technical, technician (m./f.)
TELE + PATHIA	telepatía	telepathy
THEATRUM	teatro	theater
THEOLOGIA	teología	theology
THEORIA	teoría	theory
THERAPIA	terapia	therapy
THRONUS	trono	throne
	entronizar	(to) enthrone

MPH → *nf*

AMPHIBIOS	anfibio	amphibious, amphibian (m.)
EMPHASIS	énfasis (m.)	emphasis
	enfático	emphatic
	enfatizar	(to) emphasize
SYMPHONIA	sinfonía	symphony

---

[6] The ultimate origin of *rima* / *rhyme* is debated. Some see it as representing a "popular" deformation of RHYTHMUS, others as having a Germanic source, with the English spelling subsequently being influenced by *rhythm* (*rime* remains an accepted variant of *rhyme*).

Note that Greek *-ia* (and Latin *-IA*) has often become English *-y: dynasty, pharmacy,* etc. Similarly:

aristocrac**ia**	aristocracy
autop**sia**	autopsy
controver**sia**	controversy, debate
democrac**ia**	democracy
energ**ía**	energy
epilep**sia**	epilepsy
genealog**ía**	genealogy
modes**tia**	modesty
org**ía**	orgy
parod**ia**	parody
penur**ia**	penury

"Post-Classical" (non-Greek) examples include:

artiller**ía**	artillery
bater**ía**	battery (elec., mil., music: percussion), kitchen utensils
loter**ía**	lottery

In about half of such words, the stress accent falls on the *-i* (*an•to•lo•gí•a, sin•fo•ní•a*), which therefore has a written accent, while in the remainder the stress is on the preceding syllable and the *-ia* is pronounced as a diphthong (*far•ma•cia, pe•ri•fe•ria*).

PS became *s* in

PSALMUS	salmo	*psalm*

but has remained in words like *pseudónimo, psoriasis, psiquiatría, psicoanálisis, psicología, and psicopático.* These are also frequently found without the initial *p.*

Among the more common Greek endings are the following:

(1) *-logía / -lógico / -logo*
(2) *-grafía / -gráfico / -grafo*
(3) *-sis / -tis*
(4) *-ema / -oma*
(5) *-tico / -tica*

1. -logía / -lógico / -logo

The standard pattern is shown below corresponding to English *biology* and *geology:* the Spanish noun (feminine) ends in *-logía,* the adjective in *-lógico* (feminine: *-lógica*), and the "performer" in *-logo* (feminine: *-loga*).

biología	biológico	biólogo	biology	biologic(al)	biologist
geología	geológico	geólogo	geology	geologic(al)	geologist

Note that in Spanish the word stress falls on a different syllable in each of the three words: for the adjective and the performer, the same syllable is stressed as in English, while for the "subject", the stress is moved forward two syllables:

	Spanish	English
geología	*ge•o•lo•**gí**•a*	ge•**ol**•o•gy
geológico	ge•o•**ló**•gi•co	ge•o•**log**•i•cal
geólogo	ge•**ó**•lo•go	ge•**ol**•o•gist

There are several words for which the performer is a *-logista* rather than a *-logo / -loga:*

apologista	apologist
ecologista[7]	ecologist
etimologista	etymologist
genealogista	genealogist
mineralogista	mineralogist

Note that Spanish *apología* makes use of the secondary English definition "formal justification or defense", rather than the more common "acknowledgment expressing regret or asking pardon for a fault or offense".[8] Hence an *apologista* is "one who defends by argument", rather than "one who offers or asks for forgiveness".[9]

---

[7] *Ecólogo (-loga)* also exists, but is relatively rare.

[8] Spanish in fact conserves the "original" meaning: the first use in English with the sense of "expressing regret" is attributed to Shakespeare (1594).

[9] This is the definition of English *apologist* as well, where the emphasis is on defending and justifying—an "apologist for slavery" defended the practice rather than asking for forgiveness.

Other words following the *biología—biológico—biólogo* pattern include:

analogía[10]	analogy
antropología	anthropology
arqueología	archaeology
astrología	astrology
cardiología	cardiology
cosmología	cosmology
criminología	criminology
dermatología	dermatology
embriología	embryology
entomología	entomology
espeleología	speleology
filología	philology
fisiología	physiology
geología	geology
ginecología	gynecology
ideología	ideology
meteorología	meteorology
odontología	odontology, dentistry
paleontología	paleontology
patología	pathology
psicología	psychology
radiología	radiology
sociología	sociology
tautología	tautology
tecnología	technology
teología	theology
terminología	terminology
toxicología	toxicology
urología	urology
zoología	zoology

As in English, there are a few *-logo* words referring not to a performer but to an object:

catálogo	catalog(ue), list
decálogo	Decalog(ue), Ten Commandments
diálogo	dialog(ue)

---

[10] *Análogo* means "analogous" (adj.) rather than "one who makes analogies", while *analógico* means "analog".

epílogo	epilog(ue), recapitulation
monólogo	monolog(ue)
prólogo	prolog(ue), preface

Two groups of words follow a similar pattern, but end with *-gogo* rather than *-logo:*

demagogia	demagógico	demagogo	demagogy	demagogic(al)	demagogue
pedagogía	pedagógico	pedagogo	pedagogy	pedagogic(al)	pedagogue

Note that *demagogia* (de•ma•**go**•gia) has a different stress compared to *pedagogía* and the *-logía* words, while both *demagogo* (de•ma•**go**•go) and *pedagogo* (pe•da•**go**•go) are stressed differently from the *-logo* words.

2. *-grafía / -gráfico / -grafo*

This is analogous to *-logía / -lógico / -logo:* the Spanish noun (feminine) ends in *-grafía,* the adjective in *-gráfico* (feminine: *-gráfica*), and the performer in *-grafo* (feminine: *-grafa*). The standard pattern is shown below corresponding to English *biography* and *geography:*

biografía	biográfico	biógrafo	biography	biographic(al)	biographer
geografía	geográfico	geógrafo	geography	geographic(al)	geographer

There are a few cases where *-grafo* refers to an instrument rather than a person, e.g.,

(electro)cardiógrafo	(electro)cardiograph
cinematógrafo	movie projector, movie theater, cinematograph
telégrafo	telegraph

The operator of a *telégrafo* is a *telegrafista.* Other examples following the "normal" pattern include:

bibliografía	bibliography
caligrafía	calligraphy
cartografía	cartography
coreografía	choreography
criptografía[11]	cryptography

---

[11] *Criptógrafo* ("cryptographer") doesn't exist (according to the *DRAE* and Moliner), but is nonetheless occasionally found.

dactilografía	typewriting	[*dactylography*]
fotografía	photography, photograph	
demografía	demography	
lexicografía	lexicography	
mecanografía	typewriting (~ *dactilografía*)	
oceanografía	oceanography	
paleografía	paleography	
pornografía	pornography	
taquigrafía	stenography, shorthand	

A point of frequent confusion for native English speakers is that a *fotógrafo* is a "photographer", not a "photograph". A "photo" is *una fotografía* or, more commonly (especially in the spoken language), *una foto*.

3. -sis / -tis

Words with -*sis* and -*tis* endings are nouns, the vast majority of which are feminine. The only exceptions (i.e., masculines) among commonly used words are the following:[12]

análisis (m.)	analysis
apocalipsis (m.)	apocalypse
énfasis (m.)	emphasis
éxtasis (m.)	ecstasy
oasis (m.)	oasis
paréntesis (m.)	parenthesis
psicoanálisis (m.)	psychoanalysis

The plurals, for both feminines and masculines, are identical to the singulars. Other examples (all feminines) are:

-sis

antítesis	antithesis
arteriosclerosis, -esclerosis	arteriosclerosis, hardening of the arteries
cirrosis	cirrhosis
crisis	crisis
diagnosis (~ diagnóstico)	diagnosis (medical)

---

[12] In addition, there are a few masculines among the relatively small number of non-Greek -*sis* / -*tis* words (see Annex A).

diálisis	dialysis
dosis	dose, dosage
electrólisis	electrolysis
génesis	genesis, origin, Genesis (*m.,* cap.)
hipnosis	hypnosis
hipótesis	hypothesis
osteoporosis	osteoporosis
prognosis (~ pronóstico)	prognosis, prognostication
prótesis	prosthesis (med.), prothesis (gram.)
sinopsis	synopsis, abstract, summary
síntesis	synthesis
sobredosis	overdose
tesis	thesis
tuberculosis	tuberculosis

Many of these nouns have corresponding adjectives ending in *-tico* (no. 5 below), e.g., *antitético, crítico,* and *hipnótico.*

-tis (medical terms, all feminine)

apendicitis	appendicitis
artritis	arthritis
bronquitis	bronchitis
conjuntivitis	conjunctivitis
dermatitis	dermatitis
gastritis	gastritis
hepatitis	hepatitis
laringitis	laryngitis
meningitis	meningitis
sinusitis	sinusitis

4. *-ema / -oma*

These are nouns, the large majority of which are masculine, in marked contrast to the general Spanish rule that nouns ending in *-a* are feminine. In the lists below, masculine nouns are shown first.

-ema

anatema (m./f.)	anathema	
cinema (m.)	cinema, movie theater	(short form: *el cine*)

dilema (m.)	dilemma
ecosistema (m.)	ecosystem
edema (m.)	edema (inflammation due to fluid accumulation)
emblema (m.)	emblem
enema[13] (m.)	enema
enfisema (m.)	emphysema
esquema (m.)	*scheme,* outline, sketch
fonema (m.)	phoneme
lema (m.)	lemma, motto
poema (m.)	poem
problema (m.)	problem
sistema (m.)	system
tema (m.)	theme
teorema (m.)	theorem
crema	cream
diadema	diadem (a crown worn as a sign of royalty)
estratagema	stratagem, deception, trick
flema	phlegm, calmness, imperturbability
gema[14]	gem, precious stone, gemma (bud)
—yema	—bud, yolk, gemma

-oma

aroma (m.)	aroma
axioma (m.)	axiom
carcinoma (m.)	carcinoma
coma (1) (m.)	coma
cromosoma (m.)	chromosome
diploma (m.)	diploma
genoma (m.)	genome
glaucoma (m.)	glaucoma
hematoma (m.)	hematoma, bruise

---

[13] There is some confusion concerning the gender of *enema:* until 1984, the RAE differentiated between the "traditional" *enema,* which was feminine, and a second definition of "astringent and drying substance used on wounds", which was masculine. Since 1984, all enemas, of whatever type, have (at least according to the RAE) been masculine.

[14] *Gem* is of Latin rather than Greek origin, coming from Latin GEMMA ("bud", hence—due to the similarity in form and color—"precious stone"). *Yema* is the corresponding "popular" Spanish word.

idioma (m.)	language	[*idiom*]
melanoma (m.)	melanoma	
síntoma (m.)	symptom	

broma[15]	joke, jest	[*bromide*]
—abru**m**ar	—(to) overwhelm or crush	
—abrumador	—overwhelming, crushing, oppressive	
coma (2)	comma	
—comillas (pl.)	—quotation marks	
goma	*gum*, rubber, rubber band, eraser	
paloma[16]	dove, pigeon	
poma	pome, apple (botanical), perfume box	

5. -tico / -tica

Words ending in -*tico* are of both Greek and Latin origin. They are almost always masculine adjectives with corresponding feminines ending in -*tica*. In many cases, they can also be used as nouns, e.g.,

	diplomático (adj.)	diplomatic
	el diplomático (n.m.)	the diplomat (masculine)
	la diplomática (n.f.)	the diplomat (feminine)
also:	diplomacia	diplomacy, tact

Very rarely (e.g., *gramático, pronóstico*), words ending in -*tico* are nouns rather than adjectives. A more frequent occurrence is an abstract feminine noun ending in -*tica*, e.g., *acústica*.

For all of these words there is a written accent on the *preceding* vowel, e.g., *diplomático* (pronounced *di•plo•má•ti•co*).

A sampling of these words (adjectives, unless otherwise indicated) is given below:

acróstico		acrostic (adj. & n.m.)
acuático		aquatic
acústico	acústica (n.f.)	acoustic, acoustics (n.f.)
adriático		Adriatic

---

[15] English *bromide* and *bromine* come from Greek *bromos* ("stench"), while Spanish *broma* likely comes from a closely related Greek word meaning "rottenness".

[16] *Paloma* and *poma* are of Latin, not Greek, origin.

agnóstico		agnostic (adj. & n.m./f.)
alfabético		alphabetical
analítico	analítica (n.f.)	analytic, analytical, analytics (n.f.)
anecdótico		anecdotal, anecdotic
antártico		antarctic [the continent is gen. *Antártida*]
antibiótico		antibiotic (adj. & n.m.)
antidemocrático		undemocratic
antiestético		un(a)esthetic, ugly
antipático		antipathetic, disagreeable
antipatriótico		unpatriotic
antisemítico		anti-Semitic
antiséptico		antiseptic (adj. & n.m.)
antitético		antithetical, opposing
apático		apathetic
apocalíptico		apocalyptic
apolítico		apolitical
aristocrático		aristocratic
aritmético	aritmética (n.f.)	arithmetical, arithmetic (n.f.)
aromático		aromatic
ártico		arctic
artístico		artistic
ascético	ascética (n.f.)	ascetic, asceticism (n.f.)
asiático		Asiatic (adj. & n.m./f.), Asian
asmático		asthmatic (adj. & n.m./f.)
atlántico		Atlantic
atlético		athletic
auténtico		authentic
autocrático		autocratic
automático		automatic
báltico		Baltic
caótico		chaotic
característico	característica (n.f.)	characteristic (adj. & n.f.)
carismático		charismatic
catedrático (n.m.)	catedrática (n.f.)	professor (UK: *chair*)
cáustico		caustic (adj. & n.m.)
céltico		Celtic, Celtic language (n.m.)
ciático	ciática (n.f.)	sciatic, sciatica (n.f.)
cibernético	cibernética (n.f.)	cybernetic, cybernetics (n.f.)
cosmético	cosmética (n.f.)	cosmetic (adj. & n.m.), cosmetology (n.f.)

cósmico		cosmic
críptico		cryptic
crítico	crítica (n.f.)	critical, critic (n.m./f.), critique/criticism (n.f.)
cromático		chromatic
cuadrático		quadratic
democrático		democratic
diagnóstico		diagnostic (adj. & n.m.), diagnosis (n.m.)
didáctico	didáctica (n.f.)	didactic, educational, didactics (n.f.)
diurético		diuretic (adj. & n.m.)
dogmático		dogmatic
doméstico		domestic (adj. & n.m./f.)
dramático	dramática (n.f.)	dramatic, dramatist or actor/actress (n.m./f.), dramatic arts (n.f.)
drástico		drastic, medicinal purge (n.m.)
eclesiástico		ecclesiastical, ecclesiastic (n.m.)
elástico		elastic (adj. & n.m.)
emético		emetic (adj. & n.m.)
energético	energética (n.f.)	pertaining to energy, science of energy (n.f.)
—enérgico		—energetic (possessing or displaying energy)
enfático		emphatic
enigmático		enigmatic
epiléptico		epileptic (adj. & n.m./f.)
erótico	erótica (n.f.)	erotic, erotica (n.f.)
errático		wandering, vagrant, erratic
escéptico		skeptical, skeptic (n.m./f.)
escolástico	escolástica (n.f.)	scholastic (adj. & n.m./f.), Scholasticism (n.f.)
estadístico	estadística (n.f.)	statistical, statistician (n.m./f.), statistics (n.f.)
estático	estática (n.f.)	static (adj.),[17] statics (n.f.)
estético	estética (n.f.)	esthetic (adj.), esthetics (n.f.)
estilístico	estilística (n.f.)	stylistic, stylistics (n.f.)
ético	ética (n.f.)	ethical, ethics (n.f.)
exótico		exotic

---

[17] The Spanish noun for "static" is *interferencia* or *parásitos* ("parasites").

fanático		fanatical, fanatic (adj. & n.m./f.)
farmacéutico		pharmaceutical, pharmacist (n.m./f.)
flemático		phlegmatic, unemotional
fonético	fonética (n.f.)	phonetic, phonetics (n.f.)
genético	genética (n.f.)	genetic, genetics (n.f.)
gimnástico	gimnástica (n.f.)	gymnastic, gymnastics (n.f.)[18]
gótico (adj. & n.m.)		Gothic (style, people, language, print)
gramático (n.m.)	gramática (n.f.)	grammarian (n.m./f.), grammar (n.f.)
hermético		hermetic, airtight
hipnótico		hypnotic, sleeping pill (n.m.)
hipotético		hypothetical
informático	informática (n.f.)	data processing (adj.), computer expert (n.m./f.), computer science (n.f.)
lingüístico	lingüística (n.f.)	linguistic, linguistics (n.f.)
logístico	logística (n.f.)	logistical, logistics (n.f.)
magnético		magnetic
místico	mística (n.f.)	mystical, mystic (n.m./f.), mysticism (n.f.)
monolítico		monolithic
narcótico		narcotic (adj. & n.m.)
neolítico		Neolithic (adj. & n.m.)
neumático		pneumatic, tire (n.m.)
neurótico		neurotic (adj. & n.m./f.)
numismático	numismática (n.f.)	numismatic, numismatist (n.m./f.), numismatics (n.f.)
onomástico	onomástica (n.f.)	onomastic, onomastics (n.f.), saint's day (n.f.)
óptico	óptica (n.f.)	optic, optical, optician (n.m./f.), optics (n.f.), optical shop (n.f.)
paleolítico		Paleolithic (adj. & n.m.)
patético		pathetic
patriótico		patriotic

[18] For "gymnastics", *gimnasia* is more common (*gimnasio* is "gymnasium").

peripatético		peripatetic (Aristotelian),[19] ridiculous or outlandish
plástico	plástica (n.f.)	plastic (adj. & n.m.), plastic arts (n.f.)
poético	poética (n.f.)	poetic, poetics (n.f.)
político	política (n.f.)	politic, political, in-law,[20] politician (n.m./f.), politics (n.f.), policy (n.f.)
práctico	práctica (n.f.)	practical, practiced (i.e., skillful), harbor pilot (n.m.), practice (n.f.)
pragmático	pragmática (n.f.)	pragmatic, interpreter of the laws (n.m./f.), pragmatics (n.f.)[21]
problemático	problemática (n.f.)	problematic, collective problems (n.f.)
pronóstico (n.m.)		prognosis, prognostic, prediction
quiropráctico (n.m.)	quiropráctica (n.f.)	chiropractor (n.m./f.), chiropractic (n.f.)
reumático		rheumatic (adj. & n.m./f.)
rústico		rustic (adj. & n.m./f.)
sarcástico		sarcastic
semántico	semántica	semantic, semantics (n.f.)
sintético		synthetic
sintomático		symptomatic
sistemático		systematic
socrático		Socratic
táctico	táctica (n.f.)	tactical, tactician (n.m./f.), tactics (n.f.)
teorético		speculative, theoretical[22]
transatlántico		transatlantic, (ocean) liner (n.m.)
traumático		traumatic
viático (n.m.)		viaticum,[23] travel allowance

---

[19] English *peripatetic* normally means "walking about from place to place; traveling on foot", a meaning not shared by Spanish peripatético. Both words maintain the formal (original) definition "of or relating to the philosophy of Aristotle, who conducted discussions while walking about in the Lyceum of ancient Athens".

[20] See Section 4.8.

[21] *Pragmatics* means "the study of language as it is used in a given context". Spanish *pragmática* (n.f.) has a second definition as well, analogous to that of English *pragmatic sanction*: "an edict or a decree issued by a sovereign that becomes part of the fundamental law of the land".

[22] *Teórico* is far more common, as the use of *teorético* in the sense of "theoretical" is widely viewed as an *anglicismo*.

[23] Latin VIATICUM is also the origin of both English *voyage* and Spanish *viaje*.

PART III

POPULAR VOCABULARY: THE *SHAPE* OF SPANISH

Consider the following lists of words:

Language 1	Language 2	Language 3	English
viejo	vieux	vecchio	old
escuela	école	scuola	*school*
verde	vert	verde	green
bueno	bon	buono	good
puente	pont	ponte	bridge
público	public	pubblico	*public*
libertad	liberté	libertà	*liberty*
harina	farine	farina	flour, *farina*
seguro	sûr	sicuro	*sure, secure*

Even if one has not already studied a Romance language, it is not too difficult to guess that Language 1 is Spanish, Language 2 is French, and Language 3 is Italian. All languages have a certain "feel" to them, and the Romance languages are no exceptions.

The aim of Part III is to further develop this inherent "feel" for the nature of Spanish so that it can effectively be used as a tool in the acquisition of new vocabulary.

Addition of "Helping" *e: esnob = snob*

The Vulgar Latin grammarians noted an inconsistency in the Latin phonetic system. In the interior of a word, the combination *s* + consonant was *always* divided between different syllables and was never pronounced as a single "sound". Thus,

		Spanish	English
JUSTITIA	JUS•TI•TI•A	jus•ti•cia	jus•tice
MONSTRUM	MONS•TRUM	mons•truo	mon• ster

As the example shows, this is *not* a feature of English, where in many words like *monster* the consonant combination *st* is pronounced jointly.

If a syllable within a word could never begin with *s* + consonant, why should it be any different at the *beginning* of a word? The Vulgar Latins decided that there was no good reason for such difference, and that what was required was the addition of a "helping" (*prothetic*) vowel to permit *s* and the following consonant to be placed in separate syllables:

	Spanish	English
SPI•NA → ES•PI•NA	espina	thorn, *spine*

Italian subsequently gave up the initial *e,* Spanish has maintained it, while French has generally eliminated the *s,* which was the justification for the *e* in the first place.

Latin	Spanish	French	Italian	English
SCALA	escala	échelle	scala	*scale*
SCUTUM	escudo	écu	scudo	*escutcheon,* shield
SPIRITUS	espíritu	esprit	spirito	*spirit*
SPONSA	esposa	épouse	sposa	*spouse,* wife
STATUS	estado	état	stato	*state*

Examples:

esbelto	*svelte* (slender, graceful)
escala	ladder, *scale,* proportion, port of call, stop (airplane)

—escalera	—staircase, stairs	
—escalar	—(to) climb, (to) *scale*	
—escalador	—(mountain) climber	
—escalada	—climb, rapid increase, rise, *escalade*	
—escalón	—step (of a stair), stepping stone	[*echelon*]
—escalafón	—roster of employees (by rank)	
escalpelo	*scalpel*	
escama	scale (of fish, snake), flake (of soap), *squama*	
—escamoso	—scaly, flaky, *squamous*	
escándalo	*scandal*	
—escandaloso	—*scandalous*	
—escandalizar	—(to) *scandalize*	
Escandinavia	*Scandinavia*	
—escandinavo	—*Scandinavian*	
escandir	(to) *scan* (verse)	
escápula	*scapula* (shoulder blade)	
escarbar	(to) scrape, (to) scratch, (to) dig into	[*scarify*]
escarlata	*scarlet*	
—escarlatina	—*scarlatina, scarlet* fever	
escarnecer	(to) mock, (to) ridicule	[*scorn*]
—escarmentar	—(to) punish severely, (to) learn one's lesson	
—escarmiento	—lesson, punishment	
escarpa	*scarp,* steep slope, *escarpment*	
—escarpado	—steep, sheer, craggy	
escatológico (1)	*scatological*	
—escatología (1)	—*scatology*	
—escatología (2)	—*eschatology*	
—escatológico (2)	—*eschatological*	
escayola	plaster, plaster cast, *scagliola*	[fish *scale*]
escena	*scene,* stage	
—escenario	—stage, scene, setting	[*scenario*]
—escénico	—*scenic* (of or relating to the stage)	
escéptico (adj. & n.)	*skeptical, skeptic*	
—escepticismo	—*skepticism*	
esclavo	*slave*	(see appendix)
—esclavitud	—*slavery*	

—esclavizar	—(to) *enslave*	
—eslabón	—link (of a chain)	
—eslavo	—*Slav*	
—Eslovaquia	—*Slovakia*	
—eslovaco	—*Slovak*	
—Eslovenia	—*Slovenia*	
—esloveno	—*Slovene, Slovenian*	
esclerosis	*sclerosis*	
—esclerosis múltiple	—multiple sclerosis	
esclusa	(canal) lock, *sluice, sluice gate*	
escoba	broom	[*scopula*]
—escobilla	—brush	
Escocia	*Scotland*	
—escocés (-esa)	—*Scottish*	
escolar (adj. & n.)	*scholastic, school* (adj.), student, pupil	
—escuela	—*school*	
escorbuto	*scurvy*	[*scorbutic*]
escoria	*scoria* (slag, dross, lava fragments)	
—El Escorial	—Escorial (monastery & palace near Madrid)	
escribir	(to) write	[*scribble*]
—escriba (m.)	—*scribe*	
—escribano	—*scrivener*, notary	
—escrito (p.p.)	—writing (report, etc.), writ (law)	[*script*]
—por escrito	—in writing	
—escritor	—writer, author	
—escritorio	—desk, office	[*scriptorium*]
—escritura	—handwriting, *Scripture* (cap., freq. pl.)	
escrúpulo	*scrupule*	
—escrupuloso	—*scrupulous*	
—sin escrúpulos	—*unscrupulous* (~ *inescrupuloso*)	
escrutar	(to) *scrutinize*, (to) count votes	
—escrutinio	—*scrutiny*, (official) vote count	
—escudriñar[1]	—(to) *scrutinize*	

---

[1] Formerly *escrudiñar*.

escuadra	triangle (for drawing), *squad, squadron,* fleet	
—escuadrón	—*squadron* (military) [2]	
escuálido	skinny, emaciated, *squalid*	
escudo	shield, *escutcheon, escudo*	
—escudo de armas	—coat of arms	
—escudar	—(to) shield	
—escudero	—*squire,* shield-bearer	
esculcar	(to) delve into, (to) spy	[*skulk*]
escultura	*sculpture*	
—escultor	—*sculptor*	
—esculpir	—(to) *sculpt,* (to) engrave	
escupir	(to) spit	
—escupidera	—spittoon, *cuspidor,* urinal (Amer.)	
esfera	*sphere,* dial or face (e.g., watch)	
esgrimir	(to) brandish, (to) fence	[*scrimmage*[3]]
—esgrima	—fencing, swordplay	
—escaramuza	—*skirmish,* dispute	[*Scaramouch*]
esmalte	enamel	[*smelt*]
—esmalte de uñas	—nail polish	
—esmaltar	—(to) enamel, (to) adorn	
esmoquin (< Eng.)	tuxedo, dinner jacket	[*smoking*]
esnob (< Eng.)	*snob*	
espacio	*space*	
—espacioso	—*spacious,* slow, deliberate	
—despacio	—slowly (~ *lentamente*)	[of *space*]
esparcir	(to) scatter, (to) spread, (to) amuse	[*sparse*]
—esparcimiento	—scattering, recreation, leisure activity	
espátula	*spatula*	
especia	*spice*	
—especie	—*species,* kind, sort	

---

[2] An army *escuadrón* is generally larger than an *escuadra;* the former is commanded by a *capitán* (captain), the latter by a *cabo* (corporal).

[3] *Scrimmage* was previously *scrimish,* itself a "deformation" of *skirmish.* Thus, both Spanish *esgrimir* and English *scrimmage* have "moved" the *r* from its "original" place (cf. Section 3.5, no. 8).

especial	*special*
—especialidad	—*specialty*
—especialista	—*specialist*
—especializar	—(to) *specialize*
específico	*specific*
—especificación	—*specification*
—especificar	—(to) *specify*
espécimen (pl.	*specimen*
especímenes)	
espectáculo	*spectacle*, show
—espectacular	—*spectacular*
—espectador	—*spectator*
espectro	*specter, spectrum*
especular	(to) *speculate* (meditate, think about, buy and sell)
—especulación	—*speculation*
—especulativo	—*speculative*
—especulador	—*speculator*
esperma (m./f.)	*sperm,* spermaceti [4]
espeso	thick, dense [*inspissate*]
—espesor	—thickness
—espesura	—denseness, thicket, dense wood
espina	thorn, fish bone, splinter, *spine* (bot.)
—espina dorsal	—*spine,* backbone, spinal column
—espina bífida	—*spina bifida*
—espinal	—*spinal*
—espinazo	—*spine,* backbone
—espino	—hawthorn, thornbush
espiral (adj. & n.f.)	*spiral*
espíritu	*spirit*
—espiritual	—*spiritual*
esplendor	*splendor*
esponja	*sponge*
—esponjoso	—*spongy*
espontáneo	*spontaneous*
—espontaneidad	—*spontaneity*
esporádico	*sporadic*

---

[4] Spermaceti is a white waxy substance found in the *head* of *sperm* whales (the whale name arising from either a deficient anatomical understanding or a somewhat off-color sense of humor).

espuma	foam, froth, lather, *spume*	
—espumoso	—frothy, foamy, sparkling (wine), *spumous*	
esqueleto	*skeleton*, framework	
esquema (m.)	outline, sketch, *scheme*	
—esquemático	—*schematic*	
esquí	*ski, skiing*	
—esquí alpino / de fondo	—alpine skiing / cross-country skiing	
—esquiar	—(to) *ski*	
esquimal (adj. & n.)	*Eskimo*, Eskimo language (m.)	
esquina	corner	[*shin, chine*]
esquizofrenia	*schizophrenia*	
—esquizofrénico	—*schizophrenic* (adj. & n.)	
estaca	*stake*, post	
—estacada	—picket fence, *stockade* (< Sp.)	
—dejar (s.o.) en la estacada	—(to) leave someone in the lurch	
estampa	print, engraving, likeness or image	
—estampar	—(to) print, (to) *stamp*, (to) engrave	
—estampida	—*stampede*	
—estampido	—loud noise (as from an explosion)	
—estampilla	—rubber *stamp*, postage *stamp* (Amer.)	
estanco	watertight (adj.), tobacconist (n.)	[*staunch*]
—estancar	—(to) *stanch*, (to) monopolize (block the free sale of)	
—estanque	—pond, basin, reservoir	[*tank*[5]]
—tanque (< Eng.)		
estelar	*stellar*	
—estrella[6]	—*star*	
—estrella de mar	—*starfish*	

---

[5] English *tank* ("container") comes, in the first instance, from one of the languages of India, though it has also been influenced by the Romance word. It may well be the case that the Indian word comes from the Romance one via the Portuguese, who were India's first European colonizers.

[6] *Estrella* likely comes from a "mixing" of **astro** (originally from Greek) with Latin sᴛᴇʟʟᴀ ("star").

—estrella fugaz	—shooting star	
—estrellar	—(to) fill with stars, (to) smash to pieces, (to) fail	
—con**stela**ción	—constellation	("with stars")
—destellar	—(to) twinkle, (to) sparkle, (to) flash	(unrelated)
—destello	—flash (of light), twinkle	
estéril	*sterile* (barren, unproductive, bacteria-free)	
—esterilidad	—*sterility*	
—esterilizar	—(to) *sterilize*	
—esterilización	—*sterilization*	
(libra) esterlina	(pound) *sterling*	
estibador	longshoreman, *stevedore*	
—estibar	—(to) stow, (to) load or unload, (to) stuff	[con*stipate*]
estigma (m.)	*stigma* (incl. bot. and biol.), *stigmata* (pl.)	
—estigmatizar	—(to) *stigmatize*	
estilo	*style* (incl. bot.), *stylus,* fashion	
—estilográfica	—fountain pen	
estímulo	*stimulus, stimulation*	
—estimular	—(to) *stimulate,* (to) encourage	
—estimulante (adj. & n.)	—*stimulating, stimulant*	
estipendio	*stipend*	
estipular	(to) *stipulate*	
—estipulación	—*stipulation,* condition	
estirpe (f.)	ancestry, lineage, *stirps*	
—extirpar	—(to) *extirpate,* (to) remove, (to) eradicate	[*ex* + *stirps*]
estoico (adj. & n.)	*stoical, stoic*	
estola	*stole*	
estoque	rapier, sword	[*stoke, stock*]
—estocada	—stab, thrust	
estrangular	(to) *strangle,* (to) *strangulate*	
estrategia	*strategy*	
—estratégico	—*strategic*	
—estratega (m./f.)	—*strategist*	
—estratagema	—*stratagem*	
estrato	*stratum, stratus* (cloud), layer	[*street*]

—estratosfera	—*stratosphere*
—estrado	—dais (raised platform), halls of justice (pl.)
estría	groove, stretch mark (skin), *stria*
—estriado	—*striated*
estridente	*strident*
estrofa	stanza, *strophe*
estructura	*structure*
—estructural	—*structural*
—estructurar	—(to) *structure*, (to) organize
—infraestructura	—*infrastructure*
estudiante (m./f.)	*student*
—estudiar	—(to) *study*
—estudio	—*study* (act, place), *studio* (workshop, apartment)
—estudioso (adj. & n.)	—*studious*, specialist
estupefaciente	*stupefacient* (drug), narcotic
estupendo	*stupendous*
—estupor	—*stupor*, astonishment
estúpido (adj. & n.)	*stupid*, foolish (or such a person)
—estupidez	—*stupidity*

Appendix
On *Slavs* and *Slaves*

The name used by the east European Slavs to describe themselves was taken into Medieval Latin in two different forms: SCLAVUS and SLAVUS. It came to mean "slave" as well as "Slav", the association arising from the the large number of Slavic slaves in both the eastern Roman Empire and the Germanic territories. Eventually, SCLAVUS specialized in "slave", and SLAVUS in "Slav", a distinction carried on in modern Spanish and in other Romance languages, as well as in German (but not in Dutch). It was also the case in English (*sclave*) until the sixteenth century, when the "unnatural" (for English) *scl* combination was reduced to *sl* (as happened also in *slander, slice,* and *sluice*), leaving *slave* and *Slav* to be distinguished only by their respective vowels.

	Slav	slave
Dutch	Slaaf	slaaf
German	Slawe	Sklave
Spanish	eslavo	esclavo

| French | slave | esclave |
| Italian | slavo | schiavo |

In "mainstream" Italian, sclavus became *schiavo* (pronounced [skyavo]), while in the Venetian dialect a shortened variant, *ciao* (pronounced [chao]), came to be used as an informal greeting or farewell in the sense of "I am your humble servant". This was then exported to Spanish, where *chao* is used only as a farewell (¡ *Adiós* ! ¡ *Hasta luego* ! ¡ *Chao* !). Hence the correspondence:

| chao | *ciao,* adios |

SECTION 3.2

Initial *f* → *h: higo* = *fig*

The presence of (unpronounced) *h* arising from Latin F is one of the most distinctive features of Spanish, setting it apart not only from French and Italian but also from the other Iberian Romances (Portuguese/Galician, Catalan).

Latin	Spanish	Portuguese	French	Italian	*English*
FALCO(N)	**h**alcón	falcão	faucon	falco	*falcon*
FARINA	**h**arina	farinha	farine	farina	*farina,* flour
FICUS	**h**igo	figo	figue	fico	*fig*

Examples include:

FABULARI	hablar	(to) speak, (to) talk	[*fabulate*]
	habla	speech, language, dialect	[*fable*]
	hablador (adj. & n.)	talkative, gossipy, chatterbox	[*confabulator*]
	fábula	*fable*	
	fabuloso	*fabulous* (barely credible, extraordinary)	
FACERE	hacer	(to) do, (to) make	[*factory*]
	deshacer	(to) undo, (to) take apart	[*defeat*]
	hacia	toward	[*face* to]
	hacienda	ranch, *hacienda,* public finance	
	rehacer	(to) redo, (to) remake	[*refect*]
	hecho (p.p.)	*fact*	
	cohechar	(to) bribe	[*confect*]
	cohecho	bribe, bribery	[*confetti*]
	quehacer	chore, task, occupation	(que + hacer)
	facsímil, facsímile	facsimile	(fac + *similar*)
	faena (< Cat.)	task, toil, dirty trick	
	faenar	(to) fish (at sea), (to) slaughter (animals), (to) toil	
FACIES	haz (1) (f.)	*face,* sur*face* (e.g., of leaf, fabric)	

FAEX (pl. FAECES)	hez (pl. heces)	*feces* (pl.), dreg(s)	
FAMINEM (acc.)	hambre (f.)	hunger, *famine*	
	hambriento	hungry, *famished*	
	famélico	hungry, *famished*, scrawny	
FARINA	harina	flour, *farina*	
	harina de otro costal	"horse of a different color"[1]	
	harinoso	mealy, *farinaceous*	
FARTUS	harto	fed up, full	[*farci*]
	hartar	(to) satiate, (to) glut,	[*farce*]
		(to) get fed up	
	infarto	*infarct*, heart attack	
		(~ *ataque cardíaco*)	
FASCIS	haz (2)	bundle, sheaf, (light) beam	[*fascia,*
			fascist]
FASTIDIUM	hastío	weariness, annoyance,	[*fastidious*]
		boredom	
	hastiar	(to) annoy, (to) weary,	
		(to) cause disgust	
	fastidiar	(to) annoy, (to) tire,	
		(to) bore	
	fastidioso	annoying, tiresome	
	fastidio	annoyance, nuisance	
FATUM	hado	*fate*, destiny	
	hada	*fairy,*[2] *fay*	
	cuento de hadas	fairy tale	
	hada madrina	fairy godmother	
FEMINA	hembra (n.)	*female* (animal)	
	femenino	feminine, female (adj.)	
	fémina (n.)	female (human)	
	feminismo	feminism	
	feminista	feminist	
FENUM	heno	hay	[*fennel,*
			sain*foin*]
	fiebre del heno	hay *fever*	

[1] Literally "flour from a different sack".

[2] Latin FATA became *fée* in French (and *hada* in Spanish), while *faerie* (Modern French *féerie*) was "fairyland". The French words were imported into English as *fay* and *fairy,* with their original meanings intact; subsequently, *fairy* altered its sense to that of *fay,* its original meaning being assumed by the new term *fairyland* (which first appeared as "Fairy Land" in Shakespeare's *A Midsummer Night's Dream*). English *faerie* (an alternative spelling of *fairy*) maintains the original definition of "land or realm of the fairies".

FERIRE	herir	(to) wound, (to) injure, (to) hurt	[inter*fere*]
	herido (p.p.)	injured person (m./f.), casualty (m./f.)	
	herida	wound, injury	
FERRUM	hierro	iron, brand (mark on animal)	[*ferrous*]
FERVERE	hervir	(to) boil	
	hervor	boiling (n.)	[*fervor*]
	agua hirviendo	boiling water	
	hirviente³	boiling (adj.)	[*fervent*]
	fervor	fervor	
	ferviente	fervent	
	efervescencia	effervescence, agitation	
FIBRA	hebra	thread, *fiber,* grain (of wood)	
FICUS	higo	*fig*	
	higuera	fig tree	
FIGICARE	hincar	(to) thrust, (to) drive in(to)	[*fix, affix*]
	hacer hincapié en	(to) drive the foot (*pie*) in, (to) emphasize	
	ahínco	eagerness, determination, zeal	
	finca	rural property, country estate, *finca*	
FILIA	hija	daughter	[*filial*]
FILICTUM	helecho	fern	[bot. *filix*]
FILIUS	hijo	son	
FILUM	hilo	thread	[*filament*]
	hilar	(to) spin (wool, silk, spiderweb, etc.)	
	hilandero	spinner, spinster (in the original sense)	
	hilera	row, line	
	retahíla	(monotonous) list or series of things	
FINDERE	hender	(to) crack, (to) split	[*fission*]
	hendidura	crack, *fissure*	

---

³ *Hirviente* is in danger of extinction, having been largely replaced by the present participle *hirviendo*; thus, *agua hirviendo* is today far more common than *agua hirviente*.

FIXUS, FICTUS	hito	boundary stone, milestone	[*fixed*]
FOETOR	hedor	stench, *fetor*	
	heder	(to) stink	
	fétido	*fetid,* foul	
FOLIA	hoja	leaf, sheet	[*folio*]
	hojear	(to) leaf through	
FORMA	horma	*form* (mold), shoe tree	
FORMICA	hormiga	ant	[*formic acid*]
	hormigueo	tickling or tingling sensation (pins and needles)	
	hormiguero	anthill, ant nest	
	oso hormiguero	anteater	
	hormiguear	(to) have pins and needles, (to) swarm	
	hormigo[4]	corn flour mush, nougat (pl.)	
	hormigón	concrete	
	hormigón armado	reinforced concrete	
	hormigonera	cement mixer (machine or truck)	
FORMOSUS	hermoso	beautiful, lovely, handsome	[*Formosa*]
	hermosura	beauty, handsomeness	
FOVEA	hoya	pit, grave, valley	[*fovea*]
	hoyo	hole (e.g., golf), pit	
FUGERE	huir	(to) flee	[*fugitive*]
	ahuyentar	(to) frighten or chase away	
	fugaz	fleeting, *fugacious*	[*fugue*]
	fugitivo (adj. & n.)	fugitive	
	prófugo	escapee, fugitive (from justice), military deserter	
FUMUS	humo	smoke, *fume,* airs or conceit (pl.)	
	humear	(to) *fume,* (to) smoke, (to) steam	
	fumar	(to) smoke (a cigarette)	
	fumador	smoker	

---

[4] *Hormigo* apparently is due to the similarity between grains of flour bubbling in boiling corn flour mush and the bustling of ants in an ant nest. *Hormigón* then followed naturally due to the resemblance in form between mush and concrete.

FUNDERE	hundir	to sink, (to) knock or fall down	[*fondue*]
	hundimiento	sinking, collapse, subsidence	
FUNDUS	hondo	deep	[*fund*]
	profundo	deep, *profound*	
FUNGUS	hongo	*fungus*, mushroom	
FURCA	horca	gallows, pitch*fork*	
	ahorcar	(to) hang (a person)	
	horquilla	hairpin, fork (bicycle, slingshot)	
FURNUS	horno	oven, kiln, *furnace*	
FURTUM	hurto	petty theft, pilfer	[*furtive*]
	hurtar	(to) steal, (to) pilfer	
	a hurtadillas	*furtively*, on the sly	
	furtivo (adj. & n.)	furtive, stealthy, poacher	
FUSCUS	hosco	sullen, surly (person or weather)	[ob*fuscate*]
FUSTIGARE	hostigar	(to) whip, (to) harass	[*fustigate*]

Also:

DEFENSA	dehesa	pasture, meadow	[*defense, fence*]
OFFOCARE	ahogar	(to) drown, (to) suf*focate*	
	desahogar	(to) relieve, (to) alleviate, (to) vent one's feelings	
	sofocar	(to) *suffocate* or smother (person, flames)	
REFUSARE	rehusar	(to) *refuse*	

Historical Note

In its road from local dialect to Modern Spanish, Castilian adopted various forms of speech and a portion of its vocabulary from the other forms of Romance spoken in Spain, including Mozarabic, the Romance spoken by Christians in the parts of Spain under Muslim control. At the same time, due to Castile's steadily increasing political importance, a number of purely "Castilian" forms of speech, initially native to only a very small area and on occasion ridiculed by contemporaries as primitive or uncultured, were able to become the accepted norm in Modern Spanish. The noted Spanish scholar Ramón Menéndez Pidal (1869–1968), author of several of the classic works on the history of the Spanish language, expressed this conclusion somewhat less delicately. Referring specifically to the change of initial *f* to *h*, he wrote:

> La *h* no fué (*sic*[5]) en un principio más que un barbarismo dialectal propio de la gente menos culta en el Norte de Castilla y tierras limítrofes, uno de tantos casos . . . de particularidades castellanas, primero muy restringidas y que después, con el crecimiento de Castilla, llegan a difundirse por casi toda la Península.[6]

> The *h* initially was simply a dialectical barbarism characteristic of the less educated inhabitants in northern Castile and adjoining areas, one of many instances . . . of Castilian peculiarities, at first very limited in scope, which subsequently, with the expansion of Castile, were extended to the quasi totality of the (Iberian) Peninsula.

The *f* ⟶ *h* change is only one of several peculiarly Castilian characteristics that have been attributed (by Menéndez Pidal and others) to the influence of the Basques, as the Basque language did not have the [f] sound. This explanation is by no means universally accepted, and numerous competing theories have been advanced. What does not seem disputed is that the development *f* ⟶ *h* occurred in two phases, both originating from the Castilian "heartland"[7] and gradually expanding through the rest of Castilian-speaking Spain (the first also extended to the Gascon branch of the Occitan language in southwest France):

(a) *f* ⟶ aspirated *h* (as in **h**istory, **h**otel)
   There is evidence that Latin *F* was pronounced [h] in zones contiguous with Basque territories as early as the ninth century. This aspirated pronunciation then expanded southward, paralleling the expansion of Castile. There was initially no change in spelling; those using aspirated *h* continued to write "*f*" (e.g., *fablar* pronounced [hablar]).
(b) aspirated *h* ⟶ ø
   The same areas that had initially propagated the aspirated *h* in place of *f* subsequently lost the aspiration, and this new pronunciation (or lack

---

[5] Until 1959, *fue* (the simple past third person singular for *ser*) was generally written *fué*, and it is not uncommon to encounter this form well after this date.

[6] Menéndez Pidal (1956), 220.

[7] Castilian Spanish originated in a very small area in north-central Spain (between Santander and Burgos) known as Cantabria, contiguous with Basque territories and one of the last parts of Spain to be "Romanized". It is likely that the Latin spoken there diverged even more than the "typical" Vulgar Latin from the Classical norms. The name Castilla comes from the *castillos* ("castles") that were a prominent feature along its frontier; *castellano* means both "Castilian" Spanish and "castellan" (i.e., "lord of the castle").

thereof) then spread in a similar manner throughout Castilian-speaking Spain. By the late sixteenth century, the unaspirated pronunciation of Modern Spanish had been firmly established.

Nonetheless, *most* words have retained their initial *f.* These include:

(1). WORDS FROM LATIN *FL-*[8] OR *FR-*, e.g.,

FLACCUS	flaco	skinny, lean, weak	[*flaccid*]
FLATUS	flato	*flatus*, wind (intestinal gas)	[*inflation*]
	flatulencia	*flatulence*	
FLOREM (acc.)	flor (f.)	*flower*	
FLUXUS	flujo	*flux*, flow	
FRAUDEM (acc.)	fraude	*fraud*	
	fraudulento	*fraudulent*	
	defraudar	(to) *defraud*, (to) disappoint	
FRENUM	freno	brake	[*frenum*]
	frenar	(to) brake, (to) restrain	
	refrenar	(to) restrain, (to) curb, (to) rein	[*refrain*]

(2). WORDS FROM LATIN *FO-*, WHERE THE o *DIPHTHONGED* TO BECOME SPANISH *ue* (SEE SECTION 3.3),[9] e.g.,

FOCUS	fuego	fire	[*focus*]
FONTEM (acc.)	fuente (f.)	*fountain*, source, *fount*	
FORAS	fuera	out, outside, without	[*forum*]
FORTIS	fuerte	strong	[*fort, forte*]

(3). "LEARNED" (OR "SEMI-LEARNED") WORDS, E.G.,

FATALIS	fatal	*fatal, fateful*	
FATALITAS	fatalidad	*fatality* (= fate or misfortune, not death)	
FEBRIS	fiebre (f.)	*fever*	
FIDES	fe (f.)	*faith*	[Santa *Fe*]
FIGURA	figura	*figure*	
FINGERE	fingir	(to) pretend, (to) *feign*	

---

[8] One word beginning with FL- has undergone an altogether different transformation: Latin FLAMMA ("*flame*") has become *llama*, thus making it a homonym with the Andean animal as well as with the third person singular of the verb *llamar* ("to call"): Se *llama* José.

[9] The few exceptions are closely linked to verbs in which most of the forms "naturally" developed an undipthonged *ho-* (the diphthong occurring only in stressed syllables). Hence the noun *huelga* is associated with the verb *holgar* (from Latin FOLLICARE), which in turn has nine of its forty-seven "simple" conjugations with *hue-* (*huelgo, huelgas,* etc.).

FINIS	fin	end, *finish*	
FIRMARE	firmar	(to) sign	[*affirm, farm*]

Until the late fifteenth century, words with aspirated *h* (in process of disappearance) and those with "real" *f* were both written with *f*. By this time, there were many couplets with different meanings and pronunciations but identical written form, one pronounced with aspirated (or no) *h*, the other with *f*. Some of these came from the same Latin word, while others had arisen by phonetic accident. To distinguish between these in written as well as spoken Spanish, those with the *h* (or no) sound had their initial *f*- changed to *h*-. Examples of such couplets are:

(1)	(2)	(1)	(2)
hallar	fallar	(to) find	(to) render judgment, (to) fail
hecha	fecha	done, made	date
hiel (f.)	fiel	bile	*faith*ful
hijo	fijo	son	*fix*ed
hilo	filo	thread	sharp edge

As a result of these somewhat haphazard developments, the same Latin root has often wound up with *both* pronunciations in Modern Spanish:

	Spanish	English	Spanish	English
FERRUM				
	herradura	horseshoe	férreo	*ferrous*
	herramienta	tool	ferrocarril	railroad
	herrería	blacksmith's shop	ferretería	hardware store
	herrumbre	rust	ferroviario	railroad (worker)
FILIUS				
	hijo	son	filial (adj. & n.f.)	*filial*, subsidiary
	hija	daughter	filiación	*filiation, affiliation*
	hijastro	stepchild	afiliación	*affiliation*
	hidalgo	nobleman	afiliado	*affiliate*, member
FUNDUS				
	hondo	deep	fondo	bottom (n.)
	hondamente	deeply, profoundly	fundamental	*fundamental*
	hondonada	hollow, dale	fundar	(to) *found*, (to) base
	hondura	depth	fundación	*foundation, founding*
	Honduras	*Honduras*	fundamento	*foundation* (base)

Vowel Changes: *e* → *ie, o* → *ue*, etc.

Perhaps the single feature making Spanish the easiest—or least difficult—of any foreign language that an English speaker might seek to learn is the simplicity of its vowel system. Consider the European languages most commonly studied by English speakers (other than Russian, which uses a different alphabet). A reasonably consistent estimation of the "pure" vowels for each language, and the number that are "new" to English speakers, is shown below:

	No. of Vowels	"New"
German	16	4
French	16	8
Portuguese	14	6
Italian	7	0
Spanish	*5*	*0*

Spanish thus has not only the fewest vowels, all of which are familiar to English speakers, but *it is the only language that can offer a one-to-one correspondence between vowel sounds and letters (a, e, i, o, u)*. It would be difficult to overestimate the importance of this to the learner of a new language.

This simplicity is partly masked, however, by the fact that pronunciation of English vowels in most cases differs significantly from that of the corresponding Spanish vowel. For example, Spanish *republicano* and English *republican* have four vowels in common (*e, u, i, a*), not one of which has the same pronunciation in the two languages.

Spanish	Pronounced Like
republicano	ray•poo•blee•cah•no

This difference reflects the fact that since the days of "Old English" virtually all English vowels have changed their pronunciations (see appendix), while Spanish vowel pronunciation has changed remarkably little since Classical Latin times.

Although Spanish vowel *sounds* have essentially remained constant, the vowels in many individual "popular" words have shifted, albeit to a relatively limited extent. Fortunately, these shifts were linked to a corresponding change in spelling, so that the one-to-one correspondence between spoken and written forms has, with very few exceptions, been preserved.

This is illustrated in the table below, where the vowel affected is highlighted in bold.

OCCASIONAL MODIFICATIONS IN SPANISH VOWELS ("POPULAR" WORDS)				
		Latin Root	Spanish	English
1.	*I → e*	MINUS	menos	minus
2.	*E → i*	SERVIENTEM	sirviente	servant
3.	*E → ie*	CENTUM	ciento	cent
4.	*A → e*	TRACTUS	trecho	tract
5.	*O → ue*	PORCUS	puerco	pork
6.	*O → u*	COMPLERE	cumplir	complete, accomplish
7.	*U → o*	TRUNCUS	tronco	trunk
8.	*AU → o*	TAURUS	toro	Taurus

These changes occur with varying frequency: nos. 3, 5, and 7 are the most common; nos. 4 and 6, the least. In corresponding English "learned" words, the original Latin vowel generally remains unchanged (as in all the examples above), while in "popular" words (normally via French), it has frequently been altered. In some cases, the alteration is identical to that which took place in Spanish, thus facilitating the comparison, e.g.,

INTRATA   entrada   entry

Diphthongs

In two cases (nos. 3 and 5), the "new" vowel is in fact a *diphthong:*
3. *ie*   pronounced like "ye" in *yet*[1]
5. *ue*   pronounced like "we" in *wet* (sometimes more like "wei" in *weight*)
From the point of view of learning vocabulary, there are two important points to note:

a). With very few exceptions, these two diphthongs occur *only* when the vowel in question is located in the *stressed* syllable. Related words where

---

[1]At the beginning of a word or syllable, the *ie* diphthong in much of the Spanish-speaking world is pronounced either like the *s* in *pleasure* or the *j* in *judge*, while after a consonant the [ye] sound is maintained.

the stress falls on a different syllable will therefore generally not display the diphthong. Thus, from Latin TEMPUS come the following (where, in the middle column, the stressed syllable is highlighted in bold):

tiempo	**tiem•po**	time
temporario	tem•po•**ra**•rio	*temporary*
temporal	tem•po•**ral**	*temporal*

b). This situation occurs with respect to a large class of verbs known as *diphthong* verbs. Thus, for the verbs *pensar* ("to think") and *mover* ("to move"), one says:

(yo)	pienso	**pien•**so	I think
(nosotros)	pensamos	pen•**sa•**mos	we think
(yo)	muevo	**mue•**vo	I move
(nosotros)	movemos	mo•**ve•**mos	we move

Diphthongs occur in precisely those conjugations where the stress accent falls on the "stem" syllable.[2]

Examples are presented below for each of the eight different types of vowel change noted above. In many cases, related words that do not have the vowel change are shown. "Diphthong" verbs are marked with an asterisk.[3]

1. *I → e*

CIRCA	cerca (1)	near, close	[*circa*]
	cerca de	nearly, close to (place, time, quantity)	
	de cerca	close up, closely	
	acercar	(to) approach, (to) bring near	
	cercano	close, nearby	
	cercanía	proximity, vicinity (pl.), surroundings (pl.)	
CIRCUS	cerco	circle, ring, halo (e.g., sun), siege	
	cercar	(to) fence, (to) surround	[*search*]

---

[2] For further details, see Brodsky (2005, 22–28, 99).

[3] Where the diphthong forms are "optional", the asterisk is in parentheses.

	cerca (2)	(surrounding) fence or wall	
	circo	circus	
	círculo	circle	
DICERE	decir (p.p. dicho[4])	(to) say	[*dictate*]
	bendecir	(to) bless	[*benediction*]
	contradecir	(to) *contradict*	
	contradicción	contradiction	
	contradictorio	contradictory	
	desdecir	(to) not be in keeping with, (to) unsay (retract)	
	maldecir	(to) curse, (to) speak ill of	[*malediction*]
	predecir	(to) *predict*	
	predecible	predictable	
	predicción	prediction	
VERUM (truth) +	verídico	true, truthful, *veridical*	("to say the truth")
	veredicto (< Eng.)	*verdict*	("true said")
DIS-	des-	dis-	
	desfigurar	(to) disfigure	
	desmantelar	(to) dismantle	
FIDES	fe (f.)	*faith*	[*fidelity*]
IN	en	in, into, on	
INTRARE	entrar	(to) enter	[*intra*]
	entrada	entry, entrance, *entrée*[5]	
	entre	between, among	[*inter*]
	dentro (de)	inside, within	(< DE + INTRO)
	dentro de una semana	in a week's time	
	adentro	within, inside	

---

[4] The *-decir* verbs have past participles ending in *-dicho*, with the exception of *bendecir* and *maldecir*, which have regular past participles (*bendecido, maldecido*).

[5] In terms of meals, Spanish *entrada*—"a dish served before the main course"—preserves the sense of *entry*, while English *entrée* (which technically maintains this definition) is now normally used to refer to the main course itself.

MINOR	menor	smaller, younger, *minor* (adj. & n.)	
	al por menor	retail (~ *al detalle*)	
	pormenor	detail, details (pl.)	
	pormenorizado	detailed (specified in detail)	
	minoría	minority	
MINUS	menos	*minus,* less, fewer, least, fewest	
	al menos	at least (~ *por lo menos*)	
	a menos que	unless	
	minúsculo (adj.)	minuscule, tiny, lowercase (letter)	
	minúscula (n.)	lowercase letter, minuscule	
NAVIGARE	navegar	(to) navigate, (to) sail	
	navegación	navigation, voyage in a boat	
	navegable	navigable	
	navegante (m./f.)	navigator, seafarer	
PILUS	pelo	hair	[*pilosity*]
PRO + MITTERE	prometer	(to) *promise*	
	promesa	*promise*	
SICCUS	seco	dry	[Dry *Sack*[6]]
	secar	(to) dry	[de*siccate*]
	secado (p.p.)	drying (n.)	
	secador, -ora	dryer (hair, hand, clothes)[7]	
	secano	unwatered or unirrigated land	
	sequía	drought	
	sequedad	dryness	
	desecar	(to) dry up, (to) *desiccate*	

---

[6] English *sack* refers to various dry white wines imported to England from Spain and the Canaries in the sixteenth and seventeenth centuries, and initially had the form *seck* (from French *vin sec*). It became confused with the ordinary *sack* ("bag"), which at that time had an alternative form, *sek*, and when *sek* finally settled on the form *sack*, so did the dry wine. Dry *Sack,* a trade name for various types of sherry, thus literally means "dry dry".

[7] To dry one's hair or hands, most frequently a *secador* is used, while a clothes dryer can be either a *secador* or *secadora* (see appendix to Annex A).

	resecar	(to) dry out	
	reseco	dried up, parched	
SINUS	seno	*sinus,* breast, womb	
TIMOR	temor	fear	[*intimidation*]
	temer	(to) fear, (to) be afraid	
	temeroso	fearful (causing fear), *timorous*	
	tímido	timid	
	timidez	timidity	
VICINUS	vecino (adj. & n.)	neighboring, neighbor	[War*wick*]
	vecindad	*vicinity,* neighborhood	
	avecinar(se)	(to) approach (e.g., storm)	
VINCERE	vencer	(to) *vanquish,* (to) defeat	
	invencible	*invincible*	
	convencer	(to) *convince*	
VINDEMIA	vendimia	grape harvest, *vintage*	[*vine*]

2. *E → i*

In several of the following examples, the change *E → ie* (no. 3) also occurs (the corresponding vowels are italicized).

AFFECTIO(N)	afición	fondness, hobby, (sports) fans	[*affection*]
C(A)EMENTUM[8]	cim*ie*nto	basis, foundations (e.g., of house—gen. pl.)	
	cimentar *	(to) lay the foundations of	
	cemento	cement	
	cementerio[9]	*cemetery*	
DECEMBER	dic*ie*mbre	December	
(A)EQUALIS	igual	*equal,* the same	
	igualmente	equally	
	igualar	(to) equalize, (to) equal	
	igualdad	equality	
	igualitario	egalitarian	
	desigual	unequal, uneven (terrain, character, etc.)	

---

[8] At a relatively early stage, Latin AE merged with (Vulgar) Latin (short) E.

[9] *Cementerio* has nothing to do with *cemento,* but its "superfluous" *n* may possibly be due to "popular" association of the two words.

	desigualdad	inequality	
FERVENTEM (acc.)	hirviente	boiling	[*fervent*]
	hervir[10]	(to) boil	
LEVIANUS	liviano	light, slight, frivolous	[*levity*]
RENIO(N)	riñón	kidney	[*renal*]
SEMENTEM (acc.)	simiente (f.)	seed (~ *semilla*)	[*semen*]
SEQUENTEM (acc.)	siguiente	following, next, *sequent*	
	seguir[11]	(to) follow, (to) continue	[*segue*]
	subsiguiente	subsequent	
TEPIDUS	tibio	*tepid*, lukewarm	

3. E → ie

APERTUS	abierto	open	[*aperitif*]
	abertura	*aperture*, opening (physical: e.g., window)	
BENE	bien	well, fine, good (n.), goods (pl.)	
	bienestar	well-being, welfare	
	benevolencia	*benevolence*	
	benévolo	benevolent, volunteer (Amer.)	
tan + bien	también	also, too	
C(A)ECUS	ciego	blind	[*cecum—* "blind gut"]
	ceguera	blindness	
C(A)ELUM	cielo	sky, heaven	
	celeste	sky blue, *celestial*	
	celestial	celestial, heavenly	
CALENTEM (acc.)	caliente	hot	[non*chalant*]
	calentar *	(to) heat, (to) warm up	[*calenture*]
	calefacción	heating, heat	
	recalentar *	(to) reheat, (to) overheat	[*recalescence*]

---

[10] In eleven (of the basic forty-seven) conjugations, the vowel in *hervir* shifts from *e* to *i* (e.g., present participle *hirviendo*), while in the nine conjugations in which it is stressed, it becomes the diphthong *ie* (present tense *yo hiervo*). This pattern is common to *-ir* verbs with stem vowel *e* that is followed directly by either *r* or *nt*; among the few exceptions is *servir* (see following note).

[11] In twenty (of the basic forty-seven) conjugations, the vowel in *seguir* shifts from *e* to *i* (e.g., present participle *siguiendo* and present tense *yo sigo*). Apart from *venir*, this pattern is common to *-ir* verbs with stem vowel *e* that is *not* followed directly by *r* or *nt*, plus *servir*. For further details on this and the previous footnote, see Brodsky (2005, 28–31, 99–100).

	recalentamiento	reheating, overheating	
CENTUM	ciento	hundred	[*centennial*]
	centavo	hundredth part, *cent*	
	centenar ~ centena	a hundred (group)	
	centímetro	centimeter	
CERTUS	cierto	*certain,* sure	
	acierto	good shot ("hit"), good choice, good guess	
	desacierto	mistake, error	
	certeza	*certainty, certitude*	
	acertar *	(to) hit (the mark), (to) guess right	
	acertijo	riddle	
	concierto	*concert, concerto,* accord	
	concertar *	(to) harmonize, (to) *concert,* (to) agree	
	desconcierto	confusion, disorder	
	desconcertar *	(to) disconcert	
	desconcertante	disconcerting	
IN-COMMENDARE	encomendar *	(to) entrust, (to) *commend*	
	encomienda	commission, charge	
	recomendar *	(to) recommend	
	recomendación	recommendation	
CREPARE	quebrar *	(to) break, (to) go bankrupt	[*crepitate*]
	quiebra	bankruptcy, breakdown (values)	[*crevice*]
	quebrantar	(to) break, (to) violate, (to) weaken	
	quebrantahuesos[12]	osprey, ossifrage (bearded vulture)	
	resquebrajar	(to) crack (wall, pottery)	

---

[12] A *quebrantahuesos* is literally a "bone breaker": *quebrantar* + *huesos*. Likewise, an English *ossifrage* (Latin OSSIFRAGA) is a *fracturer* of bones (OSSA). *Osprey* (a fish-eating hawk) is seen by some as representing a "popular" form of the same word (via French), while others believe it comes from Medieval Latin AVIS PREDE ("bird of *prey*").

	decrépito	decrepit
	increpar	(to) upbraid, (to) scold
DECEM	di**e**z	ten
	di**e**zmar[13]	(to) *decimate*, (to) tithe
	decimal	decimal
DESERTUS	des**ie**rto (adj. & n.)	*deserted, desert*
	desértico	deserted, desert-like (e.g., climate)
	desertar	(to) desert (from military, or from obligation)
	desertor	deserter
	deserción	desertion
DEXTRA	di**e**stra	right hand
	di**e**stro	right (adj.), right-handed, *dexterous*, matador
	destreza	*dexterity*, skill
	adi**e**strar[14]	(to) train, (to) drill, (to) become skilled
	adi**e**stramiento	training
EMENDARE	enmendar *	(to) *emend*, (to) *amend*
	enm**ie**nda	correction, *emendation*, *amendment*
	remendar *	(to) *mend*, (to) patch, (to) darn
	rem**ie**ndo	patch, provisional repair
EQUA	**ye**gua[15]	mare *[equestrian]*
(H)EREMUS	**ye**rmo (adj. & n.)	barren, uninhabited, wasteland
	ermita	*hermitage*
	ermitaño	*hermit* (~ *eremita* m.)
ERRARE	errar *	(to) *err*, (to) wander

---

[13] *Diezmar,* which has a diphthong in an unstressed syllable, is the exception that proves the rule. The verb was initially *dezmar,* with diphthongs only in those conjugations where the stress fell on the stem syllable (e.g., *yo diezmo*), and no diphthongs in the other conjugations (including the infinitive). In relatively recent times, the verb was "regularized", so that all conjugations now show diphthongs, even in unstressed syllables.

[14] As for *diezmar* (see preceding footnote), the original verb *adestrar* has been regularized by extending diphthongs to unstressed syllables.

[15] Spanish does not allow a word to start with *ie*, so the diphthong *ie* is written *ye*.

	error ~ **ye**rro	error, mistake	
	errado (p.p.)	erroneous, mistaken	
	errante	errant (wandering)	
	errata	misprint, erratum	
	erróneo	erroneous	
	aberrante	aberrant	
FERRUM	h**ie**rro	iron	[*ferrous*]
	herrero	blacksmith	[*farrier*]
	herrar *	(to) shoe a horse, (to) brand	
	aferrar	(to) grasp, (to) cling to	
FERUS	f**ie**ro (adj.)	wild, *fierce*	
	f**ie**ra (n.)	wild animal	
	feroz	*ferocious*	
	ferocidad	ferocity, *fierceness*	
FESTA	f**ie**sta	party, *fete,* holiday, holy day, *festival, fiesta*	
	festín	banquet, *feast*	
	festividad	festivity	
	festival	festival	
	festivo	festive, humorous	
	festejo	celebration, festivities (pl.)	
	festejar	(to) *fete,* (to) celebrate	
GELU	h**ie**lo	ice	[*gelid, gel*]
	helar *	(to) freeze	
	helado	frozen, freezing cold, ice cream (m.)	
	congelar	(to) freeze, (to) *congeal*	
	congelador	freezer	
GR(A)ECUS	gr**ie**go (adj. & n.)	*Greek*	
	i gr**ie**ga	"y" ("*Greek*" *i—* penultimate letter of alphabet)	
	Grecia	Greece	[*Grecian*]
	gringo[16]	gringo	

[16] While labeled in many *English* dictionaries as "Offensive Slang" (the same category as the "*n*"-word or *dago*), Spanish *gringo* is in fact generally used as a relatively harmless term to refer to foreigners (and not always to "*norteamericanos*"). It is a deformation of *griego*: the original sense was in reference to those speaking an unintelligible language, i.e., analogous to the English expression "it's all *Greek* to me". This latter expression corresponds in turn to Spanish *hablar en griego/gringo* or, more commonly, *hablar en chino.*

GUBERNARE	gobernar *	(to) *govern,* (to) steer (nautical)[17]	
	gobierno	government, rudder, helm	
	gobernador	governor	
	gobernadora	lady governor, governor's wife	
	gobernante	governing, ruling, ruler (m./f.)	
	gubernamental	governmental	[*gubernatorial*]
helm (Germanic)	**ye**lmo	*helmet*	
HERBA	h**ie**rba, **ye**rba	grass, weed, *herb*	
	yerba mate	yerba maté	
	herbáceo	herbaceous	
	herbario	herbal, herbarium (dried plant collection)	
	herbicida (m.)	herbicide	
	herbívoro (adj. & n.)	herbivorous, herbivore	
HIBERNUM	inv**ie**rno	winter	(OldSp. *ivierno*)
	invernar (*)	(to) winter	[*hibernate*]
INCENDERE	encender *	(to) light, (to) switch on, (to) inflame	
	encender la luz	(to) turn on the light (turn off = *apagar*)	
	incendiario	*incendiary,* arsonist (m./f.)	
	incendio	fire (large-scale, destructive)	
	incendiar	(to) set on fire	
INCENSUM	inc**ie**nso	*incense*	
	incensar *	(to) incense (perfume with incense), (to) flatter	
	incensario	censer (for burning incense)	

---

[17] The nautical senses preserved in *gobernar* and *gobierno* are in fact the original meanings, going back to Greek *kubernan* (Latin GUBERNARE), which meant "to steer or pilot a ship".

INFERNUS	infierno	hell, *inferno*	
	infernal	infernal, hellish	
LEPOREM (acc.)	liebre (f.)	hare, rabbit	[*leporine*]
		(pacemaker)	
MANIFESTUS	manifiesto (adj. & n.)	*manifest* (obvious), *manifesto*	
	manifestar *	(to) *manifest*, (to) demonstrate	
	manifestación	manifestation, (public) demonstration	
	manifestante	demonstrator (m./f.)	
MEL	miel (f.)	honey	
	melifluo	*mellifluous*	
MEMBRUM	miembro	*member*, limb, penis	
	desmembrar *	(to) *dismember*, (to) break up	
	membrana	membrane	
MERENDA	merienda	light afternoon refreshment, tea (UK)	
	merendar *	(to) have a *merienda*	
METUS	miedo	fear	
	miedoso	fearful (easily frightened)	
	amedrentar	(to) frighten, (to) intimidate	
	meticuloso	*meticulous*	
NEBULA	niebla	fog, mist	[*nebula*]
	neblina	light fog, mist	
	nebuloso (adj.)	cloudy, foggy, hazy, *nebulous*	
	nebulosa (n.)	*nebula*	
NEGARE	negar *	(to) de*ny*, (to) *negate*	
	negación	denial, refusal, negative (gram.), negation	
	negativo (adj.)	negative (adj.)	
	negativa (n.f.)	negative (response), denial, refusal	
	negativo (n.m.)	negative (photo)	
	denegar *	(to) *deny* (refuse)	
	denegación	denial, refusal, *denegation*	

	renegar	(to) deny vigorously, (to) renounce	[*renege*]
	renegado (p.p.)	*renegade* (< Sp.), apostate	
	reniego	blasphemy, curse (lit., "I renege")	
NOVEMBER	noviembre	November	
PARENTEM (acc.)	pariente	relation, relative	[*parent*]
	emparentar (*)	(to) be or become related to	
	emparentado (p.p.)	related (to)	
PEDEM (acc.)	pie (m.)	foot	
	bípedo	biped	
PELLIS	piel (f.)	skin, *pelt*	[*pelisse*]
	película	film, movie, *pellicle*	
PETRA	piedra	stone	[*Peter, Pierre*]
	piedra angular	cornerstone	
	pedrada	throw of a stone (or blow from stone)	
	pedregoso	stony, rocky	
	pétreo	stone (adj.), *petrous,* stony (hard)	
	petrificar	(to) *petrify* (lit. & fig.)	
	apedrear	(to) stone	
	empedrar *	(to) pave with stone	
	empedrado	cobbled, stone pavement (m.)	
	empedernido	hardened (e.g., smoker), inveterate	
PIGMENTUM	pimiento	pepper plant, *pimento*	[*pigment*]
RECENTEM (acc.)	reciente	*recent*	
(before p.p.)	recién llegado	recently arrived	
	recientemente	recently	
SECARE ("to cut")	segar *	(to) reap, (to) mow, (to) cut down	[*secant*]
	siega	reaping, harvest (time)	
SEDENTARE	sentar *	(to) seat, (to) sit	[*sedentary*]
	asiento	seat	

	asentar *	(to) set, (to) place, (to) assert	
SEMINARE	sembrar *	(to) sow, (to) seed	[*inseminate*]
	siembra	sowing, sowing season	
	semental	breeding, breeding animal (stud)	
	semilla	seed (~ *simiente*)	
	semillero	seedbed, plant nursery	
	semen	semen, seed (bot.)	
	seminal	seminal (pert. to semen or seed ONLY)	
SEMPER	siempre	always	[*Sic Semper Tyrannis*]
	sempiterno	*sempiternal* (eternal)	
SENTIRE	sentir[18]	(to) feel, (to) *sense* (hear), (to) regret	
	lo siento (mucho)	I am (very) sorry	
	sentido (p.p. & adj.)	sensitive (quick to take offense)	
	sentido (n.)	*sense,* direction	
	sentido del humor	sense of humor	
	sentimiento	sentiment, feeling, regret	
	sentimental	sentimental	
	presentir	(to) have a feeling (that something will happen)	
	presentimiento	premonition, *presentiment*	
SEPTEM	siete	seven	[*septuple*]
SEPTEMBER	septiembre	*September*	
SERPENTEM (acc.)	serpiente (f.)	serpent, snake	
—SERPENS (nom.)	—sierpe (f.)	—serpent, snake	
SERRA	sierra	saw, mountain range, *sierra*	
	serrar *	(to) saw	
	serrano	mountain, highland	

---

[18] *Sentir* (as well as *asentir, consentir, disentir,* and *presentir*) is conjugated analogously to *hervir* (see footnote no. 10).

SER(R)ARE	cerrar *	(to) shut, (to) close	[*serried*]
	cerradura	lock	
	cerrojo	bolt, latch	
	cerrajero	locksmith	
	cierre	snap, clasp, closing	
	encerrar *	(to) shut in, (to) enclose, (to) contain	
	encierro	confinement, seclusion	
SEXTA ("sixth")	siesta	siesta	
	sestear	(to) take a siesta, (to) rest in the shade (cattle)	
TENDA	tienda	store, shop, *tent*	
	tendero	shopkeeper, storekeeper	
	trastienda	back room (of a shop), cunning (n.)	
TENDERE	tender *	(to) stretch, (to) lay out, (to) *tend* (toward)	
	tendido (p.p. & adj.)	full (gallop), extended, lying down	
	tendido (n.)	electrical installation, bleachers (bullfight)	
	tendencia	tendency, trend	
	atender *	(to) pay *attention* to, (to) *attend* to	
	desatender *	(to) neglect, (to) not pay attention to	
	contender *	(to) contend, (to) compete	
	contendiente	contending, contender or contestant (m./f.)	
	contienda	battle, fight, quarrel	
	entender *	(to) understand	[*intend*]
	entendimiento	understanding	
	entente	entente (accord among countries)	
	desentender(se) *	(to) ignore, (to) take no part in	
	extender *	(to) extend, (to) spread	

	pretender	(to) try to, (to) aspire to, (to) *pretend*	
TENERUM (acc.)	tierno	*tender,* affectionate	(*nr → rn*)
	ternura	*tenderness*	
	enternecer	(to) soften, (to) move (stir emotions)	
TERRA	tierra	earth, land, soil	
	tierra de nadie	no man's land	
	globo terráqueo	*terrestial globe,* the earth	[+ *aqueous*]
	terraplén	embankment, terrace, *terreplein*	
	terraza	*terrace*	
	terrateniente	landowner	[*tenant*]
	terremoto	earthquake	
	terrenal	earthly, worldly, terrestrial	
	terreno (adj. & n.)	terrestrial, *terrene, terrain,* ground	
	subterráneo (adj. & n.)	subterranean, underground passage	
	terrestre	terrestrial	
	territorio	territory	
	territorial	territorial	
	aterrar * (1)	(to) cover with earth, (to) demolish, (to) land	
	aterrar[19] (2)	(to) frighten, (to) *terrify*	
	aterrizar	(to) land (an aircraft)	
	aterrizaje	landing	
	desterrar *	(to) exile, (to) banish	
	destierro	exile, banishment	
	enterrar *	(to) *inter,* (to) bury	(IN + TERRA)
	entierro	burial, *interment* (~ *enterramiento*)	
	desenterrar *	(to) *disinter,* (to) exhume, (to) unearth	
VENTUS	viento	wind	

---

[19] *Aterrar* (2), which has no diphthongs, has a different origin: Latin TERRERE ("to *terrify*").

	vendaval	strong (SW) wind, gale	(viento -de -a-valle)
	ventana	window	
	ventanilla	small window (car, plane, ticket office, etc.)	
	ventilar	(to) *ventilate,* (to) air	
	ventilador	fan, *ventilator*	
	ventisca	blizzard	
VETULUS	viejo	old	[*veteran*]
	vejez	old age	
	envejecer	(to) age, (to) grow old	
	envejecimiento	aging	
	veterano (adj. & n.)	veteran	
	vetusto	very old, ancient	[† *vetust*]

4. A → e

FACTA	fecha	date	[*fait* accompli]
JANUARIUS	enero	*January*	
LACTEM (VL acc.)	leche (f.)	milk	[*lactic* acid]
LAXIUS	lejos	far, far off	[*lax*]
MANSIO(N)	mesón	inn, tavern	[*mansion*]
PRIMARIUS	primero	first (adj., adv.)	
	primario	primary	
SATISFACTUS	satisfecho	*satisfied*	[*satisfaction*]

5. o → ue

BONUS	bueno	good	[*bonus*]
	bondad	goodness, kindness	[*bounty*]
	bondadoso	kind, good	[*bounteous*]
	bonito (1)	pretty, nice, good	
	bonito (2)	(small) tuna, *bonito*	
	bonanza	fair weather at sea, prosperity, *bonanza* (ore)	
	bombón	*bonbon,* small chocolate, "dish" (person)	

	abonar	(to) fertilize, (to) credit, (to) pay ("make good")	
	abonar(se) [20]	(to) subscribe	
	abono	fertilizer, manure, subscription, season ticket	
	hierbabuena	mint (plant)	("good herb")
BOVEM (acc.)	buey	ox, steer, bullock	
	bovino	bovine	
CHORDA	cuerda	*cord*, rope, string, *chord* (geom.), watch spring	
	cordón	shoelace, cord (as belt), electric cord, *cordon*	
COLLUM	cuello	neck, *collar* (shirt, suit, etc.)	
	collar	necklace, *collar*	
	degüello	throat-cutting, *decollation*	[*décolleté*]
	degollar *	(to) cut the throat, (to) *decollate* (behead)	
COMPUTUS	cuento	story, tale	
	cuenta	*count*, calculation, bill or check, *account*	
	tener en cuenta	(to) take into account	
	contar *	(to) *count*, (to) tell	[*compute*]
	contable (adj. & n.)	*countable, accountant*	
	contador	meter, *counter* (e.g., Geiger), *accountant*	
	descuento	*discount*	
	descontar *	(to) *discount*, (to) deduct	
CONCHA	cuenca	eye socket, river basin, valley	[*concha*]
	cuenco	earthen bowl, hollow or concavity	
	concha	shell, seashell, *conch*	

---

[20] *Abonar(se)* is originally unrelated to the other words.

CONSOLARE	consolar *	(to) console, (to) comfort	
	consuelo	consolation, alleviation, comfort	
	consolación	consolation (e.g., *premio de consolación*)	
	desconsolado	*disconsolate*	
(IN) + CONTRA	encontrar *	(to) find, (to) *encounter*, (to) meet	
	encuentro	meeting, *encounter*, match (sports)	
CORIUM	cuero	leather, hide	[*corium*, *currier*]
	excoriar / escoriar	(to) *excoriate* (tear or rub away the skin)	
	coraza	*cuirass*, breastplate, armor plating, shell (animal)	
	acorazar	(to) armor (ships, forts, etc.)	
	acorazado (p.p.)	ironclad (adj. & n.), battleship	
CORNU	cuerno	horn, antler	[uni*corn*]
	corneta	*cornet*, bugle	
COSTA	cuesta	hill, slope	[*coast*]
	cuesta arriba	uphill	
	cuesta abajo	downhill	
	costa	*coast*, shore [21]	
	costero	*coastal*	
	costilla	rib	[*costa*]
	costal	costal (pertaining to ribs), large sack	
	costado	side, flank	
	acostar (1) *	(to) put to bed	[*accost*]
	acostar (2)	(to) reach the *coast*	[*accoast* [22]]
	guardacostas	coast guard cutter	
	recostar *	(to) lean (back), (to) recline	

---

[21] Also, *"cost"*, "expense", although this has a completely different origin (see Section 4.5).
[22] Obsolete variant of *accost*.

COVA (CAVA [23])	cueva	*cave*	
	covacha	small cave, shack	
	caverna	cavern, cave	
DOMINA	dueña	owner, mistress, landlady	[*Donna*]
	doncella	maiden, maid	[*damsel*]
	dominar	(to) *dominate,* (to) master	
	dominación	domination	
	dominante	dominant, domineering	
	dominio	dominion, control, mastery, *domain*	
	dominó, dómino	dominoes (game), domino (costume)	
	predominar	(to) predominate	
	predominante	predominant	
	predominio	predominance	
	adueñar(se)	(to) seize, (to) take possession of	
DOMINUS	dueño	owner, master, landlord	
	doncel	young nobleman, male virgin	
[dueño de casa]	duende	goblin, elf, ghost, *duende* (magnetism, charm)	
FOCUS ("fireplace")	fuego	fire	
	fuegos artificiales	fireworks	
	alto el fuego	ceasefire	[*halt* the fire]
	foco	*focus,* center, light (head- or spot-)	
	enfoque	*focus* (camera), approach (to a matter)	
	enfocar	(to) *focus* (light, camera, thoughts)	

[23] The earliest Latin form was COVA, another example where Spanish has preserved an "older" form of the language.

	fogata	bonfire, campfire	
	fogón	stove, hearth	
	fogoso	fiery, spirited, ardent	
	hoguera	bonfire	(Section 3.2: *f* → *h*)
	en la hoguera	(burned) at the stake	
	hogar	hearth, fireplace, home	[*foyer*]
	rehogar	(to) fry lightly	
FOLLIS	fuelle	bellows	[*fool* = "windbag"]
	holgar *	(to) be idle, (to) rest	
	huelga decir que	"it goes without saying that . . ."	
	holgazán (-ana)	idle, lazy (and such a person)	
	huelga	strike	[*folly*]
	huelga de hambre	hunger strike	
	juerga ~ jolgorio²⁴	revelry, carousing	(*l* → *r*)
FONTEM (acc.)	fuente (f.)	*fountain*, source, *fount*, serving dish	
	fontana	*fountain*	
	fontanería	plumbing	
	fontanero	plumber	
FORAS	fuera	out, outside, without	[*forum*]
	afuera	outside, outskirts (pl.)	
	foráneo	*foreign*	
	forastero	stranger, outsider (also adj.)	[*forester*]
FORTIA	fuerza	*force*, strength	
	forzar *	(to) *force*	
	fortaleza	strength, *fortitude*, *fortress*	
	fortalecer	(to) strengthen, (to) *fortify*	

²⁴ *Juerga* is a variant from Andalusia, where the aspirated *h* (written *j*) continued to be pronounced even after it had disappeared from "standard" Castilian. *Jolgorio* is a more "expressive" form of the original *holgorio;* a similar "expressiveness" accounts for the initial *j-* (rather than *h-*) in the Spanish "*f*"-word (< Latin FUTUERE).

	esforzar *	(to) give strength, (to) exert, (to) strain	
	esf**ue**rzo	*effort*	
	reforzar *	(to) *reinforce,* (to) strengthen	
	ref**ue**rzo	*reinforcement*	
FORTIS	f**ue**rte (adj. & n.)	strong, *fort, forte*	
	forte (<It.)	*forte* (musical)	
FORUM	f**ue**ro	rights and privileges, code of laws	
	f**ue**ro interno	conscience, heart of hearts	
	foro	*forum,* bar (legal profession)	
	forense	forensic, forensic doctor (m./f.)	
	desaf**ue**ro	excess, outrage, violation	
	desaforado	reckless, lawless, enormous	
GROSSUS	gr**ue**so (adj. & n.)	corpulent, thick, thickness, bulk	[gross]
	gr**ue**sa	*gross* (a group of twelve dozen)	
	grosero	coarse, uncouth, rude	
	engrosar (*)	(to) thicken, (to) swell, (to) increase	[*engross*]
HORTUS	h**ue**rto	orchard, vegetable garden	
	h**ue**rta	large vegetable garden, irrigated region	
	horticultura	*horticulture*	
	hortaliza	vegetable (~ *verdura*)	
HOSPITEM (acc.)	h**ué**sped (m.)	guest	[*host;* see Section 4.8]
	hospedar	(to) put up, (to) lodge	
JOVIS	j**ue**ves	Thursday	[*Jove's* day]
	jovial	*jovial*	
(IN) LOCO	l**ue**go	then, afterward, therefore	[*locus*]
	desde l**ue**go	naturally, of course	

MOBILIS	mueble	piece of furniture	[*mobile*]
	amueblar[25]	(to) furnish	
	inmueble	property, building	[*immobile*]
	bienes inmuebles	real estate	
	mobiliario ~ moblaje	household furniture	
	inmobiliario	real estate (adj.)	
	inmobiliaria	real estate (agency)	
MOLA	muela	millstone, grindstone, *molar* (tooth)	
	muela del juicio	wisdom tooth	
	moler *	(to) grind, (to) *mill*	
	molino	*mill*	
	molino de viento	windmill	
	molienda	grinding, *milling*	
	remolino	whirlwind, whirlpool, cowlick	
MOLES "mass"	muelle (1)	wharf, pier, dock	[*mole*[26]]
	mole (f.)	mass, bulk	
	molécula	molecule	
	molecular	molecular	
	demoler *	(to) *demolish*	
	demolición	demolition	
	demoledor	devastating	
MOLLIS	muelle (2)	soft, comfortable, spring (mechanical)	[*mollify*]
	mullir	(to) fluff, (to) soften	
	mullido (p.p.)	soft, fluffy, springy	
	molusco	mollusk (or mollusc)	
MONSTRUM	muestra	sample, specimen, sign	[*monster*]
	mostrar *	(to) show, (to) *demonstrate*	
	demostrar *	(to) *demonstrate,* (to) prove	
MORDERE	morder *	(to) bite	

---

[25] As for *diezmar* and *adiestrar* (see earlier footnotes), the original verb *amoblar* has been regularized by extending diphthongs to unstressed syllables.

[26] Mole[3] (*AHCD*): 1. A massive, usually stone wall constructed in the sea, used to enclose or protect an anchorage or harbor. 2. The anchorage or harbor enclosed by a mole.

	mordaz	biting, caustic, *mordant*	
	mordisco	bite	
	remorder *	(to) bite repeatedly, (to) cause *remorse*	
	remordimiento	*remorse*	
	alm**ue**rzo	lunch, midmorning snack	(cf. "a bite to eat")
	almorzar *	(to) consume one's *almuerzo*	
MORTIS (genit.)	m**ue**rte (f.)	death	[rigor *mortis*]
	m**ue**rto	dead	
	mortal	mortal, fatal	
	mortalidad	mortality	
	morir[27]	(to) die	
	moribundo	moribund, dying	
	mortificar	(to) mortify	
	amortiguar	(to) cushion, (to) muffle	
	amortiguador	shock absorber (auto)	
	amortizar	(to) amortize, (to) redeem	
	amortización	amortization	
NOSTRUM	n**ue**stro	our	[*nostrum*[28]]
	nosotros	we	
	N**ue**stra Señora	*Notre* Dame	
NOVEM	n**ue**ve	nine	[*November*]
	noveno	ninth	
	(hora) nona	*nones* (eccl., Roman)	[*noon*[29]]
NOVUS	n**ue**vo (adj.)	new	
	n**ue**va (n., gen. pl.)	news, tidings	
	n**ue**vamente	again (~ *otra vez, de nuevo*)	

---

[27] *Morir* has *ue* diphthongs in the nine (of forty-seven) conjugations in which the stress is on the stem syllable; in eleven other conjugations the *o* becomes *u*. The pattern is thus analogous to verbs like *hervir* (see footnote no. 10).

[28] From NOSTRUM REMEDIUM ("our remedy"), i.e., prepared by the person recommending it.

[29] Latin NONA originated as a shortened form of NOVENA. Originally *noon* was the *ninth* hour of daylight, or 3 P.M. When the time of church prayers shifted from the ninth to the sixth hour, *noon* became 12 P.M.

	nova	nova (suddenly bright star)
	novedad	*novelty,* news
	novel (adj.)	novel
	novela (n.)	novel, fiction
	novelista	novelist
	renovar *	(to) renew, (to) *renovate*
	renovación	renewal, renovation
	innovar	(to) innovate	(no diph- thongs !)
	innovación	innovation
	innovador (adj. & n.)	innovative, innovator
ORPHANUS	huérfano [30]	*orphan*
	orfanato	orphanage
OSSUM (CL os)	hueso	bone, pit or stone (fruit), *os*
	osificar	(to) *ossify*
	deshuesar [31]	(to) bone (meat), (to) stone or pit (fruit)
OVUM	huevo	egg	[*ovum*]
	hueva	roe (e.g., caviar)	[*ova*]
	ovulación	ovulation
	óvalo	oval
PONTEM (acc.)	puente	bridge
	pontón	*pontoon* (bridge or boat)
	pontífice	*Pontiff,* Pope	[*pontifex*]
	pontificado	pontificate (reign of Pope)
POPULUS	pueblo	small town, village, *people*
	poblar *	(to) *populate,* (to) inhabit
PORCUS	puerco	pig, hog (~ *cerdo*)	[*pork*]
	porquería	dirt, filth, "pig pen"

---

[30] An initial *h-* was added to *huérfano, hueso,* and *huevo,* since Spanish does not "permit" a word to start with *ue-*.

[31] As for *diezmar, adiestrar,* and *amueblar* (see earlier footnotes), the original verb *desosar* has been regularized by extending diphthongs to unstressed syllables.

PORTA	puerta	door
	portal	entrance hall, vestibule, *portal*
	portero	porter (doorkeeper), goalkeeper
	pórtico	portico
	portada	title page, front page or cover, facade
	porche	porch
PORTUS	puerto	*port,* mountain pass
	aeropuerto	*airport*
	aportar (1)	(to) make port (~ *arribar*)
	aportar (2)	(to) contribute
	aportación	contribution (money, goods, ideas)
POS(I)TUS	puesto (p.p. & adj.)[32]	set, laid, dressed or attired (w/ qualifying adj.)
	puesto (n.m.)	*post, position,* place, stall or stand (market)
	puesta (n.f.)	setting (e.g., *la puesta del Sol*), laying (eggs)
	puesto que	since, inasmuch as
	posición	position
	postal	postal, postcard (f.)
	poste	*post,* pole
	postizo[33]	false, artificial (hair, teeth), *postiche*
	apuesto (p.p.)	handsome, good-looking [*apposite*]
	apuesta	bet, wager
	apostar (1) *	(to) bet, (to) wager
	apostar (2)	(to) station or *post*
	compuesto (p.p.)	*composed, compound* (adj. & n.)

---

[32] Apart from other definitions they might have, words ending in *-puesto* are past participles of verbs ending in *-poner* (e.g., *poner, componer, disponer, oponer*), corresponding to English words ending in *-pose* (*pose, compose, dispose, oppose*). These verbs can be found in Section 4.10.

[33] Something (artificial) *positioned* to make up for whatever is lacking.

composición	composition
compositor	*composer*
decomposición	decomposition
deposición	deposition, bowel movement
disp**ue**sto (p.p.)	*disposed,* ready, apt
disposición	disposition, arrangement, decree, will
dispositivo	device, mechanism
exp**ue**sto (p.p.)	*exposed,* unprotected, dangerous or risky
exposición	exposition, exhibition, *exposure* (photo, sun)
imp**ue**sto (p.p.)	tax
imposición	imposition, deposit (in a bank)
impostor	impostor, slanderer
indisp**ue**sto (p.p)	*indisposed,* mildly ill, on bad terms
indisposición	indisposition, minor ailment
op**ue**sto (p.p.)	*opposite,* contrary
oposición	opposition, competitive entrance exam (gen. pl.)
presup**ue**sto (p.p.)	budget
prop**ue**sta	*proposal*
proposición	proposition, proposal
a propósito	by the way, *a propos*
rep**ue**sto (p.p.)	spare (held in reserve), spare part
reposición	replacement, revival (theater), repeat (TV)
sup**ue**sto (p.p.)	*supposed,* so-called, *supposition* (m.)
por sup**ue**sto	of course, naturally
suposición	supposition, assumption
POST p**ue**s (conj.)	since, then, well (interjection) [*post*]
desp**ué**s	after, afterward

PROBARE	probar *	(to) *prove,* (to) try, (to) taste (sample)	
	pr**ue**ba	*proof,* test, ordeal	
RESOLUTUS	res**ue**lto (p.p.)	*resolute*	
	resolver *	(to) resolve, (to) solve	
	resolución	resolution, *resolve*	
ROGARE	rogar *	(to) request, (to) plead (appeal earnestly)	
	r**ue**go	request, plea, entreaty	
	interrogar	(to) *interrogate*	
	abrogar	(to) *abrogate*	
	arrogar(se)	(to) *arrogate* to oneself, (to) usurp	
	derogar	(to) repeal or revoke	[*derogate*]
	prorrogar	(to) extend, (to) defer	[*prorogue*]
	prórroga	extension, overtime (sports)	
	subrogar	(to) *subrogate,* (to) *surrogate*	
ROTA	r**ue**da	wheel	[*rota*]
	r**ue**da de prensa	press conference	
	rodar *	(to) *roll,* (to) film, (to) *rotate* (~ *rotar*)	
	rodaje	shooting or filming (motion picture)	
	rodear	(to) surround, (to) take the long way around	
	rodeo	roundabout way, *rodeo*	
	r**ue**do	bullring, border or fringe (round)	
	rotación	rotation	
	rotar	(to) *rotate*	
SOCCUS ("slipper")	z**ue**co	clog, sabot (wooden shoe)	[*sock*]
SOLEA	s**ue**la	*sole* (of a shoe)	
SOLERE	soler *	(to) be used to, (to) be in the habit of	

	insólito	unusual, uncommon, unheard-of	
	insolente[34]	insolent	
	insolencia	insolence	
SOLIDUS	**sue**ldo	salary	[*sou, solidus*]
	soldado	*soldier*	
	sólido	solid (adj. & n.)	
	solidez	*solidity*	
	solidario	supportive, making common cause	
	solidaridad	solidarity	
	soldar *	(to) *solder*, (to) weld	
	soldador	welder or *solderer, soldering* iron	
	soldadura	*soldering* or welding, solder	
SOLUM	**sue**lo	floor, ground, *soil*	[*solum*]
	sub**sue**lo	*subsoil*	
	solar (1)	plot (of land), lot	
	solar * (2)	(to) floor, (to) pave	
	(unrelated)	solar (3)	solar (pertaining to the sun)
SOMNIUM	**sue**ño (1)[35]	dream	
	soñar *	(to) dream	
	soñador	dreamer	
	en**sue**ño	illusion, fantasy, dream	
SOMNUS	**sue**ño (2)	sleep, sleepiness	
	insomnio	insomnia, sleeplessness	
	sonámbulo	somnambulist, sleepwalker	
	somnoliento	somnolent (sleepy)	
	soñoliento		

---

[34] In Latin, an *insolent* person was initially one who acted in a manner contrary to custom; from this developed the "modern" notion of insolence.

[35] Latin "sleep" and "dream" were two closely related words that by phonetic "accident" have coalesced in Spanish. They have been maintained apart in French, Italian, and Portuguese.

	somnolencia	somnolence, drowsiness	
	somnífero (adj. & n.)	somniferous (~ *soporífero*), sleeping pill	
SORTEM (acc.)	su**e**rte (f.)	luck, fate, lot, *sort*	
	sortear	(to) draw lots for, (to) evade (a problem)	
	sorteo	raffle, drawing of lots	
	sortilegio	*sorcery,* magic spell, *sortilege*	
	consorcio	*consortium,* association	
	consorte	*consort,* spouse	("sharing same fate")
	resorte	spring (elastic), *resort* (means to attain something)	
TONARE	tronar *	(to) thunder	(*o—r → ro*)
	tru**e**no	thunder	
	atónito	thunderstruck, *astonished, astounded, stunned*	
	estr**ue**ndo	thunderous noise, uproar	
	detonación	detonation	
	detonar	(to) detonate	
	detonante	detonator	
	detonador		
TORQUERE	torcer *	(to) twist	[*torque*]
[TORTUS (p.p.)]	tu**e**rto	one-eyed (adj. & n.)	
	entu**e**rto	injustice, wrong, afterpains (pl.)	[*tort*]
	torcido (p.p.)	twisted, bent, crooked (tie, picture)	
	torsión	twisting, *torsion*	
	tormento	torment, *torture*	
	tormenta	storm, tempest	
	atormentar	(to) *torment,* (to) *torture*	
	tortura	torture	

	tortuoso	tortuous (winding, twisted, circuitous, devious)	
TROCARE	trocar *	(to) exchange, (to) barter, (to) *truck*	
	trueque	exchange, barter, *truck*	
VOLARE	volar *	(to) fly, (to) disapp-ear, (to) blow up	
	vuelo	flight	[*vol-au-vent*]
	volador	flying	
	volátil	*volatile*	
	volante (adj. & n.)	flying, steering wheel	[*volant*]
	ovni	UFO	(objeto volador no identificado)
	voleibol, vóleibol	*volleyball*	
VOLVERE	volver *	(to) turn, (to) return	
	vuelto (p.p.)	verso (back side), change (Amer.)	
	vuelta	turn, curve, tour, return, stroll	[*volute*]
	ida y vuelta	roundtrip	
	voltear	(to) turn over, (to) toss	
	voltereta	somersault, tumble	
	desenvolver *	(to) unwrap, (to) develop, (to) unfold	
	desenvoltura	ease, confidence, poise	
	devolver *	(to) return, (to) give back	[*devolve*]
	envolver *	(to) envelop, (to) wrap, (to) cover	[*involve*]
	envoltura	wrapper, wrapping	
	revolver *	(to) stir (up), (to) turn (around), (to) *revolve*	
	revólver (< Eng.)	revolver	
	revolución	revolution	
	revolucionario	revolutionary (adj. & n.)	

revolucionar	(to) revolutionize, (to) stir up
rev**ue**lta	*revolt*, disturbance
rev**ue**lto (p.p.)	disordered, scrambled, unsettled, stormy
huevo rev**ue**lto	scrambled egg

It is interesting to observe that the language of animals is subject to the same evolutionary forces:

CLOC (onom.)	cl**ue**ca	broody hen
	clocar *	(to) cluck (~ *cloquear*)
	en cuclillas	squatting, crouching (OldSp. *cluquillas*)

English is not immune to such changes: until at least the seventeenth century, English-speaking chickens *clocked,* while now (apart from some northern English dialects) they *cluck.*[36]

6. *o → u*

COGITARE	c**ui**dar[37]	(to) care for, (to) look after	[*cogitate*]
COGNATUS	c**u**ñado	brother-in-law	[*cognate*]
DORMIENTEM (acc.)	d**u**rmiente	sleeping, *dormant*	
	la Bella Durmiente	Sleeping Beauty	
	dormir[38]	(to) sleep	
	d**ue**rmevela	light or restless sleep	
JOCARI	j**u**gar[39]	(to) play	
	j**u**gador	player, gambler	
	j**u**guete	toy	
	j**ue**go	game	[*joke*]
	j**o**coso	humorous, *jocose, jocular*	
	joya (< Fr.)	*jewel,* jewelry (pl.)	
	joyería	jewelry store, jewelry trade	

---

[36] Spanish-clucking chickens have undergone a further "popular" phonetic change, described in Section 3.5 (*cl → ll*), so that a *clueca* is also known as a *llueca.*

[37] Following the disappearance of the intervening *g* (Section 3.4), the *u* combined with *i* to form a diphthong: [kwi•dar].

[38] Like *morir* (see footnote 27), *dormir* has *ue* diphthongs in the nine (of forty-seven) conjugations in which the stress is on the stem syllable; in eleven other conjugations the *o* becomes *u.*

[39] For the verb *jugar,* the stressed syllables have diphthongs (*yo juego*), the unstressed syllables have *u* (*nosotros jugamos*).

	joyero	jeweler (m./f.), jewel case	
JOCULARIS	juglar	minstrel, jester	[*juggler, jocular*]
OCTOBER	octubre	October	
POLIRE	pulir	(to) *polish,* (to) polish up	
POTENTEM (acc.)	pudiente	rich, wealthy	[*potent*]

7. u → o

The vast majority of Spanish nouns and adjectives ending in -*o* were derived from Latin words ending in -*us* or -*um*. Corresponding English nouns have frequently preserved the original ending, while for adjectives it has become -*ous*.

ABACUS	ábaco	abacus
ATRIUM	atrio	atrium, portico (church, palace)
CENSUS	censo	census
CUMULUS	cúmulo	cumulus (pile or heap, cloud)
EUCALYPTUS	eucalipto	eucalyptus
ODIUM	odio	odium
STIMULUS	estímulo	stimulus
ERRONEUS	erróneo	erroneous
FAMOSUS	famoso	famous
FORTUITUS	fortuito	fortuitous
FRIVOLUS	frívolo	frivolous
HETEROGENEUS	heterogéneo	heterogeneous
PRAEVIUS	previo	previous
SERIUS	serio	serious

Examples of more "popular" words include:

CUM	con	with	(*cum* laude, con-)
CURRERE	correr	(to) run	[*course*]
	correo	mail, post office (gen. pl.)	[*courier*]
	corriente (adj.)	*current,* ordinary, running (e.g., water)	
	corriente (f.)	*current* (water, air, electricity)	
	estar al corriente	(to) be up-to-date, well-informed	
	corriente eléctrica	*electric current*	

	corredor (adj. & n.)	running, runner, *corridor,* broker	
	corrida	race, bullfight, *corrida*	
	recorrer	(to) travel (across), (to) scan	[*recur*]
	recorrer a pie	(to) walk	
	recorrido (p.p.)	distance traveled, route, journey	
	recurrir	(to) have *recourse,* (to) resort, (to) appeal	
	recurrente	*recurrent*	
	recurso	*recourse,* resort, appeal (legal), resources (pl.)	
	socorrer[40]	(to) *succor,* (to) give help or relief to	
	socorro	help, aid, relief, *succor*	
	sucursal (f.)	branch (office)	
	transcurrir / tras-	(to) elapse, (to) pass	[*transcurrent*]
CURTARE	cortar	(to) cut	
	corto	short	[*curt*]
	corte	cutting, cut (n.)	
	corte de pelo	haircut	
	El Corte Inglés	"The English Cut"	(Sp. dept. store chain)
	cortina	*curtain*	
	cortina de humo	smokescreen	
	recortar	(to) trim, (to) cut (reduce)	
	recorte	clipping (newspaper), cutting (reduction)	
(unrelated)	corte (f.)	*court* (royal, law)	

---

[40] From Latin SUCCURRERE (= SUB + CURRERE), literally "to run under", i.e., to support.

FURNUS	horno	*furnace,* oven, kiln	
	hornillo	small stove	
JUVENIS	joven (adj. & n.)	young, young person	[*junior*[41]]
	juventud	youth (period of life), young people	
	juvenil	*juvenile,* youthful	
	rejuvenecer	(to) *rejuvenate*	
MUTILARE	motilar	(to) give a haircut to	
	mutilar	(to) mutilate	
PLUMBUM	plomo	lead	[*plumb*]
	plomero	lead worker, *plumber* (Amer.)	
	plomería	lead roofing, plumbing (Amer.)	
	plomizo	lead-colored	
	aplomo	*aplomb,* poise	
	desplomar	(to) get out of *plumb,* (to) collapse, (to) topple	
	desplome	collapse (e.g., of a building)	
PULVIS	polvo	dust, *powder*	
	polvoriento	dusty	
	pólvora	gun*powder,* fireworks	
	pulverizar	(to) *pulverize,* (to) spray (with an atomizer)	
RUMPERE	romper	(to) break, (to) smash, (to) tear	[*erumpent*]
	corromper	(to) *corrupt*	
	derrumbar	(to) knock down, (to) collapse	
	derrumbe	collapse (building, wall, idea)	

---

[41] The Latin comparative of JUVENIS was initially JUVEN-IOR ("younger"), subsequently shortened to JUNIOR.

RUPTUS (p.p.)	roto (p.p.)	broken, torn	[*rout, route*]
RUPTURA	rotura	breakage, fracture (bone), crack (e.g., pipe)	
	ruptura	*rupture,* breakup (relationship)	
	erupción	eruption	
SUBMITTERE	someter	(to) subject, (to) *submit*	
	sumiso	*submissive,* obedient, *submiss*†	
SUBORNARE	sobornar	(to) *suborn,* (to) bribe	
	soborno	bribe, bribery, subornation	
SUB POENA	so pena de	under *pain* (or *penalty*) of	[*subpoena*]
SUPER	sobre	over, above, about, envelope (n.)	[*super*]
TRUNCUS	tronco	*trunk* (tree, body, etc.)	
	troncho	stem or stalk (cauliflower, lettuce, etc.)	
	tronchar	(to) break or fall off (branch, stem, etc.)	
	truncar	(to) truncate, (to) leave incomplete (phrase, life)	
	entroncar	(to) connect or relate to (person, idea)	
UNDA	onda	wave, ripple	
	ondear	(to) *undulate,* (to) ripple	
	ondulación	*undulation*	
	ondular	(to) *undulate,* (to) wave (the hair)	
	(horno) microondas	microwave (oven)	
URTICA	ortiga	(stinging) nettle	
	urticaria	urticaria, hives	

| | urticante | urticant (causing itching or stinging) | |

8. *AU* → *O*

AUDIRE	oír	(to) hear, (to) listen	[*oyez*]
	oído	hearing, ear	[*audit*]
	audible	audible	
	inaudito	unheard-of, outrageous	[*inaudible*]
AURICULA	oreja	ear (external part)	[*auricle*]
	auricular	receiver (telephone), headphones (pl.)	
AURUM	oro	gold	[*oriole*]
	orfebre	goldsmith, silversmith	[gold *forger*]
	orfebrería	gold or silver work	
AUSARE	osar	(to) dare	
	osado (p.p.)	daring (adj.), impudent, disrespectful	
	osadía	daring (n.), *audacity*	
	audaz	audacious, bold	
	audacia	audacity, boldness	
AUTUMNUS	otoño	*autumn*	
CAUSA	cosa	thing, matter	
	causa	*cause,* reason, case (legal), lawsuit	
GAUDIUM	gozo	*joy*	
	gozar	(to) *enjoy,* (to) have the benefit of	
	gozoso	*joyous, joyful*	
	goce	enjoyment, pleasure	
	regocijar	(to) gladden, (to) *rejoice*	
	regocijo	delight, *rejoicing*	
LAUDARE	loar	(to) *laud,* (to) praise	
MAURUS	moro	*Moorish, Moor*	
	moreno	swarthy, dark-skinned, tanned, brunette	
	Mauritania	Mauritania	
PAUCUS	poco	little, few	[*paucity*]
	poco a poco	little by little, gradually	
	poquito	very little, very small amount	
tan + poco	tampoco	neither, nor	

TAURUS	toro	bull	[*Taurus*]
	torero	*torero* (bullfighter), *toreador*[42]	
	tauromaquia	art of bullfighting	[rare *tauromachy*]
THESAURUS	tesoro	*treasure, Treasury, thesaurus*	
	tesorero	treasurer	
	tesorería	treasury (of an entity, not necessarily the state)	

Appendix

English Vowels—A Historical Note

Many native English-speaking students of "continental languages" (Romance, Germanic, Slavic) initially find themselves puzzled by the names given to some of "our" vowels by these other languages. Specifically:

Spanish			English	
the name of the letter *e*	is pronounced	*a*	as in *mate*	
the name of the letter *i*	is pronounced	*e*	as in *me*	

and the sounds represented by these vowels are similarly represented (or, one might think, misrepresented). Hence

Latin/Spanish	is pronounced much like	English
de		day
mi		me

The explanation for these divergences lies in the fact that over the past six hundred years *English* vowel pronunciation has undergone a dramatic transformation—known, not surprisingly, as "The Great Vowel Shift"—while "Continental" vowels continue to be pronounced as they have "always" been. This can be illustrated by contrasting the vowel sounds in the following pairs of cognate Spanish and English words:

	Spanish		English	
a	natura	natural	nature	natural
e	legión	legendario	legion	legendary

---

[42] Spanish *toreador* exists, but it is rare.

i	mil	milenio	mile	millennium
o	probar	probable	prove	probable
u	profundo	profundidad	profound	profundity

For each pair of English words, the two vowels marked in bold used to have the same sound but now differ markedly, while in Spanish the corresponding vowels continue to be pronounced identically.

In the "old" days, English vowel pronunciation was very similar to that of Classical Latin: each vowel had a *short* and a *long* variant, which were distinguished by their *length* of articulation rather than by any fundamental difference in their pronunciation. In the above list, the highlighted vowel in the first English word (i.e., *nature*) was *long*, while in the second (*natural*) it was *short*. Between the times of Chaucer and Shakespeare, the pronunciation of all *long* vowels—and most short ones as well—shifted, so that in "Modern" English there is no direct correspondence between "long" and "short" vowel sounds: one can extend the pronunciation of a "short" vowel for as long as one likes, but it will never sound even remotely like the corresponding "long" vowel. As a result, the natural linkage between the vowel sounds in pairs like *nature—natural* has been irretrievably broken.

Spanish vowel pronunciation remains very close to that of Middle English, so that a native Spanish speaker today would pronounce a text by Chaucer (at least the vowels) with considerably more accuracy than would a native English speaker.

Basic Consonant Changes: *p/b, t/d, c/g*

In this section we will focus on what are called *stop* consonants or *occlusives,*
i.e, those in which the outgoing flow of air is temporarily blocked: *p, b, t, d, c,
g,* where "*c*" and "*g*" refer to the "hard" pronunciations of these consonants (*cat*
and *go*). The varying treatment of stop consonants during the transition from
Latin is one of the principal features distinguishing the modern Romance languages. This can be illustrated by the comparisons in the following table, where
(ø) denotes that the consonant in question has disappeared.

	Latin	Italian	Spanish	French	English
P	SAPERE	sapere	saber	savoir	savant, sapient
T	MONETA	moneta	moneda	monnaie (ø)	money, monetary
C	SECURUS	sicuro	seguro	sûr (ø)	sure, secure
B	PROBARE	provare	probar	prouver	prove, probatory
D	CRUDELIS	crudele	cruel (ø)	cruel (ø)	cruel, crudity
G	LIGARE	legare	liar (ø)	lier (ø)	liaison, ligament

The following are common features of the treatment of *interior* stop consonants in "popular" words:

1. Latin *в* changed to *v* in Italian and French; its pronunciation in Spanish
   also changed to *v*, although the written form *b* has been maintained.[1]
2. In Spanish, the other five consonants have either changed (*P, T, C*) or
   (frequently) disappeared (*D, G*).
3. In Italian, apart from the change *в* → *v*, the stop consonants generally
   remained unchanged.
4. In French, both *P* and *в* became *v*; the other four consonants generally
   disappeared without a trace.
5. English "popular" forms show the French pattern, while "learned" ones
   preserve the original Latin consonants.

Before considering Spanish stop consonants in greater detail, we will first look
at what happened to double consonants of whatever type.

---

[1] Spanish *b* is pronounced [b] at the beginning of a word or following *m* (*cambiar*); otherwise
it is pronounced [v] (see Section 3.5, no. 9).

Double Consonants

In Latin (as in Old English), there was a distinction in pronunciation between single and double consonants. This remains an important feature in Italian, where, for example, *papa* ("Pope") and *pappa* ("pap", i.e., "baby food") are pronounced differently. In Spanish, the various outcomes of Latin double consonants are illustrated in the following examples; the corresponding English word in each case maintains a *written* double consonant.[2] For *cc*, it is necessary to take into account the nature of the letter that follows: *back* vowel (*a, o, u*), consonant, or *front* vowel (*e, i*).

BB	ABBREVIARE	abreviar	abbreviate
CC			
+ *a/o/u*	ACCUSARE	acusar	accuse
+ consonant	ACCLAMARE	aclamar	acclaim
+ *e/i*	ACCIDENTEM (acc.)	accidente	accident
	ACCENTUS	acento	accent
DD	ADDICTUS	adicto	addict
FF	AFFIRMARE	afirmar	affirm
GG	AGGRAVARE	agravar	aggravate
LL	VALLIS	valle	valley
	ILLEGALIS	ilegal	illegal
MM	COMMA	coma	comma
	IMMINENTEM (acc.)	inminente	imminent

---

[2] In Modern English, *spoken* "double" consonants exist only in a few compound words where the separate words have maintained their identity:

unnatural	un•natural	
bookkeeper	book•keeper	
doggone	dog•gone	(cf. the *dog on* the roof)
rattail	rat•tail	(cf. *rat ale*)

or in expressions pronounced as single words:

bus stop	bus•stop
stop payment	stop•payment

NN	ANNUS	año	year
	INNOCENTEM (acc.)	inocente	innocent
	INNOVARE	innovar	innovate
PP	APPLICARE	aplicar	apply
RR	IRRITARE	irritar	irritate
SS	MASSA	masa	*mass*, dough
TT	LITTERA	letra	*letter*

Seven double consonants plus *cc* followed by *a/o/u* or by a consonant have thus been totally eliminated from Spanish:

> **Rule:** In *native* Spanish words, *b, d, f, g, p, s,* and *t* are never "double". This holds as well for *c* when followed by a "back" vowel (*a/o/u*) or consonant.[3]

Of the remaining five consonants that could be doubled in Latin, RR became the *trilled r* (distinct from "simple" *r*), while for CC (+ *e/i*), LL, MM, and NN there were divergent outcomes:

(a) CC (+ *e/i*) was maintained in three "groups" of words; in all others it was simplified to *c*.[4]
The three groups that maintained the double *c* are:

ACCEDERE	acceder	(to) accede, (to) have *access* to
ACCESSUS	acceso	access (incl. "outburst or onset", e.g., fever)
	accesorio	accessory (secondary), accessory (m.)
	accesible	accessible
	accesibilidad	accessibility

---

[3] There are a very limited number of exceptions, all in "non-native" words: e.g., *hobby, yiddish, sheriff, jogging, hippie, topless, watt, staccato*.

[4] The double *c* also appears in several scientific and medical terms (e.g., *cóccix* and *occipital*) and in the alternative spellings *fláccido* and *flaccidez* for the "preferred" *flácido* and *flacidez* ("flaccid", "flaccidity").

	accésit	consolation prize	("nearly got there")
	inaccesible	inaccessible	
	inaccesibilidad	inaccessibility	
ACCIDENTALIS	accidental	accidental	
	accidente	accident	
	accidentado	uneven, hilly, eventful, accident victim (m./f.)	
OCCIDENTALIS	occidental	western, occidental, Westerner (m./f.)	
	occidente	occident, west, the West	

Examples of simplification of CC (followed by a front vowel *e/i*) to a single *c* include:

ACCELARE	acelerar	(to) accelerate	
	aceleración	acceleration	
	acelerador	accelerator	
	desaceleración	deceleration	
	celeridad	celerity (swiftness, speed)	(CELER = "swift")
ACCENTUS	acento	accent	
	acentuar	(to) accent, (to) accentuate	
ACCEPTARE	aceptar	(to) accept	
	aceptable	acceptable	
	inaceptable	inacceptable	
	aceptación	acceptance (favorable reception), acceptance	
	acepción	acceptation (meaning [of a word])	
SUCCESSUS	suceso	event, occurrence	
	sucesor	successor	
	sucesión	succession	
	sucesivo	successive	
	suceder	(to) succeed (follow), (to) happen	
	sucedáneo	succedaneum (substitute)	

This different treatment represents a real difference in pronunciation, not only in spelling, since *cc* is pronounced as two *separate and distinct* sounds, "hard" *c* followed by "soft" *c:*

acento	a•cen•to	[a•cen•to] *not* like English [ak•sent]

versus

acceso	ac•ce•so	[ak•ce•so] like English [ak•ses]

Recall also from Section 2.1 that there are a large number of Spanish words ending in *-cción* (e.g., *acción*) that correspond to English *-ction* words (both coming from Latin words ending in *-CTION*).

(b) In *compound* words, LL was reduced to a single consonant (as in *ilegal*, originally from IN + LEGALIS), while in most other words it became a *palatized l*, written *ll*. This is theoretically pronounced much like the [ly] sound in *million*, but for most modern Spanish speakers it is pronounced indistinguishably from *y:*[5]

calló	[caλo] *or* [caYo]	he silenced (or became silent)
cayó	[caYo]	he fell

Thus:

ALLEGORIA	alegoría	allegory
ALLUSIO(N)	alusión	allusion
	aludir	(to) allude
BULLA	bula	(Papal) *bull*
COLLABORARE	colaborar	(to) collaborate
	colaboración	collaboration
COLLEGIUM	colegio	*college*, school
	colega	*colleague*
ILLICITUS	ilícito	illicit, unlawful
ILLUSIO(N)	ilusión	illusion, hope, happiness (thinking of something)
	ilusionar	(to) have high hopes for
	ilusionista	illusionist, magician
	desilusión	disillusion, disillusionment, disappointment

---

[5] Which itself can have a range of pronunciations, ranging from "pure" *y* (as in *yet*) to a sound very much like English "soft" *g*.

ILLUSTRARE	ilustrar	(to) illustrate, (to) enlighten	
	ilustración	illustration, the Enlightenment (cap.)	
	ilustre	illustrious, distinguished	
POLLEN	polen	pollen	
but:			
BELLUS	bello	*beautiful*	
BULLIRE	bullir	(to) *boil*	[*ebullient*]
	bulla ~ bullicio	hubbub, uproar, racket	
CASTELLUM	castillo	*castle*	[*chateau*]
SIGILLUM	sello	*seal,* stamp, postage stamp	
VALLA	valla	fence, hurdle (track), billboard	[*wall*]
	vallar	(to) fence in	
	vallado ~ valladar	fence, defensive enclosure	[*vallation*]
	intervalo	interval (orig. "between the ramparts")	
	circunvalación	beltway, circumvallation	
VILLUS	vello	fuzz (body, fruit), body hair	[*villi, velour*]
	velloso	fuzzy, downy	[*villous*]
	velludo	hairy (lots of fuzz or down)	[*velvet*]
	vellón	fleece	

(c) In compound words where MM had arisen from IN (either in the negative sense or meaning "in") + M-, Spanish went back to the *original* (pre-Classical) Latin form. Words in which the MM had arisen from CUM- ("with") + M- were reconstituted as *conm-,* due to the influence of *con* (< CUM).

		Classical Latin	Spanish	English
IN-MATERIALIS	→	IMMATERIALIS	inmaterial	immaterial
CUM-MOTIO(N)	→	COMMOTIO(N)	conmoción	commotion

Similarly,

conmemorar	(to) commemorate
—conmemoración	—commemoration
—conmemorativo	—commemorative

conmiseración	commiseration
conmutar	(to) commute (exchange; reduce a judicial penalty)
—conmutación	—commutation
inmaculado	immaculate
inmaduro	immature, unripe
—inmadurez	—immaturity
inmediato	immediate
inmemorial	immemorial
inmenso	immense
—inmensidad	—immensity
inmersión	immersion
—inmerso	—immersed
inmigrar	(to) immigrate
—inmigrante (adj. & n.)	—immigrant
—inmigración	—immigration
inminente	imminent
inmoderado	immoderate
inmodesto	immodest
inmolar	(to) immolate, (to) sacrifice
—inmolación	—immolation, sacrifice
inmoral	immoral
—inmoralidad	—immorality
inmortal	immortal
—inmortalidad	—immortality
—inmortalizar	—(to) immortalize
inmune	immune
—inmunidad	—immunity
—inmunizar	—(to) immunize
—inmunología	—immunology
inmutable	immutable

In virtually all other words, MM was reduced to simple *m:*

COMMENTARE	comentar	(to) comment (on)
COMMODUS	cómodo	comfortable, *commodious*
DILEMMA	dilema (m.)	dilemma
GAMMA (UT)	gama	*gamut,* range, scale (musical)
	gamma	gamma (letter, ray, 10^{-6} gram)
SUMMARIUM	sumario (adj. & n.)	summary
	somero	shallow (e.g., waters), superficial

(d) In *compound* words, NN was usually maintained as *nn*,[6] sometimes reduced to simple *n,* but never palatized to *ñ.*

CONNIVENTIA	connivencia	connivance
INNATUS	innato	innate, inborn
INNUMERABILIS	innumerable	innumerable

but

INNOCUUS	inocuo	innocuous (harmless, insipid)

In *non-compound* words, it was generally palatized to *ñ:*

ANNUS	año	year	[per *annum*]
	añejo	old, aged (wine, cheese, etc.)	
CANNA	caña	*cane,* reed	
	caña de azúcar	sugar cane	
	caña de pescar	fishing rod	
	caño	pipe, short tube, spout	
	cañería	pipe(s), plumbing	
	cañaveral	cane field	[Cape *Canaveral*]
	cañón (1)	*cannon,* gun barrel	
	cañón (2)	*canyon*	
CAPANNA	cabaña	*cabin*	[*cabana*]
PANNUS	paño	cloth (fabric or piece)	[*pane, panel*]
	pana (< Fr.)	corduroy, velveteen	
PINNA	peña	large rock, rocky terrain	[*pinnacle*]
	peñasco	large rock, crag	
	peñón	rocky prominence (e.g., Gibraltar)	
STANNUM	estaño	tin	[*stannous*]

(e) In both compound and "regular" words, RR generally became the Spanish trilled *r,* written *rr.*[7]

CARRUS	carro	*car, cart*	
CIRRUS	cerro	(big) hill, neck (of animal)	[*cirrus*]
CORRUMPERE	corromper	(to) *corrupt*	

---

[6] In these cases, the pronunciation frequently retains a certain degree of the original doubled pronunciation (analogous to English *unnatural*); thus *innato* is generally represented phonetically as [in•na•to] or [i[n]•na•to].

[7] A single *r* has the trilled *r* pronunciation (a) at the beginning of a word (*radio*), and (b) in the interior following *l* (*alrededor*), *n* (*sonrisa*), or *s* (*israelí*).

	corrupto	corrupt, corrupted	(old p.p.)
	corrupción	corruption	
IRREGULARIS	irregular	irregular	
	irregularidad	irregularity	

The contrast between *r* and *rr* distinguishes a number of pairs of words, e.g.,

Con [r]	Con [rr]	With [r]	With [rr]
bario	barrio	*barium*	*barrio*, neighborhood
cero	cerro	*zero*	hill
coro	corro	*choir*	circle, ring of people; also "I run" (verb *correr*)
encerar	encerrar	(to) wax	(to) shut in
moro	morro	*Moor*	snout
para	parra	for	vine
pero	perro	but	dog
quería	querría	1s/3s[8] imperfect (verb *querer*)	1s/3s conditional (verb *querer*)

Simplification of Stop Consonants: *p, b, t, d, c, g*

In the evolution from Latin to Spanish, stop consonants in "popular" words have undergone a systematic and far-reaching transformation that continues to this day, at least in certain regions. The transformation is depicted below; for *c* and *g* we restrict ourselves for the moment to the "hard" forms followed directly by *a/o/u* or a consonant.

Latin		Spanish
PP	→	*p*
P	→	*b*
TT	→	*t*
T	→	*d*
D	→	ø
CC	→	*c*
C	→	*g*
G	→	ø
BB, DD, GG	→	*b, d, g*

---

[8] First and third person singular, respectively.

The transformation thus consisted of three stages, the first two of which occurred more or less contemporaneously:

I. double consonants	→	single consonants
II. P, T, C	→	b, d, g
III. D, G	→	ø

The first stage has already been considered above, where we saw that it affected various consonants in addition to *p, b, t, d, c, g*. The third stage continues to the present day.

Linguistic Note: *Voiced* versus *Unvoiced* Consonants

The series of consonant changes portrayed above was by no means random. To see this, it is necessary to introduce the notion of *voiced* and *unvoiced* consonants. During the articulation of a voiced consonant (or vowel) the vocal cords vibrate, whereas for a voiceless consonant there is no such vibration. One way to convince yourself of the reality of this difference is to cover your ears and utter the sounds: you should be able to hear a resonance for the voiced consonants that is lacking for the voiceless ones.[9]

The six occlusives are in fact divided into three pairs—*p/b, t/d, c/g*—whose elements are articulated identically, apart from the fact that while the first is voiceless, the second is voiced. The three stages in the evolution of Spanish *voiceless* stop consonants can thus be portrayed as elements of a uniform overall process:

voiceless double → voiceless single → voiced single → ø

The second stage, that is, voicing of unvoiced consonants, also affects "casual" English speech, where *atom* and *latter* are often pronounced indistinguishably from *Adam* and *ladder*.

We will now provide illustrations of these changes as they affected the consonant pairs *p/b, t/d,* and *c/g*.

---

[9] The difference can most easily be detected for the fricative (or hissing) consonants *s* and *z*, e.g., *sssssss* (no vibration) versus the bumble-bee sound *zzzzzzz* (vibration). *S* is thus voiceless, and *z* is voiced.

Stage I: Double Consonants to Single Consonants

a. *PP → p*

APPLAUDERE	aplaudir	(to) applaud	
	aplauso	applause	
CAPPA	capa	*cape,* coat (layer)	
OPPOSITIO(N)	oposición	opposition, competitive examinations (pl.)	
	oponer	(to) *oppose*	[*opponent*]
SUPPORTARE	soportar	(to) *support,* (to) tolerate	
	soportable	supportable, tolerable, bearable	
	insoportable	insupportable, unbearable	

b. *TT → t*

ATTRACTIO(N)	atracción	attraction	
	atractivo	attractive, charm or attractiveness (m.)	
	atraer	(to) *attract*	
GLUTTO(N)	glotón (-ona)	gluttonous, glutton	
	glotonería	gluttony	
GUTTA	gota	drop, *gout*	
	gotear	(to) drip	
	gotera	leak (roof or wall)	[*gutter*]
	agotar	(to) exhaust, (to) use up completely	
	agotado (p.p.)	exhausted, worn out, sold out, out of print	
	inagotable	inexhaustible	
LITTERA	letra	*letter*	
SAGITTARIUS	sagitario	Sagittarius	

c. *CC → c*

We saw earlier that when followed by a front vowel (*e, i*), CC was generally reduced (*acento*) but occasionally maintained (*acceso*). It is always reduced before a back vowel (*a, o, u*) or consonant. Some examples follow:

ACCOMODARE	acomodar	(to) accommodate, (to) adapt, (to) place

	acomodado (p.p.)	well-off, well-to-do, reasonable (moderate)
	acomodación	accommodation (gen. adaptation, not lodging)
	acomodador (-ora)	usher, usherette (theater)
ACCUSARE	acusar	(to) accuse
	acusar recibo (de)	(to) acknowledge receipt (of)
	acusado (p.p.)	notable or marked, accused (m./f.), defendant (m./f.)
	acusación	accusation, prosecution (legal)
	acusativo	accusative (gram.)
ECCLESIASTICUS	eclesiástico	ecclesiastical, ecclesiastic
OCCASIO(N)	ocasión	occasion, opportunity
	ocasional	occasional, *chance* (adj.)
	ocasionar	(to) occasion, (to) cause
	ocaso[10]	sunset (~ *puesta del Sol*), decline
OCCULTUS	oculto	occult (hidden from view, concealed)
	ocultar	(to) occult (hide, conceal)
	ocultismo	occultism
OCCUPATIO(N)	ocupación	occupation
	ocupar	(to) occupy
	ocupante	occupying, occupant (m./f.)
	ocupado	busy (person, telephone), occupied
OCCURRERE	ocurrir	(to) occur
	ocurrencia	occurrence, (bright) idea
	ocurrente	witty
PRAEOCCUPARE	preocupar	(to) preoccupy, (to) be concerned
	preocupado	preoccupied, worried, concerned
	preocupación	preoccupation, worry, concern
	despreocupar(se)	(to) stop worrying, (to) stop paying attention to
	despreocupado (p.p.)	unconcerned, carefree, careless
	despreocupación	lack of concern, carelessness
SACCUS	saco	*sack,* jacket, sweater, *sac*

---

[10] *Ocaso* and *ocasión* are both derived from the Latin verb CADERE ("to fall", Spanish *caer*): *ocasión* is a falling of things together; *ocaso* is the falling of the sun.

Double *voiced* consonants were much rarer in Latin than double unvoiced ones:

d. BB → *b*

ABBATEM (acc.)	abad (m.)	abbot	
SABBATUM	sábado	Saturday	[*Sabbath*]

e. DD → *d*

ADDITIO(N)	adición	addition
ADDUCERE	aducir	(to) adduce

f. GG → *g*

AGGRESSIO(N)	agresión	aggression
	agre**d**ir	(to) assault, (to) attack, (to) *aggress*
	agresivo	aggressive
	agresividad	aggresivity
	agresor	aggressor
EXAGGERARE	exagerar	(to) exaggerate
	exageración	exaggeration
SUGGESTIO(N)	sugestión	suggestion (esp. "power of suggestion")
	suge**r**ir	(to) suggest
	sugerencia	suggestion
	sugestivo	suggestive, appealing

Stage II: Voiceless to Voiced Consonants

The change from a voiceless to a voiced pronunciation affected P, T, and C between vowels, or between a vowel and a following R or L.

a. P → *b*

APERTUS	abierto (p.p.)	open	[pert]
	abrir	(to) open	[*aperient*]
	abertura	*aperture*, opening (physical: e.g., window)	
	a**p**ertura	opening (abstract: inaugural, political, chess)	

APOTHECA	bodega[11]	(wine) cellar, ship's hold, *bodega*	
	bodegón	cheap restaurant, still life (painting)	
	botica	pharmacy, drugstore	[*boutique*]
	boticario	pharmacist, *apothecary*	
	botiquín	medicine chest, first aid kit	
	boutique (f.)	boutique	(< Fr.)
APRILIS	abril	*April*	
CAPILLUS	cabello	hair	[*capillary*]
CAPRA	cabra	goat	[*Capricorn*]
CAPUT ("head")	cabo	end, *cape,* corporal	(see Section 4.9)
	cabeza	head	
	caber	(to) fit, (to) hold (be contained in)	
-CIPERE	recibir	(to) *receive*	
	apercibir	(to) prepare, (to) warn, (to) *perceive*	[*aperçu*]
	desapercibido	unprepared, unaware, unnoticed	
	percibir	(to) *perceive,* (to) receive (salary, etc.)	
	concebir	(to) *conceive*	
	concebible	*conceivable*	
	inconcebible	*inconceivable*	
COOPERIRE	cubrir	(to) *cover*	[*oper*culum]
	cubierta	cover (book, bed, etc.)	
	cubierto (p.p.)	place setting, meal (fixed price)	
	descubrir	(to) *discover,* (to) reveal, (to) uncover	
	descubierto (p.p.)	uncovered, deficit or overdraft (m.)	
	descubrimiento	discovery	
	descubridor	discoverer, scout (mil.)	
	encubrir	(to) conceal, (to) cover up (a misdeed)	

---

[11] Note that *bodega* incorporates all three changes: P → b, (TH →) T → d, and C → g.

	recubrir	(to) *cover* (a surface, e.g., rust), (to) *re-cover*	
CUPA (CUPPA)	cuba	cask, barrel, vat	[*coop, cooper*]
	co**p**a	*cup* (goblet, trophy), drink (alcoholic)	
	cúpula	*cupola,* dome	
	cubo (1)	bucket, hub (wheel)	
(unrelated)	cubo (2)	cube	
	cúbico	cubic	
CUPRUM	cobre	*copper*	[*Cyprus*]
DUPLARE	doblar	(to) *double,* (to) fold, (to) *dub* (movies)	
LUPUS	lobo	wolf, *lobo*	
	lu**p**us	lupus (disease)	
	lu**p**anar	brothel	
OPERA	obra	work, construction, *opus*	[*opera*]
	obra de arte	work of art	
	obra de teatro	play (~ *obra teatral*)	
	obra(s) pública(s)	public works	
OPERARI	obrar	(to) work, (to) act, (to) defecate[12]	[*operate*]
	obrar en poder	(to) be in the hands of (letter, document, etc.)	
	obrero	working, worker (m./f.)	
	ó**p**era	opera	
	o**p**erar	(to) operate	
	o**p**eración	operation	
	o**p**erable	operable	
PAUPER	pobre	*poor, pauper* (m./f.), the poor (pl.)	
PIPER	pebre (m./f.)	*pepper* sauce (with garlic, parsley, and vinegar)	
POPULATIO(N)	población	*population,* town	
	poblar	(to) populate, (to) *inhabit*	

---

[12] This more "popular" definition of *obrar* has an interesting parallel in English, where *manure* is a deformation of *maneuver,* from MANU OPERARI ("to *operate* by hand").

RECUPERARE	recobrar ~	(to) *recover*, (to) get	
	recu**p**erar	back, (to) *recuperate*	
	cobrar	(to) get paid, (to) charge (a price)	
RIPARIA	ribera	shore, bank	[*river, Riviera*]
	ribereño	*riparian, riverine*	
	ribazo	steep bank, slope	
AD + RIPA	arriba	above, up, upstairs	("toward shore")
	arribar	(to) put into port, (to) *arrive* (~ llegar)	
DE + RIPA	derribar	(to) tear down or demolish, (to) topple (govt.)	
	derribo	destruction, demolition	
SAPERE	saber	(to) know	[*sapient*]
	sabio (adj. & n.)	wise, learned, *sage*, learned person	
	sabiduría	wisdom, learning	
	sabor	taste, *savor*, flavor	
	sabroso	*savory*, flavorful, tasty	
	saborear	(to) relish, (to) enjoy, (to) *savor*	
	sa**p**iencia	sapience, wisdom	
	Homo sa**p**iens	Homo sapiens	
	ins**í**pido	insipid (lit. "without taste")	
	resabio	unpleasant aftertaste, bad habit	
	quizá, quizás	maybe, perhaps	(quién + sabe)
SUPER	so**b**re	over, above, concerning, envelope (n.)	
	sobra	*sur*plus (n.), remainder, leftovers (pl.)	
	sobrante	surplus (adj. & n.)	
	sobrar	(to) be in excess, (to) be superfluous, (to) remain	
	soberano (adj. & n.)	*sovereign*	

	soberanía	*sovereignty*	
	soprano	soprano (voice: m.; singer: m./f.)	(< It.)
	superfluo	superfluous, unnecessary	
	superar	(to) *sur*pass, (to) *sur*mount	
	insuperable	insuperable, insurmountable	
	superávit	surplus	(Lat. SUPERA-VIT: "it has surpassed")
SUPERBUS	soberbio	arrogant, haughty, *superb*	
	soberbia	pride, haughtiness, arrogance	
VIPERA	víbora	*viper*	

b. T → d

ADVOCATUS	abogado[13]	lawyer, attorney	[*advocate*]
	abogar	(to) plead (in favor or defense of)	
ARMATURA	armadura	*armor, armature*	
CATENA	cadena	*chain,* TV or radio network	
	cadena perpetua	life imprisonment	
	encadenar	(to) chain, (to) *enchain*, (to) link, (to) con*catenate*	
	desencadenar	(to) unchain, (to) unleash	
CATENATUS	candado	padlock	(< cadenado)
COMITEM (acc.)	conde	*count,* earl	
	condesa	*countess*	
COMITATUS	condado	*county,* earldom (title, territory)	
CONVITARE[14]	convidar	(to) *invite* (to a fiesta; to encourage)	

---

[13] Note that *abogado* incorporates both the changes T → d and C → g. The initial b (rather than v) is an example of the "confusion" between the two letters resulting from the coalescing of the [b] and [v] sounds (see Section 3.5, no. 9).

[14] CONVITARE was formed by replacing the prefix IN- of Classical Latin INVITARE with CON-, probably due to association with the (unrelated) words CONVIVIUM ("banquet") and CONVIVI-ALIS ("convivial"). *Invitar* also exists and is synonymous with *convidar*.

	convite	*invitation,* banquet, feast	
	convidado (p.p.)	guest (particularly at a *convite*)	
FATUM	hado	*fate,* destiny	
	fatídico	*fateful,* ominous, *fatidic*	
	enfado	annoyance, vexation	
	enfadar	(to) annoy, (to) develop a mutual dislike	
LATER	ladrillo	brick	[*laterite*]
LATINUS	ladino	cunning, crafty, *Ladino* (Judeo-Spanish)	
	latín	Latin (language)	
	latino	Latin (adj.), *lateen* (sail)	
LATRO(N)	ladrón (-ona)	thieving, thief or *larcenist,* multiple plug (m.)	
	ladrar[15]	(to) bark	
	ladrido	bark, barking	
MARITUS	marido	husband	[*marital*]
MATER	madre (f.)	mother	[*maternal*]
MATERIA	madera	wood	[*matter*]
	madeira, Madeira	Madeira (wine, islands)	(< Port.)
MATURUS	maduro	ripe, *mature*	
	madurar	(to) ripen, (to) mature	
	madurez	ripeness, maturity	
	prematuro	premature	
METIRI	medir	(to) *measure*	[*meter*]
	medida	measure, measurement	
	desmedido	excessive, immoderate	
MINUTUS	menudo	small, *minute* (adj.)	
	a menudo	often, frequently	
	minuto	minute (time), minute (sixtieth part of a degree)	
	minuta	minute (memorandum), bill (lawyer)	
MONETA	moneda	*money,* coin	

---

[15] Thieves rarely bark; *ladrar* comes from a different Latin word very similar in form to that which produced *ladrón. Ladrar*'s relatives in English (*latrant, latrate, latrator,* etc.) have long since died out.

	monedero	change purse (~ *portamonedas*)	
	monetario	*monetary*	
MUTARE	mudar	(to) change, (to) *molt*, (to) move	[*mutate*]
	muda	change of clothes (underwear), *molting*	
	mudanza	move (change of residence)	
	mutar	(to) mutate	
	mutación	mutation	
	mutante	mutant	
MUTUS	mudo	*mute,* dumb, silent	
	mudez	muteness, silence	
	tartamudo[16]	stuttering, stammering, stutterer or stammerer (m./f.)	
	tartamudear	(to) stutter, (to) stammer	
	enmudecer	(to) become silent, (to) silence	
NATARE	nadar	(to) swim	
	nadador	swimmer	
	natación	natation, swimming	
NATIVITAS	Navidad	Christmas, *Nativity*	(acc. NAVITAT-EM)
NUTRIX	nodriza	wet *nurse*	[*nutrition*]
PATER	padre	father	[*paternal*]
PETERE	pedir	(to) request	[*petition*]
	pedido (p.p.)	request, order (goods, restaurant)	
	despedir	(to) dismiss, (to) bid farewell, (to) throw, (to) emit	
	despedida	farewell, parting	
PUTARE	podar	(to) prune (plant, budget)	[am*putate*[17]]
PUTRERE	pudrir	(to) rot, (to) *putrefy*	

---

[16] *Tarta-* represents a stuttering or stammering sound.

[17] Latin AMPUTARE was formed from *AMBI-* ("on both sides", "around") and PUTARE ("to prune"), so that an amputation was an extensive "trimming" or "pruning".

	podrido (p.p.)	*putrid,* rotten	(irregular p.p.)
	putrefacción	putrefaction, rotting	
	putrefacto	putrefied, rotten, putrid	
QUADRATUS	cuadrado (adj. & n.)	square, *quadrate*	
ROTA	rueda	wheel	[*rotate*]
ROTUNDUS	redondo	*round*	
	redondear	(to) make *round,* (to) *round* (up or down)	
	rotundo	categorical, expressive (language), *rotund*	
(unrelated)	ronda	round(s), patrol, group of serenaders	
	rondar	(to) make the rounds, (to) prowl, (to) hover around	
SAETA ("bristle")	seda	silk	[*seta*]
	sedoso	silky	[*setose, setaceous*]
	sedal	fishing line	
SALUTEM (acc.)	salud	health	
	saludable	*salutary,* healthy, healthful	
SALUTARE	saludar	(to) greet, (to) *salute*	
	saludo	greeting, salutation, *salute*	
	salutación	greeting, salutation (~ *saludo*)	
STERNUTARE	estornudar	(to) sneeze	[*sternutation*]
	estornudo	sneeze	
TITULUS	tilde (f.)	tilde (~), written accent (')	(*dl* → *ld*)
	tildar	(to) put a tilde on, (to) label or brand as (negative)	
	título	title	
	titular (1)	*title*holder, incumbent, headlines (pl.)	
	titular (2)	(to) title, (to) entitle, (to) obtain an academic title	
TOTUS	todo	all, every, whole	[*tutti-frutti*]
	todopoderoso	all-powerful, almighty	
	sobre todo	above all, especially	
	sobretodo	overcoat, smock/overall (~ *overol*)	("over all")

	total	total	
	totalidad	totality	
	totalitario	totalitarian	
VERACITAS	veracidad	veracity, truthfulness	(acc. -TATEM)
	veraz	truthful, *veracious*	
VERITAS	verdad	truth, *verity*	(acc. VERITAT-EM)
	verdadero	true, real	
VETARE	vedar	(to) prohibit, (to) forbid	
	veda	prohibition, closed season (hunting)	
	vetar	(to) *veto*	
	veto[18]	*veto*	
VITA	vida	life	[*vita, CV*]
	salvavidas	life preserver	
	vital	vital	
	vitalidad	vitality	
	vitalicio	for life, lifelong	
	vitamina	vitamin	
VITREUM	vidrio	glass	
	vítreo	*vitreous*, glassy, glass-like	
	vitrina	display (glass) case, *vitrine,* shop window	
VOTA	boda	wedding	[*vote, vows*]

The ending *-TOR* generally referred to an *actor* or *agent*. When preceded by a vowel, it has frequently become Spanish *-dor:*

IMPERATOR	emperador	emperor
GLADIATOR	gladiador	gladiator

c. *c(a, o, u)* → *g*

When followed immediately by *e* or *i,* the *c* was maintained in spelling but became "soft" in pronunciation; in most of Spain it is pronounced as [th] (as in *thin,* not *this*), elsewhere as [s], e.g.,

CICERO ("kikero")   Cicerón   Cicero   [thitheron] *or* [siseron]

---

[18] VETO was the first person singular of the verb VETARE and thus meant "I forbid"; it was the ritual word used by Roman tribunes to oppose measures of the Senate or actions of the magistrates.

After a vowel, and when followed by either a back vowel (*a, o, u*) or a "liquid" consonant (*r* or *l*), a "hard" *c* frequently became Spanish *g*:

ACRUS (CL ACER)	agrio	sour, *acid,* citrus fruits (pl.)	
	acre	*acrid,* tart, *acrimonious*	[*eager*]
ACUTUS	agudo[19]	sharp, *acute*	[*ague*]
ALACRIS	alegre	cheerful, happy	[*alacrity*]
	alegría	happiness, joy	
	alegrar	(to) make happy or glad, (to) enliven	
	alegro	*allegro* (music)	
AMICUS	amigo	friend	
	amigable	*amicable,* friendly	
CARRICARE	cargar	(to) load, (to) *charge,* (to) *carry* (Amer.)	
	carga	loading, *charge* (military, electric, tax, etc.), burden, load, *cargo* (< Sp.)	
	cargo	post (job), *charge* (duty or task, accusation, debit)	
	cargamento	cargo	
	descargar	(to) unload, (to) *discharge,* (to) download (~ *bajar*)	
	descarga	unloading, *discharge* (electricity, firearm)	
	descargo	discharge (of responsibility or obligation)	
	encargar	(to) entrust, (to) take *charge* of	
CLERICUS	clérigo	*clergy*man, *cleric*	[*clerk*]
	clerical	clerical (pertaining to the clergy)	

---

[19] Note that *agudo* incorporates both the changes C → g and T → d.

COLLOCARE	colgar	(to) hang (clothes, criminal) or hang up (phone)	
	colgante	pendent (hanging), pendant (jewelry)	[*couch*]
	colocar	(to) place, (to) set, (to) *collocate*	
	descolgar	(to) take down, (to) pick up (telephone)	
DELICATUS	delgado	thin, *delicate*	
	delgadez	thinness, slenderness	
	adelgazar	(to) lose weight, (to) slim	
	delicado[20]	delicate	
	delicadeza	delicacy, tactfulness, considerateness	
DRACO(N)	dragón	*dragon, dragoon*	
	draconiano	draconian	
E(C)CLESIA	iglesia	church	
	eclesiástico	ecclesiastic	
FRICARE	fregar	(to) scrub, (to) scour	[*friction*]
	friega	rubdown	
	fregadero	(kitchen) sink	
	refriega	skirmish, encounter	[*fray* vb.]
GALLICUS	galgo	greyhound	[*Gallic*]
INIMICUS	enemigo	*inimical, enemy* (adj. & n.)	
	enemistad	*enmity,* hostility	
LACRIMA	lágrima	tear, teardrop	
	lagrimal	*lachrymal* (relating to tears)	
	lacrimoso	*lachrymose,* tearful	
	lacrimógeno	tear-producing, tearjerker (movie)	
	gas lacrimógeno	tear gas, *lachrymator*	
LACUNA	laguna	*lagoon, lacuna* (gap)	
LACUS	lago	*lake*	

[20] *Delicado* is a "mixed form" word: it has undergone the change $T \rightarrow d$ but not $C \rightarrow g$; by contrast, *delgado* has undergone both and has also lost a vowel.

LAICUS	lego (adj. & n.)	*laic, lay,* inexperienced, ignorant, layperson	
	laico (adj. & n.)	*laic, lay,* layman/ woman	
LUCRUM	logro	accomplishment, gain	
	lograr	(to) attain	
	lucro	gain, profit, *lucre*	
	lucrativo	lucrative	
mal + lograr	malograr	(to) go wrong, (to) waste (a chance)	
MACRUM (acc.)	magro	lean (person or meat), pork loin (m.)	[*meager*]
MENDICUS	mendigo	beggar	
	mendigar	(to) beg	
	mendicidad	beggary, *mendicity* (*mendicancy*)	
	mendicante	mendicant (adj. & n.), beggar	
PACARE	pagar[21]	(to) *pay*	
	pago	*payment*	
	pagaré	promissory note, IOU (lit. "I will pay")	
	apagar	(to) extinguish, (to) turn off, (to) quench	[*appease*]
	apagado (p.p.)	turned off, dull (color, person)	
PLICARE	plegar[22]	(to) fold, (to) *pleat*	[*ply*]
	plegable	folding, collapsible (e.g., umbrella)	
	desplegar	(to) unfold, (to) *deploy,* (to) *display*	
	pliegue	fold, crease, *pleat, plait, plica*	
	pliego	sheet of paper, official communcation	
	pliego de cargos	specification of charges (vs. public official)	

---

[21] PACARE meant "to *pacify* or *appease*"; the notion of *payment* initially arose from the idea of pacifying one's creditors. One "pacifies" an electric applicance by turning it off (*apagar*).

[22] A "doublet" of *plegar* is *llegar* ("to arrive"); see Section 3.5, no. 1.

	pliego de	(contractual)	
	condiciones	specifications	
	despliegue	*display(ing),*	
		deployment (mil.)	
	replegar(se)	(to) retreat or fall back	[*reply*]
		(in orderly fashion)	
	repliegue	retreat, withdrawal,	[*redeployment*]
		double fold	
SACRATUS	sagrado	*sacred*	
	consagrar	(to) *consecrate,* (to)	
		devote	
	sacro	sacred, sacrum	(see Section 4.7)
		(base of spine)	
SECARE ("to cut")	segar	(to) reap, (to) mow,	
		(to) cut down	
	siega	reaping, harvest (time)	
	segador	reaper, harvester	
	segadora	reaper or harvester	
		(female, or machine)	
	disección	dissection	
SECUNDUM	según	according to	[*second*]
SECUNDUS	segundo	*second* (adj.), *second*	
		(unit of time)	
	segundero	*second* hand (of	
		a watch)	
	secundario[23]	*secondary*	
SECURUS	seguro (adj. & n.)	*secure, sure, insurance,*	
		safety catch	
	seguridad	*security,* safety	
	seguridad social	social security	
	seguramente	*surely*	
	asegurar	(to) *secure,* (to) *assure,*	
		(to) *insure,* (to) *ensure*	
	inseguro	insecure, *unsure*	
	inseguridad	insecurity	
SPICA	espiga	*spike* or ear of grain	
STOMACHUS	estómago	*stomach*	
UMBILICUS	ombligo	navel	

---

[23] Very rarely *segundario.*

	umbilical	umbilical	
		umbilical	
URTICA	ortiga	(stinging) nettle	[*urticaria*]

A similar change occurred in a number of cases with respect to word-interior QU, which was essentially a graphic means for representing the sound combination c + w. The [w] sound was maintained when a back vowel (*a, o, u*) followed; otherwise it was lost, although a written *u* is maintained in the spelling to signify that the preceding *g* has a hard rather than a soft sound (see Section 3.5, no. 14).

ALIQUEM	alguien	somebody, someone	(cf. **quien**, "who")
ANTIQUUS	antiguo	ancient, old	[*antique*]
AQUA	agua	water	[*aquatic*]
EQUA	yegua	mare	[*equestrian*]
(A)EQUALIS	igual	*equal*	
EX-QUINTIARE	esguince	sprain, dodge (to avoid blow)	[to part into five]
SEQUENTEM (acc.)	siguiente	following, next, *sequent*	

In a few cases, an *initial* c (or QU-) has also become *g*:

cabinet (Fr.)	gabinete	study, office, *cabinet* (of ministers)	
	cabina	cabin, cockpit, cab, *cabana*	
	cabina telefónica	telephone booth	
caraffa (It.)	garrafa	*carafe*	
CATTUS	gato	*cat*	
COLAPHUS	golpe	blow, bump, knock, *coup*	
	golpe de Estado	*coup d'état*	
	golpe de gracia	*coup de grâce*	
	golpear	(to) beat, (to) strike, (to) knock	[*cope*]
CRASSUS	graso	*greasy*, oily, fatty	[*crass*[24]]
	grasa	*grease*, fat	
	grasiento	*greasy* (containing grease; soiled with grease)	

---

[24] Latin CRASSUS meant "thick", "dense", "fat". The original meaning of English *crass* was "coarse", "dense", "thick", before acquiring its modern sense of "crude and unrefined".

	engrasar	(to) lubricate, (to) oil, (to) make *greasy*	
QUIRITARE	gritar	(to) shout, (to) *cry* (out)	
	grito	shout, *cry*	
al qutun (Arabic)	al**g**odón	*cotton*	(also *t → d*)

Stage III: The Disappearance of "Voiced" Consonants

B, arising either from Latin *b* or *p,* has not participated in Stage III.

a. *D → Ø*

AUDIRE	oír	(to) hear, (to) listen	[*audio*]
	oyente	listener, hearer	[*audience*]
CADERE	caer	(to) fall	[*cadence*]
	caído (p.p.)	the fallen (in battle, gen. pl.)	
	caída	fall, downfall	[*chute*]
	paracaídas	*parachute*	
	paracaidista	*parachutist,* paratrooper	
	decaer	(to) *decay,* (to) decline	
	deca**d**ente	decadent	
	deca**d**encia	decadence, decline	
	recaer	(to) relapse, (to) fall on (e.g., suspicion)	
	acaecer	(to) happen, (to) come to pass	[*chance*]
	acaecimiento	occurrence, event (~ *suceso*)	
CONFIDARE	confiar	(to) have *confidence* (in), (to) *confide*	
	confiado (p.p.)	trusting, unsuspecting, *confident*	
	confianza	*confidence,* self-confidence, liberties (pl.)	
	en confianza	in confidence, confidentially	
	confi**d**ente	*confidant(e),* secret informer, love seat (m.)	
	desconfiar	(to) distrust, (to) have no confidence (in)	

CREDERE	creer	(to) believe	
	creencia	belief	[*credence*]
	creyente	believing, believer	
	credo	*credo, creed*	(Lat. "I believe")
	creíble	*credible*	
	increíble	*incredible*	
	acreedor	deserving, *creditor* (m./f.)	
CRUDELIS	cruel	*cruel*	
EXCLUDERE	excluir	(to) *exclude*	
FIDARE	fiar	(to) sell on credit, (to) act as guarantor, (to) entrust	
	desafiar	(to) *defy,* (to) dare, (to) challenge	
	desafío	challenge, *defiance,* duel	
	fianza	guaranty, down payment	[*fiancé*]
	bajo fianza	on bail	
	afianzar	(to) strengthen, (to) reinforce	[*affiance*]
FIDELIS	fiel	*faithful* (adj.), faithful (n., gen. pl.) needle on a balance scale	
	infiel	*unfaithful, faithless, infidel*	
	fidelidad	fidelity, faithfulness, *fealty*	
	infidelidad	infidelity, unfaithfulness, faithlessness	
FIDES	fe (f.)	*faith*	
fe + hacer	fehaciente	authentic, genuine	("making faith")
	fidedigno	trustworthy, reliable	(+ digno)
	porfía	insistence, stubbornness	[*perfidy*]
	perfidia	*perfidy,* treachery	
	pérfido	*perfidious,* treacherous	
FOEDUS	feo	ugly	
	fealdad	ugliness	
INCLUDERE	incluir	(to) *include*	
JUDICEM (acc.)	juez, jueza	*judge*	
LAUDARE	loar	(to) *laud,* (to) praise	[*allow*]
	loa	praise, *laud*	
	loable	*laudable,* praiseworthy (~ *laudable*)	

LIMPIDUS	limpio	clean	
	limpiar	(to) clean, (to) cleanse	
	limpieza	cleanliness, cleaning	
	límpido	*limpid* (clear, transparent)	
MEDULLA	meollo	essence, heart of the matter	
	médula / medula	marrow, *medulla*	
PROVIDERE	proveer	(to) *provide,* (to) fill (a job), (to) *purvey*	
	provisto (p.p.)	*provided,* stocked, supplied	
	desprovisto	lacking (in), without, devoid	
RADERE	raer	(to) scrape, (to) *abrade*	[*erase, raze*]
(from p.p.)	abrasión	*abrasion*	
RADIX	raíz (f.)	root	[*radish*]
	enraizar	(to) take root, (to) put down roots	
	radical	radical (adj. & n.), root or stem (linguistics)	
AD + RADICARE	arraigar	(to) take root, (to) become established	
	arraigado (p.p.)	deeply rooted, established, well-entrenched	
	radicar	(to) take root, (to) reside, (to) consist in	
	erradicar	(to) eradicate	
RANCIDUS	rancio	of old (smelly) food,[25] age-old	[*rancid*]
RIDERE	reír	(to) laugh	[*riant, deride*]
(from p.p.)	risa	laugh, laughter	[*risible*]
	risueño	smiling, *riant* (cheerful, mirthful)	
	sonreír	(to) smile	
	sonrisa	smile	
	sonriente	smiling	
RODERE	roer	(to) gnaw, (to) eat away	[*erode*]
	roedor	*rodent*	
	corroer	(to) corrode	

---

[25] Not always in a negative sense (e.g., aged cheese or wine).

(from p.p.)	corrosión	corrosion	
	corrosivo	corrosive	
SUCIDUS	sucio[26]	dirty, filthy	[*succulent*]
	suciedad	dirt, filth	
	ensuciar	(to) soil, (to) make dirty	
TURBIDUS	turbio	*turbid,* confused (situation), shady (business)	
VIDERE	ver	(to) see	[*video*]
	vídeo, video	video, VCR	(< Eng.)
	vidente	sighted (person), clair*voy*ant	
	invidente	blind, blind person	

b. G → Ø

Latin interior G has frequently disappeared, although much more rarely before a back vowel (*a, o, u*) than a front one (*e, i*):

Back Vowel

LEGALIS	leal	*loyal*	[*legal*]
	lealtad	*loyalty*	[*legality*]
	desleal	*disloyal*	
	deslealtad	*disloyalty*	
	legal	legal	
LIGARE	liar	(to) embroil, (to) roll or wrap up	[*ligament*]
	lío	mess, tangle, bundle, *liaison* (affair)	
	ligar	(to) bind, (to) *alloy,* (to) *ligate*	[*ally*]
	desligar	(to) untie, (to) separate, (to) disentangle	
LITIGARE	lidiar[27]	(to) battle, (to) contend (with)	[*litigate*]
REGALIS	real	*royal*	[*regal*]

Front Vowel

COGITARE	cuidar	(to) care for, (to) look after	[*cogitate*]
	cuidado (p.p.)	care, carefulness (~ *cuido*)	
	¡cuidado!	look out! watch out! be careful!	
	cuidadoso	careful	
	descuidar	(to) be careless, (to) neglect	

---

[26] Latin SUCIDUS meant "sappy" or "juicy" (from SUCUS: "sap", "juice") and was commonly used to refer to freshly shorn lamb's wool that was still "sappy" with sweat.

[27] *Lidiar* has also undergone the change T → d.

	descuidado (p.p.)	careless, negligent, untidy	
	descuido	carelessness, negligence	
FRIGERE	freír	(to) *fry*	
	frito (p.p.)	*fried* food (gen. pl.)	[*Fritos*®]
	patatas fritas (pl.)	French *fries*	
FUGERE	huir	(to) flee	[*fugitive*]
	huida	flight, escape	
	fuga	escape, flight, leak, *fugue* (musical)	
LEGERE	leer	(to) read	
	legible	legible	
	ilegible	illegible, unreadable	
LEGIO(N)	León	León (city and region)	[Roman 7th *legion*]
	legión	legion	
LEX (acc. LEGEM)	ley (f.)	law	[*legal*]
	legítimo	*legitimate*	
MAGIS	más	more	[*master*]
	mas	but (~ *pero*)	
MAGISTER	maestro	teacher, *master, maestro*	
	maestría	*mastery,* master's degree	
REGINA	reina	queen	
	reino	*realm,* kingdom	[*reign*]
	reinar	(to) *reign*	
	reinado (p.p.)	*reign*	
REX (acc. REGEM)	rey	king	[T-*rex*]
	los reyes	the king and queen	
	los reyes católicos	The Catholic Kings (Ferdinand and Isabella)[28]	
	realeza	*royalty*	
SAGITTA	saeta	arrow, dart	[*Sagittarius*]

---

[28] They were awarded the honorary title of "Catholic" by Pope Alexander VI (himself a Spaniard) in 1494, "in recognition of their reconquest of Granada from the Moors (1481–1492), their New World discoveries (1492), and their strengthening of the church by such agencies as the Spanish Inquisition and such measures as compelling Jews to convert to Christianity or face exile (1492)" (*Encyclopædia Britannica*).

SIGILLUM	sello	*seal,* stamp, postage stamp	[*sigil*]
	sellar	(to) stamp, (to) *seal* (lips, deal, etc.)	

Stage III continues to function today with regard to interior *d* that originated from Latin *T*. In words like *cuidado* (Latin COGITATUS), the pronunciation often is more like **cuidao;* the first *d* has weakened as well (to the *th* in *this*), so that it often seems more like **cuithao* or even **cuiao.*

A number of words (including **bodega, agudo, delgado, lidiar,** corresponding to English **apothecary, acute, delicate, litigate**) have already been noted as having undergone these changes with respect to not one but two or more interior consonants. Further examples are noted below where two interior consonants have been affected, one of which has disappeared; for Latin FRIGIDUS both have vanished:

DIGITUS	dedo	finger, toe	[*digit*]
TEPIDUS	tibio	*tepid,* lukewarm	
	tibieza	tepidness, lack of enthusiasm	
TRITICUM	trigo	wheat	[*triticale*]
	trigal	wheat field	
FRIGIDUS	frío	cold (adj.), cool, cold or chill (m.)	
	escalofrío	shiver	(ex + calor + frío)
	frialdad	coldness, coolness, *frigidity*	
	frígido	frigid	
	frigidez	frigidity	
	frigorífico	frigorific, refrigerating, refrigerator (m.)	
	enfriar	(to) cool, (to) chill, (to) catch cold	
	resfriar(se)	(to) catch a cold (~ *constipar[se]*)	
	resfriado ~ resfrío	cold (minor illness)	
	refrigerar	(to) cool, (to) refrigerate	
	refrigerador	cooling, refrigerating, refrigerator (~ *nevera*)	
	fiambre	cold cut (cooked meat)	(< friambre)

SECTION 3.5

Other Distinctive Consonants (or Lack Thereof)

Consider the following pairs of Spanish words:

Spanish 1	Spanish 2	English Cognate	Change
1. pleno	lleno	plenum, plenty	$pl \rightarrow ll$
2. tracto	trecho	tract	$ct \rightarrow ch$
3. artículo	artejo	article, articulate	$cul \rightarrow j$
4. anexo	anejo	annex	$x \rightarrow j$
5. concilio	concejo	council	$li + vowel \rightarrow j$
6. reverso	revés	reverse	$rs \rightarrow s$
7. captar	catar	capture	$pt \rightarrow t$
8. parábola	palabra	parable, parabola	$r \longleftrightarrow l$
9. baron	varón	baron	$b \rightarrow v$

In each case, the first Spanish word is easily associated with its English cognate. The Spanish words in the second column are also cognates but are far less easily recognizable, as in each case they have undergone one or more consonantal changes as part of their "popular" evolution from Latin to Spanish. As we will see below, the definitions of all of these words are easily understandable, given knowledge of the cognate, although those in the first column tend to correspond more directly to the definition of the corresponding English word.

Each of the consonant changes illustrated above has occurred in numerous cases, although some are much more common than others. In this section, we will present a selection of words that have undergone these, and several other, consonant changes.

1. PL, FL, CL $\rightarrow$ ll

A relatively small number of words in Spanish have undergone this change. Similar changes occurred in both Portuguese ($\rightarrow$ ch) and Italian ($\rightarrow$ pi, fi, chi) but on a much wider scale.[1]

---

[1] The Italian "deformation" is reflected in several English words imported from Italian, including fiasco, piano, and chiaroscuro.

Latin	Spanish	Portuguese	Italian	*English Cognate*
PLICARE	llegar	chegar	piegare	ply, implicate
FLAMMA	llama	chama	fiamma	flame
CLAMARE	llamar	chamar	chiamare	claim, clamor

Some of the more common examples are:

CLAMARE	llamar	(to) call	[*claim*]
	¿Cómo te llamas?	What is your name?	
	Me llamo José.	My name is José.	
	llamar por teléfono	(to) telephone	
	llamada	call	[rare *chamade* < Port.]
	llamativo	attracting attention, showy, flashy	
CLAUSA	llosa	enclosed field	[*close*]
CLAVIS	llave (f.)	key, faucet, wrench	[*clavier*]
	llave inglesa	monkey wrench	
	clave (f.)	key (decisive), *clef*, password	
	clave de sol	treble *clef*	
FLAMMA	llama	*flame*	
	llamear	(to) *flame*, (to) blaze	
	llamarada	sudden blaze, flare-up	
	flama	*flame*, intense heat	
	flamante	brand-new, brilliant	[*flaming*]
	inflamar	(to) inflame (set on fire, arouse)	
	inflamable [2]	inflammable, flammable	
	inflamatorio	inflammatory	
PLAGA	llaga	sore, ulcer	
	plaga	*plague*	

---

[2] In Spanish there is no word *flamable*. English *flammable* and *inflammable* mean exactly the same thing, though the prefix *in-* ("in") is interpreted erroneously by many as having a negative sense.

	plagar	(to) *plague,* (to) be overrun with	
PLANTAGINEM (acc.)	llantén	*plantain* (weed)	
PLANUS	llano (adj. & n.)	level, flat, *plain* (simple, flatland), *llano*	
	llana (n.)	trowel	
	llanura	*plain,* flatland	
	plano (adj. & n.)	level, flat, smooth, *plane,* map or *plan*	
	plana (n.)	page (side), senior staff (*plana mayor*)	
	primera plana	front page	
	allanar	(to) level, (to) raze, (to) break and enter	
PLENUS	lleno	full	[*plenty*]
	llenar	(to) fill	
	pleno (adj. & n.)	full, *plenum* (assembly)	
PLICARE	llegar	(to) arrive	[*ply, plié*]
	llegada	arrival, finish (sports)	
	allegar	(to) bring near, (to) gather	[*apply*]
	allegado (p.p.)	close, close friend or relative (m./f.)	
PLORARE	llorar	(to) cry, (to) weep	[*deplore*]
	llorón (-ona)	weeping, crybaby (m./f.)	
	lloroso	tearful, weeping, sad	
	deplorar	(to) deplore, (to) lament	
	deplorable	deplorable	
	implorar	(to) implore	
PLUVIA	lluvia	rain	[*pluvial*]
	lluvioso	rainy, *pluvious*	
	llover	(to) rain	
	llovizna	drizzle	
	lloviznar	(to) drizzle	
	pluvial	pluvial, rain (adj.)	
PLANCTUS (unrelated)	llanto	weeping	[*plaint*]
	llanta	tire, wheel rim	

Llama is the only example of a Latin *FL-* word with *ll-* in Spanish. In Old Spanish, one other word was affected but has since changed the initial *ll-* to *l-*:

FLACCIDUS	lacio	lank (hair), wilted, *flaccid*	(OldSp. *llacio*)
	flácido / fláccido	flaccid, flabby	
	flacidez / flaccidez	flaccidity, flabbiness	

Note that *lacio* also displays two of the changes noted in Section 3.4: the double consonant *CC* has become simple *c,* and the *D* has vanished.

In a few words, *interior CL, FL,* and *PL* underwent a similar transformation but with a different outcome: *ch* instead of *ll.*

AMPLUS	ancho (adj. & n.)	wide, broad, width, breadth	
	anchura	width, breadth	
(ex → ens)	ensanchar	(to) widen or enlarge, (to) let out (clothes)	
	ensanche	extension, widening, expansion (town)	
	amplio	spacious, extensive, *ample*	
	ampliar	(to) enlarge, (to) *amplify*	
CONCLAVARE	conchabar	(to) unite, (to) mix (wool), (to) conspire	
	cónclave	*conclave*	
IMPLERE	henchir	(to) fill, (to) stuff	[*implement*]
INFLARE	hinchar	(to) *inflate,* (to) swell	
	hinchado	swollen, inflated, pompous	
	hinchazón (f.)	swelling, conceit, pomposity	
	hincha	fan or supporter (m./f.), grudge or dislike (f.)	
	hinchada	fans, supporters	
	inflar	(to) *inflate*	

2. *CT → ch*

This outcome is distinct to Spanish; as shown in the table below, the other major Romance languages transformed *CT* into either *(i)t* or *(t)t.*

Latin	Spanish	Portuguese	Italian	French
LACTEM	leche	leite	latte	lait
DESPECTUS	despecho	despeito	dispetto	dépit

DICTUS	dicho	dito	detto	dit
OCTO	ocho	oito	otto	huit
LUCTARE	luchar	lutar	lottare	lutter

Examples:

bizcocho	*biscuit,* sponge cake	[twice-*cooked*]
—sancocho	—parboiled meat, stew (Amer.)	[con*coct*]
derecho (adj.)	right, right-hand, straight, upright	[*direct*]
—derecho (n.)	—right, law, rights (copyright, royalties—pl.)	
—derecha (n.)	—right hand, right-hand side, right (politics)	
—derecho (adv.)	—*directly,* straight	
despecho	*spite*	[re*spect*]
—a despecho de	—*despite,* in spite of (~ *a pesar de*)	
dicho	said (p.p. *decir*), saying or proverb (m.)	[*dictum, ditto*]
—antedicho	—aforesaid, aforementioned	
—dicha	—good fortune, happiness	
—dichoso	—happy, fortunate, "blasted" (fam.)	
—desdicha	—misfortune, calamity	
—desdichado (adj. & n.)	—unfortunate, wretched, wretch	
—entredicho	—doubt or question (hanging over), *interdict*	
ducha	shower	[*duct, douche*]
—duchar	—(to) give a shower to, (to) take a shower	
echar	(to) *eject,* (to) throw or toss, (to) cast	
—echar de menos[3]	—(to) miss, (to) note the absence of	
—desechar	—(to) *reject,* (to) exclude, (to) cast aside	[rare *disject*]
—desecho	—remainder, waste or debris (freq. pl.)	
—desechable	—disposable (e.g., syringe, razor blade)	
estrecho	narrow, tight, *strait*	[*strict*]
—estrechez	—narrowness, tightness, predicament, penury, "dire straits"	
—estrechar	—(to) narrow, (to) tighten (bonds, etc.)	[*straiten*]
—estrechar la mano	—(to) shake hands	

---

[3] *Echar de menos* comes from Portuguese *achar (de) menos,* and the "echar" thus has no connection with the normal Spanish *echar. Achar* is derived from the same latin root (ADFLARE) that produced Spanish *hallar,* thus the meaning "to find missing", "to miss".

fecha	date	[*fact*]
—fechar	—(to) date (e.g., a letter)	
—hecho (p.p.)	—*fact*	[*feat*]
—de hecho	—in *fact, de facto*	
—bienhechor (adj. & n.)	—*beneficent, benefactor* (~ *benefactor*)	
—cohecho	—bribery	[*confetti*]
—contrahecho	—deformed, hunchbacked	[*counterfeit*]
—deshecho[4] (p.p.)	—unmade (e.g., bed), devastated, exhausted	
—hechizo	—charm, enchantment	[*fetish*]
—hechizar	—(to) bewitch, (to) charm	
—hechicero	—sorcerer, sorceress, witch	
—hechura	—creation, shape or form, workmanship	[*feature*]
—malhechor	—*malefactor* (evildoer, criminal)	
—provecho	—benefit, *profit*	
—¡buen provecho!	—bon appetit!	
—provechoso	—*profitable*, beneficial, advantageous	
—aprovechar	—(to) make use of, (to) *profit* from	
leche (f.)	milk	[*lactation*]
—lechero	—dairy (adj.), milk (adj.), milkman (or woman)	
—lechoso	—milky[5]	
—lechuga	—*lettuce*	
—lechuza[6]	—owl	
—lecho[7]	—bed (~ *cama*), riverbed (~ *cauce*)	[wagon-*lit*]
lucha	fight, strife, wrestling	[*ineluctable*]
—luchar	—(to) fight, (to) wrestle, (to) struggle	[*reluctant*]
—luchador	—fighter, wrestler	
noche (f.) [8]	night	[*nocturnal*]

---

[4] Note that *deshecho* is pronounced identically to *desecho* ("debris"; see above under *echar*).

[5] However, the Milky Way is "la Vía *Láctea*".

[6] Latin for *owl* was NOCTUA (literally "'night' bird"), which would have become Spanish *nochua* or, as a pejorative variant, *nochuza*. *Lechuza* apparently resulted from a cross between *nochuza* and *leche*, due to the popular belief of the time that owls came at night to give milk to babies.

[7] *Lecho* (Latin LECTUS) is unrelated to *leche*, sharing instead a common Indo-European root with English *lie, ledge,* and *low*. *Lecho* corresponds to French *lit* (hence *wagon-lit*).

[8] *Noche* comes from Latin NOX (acc. NOCTEM), which shares a common Indo-European root with English *night*.

—anoche	—last night	
—medianoche (f.)	—midnight	
—Nochebuena	—Christmas Eve	
—Nochevieja	—New Year's Eve	
—trasnochar	—(to) stay up late, (to) have a sleepless night	
ocho	eight	[*octet*]
—ochenta	—eighty	[*octogenarian*]
—ochocientos	—eight hundred	
pecho	chest, breast	[*pectoral*]
—pechuga	—breast (of chicken, etc.)	
satisfecho	*satisfied*	[*satisfaction*]
—insatisfecho	—dissatisfied, unsatisfied	
sospechar	(to) *suspect*, (to) be *suspicious* (of)	
—sospecha	—suspicion	
—sospechoso	—suspicious (arousing suspicion), suspect (adj. & n.)	
—suspicaz	—suspicious (given to suspicion), distrustful	
—suspicacia	—suspiciousness (distrustfulness)	
techo	roof, ceiling	[*tectum, thatch*[9]]
—techar	—(to) roof	
—techumbre	—roof, roofing	
trecho	distance, stretch, *tract* (expanse of land)	
—tracto	—*tract* (digestive, urinary, etc.)	
trucha	*trout*	(Lat. TRUCTA)

One common Spanish word that has undergone the "Portuguese" treatment is

AFFECTARE	afeitar	(to) shave	[*affectation*]
	afeite	cosmetics, makeup (freq. pl.)	

The combination *LT* also on occasion evolved to *ch*:

AUSCULTARE	escuchar	(to) listen (to)	[*auscultate*]
	escucha	listening (act), wiretap, military *scout* (m.)	

---

[9] *Techo—tectum* comes from the same Indo-European root as Germanic *thatch*.

CULTELLUS	cuchillo	knife	[*cutlass*]
MULTUS	mucho (adj.)	much, a lot of, many (pl.)	
	muy (adv.)	very	

The similarity in form between *mucho* and *much* is coincidental, as etymologically they are unrelated.

3. *CUL → j*

CULUS and CULA were Latin *diminutive* endings, much like -*let* in English (*piglet, hamlet, bracelet,* etc.) and enjoyed rapid growth in Vulgar Latin. They have contributed to the Romance names of many animals, family relations, parts of the body, etc. In some cases, they have undergone a popular treatment resulting in Spanish *j*, while in other cases they have preserved a more "learned" Latin form. Examples of the latter include:

Latin	*Meaning*	*Diminutive*	*Spanish*	*English*
AVUS	grandfather	AVUNCULUS	—	avuncular, uncle
CALCEM (acc.)	pebble	CALCULUS	cálculo	calculus
CORPUS	body	CORPUSCULUM	corpúsculo	corpuscle
MINUS	less	MINUSCULUS	minúsculo	minuscule
MUS	mouse	MUSCULUS	músculo	muscle
PARTEM (acc.)	part	PARTICULA	partícula	particle

Examples of "popular" treatment resulting in Spanish *j* include:

ACUCULA	aguja	needle, steeple, spire	[*acicula, aiguille*]
	agujero	hole	
APICULA	abeja	bee	[*apian, apiary*]
ARTICULUS	artejo	joint or *articulation* (finger, arthropod)	
	artículo	*article*	
AURICULA	oreja	ear	[*auricle*]
CLAVICULA ("little key")	clavija	peg, pin, electric plug	[*clavicle*]
	clavícula	*clavicle* (collarbone)	
CUBICULUM	cobijo	shelter, protection	[*cubicle*]
	cobija	blanket (Amer.)	
	cobijar	(to) shelter, (to) harbor (ideas)	

CUNICULUS	conejo	rabbit	[*Coney* Island]
FENUCULUM	hinojo (1)	*fennel*	
GENUCULUM	hinojo (2)	knee (~ *rodilla;* used gen. only as below)	
	de hinojos	on one's knees, kneeling	
	genuflexión	*genuflection*	
LENTICULA	lenteja	*lentil*	
	lente	*lens* (gen. f.), glasses (pl., gen. m.)	(lentil-shaped)
	lentilla	contact lens (~ *lente de contacto*)	
MUSCULUS	mejillón	*mussel*	[*muscle]*
OCULUS	ojo	eye	[*ocular*]
	ojear	(to) eye, (to) regard	[Germ. *ogle*]
	ojeada	glance	
	oculista	oculist	
PARICULA	pareja	couple, *pair* (people, animals, etc.)	
	parejo (adj.)	equal, alike, flat (land)	[non*pareil*]
	aparejo	preparation, gear, harness, rigging, tackle	
	aparejar	(to) prepare, (to) rig	
	aparejado (p.p.)	apt, suitable	
	traer aparejado	(to) entail or involve (~ *llevar aparejado*)	
	emparejar	(to) match, (to) *pair* (off)	
PEDICULUS (PEDU-)	piojo	louse	[*pedicular*]
	piojoso	lousy (full of lice)	
SPECULUM	espejo	mirror	
	espejismo	mirage	
	espéculo	*speculum*	
VERMICULUS	bermejo	bright red, *vermilion* (adj.), *vermeil* (adj.)	

The much rarer Latin GUL also had the same "popular" result:

COAGULARE	cuajar	(to) *coagulate,* (to) curdle
	cuajo	rennet
	cuajada	curd (*coagulated* milk)

TEGULA	teja	roof *tile*
	tejar	(to) *tile* (roof), *tile* or brick factory (n.)
	tejado (p.p.)	roof, esp. *tiled* roof

4. x → j

Dating back to Latin times, the letter *x* has been a "shorthand" symbol representing the combined sound [ks].[10] In the transition to Spanish, this underwent a major transformation, which occurred in two separate stages:

1. [ks] → [sh], still written *x*
2. [sh] → [h*],[11] subsequently written *j*

The first transformation occurred during the early stages of the evolution from Latin to Spanish (well before AD 1000), while the second transformation took place only after *Don Quijote* (formerly *Don Quixote*) was published (1605)—and after *sherry* (Spanish *Jerez,* formerly *Xerez*) had become an English word (Shakespeare: 1597).

ANNEXUS	anejo ~ anexo	attached, *annex,* attachment (email)
	anexar / anejar	(to) annex, (to) join
	anexionar	(to) annex (esp. territory)
AXIS	eje	*axis,* axle, crux, *Axis* (cap.)
COMPLEXUS	complejo	*complicated, complex* (adj. & n.)
	complejidad	*complexity*
COXINUM	cojín	*cushion*
	coxal (adj.)	coxal (pertaining to the hip or hip joint)

---

[10] In Classical Greek, the letter represented by the symbol X (chi) had the sound [kh], but in the Greek of Italy, from which the Latin alphabet was derived, it had the sound [ks].

[11] Most books and dictionaries denote this sound [x] instead of [h], [x] being the phonetic symbol for the sound represented by the *ch* in Scottish *loch* or German *Achtung.* It is undoubtedly true that many Spanish speakers have a *slightly* greater degree of aspiration of this sound than is characteristic of English (aspirated) *h.* The emphasis is on *slightly:* an English speaker attempting to transplant his or her version of Scottish or German *ch* to words like *general* will in most cases sound far less "Spanish" than if he or she simply pronounced it [*heneral*]. We will therefore use [h*] to represent this sound.

EXECUTIO(N)	ejecución	*execution* (various senses)	
	ejecutar	(to) *execute*	
	ejecutivo	*executive* (adj. & n.)	
EXEMPLUM	ejemplo	*example*	
	por ejemplo	for *example*	
	ejemplar	*exemplary, exemplar, example* (specimen)	
	ejemplificar	(to) *exemplify*	
EXEMPLI GRATIA	p.ej. = p.e.	*e.g.* ("for the sake of an example")	
EXERCITIUM	ejercicio	*exercise,* practice, drill	
EXERCITUS	ejército	army	
FIXUS	fijo	*fixed,* firm	(old p.p.)
	fijar	(to) *fix,* (to) set	
	fijación	*fixation,* setting (e.g., date)	
	fijador	*fixative,* hair spray or gel	
	prefijo	*prefix,* dialing (area) code	
	sufijo	*suffix*	
FLUXUS	flujo	flow, *flux*	
	influjo	*influence* (~ *influencia*)	[*influx*]
	reflujo	ebb (tide), *reflux*	
	flojo	loose, slack, weak	
	flojear	(to) weaken, (to) slacken	
	aflojar	(to) loosen, (to) weaken, (to) let up	
LAXARE	dejar	(to) let, (to) leave	(OldSp. *lejar*)
	dejar de fumar	(to) stop smoking	
	dejadez	laziness, carelessness, slovenliness	
	laxitud	laxity, laxness	
	laxante	laxative	
LAXIUS	lejos (adv.)	far, far away	[*lax*]
	lejano (adj.)	distant, far-off	
	lejanía	distance, remoteness	
	alejar	(to) move away (from)	
LUXUS	lujo	*luxury*	
	lujoso	*luxurious*	
	de lujo	*deluxe*	
	lujuria	lust, lechery	[*luxury*]
	lujurioso	lustful, lecherous, lewd	[*luxurious*]

MAXILLA	mejilla	cheek	[*maxillary*]
PARADOXA	paradoja	*paradox*	
	paradójico	*paradoxical*	
PARALLAXIS	paralaje (f.)	*parallax*	
PERPLEXUS	perplejo	*perplexed*	
	perplejidad	*perplexity*	
PROLIXUS	prolijo	*prolix,* excessively detailed, tedious	
PROXIMUS	prójimo	fellow human ("neighbor")	[*proximity*]
Don Quixote (1605)	Don Quijote	Don Quixote	
	quijote	a Don Quixote (impractical idealist)	
	quijotesco	quixotic	
REFLEXUS	reflejo (adj. & n.)	*reflected, reflection, reflex*	
	reflejar	(to) *reflect,* (to) mirror	
RELAXARE	relajar	(to) *relax,* (to) become *lax*	
	relajación	relaxation, (moral) laxity	
	relajante	relaxing	
SAXONES	sajón (-ona)	Saxon	
	anglosajón (-ona)	Anglo-Saxon	
TEXERE	tejer	(to) weave, (to) knit	
	tejido (p.p.)	fabric, *textile, tissue,* weave	
	entretejer	(to) interweave, (to) interlace	
	textil	textile	
	texto	text, textbook	
	textura	texture	
VEXARE	vejar	(to) *vex*	
	vejación	*vexation*	

One case worth noting, in which the sound [ks] avoided a major transformation by shedding [k] at an early stage, is:

TAXARE	tasar	(to) appraise, (to) fix (price, quantity)	
	tasa	rate (%), fee, *tax*	
	tasación	valuation	[*taxation*]
	taxi	taxi	
	taxista	taxi driver	

The combination *ss* on a number of occasions has also become Spanish *j*:

ambaissada (Occitan)	embajada	*embassy*	
	embajador	*ambassador*	
BASSUS	bajo (adj.)	low, short, *base* (vile)	
	bajo (adv.)	low (softly, quietly)	
	bajo (prep.)	under (~ *debajo de*)	
	bajo (n.)	*bass* (voice, instrument), *bass* guitar	
	contrabajo	double *bass* (*contrabass*)	
	bajón	*bassoon*	
	bajar	(to) descend, (to) lower, (to) download	
	abajo	down, below, downstairs	
	debajo	underneath, below	
	rebajar	(to) lower (price, self-esteem, etc.)	
	rebaja	reduction, discount	
	altibajos (pl.)	ups and downs, vicissitudes	
CESSARE	cejar	(to) back up, (to) give up	
	cesar	(to) *cease*, (to) stop	
PASSER	pájaro	bird	[*passerine*]
QUASSARE	quejar(se)	(to) complain	[*quash, squash*]
	queja	complaint	
	aquejar	(to) afflict, (to) distress	
RUSSUS	rojo	red	[*russet*]
	pelirrojo	red-haired, redhead (m./f.)	
	enrojecer	(to) redden (make or become red, blush)	

In a few cases, a single *s* at the beginning of a word or syllable was (mis)pronounced as [sh] and hence has wound up as *j*:

INSERTARE	injertar	(to) graft (plant or medical)	[*insert*]
	injerto	graft	
(unrelated)	injerencia	interference, meddling	[*ingest*]
	insertar	(to) insert	
	inserción	insertion	

SAPO(N)	jabón	soap	[*saponification*]
SUCUS	jugo	juice	[*succulent*]
	suculento	succulent, juicy	
SYRINGA	jeringa	*syringe*	
VESICA	vejiga	bladder, *vesica*	
	vesícula	*vesicle*	
	vesícula biliar	gall bladder	

Finally, in a small number of isolated cases, other consonant combinations involving *s* have also wound up as Spanish *j*:

CAPSA	caja	box, *case, cashier's* desk	
	caja de ahorros	savings bank	
	caja fuerte	safe, strongbox	
	cajero	*cashier*	
	cajón	drawer, crate (gen. without top)	[*caisson*]
	cápsula	capsule	
	encajar	(to) fit in, or together	[*encase*]
	encaje	lace, socket, fitting in (insertion)	
	casete / cassette (m./f.)	*cassette*	(< Fr.)
FASCIA	faja	girdle, sash, strip or band, *fascia* (arch.), *fess* (heraldry)	
	fajita	*fajita* (Mex. food)	
PULSARE	pujar (1)	(to) *push* (intransitive)	
	puja (1)	*push* (stimulus)	
	empujar	(to) *push* (transitive), (to) *propel*	
	empujón	*push,* shove (brusque)	
	empuje	*push, impulse,* thrust	
(unrelated, < Cat.)	pujar (2)	(to) offer a higher bid	[*podium*]
	puja (2)	(higher) bid	
(unrelated, < Fr.)	pujante	strong, vigorous	[*puissant*]
	pujanza	vigor, strength	[*puissance*]
VASCELLA (< Cat.)	vajilla	tableware	[*vase, vessel*]
	vascular	vascular (pertaining to the *vessels*)	

Historical Note: *México* or *Méjico? Texas* or *Tejas?*

"Mexico" and "Texas" are special cases. Historically, these words entered Spanish at a stage when *x* was still pronounced [sh]. They have never been pronounced by native Spanish speakers as [meKSico] or [teKSas], this being a later innovation by *gringos*. After Spanish [sh] had evolved to [h*], *México* and *Texas* had their *x* changed to *j*, analogous to *Quixote* → *Quijote*, but not in the Americas, where the locals remained attached to the original spelling (but not the original pronunciation) of the two names.

Throughout most of its history, the RAE has unsuccessfully tried to convince Mexico (and the world) that the correct spellings were *Méjico* and *mejicano*. In 1992 it still listed them as the preferred forms. Only with the publication of its 2001 dictionary has it conceded defeat and accepted *México* and *mexicano*—as well as *Texas* and *texano*—as the preferred forms, although *tejanos* remains the only accepted spelling in the sense of "blue jeans".

5. *ll* + vowel → *j*

This change was the result of several separate transformations, the last of which was not concluded until the mid-seventeenth century. The Spanish outcome contrasts markedly with those of the other principal Romance languages, in which the transformation stopped at the stage of palatized *l* (i.e., the equivalent of Spanish *ll*):

Latin	Spanish	Portuguese	Italian	French
FILIA	hija	filha	figlia	fille
MELIOR	mejor	melhor	migliore	meilleur
PALEA	paja	palha	paglia	paille

Examples:

ALIENUS	ajeno	another's, *alien* or foreign	
	enajenar	(to) drive insane, (to) *alienate* (a person, or transfer a property right)	
AL(L)IUM	ajo	garlic	[*allium*]
CILIA	ceja	eyebrow	[*cilia*]

CONCILIUM	concejo	city *council,* city council meeting	
	concejal (-ala)	city *councilor,* alderman	
	concilio	*council* (esp. religious)	
	conciliación	conciliation	
	conciliar	(to) conciliate, (to) reconcile	
	reconciliación	reconciliation	
	reconciliar	(to) reconcile	
CONSILIUM	consejo	*counsel,*[12] advice, council	
	Consejo de Ministros	Council of Ministers	
	consejero	*counselor,* advisor, councilor	
	aconsejar	(to) *counsel,* (to) advise	
	desaconsejar	(to) advise against	
DESPOLIARE	despojar	(to) *despoil,* (to) divest	
	despojo	*despoliation, spoils* (pl.), offal (pl.), mortal remains (pl.)	
FILIUS	hijo	son	[Fitz-[13]]
FOLIA	hoja	leaf, sheet	[*foil, folio*]
	folio	folio	
	foliar	(to) number (pages)	[*foliate*]
	follaje (< Occitan)	foliage	
	folleto	pamphlet, brochure, leaflet	
	folletín	*feuilleton,* melodrama (often published serially)	
MELIOR	mejor	better	[*amelioration*]
MILIUM	mijo / millo	*millet*	[*mealie, milium*]
MOLLIARE	mojar	(to) wet, (to) moisten	[*emollient*]
	mojado (p.p.)	wet, damp, soaked	
	remojar	(to) soak	
MULIER	mujer (f.)	woman, wife	[*muliebrity*]
	mujeriego	womanizer	

---

[12] English *counsel* and *council* are distinct words, albeit frequently confused, with separate Latin origins: CONSILIUM (related to *consult*) and CONCILIUM (lit. "to call together").

[13] Modern French *fils* ("son") formerly was pronounced [fits] and was brought in this form to England by the Norman French and from there to Ireland (hence John **Fitz**gerald Kennedy). *Fitz-* is thus equivalent to Scottish and Irish *Mac-* and *Mc-,* as well as to the "native" English suffix *-son.*

PALEA	paja	straw	[*paillasse*]
	payaso (< It.)	clown	
SIMILIARE	semejar	(to) *resemble*, (to) be *similar* to	
	semejanza	*similarity, resemblance*	
	semejante	*similar*, like, such (a)	
	semblante	face, countenance, aspect	
	semblanza	biographical sketch	[*semblance*]
	similar	similar	
	símil	*simile*	
TALIARE	tajar	(to) cut or slice (e.g., meat)	[*tailor*]
	tallar (<It.)	(to) cut, (to) carve	
(unrelated)	talar (1)	(to) cut a tree (at the base), (to)	
	(< Germ.)	devastate	
(unrelated)	talar (2)[14]	full length, reaching to the ankles	[*talus*]
TRIPALIUM	trabajo	work	[*travail, travel*]
	trabajar	(to) work	
	trabajador	hard-working, worker (m./f.)	

6. *NS, RS, PS → S*

EXAMPLES OF *ns → s*

ANSA	asa	handle	[*ansate*]
	asidero	grip (handle), grab bar (shower)	
	asir	(to) grasp (rope, opportunity)	
CONSTARE	costar	(to) *cost*	
	constar	(to) consist (of), (to) be clear or evident, (to) be recorded in (document)	
	me consta (que)	I am sure . . . , I know for certain (that) . . .	
CON + SUTURA	costura	sewing, seam	
	alta costura	*haute couture*	
	coser	(to) sew	

---

[14] The literal meaning is "extending to the *talón* (heel)", e.g., a cassock or a toga.

INSULA	isla	island,[15] *isle*	
	islote	*islet*	
	insular	insular	
	insulina	insulin	
a + isla	aislar	(to) *isolate*, (to) *insulate*, (to) *enisle*	
	aislamiento	*isolation, insulation*	
	aislante (adj. & n.)	*isolating, insulating, insulator*	
MANSIO(N)	mesón	inn, tavern	[*mansion*]
	remanso	still water, haven or oasis	[*remnant*]
MENSA	mesa	table	[*Mesa* Grande]
	mesilla (de noche)	night table	
	sobremesa	time immediately following a meal	
	de sobremesa (adj.)	after-dinner, tabletop, desktop	
MENSIS	mes	month	
	mensual	monthly	
MONSTRARE	mostrar	(to) show, (to) de*monstrate*	
	demostrar	(to) *demonstrate*, (to) prove	
	demostración	demonstration	
PENSARE	pesar (1)	(to) weigh	[com*pensate*]
	pesado (p.p.)	heavy, irksome, deep (sleep)	
	pesar (2) (n.)	sorrow, regret	
	a pesar de ~ pese a	despite, in spite of	
	a pesar de que ~ pese a que	despite (in spite of) the fact that	
	a pesar de todo	despite everything	
	pesadilla	nightmare	

---

[15] English *island* originally had nothing to do with *isle*. The Middle English form was *iland* or *yland* (the first syllable being of Germanic origin and equivalent to that in *Eaton* and *Eton*, meaning "water"). This was then changed to *ile-land* due to association with the French word *ile* (like Spanish *isla*, from Latin INSULA), and at a still later stage an "etymological" *s* (never pronounced) was added.

	pesadez	heaviness, nuisance	
	pésame	condolence(s)	
	pesa	weight (for scales, barbell), counterweight	
	peso	weight, *peso,* shot put	
	peseta	peseta (former Spanish currency)	
	pensar	(to) think	
	pensamiento	thought, *pansy*[16]	
	pensativo	*pensive*	
SENSUS	seso	wit or good *sense,* brains (gen. pl.)	
	devanar(se) los sesos	(to) rack one's brains	
	sesudo	*sensible,* sage	
SPONSA	esposa	wife, *spouse*	
	esponsales (pl.)	engagement, betrothal	[*spousals*]
TENSUS	tieso	stiff, rigid, firm	
	tesón	*tenacity,* perseverance	[*tension*]
TRANS	tras (prep.)	after, behind	[*trans-*]
	trasero	back (adj.), rear, "rear end" (m.)	
	detrás (adv.)	behind, back, *in* the rear	
	atrás (adv.)	behind, back, *to* the rear, ago	
	atraso	delay, backwardness, arrears (pl.)	
	atrasar	(to) delay, (to) set back or lose time (clock)	
	retrasar	(to) delay, (to) set back or lose time (clock)	
	retraso	delay, backwardness	
	retrasado (p.p.)	behind (schedule), backward or retarded	
	trasplantar[17]	(to) *transplant*	

---

[16] From French, in the same fanciful sense as "forget-me-not" (a type of plant with small blue flowers).

[17] The distribution between *tras-* and *trans-* is somewhat haphazard, with the four examples in the text illustrating the possible patterns: *tras-* only; both (with *tras-* "preferred"); both (with *trans-* "preferred"); *trans-* only.

traslación / trans-	*translation* (uniform movement)
transatlántico / tras-	*transatlantic,* transatlantic ship
transacción	*transaction,* compromise

EXAMPLES OF *RS* → *s*

AVERSUS	avieso	twisted, malicious	[*averse*]
	aversión	*aversion*	
EXCAR(P)SUS	escaso	*scarce,* scanty	
	escasamente	*scarcely*	
	escasez	*scarcity,* shortage, poverty	
	escasear	(to) be *scarce*	
INDORSARE	endosar	(to) *endorse*	
	dorso	back (of hand, page, etc.)	[*dorsum*]
	dorsal	dorsal	
REVERSUS	revés	*reverse* (n.), other side, backhand	
	reverso	reverse (n.), other (or back) side	
SURSUM + DICTUS	susodicho	aforesaid (~ *antedicho*)	
TRANSVERSA	traviesa (n.)	railroad tie	[*traverse*]
	travieso (adj.)	mischievous, naughty	
	travesura	mischief, prank	
	travesía	small (connecting) road, part of road *traversing* a town, voyage (air, sea)	
	través	slant, inclination (tilt)	
	a través de	through	
	atravesar	(to) cross (over), (to) pierce	
	transversal	transverse (~ *transverso*)	
URSUS	oso	bear	[*ursine*]
	Osa Mayor	*Ursa* Major (constellation with Big Dipper)	

FINALLY, IN A FEW CASES, *PS* BECAME *s:*

GYPSUM	yeso	plaster, plaster cast, *gypsum*
PSALMUS	salmo	*psalm*
PSEUDONYMOS	seudónimo	*pseudonymous, pseudonym,* pen name

7. *PT* → *t*

AEGYPTANUS	gitano	*gypsy*	
	egipcio	*Egyptian* (adj. & n.)	
APTARE	atar	(to) tie	[*apt, lariat*]
CAPTARE	catar	(to) taste, (to) sample	[*capture, catch*]
	catalejo	(small) telescope, spyglass	(catar + lejos)
	acatar	(to) comply with, (to) obey	[*cater*]
	percatar(se)	(to) notice, (to) realize	[*perception*]
	recato	modesty, reserve (caution)	
	recatado	modest, reserved	
	captar	(to) pick up (signal, sound),	
		(to) *capture* (water, attention),	
		(to) *catch* (meaning)	
	capturar	(to) *capture*, (to) *catch*	
	recaudar	(to) collect (e.g., taxes)	(*pt* → *ud*)
	recaudador	(tax) collector	
	recaudación	takings, collection, gate	
		(paid attendance)	
RE + EX +	rescatar	(to) rescue, (to) ransom, (to)	
CAPTARE		recover	
	rescate	rescue, ransom	
PROMPTUS	pronto	adj.—quick, *prompt;* adv.—	
		promptly, soon	
	prontitud	*promptness, promptitude*	
RECEPTA	receta	*recipe,* prescription (medical)	[*receipt*]
	recetar	(to) prescribe (medical)	
RUPTUS	roto	broken (p.p. of *romper*)	[*rupture*]
	derrota	defeat, *rout,* path, ship's	
		course or *route*	
	derrotar	(to) defeat, (to) *rout*	
	derrotero	*route,* way, ship's course or	
		track	
	ruta	*route*	
	rutina	*routine* (n.)	
	rutinario	*routine* (adj.)	
SCRIPTUS	escrito	written (p.p. of *escribir*),	
		writing (m.)	
	escritura	handwriting, *Scripture* (cap.,	
		freq. pl.)	

SAEPTUM	seto	hedge, fence	[*septum*]
SEPTEM	si*e*te	seven	
	septuagenario	*septuagenarian* (adj. & n.)	
SYMPTOMA	síntoma (m.)	*symptom*	

8. Shifts of R and L

The sounds [r] and [l] are phonetically very similar, and it is therefore not surprising that they are frequently interchanged or substituted one for the other. One prominent English example is *mulberry:* the first component of the word was a very early import from Latin MORUM (Spanish *mora*), and in Old English the word was *morberie.* A second example is *pilgrim,* which ultimately comes from Latin PEREGRINUS—in this case the "switch" was carried out in French and then imported into English. The original form is preserved in English *peregrine* (as in *peregrine* falcon). Finally, Latin PRUNA has produced both the "learned" English *prune* and the more "popular" *plum.*

In the first two examples cited above, the combination R—R was changed to L—R, probably due to a (perhaps subconscious) desire to distinguish more clearly the two syllables—a process linguists call *dissimilation.* This change has occurred in Spanish with considerably greater frequency than in English.

a) R—R → r—l

ARBOR	árbol	tree	[*arboretum*]
	arbolado	wooded, woodland (m.)	
	arbóreo	*arboreal, arboreous*	
	arbusto[18]	bush, shrub	
CARCER	cárcel (f.)	prison	
	carcelario	prison (adj.)	
	carcelero	prison (adj.), jailer, warden	
	encarcelar	(to) *incarcerate,* (to) imprison	
FRATER	fraile	*friar,* monk	
MARMOR	mármol	*marble* (< Fr. *marbre*)	

---

[18] The *s* in *arbusto* reflects the fact that at an earlier stage, Latin ARBOR had been ARBOS—the *s* then changed to R due to *rhotacism* (see Section 1.3), initially only in those forms of the word where it found itself between vowels (e.g., the accusative ARBOSEM), and eventually by analogy in the nominative case as well.

	marmóreo	*marble* (adj.), *marmoreal* (marble-like)	
MERCURII DIES	miércoles	Wednesday	[*Mercury's* day]
MURMURIUM	murmullo	*murmur, murmuring,* rustling (leaves)	
	murmurar	(to) murmur, (to) mutter, (to) rustle	
quartier (Fr.)	cuartel	*quarter, quarters,* barracks	
recruter (Fr.)	reclutar	(to) *recruit*	
STERCORIS	estiércol	dung, manure	[*stercoraceous*]
	estercolero	manure pile, dunghill	

For *purple,* it is English that has altered the original:

PURPURA	púrpura	purple, purpura (med.) [OldEng. *purpure*]	

The reverse pattern has occurred in several cases:

b) R—R → l—r

haribergon (Germ.)[19]	albergar	(to) house, (to) shelter, (to) *harbor*	
	albergue	lodging, inn, shelter	
ARBITRIUM	(libre) albedrío	(free) will, desire, whim	
	arbitrio	(free) will, discretion (choice), judgment	
	arbitrario	arbitrary	
	árbitro	*arbiter, arbitrator,* judge, referee	
	arbitraje	arbitration, refereeing, umpiring, *arbitrage*	
brandir (Fr.)	blandir	(to) *brandish*, (to) wave	
CORIANDRUM	cilantro, culantro	*coriander, cilantro* (< Sp.)	
PRECARIA	plegaria	*prayer,* supplication	[*imprecation*]
	precario	*precarious*[20]	

---

[19] *Hari-* was Germanic for "army" (appearing also in *Harold, harry, herald, harbinger*), and *bergian* meant "shelter" (one means being to *bury*).

[20] The literal meaning of *precarious* is "obtained through entreaty or *prayer*".

TEMPERARE	templar	(to) *temper*, (to) warm up, (to) tune (guitar, etc.)	
	temple	*temper* (metal, person), *temperament*, courage, tuning (music), *tempera* (art)	
	intemperie	bad weather	[*intemperate*]
	a la intemperie	in the open air, exposed, unsheltered	

Similar dissimilations occurred with respect to the *L—L* combination:

c) *L—L* → *r—l* OR *l—r*

colonnello (It.)	coronel	*colonel*	
LILIUM	lirio	*lily*, iris	
LOCALIS	lugar	place	(OldSp. *logar*)
	en lugar de	in *lieu* of	
	lugarteniente	deputy, substitute, *lieutenant*	
	local	local, premises (m.)	
	localidad	locality, seat (theater), ticket (entry)	
	localizar (to) localize	(to) locate,	

Spanish *lugarteniente* applies to civilians, the military term being simply *teniente.*

In the sixteenth century, Italian *colonnello* (head of a *column* of soldiers) was imported by French, and for some time thereafter two competing forms coexisted: the "correct" (and modern French) *colonel* and a second form with dissimilation, *coronel.* It was this second form that was exported to both English and Spanish. The *r—l* spelling continued in English until the mid-seventeenth century, when "purists" succeeded in restoring the etymologically "correct" *colonel.* They were unsuccessful, however, in their attempts to "reform" the pronunciation, which is why today we continue to pronounce *colonel* as [keR•nel].

In one case (imported from French or Catalan), *l—l* became *n—l*:

LIBELLA	nivel	*level*
	nivelar	(to) level (even, equalize)
	desnivel	drop, difference in *level,* unevenness

In some cases, instead of a dissimilation, the combination R—R has been reduced to a single r:

d) R—R → r

APPROPRIARE	apropiar(se)	(to) appropriate (take possession [of])	
	apropiado (p.p.)	appropriate	
	apropiación	appropriation (taking as one's own)	
OPPROBRIUM	oprobio	opprobrium	
ORCHESTRA	orquesta	orchestra	
	orquestal	orchestral	
	orquestar	(to) orchestrate	
	orquestación	orchestration	
PROPRIUS	propio	one's own, *proper* (suitable, characteristic)	
	impropio	improper, unsuitable	
	propiedad	*property, proprietorship*	*[propriety]*
	propietario (adj. & n.)	*proprietary,* owner, *proprietor*	
	expropiar	(to) expropriate	
	expropiación	expropriation	

In each of the above examples it is the second r that has disappeared. The first r disappeared in:

CREMARE	quemar	(to) burn	*[cremate]*
	quemadura	burn, sunburn	
	quemador	burner (cooking, CD, etc.)	
	quemazón (f.)	burning (sensation)	
	a quemarropa[21]	point-blank, at point-blank range	
PROSTRARE	postrar	(to) *prostrate,* (to) humble	
	postrado (p.p.)	prostrate	
	postración	prostration	
RETRO-guardia	retaguardia	*rear guard, rear* (n.), *rearward* (n.)	
SCRUTINIARE	escudriñar	(to) *scrutinize*	

---

[21] From *a* + *quemar* + *ropa*, literally "[close enough] *to cremate* [their] *robes*".

In several cases, R and L have reversed positions, a phenomenon known as *metathesis:*

Algeria	Argelia	*Algeria*	
LIQUIRITIA	regaliz	*licorice*	
MIRACULUM	milagro	*miracle*	
	milagroso	*miraculous*	
PARABOLA	palabra	word	
	palabrería	*palaver* (idle chatter)	(Eng. < Port.)
	parábola	*parable, parabola*	
PERICULUM	peligro	danger, *peril*	
	peligroso	dangerous, *perilous, parlous*	
	peligrar	(to) be in danger	
	poner en peligro	(to) *imperil*	

In several cases, R—L lost the R:

TREMULARE	temblar	(to) *tremble*, (to) shake
	temblor	*tremble, tremor,* quake, *temblor* (< Sp.)
	tembloroso	*trembling, tremulous,* shaking
	estremecer	(to) shake, (to) *tremble*
TRIPLUM	tiple	*treble* or soprano (voice), soprano (singer), musical instrument (similar to guitar)

In a number of cases, a single R has changed to *l,* or vice versa.

ANCORA	ancla	*anchor*
	anclaje	*anchorage*
	anclar	(to) anchor, (to) cast anchor
BURSA	bolsa	bag (shopping, trash), pouch, *purse, burse,* stock market, stock exchange, *bursa*
	bolso	*purse,* ladies' handbag
	bolsillo	pocket

	embolsar	(to) pocket, (to) be paid (money)	[† *imburse*]
	reembolsar	(to) *reimburse*	
	bursátil	stock-market (adj.)	
	bursitis	bursitis	
CATHARINA	Catalina	*Catherine, Katharine*	(< Gk.)
CHRISTOPHORUS	Cristóbal	Christopher	(< Gk.)
cramp (Germ.)	calambre	*cramp,* electric shock (sensation)	
fret (Fr.)	flete	*freight,* cargo, freight charge	
	fletar	(to) charter (ship, etc.), (to) *freight* (load)	
PAPYRUS	papel	*paper,* role (part)	
	papiro	*papyrus*	
PRACTICA	plática	chat, conversation, brief sermon	[*practice*]
	platicar	(to) chat, (to) converse	
qirat (< Arab < Greek)	quilate	*carat*	
Säbel (German)	sable [22]	*sabre / saber*	
scorta (It.)	escolta	*escort*	
	escoltar	(to) *escort*	
spora (Germ.)	espuela	*spur*	
	espolear	(to) *spur,* (to) *spur* on	
	espolón	*spur* (bone, bird), breakwater, jetty	
TEMPERANTIA	templanza	*temperance,* moderation	
TENEBRAS	tinieblas (pl.)	darkness, *Tenebrae* (eccl.)	
	tenebroso	*tenebrous* (dark and gloomy)	
FLASCO (< Germ.)	frasco	*flask,* vial	
	fiasco	fiasco	(< It.)

---

[22] In this case it is French (and hence English) that has made the "mistake", changing the *l* of German *Säbel* (itself of Hungarian origin) to *r*.

h) R: SHIFT IN POSITION

Finally, on a few occasions, R shifted place within the word. This is a phenomenon that has also occurred occasionally in English, two prominent examples being:

Old English	Modern English
brid	bird
thridda	third

Spanish examples include:

ABBRACCHICARE	abarcar[23]	(to) *embrace*, (to) encompass, (to) take in	
CREPARE	quebrar	(to) break, (to) go bankrupt	[*decrepit*]
CROCODILUS	cocodrilo	*crocodile*[24]	
CRUSTA	costra	*crust*, scab	
	crustáceo	crustacean (lobsters, crabs, etc.)	
	incrustar	(to) *encrust*, (to) inlay	
INTEGRARE	entregar	(to) deliver, (to) hand over	
	entrega	delivery	
	integrar	(to) *integrate* (various senses)	
MATURICARE	madrugar	(to) get up early	[*mature*]
	madrugada	dawn, early morning (12 A.M.—daybreak)	
skirmyan (Germ.)	esgrimir	(to) brandish, (to) fence	[*skirmish*]

A similar change occurred with respect to L in one very common word:

OBLITARE	olvidar	(to) forget
	olvido	forgetfulness, oversight, *oblivion*
	olvidadizo	forgetful, absent-minded

---

[23] In Latin, the word for "arm" could have two forms, BRACHIUM or BRACCHIUM. The first gave rise to *brazo* and *abrazar* ("to embrace"), as well as to English *brace*; the second, to *abracar* (still found in some dictionaries), which later became *abarcar*.

[24] In English, it was also *cocodrille* until the "classicists" restored the "correct" form in the sixteenth century. A similar attempt was made in Spanish, but without success (although *crocodilo* can still be found as a variant in some dictionaries).

Such interchanges of letters were not limited to *r* and *l*; they occasionally occurred when an interior vowel disappeared and thereby produced a combination of consonants difficult to pronounce, e.g.,

TENERUM	→	TEN_RUM	→	tienro	→	tierno	(*nr* → *rn*)
TITULARE	→	TID_LARE	→	tidlar	→	tildar	(*dl* → *ld*)

9. *b* = *v*

One feature of Spanish that English speakers often find somewhat surprising is that there is absolutely no difference in pronunciation between the sounds represented by the letters *b* and *v*. They are *both* pronounced as follows:

Initial	Interior	
	Following m/n	*Otherwise*
[b]	[b]	[v]
balcón	ambiguo	labor
blanco	sombrero	doble
valor	invención [25]	grave
vino	convexo	larva

As a result of this "confusion" between *b* and *v*,[26] many originally distinct words are now pronounced indistinguishably. Examples include:

baca	vaca	roof rack	cow
basto	vasto	coarse, rough	vast
bello	vello	beautiful	down, fuzz
botar	votar	(to) fling	(to) vote
grabar	gravar	(to) engrave	(to) tax
haber	a ver	(to) have [27]	"let's see"

---

[25] In this case (and for *convexo* as well), the [b] that follows the *n* causes the latter to change its pronunciation to [m]; the same principle accounts for English *imbalance* (not **inbalance*) and *combat* (not **conbat*).

[26] The mixing of *b* and *v* in the *interior* of words was common to all the Romance languages; thus, to English *describe*, which maintains the original B from Latin DESCRIBERE, correspond Italian *descrivere* and Portuguese *descrever* (and French *nous décrivons*). Spanish was unique in extending the *b/v* equality to the beginning of the word.

[27] Only as an auxiliary verb (e.g., *he escrito* = I *have* written). In the sense of possession, "have" is translated by *tener*.

Nobel	novel	Nobel	novel (adj.)
sabia	savia	wise	sap
tubo	tuvo (verb. *tener*)	tube	"he had"

Some Spanish words have initial *v* where in English (and other Romance languages) they begin with *b*, and conversely:

claire-voie (Fr.)	claraboya²⁸	skylight	
VERONIX	barniz	*varnish*	[*Bernice, Veronica*]
	barnizar	(to) *varnish*	
vogue (Fr.)	boga	*vogue,* fashion	
VOTA	boda	wedding	[*vows*]
VULTUR	buitre	*vulture*	

baron (Germ.)	varón	male, male person	[*baron*]
	varonil	manly, virile	
	barón, baronesa	baron, baroness	
binda (Germ.)	venda	*bandage*	
	venda en los ojos	blindfold (figurative)	
	vendaje	*bandage,* dressing	
	vendar	(to) *bandage*	
Bizkaia (Basque)	Golfo de Vizcaya	Bay of *Biscay*	

Spanish has *restored* a written *b* (pronounced [v]) in a few words to make them more etymologically "correct"; the corresponding English words (via French) have a *v*. Examples include:

CABALLUS	caballo	horse, knight (chess)	(OldSp. *cavallo*)
	caballero	cavalier, knight, gentleman	
	caballería	cavalry	
	cabalgata	cavalcade	
GUBERNARE	gobernar	(to) *govern,* (to) steer (nautical)	(OldSp. *governar*)
TABERNA	taberna	tavern, bar	(OldSp. *taverna*)
	tabernero	tavern keeper, bartender	

---

²⁸ The *boya* comes ultimately from Latin VIA ("way", "road") and corresponds to the *-voy* in English *envoy* and *convoy*. Since VIA is cognate with Germanic *way,* a *claraboya* is etymologically a "*clear way*".

In *grabar,* taken from French *graver* (of Germanic origin), modern Spanish has also "restored" *b:*

graver (Fr.)	grabar	(to) *engrave,* (to) record (disk, etc.)
	grabado (p.p.)	engraving
	grabación	recording (of program, etc.)

French *javeline* was likewise transformed, thus producing confusion between a *javelin* and a female wild boar (the male being a *jabalí*):

javeline (Fr.)	jabalina	*javelin,* female wild boar

Spanish has not restored the Latin B in *móvil,* presumably due to the influence of the related verb *mover:*

MOBILIS	móvil	mobile, mobile phone
	automóvil	automobile
MOVERE	mover	(to) move

Finally, the *b* in English "**Basque**" corresponds to a Spanish *v:*

vasco	*Basque* (adj., inhabitant, language—m.)
vascuence	*Basque* (language)

Pronunciation Note

The typical Spanish pronunciation of *v* differs marginally from that of English: in Spanish, it is pronounced with the lips together (as with *b* in both languages), whereas in English (and the other Romance languages), it is articulated with the lower lip against the upper teeth. For a linguist, the difference is between a *bilabial* fricative (Spanish) and a *labiodental* one (English). The standard phonetic symbol for the Spanish *v* pronunciation is β, and this is what is generally shown in dictionaries that provide pronunciations for Spanish words. The use of the Greek symbol β can be a bit confusing in this context, however, since this sound corresponds neither to the pronunciation of Classical Greek β (*beta*), which was [b], nor to that of Modern Greek β, which is [v].

10. *NCT* → *nt*

The change from *NCT* to *nt* is a universal change, occurring in "learned" as well as "popular" words.[29]

DEFU**NCT**US	di**f**un**t**o	*defunct,* dead, deceased (adj. & n.)	
	defunción	death, demise	[*defunctness*]
DISTI**NCT**US	disti**nt**o	distinct, different	[old p.p.]
	disti**nt**ivo	distinctive, badge or distinguishing mark	
	distinción	distinction, honor	
	distinguir	(to) *distinguish,* (to) honor	
EXTI**NCT**US	exti**nt**o	extinct, extinguished	(old p.p.)
	exti**nt**or	fire extinguisher	
	extinguir	(to) *extinguish,* (to) become extinct	
	extinción	extinction (fire, animal)	
INSTI**NCT**US	insti**nt**o	instinct	
	insti**nt**ivo	instinctive	
PU**NCT**A	pu**nt**a	*point* (sharp or tapering end), tip	
	pu**nt**apié	kick	(punta + pie)
	pu**nt**ería	aim, marksmanship	
	apu**nt**ar	(to) *point,* (to) aim, (to) make a note of	
	apu**nt**e	note, rough sketch, notes (pl.)	
PU**NCT**UM	pu**nt**o	*point* (dot, idea, unit of scoring, etc.)	
	pu**nt**uación	punctuation	
	pu**nt**uar	(to) punctuate	
	pu**nt**ual	punctual	
SA**NCT**US	sa**nt**o	*saintly,* holy, *saint* (m./f.)	
	sa**nt**idad	sanctity, holiness, saintliness, sainthood	
	sa**nt**uario	sanctuary	
SUBJU**NCT**IVUS	subju**nt**ivo	subjunctive (adj. & n.)	
SUCCI**NCT**US	suci**nt**o	succinct, brief	
TI**NCT**A	ti**nt**a	ink	
	ti**nt**a china	India ink	

---

[29] There are only a handful of exceptions, the most common being *planc**t**on* ("plankton").

tinte	dyeing, dye, *tint, tinge*	
tinto	red (wine), black coffee	
	(Amer.)	(old p.p.)
tintura	*tincture*	
tintorería	dry cleaner's (also for dyeing)	
teñir	(to) dye, (to) *tint,* (to) *tinge*	(see 13b below)

11. *sc(i) → c*

The treatment of Latin *sc(i)* was far from uniform:

centella	lightning, *scintilla* (spark, flash)	(Lat. SCINTILLA)
—centellear	—(to) *scintillate,* (to) sparkle	
ciencia	*science*	
—científico	—*scientific, scientist* (m./f.)	
ciático	*sciatic*	
—ciática	—*sciatica* (pain in the sciatic nerve)	
necio	foolish, inane, stupid (or such a person)	[*nice, nescient*]
—necedad	—foolishness, inanity, stupidity	[*nicety, nescience*]

For an explanation of the rather startling difference in meaning between Spanish *necio* and English *nice,* see the appendix.

suscitar	(to) provoke, (to) stir up	[† *suscitate*]
—susceptible	—susceptible	
—resucitar	—(to) *resuscitate*	
—resucitación	—*resuscitation*	

Also:

cisma (m.)	*schism,* split

The case of "consciousness" is particularly confusing:

consciente	conscious ("aware"—with *ser;* "awake"—with *estar*)[30]
inconsciente	unconscious ("unwitting"—with *ser;* "senseless"—
	with *estar*)
consciencia	consciousness

---

[30] This convenient division does not always hold in the Americas, where *estar consciente* is not infrequently used in the sense of "to be aware".

inconsciencia	unconsciousness (lack of awareness, medical state), thoughtlessness
subconsciente (adj. & n.)	subconscious
conciencia	conscience, consciousness
—a conciencia	—conscientiously (~ *concienzudamente*)
—objetor de conciencia	—conscientious objector
concienzudo	conscientious, thorough (done conscientiously)
concienciar, concientizar	(to) make aware, i.e., make someone *conscious* of something

Most other words have conserved *sci,* e.g.,

discípulo	disciple, pupil	
—disciplina	—discipline (academic subject, rules, training)	
fascículo	*fascicle* (one of the parts of a book published in installments)	
fascinación	fascination	
—fascinar	—(to) fascinate (incl. obsolete Eng. sense "to bewitch")	
—fascinante	—fascinating	
fascismo	fascism	
—fascista	—fascist (adj. & n.)	
lascivo	lascivious	
—lascivia	—lasciviousness	
oscilación	oscillation, fluctuation	
—oscilar	—(to) oscillate, (to) fluctuate	
piscina	swimming pool	[*piscina*]
plebiscito	plebiscite	

12. *-mbre*

The *-mbre* ending has two principal sources:

(a). A number of Spanish *feminine nouns* that "should" end in *-tud* (Section 2.1) instead have a more "popular" form ending in *-dumbre.*

certidumbre	*certitude*	
costumbre	*custom,* habit, *consuetude*	[*costume*]
—acostumbrar	—(to) *accustom,* (to) be accustomed to	

—consuetudinario	—*customary*, habitual, *consuetudinary*	
—derecho consuetudinario	—common law	
incertidumbre	*incertitude*	
mansedumbre	gentleness, tameness, *mansuetude*	
muchedumbre	*multitude* (of people, objects, animals)	
—multitud	—multitude	
pesadumbre	grief, sorrow	("heavy" feeling)
podredumbre	rottenness, *putrefaction*	[† *putritude*]
servidumbre	*servitude,* subjection, servants (household)	

(b). MIN → *mbr*

In a number of words, the *I* between vowels disappeared at the Vulgar Latin stage, and the resulting consonant combination MN was subsequently replaced by *mbr*, which was easier to pronounce. Thus, for NOMEN ("name"):

NOMINEM (VL ACC.) → nom _ NEM → no**mbr**e

Words with similar origin include:

ALUMINEM	alu**mbr**e (m.)	*alum*	
	aluminio	*aluminum*	(UK *aluminium*)
FAMINEM	ha**mbr**e (f.)	hunger, *famine*	
FEMINA	he**mbr**a	*female* (animal)	[*feminine*]
FERRUMINEM	herru**mbr**e	rust	[*ferrous*]
HOMINEM	ho**mbr**e	man	[*homo, hominid*]
	ho**mbr**ía	moral qualities: fortitude, etc.	
	gentilho**mbr**e	*gentle*man	
	superho**mbr**e	*super*man	
LEGUMINEM	legu**mbr**e	*legume*, vegetable	
	leguminoso	leguminous	
LUMINEM	lu**mbr**e	light, fire	
	lumen	lumen (unit of light)	
	luminoso	luminous	
	alu**mbr**ar	(to) *illuminate,* (to) give birth	
	alu**mbr**amiento	childbirth	

	deslu**mbr**ar	(to) dazzle, (to) blind (with light)	
	deslu**mbr**ante	dazzling	
	relu**mbr**ar	(to) shine brightly	
	vislu**mbr**ar	(to) glimpse, (to) begin to see	
	vislu**mbr**e	glimpse, glimmer	
NOMINEM	no**mbr**e	name,[31] *noun*	
	no**mbr**ar	(to) appoint, (to) name, (to) *nominate*	
	prono**mbr**e	*pronoun*	
	reno**mbr**e	*renown*	
	sobreno**mbr**e	*surname* (e.g., William *the Conqueror*)	
	nomenclatura	nomenclature	
SEMINARE	se**mbr**ar	(to) sow	
	se**mbr**ador	sower (person)	
	se**mbr**adora	sowing machine, female sower	
	seminario	*seminary, seminar*	
	diseminar	(to) *disseminate*	
CULMINEM	cu**mbr**e	summit (peak, conference)	[*culminate*]
	encu**mbr**ar	(to) elevate, (to) exalt	[≠ *encumber !*]
	culminar	(to) culminate	
	culminante	highest, culminating	
	culminación	culmination	

Note the elimination of *L* as well in the final example.

Latin HUMERUS ("shoulder", "upper arm") underwent a similar transformation:

HUMERUS → HUM_RUS → ho**mbr**o   shoulder   [*humerus*]

Spanish *nombre* is a source of potential confusion for English speakers, especially those who know some French. In French, Latin NUMERUS ("number")

---

[31] English *name* is of Germanic origin and comes from the same Indo-European root as Latin NOMEN—NOMINEM.

underwent a transformation analogous to that of HUMERUS in Spanish and became *nombre,* the source of English *number.* Hence:

Spanish	French	English
nombre	nom	name
nombrar	nommer	(to) name
número	*nombre,* numéro	number
numerar	(dé)*nombrer*	(to) number

13. *ñ*

Probably the most striking figure of Spanish orthography for a foreigner learning the language is the presence of an altogether new character: ñ. This represents a *palatized* nasal consonant, essentially a combination of the sounds [n] and [y]. The pronunciation is similar to that in English *canyon* (which comes from Spanish), but with the important difference that in Spanish the [ny] sound is restricted to a single syllable:

English	canyon	[can•yon]
Spanish	cañón	[ca•ñón]

The palatized [n] is common to all the major Romance languages (apart from Romanian), but the similar pronunciations are masked by a variety of different symbols:

Spanish	**Portuguese**	**French**	**Catalan**	**Italian**	*English*
España	Espanha	Espagne	Espanya	Spagna	Spain, spaniel
señor	senhor	seigneur	senyor	signore	senior, sir, sire

The palatized [n] sound arose from at least four different combinations of sounds:

a) *NE, NI* + vowel

ARANEA	araña	spider	[*arachnophobia*]
BALNEUM	baño	bath, bathtub, bathroom	[*balneal, bagnio*]
	bañera	bathtub	
	bañar	(to) bathe	
	balneario	public baths (esp. medicinal), spa (~ *baños*)	

	rebañar[32]	(to) gather up remnants (esp. of meal, using a piece of bread)	
	rebaño	flock, herd	
CAMPANIA	campaña	*campaign*	
CASTANEA	castaña	*chest*nut (fruit)	
	castañeta	snapping of the fingers, *castanet*	
	castañuela	*castanet* (freq. pl.)	
	castaño	*chestnut* (tree, wood, color)	
COMPANIA	compañía	*company* (commercial, social, military unit)	
	compañero	*companion*	
CUNEUS	cuño	die (for stamping *coins*, medals, etc.)	
	cuña	wedge, bedpan	[*quoin*]
	acuñar	(to) *coin*, (to) mint	
EXTRANEUS	extraño	*strange*, foreign (object), *stranger* (m./f.)	
	extrañar	(to) find *strange* or odd, (to) miss	
	me extraña que . . .	it surprises me that . . . ("seems *strange* to me")	
	te extraño mucho	I miss you a lot ("feel *estranged*")	
	extrañeza	*strangeness*, surprise (caused by something *strange*)	
	extranjero	foreign, foreigner (m./f.)	[*stranger*]
	(en) el extranjero	abroad	
HISPANIA	España	*Spain*	
	español (-ola)	*Spanish* (adj. & n.), *Spanish* language (m.)	
	hispánico	*Hispanic, Spanish*	
	hispanohablante	*Spanish*-speaking, *Spanish* speaker (m./f.)	

---

[32] *Rebañar* and *rebaño* are unrelated to *baño*, but for the former, one can easily derive a "folk etymology", i.e., "bathing" a piece of bread to soak up the remnants of a meal.

PINEA	piña	*pine*apple, *pine* cone	
SENIOR	señor	Mister, *sir,* gentleman, lord, the Lord (cap.), *seigneur, seignior, sire, señor, signor, monsieur, Messrs.* (pl.)	
	señora	woman, lady, Mrs., Madam, *señora, signora*	
	señorita	young woman, Miss, *señorita*	
	señorío	dominion, domain, lordship, *seigniory*	
	monseñor	*Monsignor (Msgr.), Monseigneur*	

b) GN, NG

COGNATUS	cuñado	brother-in-law	[*cognate*]
CONSTRINGERE	constreñir	(to) *constrain,* (to) *constrict,* (to) *constringe*	
DESIGNARE	diseñar	(to) *design*	
	diseño	design	
	diseñador	designer	
	designar	(to) *designate*	
	designación	designation (incl. "nomination or appointment")	
	designio	design (idea, intention)	
DIS-DIGNARE	desdeñar	(to) *disdain*	
	desdeñoso	*disdainful*	
	desdeñable	contemptible, insignificant (gen. used with negative, hence "not insignificant", "not to be *disdained*")	
	desdén	*disdain*	
INSIGNIA	enseña	*ensign* (flag, banner)	
	enseñar	(to) teach, (to) show	
	enseñanza	teaching, education	
	insignia	insignia, banner	
	insigne	renowned, famous	

LIGNUM	leño	log	
	leña	firewood	
	leñador	woodcutter, lumberjack	
	leñera	woodshed	
	lignito	*lignite* (brown coal)	
PRAEGNARE	preñar	(to) *impregnate*	
PUGNUS	puño	fist, cuff (shirt), hilt	[*pugnacious*]
SIGNA	seña	*sign* (gesture), description (pl.), address (pl.)	
	lenguaje de señas	*sign language* (~ *lenguaje de signos*)	
	señal (f.)	*signal, sign,* (distinctive) mark	
	señalar	(to) *signal,* (to) mark	
	señalización	signalization, (system of) traffic signals	
	señuelo	decoy, lure, enticement	
	signatario	signatory (~ *firmante*)	
	signo	sign, mark	
	signo de admiración [33]	exclamation point (¡ . . . !)	
	signo de interrogación	question mark (¿ . . . ?)	
	contraseña	password, *countersign*	
	reseña	brief description, review (published)	
	reseñar	(to) give a brief description, (to) review	
	resignación	resignation (acceptance of one's fate, less frequently from a job)	
	resignar	(to) resign, (to) resign oneself	
STRINGERE	estreñir	(to) constipate	[*stringent*]
TAM MAGNUS	tamaño	very big, such a large, size (m.)	[*magnitude*]

---

[33] In English, the *exclamation point* was for a long time known as a *note of admiration*. This definition was still in use in the early twentieth century, as attested by the following entry from *Webster's Revised Unabridged Dictionary* (1913): "Note of admiration, the mark (!), called also exclamation point."

| TANGERE | tañer | (to) play a musical instrument | [*tangible*] |
| TINGERE | teñir | (to) dye or *tint* | |

c) MN

AUTUMNUS	otoño	*autumn*	
DAMNARE	dañar	(to) *dam*age, (to) harm, (to) spoil (fruit, harvest)	
	dañino	harmful, damaging (~ *dañoso*)	
	daño	*damage*	
SOMNIARE	soñar	(to) dream	
SOMNIUM	sueño (1)	dream	
SOMNUS	sueño (2)	sleep, sleepiness	[*somnolent*]

In several cases, the MN combination arose through the disappearance of an intervening I:

DOM(I)NUS	dueño	owner, master, landlord	[*Dom, Don*]
	don	title of respect (with first name: *don Juan*)	
	don nadie	Mr. Nobody	
DOM(I)NA	dueña	owner, mistress, landlady	[prima *donna*]
	doña	title of respect (with first name: *doña Beatriz*)	

d) NN

| ANNUS | año | year |

(Additional examples of NN → ñ are given in Section 3.4.)

14. Orthographic Changes due to Nature of Following Vowel

In Spanish, the letters *c* and *g,* as well as the combination *gu,* each represent two completely different sounds depending on the nature of the following vowel. This is illustrated below, where the English correspondences of the two sounds are given as well as examples of Spanish words with the contrasting pronunciations.

Spanish	(1) back—*a/o/u*	(2) front—*e/i*	(1)	(2)
c	[k], as in *cat*	[θ], as in **thin** or [s], as in **sin**	cana	cena
g	[g], as in **go**	[h*], as in **hotel**	gol	gel
gu	[gw], as in *linguistic*	[g], as in **go**	**gu**arda	**gu**erra

The large majority of the Spanish-speaking world pronounces "soft" *c* as [s] rather than [θ]. Note that there are a total of five consonant sounds involved: [k], [θ] or [s], [g], [gw], [h*].

To maintain a consistent pronunciation of these five sounds in related words where the following vowels may differ in nature (front or back), a series of *regular orthographic modifications* takes place. This is illustrated in the table below:

REGULAR ORTHOGRAPHIC MODIFICATIONS

Sound	(1) *a/o/u* or consonant, or at end of word	(2) *e/i*	(1)	(2)
[k]	*c*	*qu*	monarca	monar**qu**ía
[θ] / [s]	*z*	*c*	pez	pe**c**es (pl.)
[g]	*g*	*gu*	despe**g**ar	despe**gu**e
[gw]	*gu*	*gü*	len**gu**a	bilin**gü**e
[h*]	*j*	*j* or *g*	eri**j**o ("I erect") tejo ("I weave")	eri**g**ir (inf.) te**j**er (inf.)

The written form for the first four of these sounds is *always* determined *uniquely* by the nature of the following letter. For [h*] there is a well-defined rule for back vowels, but before front vowels there is ambiguity.

Note that as a result of this rule, the letter combinations *ze* and *zi* theoretically should never occur. Hence the following contrasts between English and Spanish:

bronce	bronze	
celo	zeal, ardor, heat (animals)	
—celoso	—zealous, jealous	(Lat. ZELOSUS)

cero   zero
chimpancé   chimpanzee

Nevertheless, in a number of common "international" words like *zebra* and *zinc*, the *ze/zi* forms coexist with the *ce/ci* ones. The RAE generally prefers the forms with *ce/ci*:

acimut, azimut	azimuth	
bencina / benzina	benzine	
cebra / zebra	zebra	
cenit / zenit	zenith	(*also* cénit / zénit)
cinc / zinc	zinc	
eccema / eczema (m.)	eczema	
zeta / (ceta[34])	zeta, the letter "z", *zed* (UK)	
kamikaze / camicace	kamikaze	

Notwithstanding the RAE's preference, apart from *bencina* and *cebra,* the *ze/zi* forms seem to be more common.

Some words have resisted all efforts at normalization and offer only the *ze/zi* possibility:

enzima[35]	enzyme	
jacuzzi[36]	jacuzzi	
nazi	Nazi	
neozelandés[37] (-esa)	New Zealander	
pizzería	pizzeria	
—pizza	—pizza	
zen	zen	
zepelín	Zeppelin (dirigible)	
Zeus	Zeus	
zigzag	zigzag	(both from French)
—zigzaguear	—(to) zigzag	

Spanish has imported a number of *-age* words from French. While these *could* have been spelled with *-age,* the ending chosen was *-aje* (with no effect on the

---

[34] *Ceta* was eliminated in 2001 from the RAE's *Diccionario,* though it is still found frequently in other dictionaries.

[35] If a *c* were used rather than *z,* it would become indistinguishable from the extremely common adverb *encima* ("over", "above").

[36] The RAE has recently proposed *yacusi* as a substitute for the decidedly un-Spanish-looking *jacuzzi.*

[37] Formerly *neocelandés.*

pronunciation). Hence the correspondence between English *-age* words (all from French) and Spanish *-aje* ones. Examples include:

fuselaje	*fuselage*
homenaje	*homage*
maquillaje	makeup, *maquillage*
mensaje	*message*
—mensajero	*—messenger*
pasaje	*passage,* ticket (boat, airplane), *passengers* (as group)
—pasajero	*—passing* (temporary), *passenger* (m./f.)
pillaje	*pillage,* looting
potaje	*pottage* (vegetable stew), hodgepodge
sabotaje	*sabotage*

Appendix

Semantic Evolution: How "nice" is *nice?*

Spanish *necio* and English *nice* both come from Latin NESCIUS ("unknowing", "ignorant"). *Nice* is the archetype of a word undergoing major semantic evolution, as shown by a *partial* listing of its various English meanings over the past seven hundred years:

(1) foolish, stupid (i.e., *necio*)
(2) wanton, lascivious
(3) extravagant
(4) elegant
(5) rare
(6) lazy
(7) effeminate
(8) delicate
(9) luxurious
(10) shy
(11) dainty
(12) fastidious
(13) cultured
(14) intricate
(15) subtle
(16) slender
(17) trivial
(18) pleasant and agreeable (i.e., "nice").

Nicety has undergone a similar evolution in sense—from "foolish or irresponsible conduct" to "delicacy of character or feeling".

English *nescience* ("ignorance") from Latin NESCIENTIA—literally "not science"—and *nescient* ("ignorant") preserve the original Latin meanings.

PART IV

SELECTED TOPICS

SECTION 4.1
Goths and Other Germans

In the late fourth and early fifth centuries, the Western Roman Empire was devastated by numerous attacks by "barbarians", for the most part Germanic tribes that had previously been allied to Rome and had served a key role in guarding the frontier. Rome was sacked by the Visigoths in 410, and in 476 the Western Roman Empire came to an end when the Germanic warrior Odoacer deposed Romulus Augustulus, the last of the (western) emperors.

The Iberian Peninsula (Spain and Portugal) was controlled by a succession of Germanic tribes for three centuries, from the waning years of the Western Roman Empire to the arrival of the Arabs in 711. The first of the Germanic tribes to reach Spain were the *Vandals* in 409.

vándalo	Vandal, vandal
vandalismo	vandalism
—acto vandálico	—act of vandalism

The Vandals' twenty-year passage through Spain on their way to Africa left little mark, except (probably) the name of *Andalucía,* whose origin is generally seen as "Portus *[V]andalus*". The Vandals were followed by the Visigoths, who remained in control of most of Spain until 711, establishing their capital at Toledo and their most important settlements in the central *meseta* ("tableland").

godo	Gothic (people), Goth	
—gótico	—Gothic (artistic style, people, language, print)	
visigodo	Visigothic, Visigoth	[*west Goth*]
ostrogodo	Ostrogothic, Ostrogoth	[*east Goth*]

For the first century and a half of their presence in Spain, the Visigoths did not mix very much with the locals—who are estimated to have outnumbered them by about thirty to one—largely because of religious differences; though both they and the local Hispano-Roman inhabitants were Christians, the Visigoths adhered to the Arian "heresy" that denied the divinity of Christ. In retrospect, this separation had its positive aspects, particularly for the relatively large Jewish community: following the "abjuration" of the Arian faith by the Visigothic king Recared in 589, a theocracy was established that exhibited a degree of religious intolerance and persecution exceeding that of the later, and more famous, Spanish Inquisition. A series of anti-Jewish laws in the late seventh century, for example, forbade circumcision under penalty of castration (for circumcisee and circumciser alike). In 694 a law was approved under which all Spanish Jews were to be reduced to slaves and distributed among the rich and pious, with Jewish children up to the age of seven separated from their parents so they would receive a proper Christian education.[1]

The Visigoths ("Western Goths") had spent several centuries passing through various parts of Western Europe before crossing the Pyrenees into Spain in 415. They had already been largely "Latinized", so instead of imposing their Germanic language on their Spanish subjects they saw it disappear. The linguistic heritage of the Visigoths was thus very limited, although they did introduce a number of proper names to Spain (and subsequently to Spanish), including:

> Alfonso, Álvaro, Elvira, Fernando, Gonzalo, Ildefonso, Ramiro, Rodrigo

In the development of the Spanish language, the Visigothic period is the least well known, reflecting the relative scarcity of written documents from the period. While there are a significant number of words of Germanic origin in Spanish, it is generally difficult to distinguish between those that are the result of the Visigothic presence in Spain and those that

> (a) had been previously "Latinized" from Germanic languages (including Visigothic) in other parts of the Empire, or
> (b) came to Spain at a later stage through France, during the reign of (the Germanic) Charlemagne and his successors.

Spanish words believed to be of Visigothic origin include:

bregar	(to) toil, (to) struggle	[*break*]
brotar	(to) sprout, (to) gush,	
	(to) break out	
—brote	—bud, shoot, outbreak	
	(fire, disease, etc.)	
espía	*spy* (m./f.)	
—espiar	—(to) *spy*	

---

[1] Bonnassie et al., 43–45. For a woman circumciser, the penalty was loss of her nose.

—espionaje	—*espionage*	
esquilar	(to) *shear* (wool or hair)	($r \rightarrow l$, Section 3.5)
gaita	bagpipes	[*goat*]
ganso	*goose*	
tregua	*truce*	
—sin tregua	—without a break, nonstop	

Before introducing "general" Germanic words, two features can be observed:

1) Germanic *h* has in most cases been dropped from the spelling. This contrasts to the large majority of *h*- words from Latin (*habitante, heroísmo, honesto,* etc.) in which the *h,* which had initially been dropped, has been restored to the spelling (but not to the pronunciation). Thus:

albergar	(to) *h*arbor or lodge	(r-$r \rightarrow l$-r)
alto (2)[2]	*h*alt, stop (both interjection and noun)	
arenga	*h*arangue (gen. w/out neg. connotation), speech	
arenque	*h*erring	
arnés	*h*arness (incl. archaic "armor"), equipment (climbing, etc.)	
arpa	*h*arp	
arpón	*h*arpoon	
Enrique	*H*enry	
izar	(to) *h*oist, (to) raise (e.g., flag)	[*heist*]
obús (via Fr.)	*h*owitzer, artillery shell	
yelmo[3]	*h*elmet	

2) Germanic words beginning with *w-* generally appear in Spanish with initial *gu-*. These frequently correspond to English words beginning with *w-, gu-,* or *ga-*.

| guarda | *guard* (m./f.), safekeeping or custody (f.) |
| —guardar | —(to) *guard,* (to) keep or store, (to) watch over |

---

[2] To be distinguished from *alto* (1) meaning "tall", "high", which comes from Latin ALTUS.

[3] The *ye* in *yelmo* represents a normal "diphthong" of the vowel *e* in *helmet* (see Section 3.3), with the diphthong *ie* written *ye* at the beginning of a word.

—aguardar	—(to) wait, (to) await
—guardaespaldas (m./f.)	—body*guard* (literally "back-guard")
—guardacostas	—coastguard vessel
—guardarropa	—cloakroom, *wardrobe*
—guardería	—nursery (school), daycare center
—guardia	—*guard* (group—f.; person —m./f.), safekeeping (f.)
—la Guardia Civil	—*Civil Guard* (rural police)
—guardián (-ana)	—*guardian*, watchman (or -woman)
—resguardar	—(to) protect, (to) protect against (cold, rain, etc.)
—retaguardia[4]	—*rear guard, rear* (n.), *rearward* (n.)
—vanguardia	—*vanguard, avant-garde*
guarnecer	(to) *garnish*, (to) equip, (to) *garrison*
—guarecer	—(to) shelter, (to) protect
—garaje (< Fr.)	—*garage*
—garita (< Fr.)	—sentry box, gatekeeper's box [*garret*]
guerra	*war*
—guerrero	—martial, *war*-like, *warrior*
—guerrilla	—guerrilla warfare, guerrilla force or band
—guerrillero	—guerrilla fighter
guiño	*wink*
—guiñar	—(to) *wink*
—guiñol	—puppet show [Grand *Guignol*]
guisa	manner, mode [*guise, wise*]
guía	*guide* (m./f.), guidance (f.), guide(book) (f.)
—guiar	—(to) *guide*
—guion, guión (m.)	—outline, film script, hyphen

---

[4] Spanish *retaguardia* was initially **retroguardia** and corresponds to English (via French) *rear guard* and *rearward*. English *rear* is a shortened form of *rearward* ("the *rear guard* of an armed force", "at the *rear*").

Historical Note

When French and Spanish sought to adopt Germanic words beginning with the sound [w], they faced a common problem: although this sound had existed in Classical Latin (written *v*[5]), it had disappeared from their respective languages many centuries before. But both languages still maintained the [gw] sound of Classical Latin, represented by the letter combination *gu*. So in the absence of a "true" [w], they used the next best thing, hence the *gu-* in words such as *guerra, guardar,* etc. "Central" French subsequently lost the [w] element in the pronunciation of [gw], while in Spanish the [w] element was preserved only when the following vowel was *a* or *o*.[6]

Norman French, on the other hand, *did* have the [w] sound, and it was the Normans who conquered England in 1066 and maintained their version of "Anglo-Norman" French for some time thereafter. A number of Germanic *w* words arrived in English via Norman French with the [w] sound and spelling intact, only to be joined at a later date by the same word displaying the trademark central French *gu,* which by that time was pronounced simply [g]. Thus in English one has the doublets:

guard	ward (<Old Eng.)
guardian	warden
guarantee	warranty
guardroom	wardroom
rear guard	rearward
guile	wile
guise	-wise (as in "like*wise*"; <Old Eng.)

In *gua-* words, French subsequently dropped the *u-* from the spelling as well (thus English *guard* corresponds to French *garde*), and some English words reflect this change:

gage and en**g**age (vs. *wage*), garage (cf. rabbit *warren*), garderobe (vs. *wardrobe*), garment, garnish, garret, garrison, re**g**ard (vs. *guard* and *reward*), etc.

---

[5] Thus Caesar's famous victory announcement VENI VIDI VICI ("I came, I saw, I conquered") was pronounced [weni widi wiki].

[6] Hence *guardar* is pronounced with initial [gw], *guisa* with initial [g]. In the rare situation in which *gue* or *gui* is pronounced in Spanish with [gw], this is indicated by adding a dieresis (two dots) to the *u*, e.g., *lingüista* (see Section 3.5, no. 14).

Other common words of Germanic origin, Visigothic or otherwise, include:

alemán	German (adj. & n.), German language	[*allemande*]
—*Alemania*	—Germany	[*Alemanni*]
germánico	Germanic (less frequently: German)	
—germano	—Germanic, German	

In Classical times, the Romans referred to the barbarians to the north as GER-
MANI and to their country or region as GERMANIA, and these are the names
that subsequently entered English. The ALAMANNI (or ALEMANNI) were a
loosely knit confederation of Germanic peoples, first mentioned by the Romans in AD 213, who in the fifth century expanded into Alsace and northern
Switzerland before being conquered by the Frankish king Clovis and absorbed
into his dominions. They bequeathed their name—which probably comes from
all + *man*—to French, Spanish, and Portuguese,[7] while the Italians refer to the
Germans as *Tedesco* (from THEODISCUS, the Medieval Latin form of *Deutsch*,
which also gave rise to English *Dutch*).

banca	*banking*, banking system, bank (gambling), *bench*	
—bancario	—*banking* (adj.)	
—bancarrota[8]	—*bankruptcy*	[*ruptured bench*]
—banco	—*bench*,[9] *bank*, school (of fish)	
—banco de arena	—sand*bank*, sandbar, shoal	
—banco de datos	—data *bank*	
—banquero	—*banker*	
—banqueta	—stool (~ *taburete*), footstool	[*banquette*]
—banquete	—*banquet*, feast	(< Fr.)
banda (1)	*band* (musicians, people, animals), side or border	
—bandada	—flock (of birds; also fish, people)	
—bandazo	—lurch (ship, car, point of view)	
—bandera	—flag, *banner*	

---

[7] In English, "Alemannic" refers to the dialects of German spoken in Switzerland, Alsace, and
southwestern Germany.

[8] From Italian, where it is said that the benches of insolvent bankers/merchants were broken
to show that they were no longer in business. The idea, if not the origin, is parallel to the English
expression "to be broke".

[9] In the sense of an object for sitting, a *banco* may (or may not) have a back support, whereas
(according to the *DRAE*) a *banca* does not, at least in Spain.

—banderola	—*banderole,* pennant, signal flag	
—bandeja[10]	—tray (≠ *bandage* !)	
—desbandada	—scattering, *disbanding, disbandment*	
—a la desbandada	—in disorder, pell-mell (~ *en desbandada*)	
banda (2)	scarf, sash, strip, ribbon (award), *band* (range)	
—banda sonora	—sound track (cinema)	
bando (1)	edict, proclamation	[*ban, banns*]
—contrabando	—smuggling, *contraband*	
—contrabandista	—smuggler	
—bandido	—*bandit*	
bando (2)	faction or side (of a dispute)	
—bandolero	—*bandit*	
—bandolera	—*bandolier / bandoleer* (cartridge belt worn across chest)	

Banda (1) was initially a group of armed men (rallying around the *bandera*) before acquiring the more general meaning of a group of people. A Spanish *desbandada* generally involves more disorder than its English etymological equivalent.

blanco	white, target	[*blank*]
brecha	*breach,* gap, head wound	
brindis (pl. brindis)	a toast (that one offers)	

This corresponds directly to German *ich bring dir's,* "I *bring* it to you". It can also be used more generally.

—brindar	—(to) toast, (to) offer, (to) present

Brindó su amistad al recién llegado.
"He *offered* his friendship to the new arrival."

esquivar	(to) dodge or avoid, (to) *shy* away from, (to) *eschew*

---

[10] This comes from Portuguese, where a *bandeja* was an instrument for winnowing grain—i.e., separating it into two *bands* (the wheat and the chaff). In appearance a *bandeja* was similar to a serving tray, and the definition was subsequently expanded to include this as well. This secondary definition was then exported to Spanish.

—esquivo	—aloof, unsociable	[*shy*]
falda	skirt (clothing), lower part of a mountain	[*faldstool*]
—minifalda	—miniskirt	

Falda comes from the same Germanic root that produced English *fold* (*fald* in Middle English).

feudal	*feudal*
—feudo	—*fief, fee* or *feud* (in feudal law)
franco (adj.)	*frank,* free (of obstacle, charge), *Frankish, Franco-*
—francamente	—*frankly*
—franco (n.)	—*franc* (currency), the *Franks* (pl.)
—Francia	—France
—francés (-esa)	—French, Frenchman/Frenchwoman
—francotirador	—sniper
—franquear	—(to) free (remove obstacle), (to) get over or across, (to) pay postage on—i.e., (to) *frank* a letter
—franqueo	—postage
—franquicia	—*franchise* (incl. exemption or immunity)
—franqueza	—*frankness*
fresco (adj. & n.)	*fresh* (incl. "impudent"), cool, coolness, *fresco*
—fresca	—cool air (morning, evening), *fresh* remark
—frescor	—*freshness,* coolness
—frescura	—*freshness* (incl. "impudence"), coolness
—refrescar	—(to) *refresh,* (to) cool
—refresco	—*refreshment,* soft drink [*alfresco*]

While *fresco* is associated with Italian (painting on fresh plaster), by origin it is Germanic.

gabardina	*gabardine,* raincoat	
gajes del oficio (pl.)	occupational hazards (or pains)	[*wages* of *office*]
ganar	(to) win, (to) earn	[*gain*]
—gana	—desire, inclination	

Esta mañana no tengo ninguna *gana* de levantarme de la cama.

This morning I have no *desire* to get out of bed.

He dejado un poco de la comida en el plato porque no tengo más *ganas*.

I have left some food on my plate because I have no further *inclination* to eat (I'm full).

—ganancia	—*gain*, profit
—ganador (adj. & n.)	—winning, winner (m./f.)
—ganado (p.p.)	—livestock
—ganado vacuno/bovino	—cattle
—ganado ovino	—sheep
—ganado porcino	—pigs, swine
—ganadería	—animal husbandry, livestock (of region, country)

For *ganar,* the original Germanic meant "to obtain food", "to graze cattle". This subsequently acquired the broader meaning of obtaining a material profit by work, by good fortune, or by gambling. The agricultural sense is no longer associated with English *gain*[11] but is preserved in Spanish *ganado* and *ganadería*.

gris	*gray*	[*grizzly, grisaille*]
guante	glove	
—guantelete	—*gauntlet* (protective glove worn with medieval armor)	
—aguantar	—(to) support, (to) tolerate, (to) bear	
—aguante	—endurance, stamina	

The English expression *to throw down the gauntlet* (or *gantlet*) thus literally means to throw one's glove in front of one's adversary in order to initiate a challenge.[12]

In a few cases an original *gua* has subsequently become *ga:*

galardón	*guerdon* (reward, recompense)
—galardonar	—(to) *guerdon* (reward, recompense)
garantía	*guarantee, warranty, guaranty*

---

[11] The obsolete English word *gainage* meant "profit or produce derived from the tillage of land".

[12] The expression "to run the *gauntlet* (or *gantlet*)" has nothing to do with gloves, however. It comes from a traditional Swedish military punishment known as the *gatlopp* (from Swedish *gata,* "street" + *lopp,* "race"), and its initial English form—already showing the "corrupting" influence of *gauntlet*—was *gantelope*.

—garantizar	—(to) guarantee, (to) warrant
gastar	(to) spend, (to) use up, (to) *waste*
—gasto	—expenditure, expense
—desgastar	—(to) wear away, (to) wear down (or out)
—desgaste	—wear, wear and tear
—malgastar	—(to) *waste* (money, time, effort)

Spanish *gastar* and English *waste* both represent a mixture of related Latin and Germanic words: the basic source was Latin VASTARE ("to *devastate*"), but the initial *v-* was altered due to the influence of the corresponding Germanic word. The original Latin *v* remains in several "learned" Spanish (and English) words.

vasto[13]	vast
—devastar	—(to) devastate
—devastación	—devastation
—devastador	—devastating

hacha	ax, *hatchet*
jabón	*soap*
—jabonera	—soap dish

The Germanic word for *soap*—initially a substance used to dye the hair red before a battle—was taken into Medieval Latin as SAPO(N), and this should have become *sabón* in Spanish (*cf.* French *savon*, Italian *sapone*, Portuguese *sabão*, Old English *sape*). However, the initial *s* came to be pronounced [sh], a phenomenon that occurred for several other words as well (see Section 3.5, no. 4), hence Old Spanish *xabón*. When Spanish [sh] changed to its "modern" pronunciation [h*], the spelling became *jabón*.

marcar	(to) *mark*, (to) dial (telephone), (to) score
—marca	—*mark*, brand, record (sports)
—marcha (< Fr.)	—*march*, departure
—poner en marcha	—(to) start (put in operation)
—marchar	—(to) *march*, (to) walk, (to) function
—demarcación	—*demarcation*
—comarca	—region, district
—marcador	—scoreboard, *marker* (medical, scientific)
—marqués	—*marquis, marchese*

---

[13] The initial idea of "vast" was an empty or *devastated* place.

—marquesa	—*marchioness, marchesa*	
—marco	—frame (door, picture), framework, *mark* (currency)	

The Germanic roots of *marcar* have left a significant mark on English and the Romance languages. In its remote origin, *marka* signified a "sign *marking* a boundary or frontier", hence a neighboring territory. A related form of the word came to signify the act of placement of border markers, whence French *marcher* and English *to march*. *Marches* are a border region: thus the *Welsh Marches* is a historical name for the parts of England along the border of Wales, while the *Spanish March* (*Marca Hispánica*) was the name given to Catalonia when it was under the control of the Franks following its recapture from the Muslims. A *marquis* was originally the ruler of border or frontier districts, and his Germanic equivalent was a *margrave*. A *mark* was a coin bearing an official mark attesting to its value.

mariscal	*marshal*	(lit. "*mare* servant")
quilla	*keel* (ship, bird)	
rango	*rank*	
rico	*rich*, delicious	[Third *Reich*]
—riqueza	—*riches*,[14] wealth	
—enriquecer	—(to) *enrich*, (to) become rich	
robar	(to) *rob*	
—robo	—*robbery*	
ropa	clothes, clothing	[*robe*]
—ropa interior	—underwear	
—ropa sucia	—(dirty) laundry	

English *robe* and Spanish *ropa* come from the respective verbs *rob* and *robar* and originally had the sense of "spoil" or "booty"—thus one acquired one's *robes* through *robbery*.

saga	saga	
sala	living room, large room for public activities	[rare *salle*]
—salón	—living room, *salon,* restaurant/hotel dining room	[*saloon*]
sopa	*soup*	

---

[14] Note that *riqueza* is singular, whereas its English cognate *riches* is plural. This is due to the fact that when French *richesse* arrived in English, it was mistakenly perceived as a plural because of its final [s] sound.

Appendix

1. North, South, East, West

norte	north
este	east
sur	south
oeste	west
—noreste, nordeste	—northeast
—noroeste	—northwest
—sudeste, sureste	—southeast
—sudoeste, suroeste	—southwest

Note that while "south" is *sur,* in combinations *in which the following word begins with a vowel,* it is more commonly *sud-:*

sudafricano / surafricano	South African	
—Sudáfrica / Suráfrica	—South Africa	
—África del Sur	—southern Africa	
sudamericano, suramericano	South American	
—Sudamérica, América del Sur	—South America	(also *Suramérica*)

but

surcoreano	South Korean

Similarly, before a word beginning with a vowel, *nor-* sometimes becomes *nort(e)-*

norteamericano (only)	North American (frequently used for "U.S.")
norteafricano, norafricano (rare)	North African
norirlandés (only)	Northern Irish

All of the major Romance languages at an early stage took their directional words from Germanic (probably English), largely supplanting the previous Latin forms. In Spanish, the Latin directional words remain but are rarely used in a purely directional sense: *septentrión, oriente, austro, occidente. Oriente* and *occidente* have acquired a more general meaning ("the East", "the West"), while all four of the words have given rise to adjectival forms that are frequently used:

septentrional	northern, septentrional
oriental	eastern, oriental, Oriental
—orientación	—orientation
—oriente, Oriente	—east, Orient
—Medio Oriente	—Middle East
—orientar	—(to) orient (locate, align, make familiar)

—oriundo	—coming (from), native (of)
austral	southern, austral
occidental	western, occidental, Westerner
—occidente	—west, Occident, Western countries

2. Sharing Bread with Friends

An expression used by Germanic soldiers serving in the legions guarding the frontiers of the Roman Empire to refer to their companions was *ga-hlaiba,* which literally meant "with bread",[15] i.e., those with whom one shared one's bread (Spanish *pan*). This was translated directly into Latin as[16]

| CUM | + PANI(S) | COMPANIO(N) |
| with | bread | |

which over time came to replace CONTUBERNALIS—with whom one shared one's hut (TABERNA) or tent (TABERNACULUM)—which had come to imply a more intimate type of relationship. It has produced a number of common words in Spanish and English:

compañero	companion
—compañerismo	—companionship, comradeship
—compañía	—company (commercial, social, military unit)
—acompañar	—(to) accompany (to be or go with; musically)
—acompañante	—accompanist, escort
—acompañamiento	—accompaniment, retinue

3. On *Bigots* and *Bigotes*

bigote	mustache (sometimes *los bigotes*)
—bigotudo	—mustached, mustachioed
[intolerante]	intolerant, bigoted, bigot (m/f)
[intolerancia]	intolerance, bigotry

The similarity between Spanish *bigote* and French/English *bigot* has been the subject of much historical investigation and speculation. While in neither case is the etymology

---

[15] *Hlaiba* being cognate with Old English *hlaf* (Modern English *loaf*) and *ga* with Latin CUM ("with").

[16] The process by which a word or expression is formed by translation of a corresponding word or expression from another language is known as "loan translation", or *calque* (Spanish *calco*). Another example is Spanish *rascacielos* = *rascar* ("scrape") + *cielos* ("skies"), formed from English "skyscraper".

beyond dispute, it is at least moderately likely that *bigote* and *bigot* share a common origin:

1. The term *bigot* was a derogatory nickname applied by the French to the Normans, and by extension to the English, from very early times until the seventeenth century. Its early usage is attested by the twelfth-century Anglo-Norman chronicler Wace.

2. *Bigot* was, and still is, a Norman surname. Guillaume (William) Bigot and Robert Bigot accompanied William the Conqueror[17] to England in 1066, and two of the twenty-five barons designated as "guarantors" for the English Magna Carta in 1215 were Roger Bigot and Hugh Bigod.

3. From about 1425, *bigot* came to be used in French to refer to a "hypocritical or superstitious adherent of religion", and this is the definition with which it entered English (first attested in 1598). Only later did English *bigotry* acquire its present definition of "intolerance" in a more general sense, a definition absent from Modern French *bigoterie*.

4. The first recorded use of *bigote* for a Spanish mustache was in the late fifteenth century. Some very reputable authorities believe that the custom may well have been introduced by Swiss soldiers fighting alongside the Spanish at the siege of Granada, and that the word *bigote* is simply the name given by the locals to the (mustachioed) foreign soldiers.

Why was the term *bigot* (or *bigote*) applied at various times, both as a group name and individually, to the Norman French, Anglo-Normans, English, and, apparently, German-speaking Swiss? Presumably because of their custom of frequently uttering the curse *bi Got* ("by God"). Although this explanation might seem somewhat fanciful, there is a historical parallel in the word *godon* (or *goddon*), used by the French (including Joan of Arc) in the fourteenth and fifteenth centuries to refer to the English and derived from the latter's frequent use of *goddamn*.

The "by God" origin for the word *bigot* would, on the surface, seem to provide a reasonable explanation for its (initial) application to people of excessive (or false) religious faith. However, why the French would have chosen this form rather than the corresponding French expression (*bon dieu*) is unclear.[18]

---

[17] Though today *surname* and *family* name are used interchangeably, throughout most of the Middle Ages a surname was a name given to a person during the course of his life that might or might not be passed on to his children—Charles the Bald, Wilfrid the Hairy, and Charles the Simple are the names by which three important historical figures were known to their contemporaries. A surname could even be changed during one's lifetime. Thus, prior to conquering England, William had been known as William the Bastard, a surname that in those days had no pejorative sense (being applied only to those of "high birth" entitled to a portion of their natural father's estate).

[18] In a case of *déjà vu*, in the nineteenth century the French coined the word *bondieuserie* to refer to piety that is excessive or in bad taste.

SECTION 4.2
Arabs and Muslims

A contingent of Arabs crossed the Strait of Gibraltar[1] in 711 after having been invited by one faction of Visigoths to overthrow Roderick (Rodrigo), the newly installed king. By 718, virtually the whole of the Iberian Peninsula was under their control. This expansion did not stop at the Pyrenees, as the Arabs advanced as far as Poitiers in central France before being defeated in 732 by Charles Martel ("Charles the Hammer"), the de facto ruler of the Frankish kingdom.

The *Reconquista* ("Reconquest") of Spain by the Christian states in the north, principally Castile, Aragon, and Catalonia, is the central unifying element in Spanish history, for better or for worse. By tradition, the Reconquista began with the battle of Covadonga in Asturias in about the year 720 in which, according to later chronicles, 124,000 Muslims were miraculously killed when their weapons reversed course in mid flight and attacked their masters; the survivors (63,000) were then buried by a landslide while retreating across the mountains. In reality, the Reconquista did not get up much steam until the eleventh century, when:

(a) The unity of Muslim Spain collapsed as the central authority of the caliphate of Córdoba was replaced by a patchwork of more than twenty independent kingdoms (known as *taifas*). This anarchy was finally overcome at the end of the eleventh century by a second Muslim invasion from North Africa, this time by a confederation of Berber tribes known as the Almoravids.

(b) The crusading spirit took hold in Europe (the first Crusade was launched at the end of the century).

From this point on, until the final surrender of Granada in 1492, there was a steady southward advance of the Christian kingdoms. The old Visigothic capital of Toledo was recaptured in 1085, Saragossa (Zaragoza) in 1118, and Córdoba in 1236.

The Muslim influence on Spain was enormous, which is not surprising if one considers that many areas of Spain remained under Muslim rule for longer

---

[1] Gibraltar derives its name from Jabal Tariq (Mount Tarik), Tariq ibn Ziyad being the general who led the invasion.

than they had been under Roman rule, and that only in 2273 will the city and region of Granada have been "Spanish" for as long as they were Muslim. Most of Spain was under Muslim control for periods of between three and eight centuries, and throughout much of this period "Spain" meant *Muslim* Spain.

Until the Renaissance, the level of Muslim culture and science was far in advance of that of Christian Europe, and Muslim Spain was no exception.[2] Perhaps even more exceptional was the degree of relative religious tolerance among ruling Muslims and native Christians and Jews that seems to have prevailed until the arrival of the extremist Almohads who displaced the (already rather extreme) Almoravids in the mid-twelfth century. The high point of Spanish Muslim culture is exemplified by the philosopher, doctor, and jurist Averroës (Ibn Rushd, 1126–1198). When his commentaries on Aristotle were translated into Latin in the first part of the thirteenth century, they were held in such uniformly high esteem that he was referred to simply as "the Commentator".

Not surprisingly, the influence of Arabic was far greater on Spanish than on other Romance languages, with numerous words—and many place-names— taken directly from Arabic. Some of these in turn were "Arabized" forms of words previously adopted from other languages, chiefly Persian, Greek, and Latin.

About half of the words of Arabic origin in Spanish begin with *a-*, and most of these with *al-*. This reflects the fact that Spanish frequently incorporated the Arabic definite article *al* as part of the word itself.[3] Thus when one says *la alcoba* or *el atún,* one is really saying "the the alcove" or "the the tuna". There is no fully satisfactory explanation as to why this occurred so often in Spanish and Portuguese but only infrequently in borrowings from Arabic by other Romance languages. Thus one has the following contrasts:

Spanish	French	Italian	English
alcanfor	camphre	canfora	*camphor*
algodón	coton	cotone	*cotton*
alminar	minaret	minareto	*minaret*
alquitrán	goudron	catrame	tar (road surface)
azafrán	safran	zafferano	*saffron*
azúcar (m./f.)	sucre	zucchero	*sugar*
arroz	riz	riso	*rice*
atún	thon	tonno	*tuna*

[2] See, for example, Turner, *Science in Medieval Islam.*
[3] Before words beginning with what in Arabic are known as "solar" (English *dental* and *liquid*) consonants (*d, t, n, s, z, sh, l, r*), the *l* of the article disappeared; in a handful of cases (e.g., *aldea*) Spanish has restored it.

The last two words went from Greek (via Latin) to French and Italian, while in Spanish they transited through Arabic.[4]

A number of common words of Arabic origin are presented below, with the presentation divided into three parts: (a) general words; (b) words specifically related to mathematics and science; and (c) the appendix, which covers several special topics (*scarlet, orange, chess*).

General Words of Arabic Origin

aceite	oil, olive oil
—aceituna	—olive

In Latin, OLIVA was used for both "olive tree" and "olive", while the related word OLEUM[5] was "olive oil" (and oil in general). The normal phonetic evolution of OLEUM (source of English *oil*) would have been *ojo*, which was presumably ruled out, since *ojo* already meant "eye" (from OCULUS); hence the adoption of Arabic *aceite* and *aceituna*. The "learned" form *olivo* was retained for "olive tree"; *óleo* also exists, referring to oil-based paints and oils used in religious ceremonies.

acequia	irrigation ditch or canal, *acequia*[6]
ademán	gesture, attitude (posture)
adobe	*adobe*
adoquín	paving stone
ahorrar	(to) save, (to) economize
—ahorro	—saving, savings (pl.)
albahaca	basil
albañil	mason
albaricoque	*apricot*

---

[4] The Greek word for "rice" came from India or Persia; it is very likely that the Arabic word, subsequently passed on to Spanish, has the same origin. For *atún*, the path was Greek → Arabic → Spanish.

[5] OLEUM and OLIVA had been OLEIVOM and OLEIVA at an earlier stage; however, the sound combination *w* + *o* (represented by VO) was unstable in Latin and the first element disappeared. A similar explanation underlies the disappearance of *v* from DEUS (Spanish *dios*), earlier DEIVOS, compared to the adjective DIVINUS (Spanish *divino* and English *divine*). An analogous process occurred in English: e.g., *two* and *who* (Middle English *hwo*), where the *w* used to be pronounced.

[6] The name used for the still-functioning irrigation system introduced in the southwestern United States by the early Spanish missions.

Historical Note: The Globe-trotting Apricot

Apricot is an early product of globalization. Its ultimate origin is Latin
PERSICUM PRAECOQUUM ("*precocious* peach",[7] literally a *precooked* one), which
then followed a circuitous course to arrive in English after passing through
Greek, Arabic, Spanish, and French:

PERSICUM *PRAECOQUUM*	→	*praikokion*	Greek
	→	*al-barquq*	Arabic
	→	*albaricoque*	Spanish
	→	*abricot*	French
	→	*apricot*	English

albóndiga	meatball, fishball	
albornoz	bathrobe	[*burnoose*]
alcachofa	*artichoke*	
alcalde	*alcalde* (mayor)	
—alcaldía	—mayoralty (term of office, city hall)	
álcali	*alkali*	
—alcalino	—*alkaline*	
—alcalinidad	—*alkalinity*	
alcantarilla	sewer, culvert	
—alcantarillado	—sewage system	
alcatraz	pelican, gannet	[*albatross*]

English *albatross* was derived from *alcatraz* sometime in the late seventeenth
century by English seafarers with limited ornithological training. *Alcatraz* Island in San Francisco Bay was so named by a Spanish explorer in 1775 because
it was inhabited by pelicans.[8]

alcázar	*alcazar* (fortress or palace)

The ultimate source for this was Latin CASTRUM ("fort"), whose diminutive
CASTELLUM provided Spanish *castillo* as well as English *castle* and *chateau*.

alcoba	bedroom	[*alcove*]
alcohol	*alcohol*	

---

[7] PERSICUM was itself a shortened form of MALUM PERSICUM ("*Persian* apple", i.e., *peach*).

[8] It is perhaps fortunate that the Spanish got there first, as most would agree that *Escape from Alcatraz* has a better sound to it than *Escape from Pelican*—and is far superior to *Escape from Albatross* (!).

—alcohólico   —*alcoholic* (adj. & n.)
—alcoholismo   —*alcoholism*

Some will be surprised to learn that until at least the mid-eighteenth century English *alcohol* meant:

A fine powder produced by grinding or esp. by sublimation.

Alcohol entered Spanish in the thirteenth century with its original Arabic (*al-kuhl*) meaning of "powder of antimony", specifically "a fine powder used as a cosmetic by women to darken their eyelids, eyebrows, or eyelashes" (cf. English *kohl*). By the end of the fifteenth century, its meaning had been broadened to "a powder or substance obtained by trituration, sublimation, or distillation", and it is with this definition that it is first attested in English (1543). In the eighteenth century, *alcohol* was used to refer to wine and spirits, and in the nineteenth century it acquired its modern meaning in terms of chemical compounds. Until the 2001 edition of its *Diccionario,* the RAE's primary definition of *alcohol* remained unchanged from the original Arabic:

Polvo finísimo usado como afeite por las mujeres para ennegrecerse los bordes de los párpados, las pestañas, las cejas o el pelo.

aldea	hamlet, village	
—aldeano	—village (adj.), villager (m./f.)	
alfalfa	*alfalfa*	
alfarero	potter	
—alfarería	—pottery, potter's shop	
alférez	second lieutenant, ensign (navy)	
alfiler	pin, brooch	[*alfilaria*]
alfombra	floor carpet, rug	
alguacil	bailiff, constable	(< al-wazir)
—visir	—*vizier*	(< Turkish < Arabic)
alicate	pliers (freq. pl.: *alicates*)	
aljibe	cistern	
almacén	store, warehouse, *magazine* (storehouse)	
—(grandes) almacenes (pl.)	—department store, shopping center	
—almacenar	—(to) store, (to) warehouse	
almanaque	*almanac* (calendar with daily forecasts)	

almíbar   syrup (used in confectionery)
almirante   *admiral*   (Fr. *amiral*)

Arabic *amir* ("emir") meant "commander" and typically was followed by what it was that the emir commanded, e.g., *amir al-bahr* ("commander of the sea"), where *bahr* was "sea" and *al* the definite article. For Spaniards, Arabic words with initial consonant *m* typically began with *alm-* (*almacén, almanaque,* etc.), so in Spanish the initial *am-* was altered to *alm-*; at the same time, *ante* was added to the end of the word (*almir* + *ante),* in analogy with *comandante.* The term initially had no inherent connection with the sea, hence the title accorded to Christopher Columbus in 1492: *Almirante de la Mar Océana* ("Admiral of the Ocean Sea").

The French left unchanged the initial *am-* but (mistakenly) assumed that the definite article *al* that normally followed "emir" was part of the name itself, hence *amiral.* In English the initial *am-* was then altered to *adm-,* presumably because **adm**irals are normally **adm**irable.

almohada   pillow
—consultar (algo) con la almohada   —(to) sleep on something, (to) think it
                                             over
alquilar   (to) rent from or to (~ *arrendar*)
—alquiler   —rent (payment), rental
—inquilino   —tenant, *inquiline* (biol.)

Despite its similarity, *inquilino* is etymologically unrelated to *alquilar,* coming instead from Latin.

amapola   *poppy*   [Lat. PAPAVER → Arabic]
arrecife   reef   [*Recife,* Brazil]
arroba   *arroba* (weight or liquid
              measure), @ symbol
asesino   murderer, *assassin*
—asesinar   —(to) murder, (to) *assassinate*
—asesinato   —murder, *assassination*
—hachís   —*hashish*

The *Assassins* were an extreme Islamic sect who believed in terrorism as a political tool and very effectively implemented their beliefs. Operating from their main fortress of Alamut in northern Iran and a series of other forts in Iraq and Syria, from 1090 to 1256 they were a major force in the Middle East, their power extinguished only by the Mongol invasion in the mid-thirteenth century. Their Sunni opponents gave them the name *hashshash* (pl. *hashshashin*), or "hashish smokers (or eaters)", in reference to their supposed method of preparing themselves for their suicidal missions of terror. Although the historical accuracy of this description is disputed, there seems little doubt that they were *called* by this name, and that this is the origin of the term *assassin* that was brought back to Europe by returning Crusaders. The word is attested in Spanish in the mid-thirteenth century, though it seems to have fallen out of use shortly thereafter. It was revived in Italian in the sixteenth century and from there went to French, English, and back to Spanish. While the Spanish and English definitions are virtually identical, Spanish generally uses these words to refer to *any* premeditated killing, not only that of a public figure.

Asesinó a su abuelo para recibir la herencia.

He *murdered* his grandfather to get his inheritance.

atalaya	watchtower, vantage point	
ataúd (m.)	coffin	
auge	peak, apogee, rapid growth (boom)	
avería	damage, breakdown	[*average*]
—averiar	—(to) damage, (to) break down	

The source for both Spanish *avería* and English *average* is believed by many to be Arabic *awariya* ("damaged goods"). The initial definition of English *average* related to maritime damages or charges, a sense still preserved in the English legal definition (*AHCD*):

   a. The loss of a ship or cargo, caused by damage at sea.
   b. The incurrence of such damage or loss.
   c. The equitable distribution of such a loss [among concerned parties].
   d. A charge incurred through such a loss.

From the "average" paid by shipowners for damages (or other charges), the definition was broadened to its current more general meaning.

azafata   air hostess, hostess

Arabic *as-safat* was the basis for *azafate*, "wicker basket". The lady of the queen's wardrobe who brought the queen her daily perfumes and other accessories in an *azafate* then came to be called *la azafata*.

azahar	orange blossom, lemon blossom
—azar	—*hazard*, chance

—al azar   —at random
—azaroso   —*hazardous,* unlucky

Arabic *zahr* (or *zahar*) was "flower" and produced Spanish *azahar* with the typical addition of the definite article. In Arabic, *az-zahr* was a game with dice, so-called because one face of the die had a flower on it. This gave rise to Spanish *azar,* initially "a game of chance played with dice", then "an unfavorable roll of the dice", "bad luck", "risk". *Hazard* passed into English from French in the fourteenth century. The modern English and Spanish definitions are very similar, though Spanish tends to emphasize the sense of chance or randomness, English more that of risk or danger. It should perhaps be noted that those Spanish speakers who do not distinguish in their pronunciation between *s* and *z* (which includes virtually all of Spanish-speaking America) pronounce *azar* indistinguishably from *asar* ("to roast").

azote	whip, lashing, spanking	
—azotar	—(to) whip, (to) spank, (to) lash (sea, rain)	
azotea	flat roof (serving as a terrace)	
azucena	white lily	
azufre	*sulfur*	
azul	blue	[*azure: r → l*]
—azul celeste	—sky blue, *azure*	
—azul marino	—navy blue	
—azul turquesa	—*turquoise* (color)	[*Turkish*]
azulejo	glazed tile[9]	
barrio	*barrio,* quarter or district, neighborhood	
fulano	what's-his-name, so-and-so	
garra	claw, talon, paw	
—agarrar	—(to) grasp, (to) seize	
—agarradera	—handle (~ *asa, mango*)	
—desgarrar	—(to) rip, (to) break (heart or spirit)	
—desgarro	—rip or tear (fabric, muscle, tendon)	
Guadalcanal	Guadalcanal	[*wadi + canal*]
—Guadalajara	—Guadalajara (Spain, Mexico)	("river of stones")
—Guadalquivir	—Guadalquivir (river through Seville)	("great river")
—Guadalupe	—Guadalupe, Guadaloupe	(= "Río Lobo")

Arabic *wadi* ("valley", "ravine", "riverbed") was used to form the names of a number of rivers (and hence cities on rivers). In most cases, *wadi* was combined

---

[9] Not necessarily blue! There is no connection between *azulejo* and *azul.*

with a descriptive Arabic term, but in some (e.g., *Guadalcanal*) it was added to an existing name of Latin origin. The World War II battle of Guadalcanal, one of the Solomon Islands in the Pacific, owes its name to the fact that one of the leaders of the Spanish expedition that discovered it in 1568 came from Guadalcanal, Andalusia.

halagar	(to) flatter
—halago	—flattery, compliment
hasta	until, till, as far as; even
—hasta mañana	—until tomorrow
—hasta luego, hasta pronto	—see you soon
—Hasta un niño lo haría.	—Even a child could do it.

Hasta is by far the most important *grammatical* (as opposed to *lexical*) word that does not come from Latin.[10]

hazaña   exploit, feat, achievement   [*Hassan, Hussein*]

> Los romances cantan las *hazañas* del Cid.
> The romances recite the *exploits* of El Cid.

hidalgo   *hidalgo* (member of the
                    minor nobility in Spain)

This arose from imitation of Arabic expressions containing *ibn* ("son of") that commonly expressed a metaphorical value ("son of wealth", etc.). Thus, *hijo de algo* meant "son of something" (substantial, i.e., of wealth) and wound up being contracted to *hidalgo,* as in *El ingenioso hidalgo Don Quijote de la Mancha* (by Cervantes).

jabalí (m.), jabalina (f.)	*wild boar*
jaqueca	migraine
jarabe	*syrup*

Jarabe comes from Arabic *sharab* ("beverage") and until the seventeenth century was pronounced with an initial [sh] (cf. English *sherbet* and *shrub* ["drink"], from the same Arabic root).

jarra, jarro   *jar,* pitcher, jug, pot

---

[10] For a definition of *grammatical* and *lexical* words, see the first part of Section 4.10.

This comes from Arabic *jarra,* the source (via French) of English *jar.* In the past, a *jarra* was larger than a *jarro,* but they now seem to be used almost interchangeably, the difference being that while a *jarra* can have either one or two handles, a *jarro* has only one (an English *jar* has either zero or two handles).

jazmín	*jasmine*	
jinete	horseman, rider	[*jennet*]
joroba	hump (on a camel or a hunchback)	
—jorobado (p.p.)	—hunchbacked, hunchback	
—*El jorobado de Notre Dame*	—*The Hunchback of Notre Dame*	
—jorobar	—(to) annoy, (to) bother, (to) ruin	
limón	*lemon*	
—limonada	—*lemonade*	

Possibly from Arab is *loco:*

loco	*loco,* crazy, madman (-woman)	
—locura	—madness, insanity, folly, lunacy	
—enloquecer	—(to) drive insane, (to) drive crazy	
—alocado	—foolish, wild, reckless	
mezquino	miserly, small-minded, paltry	
—mezquindad	—stinginess, smallmindedness, act of pettiness	
mezquita	*mosque*	
mezquite	*mesquite* (shrub)	(unrelated to *mezquita*)
minarete (< Fr.)	*minaret* (~ *alminar*)	
noria	*noria,* waterwheel, Ferris wheel	
¡ojalá!	if only (it were so)!, I hope that . . .	

Ojalá comes from *wa sha (A)llah* ("and may it please *Allah*") and is analogous to the Modern Arabic (and occasional English) expression *inshallah* ("if *Allah* wills it"). It is used as a frequent interjection and conjunction (always requiring the verb to be in the subjunctive):

¡Ojalá que venga pronto!	I hope he (or she) comes soon!
ola[11]	wave
—ola de calor (frío)	—heat (cold) wave

---

[11] While generally considered to be of Arabic origin, *ola* may well come from the same Germanic root that produced English *hole* and *hollow.*

—oleada	—large wave, surge, swell	
—una oleada (ola) de robos	—a wave of robberies	
quilate	*carat*	[*r* → *l*]
rebato	alarm, tocsin	
—arrebatar	—(to) snatch, (to) captivate, (to) overcook or parch	
—arrebato	—outburst, fit, fury, rapture	
rincón	corner, nook	
—arrinconar	—(to) put in a corner, (to) corner (a person)	

Registraron hasta el último *rincón* de la casa.
They searched every *nook and cranny* of the house.

sandía	watermelon

Sandía comes from Arabic *sindiya*, literally meaning "from the Sind" (a region in Pakistan).

tabique	thin wall, partition, (nasal) septum
—tabicar	—(to) wall up, (to) block up (e.g., nose)
taquilla	ticket office, locker (pool, gymnasium)
—taquillero	—box-office success (adj.), ticket clerk (m./f.)
tara	*tare* (weight), defect or fault
tarea	task, job
—atareado	—busy (~ *muy ocupado*)
tarifa	schedule of prices or fees, *tariff*

Spanish *tarifa* (from the Arabic meaning "notification") is used only in the sense of a schedule of prices or rates (or the price itself), not in the sense of import duties. English *tariff* maintains both of these meanings but specializes in the second.

Las *tarifas* de teléfono han subido.   Telephone *rates* have gone up.

The Spanish words corresponding to import duties and customs also come from Arabic:

arancel	tariff, duty	
aduana	customs (importation), duty	(Persian → Arabic → Sp.)
—diván	—divan, couch	(Persian → Turkish → Sp./Eng.)

tarima	wooden platform, dais	
taza	cup, toilet bowl	[*demitasse*]
zaga	rear (n.), back (n.), defensive backfield (sports)	
—a la zaga	—behind, at the rear	
zaguán	entrance hallway (to a house)	
zanahoria	carrot	

Words Related to Mathematics and Science

álgebra	algebra
—algebraico	—algebraic

Arabic *al-jabr* meant "reduction" or "reunification" and was applied initially to the surgical procedure of setting bones. From the ninth century onward, it was also frequently applied to the solving of what we would today call *algebraic* equations, the science of "restoring what is missing and equating like with like", to quote from the title of a work by probably the most famous of Arab mathematicians,[12] Muhammad Ibn Musa Al-Khwarizmi (c. 780–c. 850). This work dealt not only with linear algebraic equations but also with quadratic equations, geometry, and the mathematics of inheritance.

Algebra initially entered the Romance languages and English only with its medical connotation ("surgical treatment of bones"), as solving algebraic equations was to this point still restricted to the Arabic-speaking world. An *algebrista* ("algebraist") was therefore a bonesetter:

> En esto fueron razonando los dos, hasta que llegaron a un pueblo donde fue ventura hallar un *algebrista,* con quien se curó el Sansón desgraciado. (*Don Quijote,* Segunda Parte, Capítulo XV)

> The two continued thus to discourse, until they came to a town where it was their good luck to find a *bonesetter,* who treated the unfortunate Samson.

---

[12] His chief competion perhaps comes from Omar Khayyam (1048–1131), better known to most for his *Rubáiyat.* Among Omar's accomplishments were: (a) a "systematic discussion of the solution of cubic equations by means of intersecting conic sections", including the discovery of "how to extend Abu al-Wafà's results on the extraction of cube and fourth roots to the extraction of nth roots of numbers for arbitrary whole numbers n"; and (b) the creation of a calendar more accurate than the current Gregorian one (*Encyclopædia Britannica*).

In Modern Spanish, this definition, though rarely used, still exists. It was not until the mid-sixteenth century that "algebra" began to be used in the West in its modern (and "old") sense as a branch of mathematics using numbers and symbols.

Scholars came in large numbers to Muslim Spain—and to Toledo after its "reconquest", where the tradition of Arabic (and Jewish) scholarship was maintained—to translate Arabic texts into Latin. When finally translated into Latin in the twelfth century, Al-Khwarizmi's works were credited with introducing the *Arabic* (or Hindu-Arabic) number system to the West. Latin ALGORISMUS, source of English *algorism* ("the Arabic or decimal system of writing numbers"), was taken from his name. In the late seventeenth century, a modified form of the word developed, *algorithm*—influenced by the *th* from *arithmetic*—which more recently has come to mean "a procedure or set of rules for calculation or problem-solving, now esp. with a computer".

algoritmo	*algorithm*	
algorítmico	*algorithmic*	
algoritmia	science of calculations (esp. with computers)	
guarismo	digit or digits forming a number	[*algorism*]

An important element of the Arabic number system was the concept of the *zero* as both a number and a placeholder (i.e., distinguishing 507 from 57). The notion of *zero* was hitherto completely unknown in the West—which explains why our modern calendar skips from 1 BC to AD 1, thus creating unending controversy as to whether the third millennium began in 2000 or 2001. Arabic *sifr* ("empty space", "zero") entered Medieval Latin in the early thirteenth century in two different forms: CIFRA (in France) and ZEPHIRUM (in Italy). Over time, the second form—which gave rise to Italian *zero*—largely displaced the first, whose primary meaning then shifted to that of *numerals* in general, as in *Arabic* (0, 1, 2, 3, . . .) and *Roman* (I, II, III, . . .). In Spanish this became *cifra* and in English, *cipher.* While *cipher* still maintains the definitions of "an Arabic numeral" and "the mathematical symbol for zero", its primary meaning today is as a secret or disguised system of writing.

cifra	numeral, *cipher,* code	
—cifrar	—(to) write in cipher, (to) reckon or *cipher*[13]	
—descifrar	—(to) *decipher,* (to) figure out	
cero	*zero*	(both < It.)

---

[13] "By and by he said he had *ciphered* out two or three ways, but there warn't no need to decide on any of them yet" (Mark Twain, *Huckleberry Finn*).

The concept of *cipher—zero* seems to have been applied at an early stage in the Romance languages and English to persons as well, in the sense of "a nonentity", "a mere nothing":

Soy un *cero* a la izquierda.	I am a *zero* to the left [of the number];
	i.e., I am a *cipher.*[14]

Many have the idea that *chemistry* comes directly from Greek, like *biology* and *physics* (the latter via Latin), presumably because it is such a serious science. However, the word actually comes from *alchemy,* which is what the science of chemistry was called during the Middle Ages. The source of *alchemy—alquimia* was Arabic *al kimiya,* the "philosophical stone". The origin of the Arabic word is disputed: some believe that it was taken from Greek *khumeia* (or *khemeia*)— which referred both to the "black" magic of transmuting metals and the (more respectable) art of alloying them—while others believe that it came directly from Coptic Egyptian or from a Semitic language.[15]

In any event, by abandoning its initial *al-*, *alquimia* gave rise in the thirteenth century to Medieval Latin CHIMIA, source for Spanish *química* and English *chemistry. Chemistry* and *alchemy* existed in parallel, without any substantive difference, until the early seventeenth century when *chemistry* began to distinguish itself in the modern sense of making deductions from experiments.

alquimia	*alchemy*
alquimista	*alchemist*
química	*chemistry*
químico (adj. & n.)	*chemical, chemist*
quimioterapia	*chemotherapy*

There was a second word in Arabic referring to the philosopical stone, *iksir,* which gave rise (*al* + *iksir*) to Spanish and English *elixir.*

elixir, elíxir	*elixir,* mouthwash	
acimut, azimut	*azimuth*	
cenit / zenit	*zenith*	(*also* cénit / zénit)
nadir	*nadir*	

---

[14] "One having no influence or value; a nonentity."

[15] The Greek word itself may well come from Coptic, as the similar *khemia* was the Greek transcription of the Coptic name for "Egypt" (designating the "black" or fertile country, as compared to the desert sand).

Arabic *samt* meant "point on the horizon", hence "path". The plural *as-sumut* gave *acimut—azimuth,* while the singular *samt (ar-ras),* "path (over the head)", is the origin of *cenit—zenith.* Arabic *nadir* meant "opposite", "vis-à-vis", so that *nadir as-samt* was "opposite the zenith", i.e., *nadir.*

Appendix

1. A Tale of Scarlet

escarlata	*scarlet*
—escarlatina	—*scarlet* fever
carmesí	*crimson*
carmín	*carmine*, lipstick
bermejo	*vermeil*
—bermellón	—*vermilion*

Many people have trouble keeping straight the differences between the colors *scarlet, crimson, carmine, vermilion,* and *vermeil.* This is not very surprising, since all are linguistic variations of an identical process for making a reddish color with an orange tint.

    Scarlet, following a similar path to *apricot,* had as its ultimate origin the classical Latin (TEXTUM) SIGILLATUM, "fabric adorned with small images"—SIGILLATUM itself coming from SIGNUM ("sign" or "mark"):

SIGILLATUM → *sigillatos* (Greek) → *siqillat* (classical Arabic) → *iskirlata* (Spanish Arabic) → *escarlata* (Spanish)

Escarlata arrived in Spanish with the original meaning intact, that of "an ornate cloth of *any* color", and English *scarlet* (from French) initially meant the same: "any rich or brightly colored cloth". Beginning in the twelfth century, *escarlatas* made in southern Spain were tinted a reddish color, and the word *escarlata* then began to acquire its current meaning of "a brilliant red color tinged with orange".

    What type of dye was used to produce the color scarlet? It came from the dried bodies of the insect known in Spanish as *quermes* and in English as *kermes.* The name for the insect came, like so much else, from Arabic (*qirmiz*). The Muslims in Spain changed the vowels so that the insect became *qarmaz,* and the associated color they called *qarmazi.* This latter word entered Spanish as *carmesí,* giving Spanish a second name for the color scarlet. *Carmesí* then had to compete against a "deviant" form—*cremesín*—which had arisen by *metathesis* (see Section 3.5, no. 8). This deviant form—which died out in Spanish—gave rise to Middle English *cremesin* and Modern English *crimson.*

    The Romans themselves had called scarlet COCCUM, their name for what they thought was the "berry" or "grain" that was the source of the dye.[16] At some point during the late Roman Empire, they decided that it was not a berry but a little *worm* that produced the dye. Hence VERMICULUS ("little worm") began to be used to denote the color scarlet and appears several places in the Vulgate Bible. This gave rise to *vermeil* (Spanish *bermejo*) and its derived form *vermilion* (*bermellón*), a third (and fourth) name for scarlet. These same little worms are the source of Italian (and English) *vermicelli,* a form of pasta:

[fideo]   vermicelli or noodle (freq. pl.), skinny person

Finally, the Romans had a similar reddish color MINIUM, which came not from an insect (or worm) but from a type of red lead with the same name. At some point in the Middle Ages, this word apparently blended with *qirmiz* (or *qarmaz*) to produce Medieval Latin CARMINIUM, presumably to indicate a color very similar to MINIUM but produced using the dried-insect technique. This is the origin of Spanish *carmín* and English *carmine.* MINIUM had a further role to play, being the ultimate source of English *miniature* and Spanish *miniatura,* which have nothing to do with size but with the medieval practice of illuminating manuscripts with a red ink made from *minium.*

minio   minium (red lead)
—miniatura   —miniature

2. Oranges, Orangemen, and William of Orange

naranja   *orange* (fruit), *orange* (color—m.)
naranjo   *orange* tree
anaranjado   orange-colored, orange (adj.)

Orange has had a very colorful history. Its ultimate origin seems to be non-Indo-European, possibly from the Dravidian family of languages, entering Indo-European Sanskrit as *naranga.* This eventually arrived in Arabic (via Persian) as *naranj,* from where it was introduced into Spanish as *naranja—naranjo* and Italian as *arancia—arancio,* with the Italian words losing the initial *n* in a manner reminiscent of English *adder* (snake), *apron,* and *umpire.*[17]

   un *narancio → un arancio

---

[16] Conquering Roman armies often received part of their tribute in the form of scarlet dye. COCCUM came from Greek *kokkos* ("grain", "seed"), which is also the origin of *coccus* ("bacteria in a spherical form")—as in *streptococcus*—due to its grain-like shape.

[17] Which earlier had been *naddre, napron, noumpere* ("non" + "peer"). In each case, the initial *n* was lost because it was mistakenly perceived as belonging to a preceding indefinite article: *a napron → an apron.*

French imported *arancia* as *orenge*, later *orange*. The initial *o-* is generally believed to have arisen from the similar-sounding name of the southern French city of *Orange* (Old French *Orenge*), which just happened to be a major transit center for oranges on their way to the north of France. The name of the city itself goes back to pre-Roman times and has nothing to do with the fruit.

The story does not end here, however, because in those days the town of Orange was not French but rather part of the Principality of Orange (acquired by France only in 1713). In 1544 the reigning prince died without a direct heir, and possession of the principality then passed to the House of Nassau, which subsequently wound up constituting the royal families (to this day) of the Netherlands and Luxembourg.

By the second half of the sixteenth century, *orange* had come to represent not only the fruit but the *color* orange. So when the now Dutch House of Orange-Nassau looked around for a symbol to represent them, the choice was not difficult: the color orange. Not wanting their monarchy to be identified with a fruit, the Dutch adopted *orange* only as a color (*oranje*), preferring "Chinese apple" (*sinaasappel*) for the fruit.

William of Orange (king of England from 1689 to 1702) made himself a hero to the Protestants of Ireland by his victory at the Battle of the Boyne against the Catholic James II, which explains why to this day the *Orangemen* of Northern Ireland march around with orange banners and why the flag of the Irish Republic has an orange stripe.

3. Chess

Chess has had an important impact on English, extending far beyond the game itself. The origins of the game are somewhat murky, but what seems reasonably clear is that the Europeans got it from the Arabs, who took it from the Persians, who took it from the Sanskrit game known as *chaturanga,* meaning the four corps of the Indian army: elephants, chariots, cavalry, and foot soldiers. The Arabs introduced the game in the tenth century to Spain and to Sicily (also under their control), from where it spread to the rest of Europe. The original name of the game remains only in Spanish *ajedrez* and Portuguese *xadrez* (from Arabic *ash-shatranj*).

	Spanish	Meaning		Chess Piece
	ajedrez (m.)	chess		
	tablero de ajedrez	chessboard		
	ajedrecista	chess player		
	ajedrezado	checkered, checked		
	alfil	elephant	→	bishop
	—marfil	—ivory		
	roque	chariot	→	*rook*
	—enrocar	—(to) castle		
or	torre (f.)	*tower*	→	castle (chess)
	peón	*peon,* unskilled laborer	→	*pawn*
	caballo	horse	→	knight (chess)

Peón, from the Medieval Latin for "foot soldier"—PEDO(N)—can be used outside of chess in a sense similar to English *peon,* an unskilled laborer. A *peón* is in a sense a *pioneer* on the chessboard, and *pioneer* in fact comes from the Old French word for "foot soldier".

pionero	*pioneer*

Roque and *alfil* come from Arabic and are used only as chess terms. The *fil,* from Arabic *al-fil,* also appears in *marfil* (elephant "bone"). The (chess) elephant in English was initially called *alfin,* and it was not until the second half of the sixteenth century that *bishop* was first used; *bishop* then successfully fended off the encroachment of *archer.*[18] At about the same time, *castle* began to be used along with the original *rook,* and, similarly, in Spanish *torre* appeared alongside *roque.*

In Arabic, the end of the game was announced by the expression *(ash) shah mat,* literally "the king is dead",[19] where *shah* came from the Persian for "king" (cf. English *shah* of Iran). In the Romance languages, the expression came to be pronounced as:

Sp.	*xaque y mate*	→	jaque mate
It.			scacco matto
Fr.	eschec et mat	→	échec et mat
Eng.		→	checkmate

Old French *eschec* entered English as *check,* to directly threaten the king. The French used the plural *esches* (Modern French *échecs*) to refer to the name of the game, hence English *chess.*

At a relatively early stage, English *check* acquired the broader meaning of "restraint" or "halt", and following this there was literally no checking its development. By the late seventeenth century it had added the meaning of "to verify by consulting a source or authority", and in the eighteenth century, that of a *check* on forgery, taking the physical form of a counterfoil or bank *check* (UK *cheque*). From there it went on to develop a variety of other forms: *checklist, check mark, checkoff, check in, check out, checkpoint, checkrein, checkroom, checkup,* etc. Some of these meanings and forms then filtered back to French, Spanish, and various other languages.

chequear	(to) *check,* (to) give a *checkup* to
chequeo	*checkup, check* (exam)
cheque	*check* (for payment)
chequera	*checkbook*

---

[18] Modern French uses *fou,* "court jester".

[19] It seems that the Arabs misinterpreted the Persian expression, which (somewhat more sensibly) meant the king is "at a loss" or "helpless" (i.e., he has been placed in a situation with no escape).

The French for "chessboard" is *échiquier,* and its distinctive pattern was the source for *checkered* (UK *chequered*) and *checked*. By coincidence, the twelfth-century Anglo-Norman Internal Revenue Service used counters positioned on tables with *chequered* tablecloths. This gave rise to the British *exchequer,* as in Chancellor of the *Exchequer*. The *checkerboard* pattern also gave rise to the game that Americans know as *checkers* and British as *draughts*. The Spanish have taken their name for this game from the French, *juego de damas* (or simply *damas*).

The *mate* from *checkmate* has also left its traces in English *stalemate,* initially restricted to chess but later extended to the more general situation of a deadlock. The traditional Spanish expression for a chess stalemate is that the king is *ahogado* ("suffocated" or "drowned") but more common now is *tablas* (literally "tables"), which, like *stalemate,* can also be used in the more general sense.

An unresolved debate is whether the *mate* in *jaque mate* bears any relation to the Spanish verb *matar* ("to kill"), the root for *matador.*

matar	(to) kill	
matadero	slaughterhouse	
matador	matador, bullfighter	
matamoscas	flyswatter, insecticide (~ *insecticida—m.*)	
matarratas	rat poison	
matasellos	postmark	
matasanos	unskilled doctor, quack	(kill + healthy people)
matanza	slaughter, massacre	
rematar	(to) kill off, (to) finish off, (to) conclude	
remate	end, conclusion, shot (e.g., soccer)	

SECTION 4.3

Numbers and Quantities

Apart from *zero,* English numbers up to a million are of Germanic origin. Although they share a common Indo-European origin with Latin (hence Spanish) numbers, in only a relatively few cases (e.g., *tres, seis*) is this correspondence readily apparent. On the other hand, virtually all English words relating to numerical operations come directly from Latin, so that the correspondence with Spanish words is far more obvious.

número	number
numeral	numeral
numérico	numerical
numéricamente	numerically
numeroso	numerous
innumerable	innumerable
numerar	(to) number (e.g., pages), to numerate (count)
numeración	numbering (e.g., pages), numeration
—numeración romana	—Roman number(s)
enumerar	(to) enumerate
enumeración	enumeration
numerador	numerator
denominador	denominator

The last word in the above list (in both Spanish and English) initially had nothing to do with numbers, coming instead from NOMEN ("name") and signifying "that which gives a name to something". Its first known application to arithmetic—"common denominator"—is recorded in French in 1484.

Cardinal Numbers—*Los números cardinales*

0	(Arabic)	cero	10	DECEM	diez
1	UNUS / UNA	uno/una	11	UNDECIM	once
2	DUO (DUOS)	dos	12	DUODECIM	doce
3	TRES	tres	13	TREDECIM	trece
4	QUATTUOR	cuatro	14	QUATTUORDECIM	catorce
5	QUINQUE	cinco	15	QUINDECIM	quince

6	SEX	seis	16	SEDECIM	dieciséis
7	SEPTEM	siete	17	SEPTEMDECIM	diecisiete
8	OCTO	ocho	18	DUODEVIGINTI	dieciocho
9	NOVEM	nueve	19	UNDEVIGINTI	diecinueve
20	VIGINTI	veinte	21	veintiuno / veintiuna	
26	VIGINTI SEX	veintiséis	28	veintiocho	

"Antiquated" forms for 16–29 "to be avoided" (RAE) are:
  diez y seis, diez y nueve, veinte y dos, veinte y siete, etc.

30	treinta	32	treinta y dos	
40	cuarenta	43	cuarenta y tres	
50	cincuenta	54	cincuenta y cuatro	
60	sesenta	61	sesenta y uno/una	
70	setenta	76	setenta y seis	
80	ochenta	87	ochenta y siete	
90	noventa	98	noventa y ocho	
100	ciento / cien	101	ciento uno/una	(CENTUM)
120	ciento veinte	131	ciento treinta y uno/una	
200	doscientos, -as	242	doscientos cuarenta y dos	
300	trescientos, -as	325	trescientos veinticinco	
400	cuatrocientos, -as			
500	*quinientos*, -as (*not* *cinco . . .*)			
600	seiscientos, -as			
700	*setecientos*, -as (*not* *siete . . .*)			
800	ochocientos, -as			
900	*novecientos*, -as (*not* *nueve . . .*)			
1000[1]	mil			(MILLE)
2000	dos mil	5000	cinco mil	
9000	nueve mil	10 000	diez mil	
100 000	cien mil	200 000	doscientos/as mil	
1 000 000	un millón	7 000 000	siete millones	

---

[1] The presentation in the text is that currently recommended by the RAE. Nonetheless, decimal *points* are frequently found between three-digit groups (e.g., 1.000, 200.000, 1.234.567).

3 000 000 000	tres mil millones
	or tres millardos
1 000 000 000 000	un billón
10^{18}	un trillón
10^{24}	un cuatrillón
1776	mil setecientos
	setenta y seis
	(*not* *diecisiete
	cientos . . .)

Notes:

1) For numbers ending in "-one", there is agreement with the gender of a following noun, the masculine taking the shortened form -*un*, the feminine -*una*:

21 rosas	veinti*una* rosas	21 roses
31 libros	treinta y *un* libros	31 books
31 rosas	treinta y *una* rosas	31 roses
1051 libros	mil cincuenta y *un* libros	1,051 books
1051 rosas	mil cincuenta y *una* rosas	1,051 books
31 000 rosas	treinta y *un mil* rosas	31,000 roses

2) Written accents are required for 16, 22, 23, 26 (since *dos*, *tres*, and *seis* end in -*s*) as well as 21 when used as a masculine adjective:

dieciséis, veintidós, veintitrés, veintiséis, veintiún libros

3) For "hundreds", there is also agreement with the gender of a following noun:

600 naranjas	seiscien**tas** naranjas	600 oranges
341 manzanas	trescien**tas** cuarenta y *una* manzanas	341 apples

4) *Mil* comes from Latin MILLE, whose descendants in English include *millennium* and *mile* (1,000 paces). Like English *thousand*, *mil* is invariable when used as a number (*five thousand / cinco mil*) or adjectivally, but when used as a noun to indicate "thousands", it has the masculine plural form *miles*:

mil dólares	one thousand dollars
cinco mil dólares	five thousand dollars
muchos miles *de* pesos	many thousands *of* pesos

5) *Millón, billón,* etc., are technically not numbers but nouns, so that when there is more than one, they take the plural form *millones, billones,* and when they are used with a following noun, the preposition *de* is required.

un millón *de* dólares	one million [of] dollars
dos millones de dólares	two million [of] dollars

But when they are used as part of a larger numeric expression, *de* is not used:

nueve *millones* setecientos sesenta y cinco mil   9,765,000

Note also that *billón* corresponds to (U.S.) English trillion (10^{12}); similarly, *trillón* corresponds to quintillion (10^{18}) and *cuatrillón* to septillion (10^{24}).[2] In an attempt to halt the growing use of *billón* in the American English sense (10^9)—leading to "dangerous confusions"—the RAE has recently "adopted" the term *millardo* from French (*milliard*) and recommended its use for 10^9.

6) 100 is *ciento* (from Latin CENTUM). However, whenever the number is used adjectivally, it is shortened to *cien,* even when the object is not specified explicitly. This shortening also occurs in compound numbers in which *ciento* is used multiplicatively (i.e., as an adjective), but not when used additively (as a noun).

cien (personas)	one hundred (people)
doscientas personas	two hundred people
ciento diecisiete	one hundred seventeen
cien mil	one hundred thousand
cien millones	one hundred million

counting: noventa y ocho, noventa y nueve, *cien* (e.g., *pesos, páginas*)

---

[2] English *-illion* numbers have had a torturous history. They originated in fifteenth-century French based on powers of a *million,* applied to the prefixes *bi-* ($\times$ 2), *tri-* ($\times$ 3), *quadri-* ($\times$ 4), etc.; thus a billion was a million million; a trillion, a million billion, etc. This is exactly how they are defined in Spanish today. In the eighteenth century, the French had second thoughts and redefined the system so that the multiplying factor was *thousands* rather than *millions.* This new nomenclature was adopted by some countries (including the United States) but not by others (including Spain and the United Kingdom). In 1961, to further confuse matters, France officially reverted to the original (i.e., Spanish) definition, whereas, in recent decades, British English use has increasingly followed the American pattern.

Ordinal Numbers—*Los números ordinales*

Ordinal numbers indicate numerical order: *first, second, third, . . . , fortieth, . . . , hundredth, . . . thousandth,* etc.

1.º	primero	11.º	undécimo	21.º	vigesimoprimero
2.º	segundo	12.º	duodécimo	22.º	vigesimosegundo
3.º	tercero, tercio	13.º	decimotercero	30.º	trigésimo
4.º	cuarto	14.º	decimocuarto	40.º	cuadragésimo
5.º	quinto	15.º	decimoquinto	50.º	quincuagésimo
6.º	sexto	16.º	decimosexto	60.º	sexagésimo
7.º	séptimo (sétimo)	17.º	decimoséptimo	70.º	septuagésimo
8.º	octavo	18.º	decimoctavo	80.º	octogésimo
9.º	noveno, nono	19.º	decimonoveno	90.º	nonagésimo
10.º	décimo	20.º	vigésimo	100.º	centésimo

Notes:

a) *Feminine* ordinal numbers replace the *-o* with *-a:*

1.ª	primer**a**	11.ª	undécim**a**

b) For *13–19* and *21–29,* the forms can be written as either one or two words. When written as one word, the *decimo-* or *vigesimo-* part remains "masculine":

decimocuarto—decim**o**cuarta *or* décimo cuarto—décim**a** cuarta

vigesimosegundo—vigesim**o**segunda *or* vigésimo segundo—vigésim**a** segunda

c) For *11–12,* it is very common to find "modern" forms:

decimoprimero—decim**o**primera *or* décimo primero—décim**a** primera

decimosegundo—decim**o**segunda *or* décimo segundo—décim**a** segunda

d) Beyond thirty, compound forms are written as two words:

trigésimo segundo—trigésima segunda

101.º	centésimo primero	105.º	centésimo quinto
200.º	ducentésimo	300.º	tricentésimo
400.º	cuadrin*gentésimo*	500.º	quin*gentésimo*

600.°	sexcentésimo	700.°	septin*gentésimo*
800.°	octin*gentésimo*	900.°	nonin*gentésimo*
1000.°	milésimo	2000.°	dosmilésimo
1 000 000.°	millonésimo	one millionth	
	último	last, final, *ultimate*	

Notes:

1) Ordinal numbers are adjectives and hence agree in gender with the noun that they modify. They can be placed before or after the noun, although for royalty and popes they are placed after.

el segundo acto / el acto segundo	the second act
Carlos Quinto (Carlos V)	Charles [the] Fifth
Juan Pablo Segundo (Juan Pablo II)	John Paul [the] Second

2) *Primero* and *tercero* are shortened to *primer* and *tercer* when used before masculine nouns, and the abbreviations are modified accordingly.

1.er	primer piso	first floor
3.er	tercer piso	third floor

3) Beyond ten, cardinal numbers are generally used instead of ordinals:

Enrique VIII (spoken: *Enrique octavo*)	Henry the Eighth
Alfonso X (*Alfonso décimo* or *diez*)	Alfonso the Tenth ("the Wise")
Luis XIV (*Luis catorce*)	Louis the Fourteenth (Louis XIV)
el piso treinta y cinco	the thirty-fifth floor
el siglo XIX , el siglo diecinueve	the nineteenth century

4) From *cuadragésima día*[3] (fortieth day) was derived *cuaresma* ("Lent").
5) From Latin CENTENI ("one hundred each") comes Spanish *centeno* ("rye"), from the belief that each grain planted would yield one hundred in return.
6) Expressions relating to a half include:

medio (adj. & n.)	half, middle, center, *means*
—medio litro	—half a liter
—promedio	—middle point, average
—media (n.)	—*mean* (average), sock, stocking, pantyhose (pl.)

---

[3] Note that *cuadragésima* (and hence *cuaresma*) is feminine, reflecting the fact that in early Spanish, *día* (now masculine) could also be feminine.

—mediano (adj.)	—median, medium, mediocre
—mediana (n.)	—median (geom., statistical)
—mediar	—(to) mediate, (to) intercede
—mediante (prep.)	—by means of
—intermedio (adj. & n.)	—intermediate, intermission, break
—intermediario	—intermediary
(la) mitad	half (n.), middle

7) Up to ten, other simple fractional expressions (i.e., with numerator equal to one) can be expressed either by the ordinal alone (masculine), or by the ordinal in conjunction with the feminine noun *parte.* For "third" as a noun, *tercio* is used rather than *tercero.*

un tercio de la torta	a third of the cake
un tercio de los alumnos	a third of the students
una (la) tercera parte de la torta	a third of the cake
una (la) tercera parte de los alumnos	a third of the students
un cuarto, una (la) cuarta parte	quarter, fourth part
un quinto, una (la) quinta parte	fifth, fifth part
un sexto, una (la) sexta parte	sixth, sixth part
un séptimo, una (la) séptima parte	seventh, seventh part
etc.	

8) Fractions in which *the denominator is no greater than ten* are expressed using cardinal numbers for the numerator and ordinal ones for the denominator—as above, masculine when used as a noun, feminine when employed as an adjective (modifying *parte,* which can be omitted).

dos quintos, dos quintas partes	two-fifths
cuatro séptimos, cuatro séptimas partes	four-sevenths

9) When the denominator exceeds ten, it takes the form of the *cardinal* number followed by the suffix *-avo,*[4] apart from hundred, thousand, and million, for which the unmodified *ordinal* number is used:

tres onceavos, tres onceavas partes	three-elevenths
una veinteava parte de la torta	a twentieth (part) of the cake
seis veintitresavos, seis veintitresavas partes	six twenty-thirds
dos centésimas (partes)	two-hundredths (e.g., of a second)

---

[4] When the cardinal number ends in *-a,* only *-vo* is added: *treintavo, cuarentavo, etc.*

tres milésimas (partes)	three-thousandths
diez millonésimas (partes) de un metro	ten-millionths of a meter
un centavo	*centavo*, cent

10) Decimal fractions are expressed by *feminine* ordinals (feminine on account of the implicit feminine noun *parte*):

0,1	una décima
0,02	dos centésimas
0,003	tres milésimas

11) Applied to the four cardinal directions, *quarter* came to mean an area in general (e.g., the French *quarter*[5]), and then an individual habitation.

cuarto (n.)	room, bedroom
—cuarto de baño	—bathroom
—cuarto oscuro	—darkroom
cuartel	*quarters,* barracks
—cuartel general	—headquarters
—sin cuartel	—without *quarter,* merciless
—acuartelar	—(to) quarter, (to) billet

Collective Numbers

ambos	both	[*ambi-*]
una docena	a *dozen*	
una quincena	a group of fifteen, a period of fifteen days (two weeks)	
una veintena, una treintena, etc.	a group of twenty, thirty, etc.	
cuarentena	group of forty, *quarantine*	
un centenar	a group of one hundred, lots	
~ una centena	("hundreds")	
—tiene centenares de admiradores	—he/she has hundreds of admirers	
un millar	a thousand, lots ("thousands" —gen. pl.)	

---

[5] In this sense, Spanish now uses *barrio*.

Operations

añadir	(to) add	
multiplicar	(to) multiply	
sustraer / substraer, restar	(to) subtract	("s" from *extract*)
dividir	(to) divide	
adición	addition, sum	
—adicional	—additional	
—adicionar	—(to) add (to)	
—aditivo	—additive	
—sumar	—(to) add, (to) sum up	
—suma (n.)	—sum, addition	
—sumo (adj.)	—supreme, extreme	[*summit*]
—a lo sumo	—at (the) most	
multiplicación	multiplication	
—multiplicador	—multiplier	
—multiplicando	—multiplicand	
—múltiple	—multiple	
sustracción / subs-, resta	subtraction	
—resto ~ residuo	—remainder (subtraction *or* division), *residue*	
división	division	
—divisor	—divisor	
—cociente / cuociente	—quotient	
—cociente intelectual (CI)	—intelligence quotient (IQ)	
—resto ~ residuo	—remainder (division *or* subtraction)	

Dating back to Indo-European times, a person *di-vided* from his or her spouse by death was a *widow* (Germanic) or VIDUUS / VIDUA. In Spanish, the *d* and *u* were interchanged, hence

viuda	*widow*
—viudo (adj. & n.)	—widowed, widower
—viudez ~ viudedad	—widowhood
—enviudar	—(to) become a widow or widower

Other Numerical Terms

coeficiente	coefficient
cuadrado (adj. & n.)	*square*

—cuadrar	—(to) *square* (multiple senses)	
—cuadra	—stable (horses), city block (Amer.)	
—cuadrangular	—quadrangular	
—cuadrante	—quadrant (90°; instrument for measuring angles)	
—cuadrático	—quadratic	
—cuadrilátero	—quadrilateral, ring (boxing)	
—cuadro	—square (n.), painting, *cadre*	
—cuaderno	—notebook	[*quire, cahier*]
entero	*entire,* whole	
—número entero	—whole number, *integer*	
—entereza	—strength of character, *integrity*	[*entirety*]
—enterar(se)	—(to) find out about, (to) become informed	[*integrate*]
fracción	fraction	
—fraccionario	—fractional	
—fraccionar	—(to) fractionate	
por ciento	percent	
—porcentaje	—percentage	
(número) primo	prime (number)	
—prima	—bonus, (insurance) premium, female cousin	
—primacía	—primacy, supremacy	
proporción	proportion (incl. "dimension", "size")	
—proporcional	—proportional	
—proporcionalidad	—proportionality	
—proporcionar	—(to) provide, (to) furnish	
—proporcionado (p.p.)	—proportionate	
—desproporción	—disproportion	
—desproporcionado	—disproportionate, out of proportion	
—porción	—portion	
gramo	gram	
—kilogramo	—kilogram	
tonelada	metric *ton* (1,000 kg), register *ton* (maritime: 100 ft.³)	
—túnel (< Eng.)	—tunnel	
—tonel	—barrel, cask, *tun*	

A *ton* was initially defined to be the space occupied by a *tun* (pronounced identically)—a cask of wine—and only later acquired the notion of weight. An English *short* ton (used in the United States) is equal to 2,000 lbs., while an English *long* ton (2,240 lbs.) is slightly heavier than a *metric* ton (1,000 kg = 2,204.6 lbs.). The diminutive of *tun* was *tunnel,* and an English *tunnel* (Spanish *túnel*) was initially a net for catching partridges or water fowl—so-called because it looked like a *tun* due to its having a pipe-like passage with a wide opening. It then passed through various meanings—including chimney flue, pipe, and funnel—before settling on its modern definition in the late eighteenth century.

hectárea	hectare (10,000 m^2 = 100 m × 100 m)	(= 100 áreas)
—área	—*area, are* (100 m^2)	
litro	liter	
—mililitro	—milliliter	
metro (1)	meter, measuring rod (or tape)	
—centímetro	—centimeter	
—milímetro^6	—millimeter	
—métrico	—metric, metrical (poetry)	
—metrónomo	—metronome	
—largometraje	—feature film (longer than sixty minutes)	
—cortometraje	—short film	
—diámetro	—diameter	
—diametralmente	—diametrically	
—parámetro	—parameter	
—perímetro	—perimeter	
—metro (2)	—metro (subway)	(< metropolitan)
—metropolitano	—metropolitan, metro (subway)	[*mother* city]
—metrópoli / metrópolis (f.)	—metropolis	
mínimo (adj. & n.)	minimal, minimum, least	
—mínima (n.)	—minimum temperature during a certain period	
—minimizar	—(to) minimize	
—mermar	—(to) *diminish* (~ *disminuir*)	(< MINIMARE)
máximo (adj. & n.)	maximal, maximum	
—máxima (n.)	—maxim (saying, rule, principle), maximum temperature	
—máxime (adv.)	—all the more so, especially	
positivo	positive	

^{6} Note that the stress in *mililitro* and *milímetro* is on different syllables: *mi•li•li•tro* as opposed to *mi•lí•me•tro.*

negativo	negative
par	even, *pair, peer, par*
impar	odd, *peerless, nonpareil*
doble	double
—doblar	—(to) double (incl. "fold in two"), (to) *dub* (movies)
—doblez (gen. m.)	—fold, crease
—doblez (gen. f.)	—*duplicity* (double-dealing) (~ *duplicidad*)
triple	triple, *treble* (numerical), three-point shot
—triplicar	—(to) triple, (to) *treble,* (to) triplicate
dimensión	dimension
—dimensional	—dimensional
volumen	volume (space, book, loudness)
—voluminoso	—voluminous
ángulo	angle, corner
—angular	—angular
rectángulo	rectangle
—rectangular	—rectangular
—recta (n.)	—straight line
—recto (adj. & n.)	—straight (~ *derecho*), recto (right-hand page), rectum
—ángulo recto	—right angle
—rectal	—rectal
triángulo	triangle
—triangular (adj. & vb.)	—triangular, (to) triangulate
pentágono	pentagon
paralelogramo	parallelogram
—paralelo	—parallel
rombo	*rhombus* (equilateral parallelogram)
—rumbo	—direction, course, bearing, *rhumb* (line)
—poner (hacer) rumbo a	—(to) sail for, (to) head for
—rumba	—rumba (dance, music) (< Amer. Sp.)
trapecio	*trapezoid* (figure, bone), *trapeze, trapezius* (muscle)

Quantities

The principal words involving quantities of things or people are presented below, divided into three basic groups. Some are used only as pronouns, other as adjectives or adverbs, while a number are able to perform in more than one capacity.

A Little, a Lot, or Just the Right Amount

mucho	much, a lot of, many	**poco**	little, few
bastante	enough, sufficient	**demasiado**	too much, too many
tanto	so much, so many	**tan**	so, as (adverb)

Mucho (as well as the adverb *muy*) is derived from MULTUS (as in *multitude*). An English cognate of *poco* (Latin PAUCUS) is *paucity*. *Bastante* comes from the verb *bastar* ("to suffice"), source of the Spanish and Italian interjection *basta!* ("enough already !"), which also has a distinguished English heritage:

Basta, content thee: for I have it full.	(Shakespeare, *Taming of the Shrew*)
If he will not consent—*basta*—I can but go away home.	(Scott, *Ivanhoe*)

Demasiado is derived from *demás* (*de* + *más*), "others", "the rest". A related derivation is *además* = *a* + *demás*:

además	besides, in addition

Tanto is related to English *tantamount*—which literally means "that *amounts to* as much", i.e., "that comes to the same thing". *Tanto* is also frequently used in the expressions *por tanto* (or *por lo tanto*), *mientras tanto,* and *entre tanto* (*entretanto*):

por (lo) tanto	therefore
mientras tanto, entre tanto, entretanto	meanwhile, in the meantime

Each and Every One or Various

cada	each, every	**cada uno, cada cual**	each one, everyone
todo	all	**todos, todo el mundo**	everybody
otro	other, another	**varios**	several

Cada corresponds to the *cata-* in English ***cata****log,* literally a collection of "each" thing,[7] while *todo* corresponds to English *total* (see Section 3.4). *Otro* comes from Latin ALTER, as in *alter ego* ("other I", "second self"). *Vario* ("varied") and *varios* (pl.) correspond to English *various;* however, the sense of "diverse" is more commonly expressed by *diversos* or *diferentes:*

Tengo *varios* libros.	I have *several* books.
Diversas personas han solicitado	*Various* persons have requested our
nuestra ayuda.	assistance.

Somebody or Something, Nobody or Nothing

algo	something, somewhat	**nada**	nothing, not at all
alguien	somebody, someone	**nadie**	nobody, no one
alguno, algún	some (pron., adj.), any	**ninguno, ningún**	none (pron., adj.)

The *al* in the positive forms comes from Latin AL- ("other"[8]), and the *go* or *gu* comes from the interrogative/relative pronouns QUIS/QUI ("who") and QUID/QUOD ("what", "which").[9] The sense was thus "someone or something else", hence "somebody", "something", "some".

Ninguno is simply the "negative" of *alguno,* the initial *n-* being a "true" negative. The origin of *nada* and *nadie* is an altogether different story, however.

Historical Note: When "Yes" Means "No"

The constant warnings of English teachers over the centuries[10] about the perils of double negatives could be strengthened by reference to Spanish (or French),

---

[7] Greek *kata* in fact had a range of meanings, most dealing with a downward motion; hence *cataclysm, catacomb, cataract,* etc.

[8] Found in English *alibi, alias, alien,* and *alter.*

[9] These Latin pronouns are found in a number of common English expressions, including *quid* pro *quo,* sine *qua* non, status *quo,* and *quod* erat demonstrandum (QED)

[10] Actually, not so many: until perhaps the eighteenth century, double negatives were an accepted manner of making emphatic statements. In the *Canterbury Tales,* for example, Chaucer says of the friar: "Ther *nas no* man *nowher* so vertuous", i.e., "There **no** was **no** man **nowhere** so virtuous." Even in Modern English, a number of double-negative constructions are considered acceptable, with meanings that frequently differ from the "simple" positive forms: *not uncommon* vs. *common, not infrequently* vs. *frequently, not without* vs. *with,* etc.

where their frequent use has completely reversed the meanings of a number of very common words:

Current Meaning	Original Meaning	
	Spanish	*French*
nothing	anything	anything
nobody	anybody	person
never	ever	ever
absolutely not	absolutely	—

Nada originated from negative expressions of the form

NON HABEO REM NATAM   I have not *anything at all,*

where REM NATAM, "born thing", was a somewhat exaggerated way of saying "anything at all". In Vulgar Latin, multiple negatives became very frequent and their profusion created a situation in which REM NATAM was misinterpreted as a *negative* element rather than a positive one. Thus when people were asked "What do you have?" the simple response was REM NATAM, "nothing". French subsequently reduced this expression to its first element, Spanish to its second:

| REM | → | rien | (Fr.) "nothing" |
| NATAM | → | nada | (Sp.) "nothing" |

A colorful way of saying *anybody* or *anyone* was HOMO NATUS, "a born person". In negative expressions like

NON VIDEO HOMINEM NATUM   I do not see *anyone,*

NATUM was taken for a negative, and hence *anybody* became *nobody*. NATUM (or more likely the nominative plural NATI) became Old Spanish *nadi* and Modern Spanish *nadie*. By a similar process, French *personne* also came to mean "nobody".

Likewise, the positive expression IAM MAGIS ("already more") has become *never* in both Spanish (*jamás*) and French (*jamais*), although it is sometimes translated by *ever:*

| *Jamás* he visto una cosa más bella. | *Never* have I seen anything more beautiful. |

Es la cosa más bella que *jamás* he visto.	It is the most beautiful thing that I have *ever* seen.
nunca *jamás*	never *ever*, never-*never* (land)

En absoluto in Spanish has come to mean "absolutely not":

No quiero *en absoluto* ir al cine.	I have *absolutely* no desire to go to the cinema.
—¿Quieres ir al cine conmigo?	—Would you like to go to the cinema with me?
—*En absoluto.*	—*Absolutely not.*

In Modern Spanish, it is not unusual to find three, or even four, negatives in a single sentence:

No confío en *nadie* para *nada.*	I don't trust (in) anybody for anything.
¡Aquí *nunca nadie* sabe *nada* de *nada!*	No one here ever knows anything about anything! (*no* one *never* knows *nothing* about *nothing*)

SECTION 4.4
Time

The Origins of "Time"

In Latin there was a fundamental distinction between a *point* or *fraction* of time, represented by TEMPUS (genitive TEMPORIS), and time in the *continuous* sense, represented by AEVUM—root of *age* (AEVITAS, shortened to AETAS) and *eternity* (AETERNITAS). TEMPUS also came to be applied to a "period" of *weather,* and then to weather in general. Initially a general period of time, TEMPESTAS later specialized in weather of the tempestuous type.

No tengo el *tiempo* para hacerlo.	I don't have the *time* to do it.
en el *tiempo* de Carlo Magno	in the *time* of Charlemagne
—tiempo muerto	—time out (e.g., sports)
—tiempo verbal, tiempo del verbo	—*verb tense* (e.g., past, future)
—matar el tiempo	—(to) kill time
—ganar tiempo	—(to) save time, (to) *gain* time
—perder (el) tiempo	—(to) waste time, (to) lose time
—gastar (el) tiempo	—(to) *waste* time
—al mismo tiempo	—at the same time, simultaneously
—con el tiempo	—over time, with time
—a su (debido) tiempo	—in due course, in good time
Siempre hace buen *tiempo* en agosto.	It's always good *weather* in August.

TEMPUS	tiempo	time, weather
	temporal (1)	temporary, temporal, tempest, rainy spell
	temporal[1] (2)	*temporal* (relating to the *temple*), *temporal* bone
	temporario	temporary (*temporal* is more
	~ temporáneo	common)
	temporada	period of time, season
	temporada alta	high season
	temporada baja	low season
	temprano	early

[1.] The anatomical *temple*—*temporal* (2) is related neither to *time* nor to the religious *temple*.

extemporáneo	untimely, inopportune	[*extemporaneous*]
[improvisado]	extemporaneous	
tempestad	tempest, storm	
tempestuoso	tempestuous, stormy	
intempestivo	untimely, ill-timed (~ *extemporáneo, inoportuno*)	
contratiempo	*contretemps*	
contemporáneo	contemporary, contemporaneous	

AETAS	edad	*age*	(acc. AETAT-EM)
	Edad Media	Middle Ages	
	medieval	medieval	
	eternidad	eternity	(acc. AETERNITAT-EM)
	eterno	eternal	
	longevidad	longevity	
	coetáneo	coetaneous, contemporary	

Coetáneo strictly speaking means "of the same age" but is now more commonly used as a synonym of *contemporáneo,* "of the same time".

The Four Seasons—*Las cuatro estaciones*

Beginning with spring, the four Latin seasons were VER (pl. VERA), AESTAS, AUTUMNUS, and HIEMS, the latter having an associated adjective HIBERNUS and sharing a common root with Sanskrit *Hima-laya* ("abode of snow"). In the major Romance languages, "spring" was replaced by expressions relating to *first* or *prime* spring (Spanish, Portuguese, and Italian *primavera*) or season (French *printemps*[2]). Spanish *primavera* initially conserved the meaning of "beginning" of spring, with *verano* referring to the end of spring—beginning of summer. When *primavera* became the general term for "spring", *verano* moved to "summer". The original Latin for "summer" survives in *estío* and *estival,* although *verano* and *de verano* are far more common.

STATIO(N)	estación	season, station
	estación de tren	train station

[2.] From PRIMUM TEMPUS.

PRIMA VERA	primavera	spring, *prim*rose	[*primavera*]
(TEMPUS) VERANUM	verano	summer	
AUTUMNUS	otoño	autumn	
(TEMPUS) HIBERNUM	inv**ie**rno	winter	
VERNALIS	vernal	vernal	
	de verano ∼ veraniego	summer (adj.)	
	veranear	(to) summer (spend the summer)	
	veraneante	(summer) vacationer, summer resident	
	veraneo	summer vacation	
(TEMPUS) AESTIVUM	estío	summer (n.)	
	estival	summer (adj.), *estival*	
AUTUMNALIS	otoñal	autumnal, autumn (adj.)	
	retoño	sprout, shoot, child (fam.)	
HIBERNALIS	invernal	hibernal, winter (adj.)	
HIBERNARE	invernar	(to) winter (in a particular place)	
	invernadero	greenhouse	
	efecto invernadero	greenhouse effect	
	hibernar	(to) hibernate	
	hibernación	hibernation	

Year

ANNUS	año	year
	año bisiesto[3]	leap year, *bissextile* (year)
ANNUALIS	anual	annual, yearly (adj.)
	anualmente	annually, yearly (adv.)
	anales (pl.)	annals
ANNUITAS	anualidad	annuity (annual payment or receipt)
	anuario	annual (yearbook)

[3.] In the Roman calendar, a leap year was an ANNUS BI(S)SEXTUS (or BI[S]SEXTILIS), since the sixth (SEXTUS) day before March 1 (what we call February 24) occurred twice (BIS).

BIENNIUM	bienio	biennium (period of two years)
BIENNALIS	bienal (adj. & n.f.)	biennial (every two years)
CENTENARIUS	centenario	centennial, centenary, centenarian
MILLENARIUS	milenario	millennial, millenary, millenarian
	milenio	millennium
PERENNIS	perenne	perennial
ANNIVERSARIUS	aniversario	anniversary
	cumpleaños	birthday (lit. one *completes* a year)
DECADA	década	decade
DECENNIUM	decenio	decennium, decade
SAECULUM	siglo	century, Age (distinctive period)
	Siglo de Oro	Golden Age (esp. Spain c. 1500–1681)
	por los siglos de los siglos	eternally, for ever and ever
(unrelated)	sigla	acronym (e.g., EE.UU. = U.S.A.)
SAECULARIS	secular	secular, (worldly; not bound by monastic restrictions; centenary)
	seglar	secular (worldly; lay; layperson)

El temor al fin del mundo es un sentimiento *secular.*
The fear of the end of the world occurs [at the end of] every century.

A SAECULUM was initially a "generation" or the duration of a generation, later becoming an "age" or "epoch", "a period of one hundred years". In Church Latin, it came to refer to life "in and of the *century*", i.e., in the *secular* world as opposed to that of monastic seclusion; *secular clergy* were those who had not taken monastic vows. Modern English *secular* continues to maintain the (alternative) definition of "occurring once in an age or century", and in scientific use, terms like *secular acceleration* and *secular variation* refer to changes occurring over a long period.

SAECULUM was also used in the Latin Bible (the Vulgate) to express the notion of "man-inhabited world", as opposed to "earth" (TERRA → Spanish *tierra*) and "universe" (MUNDUS → Spanish *mundo*). English *world* was very likely created as a direct loan translation of SAECULUM used in this sense: Old English *weor-old* or *wor-old* was formed from two separate components: the first is "man" (cf. *wer-wolf*); the second is "age" (*old*). The literal meaning of *world* is thus "age of man".[4]

Month

MENSIS	mes	month, *menses*
MENSUALIS	mensual	monthly
	mensualidad	monthly salary, monthly payment
	bimensual	twice a month
	bimestral	every two months, bimonthly[5]
	menstrual	menstrual
	menstruación	menstruation
SEMESTRIS[6]	semestre	period of six months, semester
	semestral	semiannual, lasting a semester

JANUARIUS	enero	JULIUS	julio
FEBRUARIUS	febrero	AUGUSTUS	agosto
MARTIUS	marzo	SEPTEMBER	septiembre
APRILIS	abril	OCTOBER	octubre
MAIUS	mayo	NOVEMBER	noviembre
JUNIUS	junio	DECEMBER	diciembre

Week

SEPTIMANA	semana	week (< SEPTEM = seven)
	semanal	weekly (adj.), weeklong

---

[4] The expression NOVUS ORDO SECLORUM found below the pyramid on the back of the U.S. one-dollar bill literally means "New Order of the Ages" (SECLUM, and hence the genitive plural SECLORUM, was an alternative form of SAECULUM going back to Classical Latin times). In view of the direct correspondence between SAECULUM and *world*, it can also be translated as "New World Order".

[5] English *bimonthly* is ambiguous: either every two months, or twice a month.

[6] Shortened from the original SEX-MENSTRIS ("of six months").

semanalmente	weekly (adv.)	
semanario	weekly (publication)	
por semana	per week	
por semanas	by the week (e.g.,	
rental)		
fin de semana	weekend	
la semana pasada	last week	
la semana que viene	next week (~ *la semana*	
	próxima / entrante)	
la semana siguiente	the next week	

The words relating to *week* are derived from Latin SEPTEM (seven).

Day

DIES	día (m.)	day	
	día festivo	holiday	
	día laborable	workday, weekday	
	día de trabajo	weekday, workday	
	día hábil[7]	weekday, workday	
	día lectivo	school day	[*lesson* day]
	ocho días	a week	
	quince días	a fortnight (fourteen	
	~ quincena	days)	
	quincenal	fortnightly	
	al (el) día siguiente	(on) the next day	
	al otro día	(on) the next day	
	el otro día	the other day	
	mediodía (m.)	midday, noon, south	
MERIDIANUS[8]	meridiano	meridian (adj. & n.),	
		bright or dazzling	
	meridional	southern, meridional	

[7.] Technically, *un día hábil* is a day on which public offices and courts are open.

[8.] In Latin, the original form for midday, MEDI-DIES, was changed to MERIDIES (hence the adjective MERIDIANUS), presumably to avoid the two D's in succession. Spanish *mediodía* is a reformulation of the original concept. The meaning "south" arose from the fact that at midday in the Northern Hemisphere the sun is directly to the south (which is why the south of France is called the *Midi*).

DIARIUM	diario (adj. & n.)	daily, diary, *journal*, daily (newspaper)	
QUOTIDIANUS	cotidiano	daily, *quotidian*	
DIES MALI	[sombrío, lúgubre]	*dismal*	(lit. "evil days")
DIURNUS	diurno	*diurnal*, daytime (adj.)	
	jornada	(day's) *journey*, (working) day	
DIURNALIS	jornal	day's wages, day's work	[*journal*]
	jornalero	day laborer	
	[periodismo]	journalism	
MATUTINUS	matutino	morning (adj.), *matutinal*	
	matinal	morning (adj.), *matinal*	(< Fr.)
VESPERA	víspera	eve, *Vespers* (pl.)	
	en vísperas de	on the eve of	
	vespertino	evening (adj.), *vespertine*	

The constructions *ocho días* and *quince días* strike many as illogical: first, because one normally thinks of a week as having a length of seven days, and second, because two weeks are usually twice as long as one week. In fact, such expressions are found in many of the Romance languages, and their origin can be traced back to the manner in which days were counted in Classical Latin times: today is given the number 1, tomorrow is thus day number 2, etc., so that in one week the number will be 8, and in two weeks it will be 15.

In the Roman calendar, there were no weeks as such and no individual names for the days, both of these being "Eastern" inventions that arrived in the Roman Empire only in the early years of the modern era. The seven-day week was not established as part of the official Roman calendar until AD 321 under the emperor Constantine, who designated the first day of the week to be dedicated to the Sun, followed by the Moon, Mars, Mercury, Jupiter, Venus, and Saturn. English *Saturday* maintains the original Latin nomenclature, *Monday* and *Sunday* represent direct translations from Latin into (Old) English, while the English names for the remaining four days were obtained by replacing the Latin gods with their Germanic "equivalents" (e.g., the Norse god of thunder *Thor* for *Jupiter*).

SOL	Sol, sol	Sun, sun	
	solar	solar	

	insolación	*insolation* (sunstroke, solar radiation)
	parasol	parasol, sunshade (auto)
LUNA	Luna, luna	Moon, moon, plate glass
	lunar (adj. & n.)	lunar, mole, blemish, polka dots (pl.)
	luna de miel	honeymoon
	luna creciente	crescent (waxing) moon
	luna llena	full moon
	luna menguante	waning moon
	luna nueva	new moon
	media luna	half-moon
	lunático	lunatic
MARS (acc. MARTEM)	Marte	Mars
	marcial	martial
	artes marciales	martial arts
	marciano	Martian
MERCURIUS	Mercurio, mercurio	*Mercury, mercury*
JUPITER (acc. JOVEM)	Júpiter	Jupiter
	jovial	jovial
VENUS	Venus	Venus
SATURNUS	Saturno	Saturn

Also:

URANUS	Urano	Uranus
	uranio	uranium
NEPTUNUS	Neptuno	Neptune
PLUTO(N)	Plutón	Pluto
	plutonio	plutonium
	plutocracia	plutocracy

The early Church did not approve of such pagan names and did its best to eliminate them, as suggested in the following extract from a sermon of St. Cesarius (c. 470–542), bishop of Arles in southern France:

> Some fall into this error, of observing attentively which day they are going to begin their journey, honoring the sun, or the moon, or Mars, or Mercury, or Jupiter, or Venus, or Saturn . . . Above all, my brothers, flee from these

sacrileges, avoid them like fatal poisons of the devil . . . Because Mercury
was a miserable man, avaricious, cruel, impious, and haughty; as for Venus,
she was the most shameless harlot . . . For us, my brothers . . . let us disdain
these most repugnant of names and let us never say "day of Mars", "day
of Mercury", "day of Jupiter"; but let us say them as they are written, first,
second, or third *feria* [i.e., weekday].[9]

Such sentiments carried the day in Portuguese, and in the other major Romance languages led to the replacement of *Saturn* and the *sun* by more digni-
fied names—*Sabbath* day and *master / lord's* day.[10]

		Spanish	French	Italian	Portuguese
Mon.	LUNAE (DIES)	lunes	lundi	lunedì	segunda-feira
Tue.	MARTIS (DIES)	martes	mardi	martedì	terça-feira
Wed.	MERCURII (DIES)	miércoles	mercredi	mercoledì	quarta-feira
Thu.	JOVIS (DIES)	jueves	jeudi	giovedì	quinta-feira
Fri.	VENERIS (DIES)	viernes	vendredi	venerdì	sexta-feira
Sat.	SABBATUM	sábado	samedi	sabato	sábado
Sun.	DOMINICUS (DIES)	domingo	dimanche	domenica	domingo

The Latin names took the form *day of,* with the name of the appropriate im-
mortal preceding in the genitive (possessive) case. Spanish *martes, jueves,*
and *viernes* come directly from the corresponding Latin genitives, while *lunes*
and *miércoles* have adopted by analogy the *-es* ending. In contrast to Spanish,
both French and Italian have maintained "day" as an explicit part of the name.
Lunes to *viernes* have invariable plurals (*los lunes,* etc.), reflecting their origin
as genitives: just as in English one says "Mondays" rather than "Monday", in
Spanish the plural affected only the portion that has disappeared (DIES), while
the part that remains is invariable. *Sábado* and *domingo* have regular plurals
(*los sábados, los domingos*). The Spanish week generally commences on Monday, not Sunday.

[9.] Latin text from D. Germani Morin, *Sancti Caesarii Arelatensis Sermones, Pars Altera* (Turn-
holti: Typographi Brepols Editores Pontificii, 1953), 785.
[10.] The only European languages that appear to have preserved the original seven "pagan"
names are English, Welsh, and Breton (the Celtic language spoken in Brittany in France, which,
however, is of *British,* not continental, origin).

Hour

HORA	hora	*hour*	
	hora punta,	rush hour,	
	hora pico[11]	peak hour	
HORARIUS	horario	hourly, timetable or	[*horary*]
	(adj. & n.)	schedule	
HOROLOGIUM	reloj	clock, watch,	
		horologe	
	reloj de sol	sundial	
HOROSCOPUS	horóscopo	horoscope	
IN + HORA +	enhorabuena	congratulations	(lit. "in good time")
BONA			

The unusual ending of *reloj* reflects the fact that it was taken from Catalan.

Minute

MINUTUS	minuto	minute (time,	
		geometry)	
	menudo	*minute* (small, insignificant)	
	a menudo	often, frequently	
(via Fr.)	menú	menu	
MINUTIA	minucia	minutia (small or trivial	
		detail), trifle	
	minucioso	meticulous, *minute* (detailed)	
	minuciosamente	*minutely* (with attention to	
		small details)	
	diminuto	minute (tiny), diminutive	
	diminutivo	diminutive (gram.)	
	disminuir	(to) diminish, (to) reduce	
	disminución	diminution, reduction	
	disminuido (p.p.)	handicapped, handicapped person	
	menguar	(to) diminish, (to) wane (e.g., Moon)	

[11.] The respective plurals are *horas punta* and *horas pico,* reflecting the fact that *punta* and *pico* are nouns, not adjectives. The second expression is widespread in the Americas, with the notable exception of Chile, where "la palabra *pico* es tabú lingüístico por designar el órgano sexual masculino" (RAE, *Diccionario panhispánico de dudas*).

	menguante	diminishing, waning
	desmenuzar	(to) crumble, (to) *mince*, (to) examine *minutely*

Menú comes from French, where, in addition to "minute (tiny)", it came to mean "detailed list of courses of a meal".

Second

By origin, *second* has nothing to do with the number *two*. Rather, it is "the one that *follows*", SECUNDUS originally being a participle of the verb SEQUI ("to follow"). The *second* division of the hour, after the *minute,* is a *second.*

SECUNDUS	segundo (adj. & n.)	second (in order), second (of time)	
SECUNDUM	según	according to	
SECUNDARIUS	secundario	secondary	
SEQUERE (CL SEQUI)	seguir	(to) follow, (to) continue	[*segue*]
	enseguida / en seguida	at once, immediately	[*ensue*]
	seguidor	follower	[*suitor*]
	exequias	ob*sequies,* funeral rites	
SEQUENTEM (acc.)	siguiente	following, next, *sequent*	
	séquito	retinue, entourage	
SEQUENTIA	secuencia	sequence	
CON + seguir	conseguir	(to) obtain, (to) succeed in	
CONSEQUENTIA	consecuencia	consequence	
	consecutivo	consecutive	
CONSEQUENTEM (acc.)	consecuente	consequent, consistent (conduct)	
	consiguiente	consequent (following, resulting)	
	por consiguiente	consequently, therefore	
	en consecuencia	consequently, accordingly	
INCONSEQUENTEM (acc.)	inconsecuente	inconsistent (adj. & n.)	

> Esto no sólo es *inconsecuente* con los estándares de derechos humanos . . .
> This is not only *inconsistent* with human rights standards . . .

Juan es un *inconsecuente:* dice que es vegetariano y come pollo.
Juan is (an) *inconsistent:* he says he is vegetarian yet he eats chicken.

OBSEQUIUM	obsequio	gift, present	[*obsequious*]
	obsequiar	(to) make a present of, (to) regale	
PER + seguir	perseguir	(to) pursue, (to) *persecute*	
	perseguidor	pursuer, persecutor	
	persecución	persecution, pursuit	
PRO + seguir	proseguir	(to) *prosecute* (carry on, *pursue*)	
	prosecución	prosecution (nonjudicial senses)	
SEQUELA	secuela	sequel, sequela	
SEQUAX	secuaz	follower, henchman	[*sequacious*]
SECTA	secta	sect	

Moment

MOMENTUM	momento	moment, momentum (physics)	
	momentáneo	momentaneous	
RAPTUS	rato	brief period of time, while (n.)	[*rapt*]
	a ratos	at times, occasionally	
	rapto	kidnapping, *ravishment,* fit, *rapture*	
	raptar	(to) abduct, (to) kidnap	
RAPIDUS	rápido	rapid	
	rapidez	rapidity, swiftness	

The initial meaning of *rato* was "instant" or "moment"—a meaning still preserved in much of the Americas—before undergoing an evolution in meaning similar to that of *ahora* (i.e., from "now" to "some point in the not-too-distant future").

Adverbs of Time

HAC HORA (at this hour)	ahora	now
AD + NOCTEM (at night)	anoche	last night
ANTE	antes	before
ANTE + ANNUS (before + year)	antaño	in the old days, long ago
ADHUC (until this point)	aún	yet, still
HERI	ayer	yesterday
ANTE + HERI (before + yesterday)	anteayer	the day before yesterday

DE + EX + POST (from + from + after)	después	after
IN + TUNC (in + then)	entonces	then
HODIE (< HOC DIE, "on this day")	hoy	today
JAM (now, already)	ya	already
JAM MAGIS (ya más = "now more")	jamás	never
(IN) + LOCUS (place)	luego	next, right away
(CRAS) MANEANA (tomorrow morning)	mañana	tomorrow
	pasado mañana	the day after tomorrow
NUNQUAM	nunca	never
PRIMARIUS	primero	first, to begin with
PROMPTUS	pronto	soon, quickly, *promptly*
RECENTE(M) + MENTE	recientemente	*recently*
SEMPER	siempre	always
TARDE (slowly, tardily)	tarde	late
TEMPORANEUS (timely)	temprano	early
TOTA + VIA (all + way)	todavía	still

Notes:

(1) As an adverb, *mañana* means "tomorrow". *El mañana* is a *masculine* noun meaning "morrow" or "future", hence *pasado mañana* ("the day after tomorrow"). *La mañana* is a *feminine* noun meaning "morning", so that *mañana por la mañana* is "tomorrow morning".[12]

(2) *Mañana* is known as an expression associated with a lack of urgency. *Ahora* is similar, essentially meaning some point in the future starting from now. To express a more immediate "now", various strengthened expressions are employed, with different nuances in different regions: *ahora mismo, ahorita, ahorita mismo,* etc. (*mismo* in this context means "exactly" or "right", as in "right now").

(3) *Tarde* is also a feminine noun meaning "afternoon". So *muy tarde por la tarde* means "very late in the afternoon".

buenos días	good day, good morning
buenas tardes	good afternoon
buenas noches	good evening, good night

---

[12] English *morrow* formerly had a similar double employ: "morning" (now archaic) and "the next day"; both senses are still preserved in German *morgen* ("tomorrow") / *Morgen* ("morning").

(4) As for *jamás* (see Section 4.3), in certain constructions the translation of *nunca* can be "ever" rather than "never".

La situación es más grave que *nunca*.   The situation is more serious than *ever.*

(5) *Aún* (with written accent) is to be distinguished from *aun* (without), the latter meaning "even" (adverb). Theoretically, there is a difference in pronunciation as well as spelling:

aún	a•un	*2 syllables, a* and *u* are separate vowels
aun	aun	*1 syllable, a* and *u* form a diphthong

A simple aid for keeping them straight: *still . . .* has the *longer* pronunciation. In practice, though, particularly in the Americas, the two are often pronounced the same, and the RAE has given up and no longer insists that the words be distinguished orally.

SECTION 4.5
Ser and *Estar*

Distinguishing between the uses of *ser* and *estar* is one of the greatest challenges facing the student of Spanish. The Latin origins of these verbs can provide some assistance in understanding their different uses:

(a) *Ser* represents a merger of the Latin verbs "to be" (ESSE) and "to be seated" (SEDERE). ESSE is the ultimate origin of English *essence* and *essential;* SEDERE, that of *sedentary* and *residence.*

(b) *Estar* comes from the Latin verb "to stand" (STARE), the origin of English *state* and *status* and, via Old French, the verb *stay.*

Thus one can think of *ser* as applying to the *essence* of an object, a characteristic that is *seated* or innate, as opposed to the less permanent *state* (or *status*) of an object represented by *estar.*

In this section we will introduce some of the very large number of Spanish (and English) words etymologically related to *ser* and *estar.*

1. *Ser*

As noted above, Spanish *ser* represents an amalgam of Latin ESSE and SEDERE, each of which individually contributed numerous words to Spanish and English.

A. ESSE

Like its English counterpart *to be,* ESSE was itself a hybrid composed of elements from different Indo-European roots: most of the forms came from the root **es-,* which produced English *is,* while others—including the future participle FUTURUS—came from the root **bheu-,* origin of *be.*[1]

| FUTURUS | futuro (~ porvenir[2]) | future |

---

[1] An initial Indo-European **bh-* corresponds to *b-* in the Germanic languages, but to *f-* in Latin, hence the correspondence FUTURUS—*be;* other such Germanic-Latin correspondences are *bloom—flower,* *brother—fraternal,* *break—fracture,* *brew—ferment.*

[2] Literally "that which is to come" (*por* + *venir*).

In early Classical Latin, ESSE had no present participle, although -SENS (acc. -SENTEM) served as a present participle for several of the composite verbs formed from ESSE (e.g., ABSENS). A later form, ENS (acc. ENTEM), is attributed by some to Caesar and is the basis for

ENTEM	ente	being, public entity (esp. TV)
ENTITAT-EM (acc.)	entidad	entity (being, corporation or association)

Not to be outdone by his contemporary (and political rival), Cicero "invented" another "pseudo" present participle (ESSENS—ESSENTEM) and used it to create the noun ESSENTIA, in analogy with the manner in which PATIENTIA ("patience") had been constructed from the present participle PATIENS of the verb PATI ("to suffer"). A new word for "essence" was necessary because the existing one (NATURA, "nature") was thought to be too general and imprecise.

ESSENTIA	esencia	essence
	esencial	essential
	esencialmente	essentially
PATIENTIA	paciencia	patience
	paciente	patient (adj. & n.)
	pacientemente	patiently
	impaciencia	impatience
	impaciente	impatient
	impacientemente	impatiently

In medieval times, the term *fifth element* was coined to refer to the ethereal element that, along with the four basic ones (air, earth, fire, water), permeated all things.

QUINTA ESSENTIA	quintaesencia	quintessence

ESSE joined forces with several prepositions to produce compound verbs, which then served as the basis for various other forms:

AB + ESSE	**ABESSE**	to be away **from:** be absent
ABSENTIA	ausencia	absence
ABSENTEM (acc.)	ausente	absent, absentee
	ausentar(se)	(to) absent oneself, (to) leave
	absentismo	absenteeism
	[distraído]	absentminded

INTER + ESSE	**INTERESSE**	to be or lie **between:** be of importance (or *interest*)
INTERESSE	interés	interest
	interesar	(to) interest, (to) be interesting
	interesante	interesting
	interesado (p.p.)	interested, selfish
	desinterés	disinterest (impartiality; lack of interest)
	desinteresado	disinterested (impartial; uninterested)
PRAE + ESSE	**PRAEESSE**	to be **before:** preside, be *present*
PRAESENTIA	presencia	presence
	presenciar	(to) be present at, (to) witness
PRAESENTEM (acc.)	presente	present, present tense
	[regalo]³	present (gift)
	[regalar]	(to) give a present, (to) *regale*
	presentar	(to) present
	presentación	presentation
	presentador	presenter (TV, radio, etc.)
	presentable	presentable
	impresentable	unpresentable (not fit to be presented)
RE-	representar	(to) represent, (to) perform (play)
	representación	representation, performance (theater)
	representativo	representative (adj.)
	representante (m./f.)	representative (person)
PRO + ESSE	**PRODESSE**	to be **at hand:** be useful or profitable

The associated adjective PRODE is the source of English *pride, proud, prude, prowess,* and *improve* (which has no etymological connection with *prove*). With the exception of *proeza,* Spanish has drawn these words from other sources:

proeza	heroic deed (~ *hazaña*)	[*prowess*]
orgullo	pride	[† *orgueil*]
orgulloso	proud	

---

³ Spanish *presente* can also mean "present (gift)", but *regalo* is far more common.

mojigato	prude	(lit. "kitty cat")
mejorar	(to) improve, (to) *ameliorate*	
mejora	improvement, *melioration*	
	(~ *mejoría, mejoramiento*)	
inmejorable	unbeatable (can't be bettered)	

ESSE also mated with the adjective POTIS to form the verb POSSE,[4] which in Vulgar Latin became POTERE. POTIS initially had the meaning "master of" or "possessor" before acquiring the more abstract sense of "being capable". Its Greek equivalent is found in the *-pot* element of *despot* (lit. "master of the house"). POTERE is the source of English *power,* via Anglo-Norman French *poër* (French *pouvoir*).

POTIS + ESSE	POSSE	to be **master** (of a situation): be able, can
POTERE	poder	can, (to) be able
	poder (n.)	*power,* authority, control
	poderoso	powerful
	todopoderoso	all-powerful, almighty
POTENTIA	potencia	potency, power
	impotencia	impotency
	superpotencia	superpower
	potencial	potential (adj. & n.)
	potenciar	(to) strengthen, (to) *potentiate*
POTENTEM (acc.)	potente	potent, powerful
	impotente	impotent
	omnipotente	omnipotent, almighty
	omnipotencia	omnipotence
	potentado	potentate
	potestad	authority, *power*
	apoderar	(to) empower, (to) seize
	apoderado (p.p.)	representative, agent
POSSIBILIS	posible	possible
	posiblemente	possibly
	posibilidad	possibility
	posibilitar	(to) make possible

---

[4] In Medieval Latin, the verb POSSE could also be used as a noun with the sense of "*power*", "force". In *British* Medieval Latin the expression POSSE COMITATUS arose, literally "force of the *county*", referring to a body of men whom the sheriff could call upon to maintain public order (i.e., a *posse*).

	imposible	impossible
	imposibilitar	(to) make impossible, (to) prevent
(< Gk.)	déspota	despot
	despótico	despotic
	despotismo	despotism

B. SEDERE

SEDERE corresponds directly to English *to sit,* as both come from the Indo-European root **sed-.* Like *sit,* it refers to the state of being seated and is distinguished from the active sense of *sitting down* ("to seat oneself"), which is represented by the related verb SIDERE. With regard to a person, SEDERE implies a notion of resting without movement; to an object, that of stability or of having been deposited (like a *sed*iment on a river bed).

Words derived directly from SEDERE include:

SEDENTARIUS	sedentario	sedentary
SEDIMENTUM	sedimento	sediment
	sedimentación	sedimentation
	sedimentar	(to) deposit (as sediment), (to) settle
SEDES	sede (f.)	seat (of power), headquarters
	la Santa Sede	the Holy *See*

English *seance* comes from the present participle of the French verb *seoir,* derived from SEDERE, so that it literally means a "sitting". The letter combination DL regularly became LL in Latin, so that the related noun for *chair,* *SEDLA—the etymological counterpart of English *settle*[5]—became SELLA:

SELLA	silla	seat, chair
	sillón	armchair

The past participle of SEDERE was SESSUS,[6] hence the related noun

SESSIO(N)	sesión	session

The **sed-* root is found in both Latin NIDUS (from *NISDUS) and English (via Germanic) *nest,* where the first element, NI—*ne,* is the same as in **nether**

---

[5] "A long wooden bench with a high back, often including storage space beneath the seat."
[6] See Section 1.3 for an explanation of the change in consonant D (SEDERE) to SS (SESSUS).

("lower", "down", *Nether*lands) and *beneath;* hence a nest is literally a place for birds to "sit down".

NIDUS	nido	*nest*
	anidar	(to) *nest,* (to) reside

Apart from SEDERE and SIDERE, there was an associated *causative* verb SEDARE, literally "to make someone sit down", e.g., to calm or *sedate* them. In an analogous fashion, the English verb *sit* has an associated causative verb *set.*

SEDARE	sedar	(to) calm, (to) sedate
	sedación	sedation
	sedante	sedative (adj. & n.)

In Vulgar Latin, a new verb form SEDENTARE was created, corresponding to the act of being seated, leading to:

SEDENTARE	sentar	(to) seat, (to) sit (transitive), (to) sit well with
sentada	sit-in, protest	
dar por sentado	(to) take for granted	
asentar	(to) set, (to) establish	
asentamiento	settlement	
asiento	seat	
el asiento *delantero /* *trasero*	front / back seat	

SEDERE and its active counterpart SIDERE combined with a range of prepositions to form compound verbs, in which those corresponding to SEDERE had more passive meanings, and those to SIDERE, more active ones. While in most cases the two compound forms *looked* alike, they were in fact distinguished in pronunciation by the nature (i.e., length) of their vowels, e.g., for the combinations with the preposition AD:

AD + SEDĒRE	→	ASSIDĒRE[7]	to be seated **near:** attend upon or assist
+ SĪDERE	→	ASSĪDERE	to sit **toward:** sit down

---

[7] The change of stem vowel ($E \rightarrow I$) reflects the regular "vowel weakening" of interior Latin short vowels, discussed in Section 1.3. Apart from the difference in vowel pronunciation, the word accent was on different syllables: AS•SI•DĒ•RE versus AS•SĪ•DE•RE.

where the line (macron) over the vowel indicates that it was a *long* vowel.

ASSESSOR	asesor	adviser, consultant	[*assessor*]
	asesoramiento	advice (esp. legal or professional)	
	asesorar	(to) advise, (to) consult (with)	
	asesoría	consultancy, consultant's office	
ASSIDUUS	asiduo	assiduous, frequent (e.g., contributor)	
	asiduidad	assiduity	
DE + SEDERE	DESIDERE	to be seated **away from:** sit idle	
+ SIDERE	DESIDERE	to sit **away from:** sink, deteriorate	
DESIDIA	desidia	apathy, laziness, carelessness	[† *desidiose*]

The Vulgar Latins created a neuter form DESIDIUM and, evidently inspired by the cautionary proverbs[8]

> An idle mind is the devil's workshop.

> Satan finds some mischief still, for idle hands to do.

came up with an altogether new meaning, that of "erotic desire". This then gave rise to:

DESIDIUM	deseo	desire, wish
	deseoso	desirous
	desear	(to) desire
	deseable	desirable
	indeseable	undesirable (person)

The similarity in form with English *desire* is (essentially) coincidental: *desire* comes from DESIDERARE, "to long for", which originally meant "waiting for what the *sidereal* bodies [i.e., stars] will bring" (or "pining for what they have taken away").[9]

DIS + SEDERE	DISSIDERE	to be seated **away from:** disagree
+ SIDERE	DISSIDERE	to sit **away from**

---

[8] A Spanish equivalent: *La ociosidad es la madre de todos los vicios* ("Idleness is the mother of all vices").

[9] Similarly, CONSIDERARE ("to *consider*") literally meant "to be with (i.e., examine attentively) the stars".

	disidir	(to) dissent[10]
	disidencia	dissidence
	disidente	dissident (adj. & n.)
IN + SEDERE	INSIDERE	to be seated **in** or **on:** be in occupation
+ SIDERE	INSIDERE	to sit **in** or **on:** occupy, be rooted in
INSIDIAE	insidia	deceit, trap or snare (pl.)
INSIDIOSUS	insidioso	insidious, deceitful
	insidiosamente	insidiously

An *insidious* person is thus literally one who lies or *sits* in wait, seeking to entrap.

OBS + SEDERE	OBSIDERE	to be seated **in front of:** occupy
+ SIDERE	OBSIDERE	to sit **in front of:** be*siege*
OBSESSIO(N)	obsesión	obsession
	obsesivo	obsessive
	obsesionar	(to) obsess, or become obsessed
	obseso	obsessive

The original Latin sense of *obsession* related to a military *siege* of a fortress, and this was the sense with which it entered English. Thus in his *History of King Richard III* (1513), Sir Thomas More could write

> They which were in the castell . . . sent also to the Earle of Richemonde to advertise [advise] hym of their sodeine [sudden] *obsession.*

Only in the seventeenth century did the (English) meaning shift to a siege of the mind (e.g., by the devil or an evil spirit), a meaning that had developed in Medieval (Ecclesiastical) Latin at a relatively early stage.

In the original sense, *obsess* and *obsession* have been replaced in both languages by other constructions derived from SEDERE:

	asediar	(to) *besiege*	(† *assiege*)
	asedio	*siege*	
PRAE + SEDERE	PRAESIDERE	to be seated **in front:** preside over, guard	

---

[10] *Dissent* is etymologically unrelated, coming instead from DIS-SENTIRE (lit. "to feel apart"). "To dissent" in Spanish is expressed far more commonly by *disentir.*

	presidir	(to) preside (over)	
PRAESIDENTEM (acc.)	presidente (m./f.)	president	(also *presi-denta*—f.)
	presidencia	presidency	
	presidencial	presidential	
	presidio	prison, penitentiary	[*presidio*]
	presidiario	convict	

PRAESIDENTEM is the present participle, so that *presidente—president* literally means "presiding" (one).

RE + SEDERE	RESIDERE	to **remain** sitting: *reside*
+ SIDERE	RESIDERE	to sink or settle **back** (or down)
	residir	(to) reside
RESIDENTEM (acc.)	residente	resident (adj. & n.)
	residencia	residence
	residencial	residential
RESIDUUM	residuo	residue, remainder
	residual	residual

A *resident* is thus one who remains sitting.

SUB + SIDERE	SUBSIDERE	to sink **under**: *subside*

This verb has been replaced in Spanish by *hundir* (from FUNDERE, "to pour", source of English *fusion* and *fondue*).

[hundir]	(to) subside, (to) sink
[hundimiento]	subsidence, sinking, collapse

The similar-sounding *subsidy* comes from the (otherwise unattested) composition of SUB with **SEDERE** and hence has the more passive meaning of "aid or support", i.e., something that is sitting underneath as opposed to something that actively sinks down. Its primary use in Latin was to refer to soldiers held in reserve ("behind the lines").

SUBSIDIUM	subsidio	subsidy (~ *subvención*)
	subsidiario	subsidiary
	subsidiar	(to) subsidize
		(~ *subvencionar*)
SUPER + SEDERE	SUPERSEDERE	to sit **above**: refrain from, omit
+ SIDERE	SUPERSIDERE	to sit **down** *on top of*

sobreseer	(to) stay a judicial case	[*supersede*]
sobreseimiento	stay of proceedings	[*surcease*]
sobreseimiento definitivo	dismissal (of a case)	

The two verbs also combined with the adjective POTIS to form verbs of possession:

POTIS + SEDERE	POSSIDERE	to be in **possession** of: *possess*
+ SIDERE	POSSIDERE	to take **possession** of
	poseer	(to) possess
	poseído (p.p.)	possessed (haunted or crazed)
POSSESSIO(N)	posesión	possession
	poseedor	possessor
	posesivo	possessive
	desposeer	(to) dispossess, (to) renounce (rights)

2. *Estar*

Unlike *ser, estar* has a sole parent, Latin STARE ("to stand"). Etymologically it corresponds to English *stay,* which was derived from the Old French equivalent of *estar.* STARE comes from the same Indo-European root **sta-* as English *stand.* Other English words derived from this root and arriving via Germanic, rather than Latin, include:

stud	place for breeding horses; male animal used for breeding
steed	horse (esp. a spirited one)
stool	small chair or footrest
standard	a flag or banner; normal, familiar, or usual
stead	the place occupied by another
steady	firm in position or place

Standard comes from Old French *estandart* (Modern French *étendard*), and the most widely held view is that it represents the Germanic *stand hard.* In those days of frequent pitched battles, each side would place its flag or banner, mounted on a pole, in the ground, which then became an immovable object to be seen by all and to be defended, i.e., it "stood hard". A contemporary account from the twelfth century suggests alternatively that the banner may have taken its name from the surrounding soldiers themselves who were "standing hard", for "it was there that valour took its stand to conquer or die". A minority see the origin as relating instead to the *extending* of the banner, i.e., derived from Latin EXTENDERE.

Whatever its precise origin, the initial use of *standard* was purely as a flag, banner, or ensign, and it is with this meaning that it passed from Anglo-Norman French to English in the twelfth century. Only several centuries later did it develop its other, now more common, meaning of "being of a specified norm or *standard*". This sense probably arose from the association of the royal *standard* (flag) with the (royal) source from which *standards* of weights and measurement were issued. Today both meanings continue in English: thus

to raise the *standard* of liberty in our battle for justice and equality

employs *standard* in its initial sense, whereas "to raise the *standard* of living" is more likely to be interpreted with its "normative" sense.

estándar (< Eng.)	standard (norm)
estandarte (< Fr.)	standard (flag or banner)
estandarizar	(to) standardize
estandarización	standardization

The large majority of **sta-* words have arrived in English via the Latin route. From the basic verb STARE and Latin root STA- came a whole host, including:

STARE	estar	(to) be	[*stay*]
	bienestar	well-being, welfare	
	estado de bienestar	welfare state	
STATUS	estado (p.p.)	status, state	
	malestar	discomfort, malaise	
	[declarar, decir]	(to) state	
	estatal	state (adj.)	
	statu quo[11]	status quo	
	estatus / status	status (economic, social)	(< Eng.)
	estante	shelf, bookcase	
	estantería	shelves, bookcase	
STATIO(N)	estación	station, season	
	estacional	seasonal	

---

[11] Note that it is *statu,* not *status. Statu* is pronounced as if it were spelled *estatu* and similarly for *status;* the latter is not recognized by the RAE but is nonetheless common.

estacionario	stationary
[papelería]	stationery store
[artículos de papelería]	stationery

English *stationery* initially referred to a shopkeeper—typically a bookseller—whose premises were *stationary*, as opposed to those of a peddler.

	estacionar	(to) station, (to) park
	estacionamiento	parking, parking lot
STATURA	estatura	stature, height
STATUA	estatua	statue
STABILIS	estable	stable (adj.)
	estabilidad	stability
	inestable	unstable
	inestabilidad	instability
	estabilizar	(to) stabilize
	desestabilizar	(to) destabilize
	estabilización	stabilization
	estabilizador (adj. & n.)	stabilizing, stabilizer
	establecer	(to) establish
	establecimiento	establishment
	restablecer	(to) reestablish (health, contact, etc.)
STABULUM	establo	stable (for animals, not only horses)

Modern Latin developed the word STATISTICUS in the seventeenth century from the Italian *statista* ("statesman") with the meaning of "relative to the state". In the mid-eighteenth century, its definition was expanded in Germany to the scientific measurement of social facts (German *Statistik*). *Statistics* arrived in English at the end of the eighteenth century, supplanting the previously used term *political arithmetic*.

estadista	statesman, stateswoman
estadística	statistic, statistics
estadístico	statistical

Medieval Latin STANTIA produced *stanza* in Italian ("standing or stopping place"), one of whose early meanings was "group of verses constituting the metric unity" of a poem or song. *Stanza* was introduced into English by Shakespeare in 1588 (*Love's Labour's Lost*) with its current English poetic sense. It had earlier been taken into French as *stance* and entered English in this form as well—initially as "standing place", subsequently as "golf *stance*", and only in the mid-twentieth century in the sense of "posture or attitude".

STANTIA	estancia	*stay* (sojourn), room, ranch, *estancia*
	[postura, posición]	*stance*
[STROPHA	estrofa]	stanza, strophe

Numerous Latin verbs were formed by prefixing prepositions to STARE, leading to many additional nouns and adjectives.

CIRCUM + STARE	CIRCUMSTARE	to stand **around:** be present, surround
	circunstancia	circumstance
	circunstancial	circumstantial
CONTRA + STARE	CONTRASTARE	to stand **against:** dispute, *contrast*
	contrastar	(to) contrast
	contraste	contrast
CUM + STARE	CONSTARE	to stand **with:** stand firm, be *constant*
	constar	(to) consist of, (to) be evident
CONSTANTIA	constancia	constancy
CONSTANTEM (acc.)	constante	constant (adj. & n.f.)
	constantemente	constantly
(< Fr.)	constatar	(to) confirm, (to) verify
	constatación	confirmation, verification

Cost also comes from CONSTARE, with the reduction NS → s frequent in "popular" words (Section 3.5, no. 6), the notion being that a price was "firmly fixed".

costar	(to) cost
costoso	costly
costo, coste, costa	cost, expense
costas del juicio	costs (judicial)
a costa de	at the expense of (gen. nonmonetary)

In terms of monetary cost, *costo* is the most common, *costa* the least (more commonly being found with the unrelated meaning of "*coast*", from COSTA, "rib").

DIS + STARE	DISTARE	to stand **away from:** be at a distance
	distar	(to) be [e.g., 80 km] distant from
DISTANTIA	distancia	distance
DISTANTEM (acc.)	distante	distant
	distanciar	(to) place at a distance, to separate

EX + STARE	EXSTARE	to stand **out:** appear, exist
EXSTANTEM (acc.)	[existente[12]]	*extant* (still in existence)
IN + STARE	INSTARE	to stand **in** or **on:** urge, press upon

BELLUM INSTAT

War is imminent. (Cicero)

	instar	(to) urge, (to) insist
INSTANTIA	instancia	application (request), instance (law)
	a instancia de	at the instance (request) of
	en primera instancia	in the first instance
	en última instancia	as a last resort
	[caso, ejemplo]	instance
INSTANTEM (acc.)	instante	instant
	instantáneo	instantaneous
	instantáneamente	instantaneously, instantly

Spanish *instar* preserves the original sense of Latin INSTARE, as do the expressions *a instancia de—at the instance of*. *Instant* arrived in English as an adjective with the meaning of "pressing or urgent",[13] a definition still found in many dictionaries.

OB + STARE	OBSTARE	to stand **in front of** or **against:** hinder, obstruct	
	obstar	(to) stand in the way, (to) hinder	
	[echar, expulsar]	(to) *oust*	(< OldFr. *oster*)
	obstáculo	obstacle	
NON OBSTANTE	no obstante	*non obstante* (notwithstanding[14]), nevertheless	
	obstaculizar	(to) hinder, (to) place obstacles in the way	

---

[12] From EX + SISTERE (see below).

[13] Thus, in the King James Version of the Bible: "And they were *instant* with loud voices, requiring that he might be crucified" (Luke 23:23). Modern versions generally replace "instant" with "urgent" or "insistent".

[14] Note that the *with-* in *withstand* maintains the archaic (original) definition of "against" (also found in *withhold* and *withdraw*), and hence *notwithstanding* is an "exact" translation of NON OBSTANTE. This is no coincidence: *notwithstanding* was "coined" by the English theologian John Wycliffe (c. 1330–1384) as a direct loan translation of the Latin expression.

OBSTETRIX, Latin for "midwife", also comes from this verb, i.e., she who *"stands in front of* the woman in childbirth to receive the baby".

OBSTETRICA	obstetricia	obstetrics
	obstétrico	obstetric
	obstetra (m./f.)	obstetrician
PRAE + STARE	**PRAESTARE**	to stand **in front:** stand out, excel

Latin PRAESTARE also incorporated meanings derived from the adverb PRAESTO ("at hand", "ready"), whose relation, if any, to the verb STARE is not clear. Hence other meanings of PRAESTARE included "to place at the disposition of", "to furnish", "to vouch for or guarantee", and (in Medieval Latin) "to lend". English formerly had a number of derived words—*prest, prestable, prestation,* etc.—but these are now found only in unabridged (or historical) dictionaries.

prestar	(to) lend	(Fr. *prêter*)
prestación	service(s) offered	
préstamo	loan	
prestamista	lender, moneylender	
prestatario	borrower	
presto	prompt, promptly, *presto* (right away, music)	
presteza	rapidity, promptness	

Spanish has no single verb corresponding to the reciprocal operation, i.e., *to borrow.*

pedir prestado ~	(to) borrow
tomar prestado	
RE + STARE	**RESTARE**	to stand **back:** *rest* (remain)

Spanish has taken the idea of "that which remains" to reformulate *restar* as "to subtract", i.e., one of the four basic arithmetic operations. English *rest* has (at least) three different meanings, each with its own origin: (a) cessation of work and period of relaxation; (b) remainder (corresponding to Spanish); and (c) a support for a lance. The first comes from Germanic, the second and third from Latin.

restar	(to) subtract, (to) take away, (to) remain[15]
resta	subtraction (~ *sustracción*)
resto	rest, remainder, leftovers or remains (pl.)

---

[15] In the sense of "being left": fifteen days *remain* before the deadline expires; it (only) *remains* to say; etc..

	restos mortales	mortal remains
	[descanso]	rest (relax)
	[descansar]	(to) rest (relax)
AD + RESTARE	arrestar	(to) arrest
	arresto	arrest
SUB + STARE	SUBSTARE	to stand **under:**
		be present, stand firm
SUBSTANTIA	sustancia	substance
	sustancial	substantial (important, essential)
	sustancioso	substantial (incl. "nourishing")
	sustantivo	substantive (incl. "noun")
	sustancialmente	substantially

These words can be spelled with or without the letter *b*, i.e., *substancia* or *sustancia,* although the latter is more common (and preferred by the RAE).

SUPER + STARE	SUPERSTARE	to stand **above** or **over**
	supérstite	surviving (e.g., spouse—legal term)
SUPERSTITIO(N)[16]	superstición	superstition
	supersticioso	superstitious

Superstitious is thus related to the idea of "standing over", though the exact sense is not clear—perhaps it had to do with "standing over in awe and amazement".

Just as the passive SEDERE had a counterpart SIDERE to express the action of sitting, SISTERE is the active counterpart to STARE, expressing "to cause to stand", "to place", "to stand still or firm". SISTERE was the basis of numerous compound verbs, including:

AD + SISTERE	ASSISTERE	to take a stand **near:**
		attend, *assist*
	asistir	(to) attend, (to) assist
	asistente (m./f.)	assistant, attendee
	asistenta	cleaning lady
	asistencia	attendance, assistance, assist (sports)

---

[16] SUPERSTITIO(N) was formed as a combination of SUPER and STATIO(N); the latter's *A* was a *short* vowel and hence became *I* in the compound word (Section 1.3).

Asistir—assist is frequently cited as an example of *falsos amigos,* as students are taught that they should translate English "assist" by *ayudar,* never by *asistir.*[17] In reality: (1) *asistir* can be, and not infrequently is, used in the sense of "ayudar"; while (2) *assist* can be, but rarely is, used in the sense of "to attend". The Spanish and English definitions are thus virtually identical, the only difference being that English has essentially chosen to ignore one of them.[18]

CUM + SISTERE	CONSISTERE	to stand **with:** stand firmly, halt, exist
	consistir	(to) consist (of, in)
	consistente	solid, firm, consistent
	consistencia	consistency, solidity
	inconsistente	weak, flimsy, unsubstantial
	inconsistencia	flimsiness, inconsistency
DE + SISTERE	DESISTERE	to stand **away from:** stop, *desist*
	desistir	(to) desist
EX + SISTERE	EXSISTERE	to step **out from:** emerge, become

EX LUXURIA EXSISTIT AVARITIA (Cicero)
From luxury is born avarice.

existir	(to) exist
existencia	existence, stock or supply (pl.)
existente	existent, extant
existencial	existential
existencialismo	existentialism
existencialista	existentialist
coexistir	(to) coexist
coexistencia	coexistence
preexistir	(to) preexist
preexistente	preexisting

IN + SISTERE	INSISTERE	to stand **in** or **on:** persist, *insist*
	insistir	(to) insist
	insistente	insistent
	insistencia	insistence
INTER + SISTERE	INTERSISTERE	to stop **in between:** pause
INTERSTITIUM	intersticio	interstice (gap)

---

[17] For example: Marion P. Holt and Julianne Dueber, *1001 Pitfalls in Spanish,* 3rd ed. (New York: Barron's Educational Series, 1997), 248.

[18] This was not always the case: in the nineteenth century, the English novelist William Makepeace Thackeray could write: "The dinner at which we have just assisted" (i.e., attended).

PER + SISTERE	PERSISTERE	to stand **for** (steadfastly): *persist,* remain
	persistir	(to) persist
	persistencia	persistence
	persistente	persistent
RE + SISTERE	RESISTERE	to stand **back**: oppose, *resist*
	resistir	(to) resist, (to) with*stand*
	resistencia	resistance, endurance
	resistente	resistant, strong, resisting
	resistor	resistor (electrical) (< Eng.)
	resistible	resistible
	irresistible	irresistible (also: unbearable [!])
SUB + SISTERE	SUBSISTERE	to stand **under**: stand firm, exist, *subsist*
	subsistir	(to) subsist (remain, live)
	subsistencia	subsistence

Another verb derived from STARE was STATUERE—"to place or set up", "to establish", "to decree"—whose past participle became English *statute:*

STATUERE	estatuir	(to) enact, (to) establish
	estatutario	statutory
STATUTUM	estatuto	statute

STATUERE joined with various prepositions to form other verbs and associated nouns. Reflecting the normal weakening of interior (short) vowels,[19] in these composites *A* became *I*: -STITUERE.

CON + STATUERE	CONSTITUERE	to set up **with**: establish, *constitute*
	constituir	(to) constitute
	constitución	constitution
	constitucional	constitutional
	constitutivo	constitutive (essential)
	constituyente (adj.)	constituent (≠ voter)
	[elector]	constituent (voter)
	[distrito electoral]	constituency (voting district)

---

[19] As discussed in Section 1.3. The compound verbs with STARE (e.g., CONSTARE) avoided this fate, since the stem vowel of STĀRE was long.

DE + STATUERE	DESTITUERE	to set **far away:** forsake, abandon
	destituir	(to) dismiss or remove (office, job)
	destitución	dismissal, removal from office
	[desprovisto]	destitute
IN + STATUERE	INSTITUERE	to set up **in:** establish, *institute,* instruct
	instituir	(to) institute
	institución	institution
	institucional	institutional
	institucionalizar	(to) institutionalize
	instituto	institute
	institutriz	governess
PRO + STATUERE	PROSTITUERE	to place **in front of:** offer publicly, expose
	prostituir	(to) prostitute
	prostitución	prostitution
	prostituta	prostitute
	prostíbulo	brothel
RE + STATUERE	RESTITUERE	to put **back** (in its original place or state): restore, *restitute*
	restituir	(to) restitute
	restitución	restitution
SUB + STATUERE	SUBSTITUERE	to put or place **under:** *substitute*
	sustituir	(to) substitute, (to) replace
	sustitución	substitution, replacement (act)
	sustituto	substitute, replacement (person)

These words can also be spelled with *b—substituir,* etc.

Finally, a standing still or stoppage (-STITIUM) of the sun (SOL) was a

SOLSTITIUM   solsticio   solstice

while a much later (fourteenth century) use in connection with ARMA ("weapons") provided

ARMISTITIUM   armisticio   armistice

Food and Animals

We treat these two topics together because animals frequently wind up being food, in which case they often (but not always) are given different names. In English, for example, *fish* is *fish*, whether dead or alive, whereas Spanish distinguishes between *pez* and *pescado*. Conversely, in English one does not generally eat *calf* but rather *veal*, while in Spanish *ternera* functions for both.

We begin with (vegetarian) food.

Food and Drink

Alimento	**Food,** nourishment, *aliment*	
—alimentar	—(to) feed, (to) nourish, (to) aliment	
—alimentación	—feeding, nourishment, alimentation	
comer	(to) eat	
—comida	—food, meal	
—comedor	—dining room, (heavy) eater	[*comedo*]
—comestible	—*comestible* (*edible*), *comestibles* (foodstuffs—*pl.*)	
—comensal[1]	—table companion, *commensal*	
—comezón (f.)	—itch, itching	
hambre (f.)	hunger, *famine*	
—tengo hambre	—I am hungry	
—hambriento	—hungry, starved, *famished*	
sed	thirst	
—tengo sed	—I am thirsty	
—sediento	—thirsty	
desayuno	breakfast	[*dinner*]

---

[1] *Comensal* is unrelated to *comer*, as it comes from CUM + MENSA, the latter the source of Spanish *mesa* ("table"). The biological definition, shared with English *commensal*, is that of an organism participating in "a symbiotic relationship between two organisms in which one derives some benefit while the other is unaffected".

—desayunar	—(to) breakfast	[*dine*]
—ayuno	—fast, fasting	[*jejune*]
—ayunar	—(to) fast	
—yeyuno	—*jejunum* (second section of small intestine)[2]	
almuerzo	lunch	[*morsel*]
—almorzar	—(to) lunch	
cena	dinner, supper	[*cenacle*]
—cenar	—(to) have dinner or supper	
—la Última Cena	—the Last Supper	

Desayuno—almuerzo—cena is the most common series of names for the three principal meals. For some, however, *almuerzo* is "breakfast", while for others *comida* can be either "lunch" or "dinner".

Desayunar means literally to "break the fast". Students who know French often have trouble with *desayuno,* since French *déjeuner* now corresponds to "lunch", having been replaced in its original sense by *petit déjeuner*. French also formed a second word from the same source, *dîner*—originally meaning "to take the morning meal"—which gave rise to English *dinner*.

plato	*plate*, dish (container or contents), course (meal)	
—primer plato	—starter (first course)	
—plato fuerte	—main course	
—platillo	—saucer, small dish, cymbal (~ *címbalo*)	
—platillo volador (volante)	—flying saucer	
—plata	—silver, money (Amer.)	
—platero	—silversmith	
entremés	hors d'oeuvre, *entremets* (side dish), short farce	[*intermission*]
—entrometer ~ entremeter	—(to) insert, (to) place between, (to) meddle	[*intromit, intermit*]
—intermitente	—*intermittent*, blinker (auto)	
manjar	food, dish, delicacy	[*manger, mangy*]
—manjar blanco	—*blancmange* (sweetened milk pudding)	

---

[2] I.e., the "fasting" intestine, so called because when dissections are performed, it is invariably found to be empty.

cuchillo	knife	[*cutlery*]
cuchara	spoon	[*cochlea*]
—cucharada	—spoonful	
—cucharilla	—teaspoon	
—cucharadita	—teaspoonful	
—cucharón	—ladle	
tenedor	fork	(< verb *tener*)
colador	strainer, *colander*	
—colar	—(to) strain, (to) slip or sneak in	[*percolate*]
escurridor	colander	[*ex + corridor*]
—escurrir	—(to) drain off, (to) slip away	[*excursion*]
—escurreplatos	dish rack	
—escurridizo	slippery (eel, soap, floor, idea, person)	
servilleta	napkin, *serviette*	

Bebida	**Beverage,** drink	
beber	(to) drink, (to) *imbibe*	[*bibulous, beer*]
—biberón	—baby bottle	[*bib*]
tomar	(to) take, (to) drink (esp. Amer.)	
—toma	—taking, capture, dose, intake, outlet (elec.)	
—toma de conciencia	—awareness, realization	
—toma de posesión	—inauguration (taking office)	
agua	water	[*aqua*]
—agua dulce	—fresh water	
—agua salada	—salt water	
—aguafiestas	—killjoy, wet blanket, spoilsport	
—aguardiente	—spirit, firewater	[*ardent* water]
—acuático	—*aquatic*	
—acuario	—*aquarium*, Aquarius (constellation)	
—acueducto	—*aqueduct*	
—acuarela	—water color, *aquarelle*	
—paraguas	—umbrella (for rain)	(parar³ + aguas)

---

³ The first component—*para* from *parar* ("to ward off or *parry*")—is found also in *parasol* (English/Spanish) and *parachute* (Spanish *paracaídas*).

aperitivo	*aperitif,* appetizer	
cacao	cacao, *cocoa*	
café	*coffee* (beverage, plant), *café*	
—café con leche	—coffee with milk	
—cafeína	—*caffeine*	
—(café) descafeinado	—decaf, decaffeinated (coffee)	
—cafetera	—coffeepot, coffeemaker	
—cafetería	—coffee shop, snack bar	[*cafeteria*]
—cafetero	—coffee (adj.), coffee grower or seller (m./f.)	
cerveza	beer	
—cervecería	—bar, alehouse, brewery	
chocolate	chocolate	
jerez (m.)	*sherry*	
ron (< Eng.)	*rum*	
sidra	*cider* (alcoholic)	
té	*tea* (beverage, plant)	
—tetera	—teapot, teakettle	
vid	vine, grapevine	[*vise*]
—viticultura	—*viticulture* (cultivation of grapes)	
vino	*wine*	
—vino tinto	—red wine	[*tinted*]
—vino blanco	—white wine	
—vino rosado	—rosé (wine)	
—viña ~ viñedo	—*vineyard*	
—viñeta [4]	—*vignette,* individual drawing in a comic strip, cartoon (political)	
—vendimia	—grape harvest, *vintage* [5]	
—vinagre	—*vinegar*	[*acrid wine*]
—vinagreta	vinaigrette	
jugo ~ zumo	juice	
—enjugar [6]	—(to) wipe off (tears, dishes, debt, etc.)	
néctar	nectar	

---

[4] Initially a decorative design in the form of *vine* tendrils.
[5] In the limited sense of "the harvesting of a grape crop".
[6] Literally "to remove the juice" (< EX-SUCUS).

botella	*bottle*	
—botellero	—bottle or wine rack	[*butler*]
—embotellar	—(to) bottle, (to) bottle up, (to) cause a bottleneck	
—embotellamiento	—bottleneck, traffic jam, gridlock	
copa	*cup*, glass (generally having stem and foot)	
—copo	—flake (snow, dust, etc.)	
—copete	—tuft or forelock, crest (bird, mountain), topping	
taza	cup (with handle), toilet bowl	[*demitasse*]
vaso	glass, vessel (anatomical)	[*vase*]
—vasija	—*vessel* (container for liquids)	
—envasar	—(to) bottle, (to) put in a container	
—envase	—container (package, bottle, can, sack)	

Miscelánea	**Miscellanea**	
batería de cocina	pots and pans	
cacerola	*casserole*, saucepan (~ *cazuela*)	
cacharro	earthenware pot or jar; crockery (pl.), rattletrap (vehicle)	
marmita	*marmite*, pot	
olla	pot	[*olla, olio*]
—olla a/de presión	—pressure cooker	
—olla podrida	—olla podrida (seasoned stew of meat and vegetables)	
—popurrí	—*potpourri*[7]	
paella	shallow pan, *paella*	[*patella*]
sartén (f.)	frying pan	
chupar	(to) suck, (to) to soak up or absorb	
dieta (1)	*diet*	

[7] *Olla podrida* and *potpourri* are equivalent expressions, both literally meaning "rotten (*putrid*) *pot*". The original idea seems to have been Spanish, which the French then took and simply translated before exporting it to English (and back to Spanish). In all three languages, "potpourri" now refers not to culinary conconctions but to various mixtures of diverse items.

—dieta (2)[8]	—per *diem* allowance (gen. pl.),
	diet (legislative body)
—la dieta de	—the Diet of Worms (1521)
Worms	
—una dieta de	—a diet of worms
gusanos	
—dietética	—dietetics (study of nutrition as it
	relates to health)
—dietético	—dietetic, dietary
—dietista	—dietitian
—dietario	—family account book
digestión	digestion
—digerir	—(to) *digest*
—digesto	—digest (esp. legal)
—indigestión	—indigestion
ebrio	drunk, *inebriated*
—ebriedad	—drunkenness, *inebriation,*
	inebriety
—embriagar	—(to) *inebriate*, (to) intoxicate
—embriagador,	—inebriating, intoxicating
embriagante	
—embriaguez	—drunkenness, *inebriation*
sobrio	*sober,* temperate, moderate
—sobriedad	—sobriety, moderation

The words that come under Spanish *ebrio* are all ultimately derived from Latin EBRIUS ("drunk"), the root of English *inebriate*. In Latin, the opposing state was SOBRIUS (literally "not EBRIUS"). Also popular in this context are *borracho* and *emborrachar,* arising from the perceived similarity in nature between the fluid contents of a *borracha* (leather wine bottle) and those of a *borracho.*

borracho	drunk, rum-soaked (e.g., cake),
(adj. & n.)	drunkard

---

[8] *Dieta* (1) comes from Latin DIAETA ("mode of living", "diet"), itself from Greek. In Medieval Latin, AE became E, and hence DIAETA became DIETA, whereby it came to assume various meanings more appropriate to the unrelated word DIES ("day"): day's march, day's work, daily liturgy, etc. The notion of a legislative assembly arose from the idea of a "day's" sitting. The German equivalent is found in *Reichstag* and *Bundestag,* where *Tag* is German for "day".

—emborrachar	—(to) make drunk, (to) get drunk	
—borrachera	—drunkenness, spree	
lamer	(to) lick, (to) *lap* (tongue, waves)	[*lambent*]
masticar	(to) chew, (to) *masticate*	
—mascar	—(to) chew, (to) mumble	
—papel maché	—*papier-mâché* (~ *cartón piedra*)	
—mascullar	—(to) mumble, (to) mutter	
caldo	broth, bouillon, juices (pl.)—incl. wine, olive oil	[*chowder*]
—cálido	—hot (climate), warm (temperature, reception, color)	(Fr. *chaud*)
—caldera	—boiler, *cauldron* (*caldron*), *caldera*	
—caldero	—kettle (= *caldera pequeña*)	
—caldear	—(to) heat up (room, spirits—not food)	
—escaldar	—(to) *scald* (incl. "heat liquid almost to boiling")	(Lat. EX-CALDARE)
gazpacho	gazpacho (cold soup) (< Sp.)	
helado	ice cream	[*jelly*]
leche (f.)	milk	
—leche pasteurizada	—*pasteurized* milk	
—productos lácteos	—dairy products	
—láctico	—lactic	
—lactar	—(to) suckle, (to) nurse	[*lactate*]
—lactancia	—lactation	
—lechuga	—*lettuce*[9]	
manteca	fat, lard	
—mantequilla	—butter	
mayonesa	mayonnaise	
mermelada	*marmalade,* jam	("honey apple")
mostaza	*mustard*	
nata[10]	cream, scum (filmy surface layer)	[*mat*]

---

[9] The name arose from the milky juice associated with the lettuce plant.

[10] *Cream* represents the *mat* or "scum" on top of the milk: *scum* and *skim* are etymologically the same word—one *skims* something by removing the *scum*.

—natillas (pl.)	—custard	
—desnatar	—(to) cream, (to) skim (~ *descremar*)	
—leche desnatada	—skim (skimmed) milk (~ *leche descremada*)	
pan	bread	[*panini*]
—panadero	—baker	
—panadería	—bakery	[*pantry*]
—panera	—breadbasket, breadbox	[*pannier*]
—empanar	—(to) bread	
—empanada	—turnover, pasty, *empanada*	
—pan tostado ~ tostada	—*toast*	
—tostar	—(to) *toast,* (to) roast (coffee)	
—tostador, tostadora	—*toaster*	
puré	*purée*	
queso	*cheese*	(both < Lat. CASEUS)
—quesadilla	—*quesadilla* (cheese-filled tortilla)	
sopa	*soup*	
yogur	yogurt	

Condimento	**Condiment,** seasoning	
condimentar	(to) season, (to) flavor	
sazonar	(to) *season* (with time, spices)	
—sazón (f.)	—ripeness or maturity, *seasoning*	
—a la sazón	—at that time, then	
—desazón	—discomfort, anxiety, uneasiness	
anís	anise (herb), anise seed, anisette (liqueur)	
azafrán	*saffron*	
canela	cinnamon	
cardamomo	cardamom	
cilantro, culantro	*coriander, cilantro*	
clavo	*clove,* nail	
comino	*cumin*	
guindilla	cayenne pepper, red pepper	
jengibre	*ginger*	

nuez moscada	*nutmeg*	[*nut* smelling like *musk*]
páprika	paprika (~ *pimentón*)	
picante	hot, spicy, *piquant*	
pimiento	pepper, *pimento/pimiento* (plant)	[*pigment*]
—pimiento verde (rojo)	—green (red) pepper	
—pimienta	—pepper, *pimento/pimiento* (condiment)	
—pimienta negra (blanca)	—black (white) pepper	
—pimentón	—ground red pepper, paprika	
—pimentero	—pepper shaker	
sal (f.)	*salt*	
—salar	—(to) salt	
—salado	—salted, salty, witty	[*salad*]
—salino	—saline	
—salina	—salt mine, salt works (pl.)	
—salsa	—*sauce*, gravy, *salsa* (music)	
—ensalada	—*salad*	
—salchicha	—*sausage*	
—salchichón	—*salami* (spiced and salted sausage)	
—salero	—salt shaker	
—soso	—lacking in salt, without taste, insipid	[so-so[11]]
—insulso	—insipid or dull (meal, person)	
—salario[12]	—salary (n.), wage	
—salarial	—salary or wage (adj.)	
—aumento salarial	—salary or wage increase	
—salpicar	—(to) sprinkle, (to) splash, (to) spatter	(sal + picar)
—salpicadura	—splash(ing), splatter(ing)	
—salpicadero	—dashboard	(lit. "sprinkled" with instruments)
tomillo	*thyme*	
vainilla	*vanilla*	

---

[11] The identity in form with English *so-so* is coincidental; Spanish *soso* comes from Latin insulsus ("unsalted"), as does *insulso*.

[12] From salarium, the allowance paid to Roman soldiers for purchasing salt (sal), hence **salary**.

Verdura	**Vegetable,** greens	[*verdure*]
hortaliza	vegetable	[*horticulture*]
legumbre	legume, vegetable	
alcachofa	*artichoke*	
berenjena	eggplant	
brócoli / brécol / bróculi	*broccoli*	
cebolla	onion	[*chive*]
col (f.)	cabbage, *cole, kale*	
—ensalada de col	—*coleslaw*	[*slaw = salad*]
—coles de Bruselas	—*Brussels* sprouts	
coliflor (f.)	*cauliflower*	
espárrago	*asparagus*	
espinaca	*spinach*	
estofar	(to) *stew*	
—estofado (p.p.)	—*stew*	
—est**u**fa	—*stove* (for heating), heater	
garbanzo	*garbanzo* (chick pea)	
guisante	pea	
guisar	(to) cook, (to) stew, (to) cook up	[*guise, disguise*]
—guisado (p.p.) ~ guiso	—stew	
haba	*fava* bean (also called: broad bean, horse bean)	
—habichuela	—bean	
frijol / fríjol / frejol / fréjol [13]	bean, *frijol(e)*	[bot. ***Phaseolus vulgaris***]
judía[14]	bean	

---

[13] *Frijol* (and variants), *judía, habichuela,* and *alubia* are all words for various types of beans from the plant known as *Phaseolus vulgaris* ("common bean"). *Frijol* is more common in the Americas. Numerous other regional names exist, including *poroto, caraota, chaucha, ejote,* and *vainita.* English names for *Phaseolus vulgaris* include: kidney bean, string bean, green bean, snap bean, pinto bean, and haricot.

[14] *Judía* also means "Jewish" (female adjective or noun), and there have been numerous and varied explanations as to how it came to be used in this context. To cite just one: "quizá porque al cocerlas salen en seguida del agua (a diferencia de los garbanzos, que permanecen en el fondo), tal como el judío no se deja bautizar . . ." (Corominas and Pascual, 3:533): "perhaps because when the beans are cooked they immediately leave the water [presumably meaning that they float on the surface] (as compared to chickpeas, which remain at the bottom), similar to the Jew who does not permit himself to be baptized." Others have attempted to explain *judía* (bean) as having evolved from a completely different (Arabic or Latin) word.

alubia	bean	
lenteja	*lentil*	
nabo	tur*nip*	[*napi*form]
patata	*potato*	(< Amer.)
—patatas fritas	—French *fries*	
—papa (1)	—potato	
—papas fritas	—French *fries*	
—papa (2)	—*pap* (bland object; semiliquid food—pl.)	
—ni papa	—not a bit, nothing (used with *saber, entender*)	
—papilla	—*pap*, mush	
—papada	—double chin	(< too much pap !)
—empapar	—(to) soak, (to) soak up	
—papa (3) (m.)	—Pope, *papa* (father), dad	(Gk. PAPPAS)
—papá (m.)	—*papa, poppa,* dad	(< Fr.)
pepino	cucumber	[*pepino*]
—pepinillo	—gherkin	
pepita	*pip* (fruit seed, bird disease) (bird disease)	
perejil	*parsley*	
puerro	leek	[bot. *Allium* **porrum**]
rábano	radish	[bot. **Raphanus** *sativus*]
—rebanar[15]	—(to) slice	
—rebanada	—slice (esp. of bread)	
zanahoria	carrot	

Cereal / *Cereal*

arroz	*rice*	
avena	oats	[bot. **Avena sativa**]
cebada	barley	
—cebar	—(to) fatten, (to) bait (fishhook, trap), (to) prime	
—cebo	—feed, bait, lure	(Lat. CIBUS, "food")

---

[15] Originally *rabanar* (as it still is in Portuguese), apparently from the manner in which radishes are sliced.

centeno	rye	[*cent*; see Section 4.3]
maíz	*maize*, corn	
—maizal	cornfield	
malta (< Eng.)	*malt*	
mijo / millo	*millet, mealie* (corn)	
sorgo	*sorghum*	
trigo	wheat	[*triticale, trite*]

Hongo	***Fungus,*** mushroom
champiñón	edible mushroom, *champignon*
seta	mushroom (with "hat")
trufa	*truffle* (edible fungi; chocolate)

Fruta	***Fruit*** (edible)	
—fruta prohibida	—forbidden fruit	
—fruto	—*fruit* (botanical, result, offspring)	(Lat. FRUCTUS)
—frutos secos (pl.)	—nuts, almonds, peanuts, etc.	
—frutal	—fruit (adj.), fruit tree	
—disfrutar	—(to) enjoy, (to) have the benefit of, (to) make use of	
—disfrute	—enjoyment, benefit	
—fructífero	—fruitful, fruit-bearing, fructuous (~ *fructuoso*)	
—infructuoso	—fruitless, unfruitful, *infructuous*	
—usufructo	—*usufruct* (legal)	
aguacate	*avocado, alligator pear, aguacate*	

The name of the fruit of the tropical American tree *Persea americana* has undergone a series of "folkloric" deformations, going all the way back to pre-Spanish times in Central America.

aguacate (Del náhuatl *ahuacatl* 'aguacate; testículo', de *ahuatl* 'encino, roble', o de *ahuacacuahuitl*, literalmente = 'arbol de los testículos', debido a que se usaba como afrodisíaco.)[16]

---

[16] From the *Diccionario breve de mexicanismos* (by Guido Gómez de Silva), available on the website of the Academia Mexicana de la Lengua.

aguacate (From Nahuatl [Aztec] *ahuacatl* "aguacate; testicle", from *ahuatl* "holm oak", "oak", or from *ahuacacuahuitl,* literally = "tree of the testicles", due to its frequent use as an aphrodisiac.)

Ahuacatl became Spanish *aguacate,* with a likely influence of *agua.* A (presumably humorous) competing version arose, *abogado*—pronounced, as today, [*avogado*]—i.e., "lawyer". Before dying out in Spanish, this form propagated itself to a number of European languages, including French (where to this day *avocat* means both "lawyer" and "avocado") and English (initially *avogato*). The *avocado pear,* as it is sometimes still called, was subsequently transformed into the *alligator pear,* from a belief that the fruit was cultivated in alligator-infested regions.

cacahuete	peanut	
∼ maní[17]		
calabaza	squash, pumpkin, gourd, *calabash*	
—calabacín	—zucchini	
cereza[18]	*cherry* (fruit), *cerise* (color)	
—cerezo	—*cherry* (tree and wood)	
coca	coca (plant, leaves), cocaine	[*Coca*-Cola]
—cocaína	—cocaine	
coco	*coco*nut, coconut tree	
fresa	strawberry (fruit, plant, color)	
kiwi	kiwi (bird and fruit)	
limón	*lemon,* lemon tree (∼ *limonero*)	
—limonada	—*lemonade*	
mandarina	tangerine, *mandarin* orange	
—mandarín	—mandarin (high public official or bureaucrat, Chinese language)	
—clementina	—clementine (seedless, deeper-red mandarin orange)	
manzana[19]	apple, city block	[*manzanita*]
—manzano	—apple tree	
—manzanilla	—camomile, camomile tea, *manzanilla* (pale dry sherry)	

---

[17] Plural: *maníes* or *manises.*

[18] English *cherry* should be *cherris* but the "s" was mistaken as a sign of a plural, hence the present form. A similar explanation accounts for the disappearance of the final "s" in *sherry,* earlier *sherris* (Spanish *jerez*).

[19] From a variety of apple known as MALA MAT(T)IANA, whose name apparently goes back to Gaius Matius, a first-century BC writer on gastronomy, renowned for his apples.

melocotón	peach	[*melon* + *quince*]
—melocotonero	—peach tree	
—durazno	—peach	(< *duro,* "hard")
—duraznero	—peach tree	
melón	melon	
mora (1)[20]	*mulberry* (fruit), blackberry	(Lat. MORA)
—moral (1)	—black *mulberry* (tree)	
—morado	—violet or *mulberry* (color)	
—mora (2)	—delay (esp. in payment), *mora* (poetry)	(unrelated)
—moral (2) (adj. & n.f.)	moral (adj.), ethics, morals, morale	(unrelated)
—moraleja	—moral (of a story)	
—moralidad	—morality	
—moralista (adj. & n.)	—moralistic, moralist	
—moralizar	—(to) moralize	
naranja	*orange* (fruit), *orange* (color—m.)	(see appendix to Section 4.2)
—naranjo	—*orange* tree	
nuez	*nut,*[21] walnut, Adam's apple	[*nux* vomica]
—nogal	—walnut (color, tree, wood)	
—núcleo	—nucleus	
—nuclear	—nuclear	
pera	*pear*	
—peral	—*pear* tree	
piña	*pine*apple, *pine* cone	
—piña colada	—piña colada	["strained *pineapple*"]
—piñata	—piñata	
—apiñado	—crammed or packed together (like a *pine* cone)	
—pino	—*pine* (tree, wood)	
—pinar	—pine grove or forest	
plátano (1)	*plantain* (1), banana	(Eng. < Sp.)
—banana	—banana	

---

[20] The *mul* in English *mulberry* comes from Latin MORUM ("mulberry"), the source as well for Spanish *mora*. In Old English, it was *morberie*.

[21] *Nut* is a Germanic cognate of Latin NUX (acc. NUCEM), the origin of Spanish *nuez*. The diminutive NUCLEUS (originally NUCULEUS) was a small nut, hence "kernel".

—plátano (2)	—*plane* tree	[genus *Platanus*]
—llantén	—*plantain* (2)—small plant (often weed)	[genus *Plantago*]
pomelo	grapefruit (fruit, tree), *pomelo* (~ *toronja*)	
sandía	watermelon	[*Sind;* see Section 4.2]
tomate	*tomato*	
uva	grape	
—úvula	—uvula	("small grape")

El postre	Dessert	[*post*-meal]
a *la* postre	in the end	
repostería	pastry shop, pastry making	[*repository*]
—repostero	—pastry cook, confectioner	
caramelo	*caramel,* candy	
chicle	chewing gum, *chicle*	[*Chiclet s*®]
dulce (adj. & n.)	sweet, mild, *dulcet,* candy or sweet, *dolce* (adv.)	
—dulzura	—gentleness, sweetness	[*douceur*]
—endulzar	—(to) sweeten, (to) *dulcify* (~ *edulcorar, dulcificar*)	
flan	flan, (caramel) custard	
galleta	cookie, biscuit	(Fr. *galette*)
miel (f.)	honey	[*mellifluous*]
—melaza	—*molasses*	
pastel	cake, pie, *pastry, pastel* (adj. & n.)	
—pastelería	—pastry shop, pastries	
—pasta	—*paste, pasta, pastry* dough	
—pasta de dientes	—toothpaste (~ *dentífrico, pasta dental*)	
tarta	*tart* (pastry), cake	
torta	cake, *torte*	
—tortilla	—omelet, tortilla	

Caloría	*Calorie*	
—calor	—heat, warmth	
—caluroso	—hot, warm (temperature, or reception)	

—escalofrío	—shiver, shudder (gen. pl.)	(< ex + calor + frío)
grasa	fat	[foie *gras*]
hidrato de carbono	*carbohydrate*	
proteína	protein	

Animals

Several animals—*turkeys, peacocks, parrots, donkeys*—are considered separately in the appendix to this section.

Gatos y perros	**Cats and Dogs**	
perro	dog	
—perrera	—kennel, dog pound	
—perrito	—puppy (~ *cachorro*), small dog	
—perrito caliente	—hot dog	
—ladrar	—(to) bark	
—ladrido	—bark, barking	
lobo	wolf	
zorro	fox	[*Zorro*]
—zorra[22]	—vixen (female fox), harlot	
gato	*cat*	
—a gatas	—on all fours	
—gato montés	—wildcat	[*mountain cat*]
—miau	—meow	
~ maullido		
—maullar	—(to) meow	
—felino	—feline	
jaguar	jaguar	
león / leona	*lion / lioness*	
—leonera	—lion's cage, untidy room	
leopardo[23]	leopard, pard	

---

[22] The initial meaning of *zorro / zorra* was apparently that of a lazy or disreputable person (of either sex), before being applied to the animal whose name was a "taboo" (in a somewhat analogous fashion, in French the name for fox is *renard,* from the cunning lead character in the medieval stories of *Reynard the Fox*).

[23] The leopard was initially thought to be a hybrid of a lion (LEO) and a panther (PARDUS), hence LEOPARDUS. In Spanish, *pardo* came to be interpreted as an adjective referring to the *color* of the animal.

—pardo	—brown, dark gray
pantera	*panther*
tigre	*tiger,* jaguar (Amer.)
—tigresa	—tigress, seductive woman

Caballos y vacas   Horses and Cows

caballo	horse	
—caballero	—*cavalier,* knight, gentleman, *chevalier, caballero*	
—caballero andante	—knight-errant	
—caballeroso	—*chivalrous,* gentlemanly	
—caballerosidad	—*chivalry,* gentlemanliness	
—caballería	—*cavalry, chivalry* (system of knighthood; medieval cavalry)	
—caballeresco	—*chivalric,* knightly, *chivalrous*	[rare *chivalresque*]
—caballeriza	—stable (~ *cuadra*)	
—cabalgadura	—riding animal, mount (~ *montura*)	
—cabalgar	—(to) ride (on horseback)	
—cabalgata	—*cavalcade,* procession	
—caballa[24]	—mackerel	
—caballete	—easel,[25] trestle	
poni (< Eng.)	*pony*	
—potro	—colt, horse (gymnastics), rack (torture)	[*puerile*]
—potra	—filly	
yegua	mare	
—ecuestre	—*equestrian*	
—equitación	—equitation (art and practice of horseback riding)	
buey	ox, steer, bullock	[*beef*]
—bovino	—*bovine*	
—bistec / bife	—*steak, beefsteak*	(< Eng.)

[24] Initially applied to "flying fish", then (due to a perceived similarity in appearance) to the mackerel.

[25] In an analogous manner, the source of English *easel* is Dutch *ezel,* the Dutch word coming from Latin ASELLUS ("little donkey").

—rosbif	—*roast beef*	(< Eng.)
filete	*fillet*	
res (f.)	head (a single animal), esp. of cattle[26]	
—carne de res	—meat (generally bovine)	
toro	bull	[*Taurus*]
vaca	cow	
—carne de vaca	—beef	
—vacunación	—*vaccination*	
—vacuna	—*vaccine, vaccinia* (cowpox)	
—vacunar	—(to) *vaccinate*	
—vacuno	—bovine (~ *bovino*)	
—vaquero	—cowboy/cowgirl (f.), blue jeans (pl. ~ *tejanos*)	
—mugir	—(to) moo (or bellow, for a *toro*)	
—mugido (p.p.)	—moo, bellow	
—ubre (f.)	—udder	(Lat. UBER)
—ex**uber**ante[27]	—lush, abundant, *exuberant* (plentiful)	
—exuberancia	—abundance, *exuberance*	
ternero	calf (~ *becerro*)	
—ternera	—veal, female calf	[*tender*loin]
hamburguesa	*hamburger,* female resident of Hamburg	
—hamburguesa con queso	—*cheeseburger*	

Ovejas y cabras	**Sheep and Goats**	
oveja	sheep, ewe (female sheep)	
—ovino	—ovine (relating to sheep)	
cordero	lamb (animal and meat; also *carne de cordero*)	
lana	wool	
—lanolina	—*lanolin*	[wool + *oil*]

[26] *Res* refers to any four-footed domesticated animal and comes from Latin RES ("thing", "property")—source of English *re* and *rebus,* and from which the adjective *real* was derived. The semantic evolution "property" → "movable possession" → "livestock" parallels that of *capital* ("wealth or property") → *chattel* ("movable personal property") → *cattle.*

[27] *Exuberante* and *exuberant* literally mean "from the breast (or *udder*)", *udder* being the Germanic cognate of Latin UBER (source of Spanish *ubre*).

—lanudo ~ lanoso	—woolly, fleecy, *lanose*	
pastor	shepherd, pastor (minister)	
—pastor alemán	—German shepherd (dog)	
—pastoral	—pastoral (of pastors, shepherds, or rural life), *pastorale*	
—pastoril	—pastoral (of shepherds or rural life)	
—pacer	—(to) *pasture*, (to) graze	
—pasto[28]	—*pasture* (grass, herbs, field), *pasturage,* fodder	[*repast*]
borrego	yearling lamb, "sheep" (timid, weak, submissive person)	
—borra	—coarse wool, fluff, dregs	
—borroso	—blurred, fuzzy (indistinct)	
—borrón	—inkblot, blemish, rough sketch	
—borrón y cuenta nueva	—"clean slate", "let bygones be bygones"	
—borrar	—(to) erase, (to) rub out, (to) delete (computer)	
—borrador	—eraser, rough draft	
cabra	goat	[*cabretta*]
—cabra montés	—*mountain* goat	
—cabrito	—kid (suckling goat)	
—cabrón	—billy goat (~ *macho cabrío*), cuckold (+ other fig. senses)	
—cabrero	—goatherd	
—cabrear	—(to) annoy, (to) make angry	
—cabriola	—*capriole,* leap, *caper*	
—Capricornio	—*Capricorn*	("goat horn")
chivo	kid (weaned), goat (not yet mature)	
—chivo expiatorio	—scapegoat (biblical and figurative)	[*expiatory* goat]
gamuza (< camuza)	*chamois* (agile goat, soft leather), *shammy*	

[28] Hence the *antipasto—before* the *pasto,* i.e., "appetizer"—found in Italian restaurants, which thus has nothing to do with *pasta* (cognate with *paste*).

Cerdos y lechones	Pigs and Piglets	
cerdo	pig, hog	
—cerda	—sow (female pig), bristle, horsehair	
—(carne de) cerdo	—pork	
chuleta	cutlet, chop	
jamón	ham	[*gammon*]
puerco	pig	[*pork*]
—puerco espín	—*porcupine*	[*spiny pork*]
—porcino	—porcine (relating to pigs)	
—porquería	—dirt, filth, junk food	
—tuerca[29]	—nut (as in *nuts and bolts*)	(OldSp. **puerca**)
—porcelana	—porcelain, china	
lechón (-ona)	piglet, suckling pig	(from *leche*)
cochino	pig	(Fr. *cochon*)
—cochinillo	—piglet, suckling pig	

Otros mamíferos grandes	Other Large Mammals	
camello	*camel* (two humps)	
chimpancé	*chimpanzee*	
ciervo, cierva	deer, stag, doe	[*cervine*]
—venado (m. only)	—deer, stag, *venison*	
dromedario	dromedary (one hump)	
cebra / zebra	zebra	
elefante	elephant	
foca	seal	[genus *Phoca*]
gorila (m.)	gorilla	
hipopótamo	hippopotamus	("river horse"[30])
—hípico (adj.)	—pertaining to (racing) horses	
—club hípico	—riding club	
—hípica (n.)	—horse racing, horse riding (sport)	

[29] Old Spanish *puerca* was derived from Latin PORCA ("female pig") and subsequently became *tuerca* through the influence of *tornillo* ("screw"); in Portuguese, "nut" is still *porca*. The explanation for this rather surprising origin—as well as that of the related word *porcelana* (English *porcelain*)—is actually quite vulgar, in the "modern" sense of the word. (For the "adult" version of *porcelain*'s origin, see *Merriam Webster's Collegiate Dictionary*; for a more "family-oriented" one, see *American Heritage College Dictionary*.)

[30] Cf. Meso*potamia,* "land between the two rivers".

—hipódromo	—*hippodrome,* racetrack (horses, bikes, etc.)	
jirafa	*giraffe*	
llama	llama	
mono (n.)	*monkey,* overalls (work clothes)	
—mono (adj.)	—pretty, cute, charming	
oso	bear	[*ursine*]
—oso polar, oso blanco	—polar bear	
—oso hormiguero	—anteater	
—Osa Mayor	—*Ursa Major,* Great Bear, Big Dipper	
—Osa Menor	—*Ursa Minor,* Little Bear, Little Dipper	
panda (1) (m.)	panda	
—panda (2)	—gang (~ *pandilla*)	(unrelated)
reno	*rein*deer	
rinoceronte	*rhinoceros*	

Roedores	**Rodents**	
ardilla	squirrel	
castor	beaver	[*castor* (oil)]
rata	*rat*	
—ratón (-ona)	—mouse (animal, computer)	
—ratonera	—mousetrap	

Otros mamíferos pequeños	**Other Small Mammals**	
conejo	rabbit, *coney* (or *cony*)	[*Coney* Island]
—conejera	—rabbit hutch, warren	
—conejito	—bunny	
—conejillo de Indias	—guinea pig (~ *cobaya*)	
erizo	hedgehog	
—erizo de mar	—sea *urchin*	
—erizar	—(to) make stand on end (e.g., hair)	
—rizo	—curl, ringlet, loop (airplane)	
—rizar	—(to) curl, (to) ripple (waves), (to) loop	

—rizar el rizo	—loop-the-loop (airplane)	
liebre (f.)	hare	
—leporino	—*leporine* (relating to hares)	
—labio leporino	—harelip	
mapache	raccoon	(< Amer.)
murciélago[31]	bat	[*murine*]
—musaraña	—shrew (animal)	["spider *mouse*"[32]]
topo	mole (animal, spy)	[*taupe*—color]

Aves y aves de corral / Birds and Poultry

ave (f.)	bird (all types)	[*avian*]
—ave rapaz ~ ave de rapiña	—bird of prey, predatory bird	[*rapacious, rapine*]
—rara avis	—rara avis ("a rare or unique person or thing")	
—avicultura	—poultry farming	[*aviculture*]
—avión (m.)	—airplane	[*avionics*]
—avión de caza	—fighter	
—aviación	—aviation	
—aviador	—aviator	
pájaro	bird (gen. smaller bird)	[*passerine*]
—pájaro carpintero	—woodpecker	[*carpenter* bird]
—matar dos pájaros de un tiro	—"kill two birds with one throw (stone)"	
ala	wing, brim (hat), *ala*	[*aisle*[33]]
—ala delta	—hang glider	
—alado	—winged, *alate*	
—aleta	—fin, flipper (gen. pl.)	
—aletear	—(to) flutter or flap the wings or fins	

---

[31] Originally *murciego,* then *murciégalo* (still exists, but rare), and finally (with interchange of *g* and *l*) *murciélago*. The literal meaning is thus "blind mouse": *mur* (obsolete for "mouse" < Latin MUS/MUREM) + *ciego* ("blind"). Germanic *mouse* and Latin MUS are Indo-European cognates.

[32] Because of a folk belief that the shrew's bite was venomous.

[33] English *aisle* owes its *-is-* to the influence of the unrelated word *isle* (which, as we have seen in Section 3.5, no. 6, also accounts for the "unetymological" *s* in *island*). The sense of "passageway" arose from a confusion with the unrelated word *alley*.

—aleteo	—flapping of wings or fins, heart palpitation
pico	beak, peak, *pick*(ax), spout (teapot, etc.)
—picar	—(to) *peck,* (to) sting, (to) mince, (to) *pique*
—picadura	—sting or bite (insect, snake, etc.)
—picadillo	—minced meat, hash, *picadillo*
—picante	—*piquant,* hot or spicy
—pique	—*pique,* resentment
—ir(se) a pique	—(to) sink, (to) fall through
—piquete	—*picket* (small military detachment labor strike)
—pica	—*pike* (spear), picador's lance, spades (cards—*pl.*)
—picador	—*picador,* horse trainer, miner (using pick)
—pícaro, pícara	—rogue, rascal, *picaro, picara*
—picaresco	—roguish, *picaresque*
—picardía	—roguishness, prank, dirty trick
pluma	feather, pen, *plume*
—plumaje	—*plumage*
—plumazo	—pen stroke
—de un plumazo	—"at a stroke", "with one stroke of the pen"
—desplumar	—(to) *deplume* (pluck), (to) fleece
águila	*eagle*
—aguileño	—*aquiline*
avestruz[34]	*ostrich*
(las Islas) Canarias[35]	*Canary* Islands

---

[34] From Latin AVIS STRUTHIO, literally "ostrich bird", where STRUTHIO was taken from the Greek for "ostrich" and also appears in English *struthious* ("of or relating to ostriches").

[35] From Latin CANARIAE INSULAE—lit. "dog (*canine*) islands"—the name given to them by the Roman naturalist Pliny the Elder (who died in the volcanic eruption at Vesuvius in AD 79) because of the large number of wild dogs reported to be native there. The name of the bird (sixteenth c.) thus comes from that of the islands.

—canario (1)	—pertaining to the *Canary* Islands, resident of Canary Islands, variety of Spanish spoken in Canary Islands (m.)	
—canario (2)	—*canary* (bird)	
cigüeña	stork	[genus *Ciconia*]
—cigüeñal	—crankshaft	
cisne	swan	[*cygnet, Cygnus*]
—canto del cisne	—swan song	
—*El lago de los cisnes*	—*Swan Lake*	
cóndor	condor (< Sp.)	
cuervo	raven, crow	[*corvine*]
—cormorán	—cormorant	(lit. "*marine crow*")
faisán	*pheasant*	
gaviota	sea gull	
golondrina	swallow	
gorrión	sparrow	
mirlo	*merle* (blackbird)	
paloma	pigeon, dove	[*palomino*]
—paloma mensajera	—carrier or homing pigeon	[*messenger* pigeon]
—palomitas (de maíz) *pl.*	—popcorn	
—palomar	—pigeon house, dovecote	[Mount *Palomar*]
—pichón (< It.)	—young *pigeon*	
pelícano	pelican	
perdiz (f.)	*partridge*	
pingüino	penguin	
ruiseñor	nightingale	
tórtola	*turtle*dove	
búho	owl	
—buhardilla	—attic	(unrelated)
lechuza	(barn) owl	(from *leche*[36])
mochuelo	owl (little owl)	

---

[36] See Section 3.5, no. 2, for an explanation.

gallo	rooster, cock	[*gallinaceous, Gallic*[37]]
—gallina	—hen, chicken	
—gallinero	—hen house, chicken coop	
pollo	young chicken, chicken (food)	[*pullet, poultry*]
—pollito	—chick	
~ polluelo		
—empollar	—(to) brood, (to) incubate (eggs or ideas)	
—pollino[38]	—(young) donkey, jackass	
ganso	*goose, gander*	(*gansa* is rare)
—hacer el ganso	—(to) play the fool	[*gonzo* ?]
pato	duck	
—pata	—foot *and* leg (animal), leg/foot (furniture)	
—a cuatro patas	—on all fours (~ *a gatas*)	
—meter la pata	—to put one's foot in one's mouth	
—mala pata	—bad luck	
—patada	—kick	
—patear	—(to) kick, (to) stamp or stomp	
—patín	—skate (ice or roller)	[*patten*]
—patinar	—(to) skate, (to) skid, (to) slip	
—patinador	—skater	
—patinaje	—skating	

Peces y mariscos	**Fish and Seafood**
pez (1) (m.)	fish (in water)
—pescado (p.p.)	—fish (for eating)
—pesquero	—fishing (adj.), fishing boat
—pescador, -ora	—fisher, fisherman (-woman)
—pescadero	—fishmonger
—pescadería	—fish market
—pescar	—(to) fish

---

[37] Latin GALLUS meant both "rooster" and "resident of *Gallia* (France)", although the relationship, if any, between the two is unclear.

[38] Latin PULLUS initially meant simply "young animal", before becoming specialized in "poultry". Spanish *pollino* and French *poulain* ("young horse of either sex") represent applications to other species.

—piscina	—swimming pool (originally "fishpond")	[*piscine, piscina*]
—piscicultura	—pisciculture (breeding and rearing of fish)	
—Pisc**is**	—*Pisces*	
—pez (2)	—*pitch,* tar	(unrelated)
marisco	shellfish, seafood (pl.)	
—marisquería	—seafood restaurant	
—marisma	—salt *marsh*	
anchoa	*anchovy*	
atún	*tuna*	
bacalao	cod	
salmón	salmon	
sardina	sardine	
tiburón	shark	
trucha	*trout*	
ballena	whale, *baleen* whale	(*mamífero*)
delfín	*dolphin*	(*mamífero*)
almeja	clam	
calamar	squid, *calamari*	
camarón	shrimp, prawn	[genus *Gammarus*]
—gamba	—(Mediterranean) prawn	
cangrejo	crab	[*Cancer*]
—cangrejo de río	—crayfish (crawfish)[39]	
—cáncer	—cancer	
—canceroso	—cancerous	
—cancerígeno	—carcinogenic	
langosta[40]	*lobster, locust*	[*langouste* (spiny lobster)]
—langostino	—(large) prawn	[*langoustine*]

---

[39] English *crayfish (crawfish)* is, of course, not a fish. Its ultimate (Germanic) origin is the same as *crab,* and it entered English in the fifteenth century (from French), spelled variously *crevesse, crevys, krevys,* etc. This was subsequently deformed to *crayfish,* a deformation made all the more easy by the fact that in those days in much of the south of England *fish* was pronounced [vish].

[40] Latin LOCUSTA meant both "lobster" and "grasshopper", presumably due to similarities in their forms. A *locust* is a specific type of grasshopper, known particularly for traveling in swarms. LOCUSTA as applied to the marine animal underwent various transformations to arrive at Spanish *langosta* and, apparently, English *lobster* (though the origin of the English word is disputed).

ostra	*oyster*	
—perla	—*pearl*	
pulpo[41]	*octopus*	(*polypod*)
—pólipo	—*polyp* (animal, growth)	
—tentáculo	—tentacle	
—pulpa	—*pulp*	(unrelated)
sepia	cuttlefish, *sepia* (color)	

Insectos y artrópodos	**Insects and Arthropods**
insecto	insect
—insecticida	—insecticide
bestia	*beast*
—bicho	—insect, vermin
—bestial	—bestial, beastly
abeja	bee
—abeja reina	—queen bee
—apicultura	—beekeeping, *apiculture*
—apicultor	—beekeeper, *apiculturist, apiarist*
avispa[42]	*wasp*
colmena	beehive
enjambre	swarm of bees, crowd, multitude
zumbar	(to) buzz or hum (insect, machine), (to) ring (ears)
—zumbido	—buzzing, humming, ringing
araña	spider, chandelier
—arácnido	—*arachnid*
—telaraña, tela de araña	—spider web, cobweb
caracol	snail, snail shell, cochlea (ear) [*caracole*]

---

[41] In Latin, "octopus" was POLYPUS, from Greek and literally meaning "many feet" (*poly* + *pous*). This became Spanish *pulpo*. English *octopus* (*octo* + *pous*) is a "modern" development, first recorded in 1758. Prior to this, *poulp, polyp,* and *polypus* had been employed, and they continued in use (alongside *octopus*) until the late nineteenth century; *polyp* continues to refer to a small invertebrate marine animal. The medical sense of *polyp* ("nonmalignant growth or tumor") goes back to Latin and arose presumably because a (nasal) polyp appeared to be attached by many "feet".

[42] From Latin VESPA (with which English *wasp* shares a common Indo-European root), with the initial *a* added through the influence of *abeja*.

—escalera de caracol	—spiral staircase	
cucaracha	*cockroach,*[43] *roach*	
escarabajo	beetle, *scarab*	
gusano	worm, worm-like creature (grub, caterpillar, maggot)	
—gusano de seda	—silkworm	
hormiga	ant	[*formic* acid]
libélula	dragonfly	[genus *Libellula*]
mariposa	butterfly	[*mariposa* lily]
mosca	fly	[*muscid*]
—mosquito	—mosquito (< Sp.)	
—mosquete	—*musket*	
—mosquetero	—*musketeer*	
—mosquitero (*or* -tera)	—mosquito net	
—moscardón	—botfly, horsefly, bluebottle (~ *moscón*)	
termes / termita	termite	[genus *Termes*]

Reptiles y anfibios	**Reptiles and Amphibians**	
reptil	reptile	
—reptar	—(to) slither, (to) crawl	[*reptant*]
serpiente (f.)	*serpent,* snake	
—serpiente de cascabel	—rattlesnake	
—cascabel	—small bell, jinglebell, rattle	[*cascabel*]
—ponerle el cascabel al gato	—"to bell the cat": to perform a daring act	
boa	boa	
culebra	snake (~ *serpiente*)	[*colubrid*]
—cobra[44]	—cobra	

---

[43] The word (perhaps the insect as well !) was brought back to England by Captain John Smith of Pocahontas fame. Initial *cacarootch,* by folk etymology it subsequently became *cockroach,* from *cock* and *roach* (the freshwater fish).

[44] The Portuguese equivalent of *culebra* is *cobra* ("snake")—this development is typical in Portuguese, where an *l* between vowels normally disappears (hence *cor* for *color*). When the Portuguese came across the cobra in India, they named it *cobra de capello* (now *cobra-capelo*), meaning "hooded (or *caped*) snake". *Cobra de capello* entered English in the seventeenth century, and only in the nineteenth century was it shortened to *cobra*. A similar process has occurred in Spanish, French, Italian, and German.

víbora	*viper*	
veneno	*venom*, poison	
—venenoso	—venomous, poisonous	
—envenenar	—(to) envenom, (to) poison	
caimán	*caiman / cayman*	
cocodrilo	*crocodile*	
rana	frog	[*ranula*]
—ranúnculo	—*ranunculus*,[45] buttercup (~ *botón de oro*), crowfoot	
—renacuajo	—tadpole	
sapo	toad	
tortuga	*tortoise, turtle*	

Marsupiales	**Marsupials**	
canguro	*kangaroo*, babysitter	
koala (m.)	koala	

Carne (f.)	**Meat,** flesh	[*carnal*]
—carnicero	—butcher	
—carnicería	—butcher shop, butchery	
—carnívoro (adj. & n.)	—carnivorous, carnivore	
—carnero[46]	—ram (male sheep), mutton	
—carnal	—carnal	
—carnaval[47]	—Carnival (feast before Lent), carnival, Mardi Gras	
—carroña	—*carrion* (dead and decaying flesh)	
—encarnar	—(to) *incarnate*, (to) personify, (to) embody	
—encarnación	—*incarnation*, embodiment	
—reencarnación	—*reincarnation*	

---

[45] A class of flowers that includes buttercups and crowfoots (*sic*). The application to flowers apparently arose from the use of RANUNCULUS ("little frog") to refer humorously to a resident of a swampy region, and subsequently to a particular class of flowers found in such regions.

[46] Initially AGNUS CARNARIUS ("sheep for meat"), but the first part disappeared (analogous to *hermano*, from FRATER GERMANUS, and to *cobra*—see above).

[47] From Italian *carnevale*, formed from *carne levare* (→ *carnelevale* → *carnevale*), where *levare* (cognate with Spanish *llevar*) means "to take off or remove"; i.e., following *Carnival*, meat is "removed" from the daily menu.

Granja	Farm	[*grange*]
—granjero	—farmer	[*granger*]
—granjear	—(to) gain, (to) earn	[*garner*]
—grano	—*grain*, (coffee) bean, (small) seed (e.g., mustard), pimple	
—granero	—*granary*, barn	
—granada (1)	—*grenade*, pome*granate* (fruit)	["seedy apple"]
—Granada (2)	—Granada (Andalusia), Grenada (Caribbean)	
—granadero	—*grenadier*	
—granito	—*granite*	
—granizo	—hail, hailstone	
—granizar	—(to) hail	
—desgranar	—(to) shell (peas, beans, corn), (to) separate out	

Appendix

1. Turkeys and Peacocks

pavo	turkey	[*pavo*nine]
—pavo real	—*peacock*	

The Romance languages (and English) generally had little problem adopting words for New World concepts like *hurricane, canoe, hammock, tobacco,* etc. For some reason, however, the *turkey* proved to be an almost insuperable challenge. At an early stage, it was confused with the African *guinea fowl,* which for centuries had been known in Europe as an "Indian" chicken, due to an apparent confusion between Ethiopia and India. Hence in France the turkey was given the name *coq d'Inde,* shortened in Modern French to *dinde.*

The turkey was likewise known for some time in England as a *cock of Ind* or *Indian cock.* At the same time, the English name of the African *guinea fowl* was *Turkey-cock*— apparently because it was imported into England from, or through, Turkish-controlled territories. The universal confusion between the guinea fowl and the American turkey led to the latter taking over the name *turkey-cock,* subsequently shortened to *turkey.*[48]

In Spain, the imported turkey usurped the name of the "old world" peacock: *pavo,* cognate with the *pea-* in English *peacock.* The denuded peacock was then forced to add

---

[48] It was not only in England that "Turkey" came to be associated with exotic American products: in Italian, *granturco* or *granoturco* ("Turkish grain") is commonly used to refer to maize (corn).

the adjective *real* to distinguish itself from the North American usurper. Contrary to what the overwhelming majority of native Spanish speakers seem to believe, *pavo real* means "*real* peacock"—to distinguish it from the turkey masquerading as a peacock—and not "*royal* turkey".[49]

Shown below are the solutions for *turkey* in several other languages:

Catalan	gall dindi	"rooster from India"
French	dinde (f.), dindon (m.)	"from India"
Italian	tacchino	(onomatopoeic: *tak tak*)
Portuguese	peru	"Peru"
Dutch	kalkoen	"from Calicut (in India)"
Turkish	hindi	"from India"

The scientific name is *Meleagris gallopavo:*

genus	*Meleagris*	"guinea fowl"
species	*gallopavo*	"rooster-peacock"

2. Parrots and Periwigs

loro ~ papagayo	parrot, chatterbox	[*popinjay* < Sp.]
perico	parakeet	
—periquito	—parakeet, budgerigar (Australian)	
peluca	peruke, periwig, wig	

Birds have not infrequently been given the names of people (e.g., *robin* and *magpie,* where the "mag" comes from *Margaret*) or of personages (e.g., *cardinal,* because of the similarity in appearance to the religious figure). *Parrots* and *parakeets* owe their names to *Peter* and its Romance equivalents. The process seems to have started in France, where *Pierrot* (or *Perrot*) was a diminutive form of *Pierre,* the French version of *Peter.* At some stage the name became associated with parrots—known in Europe since Roman times—and a further diminutive, *perroquet,* was formed to refer specifically to the bird. In the sixteenth century, during the course of which New World *parakeets* arrived in England, English took from French both the personal name *Perrot* and the diminutive form *perroquet,* thus giving *parrot* and *parakeet.*

When *parrot* arrived in English, it rapidly displaced *popinjay,* which had been used for several centuries for "parrot" and had come from Spanish *papagayo* (via Occitan and French). *Popinjay* was forced to look for a new meaning and subsequently became specialized in the sense of "a vain and overly talkative person".

In Spanish a similar process took place, except that *papagayo* was able to maintain its position as "parrot", forcing diminutives *periquito* (corresponding to English *para-*

---

[49] A "royal peacock" is thus (at least theoretically) *un real pavo real*—which could also be interpreted as a "*real* peacock", a "*real royal* turkey", or a "*real* turkey *royale*" (culinary concoction).

keet) and *perico* to compete for the sense of "parakeet". The situation in the three languages is summarized below, with the earliest attested dates in parentheses.[50]

Spanish	French	English
Pedro (Pero)—Perico	*Pierre—Perrot / Pierrot*	*Peter*
	perrot (?) "parrot"	parrot (1525)
periquito (1565) "parakeet"	perroquet (1395) "parrot"	parakeet (1581)
perico (1670) "parakeet"	perruche (1698) "parakeet"	
	pierrot (1694) "sparrow"	
from Arabic:		
papagayo (1251) "parrot"	papegai (1155, now rare)	popinjay (1310)

(→ between perico and perruche)

Where do *loro* and *papagayo* (and hence *popinjay*) come from? *Loro* comes from a Caribbean language, while the generally accepted view is that *papagayo* comes from Arabic. By folk etymology, it seems to have been modified to appear to represent a combination of two distinct words, the first being *papa* (i.e., religious father) and the second variously *jay* (the bird, as in English and Spanish), *gay* (Occitan *papagai*, also Spanish[51]), or *gallo*—"rooster" (Italian *pappagallo*).

The story does not end here, as it is likely that English *wig* and Spanish *peluca* (originally *perruca*) both took their names from the parrot: *peluca* comes from French *perruque*, which in turn was

> Probablemente extraída del francés antiguo *perruquet,* siglo XV, voz con la cual se apodaba a los funcionarios de justicia, caracterizados por sus grandes pelucas. *Perruquet* significaba propiamente "loro", con el cual se comparó al juez provisto de peluca, por la locuacidad de esta ave y las plumas de su copete y cabeza.[52]

> Probably extracted from Old French *perruquet* [Modern French *perroquet*] in the fifteenth century, a nickname given to judicial officers, who were noted for their large wigs. *Perroquet* meant "parrot", the comparison thus being to a wigged judge, in respect to the parrot's loquacity and the feathers on its crest and head.

In the sixteenth century, French *perruque* arrived in English with two different forms: *peruke* and a more popular variant *perwyke* ("modern" *periwig*). The latter subsequently gave rise to a shortened form, *wig*. In Spanish, *perruca* became *peluca*

---

[50] The use of the French name *Pierrot / Perrot* to refer to a bird is first attested only at a relatively late stage, in the *Fables* of La Fontaine, by which time it had evidently come to refer to a "sparrow".

[51] In Spanish, *gayo* initially was two separate words representing both "gay" and "jay", although the latter word is now largely obsolete.

[52] Corominas (1973), 448.

through the influence of *pelo* ("hair"). Spanish *perico* ("parakeet") at an early stage also acquired the meaning of "ornamental wig", although this usage is no longer common.

3. Asses and Donkeys

asno	*ass* (1) (~ *burro*), jack*ass* (foolish or stupid person)	
—asnal	—*asinine* (of or like an ass [1])	
—desasnar	—(to) educate, (to) polish, (to) civilize	["*de-ass*"]
burro	*burro*, donkey, ass (1); as adj.—stupid, dumb, stubborn	
—burrito (Amer.)	—burrito (Mex. food)	("small burro")
—borrico	—donkey, ass (1), jackass	
mulo[53]	*mule*, hinny	
—mulero	—muleteer (mule driver)	
—mulato	—mulatto (< Sp.)	
—muleta	—crutch, *muleta* (matador's red flag)	
culo, trasero, nalgas (pl.)[54]	ass (2), arse, bottom, behind, backside, butt, buttocks	
—culata	—butt or breach (weapon), cylinder head (auto)	[*culotte*]
—recular	—(to) *recoil* (spring/shrink/fall back)	

English *ass* (2) in the ("vulgar slang") sense of "rear end" has nothing whatsoever to do with animal *ass* (1), nor (at least in theory) with the expression "don't be an *ass!*"[55] *Ass* (1) comes ultimately from Latin ASINUS, source also of Spanish *asno; ass* (2) is an Americanized version of *arse*, a native English word that stems from an Indo-European root meaning "buttocks" or "backside". The "simplification" of *rs* to *s* was a regional American development that also produced *bust, cuss, hoss, passel* from *burst, curse, horse, parcel*. The confusion between *ass* (1) and *ass* (2) is thus primarily a North American problem.[56]

---

[53] In English, the definition of a *mule* is restricted (at least technically) to the offspring of a *male* donkey and a *female* horse, while the reverse combination (*male* horse and *female* donkey) produces a *hinny*. Spanish *mulo* applies to both combinations.

[54] Along with a multitude of others, including *donde la espalda pierde su honesto nombre* ("where the back loses its decent name").

[55] I.e., "don't be 'a vain, silly, or aggressively stupid person'", one of the definitions of *ass* (1). On the other hand, the "Vulgar Slang" *asshole* ("a thoroughly contemptible, detestable person") comes from *ass* (2).

[56] In "proper" UK English, the *r* in *arse* is no longer pronounced, but *ass* and *arse* are still distinguished by their vowels, as *arse* is pronounced with the vowel of *father, ass* with that of *cat*.

SECTION 4.7

Religion

The early universal language of the Christians was Greek. A Greek translation of the Old Testament[1] (from the original Hebrew) had existed for several hundred years, and the New Testament itself was initially composed in Greek. Scattered Latin translations began to appear by the mid-second century—the first ones in North Africa—and by the latter fourth century there were, as St. Jerome himself observed, nearly as many different versions as there were manuscripts. In 382, Jerome was commissioned by the reigning pope (Damasus) to make an "official" Latin translation of the Bible. This he did in very short order, before deciding that the Greek version of the Old Testament (Septuagint) he had used was not satisfactory. He therefore set himself the task of mastering Hebrew, and by around 405 he had completed his translation of the Old Testament from the "original" Hebrew. Jerome's translation forms the basis of the Vulgate, the official Roman Catholic version of the Bible.

Some elements of the Christian vocabulary entered the languages of Western Europe directly from Greek, without passing through Latin—English *church* being a prominent example. The major part, however, passed through Latin, and in this regard the Vulgate played an important role. Although much of the Romance (and English) religious vocabulary remains very little changed from that in the Vulgate, several frequently used words have undergone substantial remodeling, as illustrated by the following comparison:

Latin	Spanish	Portuguese	French	Italian	English
ECCLESIA	iglesia	igreja	église	chiesa	church
EPISCOPUS	obispo	bispo	évêque	vescovo	*bishop*
ARCHI +	arzobispo	arcebispo	archevêque	arcivescovo	*archbishop*
ELEEMOSYNA	limosna	esmola	aumône	limosina[2]	*alms*

In the examples above, Greek Christian terms were taken virtually unchanged into Latin. In many other cases, however, Greek terms were replaced by Latin ones: either by direct "translation", whereby an existing Latin word was given a new (religious) sense, or via the creation of an altogether new Latin

---

[1] The Septuagint—from the Latin for "seventy" (tradition held that it had been translated by seventy-two Jewish scholars).

[2] *Limosina* has now largely been supplanted by the "learned" form *elemosina*.

word. The first process is illustrated by PRAEDICARE ("to proclaim in public"), which was given the religious sense of "to *preach* the Gospel" (Spanish *predicar*); the second, by SALVATOR, which was created from the adjective SALVUS ("*safe*") to translate the Greek word corresponding to "*savior*" (Spanish *salvador*). Examples of both types are to be found in the list below.

abadía	abbey
—abad (m.)	—abbot
—abadesa	—abbess
agnóstico	agnostic
—agnosticismo	—agnosticism
altar	altar
amén	amen
—amén de	—in addition to, besides
ángel	angel
—ángel de la guarda	—*guardian angel* (~ *ángel custodio*)
—angelical ~ angélico	—angelic, angelical
—angélica	—angelica (plant)
—arcángel	—archangel
apóstol	apostle
—apostólico	—apostolic
ateo (adj. & n.)	atheistic, atheist
—ateísmo	—atheism
bautismo	baptism (sacrament), christening
—bautismo de fuego	—baptism of fire
—bautizo	—baptism (ceremony), christening
—bautizar	—(to) baptize, (to) christen
—(San) Juan Bautista	—(Saint) John the Baptist
belén	*Bethelem* (cap.), nativity scene, *bedlam*[3]
bendición	*benediction*, blessing
—bendecir	—(to) bless
—bendito	—blessed (old p.p.)

[3] English *bedlam* comes from a "popular" form of the name of the Hospital of St. Mary of *Bethlehem* in London, an institution for the mentally ill. Spanish sources explain the sense of "great confusion" as arising from the fact that this was "characteristic" of popular nativity scenes. However, given that this sense does not seem to have been present in Spanish before the nineteenth century, it is not unlikely that it comes from English.

—agua bendita	—holy water (*but:* agua **bendecida** por el sacerdote)	
Biblia	Bible	
—bíblico	—biblical	
blasfemia	blasphemy	[*blame*]
—blasfemo (adj. & n.)	—blasphemous, blasphemer	
—blasfemar	—(to) blaspheme, (to) curse	
—lastimar	—(to) hurt, (to) injure, (to) offend	
—lástima	—pity, shame	
—(es una) lástima que . . .	—it's a shame/pity that . . .	
capilla	*chapel*	
—capellán	—*chaplain,* priest	
—capa⁴	—*cape,* cloak, coat (layer)	
—escapar⁵	—(to) escape	
—escapada	—escape, escapade	
—escaparate	—shop window	(unrelated)
cardenal (1)	cardinal (religious figure, bird)	
—cardinal	—cardinal (paramount), *cardinal* number	
—punto cardinal	—cardinal point (direction: north, south, east, west)	
—virtud cardinal	—cardinal virtue (*prudencia, justicia, fortaleza, templanza*)	
—cardenal (2)⁶	—black-and-blue mark, bruise	

---

⁴ In Medieval Latin, CAP(P)ELLA (literally "little *cape*") was used to refer to the shrine in which the Frankish kings preserved part of the cloak of St. Martin of Tours, who upon encountering a beggar in the road at the height of winter had cut his cloak into two parts and given one to the beggar. The meaning was then extended to that of a private shrine within a royal palace, and over time was further enlarged to its "modern" sense. English *chapel* reflects the "central" French form of the word in which initial CA- became *ch-* : e.g., *château,* compared to English *castle* (< Latin and northern French) and Spanish *castillo.*

⁵ *Escapar* and *escape* come from Latin EX + CAPPA, literally "to get out of one's *cape* (and leave the pursuers behind)". *Escaparate* is an import from Dutch and is ultimately related to the *-scape* in English *landscape.*

⁶ Contrary to what many (if not most) native Spanish speakers seem to believe, the word for a black-and-blue mark has nothing to do with the color of the cardinal's cassock. It comes instead from Latin CARDUUS (source of English *cardoon* and *chard*), a type of wild thistle with purple flowers.

—cárdeno	—purple, violet	
catedral (f.)	cathedral	
—cátedra	—university chair, head of department (position)	
—ex cáthedra	—*ex cathedra* (lit. "from the chair", i.e., "with the authority derived from one's office or position")	
—catedrático	—university (full) professor	
católico	Catholic, catholic (religious sense; also "universal")	
—catolicismo	—Catholicism	
claustro	*cloister,* faculty (academic), faculty meeting	
—claustro materno	—womb (~ *útero*)	[*maternal cloister*]
—clausurar	—(to) *close* (officially or by order)	
—clausura	—closure, closing ceremony	
—claustrofobia	—claustrophobia	
clérigo	*clergyman, cleric*	[*clerk, Clark*]
—clerical	—clerical (relating to the *clergy*)	
—clero	—*clergy*	
comunión	communion	
—común	—common	
—comuna	—commune	
—comunal	—communal	
—comunidad	—community	
—comunicar	—(to) communicate (incl. "be connected", e.g., rooms)	
—comunicado (p.p.)	—*communiqué,* notice in the press	
—comunicado de prensa	—*press* release	
—incomunicado	—isolated, in solitary confinement, *incommunicado* (< Sp.)	
—comunicación	—communication	
—comunicativo	—communicative	
—comunista	—communist	
—comunismo	—communism	

—comulgar[7]	—(to) receive Communion, (to) share the same thought or feeling
—excomulgar	—(to) excommunicate
—excomunión	—excommunication
Cristo	Christ
—cristiano	—Christian
—cristiandad	—Christianity, Christendom
—cristianismo	—Christianity
—cretino[8]	—stupid, *cretinous, cretin* (one afflicted with *cretinism*), moron
—cretinismo	—cretinism (condition caused by thyroid hormone deficiency)

cruz (f.)	*cross,* reverse side of a coin	[*crux*]
—cruz gamada	—swastika (~ *esvástica*), *gammadion*	[*gamma cross*[9]]
—cruce	—crossing, intersection, *cross* (hybrid)	
—cruzar	—(to) *cross* (various senses), (to) *cruise*	
—cruzada (n.)	—*crusade, Crusade* (cap.)	
—cruzado (p.p.)	—*crusader*	
—crucero	—*cruise, cruiser,* transept (church)	
—crucificar	—(to) *crucify*	
—crucifixión	—crucifixion	
—crucifijo	—crucifix	
—crucigrama (m.)	—*cross*word puzzle	
—crucial	—*crucial*	

---

[7] *Comunicar* and *comulgar* are doublets, both from Latin COMMUNICARE.

[8] The word *cretin* was a "popular" evolution of CHRISTIANUS ("Christian") in certain Alpine dialects in Switzerland. The term was initially applied as a "compassionate euphemism" to those suffering from *cretinism,* a medical condition (dwarfed stature, mental retardation) frequently caused by iodine deficiency—a problem endemic to the Alps, as it is to other mountain regions throughout the world not having ready access to iodized salt. Only much later did *cretin* acquire its "modern" pejorative sense. Another example of "compassionate euphemism" is French *benêt* (< BENEDICTUS, "blessed") for "half-wit" or "simple-minded".

[9] Because a *cruz gramada* can be constructed from four Greek *gammas* (Γ).

—encrucijada	—*cross*roads (intersection, *crucial* point), difficult situation
cura (1) (m.)	priest, *curate*
—cura (2)	—*cure*, treatment
—curable / incurable	—curable / incurable
—curativo	—curative
—curar	—(to) cure, (to) treat
—curación	—cure, curing, healing
—curador (adj. & n.)	—curing, healing, caretaker or *curator*
—curandero	—healer (via natural methods or magic), quack
—incuria	—carelessness
—sinecura[10]	—sinecure (job with pay, no real work)
demonio	demon, devil
—demoníaco, demoniaco	—demonic, demoniac
diablo	*devil*
—diabólico	—diabolic, diabolical, devilish
diácono	*deacon*
diócesis	diocese
dios, Dios	god, God
—diosa	—goddess
—adiós	—adios, *adieu*, farewell, goodbye
—pordiosero	—beggar (~ *mendigo*)
—deidad	—*deity, divinity* (~ *divinidad*)
discípulo	disciple, pupil
—disciplina	—discipline (incl. branch of knowledge or teaching)
—disciplinar	—(to) teach, (to) discipline
—disciplinario	—disciplinary
—indisciplinado	—undisciplined
—interdisciplinario	—interdisciplinary (also: *interdisciplinar*)

Additional right-column annotations:

- —sinecura[10] : (*sin* + *cura* [2])
- dios, Dios : [*deus* ex machina]
- —pordiosero : (¡ por Dios !)

---

[10] Initially "an ecclesiastical benefice (church office) without cure (care) of souls".

divino	divine
—divinidad	—divinity, *deity*
—diva	—diva, distinguished performer (*m.* divo)
—adivinar	—(to) *divine*, (to) guess
—adivinación	—prediction, *divination*
—adivino	—diviner, soothsayer
—adivinanza	—riddle
eclesiástico (adj. & n.)	ecclesiastical, ecclesiastic (minister or priest, cleric)
—Eclesiastés	—Ecclesiastes (book of the Bible)
eucaristía	Eucharist
evangélico	evangelical, evangelic, Protestant
—evangelio	—Gospel, *evangel*
—evangelista (m.)	—Evangelist (author of one of the four New Testament gospels)
—evangelizar	—(to) evangelize
éxodo	exodus
exorcismo	exorcism
—exorcista	—exorcist
—exorcizar	—(to) exorcise
feligrés[11] (-esa)	parishioner, (faithful) customer, habitué
herético	heretical
—herejía	—heresy
—hereje	—heretic (m./f.)
ídolo	idol (figure or image, adored person)
—idolatría	—idolatry
—idolatrar	—(to) idolize
letanía	*litany* (liturgical prayer, repetitive enumeration)
limosna	*alms*
—limosnero (adj. & n.)	—charitable, almoner, beggar (Amer.) [*eleemosynary*]

---

[11] From FILIUS + ECCLESIA, literally "son of the Church", with the second *l* then changing to *r*.

liturgia	liturgy	
—litúrgico	—liturgical	
maldición	*malediction,* curse	
—maldecir	—(to) curse, (to) speak ill of	[† *maledict*]
—maldito	—accursed, damned	(old p.p.)
mártir	*martyr*	
—martirio	—martyrdom	
—martirizar	—(to) martyr or martyrize, (to) torment	
misericordia	mercy, pity	(see Section 4.9)
misionero (adj. & n.)	missionary	
—misión	—mission (religious or other)	
—misa	—*Mass*	[*mess*]
—misal	—missal	
—misiva	—missive (written message, letter)	
—misil	—missile	
monasterio	monastery	[West*minster*]
—monje	—*monk*	
—monja	—nun	
—monacal	—monkish, monastic	
—monástico	—monastic	
—monaguillo	—acolyte, altar boy	
Navidad	Christmas, *Nativity*	
—¡Feliz Navidad!	—Merry Christmas!	
—Navidades (pl.)	—Christmas time, Yuletide	
—navideño	—Christmas (adj.)	
—Natividad	—*Nativity*	
oración	*orison* (prayer), clause or sentence (gram.)	
—oración fúnebre	—*funeral oration*	
—orar	—(to) pray	[*orate*]
—orador	—orator, speaker	
—oráculo	—oracle	
ordenación	arrangement or ordering, *ordination*	
—orden (f.)	—order (command), religious order	

—orden (m.)	—order (arrangement, sequence, etc.)	
—ordenar	—(to) *order* (command, arrange), (to) *ordain*	
—ordenado (p.p.)	—orderly, methodical	
—ordenador (Spain)	—computer (~ *computador, computadora*)	
—ordenanza	—ordinance or regulation (gen. pl.), orderly (m./f.)	
—ordinario	—ordinary, mediocre	
—ordeñar	—(to) milk (a cow)	
—desorden	—disorder	
—desordenar	—(to) disorder, (to) mess up	
—desordenado (p.p.)	—disordered, disorderly	
pagano	pagan, heathen	
—paganismo	—paganism	
—paisano (adj. & n.)	—*paisano* (compatriot[12]), *peasant*	(G → ø; see Section 3.4)
—de paisano	—in plain (civilian) clothes (e.g., police)	
—país	—country	
—paisaje	—landscape (scenery or painting)	
papa (m.)	pope	(< Gk. *pappas*)
paraíso	paradise, heaven (~ *cielo*)	
—paraíso fiscal	—tax haven	
parroquia	*parish,* parish church	
—parroquial	—parochial (of or relating to a parish)	
—párroco	—parish priest, parson	
—parroquiano	—parishioner, habitué	
Pascua	Easter, Passover, Yuletide (12/24–1/6—*pl.*)	
—cordero pascual	—Paschal Lamb	
pecar	(to) sin	[*peccavi*]
—pecado	—sin	[*peccadillo*[13]]
—pecador	—sinner	

---

[12] Frequently in a "narrow" sense, i.e., from the same locality or region.

[13] While English *peccadillo* ("small sin")—first attested in the late sixteenth century—comes from Spanish *pecadillo,* the latter has not appeared in the RAE's dictionary since 1869; it remains in use in at least some regions, however.

—pecaminoso	—sinful	
—impecable	—impeccable, faultless	
penitente (adj. & n.)	penitent (religious), Penitente	
—penitencia	—*penance,* penitence	
—penitenciaría	—penitentiary, prison	
—arrepentir(se)	—(to) *repent,* (to) regret	
—arrepentimiento	—repentance, regret	
—de repente	—suddenly (~ *repentinamente*)	(unrelated)
—repentino	—sudden	
perdón	*pardon,* forgiveness	
—perdonar	—(to) pardon, (to) forgive	
—perdonable	—pardonable, forgivable	
—imperdonable	—unpardonable, unforgivable	
peregrinación ~ peregrinaje	*pilgrimage, peregrination*	
—peregrinar	—(to) make a *pilgrimage,* (to) *peregrinate*	
—peregrino (adj. & n.)	—wandering, migratory, *peregrine* (e.g., falcon), *pilgrim*	
piedad	*piety, pity, Pietà*	
—pío (1)	—*pious,* devout	
—piadoso	—compassionate, merciful, *pious*	
—pitanza	—daily food ration (given to the poor)	[*pittance*]
—despiadado	—merciless, *pitiless,* ruthless	
—impío	—*impious,* ungodly	
—expiar	—(to) *expiate,* (to) atone for	
—expiación	—expiation, atonement	
—pío (2)	—peep, chirp (chicks, young birds)	(onomatopoeic)
—no decir ni pío	—not to say a word, not to make a peep	
—piar	—(to) peep, (to) chirp	
plegaria	*prayer,* supplication	
predicar	(to) *preach*	[*predicate*]
—prédica	—sermon (~ *sermón*)	

—predicación	—*preaching*
—predicador	—*preacher*
—predicado (p.p.)	—*predicate* (grammar, logic)
—predicamento	—esteem, influence, predicament (*only:* Aristotelian category)
—[aprieto, apuro]	—predicament
providencia	providence, Providence (cap.), precaution, ruling (legal)
—providencial	—providential, fortunate
—prudente	—prudent, cautious
—prudencia[14]	—prudence, good sense
—imprudente	—imprudent, careless
—imprudencia	—imprudence, careless act
purgatorio	purgatory
—purgar	—(to) *purge* (organization, radiator, bowels, soul)
—expurgar	—(to) *expurgate,* (to) *purify*
resurrección	resurrection
rezar	(to) pray, (to) say or *recite* (prayer, mass)
—rezo	—prayer
rito	rite, ritual
—ritual (adj. & n.)	—ritual
romero (1)	pilgrim [*Rome, Romeo*]
—romería	—pilgrimage, saint's day festival (at hermitage or sanctuary)
—Roma	—Rome
—romano	—Roman
—románico (adj.)	—Romance (languages), Romanesque (style)
—romance (n.)	—Romance (languages), romance (love; medieval narrative)
—romanticismo	—romanticism

---

[14] Latin PRUDENTIA was a shortened form of PROVIDENTIA ("foresight"), which came to specialize in "prudence".

—romántico	—romantic	
—romero (2)[15]	—*rosemary* (plant)	
sacrilegio	sacrilege	
—sacrílego	—sacrilegious	
sacro	*sacred* (~ *sagrado*), *sacrum*[16] (bone at base of spine)	
—sacerdote	—priest	
—sacerdotal	—sacerdotal (priestly)	
—sacramento	—sacrament	[*Sacramento*]
—sacramental	—sacramental	
—sacristán	—*sexton*, sacristan	
—sacrosanto	—sacrosanct	
—sagrado	—sacred, holy	
—consagrar	—(to) *consecrate* (incl. "devote")	
—consagración	—consecration	
salvador	*savior, Savior* (cap.)	[El *Salvador*]
—salvación	—salvation	
—salvar	—(to) *save* (but not "accumulate" or "economize")	
—sálvese quien pueda	—everyone for himself!	
—salvado (p.p.)	—bran[17]	
—salvaguardar	—(to) *safeguard*	
—salvaguarda, salvaguardia	—safeguard, protection	
—salvamento	—rescue, *salvage*	
—salvo (adj.)	—*safe* (unhurt)	
—salvo (prep. & conj.)	—except, *save*	
—salva (n.)	—*salvo*	

---

[15] *Rosemary* originally had nothing to do with either *rose* or *Mary*. It comes instead from Latin ROS MARINUS (literally "sea dew") and in Middle English was *rosmarine,* a form that was subsequently "corrupted" to *rosemary. Romero (2)* comes from ROS MARIS, another name for the plant ("dew of the sea"). *Romero (1)* comes from the city of *Rome,* the site of the first pilgrimages (the name *Romeo* also means "pilgrim").

[16] *Sacrum* comes from Latin OS SACRUM ("*sacred* bone"), which was in turn a direct translation from Greek. There are a number of competing explanations for why this bone was considered "sacred", e.g., that the sacrum was used as a vessel to support the intestines in rites of animal sacrifice.

[17] The explanation for this sense is not entirely clear (and much contested): perhaps because the bran (the outer layers of a cereal grain) is removed ("saved") during the course of milling; or because it is "saved" by the sieve in the course of sifting.

santo (adj. & n.)	*saintly,* holy, *saint*	(Lat. SANCTUS)
—San Pablo	—Saint Paul	
—Santo Domingo[18]	—Santo Domingo	
—Santa María	—Saint Mary	
—en un santiamén[19]	—in an instant, in no time at all	
—santidad	—holiness, saintliness, *sanctity*	
—santificar	—(to) *sanctify*	
—santiguar	—(to) make the sign of the cross	
—santuario	—sanctuary	
—sanción	—sanction (both senses: approval; penalty)	
—sancionar	—(to) sanction (authorize; penalize)	
sermón	sermon	
—sermonear	—(to) sermonize, (to) lecture (admonish)	
sotana	cassock, *soutane*	(< SUB, "under")
—sótano	—basement, cellar	
templo	temple	
—templar[20]	—(to) *temper,* (to) warm up, (to) tune (guitar, etc.)	
—temple	—*temper,* mood, courage, tuning (music), *tempera*	
islam	Islam (~ *islamismo, mahometismo*)	
—islámico	—Islamic	
—musulmán	—Muslim / Moslem (~ *islamita, mahometano*)	

---

[18] The shortened form *San* is used in front of all masculine saints' names, apart from *Tomás / Tomé, Toribio,* and *Domingo.*

[19] From the rapid manner in which Latin prayers were enunciated—beginning and ending with the sign of the cross:

IN NOMINE PATRIS ET FILII ET SPIRITUS **SANCTI. AMEN.**

In the name of the Father, and of the Son, and of the Holy Ghost. Amen.

The origin is thus analogous to that of English *patter* (Section 4.8, appendix).

[20] *Templar* and *temple* are unrelated to *templo,* being cognate instead with *temper* (see Section 3.5, no. 8).

—Corán	—Koran
—mezquita	—*mosque*
judío (adj. & n.)	Jewish, Jew
—judaísmo	—Judaism
—judaico	—Judaic, Jewish
—rabino	—*rabbi*
—sinagoga	—synagogue
—Tora	—Torah

SECTION 4.8
The Family

In Latin, a FAMULUS was a male servant or slave, and the collection of slaves of a house was known as the FAMILIA. This subsequently expanded to include people living under the same roof—wife, children, and slaves—all under the governance of the PATER FAMILIAS. FAMILIAR-IS was the associated adjective "pertaining to the family" (initially only to household slaves). In common speech, FAMILIA gradually came to be a synonym for GENS, the traditional term for a group of people descended from a common (male) ancestor, but GENS remained the legal term.

When *family* entered English around 1400, it reverted to its original Latin definition: "the servants of a house or establishment". Though it was gradually supplanted by other definitions, the original meaning did not altogether disappear until around 1800. The semantic development of *family* paralleled that of the Latin word two thousand years before, first expanding to "a group of people living as one household, including parents and their children, boarders, servants, etc.", and then developing into the more limited notion of modern times. English *familiar* still maintains the definition "one who performs domestic service in the household of a high official", and Spanish *familiar* preserves a number of similar definitions.

FAMILIA	familia	family	
FAMILIARIS	familiar	familial, family (adj.), familiar, family member (n.m.)	
	familiarizar	(to) familiarize	
	familiaridad	familiarity	
GENS (acc. GENTEM)	gente (f.)	people, folks	[*gents*]
GENTILIS	gentil	*gentile* (pagan), *genteel*	[*gentle*]
	gentileza	grace, charm, courtesy, *gentilesse*	
	gentilicio	gentile (gram.)—expressing national or local origins: New Yorker, Danish	
PATER	padre	father	

PATRES	padres	parents, fathers	
	paternal	paternal (fatherly)	
	paterno	paternal (of the father)	
	paternidad	paternity, fatherhood	
MATER	madre (f.)	mother	
	maternal	maternal	
	—amor maternal	—motherly love (or *amor materno*)	
	materno	maternal	
	—lengua materna	—mother tongue (not *lengua maternal*)	
	maternidad	maternity, motherhood	
PARENT-EM (acc.)	pariente	relative (n.), relation	[*parent*]
	parentesco	relationship (family or things)	
	parentela	relatives, kinfolk	
	emparentar	(to) be or become related	
	parir	(to) give birth	
	partera	midwife (~ *comadrona*)	
	parto	childbirth, labor, *parturition*	
	posparto / postparto	postpartum, postpartum period	
	parturienta (adj. & n.)	parturient (woman in labor)	
	puerperio	puerperium (postpartum period)	
ADULTUS	adulto	adult	
ADOLESCENT-EM (acc.)	adolescente	adolescent	
	adolescencia	adolescence	

Los padres ("the fathers") is used to refer to *parents,* just as *los reyes* means the "king and queen". *Mis parientes* means "my relatives", not "my parents". A number of additional Spanish words related to *padre* and *madre* are provided in the appendix to this section.

In Latin, there was a very interesting relation among the infinitive, present participle, and past participle for the verbs ADOLESCERE and PARERE:

Infinitive	*Present Participle*	*Past Participle*
ADOLESCERE	ADOLESCENT-EM	ADULT-US
to grow up	growing up → *adolescent*	grown up → *adult*

PARERE	PAR(I)ENT-EM	PART-US
to give birth	giving birth → *parent*	birthed → act of delivery = Sp. *parto*

External appearance notwithstanding, *adultery* has nothing to do with *adult*. The notion of unfavorably altering (offspring, document, substance, etc.) comes instead from the verb ALTERARE ("to alter"):

AD + ALTERARE	→ ADULTERARE[1]	
	adulterar	(to) adulterate, (to) falsify
	adulterio	adultery
	adúltero (adj. & n.)	adulterous, adulterer
	adúltera (n.)	adulteress
	adulterino	adulterine (born of adultery; spurious)
FILIUS	hijo	son
FILIA	hija	daughter
	—mis hijos	—my children, my sons
	hijastro	stepson, stepchild
	hijastra	stepdaughter
	ahijar ~ prohijar	(to) adopt (~ *adoptar*)
	ahijado (p.p.)	godson, godchild
	ahijada	goddaughter
	filial (adj. & n.f.)	filial, branch (office), subsidiary
AD + FILIARE	afiliar	(to) affiliate
	afiliado (p.p.)	affiliate, member
[expressive origin]	niño	child, boy
	niña	girl
	niña (del ojo)[2]	pupil (eye)

[El *Niño*—warming]

[La *Niña*—cooling]

---

[1] See Section 1.3 for an explanation of the change of the initial A of ALTERARE to U in ADULTERARE.

[2] The use of "little girl" to represent "pupil", arising from the tiny image of oneself (like a child or a *pupil*) that can be seen reflected in the pupil of another's eye, is found in numerous languages, including Hebrew, Arabic, Greek, and Latin (whence English *pupil*, literally "little girl or *puppet*").

	niña de mis ojos	"apple of my eye"
	niñez	childhood, infancy
	niñera	nursemaid, nanny
INFANT-EM	infante	infant, infante[3] *infantry*man
	infanta[4]	(female) infant
	infancia	infancy, childhood[5]
	infantil	childish, child-like, *infantile*
	—libros infantiles	children's books
	infantería	infantry
(Eng. → Fr. → Sp.)	bebé	*baby*

An *infant* by origin is "one incapable of speaking", as it is the composition of *in-* (negative sense) plus *fantem*, the present participle of the same verb (FARI, "to speak") that is the root of FAMA ("talk", "rumor", i.e., *fame*) and ultimately Spanish *hablar* (originally, "telling *fables*"). The extension to *infantry* is an Italian innovation, due apparently to the fact that foot soldiers came to be seen as servants of those on horseback.

MARITUS	marido	husband
	marital	marital
DIVORTIUM	divorcio	divorce
	divorciar	(to) divorce
	divorciado (adj. & n.)	divorced, divorcé
	divorciada (n.)	divorcée

MARITUS is the past participle of the verb MARITARE (which, via French, produced the English verb *marry*), so that *marido* literally means "married". A *divorce* is etymologically a "turning away from", formed in pre-Classical Latin from DIS- plus VORTERE (Classical Latin VERTERE). So a divorce is literally a *diversion*, if also frequently a *vortex*.

---

[3] An *infante* is a son of a Spanish (or, formerly, Portuguese) king other than the heir to the throne, who in Spain is called the *Príncipe de Asturias* (analogous to the British *Prince of Wales*).

[4] *Infanta* refers to a daughter of a Spanish (or, formerly, Portuguese) king.

[5] Spanish *infancia* extends to puberty, whereas a child is an *infante* only until age seven. English *infant* and *infancy* in a legal sense both apply to a person under the legal age (in the United States, eighteen years).

SPONSA	esposa	wife, *spouse*
	esposo	husband, *spouse*
MULIER	mujer (f.)	woman, wife

Latin UXOR for *wife* was abandoned by Spanish in favor of SPONSA, which in Latin had meant "fiancée". SPONSA was the feminine past participle of the verb SPONDERE, "to make a solemn engagement", "to *sponsor*", the source as well for English *respond* and *response*. A *spouse* was thus literally "the promised one", "the engaged one" (provided by the *sponsor*).

DESPONSARE	desposar	(to) *espouse* (marry)
	desposorio(s)	*spousal(s)* (marriage)
	esposas (pl.)	handcuffs
SPONSARE	esposar	(to) handcuff
	esposado	handcuffed
SPONSALES	esponsales (pl.)	*espousal* (betrothal)

To *betroth* or *affiance* in Latin could take several forms, all related to the idea of making a "solemn promise": DESPONDERE, SPONSARE, DESPONSARE. The first acquired the (related ?) meaning "to abandon hope", "to give up", subsequently reflected in English *despond* and *despondent*. Spanish used DESPONSARE to form *desposar* ("to marry"); this is restricted primarily to literary use, *casar* being by far the more "popular" term. As a metaphorical allusion to the inseparable nature of marriage, *esposar* (from SPONSARE) and *esposas* came to acquire their present meanings.

> *Dicen que las esposas hacen mucho daño.*
>
> They say that handcuffs [wives] cause a lot of damage.

> *Los hombres que tienen esposas no son hombres libres.*
>
> Men with wives [handcuffs] are not free men.

The English verb *espouse* originates from SPONSARE (via French *épouser*).

NOVUS → NOVIUS	novio	fiancé, boyfriend, groom, newlywed
	novia	fiancée, girlfriend, bride, newlywed
	noviazgo	courtship, engagement (period)

Novio—novia was derived from Latin NOVUS ("new"), hence its original meaning of "newlywed". It is now used much more commonly for "boyfriend"—

"girlfriend and fiancé"—"fiancée". While being a *fiancé(e)* has something new about it, to *marry* is far more domestic, as one is "setting up *house*" or establishing a relationship of *bondage* with it (origin of *husband*[6]). For Spanish speakers outside of Spain (and some within), *casar* ("to marry") is pronounced identically to *cazar* ("to hunt").

CASA	casa	house, home	[*chez*]
	casar	(to) marry	
	casado	married, married person	
	casamiento	marriage, wedding	
	la Casa Blanca	the White House	
	Casablanca	Casablanca (city in Morocco)	
	casino	casino	
	casero (adj. & n.)	homemade, informal, landlord	
	caserío	hamlet, country house	
	caseta	cottage, cabana, stall or booth	
	casilla	pigeonhole, square (chessboard), little box, mailbox (esp. digital)	
MATRIMONIUM	matrimonio	matrimony, marriage, married couple	

Apart from various euphemisms, there are three basic words to express pregnancy: *embarazada, encinta,* and *preñada.*

embarazada (adj. & n.)	pregnant, pregnant woman	[*embarrassed*]
—embarazar	—(to) make pregnant, (to) encumber, (to) hinder	[*embarrass*]
—embarazo	—pregnancy, difficulty, embarrassment	
—embarazoso	—awkward, embarrassing	

---

[6] In Old English, "house" was *hus,* while the second element in *hus-bonda* initially meant "occupier and tiller" of the soil, only later acquiring the meaning of "one in bondage", "serf". A *husbonda* was thus the master of a house, a *husbonde* the mistress of a house. It was not until nearly 1300 that the first use of *husband* is recorded in the sense of a man joined to a woman in marriage. The original sense did not die out, however, and is still found in many dictionaries: "a manager or steward . . . a thrifty manager". Hence *animal husbandry* and *husbandman,* and the much rarer but apparently still existing *ship's husband* ("an agent representing the owners of a ship, who manages its expenses and receipts while in port").

—desembarazar	—(to) *disembarrass* (free from encumbrance or bother)
encinta	pregnant, *enceinte* (adj.)
preñada	*pregnant*
—preñez	—*pregnancy*
—preñar	—(to) *impregnate* (make pregnant)
—impregnar	—(to) *impregnate* (saturate, permeate, imbue)

By far the most frequently used in conversation is *embarazada,* correspond-ing etymologically to English *embarrassed.* Viewed from the perspective of the English word, the Spanish might seem somewhat inappropriate; however, this is not a valid comparison, since historically the Spanish word preceded the English one. The initial meaning referred in fact to a physical, not emotional, restriction, and the derivation went Portuguese → Spanish → French → En-glish. *Encinta* by popular etymology is explained by the combination *en* ("in") + *cinta* ("band" or "belt")—thus, "circled by a belt". It is very likely, however, that the original source was Latin INCIENTEM ("pregnant"), source of the En-glish adjective *enceinte.* The original meaning of *impregnate* was "to make preg-nant"; the secondary definition of "saturation" is a later development.

In *literary* use there has been a marked shift in usage in the Modern Spanish period, as illustrated by the comparison below of three versions of the Bible: Reina Valera Antigua (1602), Reina Valera (1960), and La Biblia de las Américas (1997):

	preñada	encinta	embarazada
RV Antigua	16	1	3
RV (1960)	0	18	1
Américas	0	19	0

Thus in the "old" Reina Valera—written at approximately the same time as the King James Bible[7]—by far the most commonly employed term was *preñada,* which by the twentieth century had completely disappeared, replaced by *en-cinta.* For many native Spanish speakers, *preñada* is now restricted to animals.

Both Latin and Old English had separate words for paternal and maternal aunts and uncles.[8] While Modern English has unified the paternal and mater-

---

[7] In which the word *pregnant* does not appear.
[8] In Old English: *uncles*—fædera, eam; aunts—faðe, modrige.

nal elements, Spanish has gone even further by combining all aunts and uncles into a single noun, *tío,* with masculine and feminine forms:

tío	uncle
tía	aunt
mis tíos = "my aunt and uncle" *or* "my uncles" *or* "my aunts and uncles"	
tiovivo	merry-go-round (~ *carrusel*) ("live uncle")

Modern English *uncle* and *aunt* are derived via French from the Latin for "*maternal* uncle" and "*paternal* aunt". Spanish has taken its forms from late Latin THIUS—THIA, which in turn come from Greek. In Spanish, *tío* can also be used in a general sense to mean "fellow", "guy".

[FRATER]	hermano	brother	[germane]
[SOROR]	hermana	sister	
	—mis hermanos	—my brothers and sisters, my brothers	
	hermandad	brotherhood (relation, group, fellowship), sisterhood	
FRATERNUS	fraterno	fraternal, brotherly	
	fraternal	fraternal, brotherly	
	fraternidad	fraternity, brotherhood (fellowship)	
	fraternizar	fraternize (~ *confraternizar*)	
	confraternidad	fraternity, fellowship	
	cofradía	confraternity (religious brotherhood; association)	
CUM + FRATER	cofrade	member of a confraternity	

FRATER GERMANUS meant "true" or "full" brother as opposed to one's half or stepbrother. This has a parallel in English civil law:

*brother-**german***	brother sharing two parents
uterine brother	brother sharing only same mother
consanguine brother	brother sharing only same father

The FRATER element got lost along the way, so that Spanish *brother* reflects only the "full" part.[9] Like *aunt, sister* is simply a feminized form of the masculine.

---

[9] The disappearance of the initial G from GERMANUS (the *h* in *hermano* being purely "cosmetic") was not unusual: this occurred in a number of "popular" words in which GE or GI was in an *unstressed* syllable (cf. GELARE → Spanish *helar,* English *gel*).

More traditionally derived Latin forms are used for religious brothers and sisters:

fraile	*friar,* monk
—Fray Juan	—Brother John, Friar John
Sor María	Sister Maria

The original Latin G from GERMANUS survives in one word with a rather peculiar modern meaning, presumably originating from the "brotherhood" of criminals:

germanía	slang or jargon, particularly that used by thieves

To understand the derivations of the Spanish terms for *cousin, nephew—niece,* and *grandchildren,* it is helpful to start with the corresponding Latin terms:

SOBRINUS	cousin
CONSOBRINUS	cousin (generally first)

SOBRINUS (from SOROR-INUS) was initially an adjective meaning "of the sister", so that CONSOBRINI (the plural of CONSOBRINUS) referred to "children of two sisters". Over time, the definition was extended to encompass "children of brothers and sisters", i.e., first *cousins.* SOBRINI (the plural of SOBRINUS) were in Roman law the children of CONSOBRINI, i.e., second *cousins.*

NEPOS (acc. NEPOTEM)	descendant other than son, chiefly *grandson*
NEPTIS (fem.)	analogous to NEPOS, chiefly *granddaughter*
FRATRIS FILIUS	nephew (brother's son)
SORORIS FILIUS	nephew (sister's son)
FRATRIS FILIA	niece (brother's daughter)
SORORIS FILIA	niece (sister's daughter)

The derivation of Spanish for *cousin* is similar to that which occurred for *brother.* Over time, people started using CONSOBRINUS as a general term for cousins (of whatever order), so CONSOBRINUS PRIMUS ("first cousin") was used to reinforce the original definition. In Spanish, the first part of the expression dropped out, leaving *primo* for "cousin".

primo, prima	cousin
primo hermano, prima hermana	first cousin, *cousin-german*

English *cousin* comes (via French) from CONSOBRINUS.

The ambiguous definitions of NEPOS and NEPTIS were not an invention of the Romans, reflecting instead the meaning of the Indo-European root **nepot-* ("descendant other than the son"). The plural NEPOTES was used to refer to "posterity" or "descendants", or to the "offspring" of plants and animals. Similarly, Old English *nefa,* from the same root, could mean "nephew", "stepson", "grandson", "second cousin". English *nephew* and *niece* come from French, and both French and English initially maintained the broader definitions. Thus, throughout much of its history, English *nephew* had the following accepted (additional) meanings:

(a) a grandson (until late seventeenth century)
(b) a descendant of a remote or unspecified degree of descent; a successor (until late seventeenth century)
(c) niece (until early seventeenth century)

Hence: [10]

(a) "The grandmothers also . . . love their *nephews* better than their own immediate children." (1656)
(b) "All the ancient Sages, with their Sons, and *Nephews* to the latest Posterity." (1676)
(c) "The Athenians were wont to marry the brother with the sister, but not the Uncle with the *nephew.*" (1585)

Similarly, the English definition of *niece* was originally a "granddaughter or more remote female descendant". Until the early seventeenth century, *niece* was also occasionally used to refer to a "*male* relative, especially a nephew".

nepotismo   nepotism

The word *nepotism* was taken in the seventeenth century from Italian, where the meaning was "excessive favors granted by certain popes or church dignitaries to their *nepoti*". It was the original English meaning as well, before developing into the modern sense of "favoritism shown or patronage granted to relatives". Italian *nepote* (now *nipote*) has conserved to modern times the three separate meanings of "*nephew—niece*", "grandchildren", and "posterity".

---

[10] Usage quotations from *Oxford English Dictionary.*

The feminine NEPTIS was converted in Vulgar Latin to a more feminine-looking form—NEPTA—and this then followed a normal phonetic evolution to become *nieta*, "granddaughter"; *nieto*, "grandson", was then defined by analogy. *Great-grandchildren* were obtained by adding the prefix *bis-*, "twice":[11]

NEPTA	nieta	granddaughter
	nieto	grandson, grandchild
BIS NEPTA	bisnieta / biz-	great-granddaughter
	bisnieto / biz-	great-grandson, great-grandchild
TRANSTRANS-	tataranieta	great-great-granddaughter
		(< *trastrás* = "after after")
	tataranieto	great-great-grandson, great-great-grandchild

Having defined *nieto* and *nieta* unambiguously to be "grandchildren", Spanish needed to find new words for "nephew" and "niece". SOBRINUS (formerly "[second] cousin") was available and was drafted for this purpose:

SOBRINUS	sobrino	nephew	(< Fr. *neveu* < NEPOS)
SOBRINA	sobrina	niece	(< Fr. *nièce* < NEPTIS)

AVUS	abuelo	grandfather
AVIA	abuela	grandmother
	bisabuelo	great-grandfather, great-grandparent
	bisabuela	great-grandmother
	tatarabuelo	great-great-grandfather, great-great-grandparent
	tatarabuela	great-great-grandmother

Spanish used the Vulgar Latin diminutive forms AVIOLUS (of AVUS) and AVIOLA (of AVIA) to form *abuelo* and *abuela*. AVUS survives in English only through its Classical Latin diminutive AVUNCULUS, the source of *uncle* and *avuncular*.

In-laws

familia política	in-laws (extended sense)
parientes políticos	in-laws (extended sense)

[11] The same prefix (from Latin BIS) that appears in Spanish *bizcocho* and English *biscuit* (literally "twice cooked").

	suegros	parents-in-law
SOCRUS	suegra	mother-in-law
SOCER	suegro	father-in-law
	consuegro, consuegra	father/mother in-law of one's child

Mis padres son *consuegros* de los padres de mi esposa.
"My parents are *consuegros* of the parents of my wife."

If one is referring only to one's *parents-in-law* (as in "my in-laws are visiting this weekend"), one would normally use *los suegros,* whereas the overall family of in-laws is the "political" family. It is not entirely clear whether the "politics" involved refers to its "tactful" and "diplomatic" side or to its "scheming, crafty, cunning" element. It perhaps has to do with the common desire to impress the in-laws, which might also explain the French custom of calling their in-laws "beautiful" and "handsome" (*les beaux-parents, la belle-famille*). Individual members of the "political family" can be referred to in the same way, as in *padre político* ("father-in-law"), *hijo político* ("son-in-law"), etc., but this usage is relatively rare.

SOCRUS was one of the rare feminine Latin nouns ending in -US and would have been expected to evolve into *suegro,* which is also where SOCER (acc. SOCERUM) was heading. Instead, it was "feminized" to *suegra.*

The son's wife, or *daughter-in-law,* being a member of the husband's family has a common Indo-European root, while *son-in-law* does not.[12] Latin NURUS (later NORA) corresponds to Old English *snoru* and is the source of Spanish *nuera.*[13] Latin for *son-in-law* is literally a "generic"[13] term:

| NURUS (NORA) | nuera | daughter-in-law | |
| GENER-UM | yerno | son-in-law | $(nr \rightarrow rn)$ |

The Latin terms for "brother-" and "sister-in-law" (LEVIR and GLOS) were used very infrequently and were replaced in Spanish by the equivalent of *cognate,* i.e., "related by blood", "having a common ancestor", which is of course somewhat inaccurate, since in-laws are not blood relations.[14] The principal use of

---

[12] Indo-European languages generally have common roots for relationships within the husband's family, while those for the family of the wife were left to the discretion of the individual languages.

[13] Latin GENER is from the same family as GENUS (genitive GENERIS), one of whose derivatives is *generic.*

[14] *Cuñado* initially was used to refer to members of the "familia política" in general, before coming to specialize in "siblings-in-law".

cognate is "a word related to one in another language" (e.g., English *father* and Spanish *padre* are cognates).

COGNATUS	cuñado	brother-in-law	[*cognate*]
COGNATA	cuñada	sister-in-law	

Spanish has replaced the Latin terms for "step" relations with ones derived from those relations themselves, with the addition of the "pejorative" suffix -*astro / -astra:*

padrastro	stepfather
madrastra	stepmother
hijastro	stepson, stepchild
hijastra	stepdaughter
hermanastro	stepbrother
hermanastra	stepsister

Guests—Hosts

While "guests" have not always been looked upon as exactly "family":

> Fish and visitors smell after three days. (Benjamin Franklin)
>
> El pescado y los huéspedes huelen después de tres días.

they have played an important role in the evolution of English and the Romance languages.

Anyone who has studied French has probably been confused by the fact that French *hôte,* from which English *host* is derived, signifies both "host" and "guest". Thus *l'hôte est arrivé* can mean either "the guest has arrived" or "the host has arrived". This confusing treatment did not originate with the French: while the distinction between host and guest seems a rather clear one to us, to the original Indo-Europeans the essential element was "someone with whom one has reciprocal duties of hospitality". The Indo-European root **ghos-ti* could thus mean "guest", "stranger", "host". Latin has several words that originated from this root, and that by their varied definitions recall the fundamental ambiguity of the original concept:

HOSTIS	stranger, enemy
HOSPES (genit. HOSPITIS)	host, guest, sojourner, stranger
HOSTIRE	return like for like, requite, make equal

What seems to have happened is that HOSTIS arrived in Latin with the primary meaning of "guest". HOSPITIS was then formed by combining HOSTIS with the adjective POTIS[15]—"master of"—to mean "master of the guest", i.e., *host*. For a time at least, there would have been a clear distinction between *guest* (HOSTIS) and *host* (HOSPITIS), but history repeated itself and HOSPITIS wound up acquiring the meaning "guest" as well. Having lost its meaning of "guest", HOSTIS then became "stranger" and, eventually, "enemy", hence *hostile*:

HOSTILIS	hostil	hostile
HOSTILITAS	hostilidad	hostility

How did HOSPITIS, which was clearly intended to refer to "host", wind up meaning "guest"? This is not too hard to imagine if one thinks of the sort of language that is typically exchanged between host and guest: "treat my home as if it were your own", "honored guest", etc. Indeed, a somewhat similar process has occurred in Russian, where *gost'* is the word for "guest" and *gospodin*—like HOSPITIS—was created by adding the Indo-European adjective for "master", thus producing "lord" or "master". By courtesy, *gospodin* has come to be used as a polite form of address ("Mr."), particularly to foreign "guests"—as in "Gospodin Clinton, welcome to the Kremlin", whereas it is the guests who should, in theory, be addressing their hosts as "gospodin".

huésped (m.)	guest, *host* (biological)	(Fr. *hôte*)
—huéspeda[16]	—female guest, *host* (biological)	
anfitrión (m.)	host	(Fr. *hôte*)
—anfitriona	—hostess	

Old French *hoste* (Modern French *hôte*) was derived from HOSPITIS and maintained the dual meanings of "host" and "guest". Old English already had a Germanic word for *guest*—but no word specifically for "host"—so in the thirteenth century English borrowed *hoste* from French for this purpose, thus giving English an unambiguous distinction between *guest* and *host*. Etymologically, of course, this distinction doesn't exist, since both *host* and *guest* are derived from the Indo-European root **ghos-ti*, meaning, as we have seen, "guest" and "host".

At a relatively early stage, Spanish formed *huésped* from HOSPITIS and used it for both "guest" and "host", though it has wound up specializing in the for-

---

[15] The same POTIS that is represented in Spanish *poder* and English *power* (see Section 4.5).

[16] The use of the separate feminine form is rare: *la huésped* is far more common than *la huéspeda*.

mer—in contrast to English. *Huésped* maintains a certain degree of schizophrenia, however, since not only does the "host" definition still exist (although it is *poco usada* according to the RAE) but an animal that is *host* to a parasite is called a "guest" (*huésped*)! Moreover, the associated verb *hospedar* means "to *host*".

With the increasing specialization of *huésped* as "guest", for "host" Spanish experimented with *hoste*, imported from the Italian *oste*, as well as *hospedador*. These seem not to have been a great success (although both are still found in the dictionary), perhaps because those who remembered their Latin realized that all of these words essentially meant the same thing.

The key to resolving the problem was the discovery of *anfitrión*. The *Diccionario* of the RAE sheds relatively little light on its origin:

De *Anfitrión*, rey de Tebas, espléndido en sus banquetes.

From *Amphitryon*, king of Thebes, splendid in his banquets.

This is, to put it mildly, somewhat misleading. Amphitryon was a *mythological* character who fled to Thebes from his native land after accidentally killing the father of his fiancée Alcmene. While seeming not to hold this against him, she nonetheless refused to allow their relationship to be consummated until he had avenged the deaths of her brothers (avenging that of her father presumably being out of the question). While Amphitryon was off redeeming himself, Zeus appeared in human guise in the form of Amphitryon and seduced Alcmene, for this purpose arranging with the sun that the night would last for the length of three days. From this union Hercules was born—simultaneous with his twin brother, Iphicles, fathered by Amphitryon when, upon his return from battle the following day, he belatedly claimed his marital rights.

The story of Amphitryon was recounted by numerous Greek and Roman writers and continues to be a popular theme to the present day.[17] As far as Spanish is concerned, the seminal event was Molière's *Amphitryon,* first performed in 1668. In the play there is a scene in which Amphitryon returns to his house to confront Zeus, still present in human guise as Amphitryon. It is *Zeus,* not Amphitryon, who has invited a number of guests to a banquet (to celebrate Amphitryon's victories, of course), and Amphitryon's servant is understandably confused to see two Amphitryons, each claiming to be the real one. The false Amphitryon (i.e., Zeus) declares that the matter will be sorted out in due course, and that in the meantime all should repair to the table to eat the meal

---

[17] A twentieth-century French play was entitled *Amphitryon 38*, the author ostensibly having counted the prior accounts of the story.

that has been prepared, at which point the totally bewildered servant utters the meaningless but memorable statement:

> Je ne me trompais pas. Messieurs, ce mot termine toute l'irrésolution: le véritable Amphitryon est l'Amphitryon où l'on dîne.

> I was not mistaken. Messieurs, this last word removes all doubt. The real Amphitryon is the Amphitryon where one dines.

Amphitryon subsequently entered *French* with the meaning of "one who gives dinners", i.e., "host", but it has never enjoyed wide usage outside of literary circles. It is also an English word, at least according to the *Oxford English Dictionary,* but one can safely say that its usage in English remains even more limited. The situation in Spanish was altogether different, however, and was probably affected by the fact that in 1700 Louis XIV's grandson became King Philip V of Spain and, with him, the Bourbons the royal family of Spain. It was not until 1869, however, that *anfitrión* first appeared in the RAE's *Diccionario,* and then only with the definition "he who has guests at his table and regales them in a magnificent manner". The more general definition of "someone who receives visitors in his home or country" first appeared in the RAE's dictionary in *1992.*[18]

Other words derived from HOSPITIS include:

HOSPITALIS	hostal, hostería	hostel, small hotel, inn
	hostelero	innkeeper
	hostelería	hotel business or trade
	hotel (< Fr.)	hotel
	hotelero	hotel (adj.), *hotelier* (manager or owner)
	hospital	hospital
	hospitalizar	(to) hospitalize
	hospitalidad	hospitality
	hospicio	*hospice* (shelter or lodging for travelers, pilgrims, foundlings, destitute), poorhouse
	hospitalario	hospitable, hospital (adj.), Hospitaller (religious order to care for pilgrims & needy)

---

[18] The surprising tardiness of this entry—when all evidence suggests that *anfitrión* had been in widespread use as "host" for quite some time—apparently reflected the RAE's reluctance to give up the "native" word *hospedador* in favor of the Gallic usurper. Moreover, only in 2001 did the RAE modify the definition of *hospedador* (theretofore simply "host") to include the only sense in which it seems to have been used in recent times, i.e., as a *biological* "host" rather than a social one.

hospedar	(to) lodge, (to) put up, (to) *host*
hospedar(se)	(to) lodge or stay at, (to) be a *guest*
hospedaje	lodging, (cost of) room and board
hospedería	hostel, inn, lodging in a convent

The earliest meaning of Old French *hospital* (Modern French *hôpital*) was a religious establishment caring for the poor. It then broadened in meaning to include secular establishments, but it was not until much later (sixteenth century, in English) that it acquired its current medical specialization. *Hospitality* initially meant the provision of free accommodation, as well as the charitable attitude that corresponded to caring for both the indigent and travelers. Old French *hostel* (Modern French *hôtel*) was formed in the eleventh century from HOSPITAL and initially meant "residence", "dwelling"; later it came to mean "hostelry". From this came English and Spanish *hostel—hostal,* and *hotel.* The English meaning of *hospice* as a facility caring for the terminally ill is a late-nineteenth-century development and is not shared (at least not yet) by Spanish *hospicio.*

Taking someone *hostage* is certainly a rather peculiar way of showing hospitality, but it turns out that this word has a similar origin. *Hostage* arose in Old French from *hoste* by adding the typical French noun ending *-age,* in the same manner that *esclavage* ("slavery") was formed from *esclave* ("slave"). It developed the meaning, attested in English as well as in French, of

pledge or security given to enemies or allies for the fulfillment of any undertaking by the handing over of one or more persons into their power.

Hostage was used with particular reference to treaties in which one party guaranteed its good conduct by sending a person of importance (in some cases, a child of the sovereign) to live in the residence of the other. It subsequently evolved from referring to the *condition* of this guarantee to the *person* who represented the guarantee, i.e., what we now call the *hostage.* The Spanish for *hostage* is taken from Arabic:

rehén   hostage

In addition to the "one who gives dinners", there are, of course, two other completely different meanings of *host* in English:

1. an armed company or multitude of men, an army; hence a great number, a multitude;
2. the consecrated bread of the Eucharist.

One of the definitions of HOSTIS was "enemy", and in Medieval Latin this came to be taken in a collective sense, i.e., "enemy army" and later simply "army". In English, the meaning evolved from "army" to the generic sense of "great number"; the disapperance of final *e* in English has led to a confusion in form between *host* (counterpart to guest, formerly *hoste*) and *host* (multitude). In Spanish, HOSTIS became *hueste* ("army", "body of followers") but without developing the English sense of "great number".

| HOSTIS | hueste (f.) | host, army, followers or partisans (pl.) |

HOSTIA was the expiatory "victim" offered to the gods to mollify their wrath, in contrast to the VICTIMA offered as gratitude for favors received. It is likely that this word, too, is derived from the same Indo-European root, the key element being "compensation" (a form of reciprocity). The early Christians gave HOSTIA ("sacrifice" or "offering") its religious meaning of "consecrated bread", and it subsequently arrived into English, via French, as yet another form of *host* (Modern French *hostie*). In Spain, *hostia* has acquired a multitude of pejorative meanings, but this usage does not seem to be as widespread in American Spanish.

| HOSTIA | hostia | host (consecrated bread or wafer) (Spain: smack, punch, bloody hell !, etc.) |
| VICTIMA | víctima | victim (sacrificial or otherwise) |

Appendix

Among the numerous additional words derived from *father* and *mother* are:

CUM + PADRE	compadre	godfather with respect to parents or godmother, father with respect to godparents, *compadre* (close friend, companion)
PATRONUS	patrón, -ona	boss, patron, *pattern*, patron saint
	~ patrono	
	padrón	register of people in a town
	patronal	employers' (adj.), employers' association (f.)
	patrocinar	(to) patronize (support, sponsor)
	patrocinador	patron, sponsor
	patrocinio	patronage (support), sponsorship
	patronato	patronage, foundation, council or board

	—patronato de turismo	—tourism office or board	
PATRINUS	padrino	godfather, second (at a duel)	
	padrinazgo	godfathership, support or protection	
	padrazo	doting father	
	patrimonio	patrimony (inheritance, heritage), wealth	
PATRIA	patria	fatherland	
	—madre patria	—motherland	("mother fatherland")
	patriota	patriot	
	compatriota	compatriot	
	patriótico	patriotic	
	patriotismo	patriotism	
	expatriar	(to) expatriate (exile; leave one's homeland)	
	expatriado (p.p.)	expatriate	
PATRICIUS	patricio	patrician	[*Patrick*]
PATER NOSTER	padrenuestro	paternoster (Lord's Prayer)	
PATER (NOSTER)	——	*patter* (vb.): mumble prayers mechanically, chatter glibly	
	——	*patter* (n.): meaningless talk, rapid speech, jargon	

Patter comes from the "pattering" manner—rapid and mechanical—in which Latin prayers were often repeated by non-Latin speakers.

PERPETRARE	perpetrar	(to) perpetrate
	perpetrador	perpetrator
IMPETRARE	impetrar	(to) beseech, (to) implore

PATRARE meant "to accomplish", "to effect", literally "to father" something. Combined with the preposition PER—and with the normal weakening of interior A to E in closed syllables (see Section 1.3)—PERPETRARE was "to carry through", "to bring to pass", to *perpetrate*. IMPETRARE was initally "to carry out to completion", then "to obtain".

JUPITER	Júpiter	Jupiter, Jove
JOVIALIS	jovial	jovial
JOVIS	jueves	Thursday
	[¡ por Dios !]	by Jove!

JUPITER comes from **dyew pater,* literally "Father Sky", where the first element is the Indo-European root ("to shine") found in Greek *Zeus* and in Latin DIES ("day") and

DIURNUS (*"diurnal"*). In the other grammatical cases (genitive, accusative, etc.), the "Father" element dropped out and, following a "normal" phonetic pattern,[19] what was "left" became JOV-, hence JOVIS ("of Jupiter").

PATRICIDIUM		patricide—act of murdering one's father
PATRICIDA		patricide—murderer of one's father
PARRICIDIUM	parricidio	parricide—murder of father, mother, relative
PARRICIDA	parricida (m./f.)	parricide—one who commits a parricide

While frequently linked, PATRICIDIUM and PARRICIDIUM were theoretically distinct: the former was limited specifically to murdering the father, while the latter could refer as well to the murder of citizens or to high treason. This more general meaning is preserved in English *parricide,* while Spanish *parricidio* limits the crime to murders of close family members, principally the parents. Spanish *patricidio* and *patricida* exist but are rarely used.

MATRONA	matrona	matron, midwife
CUM + MATER	comadre (f.)	godmother with respect to parents or godfather, mother with respect to godparents, midwife, a gossip[20]
	comadreja[21]	weasel
CUM + MATRONA	comadrona	midwife
MATRINA	madrina	godmother
	madraza	doting mother
ALMA MATER	alma máter	university, alma mater
MATRICIDIUM	matricidio	matricide (act)
MATRICIDA	matricida (m./f.)	matricide (person)

The concept of "mother" could be applied to plant and animal life as well. MATERIA initially meant "the substance within the trunk of a tree of which branches and leaves were the offspring". The definition was then extended to the "hard" part of the trunk, as opposed to its outer "shell", or CORTEX (source of Spanish *corteza*, "bark", and possibly English *cork*). MATRIX initially referred to a pregnant animal or one kept for breeding, before developing both the more specific meaning of "womb" and the more general one

---

[19] The basic "rule" was that -*ew*- became [u] before a consonant (JUPITER) but [ow] before a vowel (JOVIS).

[20] English *gossip* has an entirely analogous origin to *comadre* and *compadre:* it was originally *godsib,* i.e., "god sibling", specifically a godfather or godmother. Apart from its "gossipy" side, *gossip* maintains the definition of "close friend or companion", e.g., a *compadre.*

[21] I.e., "little midwife". In various other European languages the weasel was given similar names, e.g. "daughter-in-law", "sister-in-law", "young lady" (Portuguese *doninha,* Italian *donnola*), "young beauty" (French *belette*). This apparently was due to a common folk superstition that the weasel—feared as a demon—had mysterious forces, and the affectionate names were thus intended to placate it (Rohlfs, 70–72).

of "source" or "origin". Its diminutive MATRICULA took on the meaning of a "register" or "list" (of names).

MATERIA	materia	*matter*
	madera	wood
	material	material
MATRIX	matriz	uterus (~ *útero*), womb, *matrix*
MATRICULA	matrícula	license (plate), registration
	matricular	(to) register, (to) enroll, (to) *matriculate*
CORTEX	corteza	bark, crust, peel, skin, *cortex*
	descortezar	*decorticate* (remove outer layer)
	corcho	cork (material, stopper, float)
	descorchar	(to) uncork, (to) bark (a cork tree)
	sacacorchos	corkscrew (~ *descorchador*)
	alcornoque [22]	cork tree, blockhead

PATRIARCHA ("chief or head of a family") was adopted by Latin from Greek. Its female counterpart was a seventeenth-century innovation.

PATRIARCHA	patriarca (m.)	patriarch
	patriarcal	patriarchal
	patriarcado	patriarchy, patriarchate
	matriarca	matriarch
	matriarcal	matriarchal
	matriarcado	matriarchy, matriarchate

---

[22] From Arabic, the ultimate source being Latin QUERNUS ("of oak").

SECTION 4.9

Body, Spirit, and Mind

For the Romans, there was an essential series of contrasts or oppositions between *body, spirit,* and *mind.* The first portion of the presentation will consider these contrasts, following which there will be a detailed inventory of the physical parts of the body, public and private.

Body

The neuter noun CORPUS (genit. CORPORIS) referred not only to the living organism but also to the inanimate body (i.e., *corpse*). It could also be used to designate any material object, e.g., the trunk of a tree. As the body is composed of "parts", CORPUS was often applied to other entities made up of parts, as in CORPUS JURIS ("body of law").

CORPUS	cuerpo	body, corps, corpse, corpus
	cuerpo diplomático	diplomatic corps
	cuerpo a cuerpo	hand-to-hand (combat)
	cuerpo legal ~	corpus juris (body of law)
	cuerpo de leyes	
	cuerpo extraño	foreign body (medical, e.g., in the eye)
	cuerpo de bomberos	fire brigade (or department)
	tomar cuerpo	(to) take shape, (to) grow
CORPORALIS	corporal	corporal (adj.), body or bodily (adj.)
	incorporal	incorporeal, intangible
CORPOREUS	corpóreo	corporeal (of a material nature; tangible)
	incorpóreo	incorporeal (having no material body)
CORPULENTUS	corpulento	corpulent
	corpulencia	corpulence
CORPUSCULUM	corpúsculo	corpuscle
	corsé	corset

CORPUSCULUM was the Latin diminutive of CORPUS and was thus "small body" or "small particle". *Corset* comes from French, formed as a diminutive of *corps* (Old French *cors*).

CORPORATIO(N)	corporación	corporation (gen. of public nature)
	incorporación	incorporation (into), joining a group
INCORPORARE	incorporar	(to) incorporate (unite, embody), (to) join, (to) raise to a sitting position

CORPORARE was "to give a body to", "to take form", while INCORPORARE implied uniting something with something else already in existence to give them a single "corporate" form. The notion of a *corporation* as a "body of people given a legal existence distinct from the individuals who compose it" is a fifteenth-century English innovation, imported by Spanish in the nineteenth century. A money-making corporation is generally a *sociedad anónima* rather than a *corporación,* and "to incorporate (a company)" is conveyed by various expressions, including *constituir una sociedad anónima.*

Spirit

Latin had two closely related words representing the *spirit* of life as opposed to its physical manifestation in a *body:*

| ANIMUS | thinking element, reason, mind, spirit |
| ANIMA | breath, air (and by extension), soul, spirit |

ANIMUS was the superior principle to which ANIMA was subordinated; not surprisingly,[1] ANIMUS was masculine and ANIMA feminine. An effort was generally made to distinguish the two words, but over time the subordinated element, ANIMA, encroached on the domain of ANIMUS and came to be used frequently in its place. ANIMA is the origin of the Romance *soul:*

ANIMA	alma	soul	(It. *anima,* Fr. *âme*)
	ánima	soul (esp. one in purgatory)	
	desalmado	soulless, cruel, inhuman	

while ANIMUS survives in English and Spanish as the "actuating feeling" or "animating spirit":

| ANIMUS | ánimo | animus (disposition), spirit(s), energy |

---

[1] Given the mentality of the times.

In English, *animus* has acquired the negative connotation of *"animosity* shown in speech or action", as a result of contamination by *animosity*. This in turn initially had the positive meaning of "spiritedness", "ardor" (i.e., possessing lots of ANIMUS), before acquiring the definition (notably in the Vulgate Bible) of "bitter hostility or open enmity". Both definitions passed into English and Spanish, though only the negative definition is employed today.[2]

ANIMOSITAS   animosidad   animosity

Jungian psychology restored the masculine-feminine distinction between English *animus* and *anima:*

animus   the masculine inner personality, as present in women
anima   the feminine inner personality, as present in men

The verb ANIMARE was associated with both ANIMA and ANIMUS and meant "to give life to", *to animate*. An ANIMAL was a living thing that had been given ANIMA, the "breath of life".

ANIMARE	animar	(to) animate, (to) cheer up
ANIMATUS	animado (p.p.)	animate, lively
INANIMATUS	inanimado	inanimate
ANIMATIO(N)	animación	animation
DIS + ANIMUS	desánimo	discouragement, downheartedness
DIS + ANIMARE	desanimar	(to) dishearten, (to) discourage
	desanimado (p.p.)	discouraged, dispirited
ANIMAL	animal	animal
ANIMALIA ("animals")	alimaña	beast, vermin

Spanish took the plural of animal, ANIMALIA, and converted it into a feminine singular meaning animal "pest", with an interchange of the *n* and *l*.

El zorro es una alimaña que mata gallinas.   The fox is a pest that kills chickens.

Animism, meaning either the attribution of a living soul (ANIMA) to animals— somewhat tautologically, since it is their very definition—and other objects or

---

[2] The first definition can still be found in many Spanish dictionaries, including that of the RAE.

the belief that an immaterial force animates the universe, is a relatively modern innovation (eighteenth–nineteenth century).

animismo	animism
animista	animist

ANIMUS formed compounds with a number of other words:

(a) AEQUUS (*"equal"*, "even") → AEQUANIMITAS, "evenness of mind or temper"
(b) MAGNUS ("large", "great") → MAGNANIMUS, "noble-minded", "generous"
(c) PUSILLUS ("tiny") → PUSILLANIMIS, PUSILLANIMUS, "faint-hearted"
(d) UNUS ("one") → UNANIMIS, UNANIMUS, "of one mind"
(e) advertere ("to turn toward") → animadvertere, "to give attention to", "to notice", "to censure", "to punish"

AEQUANIMITAS	ecuanimidad	equanimity, impartiality
	ecuánime	even-tempered, impartial
MAGNANIMUS	magnánimo	magnanimous
	magnanimidad	magnanimity
PUSILLANIMIS / -MUS	pusilánime	pusillanimous
	pusilanimidad	pusillanimity
UNANIMIS / -MUS	unánime	unanimous
	unanimidad	unanimity
	por unanimidad	unanimously
ANIMADVERSIO(N)	animadversión	animosity

Spanish *animadversión* theoretically can be used with the English meaning of "strong criticism", but this sense is *desusado*.

Having already seen its role reduced by the increasing prominence of ANIMA, from the time of the Emperor Augustus, ANIMUS was threatened by competition from SPIRITUS as well. SPIRITUS was derived from the verb SPIRARE, "to breathe", "to blow", "to exhale an odor". Over time, SPIRARE came to acquire more figurative, or *spiritual,* meanings—"to be alive", "to be inspired"—and SPIRITUS similarly expanded its meaning from "breathing" or "breath" to "the breath of life", "spirit", "energy". The religious sense of SPIRITAL-IS (later, SPIRITUAL-IS) arose during early Christian times; before then, it had simply meant "pertaining to the act of breathing".

SPIRITUS	espíritu (m.)	spirit
	Espíritu Santo	Holy Ghost

SPIRITUALIS	espiritual	spiritual
	espiritualidad	spirituality
	espiritualismo	spiritualism
	espiritismo	spiritism (belief in spirits)

Espíritu is one of the very few Spanish words of Latin origin ending in -*u*, reflecting its constant use in a religious (hence "learned") context (a similar example is *tribu*).

The verb SPIRARE was productively combined with a number of prefixes (perhaps too many, as we shall see):

(i) AD ("to", "toward") → ASPIRARE, "to breathe (or blow) upon", "to exhale", "to strive for"

(ii) CUM ("with") → CONSPIRARE, literally "to breathe (or blow) together", used in the figurative senses "to be in agreement", "to plot against"

(iii) EX ("from") → EXSPIRARE, "to breathe out", "to exhale", "to breathe one's last"

(iv) IN ("in", "into") → INSPIRARE, "to blow upon", "to breathe or blow into", "to instill", "to excite"

(v) PER ("through", "thoroughly") → PERSPIRARE, "to blow constantly", "to breathe everywhere" (VENTI PERSPIRANTES meant "persistent winds")

(vi) RE ("again") → RESPIRARE, "to blow or breathe back", "to breathe out", "to exhale", "to catch one's breath"

(vii) SUB ("under", "beneath") → SUSPIRARE, "to draw a deep breath", "to sigh", "to exhale", "to long for"

Medieval Latin created yet another form, using the prefix TRANS ("across", "through"), to give TRANSPIRARE (literally "to breathe through").

The first thing to note is that ASPIRARE, EXSPIRARE, INSPIRARE, and RESPIRARE all referred to an *outward* flow of air. A person's *aspirations* were defined by what he breathed or blew *upon*; similarly, a person was *inspired* by having "inspiration" blown *onto* him or her. So how did the Romans refer to an *inward* flow of air into the lungs? It wasn't by *inhalation*, since the verb IN-HALARE also meant "to breathe *upon*". Inhalation was in fact described by expressions of the form "to draw, or conduct, the breath [into the lungs]", while the two-way act of breathing (what we would call *respiration*) was a "reciprocal movement" of the breath:

SPIRITUM TRAHERE / DUCERE	to draw or conduct the *spirit*
ANIMAM TRAHERE / DUCERE	to draw or conduct the *anima*
ANIMAM RECIPROCARE	to move the *anima* back and forth

In both English and Spanish, the definitions of *aspiration*—*aspiración* have evolved to include *both* inward *and* outward movements:

1. the act of breathing in; inhalation
2. expulsion of breath in speech; *"aspirated" h*
3. the process of removing fluids or gases with a suction device
4. desire for high achievement

ASPIRARE	aspirar	(to) aspire, (to) aspirate (incl. "inhale")	
	aspiración	aspiration	
	aspiradora, aspirador	vacuum cleaner	[*aspirator*]
	aspirante	aspirant (for position, honors)	
CONSPIRARE	conspirar	(to) conspire	
	conspiración	conspiracy	
	conspirador	conspirator	

English *expirar* has definitions overlapping with Spanish *espirar* (from SPIRARE) and *expirar* (from EXSPIRARE), separate verbs that many Spanish speakers pronounce identically. Until 1884 they were actually spelled the same (*espirar*), at which point the RAE tried to establish some etymological order. *Espirar* means to *exhale,* either air *from* the lungs or, rarely, an odor from the body, as well as to *infuse* with a spirit, divine or otherwise. *Expirar* has nothing to do (directly) with "air" but rather with the "end" of something.

SPIRARE	espirar	(to) expire (breathe out)
	espiración	expiration (breathing out), exhalation
EXSPIRARE	expirar	(to) expire (terminate), (to) breathe one's last
	expiración	expiration (termination)

Spanish *inspirar* and English *inspire* maintain the figurative meanings from Latin INSPIRARE—"to animate", "to infuse with spirit", etc. With regard to physical airflow, both languages have reversed the direction: to breathe *in* ("inhale") rather than *upon*.

INSPIRARE	inspirar	(to) inspire, (to) inhale
	inspiración	inspiration, inhalation
RESPIRARE	respirar	(to) respire, (to) breathe, (to) take a breather, (to) exude
	respiración	respiration, breathing, ventilation

	respiratorio	respiratory
	respiro	breath (pause), breather, respite
SUSPIRARE	suspirar	(to) sigh, (to) long for, (to) *suspire*
	suspiro	sigh, type of meringue
	—último suspiro	—last sigh (end; death)

The outward airflow represented by Latin INHALARE has also been reversed, so that *inhalar—inhale* represent the "logical" opposites to *exhalar—exhale.*

INHALARE	inhalar	(to) inhale
	inhalación	inhalation
	inhalador	inhaler *or* inhalator (med.)
EXHALARE	exhalar	(to) exhale, (to) heave (a sigh)
	exhalación	exhalation
	—como una exhalación	—rapidly, in a flash
HALITUS	hálito	breath, gentle breeze ("breath of fresh air")
	halitosis	halitosis, bad breath

In Latin, "to sweat" was SUDARE and "sweat" was SUDOR. From these, French derived *suer* and *sueur.* In addition to their direct physical meanings, French employed the two words in a large number of metaphorical senses, analogous to English "sweating blood", "to make them sweat", "to sweat over the results of an exam", etc. In the sixteenth century, a need arose for a more scientific, or elegant, way to refer to the physical act of evaporation through the skin, and French responded by coming up with not one, but two: (a) *transpirer,* from Medieval Latin TRANSPIRARE; and (b) *perspirer,* from Classical Latin PERSPIRARE.

Perspirer and *perspiration* never really caught on in French but did survive long enough to serve as the basis (in the seventeenth century) for English *perspire* and *perspiration.* These entered English with meanings very similar to *transpire* and *transpiration,* which had arrived from French sometime earlier. *Perspiration* subsequently specialized as a form of human *transpiration,* i.e., "sweat". *To transpire* can also mean "to happen or come to pass", although many style manuals frown on this usage. It transpires that this sense goes back at least to the eighteenth century and can be found, with no adverse comment, in Noah Webster's *American Dictionary of the English Language* (1828).[3] *Perspiration* never made it to Spanish, but *transpiración* did, and it, along with the

---

[3] Abigail to John Adams in a 1775 letter: "there is nothing new *transpired* since I wrote you last".

more traditional *sudar,* are the two ways of referring in Spanish to the act of sweating.

The resemblance in form between English *sweat* and Latin SUDARE is no coincidence, as both ultimately come from the Indo-European root **sweid*. While SUDARE and SUDOR were not able to displace the already well-entrenched (noun and verb) *sweat,* they did leave their mark in English in various forms, including *sudatorium* ("a sweating room"), *sudorific,* and the verb *exude* (literally "to sweat from").

SUDARE	sudar	(to) sweat
	sudor	sweat
	sudoroso	sweaty
	sudadera	sweatshirt
	sudorífico	sudorific: sweat-inducing (medication)
	sudario	(burial) shroud
EXSUDARE	exudar	(to) exude, (to) ooze out
TRANSPIRARE	transpirar	(to) perspire, (to) transpire (liquid or vapor)
	transpiración	perspiration, transpiration

Mind

Whereas ANIMUS represented the spirit and CORS (the heart) the seat of desire and of passions, Latin MENS was the *mind,* "intelligence", "intellectual faculty". It also came to represent "spirit, boldness, courage". Again, the similarity with English *mind* is not a random happenstance but a reflection of their common derivation from the Indo-European root **men-*, "to think". MENTAL-IS did not exist in Classical Latin but was formed in Medieval Latin in analogy with SPIRITAL-IS.

MENS (acc. MENTEM)	mente (f.)	mind
MENTALIS	mental	mental
	mentalidad	mentality
	mentalizar	(to) make aware (of situation, problem)
MENTIO(N)	mención	mention
	mencionar	(to) mention
	mentar	(to) mention
MENTE CAPTUS[4]	mentecato	silly, foolish, fool (m./f.)

---

[4] Literally "captured by the mind".

A *demented* person, or one who suffers *dementia,* has lost his mind:

DEMENTIA	demencia	dementia (incl. "insanity")
	demente (adj. & n.)	demented, a demented person

A person who has lost his mind in the sense of not being able to remember anything is an *amnesiac* and suffers from *amnesia,* from Greek.

amnesia	amnesia
amnésico (adj. & n.)	amnesic, amnestic, amnesiac

MENS was the source of a number of verbs having to do with the mind. MONERE[5] meant to "bring to mind", i.e., "to warn or advise", one form of this being a MONUMENTUM. The bearer of the warning was a MONITOR. A divine portent or warning was a MONSTRUM, which served very clearly to MONSTRARE, or *demonstrate,* something. MEMINISSE was "to remember", and its future imperative form (*remember!*) was MEMENTO. MINISCI, a rarely used verb ("to think", "to remember"), combined with CUM ("with") to form COMMINISCI ("to invent", "to contrive"), whose neuter past participle was COMMENTUM, literally an "invention or contrivance" rather than a *comment.* COMMENTARI meant to have in mind, i.e., "to meditate", "to reflect", and MENTIRI, "to invent in the mind", "to tell an untruth".

MONSTRARE	mostrar	(to) show, (to) display	[*muster*]
	muestra	sample, sign or token	
	mostrador	counter (flat surface)	
MONSTRUM	monstruo	monster	
	monstruoso	monstrous	
	monstruosidad	monstrosity	
DEMONSTRARE	demostrar	(to) demonstrate	
	demostración	demonstration	
	demostrable	demonstrable	
	demostrativo	demonstrative	
RE + MONSTRARE	[protestar]	(to) remonstrate	
MONUMENTUM	monumento	monument	
	monumental	monumental	
MONITOR	monitor	monitor, adviser	

---

[5] With a variation in stem vowel, from E to O, which is characteristic in Indo-European languages to mark a change in grammatical function—technically a form of *ablaut* or *vowel gradation,* another example being the vowel changes in "irregular" English verbs (e.g., *sing—sang—sung*).

	monitorizar	(to) monitor (gen. using instrument)
ADMONESTARE (VL)	amonestar	(to) admonish, (to) publish banns
	amonestación	admonishment, warning, banns (pl.)
	admonición	admonition, reprimand
MEMENTO	memento	memento (religious sense only)
COMMENTUM	comento [very rare]	comment, commentary, falsehood
COMMENTARI	comentar	(to) comment
	comentario	commentary, comment
	comentarista	commentator
MENTIRI	mentir	(to) lie
	mentira	lie, falsehood
	mentiroso (adj. & n.)	lying, deceptive, liar
("you [*vosotros*] lie")	mentís (m.)	categorical denial, refutation
	desmentir	(to) deny, (to) contradict, (to) give the lie to

MINISCI also combined with RE to form REMINISCI ("to recall to mind"), the source of English *reminisce,* which has no counterpart in Spanish, although the accompanying noun is common to the two languages:

REMINISCENTIA   reminiscencia   reminiscence

MENS has also given rise, by a process that is described in the appendix to this section, to the largest class of Romance adverbs.

One's power of *reasoning* comes from the ability to think or reckon. This was expressed in Latin by the verb RERI, whose descendants in Spanish and English are drawn from its past participle RATA (feminine) and related verbal noun RATIO(N), the latter accounting for three separate words in English, plus a naturalized French term: *reason, ratio, ration,* and *raison d'être.*

RATIO(N)	razón (f.)	*reason, ratio*
	—razón directa (inversa)	—direct (inverse) proportion
	—tener razón	—(to) be right (lit. "to have *reason*")

	—razón de ser	—*raison d'être*	
	razonable	reasonable	
	irrazonable	unreasonable	
	razonamiento	reasoning, argument (course of reasoning)	
	razonar	(to) reason	
	ración	*ration* (fixed portion, esp. of food)	
	racional	rational, reasonable	
	racionalidad	rationality, reasonableness	
	racionalizar	(to) rationalize	
	racionamiento	rationing	
	irracional	irrational	
	irracionalidad	irrationality	
PRO RATA (PARTE)	prorrata	a proportional share	[*rate*]
	—a prorrata	—pro rata, in proportion	
	prorrateo	a pro rata division, apportionment	
	prorratear	(to) prorate, (to) distribute proportionally	

A *portion* is essentially a *ration*: at an early stage in Latin the expression PRO RATIONE was shortened to PORTIONE.

PORTIO(N)	porción	portion, part

To *ratify* something is literally to confirm that it is reasonable:

ratificar	(to) ratify, (to) confirm (e.g., testimony)
ratificación	ratification, confirmation

In Latin, RATIOCINARI literally meant "to sing with reason",[6] hence "to calculate", "to deliberate".

RATIOCINARI	raciocinar	(to) ratiocinate, (to) reason
	raciocinio	reason (faculty), reasoning, ratiocination

---

[6] The second part of the word comes from the root *can-* found in CANTARE / *cantar* ("to sing"), with the regular interior vowel change ($A \to I$) discussed in Section 1.3.

Parts of the Body

We will proceed in a generally north-to-south (top-to-bottom) sense.

Not surprisingly, CAPUT figures at the head of the list in terms of the number of words bequeathed to English and the Romance languages. CAPUT became *cabo* in Spanish, which basically means "extremity" or "end" and in geographical terms is equivalent to English *cape,* itself derived from Occitan (via French) *cap.* The Spanish for "head" comes from a diminutive form, CAPITIA, which became popular in the Hispanic part of the Roman Empire. The plural of CAPUT was CAPITA, so that *per capita* literally means "by heads".

CAPUT	cabo	*cape,* extremity, corporal, *cable* (nautical)
CAPITIA	cabeza	head
PER CAPITA	per cápita	per capita, per head

Cabo is used in a figurative sense in a number of expressions, including:

al fin y al cabo	after all is said and done
al cabo de un mes	in a month, after a month
de cabo a rabo	from beginning to end (literally "from head to tail")
llevar a cabo	(to) carry out (to completion)
cabo suelto	loose end
atar cabos	(to) put two and two together

Cabeza has been used to form a number of words and expressions, a small fraction of which are shown below:

cabeza de chorlito	scatterbrain	("head of a golden plover")
cabeza de puente	bridgehead	
cabeza de playa	beachhead	
perder la cabeza	(to) lose one's head	
romper(se) la cabeza	(to) rack one's brains	
rompecabezas	(jigsaw) puzzle	
cabeza(s) de ganado	head of cattle	
cabeza de ajo(s)	bulb of garlic	
cabezazo	blow with the head, butt, header (soccer)	
cabezón	bigheaded, pigheaded [or such person]	
cabezota	large head, stubborn person	

cabecera	headboard, headwaters, header (e.g., e-mail)
cabecear	(to) nod or nod off, (to) head (soccer)
descabezar	(to) *decapitate*
descabezado (p.p.)	headless, reckless, absentminded
encabezar	(to) put a heading on, (to) head
encabezamiento	heading (letter, text, etc.)

French formed the noun *cabotage* ("trade or navigation in coastal waters"), whose origin is disputed but very likely comes from Spanish *cabo*. The meaning was subsequently expanded to include air traffic rights for foreign airlines within another country.

| cabotaje | cabotage |
| capataz | foreman, overseer (~ *mayoral*) |

CAPUT became *chief* in Old French, with the characteristic Central French palatization of CA-.[7] For a time French *chief* meant "head",[8] but it was eventually supplanted by *tête*, with *chief* maintaining its meaning as "head of". In Modern French, it has become *chef*, which developed its culinary sense in the eighteenth century. A *chef-d'oeuvre* is a "masterpiece" in English (and French) but not in Spanish.

jefe,[9] jefa	*chief*, boss, leader
—jefe de cocina	—chef (~ *cocinero*)
jefatura	headquarters, leadership (position)
[obra maestra]	chef-d'oeuvre, *master*piece, *master*work

Apart from producing "chief", CAPUT is responsible for two military ranks, *captain* and *corporal,* the latter having only an indirect connection with the "corporal" in *corporal punishment. Captain* and *capitán* come from Late Latin CAPITANEUS ("principal", "chief"), while *corporal* has a more complicated his-

---

[7] For this reason, English *cha-* words frequently correspond to Spanish *ca-* ones: *chart–carta, chamber–cámara, chase–cazar, chaste–casto, chapel–capilla,* etc.

[8] As in ker*chief* (< French *couvre-chef*), which literally means "head cover"; handker*chief* is thus etymologically a "hand head cover".

[9] Earlier *xefe,* pronounced like English *chef* with an initial [sh]; as noted in Section 3.5, no. 4, the [sh] sound subsequently shifted to [h*], and the spelling was accordingly modified to *jefe.*

tory. First attested in Italian (*caporale*) in the fourteenth century, it entered Medieval Latin as CAPORALIS ("chief of a band of soldiers"). There it suffered an apparent contamination with the unrelated word CORPUS, giving rise to a competing form CORPORALIS, presumably because a CAPORALIS was in charge of a CORPUS of soldiers. The two competing forms entered French in the sixteenth century, as *caporal* and *corporal*: the second died out, but not before giving rise to English *corporal*. The initial meaning in both French and Italian was similar to "captain" before being demoted to the "officer having the lowest rank", which is how it entered English. Italian *caporale* was also exported directly to Spanish, where as *caporal* it maintains various primarily nonmilitary meanings of "chief". A Spanish "corporal" is a *cabo*.

capitán	captain
—capitanear	—(to) captain, (to) command
cabo	corporal
caporal	chief, leader, cattle boss

Things concerning the head were CAPITALIS, and often carried the connotation of "mortal" or "fatal", as in:

POENA CAPITALIS	pena capital	capital punishment
CAPITALI PERICULO	en peligro de muerte	at risk (*peril*) of death
CAPITALIS INIMICUS	enemigo mortal	mortal enemy
PECCATUM CAPITALE	pecado mortal	mortal sin

The associated noun CAPITAL meant a *capital offense,* one subject to the punishment of removing the CAPUT. CAPITAL entered the Romance languages and English with both the connotation of "involving loss of the head or life" and that of "important, principal". A *capital* city dates from the early fifteenth century in French and somewhat later in English and Spanish. Another practical application in English was to *capital* letters (Spanish *mayúscula*). The financial sense of *capital* came from Italian *capitale,* the "principal" part of a debt as opposed to payments of interest.

capital (adj.& n.)	capital (vital, extremely serious), capital (wealth)
capital (f.)	capital (city)
capitalismo	capitalism
capitalista (adj. & n.)	capitalist
capitalizar	(to) capitalize (financial senses; turn to one's advantage)
[escribir en mayúsculas]	(to) capitalize (use capital letters)
capitalización	capitalization (financial)

To *decapitate* is "to remove the head", "to behead". Perhaps somewhat surprisingly, the word was not used by the Romans, though the practice itself was not
unknown. DECAPITARE was a Medieval Latin invention that the French took
as *décapiter* before passing it on to English (seventeenth century) and Spanish
(nineteenth century).

decapitar	(to) decapitate
decapitación	decapitation

BICEPS—with the normal modification (see Section 1.3) of the vowel A from
CAPUT—referred to something having two heads; TRICEPS and QUADRICEPS
similarly referred to things having three and four heads, respectively. In the
mid-sixteenth century, French gave *biceps* and *triceps* the anatomical meanings
of *any* muscle having two (or three) points of attachment at its upper end. It
was not until sometime later that they became specialized by referring to specific muscles. In the medical sense, *quadriceps* was an English innovation and
was never a generic term, referring from its origin to a specific muscle in the
thigh having four heads.

bíceps	biceps
tríceps	triceps
cuádriceps	quadriceps

Like many Latin diminutives, CAPITULUM, literally "little head", has been a
fertile source for new words. In Roman times, it was used for a variety of purposes, including "onion" (*head*-shaped) as well as a division of a text or law.
This latter presumably arose from the *heading* at the beginning of each section,
or *chapter*. In Medieval Latin, CAPITULUM also came to represent the convoca-
tion of canons of a religious order for the purpose of reading a *chapter* of the
Scriptures, as well as the actual text itself. In Old French, CAPITULUM became
chapitle and, with a substitution of *r* for *l*, *chapitre*. The competing forms both
passed into English, the *l* form dying out in the fifteenth century, the *r* form
becoming simplified to *chapter*.

Spanish has three forms directly derived from CAPITULUM (the third from
the plural CAPITULA):

capítulo	chapter (incl. assembly of church canons)	
cabildo	chapter (canons of a cathedral), town council	(*dl* → *ld*)
capítula	chapter (scriptural passage read after the psalms)	

CAPITULUM also was the source of Medieval Latin CAPITULARE, "to draw
up under distinct headings", "to make a report point by point", a meaning

maintained in English *recapitulate* and *recap* (as in "to recap today's top story . . ."). In the late sixteenth century, *capitulate* took on the meaning (first attested in Shakespeare) "to draw up articles of agreement", and a century later, "to surrender on agreed terms".

capitular (1)	(to) capitulate
capitulación	capitulation
recapitular	(to) recapitulate, (to) recap
recapitulación	recapitulation, recap
capitular (2)	capitular, capitulary (member of a *chapter*)

A diminutive itself, CAPITULUM had its own diminutive, CAPITELLUM, which was used to refer to the "small head" at the top of a pillar or column. This latter word is responsible for the two principal English words that refer to this element, *chapiter* and *capital*. The first comes from Old French *chapitel* (Modern French *chapiteau*), with the *l* changed to *r,* as in *chapter.* The second is from *capitel,* an Anglo-Norman form of the same word without the palatization of initial Latin CA-; the change in final vowel from *e* to *a* is an English innovation reflecting its confusion with *capital* (from CAPITAL):

capitel	capital *or* chapiter (of a pillar or column)

Another derivation of CAPITELLUM provided the title of "supreme leader" assumed by Franco in 1938 in imitation of Mussolini (*Duce*) and Hitler (*Führer*). It seems unlikely that he was aware of its etymological sense—"little little head".

caudillo	chief, military leader

Rome was built on seven hills, one of which was the CAPITOLIUM (known as MONS CAPITOLINUS, hence *Capitoline Hill*). It owes its name, at least according to Roman historians, to the fact that when digging the foundations for the giant Temple of Jupiter on the hill, workmen found a human skull (CAPUT) with its face intact—this was taken as a portent that Rome would become the "citadel of the empire" and the "head of the world". Other cities took to giving their most magnificent citadels or temples the same name. *Capitol* has thus come to mean "a citadel on top of a hill", or more specifically in the United States, the buildings occupied by the Congress and a number of state legislatures.

capitolio	elevated and majestic edifice, capitol

To finish something is, by definition, to "arrive at the end of" it. Both Spanish and French used "head" to refer to an extreme point (or "end") and created corresponding verbs and nouns:

a + cabo	→	acabar (Sp.)	(to) finish, (to) complete
		acabamiento (Sp.)	completion
a + chief	→	achever (Fr.)	(to) finish, (to) complete
		achèvement (Fr.)	completion

French *achever* and *achèvement* became English *achieve* and *achievement,* initially with the meaning of "completing" a task. Subsequently, they changed in nuance from the act of "finishing" to that of "accomplishing". Spanish *achievement* is expressed by:

| conseguir, lograr, llevar a cabo | (to) achieve |
| logro, hazaña | achievement, success |

Combined with *menos* ("less"), the result was *menoscabar;*

| menoscabar | (to) lessen, (to) impair, (to) detract from | |
| menoscabo | lessening, impairment, detriment | [*mischief*] |

Spanish *cabo* also produced *cabal,* meaning "exact" or "faultless". English *cabal* ("conspiratorial group", "intrigue") has an entirely different origin, coming instead (via Medieval Latin) from Hebrew.

cabal	exact, complete, upright (honorable)
—estar en sus cabales	—(to) be in one's right mind (gen. used negatively: *no estar . . .*)
—cabalmente	—exactly, completely
cábala	*kabbalah (cabala),*[10] divination by numbers, guess or supposition (gen. pl.), *cabal* (secret scheme or plot)

Latin combined PRAE ("before", "in front") with CAPUT to form PRAECEPS, which literally meant "head first". This was used with a variety of figurative

---

[10] *Kabbalah* refers to Jewish mysticism as it developed in the twelfth and following centuries, much of it based in Spain. To the "outside" world, it was best known as an arcane system for decoding sacred texts based on numbers, letters, syllables, etc. The sense of "secret scheme or plot" (i.e., *cabal*) seems to have first developed in France.

meanings, such as "he was thrown headfirst out of the tavern" and "headfirst (or steep) terrain". Both PRAECEPS and the derived PRAECIPITIUM came to mean a "high cliff", "a dangerous situation", a *precipice*. PRAECIPITARE was "to throw from a great height, "to fall from", *to precipitate,* while PRAECIPITATIO(N) was the "action of casting down" or "a headlong rush", which in Medieval Latin developed the sense of "ruin", "destruction". As early as the fifteenth century, English *precipitate* was used to refer to the process of separating a substance from a solution as a solid, and in the nineteenth century, it was applied to droplets of water falling headfirst from the heights during periods of inclement weather.

precipicio	precipice
precipitar	(to) precipitate (various senses)
precipitación	precipitation (various senses)
precipitadamente	precipitately, hastily
precipitado (p.p.)	precipitate (hasty, headlong), precipitate (n.)
precipitoso [rare]	precipitous (steep) (~ *escarpado*)

To end this section on a more capricious note, Latin ERICIUS, "hedgehog", became Italian *riccio*. In the fourteenth century, this combined with *capo* ("head" from CAPUT) to produce *caporiccio* and then (apparently) *capriccio*: the initial meaning was "shudder of horror", presumably from the fact that when one is scared, one's hair tends to resemble that of a hedgehog. Over time, this meaning evolved to "a sudden and unaccountable change of mind", "a whim", probably due to influence from *capra* ("goat"). The word entered French (as *caprice*) and Spanish with this meaning in the sixteenth century, and arrived in English the following century.

capricho	caprice, whim, capriccio (music)
caprichoso	capricious, whimsical
caprichosamente	capriciously

We now move on to the internal and external elements of the *cabeza:*

CEREBRUM	cerebro	brain, *cerebrum*
	cerebral	cerebral (pert. to the brain, intellectual)
	cerebelo	cerebellum
CRANIUM	cráneo	cranium, skull
CALVARIA	calavera	skull, death's head, *calvarium*

	calvario[11]	Calvary, Golgotha, calvary (ordeal)	
sinn (Germ.)[12]	sien (f.)	temple	[(Lat.) *sense*]
PILUS	pelo	hair (human or animal)	[*pile* carpet]
	terciopelo	velvet	(third + hair)
	aterciopelado	velvety	
CAPILLUS	cabello	hair (human)	[*capillary*]

Theoretically, *pelo* is one hair and *cabello* the collection of a person's hair—a distinction dating back to their Latin origins—but in practice the two words seem to be used almost interchangeably. Animals, however, do not have *cabello* but *pelo* (or *pelaje*). English *pilosity*, "covered with fine soft hair", comes from PILUS.

peludo	hairy, furry, shaggy	
pelusa	fuzz (fruits, face), fluff, lint	[*pilose*]
peluche	*plush* (fabric), stuffed toy animal	
peluca	*peruke*,[13] wig	
peluquín	toupee, hairpiece	
pelaje	*pelage* (animal coat or fur)	
peletería	fur shop, furriery	
peluquería	hairdressers, barbershop	
peluquero	barber, hairdresser	
pelagatos	penniless person, a nobody	[hair + *cats*]
pelirrojo (adj. & n.)	red-haired, redhead	
en pelotas, en pelota[14]	stark naked	
espeluznante	horrifying, hair-raising	

---

[11] The Aramaic name of the hill outside Jerusalem on which Jesus was crucified was *Gulgalta*, which meant "skull"—there are competing explanations for the origin of the name. This appears in the Latin Bible (Vulgate) as GOLGOTHA, and is also directly translated as CALVARIA: IN LO-CUM QUI DICITUR *GOLGOTHA*, QUOD EST *CALVARIAE* LOCUS (Matthew 27:33); "in (the) place that is called *Golgotha*, that is, place of (the) *skull*".

[12] Old Spanish *sen* meant "common sense" or "intelligence" and came to be used in the form *sien* as a term for "temple", thought to be the site of such activities. The diphthong (*ie*) is probably due to the influence of the verb *sentir* (*yo siento*, etc.). *Sentir* in turn comes from Latin SENTIRE ("to perceive"), which is very likely an Indo-European cognate of the Germanic *sinn* from which *sien* derives.

[13] For the origins of *peluca* and *peruke*, see Section 4.6 appendix, no. 2.

[14] There are competing explanations for the origin of this term: some (e.g., RAE, Moliner) see it as referring to someone covered only by their long hair (à la Lady Godiva); others (e.g., Corominas, Bénaben) see a somewhat less salubrious connection to *pelota* ("ball").

pelar	(to) *pluck* (hair, feathers), (to) *peel* (fruit)	
pelear	(to) fight, (to) quarrel	(pull s.o.'s hair out)
pelea	fight, quarrel	
depilar	(to) *depilate* (remove body hair)	
depilación	depilation	
horripilante	horrifying, hair-raising	
[oruga]	caterpillar	[*pilose* ("hairy") *cat*]
cabellera	head of hair, tail (of a comet)	
descabellado	preposterous, absurd	[*disheveled*[15]]

CAPILLARIS meant "pertaining to the hair, hair-like" and entered French (*cap-illaire*) and English (*capillar,* then *capillary*) with this definition. In the seventeenth century, *capillary* began to acquire its current medical meaning of "minute blood vessel", although it still maintains the more general meaning "relating to or resembling a hair; fine and slender".

capilar (adj. & n.)   pertaining to the hair, capillary
Esta loción capilar evita que se caiga el cabello.
This hair lotion prevents hair loss.
Los capilares unen las venas con las arterias.
The capillaries connect the veins to the arteries.

In Latin, one who lacked hair on his head was CALVUS, presumably because his CALVARIA was showing.

CALVUS	calvo (adj.)	bald
	calva (n.)	bald spot (head, fur, velvet, lawn, woods)
	calvicie	baldness
	calvinismo	Calvinism
	calvinista	Calvinist
	chovinismo / chauvinismo	chauvinism
	chovinista / chauvinista	chauvinist

CALVUS was also used as a Roman surname, as is *Calvo* in Spanish. A derived Roman surname was CALVINUS. In northwestern France, this became *Calvin* (or *Cauvin*); in central France, *Chauvin*. Nicolas Chauvin was a French soldier

---

[15] Literal meaning: "one's hair is out of place".

from the Napoleonic wars whose patriotism and loyalty were at first celebrated, then ridiculed.

New students of Spanish sometimes confuse *pelo* with *piel*, "skin", particularly since: (1) both are translations of English "fur" (depending upon whether the animal is alive or dead, respectively); and (2) the Spanish verb for "peel" (*pelar*) comes from the family of *pelo,* while the Spanish noun corresponding to "peel" (fruit skin) is *piel.*

PELLIS	piel (f.)	skin, hide, *pelt,* skin or peel (fruit)	
PELLICULA	película	film (incl. camera, cinema), *pellicle*	
	pellejo	hide, *pelt,* wineskin	
	despellejar	(to) skin, (to) flay	
(unrelated)	pellizcar	(to) pinch, (to) nip	
CUTIS	cutis (m.)	skin (face), complexion (~ *tez*)	
	cutáneo	cutaneous, skin (adj.)	
	subcutáneo	subcutaneous	
	cutícula	cuticle	

Both Latin PELLIS and English *film* come from the Indo-European root **pel* ("skin", "hide"), while CUTIS and *hide* (the animal skin as well as the verb) come from an Indo-European root meaning "to cover", "to conceal".

PORUS	poro	pore	
	poroso	porous	
FRONTEM (acc.)	frente (1) (f.)	forehead	
	frente (2)	*front,* battlefront	
	frente a frente	face to face (~ *cara a cara*)	
	hacer frente a	(to) face or confront	
	frontal	frontal (adj. & bone), head-on	
	enfrente (adv.)	opposite, facing, in *front*	
	enfrentar	(to) confront, (to) oppose	
	afrenta	*affront,* dishonor	
	afrentar	(to) affront	
	afrontar	(to) confront (enemy, problem)	
	confrontar	(to) compare, (to) confront (bring face to face)	
	confrontación	confrontation	
	frontera	frontier, border, boundary	
	fronterizo (adj.)	frontier, border	
CARA	cara	face, heads (coin)	[cheer]
	careta	mask (~ *máscara, antifaz*)	
	descaro	effrontery, impudence	

	descarado	impudent, brazen, shameless	
FACIALIS	facial	facial	
FACIES	facies (f.)	facies, external aspect	[*face*]
	faz (f.)	face (earth, planet, capitalism, etc.)	
	haz (f.)	right side of fabric, upper side of leaf	
	antifaz	mask	
	superficie	*surface,* area, *superficies*	
	superficial	superficial	
(unrelated)	prefacio	preface[16]	
ROSTRUM	rostro	face, beak or *rostrum* (bird, ship)	

Latin CARA was taken from Greek *kara*, "head", and, via French, gave rise to English *cheer*, which initially meant "face";[17] it has no relation to *caro* ("expensive"). FACIES is the origin of English *face* and *facies* ("general aspect or outward appearance"). Spanish *faz* also means "face" but is generally restricted to literary (especially biblical) use—*faz de la tierra, faz del planeta; haz* was formerly used in this sense as well. Latin ROSTRUM comes from the verb RODERE ("to gnaw"), source of *rodent*. It initially referred to the beak of an animal, then to the curved beak-like prow of a Roman ship, and finally (as a plural, ROSTRA) to the speaker's platform in the Roman Forum, which was adorned with the beaks of ships captured at the Battle of Antium (modern Anzio) in 338 BC. This last meaning is preserved in English *rostrum* but not in Spanish *rostro* (the nearest equivalent would be *tribuna*).

OCULUS	ojo	eye	[mon*ocle*]
	mirar de reojo	(to) look out of the corner of one's eye, (to) look askance	
	anteojo	spyglass; binoculars, glasses (pl.)	
	antojo	whim, craving, birthmark (cf. "mother's mark")	
	a su antojo	in one's own way, as one pleases	
	a tu antojo	as you like [also with *mi, nuestro, vuestro*]	

---

[16] *Preface* and *prefacio* come from Latin PRAEFATIO ("saying before"), hence the related adjective *prefatory.*

[17] Even as late as Shakespeare: "All fancy-sick she is and pale of *cheer* . . ." (*A Midsummer Night's Dream*).

	ojal	buttonhole	
	ojete	*eyelet*, grommet	(eyelet < oilet)
	ojera	ring or bag under the eyes (gen. pl.)	
OCULARIS	ocular (adj. & n.)	ocular, eyepiece	
	oculista	oculist (~ *oftalmólogo*)	
	inocular	inoculate	
	inoculación	inoculation	
PUPILLA	pupila	pupil (eye)	
CILIUM	cilio	cilium (biol.; ≠ "eyelash")	
CILIA (pl.)	ceja	eyebrow	[*cilia* = pl. *cilium*]
	entrecejo	space between the eyebrows, frown	
SUPERCILIUM	superciliar	superciliary ("above the eyebrow")	
	———	supercilious	
PALPEBRA	párpado	eyelid, *palpebra*	[*palpitate*]
	parpadear	(to) blink, (to) flicker (light, screen)	
	parpadeo	blink, blinking	
(pre-Roman)	pestaña	eyelash	
	pestañear	(to) blink	
	—sin pestañear	—1. with great attention; 2. serenely ("without batting an eyelash [*or* eye *or* eyelid]")	

CILIUM was "eyelid" (technically only the upper and lower borders), while the plural CILIA was used for both "eyelids" and "eyelashes"; SUPERCILIUM ("above the eyelid") was "eyebrow" and by extension came to mean "ridge or summit", "pride", "arrogance", hence the English adjective *supercilious*. PALPEBRA, a more popular form for "eyelid" that reflected its *palpitating* nature, is continued by Spanish *párpado*. Spanish moved CILIA upward to the eyebrow, and then reverted to an old (pre-Roman) term, *pestaña*, for "eyelash".[18]

NARES	nariz (f.)	nose
NASALIS	nasal	nasal

---

[18] The more likely explanation may be that pre-Roman *pestaña*—common to Spanish, Portuguese, and Catalan, as well as to Gascon in southern France—never gave up its role among the "common" people for *eyelash*, thus allowing SUPERCILIA (pl.) to be shortened to CILIA (which then evolved to *ceja*) for *eyebrow*, without any danger of confusion.

Latin NARIS was "nostril", and its plural, NARES, came to be used colloquially for "nose" (Classical NASUS). Having used "nostrils" for "nose", in Spanish one says things like *ventana de la nariz* ("nose window") or *fosa nasal* ("nasal cavity") for *nostril*. These constructions recall the similar origin of English *nostril*, which literally means "nose hole". The plural *narices* is used in many and varied colloquial expressions, including:

dar con la puerta en las narices	(to) shut the door in someone's face (to reject)
en sus (propias) narices	right under his nose
estar hasta las narices	(to) be fed up
meter las narices (en algo)	(to) poke one's nose into something

BUCCA	boca	mouth	(Fr. *bouche*)
	boca abajo	face-down	
	boca arriba	face-up	
	boquiabierto	open-mouthed, flabbergasted	
	bocadillo	sandwich (~ *sándwich*)	
	bucal	buccal (pert. to the mouth or cheeks)	
	desembocadura	river mouth, *debouchure*	
	desembocar	(to) flow out, (to) *disembogue*, (to) *debouch*, (to) lead to (road, etc.)	
BUCCULA (dim.)	bucle	curl, ringlet, loop	[*buckle*]
ORALIS	oral	oral (spoken, or pert. to the mouth)	
ORA	orilla	edge, (river)bank, shore	

OS (genit. ORIS), Classical Latin for "mouth", was supplanted in popular expression by BUCCA, which originally meant "cheek". ORA probably meant "river mouth" at first, before settling for "border", "edge"; Spanish *orilla* is a diminutive form.

GINGIVA	encía	gum, *gingiva*
	gingivitis	gingivitis
DENTEM (acc.)	diente	tooth
	dental	dental
	dentista	dentist
	dentadura	set of teeth

	—dentadura postiza	—set of false teeth, *dentures*	
	dentífrico	dentifrice, toothpaste	
	diente de león	*dandelion*	[*lion's* tooth]
CARIES	caries (f.)	*caries,* tooth decay, cavity	
LINGUA	lengua	tongue, *language*	
	lenguaje	*language,* speech (~ *habla*)	
	—lengua extranjera	—foreign language [not *lenguaje*]	
	—lenguaje de programación	—programming language [not *lengua*]	
	lenguado	sole (fish)	
	deslenguado	impudent, insolent, foulmouthed	
	lengüeta	tongue (shoe), reed (in music instrument)	
	lingüista	linguist	
	lingüístico	linguistic	
	lingüística	linguistics	
	bilingüe	bilingual	
SALIVA	saliva	saliva	
LABIUM	labio	lip	
	labial	labial (pert. to the lips)	
MENTUM	mentón	chin	[Germ. *mouth*]
	———	mental (pert. to the chin)	
BARBA	barba	beard	[*barber*]
	barbudo	heavily bearded	
	barbilla	point of the chin	
	barbero	barber	
	barbería	barbershop	

Barbilla is a diminutive of *barba* and has come to mean the place where the beard grows (i.e., the chin).

MANDIBULA	mandíbula	jaw, mandible	
MAXILLA	mejilla	cheek	[*maxilla*]
	maxilar (adj. & n.)	maxillary, jawbone(s)	
AURICULA	oreja	ear (external part)	[*auricle*]
	auricular (adj. & n.)	auricular, earpiece, headphones (pl.)	

AURIS was Latin for ear; AURICULA, a diminutive.

THYRSUS	torso	torso (trunk, statue without head or limbs)	
COLLUM	cuello	neck, *collar* (shirt, suit, etc.)	
DECOLLARE	degollar	(to) *decollate* (sever at the neck), (to) cut the throat	
GULA	gola	throat, *gullet*	[*gully*]
	gula	gluttony (~ *glotonería*)	
	goloso	sweet-toothed, appetizing	
	golosina	sweet (n.)	
(unrelated)	gol (< Eng.)	*goal*	
garg-	garganta	throat, gorge (ravine)	(onomatopoeia)
garg- + gula	gárgola	*gargoyle*	
	hacer gárgaras	(to) *gargle*	
BRACHIUM	brazo	arm	[*brace, brachium*]
	brazalete	*bracelet*	
	braza	fathom (~ 6 feet), breaststroke	
	abrazo	*embrace,* hug	
	abrazar	(to) *embrace,* (to) hug	

A number of other English words come from BRACHIUM and its derivatives, including *brassiere* and *pretzel* (via German *Brezel*). It is also worth noting that *arma* exists in Spanish but only with the sense of "weapon". English *arm* has two sources, both ultimately coming from the Indo-European root *ar-: (a) from Germanic, referring to the part of the body; and (b) from Latin (via French), referring to weapons or tools (giving also *army, armor, armada, armature*). *Alarm* (Spanish *alarma*) came from the Italian cry *all'arme!* ("to [the] arms!") summoning soldiers to the defense.

ARMA	arma	arm (weapon)	
	armar	(to) arm, (to) fit out (a ship), (to) assemble	
	armamento	armament	
	armada	armada, navy, fleet	[*army* < Fr.]
	—la Armada Invencible	—the Spanish Armada	[*invincible*]
	armadillo	armadillo	

	armario	wardrobe, [*armory*]
		cabinet, *armoire*
	armadura	*armor, armature*
	armazón	framework,
	(m./f.)	frame ("*armor*"
		of a building)
	armería	*armory*, gun
		shop
	alarma	alarm
	alarmar	(to) alarm
	alarmante	alarming
	alarmista	alarmist
	desarmar	(to) disarm, (to)
		dismantle
	desarme	disarmament
IN (neg.) + ARMA	inerme	unarmed,
		defenseless
HUMERUS	hombro	shoulder
	húmero	humerus (bone)
CUBITUS	codo	elbow, cubit
		(unit of measure)
	codazo	blow (or nudge)
		with the elbow
	cúbito	ulna (bone)
(unrelated)	cubito (de hielo)	ice *cube* (diminutive of *cubo*)

In Latin, CUBITUS was "elbow" and ULNA, "forearm"; the latter is cognate with Old English *eln* ("forearm"), which gave rise to *elbow* (Old English *eln-boga*). *Cubit* remains in English as an "ancient unit of measure", equal to the distance from the tip of the middle finger to the elbow. The *cúbito—ulna* is one of the two bones extending from the elbow to the wrist, the other being the *radio—radius*.

(pre-Roman)	muñeca	wrist, girl doll
	muñeco	boy doll
MANUS	mano (f.)	hand, forefoot (of quadriped), *manus*
MANUALIS	manual (adj.)	manual (by hand)
	manual (n.)	manual, handbook
A MANU ("by hand")	amanuense	amanuensis (secretary, scribe)
MANCUS	manco	missing a hand or arm
		(or with disabled use)

MANSUETUDO	mansedumbre	*mansuetude* (meekness, tameness)
	manso	meek, gentle, tame

MANSUETUDO literally meant "being accustomed to eat from the hand" (hence, "tame").

As with English *hand,* MANUS had a number of symbolic meanings beyond that of simply being "the distal part of the forelimb of a vertebrate" (definition of English *manus*). In particular, it symbolized power and control of the PATER FAMILIAS over wife, children, and slaves. For those women electing marriage CUM MANU, the expression IN MANUM CONVENIRE literally meant to "pass into the legal control" of the husband, while those opting for marriage SINE MANU remained under the legal control of the father (being only "loaned" to the husband).

	manada	flock, herd, handful	
MANUARIA	manera	manner	
MANIA[19] (VL)	maña	skill, dexterity, trick	
	amañar	(to) rig, (to) fake	
	artimaña	trick, stratagem, snare	
MANICULUS	manojo	handful, bunch	
	de antemano	beforehand	
	manecilla	clock hand	
	manija	handle (door, window, etc.)	
	manilla	handle, bracelet	[*manacle*]
MANICA	manga	sleeve, (water) hose, windsock, beam (ship's width)	
	manguera	watering hose	
	———	manicotti (pasta in large-sized tubes)	
MANICUS	mango (1)	handle (hammer, pot, etc.)	
(unrelated)	mango (2)	mango (fruit, tree)	

Both in Classical and later Latin, MANUS joined with various verbs to indicate an action done by hand:

(a) OPERARI ("to operate"), hence "to work with the hands"—the meaning was extended at the end of the seventeenth century in French to naval *maneuvers,* and subsequently to military maneuvers in general

---

[19] Unrelated to the MANIA (from Greek) that gave rise to English *mania* and Spanish *manía.*

(b) FACERE ("to make"), hence to *manufacture*

(c) SCRIPTUS (p.p. of SCRIBERE, "to write"), hence "written by hand", or *manuscript*

(d) MITTERE ("to let go", "to send off"), hence "to free" or "to set at liberty" a slave or a child, to *manumit*

(e) TENERE ("to have", "to hold"), hence "to hold in the hand", later "to protect", to *maintain*

(f) CURARE ("to care for"), hence "to care for the hands", to *manicure*

(g) DARE ("to give"), hence "to hand over", "to entrust", to give a *mandate* to, later "to order"

OPERARI	maniobrar	(to) maneuver
	maniobra	maneuver
	maniobrabilidad	maneuverability
	mano de obra	labor (versus *capital*), manpower
FACERE	manufacturar	(to) manufacture
	manufactura	manufactured good, factory
SCRIPTUS	manuscrito (adj. & n.)	handwritten, manuscript
MITTERE	manumitir	(to) manumit (free from slavery)
	manumisión	manumission
TENERE	mantener	(to) maintain, (to) sustain
	mantenimiento	maintenance, upkeep
	manutención	maintenance, support
CURARE	manicura	manicure
DARE	mandar	(to) order, (to) command, (to) send
	mandato	mandate, order, term of office
	mandatario	agent, mandatary
	[obligatorio]	mandatory
	mando	command (power), control (e.g., TV)

Manumission is, of course, very similar in meaning to *emancipation*. In Roman times both terms were used, *manumission* with regard to releasing slaves from the authority of their master, and *emancipation* with regard to the freeing of children (and wives) from the authority of the *paterfamilias*.[20] A MANCEPS— from MANUS and the verb CAPERE ("to take")—was a person who took possession of something by hand, a "purchaser", an "owner". MANCIPIUM referred both to the act of acquiring property and to the property itself; it could also mean "slave". The verb EMANCIPARE was then formed by the addition of the

---

[20] English *emancipate* maintains the legal definition "to release (a child) from the control of parents or a guardian".

prefix EX ("from"). The use of *emancipation* with regard to the manumission of slaves is an eighteenth-century innovation.

EMANCIPARE	emancipar	(to) emancipate
	emancipación	emancipation
MANCIPIUM	mancebo	youth, pharmacist's assistant

MANDARE ("to entrust", later "to order") joined forces with the prepositions CUM and DE to form the verbs COMMENDARE and DEMANDARE. The different treatment of the interior vowel *A* in the composite verbs shows that DEMANDARE is a more recent formation. COMMENDARE—"to entrust", "to commit for protection"—entered English in two separate ways: (a) *to commend,* from Classical (and Church) Latin, with the original meaning of "to entrust" subsequently expanded to that of "to present something (*commendable*) as worthy"; and (b) *to command,* from French *commander*—formed from Vulgar Latin COMMANDARE (which had taken on the later meaning of MANDARE, "to order", "*to command*").

French *commander* maintained for some time the distinct meanings of "to command" and "to commend/recommend" before the second meaning was transferred to *recommander.* English took this verb as well—in its Medieval Latin form RECOMMENDARE—giving it two similar verbs (*commend* and *recommend*). Spanish replaced the "classical" *comendar* with *encomendar* and also has *recomendar,* the two having approximately the same relationship as English *commend* ("entrust")—*recommend.*

[alabar, elogiar]	(to) commend (praise)
[alabanza, elogio]	commendation (praise)
encomendar	(to) commend (entrust, commit to the care of another)
encomienda	charge, commission, postal parcel (Amer.)
recomendar	(to) recommend
recomendable	recommendable, commendable (praiseworthy)
recomendación	recommendation
comandar	(to) command
comandante	commander, commandant, major (rank above captain)
comando	command (military authority, computer instruction), commando
mandamiento	order, commandment
—los diez mandamientos	—the Ten Commandments

DEMANDARE was initially not very clearly differentiated, meaning "to entrust", "to commit". In Medieval Latin, it developed a wide range of meanings, including "to order", "to lay claim (to something)", "to ask for urgently", "to summon to court", "to request (something)", and "to ask (a question)". English has focused primarily on the first few definitions, French on the last two, while Spanish *demandar* maintains a wide range of meanings:

demanda	demand, request, inquiry, complaint (legal)
demandar	(to) demand, (to) request, (to) ask for, (to) sue
demandante	claimant, plaintiff
demandado (p.p.)	defendant (gen. in civil case)
[exigente]	demanding

English *remand* also comes from MANDARE. The sense of "to send back" is absent from the rarely encountered Spanish *remandar* ("mandar una cosa varias veces"); Spanish uses instead various other formulations, depending on the context.

A MANIPULUS was literally a "handful" and seems to have originated from the handful of stalks that an agricultural worker grasped in one hand (normally the left) before cutting with the other. It subsequently came to represent a military unit consisting of two *centuries* (initially one hundred men each, later sixty), representing one-thirtieth of a Roman legion. A *maniple* (the English form of the word) was thus far more than a handful of soldiers; the term was initially given to the flag (or "standard") of the unit and over time came to represent the unit itself. The explanations for its origin are legion, the most common being that the standard originally consisted of a pole with a *handful* of hay at the top. In Medieval Latin, a MANIPULUS came to apply to an "ornamental silk band hung as an ecclesiastical vestment on the left arm"—possibly bearing a relation to the agricultural origin of the term—and this meaning is also found in English *maniple*.

In fifteenth-century French, *manipule* came to be used in a pharmaceutical sense to designate a *handful* of grains from plants used to concoct a remedy. Three centuries later the French verb *manipuler* arose in connection with the experimental process of seeking to improve the formulas. It was not until the nineteenth century that *manipulate* developed its current meaning of "to influence or to manage shrewdly or deviously".

manipular	(to) manipulate, (to) handle
manipulación	manipulation, handling (food, merchandise)
manipulador	manipulator, handler
manípulo	maniple (1/30th legion, eccl. vestment)

Italian *maneggiare* ("to work with the hands") yielded English *manage* and Spanish *manejar*:

manejar	(to) manage, (to) drive (a car—*Amer.*)
manejo	handling, *manège* (horsemanship)
manejable	manageable, easy to use
[gerencia, dirección]	management
[gerente, director]	manager

The initial meaning of MANIFESTUS was "grasped by the hand". This was then applied to criminals "caught in the act", whose guilt was therefore *manifest*. English *manifesto* came from the Italian, where it initially was used only as an adjective ("manifest") before developing the nominative sense of "a written declaration of principles (cultural, artistic, or political)". In the nineteenth century, "to manifest" in both Spanish and French acquired the additional meaning "to demonstrate publicly" (one's views).

manifiesto (adj. & n.)	manifest (obvious), manifesto, manifest (of a ship)		
—poner de manifiesto	—(to) make evident, (to) show plainly		
manifestar	(to) manifest, (to) demonstrate		
manifestación	manifestation, public demonstration		
manifestante	demonstrator, manifestant		
DIGITUS	dedo	*digit* (human finger *or* toe)	
	dedal	thimble	(thimble < thumb)

Dedo represents the "popular" evolution of DIGITUS. Spanish has preserved a number of "learned" forms of the word, including:

digital (adj.)	digital
digital (f.) ~ dedalera	digitalis, foxglove
dígito	digit (0, 1, 2, 3, 4, 5, 6, 7, 8, 9)
digitalizar	(to) digitalize
digitación	fingering (music)

digitado   digitate (having fingers or finger-like projections)
digitígrado   digitigrade (bearing weight on the toes—e.g., dog, horse)

Latin DIGITUS and Spanish *dedo* refer to both fingers *and* toes. A DIGITUS was also a unit of measure, being defined as one-sixteenth of a Roman "foot", or approximately 1.85 cm (a Roman foot being 29.6 cm, as opposed to the "modern" English foot of 30.5 cm). Spanish has maintained *dedo* as an unofficial unit of measure, now defined as the *duodécima parte del palmo* (twelfth part of the palm).

Each finger in Latin had its separate name or names, often of popular origin, a tradition maintained in Spanish:

#	Latin Names	Spanish Names
1 (thumb)	POLLEX	pulgar, gordo (also: *big toe*)
2	INDEX, SALUTARIS, DEMONSTRATIVUS	índice
3	MEDIUS, IMPUDICUS, INFAMIS	medio, (del) corazón, cordial
4	ANULARIS, MEDICINALIS	anular, médico
5	MINIMUS, AURICULARIS	meñique, pequeño, auricular

Pulgar is an interesting example of the force of analogy at work: it comes from Latin POLLICARIS ("measure of a thumb"), and according to the "normal" rules, it should have evolved to *polgar. But as the Spanish word for flea is *pulga,* and as one of the primary roles of the thumb was (and presumably still is) the squashing of fleas, the *u* from *pulga* became implanted in *polgar, thus giving *pulgar.*

The measure of a thumb, *una pulgada,* is an "inch". *Dedo auricular* is a "literary" name for the little finger and comes straight from Latin, relating to its usefulness for ear cleaning. The various Latin names for index finger related to its common use for signalling: INDEX was a person or object that *indicated* or "revealed" something.

INDEX (ACC. INDICEM)	índice	index, table of contents, Index (proscribed books)
	indicio	index (indication, sign)
	El humo es *indicio* del fuego.	Smoke is a *sign* of fire.
INDICARE	indicar	(to) indicate
	indicación	indication
	indicador	indicator, pointer, gauge
	indicativo	indicative (adj.), indicative (verb mood)

INDEX and INDICARE ("to indicate") are intrinsically related to DICERE ("to say"), both from the Indo-European root *deik/deig*—"to show", "to pronounce solemnly"—also found in English (Germanic) *teach*. DIGITUS itself comes from the same root, i.e., the finger was initially thought of as a "pointer".

PALMA	palma	palm (of hand; tree or leaf)	
PALMUS	palmo	palm (measure: thumb–little finger ∼ 8 in.)	
	palmada	pat or slap (with open palm), clapping (pl.)	
	palmera	palm tree	
UNGULA	uña	fingernail	[*ungulate*]
PUGNUS	puño	fist, cuff (shirt), hilt	
	puñado	fistful, handful	
	puñetazo	blow with the fist, cuff (slap)	
	puñal[21]	dagger, *poniard*	
	puñalada	stab, stab wound	

The fist, as a convenient weapon, has served as a basis for a wide range of words expressing combativeness in one form or another. The *pug-* is the same as in *pugilist*.

PUGNA	pugna	fight, strife	
	pugnar	(to) fight, (to) strive	
	impugnar	(to) *impugn* (attack as false or questionable)	
	empuñar	(to) grasp (by the hilt)	
	empuñadura	hilt, grip (racket)	
	pugnacidad	pugnacity	
	pugnaz	pugnacious	
	púgil ∼ pugilista	pugilist, boxer	
	pugilato	pugilism, boxing	
	propugnar	(to) defend, (to) advocate	[† *propugn*]
	repugnar	(to) view with repugnance, (to) disgust	
	repugnancia	repugnance	
	repugnante	repugnant	
SPATULA	espalda	back (also used in pl.)	[*spatula: dl → ld*]

---

[21] Originally *cuchillo puñal* ("fist knife"), and then the first element disappeared.

	respaldo	seatback, backing (support)	
	respaldar	(to) back, (to) endorse	
COSTA	costilla	rib	[*coast, cutlet*]
VERTEBRA	vértebra	vertebra	
	vertebral	vertebral	
	vertebrado	vertebrate	
	invertebrado	invertebrate	
THORAX	tórax	thorax, chest	
PECTUS	pecho	chest, breast, bosom	
	peto	breastplate, overalls, pinafore	(< It. *petto*)
	petirrojo	robin (redbreast)	
	parapeto	*parapet*, breastwork	(*para-* from *parasol*)
PECTORALIS	pectoral	pectoral	

From the derived verb APPECTORARE (AD + PECTORARE), Spanish formed *apretar* (with a shift in position of the first *r*):

	apretar	(to) squeeze, (to) tighten, (to) compress	
	apretado (p.p.)	tight, difficult	
	apretón	sudden squeeze, pressure	
	apretón de manos	handshake	
	aprieto	tight spot, predicament	
ABDOMEN	abdomen	abdomen	
	abdominal	abdominal	
INTERANEA	entraña (freq. pl.)	*internal* organ, guts (*innards, entrails,* core or essence)	
	entrañar	(to) involve, (to) entail	
	entrañable	most affectionate, intimate	
EXPECTORARE	expectorar	(to) expectorate (cough up and spit out)	
	[escupir]	(to) spit	[*cuspidor*]
SINUS	seno	bosom, breast, womb, lap, *sinus, sine*	

In Roman times, "to expectorate" was literally "to get something off one's chest", hence "to expel or banish from the mind" (e.g., fear). The medical sense "to clear out the chest by coughing" developed only in the seventeenth century; and the modern meaning of "to spit" (in English, not Spanish), only in the nineteenth century. SINUS initially referred to the "concave or semicircular fold of clothing in which a mother could carry her child" before taking on the more general meaning, preserved in Modern English, of "a depression or cavity formed by a bending or curving". Spanish *seno* has retained (or acquired) multiple senses: for a woman, her *breasts* or *womb;* for a person of either sex, his *sinuses;* in a nautical sense, a *gulf* or *bay;* the *sine* function in mathematics, etc. To *insinuate* oneself is to "introduce oneself *sinuously* or by devious methods"—to *worm* oneself in—or "to convey a notion by indirect suggestion".

INSINUARE	insinuar	(to) insinuate, (to) imply	
	insinuación	insinuation	
	sinusitis	sinusitis	
SINUOSUS	sinuoso	sinuous	
MAMMA	mama	mamma (breast)	
	mamá	mama, mom, mommy	(< Fr. *maman*)
	amamantar	(to) breast-feed, (to) nurse	
MAMMA + FERRE	mamífero	mammal	
MAMMARE	mamar	(to) suck (milk, from breast or bottle)	
	dar de mamar	(to) breast-feed	
	mamario	mammary, breast (adj.)	

Latin MAMMA was both "breast" (human or animal) and "mother", the latter restricted to the language of children. It comes from the near-universal *ma-* used by children (at least Indo-European ones) for their mothers, found also in MATER (*madre*).[22] In the eighteenth century, when the Swedish botanist Carolus Linnaeus created the modern (Latin) system for classifying plants and animals, he coined the name MAMMALIA to refer to the class of animals (ANIMALIA) characterized by the possession of MAMMA(s). This subsequently became English *mammal.* Spanish *mamífero* is a separate creation, an amalgam of MAMMA with the verb FERRE ("to bring"), thus literally "bearer of milk". MAMMA itself has arrived in two separate forms in Spanish: *mama* as a normal phonetic evolution from Latin, and *mamá* from French *maman.* A Hispanic *Latin* variation of MAMMA was AMMA; *ama* initially referred to the mother giving milk to her own child, and later came to refer to a wet nurse.

AMMA	ama	lady of the house, owner, landlady, wet nurse	
	ama de casa	housewife	

---

[22] And in Germanic *mother,* which comes from the same root (*mā).

	ama de llaves	housekeeper	
	amo	master (of a house), owner, landlord	
(Germanic)	teta	breast, *teat*	
	dar la teta	(to) nurse	
	destetar	(to) wean	[*"de-teat"*]
	destete	weaning	
CINCTURA	cintura	waist	[*cincture*]
	cinturón	belt	
	cinturón de seguridad	safety belt, seat belt	
	cinto	belt	
	cinta	ribbon, band, tape (adhesive or recording)	
	precinto	strap (for packing), (safety) seal	
	precintar	(to) seal, (to) seal off	[*precinct*]
	recinto	area, enclosure, *enceinte* (fortification)	
	ceñir	(to) encircle, (to) fit tightly, (to) limit oneself	
	ceñido (p.p.)	tight-fitting, clinging	[*cinch*]
CATHEDRA ("chair")	cadera	hip	[*chair, cathedral*]

Each Spanish speaker thus starts off life with two built-in chairs. A *cathedral* (Spanish *catedral*) is a church that contains a bishop's chair, while a *cátedra* is a "chaired professorship" at a university.

PELVIS	pelvis (f.)	pelvis	
INGUEN	ingle (f.)	groin	
	inguinal	inguinal	
PERNA ("ham")	pierna	leg	
	pernera	trouser leg	
	pernil	haunch (animal), ham, trouser leg	
ROTULA	rótula	kneecap, patella	[*roll*]
	rodilla	knee	
	arrodillar(se)	(to) kneel	
	rodillo	*rolling* pin, *roller*	
	rótulo	sign, label, heading, title	
	rotulador	felt-tipped pen, highlighter	

PES (ACC. PEDEM)	pie (m.)	foot	[sesqui*ped*alian[23]]
	dedo del pie	toe	
	ciempiés	*centipede*	(cie**n** + pies)
	traspié	stumble, trip	(tras + pie)
	peatón	*ped*estrian (n.)	
	peaje	toll, tollbooth	(Fr. *péage*)
	pezuña	hoof (~ *casco*)	("*uña* of the foot")
	pedestal	pedestal	
	pedestre	pedestrian (adj.)	
	pedicura	pedicure	
	pedal	pedal, treadle	
	pedalear	(to) pedal	

PERNA was "leg of ham" and replaced the less expressive Classical CRUS; *rodilla* was formed as a diminutive of ROTULA ("little wheel"), so that it literally means "little little wheel". We have already seen that *dedo* refers to toes as well as fingers, so that when one wants to be specific, one says *dedo del pie*. While *peaje* looks as if it might have something to do with "pay", it in fact refers to the "right to put one's *foot* beyond a certain point".

TUBELLUM	tobillo	ankle	[*tuber*]
TALO(N)	talón	heel	[*talon*]
	talón de Aquiles	*Achilles* heel	
	talonario	checkbook, receipt book (etc.)	
	talar (1)	full-length, reaching to the ankles[24]	[*talaria*]
(unrelated)	talar (2)[25]	(to) cut a tree (at the base), (to) devastate	
(unrelated)	tacón	heel (of a shoe)	
PLANTA	planta (1)	sole, floor or story, (floor) *plan*	[*plantar*]
	planta (2)	plant (vegetable), plant (factory)	
	planta baja	ground floor (~ *piso bajo*)	
	plantar	(to) plant	
	plantación	planting (action), plantation	
	plantear	(to) state (a problem), (to) raise (a question), (to) *plan* or outline	

---

[23] "Given to the use of long words", literally "something a foot and a half long".
[24] For example, a cassock or a toga.
[25] *Talar* (2) comes from Germanic and is related to the verbs *tajar* and *tallar* (see Section 3.5, no. 5).

planteamiento	statement (of a problem), planning, approach
plantilla	insole, roster (office staff or athletic team)
trasplantar	(to) transplant
trasplante	transplant, transplantation
implantar	(to) implant
implantación	implantation
implante	implant, implantation
suplantar	(to) supplant

PLANTA, the *sole* of the foot, comes from the same Indo-European root as English *flat*. The related verb PLANTARE referred to the action of driving in the seed for a *plant* (also PLANTA) with the PLANTA of one's foot. The application to a factory or equipment is first attested in the late eighteenth century.

OSSUM (CL OS)	hueso	bone, pit or stone (fruit), *os*	
	óseo	*osseous,* bony (consisting of bone)	
	huesudo	bony (having prominent bones)	
	osario	*ossuary*	
	osificar	(to) *ossify*	
	deshuesar	(to) bone (meat), (to) stone or pit (fruit)	
ARTICULATIO(N)	articulación	articulation (joint; vocal expression)	
	articular (1)	articular (relating to a joint)	
	articular (2)	(to) articulate (various senses)	
NERV(I)US	nervio	nerve	
	nervioso	nervous	
	ser nervioso	(to) be of a nervous state (in general)	
	estar nervioso	(to) be nervous (worried)	
TENDO(N)	tendón	tendon	
LIGAMENTUM	ligamento	ligament	
MUSCULUS	músculo	muscle	(Lat. MUS, "mouse")
	muslo	thigh	
	muscular	muscular	
LACERTUS	lagarto	*lizard,* long muscle in arm	[*alligator*]

A muscle is literally a "little mouse"—presumably a reference to the appearance created by flexing one's biceps.[26] Similarly, the long muscle in the arm (*brachialis,* from shoulder to elbow) can be viewed as a "lizard", although this use is rare.

ORGANUM	órgano	organ (bodily, musical, etc.)
	orgánico	organic
	organismo	organism, organization
	organista	organist
	organizar	(to) organize
	organización	organization
COR (genit. CORDIS)	corazón	heart (Fr. *coeur*)
	cuerdo	sane, sensible (or such a person)
	cordura	common sense, soundness of mind
CARDIACUS (< Gk.)	cardíaco	cardiac

COR and *heart* share a common Indo-European origin.[27] In Spanish, an augmented ending was added to the classical Latin form, giving rise to *corazón.*

MISERICORDIA	misericordia	mercy, pity
	misericordioso	merciful
	[despiadado]	merciless
	miseria	misery, *miserliness*
	miserable	miserable, wretched, *miserly*

MISERICORDIA was "to open one's *heart* to the *miser*able". English *mercy* is unrelated etymologically, coming instead from MERCES ("wages", "reward"),[28] ironically the root as well of *mercenary. Misericord* remains in English with a number of very specific meanings, including that of a narrow dagger used in medieval times to deliver the "coup de grace" to the seriously wounded.

To be in agreement or disagreement with someone, or something, was expressed by the position of one's heart:

CONCORDIA	concordia	concord, agreement, harmony
	concorde	in accord, in agreement

---

[26] MUSCULUS also meant *mussel* (bivalve mollusk). The identical metaphors were present in Classical Greek, where *mus* (genit. *muo-s*) meant "mouse", "muscle", and "mussel". English *myo-* and Spanish *mio-*, "muscle"—as in *myocardium* and *miocardio*—come from Greek *muo-s* (Classical Greek *u* corresponding to English *y*).

[27] Indo-European *k* and *d* shifted uniformly in the Germanic languages to *h* and *t,* part of a much larger transformation known as *Grimm's Law* (named for Jacob Grimm, a renowned linguist as well as one of the Grimm brothers of fairy-tale fame).

[28] The wages or reward that one "earns" for an act of *mercy* is received only at a later stage (i.e., in heaven).

	concordante	concordant
	concordancia	concordance
	concordar	(to) agree, (to) make agree
DISCORDIA	discordia	discord
	discordante	discordant (opinion or sound)
	discordar	(to) disagree, (to) clash (sounds)
	discordancia	discordance, disagreement
ACCORDARE	acordar	(to) agree, (to) remember
	¿Te acuerdas?	Do you remember?
	acuerdo	accord, agreement
	¡de acuerdo!	agreed!
	de acuerdo con	in agreement or accordance with
	desacuerdo	disaccord, disagreement
	acorde (adj. & n.)	in harmony, *chord* (music)
	acordeón	*accordion*
RECORDARE	recordar	(to) remember, (to) recall, (to) remind
	recuerdo	memory (of past event), souvenir
	récord (< Eng.)	record (e.g., Olympic)
	recordatorio	reminder

A musical *chord* is thus something in *accord* with the heart. Its initial form in English was *accord,* later shortened to *cord,* and only in the seventeenth century did it adopt the *h* from the unrelated word *chord* (from Greek, previously used for the "strings" of an instrument), which, to make matters even more confusing, was itself a sixteenth-century "puristic" reformulation of the original English form *cord* (which itself refused to die). English *vocal cords* (literally a "string-like" structure) can also be—and frequently are—called *vocal chords,* using *chord* in its "archaic" sense of "string",[29] a sense also found in the expression "to strike a *responsive chord* [with someone]", literally "to strike the right *(heart)string*". Likewise, *harpsichord* and *clavichord* maintain the use of *chord* in the sense of "*cord*".

The situation can be depicted as follows, where the words in bold are the "modern" uses:

Greek *khorde* ("catgut") → CHORDA → *corde* (French) → **cord (string,** line, **vocal)** → **chord** (string, **line, vocal)**

---

[29] Similarly, for both *spinal* and *umbilical,* it can be either *cord* or *chord,* though the *cord* forms are far more common. The continuing popularity of *vocal chord* undoubtedly reflects a perceived (albeit erroneous) connection with the musical *chord.*

CORS ("HEART") → *accord* (French) → accord (English) → cord → **chord (music)**

CHORDA	cuerda	*cord*, rope, string, *chord* (line), watch spring
	cuerdas vocales	vocal *cords* (or vocal *chords*)
	cuarteto de cuerda(s)	string quartet
	cordón	shoelace, cord (as belt), electric cord, *cordon*
	cordón umbilical	umbilical cord
	cordillera	mountain range, cordillera
	clavicordio	clavi*chord,* harpsi*chord*

Other derivatives of the heart include:

CORDIALIS	cordial	cordial (incl. "serving to invigorate")
	coraje	anger, fury, mettle, *courage*
	[valiente]	courageous
	El rojo emblema del valor	*The Red Badge of Courage*
	[animar, alentar]	(to) encourage
	[desanimar, desalentar]	(to) discourage

Traté de pasar por alto sus mentiras, pero el *coraje* no me lo permitió y tuve que replicar.
I tried to ignore his lies, but my *anger* didn't permit me to do it and I had to reply.

Spanish *courage* is commonly expressed by *valor. Courage* initially was a general adjective referring to the heart, without any specific connotation of bravery or valor. In English it has passed through a wide variety of meanings, including: (a) the heart as the seat of feeling; (b) purpose, desire, or inclination; (c) vital force or energy; (d) anger, wrath; (e) haughtiness, pride; and (f) sexual vigor or lust. Chaucer's *Merchant's Tale* uses *corage* (Middle English spelling), where the modern translation substitutes *rage* or *urge*:

Modern Text	**Original Text**
Now when this knight had passed his sixtieth year —Whether for holiness, or from a surge Of dotage, who can say?—he felt an **urge**	. . . but swich [such] a greet [great] *corage*
So violent to be a wedded man	Hadde this knyght to been a wedded man . . .

That day and night his eager fancies ran
On where and how to spy himself a bride,
Praying the Lord he might not be denied
Once to have knowledge of that blissful life
There is between a husband and his wife . . .[30]

SANGUIS   sangre (f.)   blood   (acc. SANGUINEM)

English *sanguine* means "blood red" or "ruddy", as well as "cheerfully confi-
dent or optimistic", the latter meaning not found in Spanish *sanguíneo*.

SANGUINARE	sangrar	(to) bleed
	sangrante	bleeding (adj.)
	sangría	bleeding (n.), sangria (wine/fruit juice concoction)
	sangriento	bloody, bloodstained
	sanguíneo	sanguine (pert. to blood, blood-red)
	—grupo sanguíneo	—blood group (O, A, B, AB)
	sanguinario	sanguinary, bloodthirsty
	sanguinolento	bloodstained, sanguinolent
	ensangrentar	(to) stain or cover with blood
CONSANGUINEUS	consanguíneo	consanguineous (having a common ancestor; of the same father)
	consanguinidad	consanguinity (blood relationship)
SANGUISUGA	sanguijuela	leech, blood*sucker*
ARTERIA	arteria	artery
VENA	vena	vein
	venero	vein (of ore), source (of water, ideas, etc.)

---

[30] *The Canterbury Tales*—translated into Modern English by Nevill Coghill (London: Penguin Books, 1977), 357.

PULSUS (VENARUM)	pulso	pulse	
	pulsar	(to) press or *push* (button, key), (to) sound out ("take the pulse of")	
	púlsar	pulsar (astron.)	
	pulsador	*push* button, buzzer	
	pulsación	pulsation, beat, keystroke	
	pulsera	bracelet (~ *brazalete*), watch strap	
	reloj de pulsera	wristwatch	
BRONCHIUM	bronquio	bronchus, bronchial tube	
	bronquial	bronchial	
	bronquitis	bronchitis	
PULMO(N)	pulmón	lung	
	pulmonar	pulmonary, lung (adj.)	
UMBILICUS	ombligo	navel	
	umbilical	umbilical	
STOMACHUS	estómago	stomach (incl. belly)	
VENTER	vientre	abdomen, belly, *venter*	
	ventral	ventral	
	ventrílocuo	*ventriloquist*	
PANTEX	panza	*paunch,* belly, rumen	[*panzer*]
FICATUM	hígado	liver	(Fr. *foie* gras)
FICUS	higo	fig	

Liver in Classical Latin was JECUR, while JECUR FICATUM was *figged liver,* i.e., "goose liver fattened with figs", the Mediterranean equivalent of French *foie gras.* Through a similar process by which FRATER GERMANUS became *hermano,* in most of the Romance languages, people today essentially have figs for livers.

BADIUS	bazo	spleen	[*baize*]
	bayo (adj. & n.)	buckskin (horse)	(grayish-yellow)
	[potro castaño]	*bay* colt	(reddish-brown)
RENALIS	renal	renal (pertaining to the kidneys)	
	adrenalina	adrenaline	
	riñón	kidney	
PANCREAS	páncreas	pancreas	
APPENDIX	apéndice	appendix (of body or book), *appendage*	

INTESTINUS	intestino (adj. & n.)	intestine (internal, civil), intestine (organ)	
	—guerra intestina	—intestine (civil) war	
	intestinal	intestinal	
UTERUS	útero	uterus	
	uterino	uterine	
URINA (VL AURINA)	orina	urine	
URINARI	orinar	(to) urinate	
	urinario (adj. & n.)	urinary, urinal	
AURUM	oro	gold (n.)	
	de oro	gold (adj.)	
	áureo	golden (of gold; also fig.)	[*oriole*]
	aureola	halo, aureole	
	aurífero	auriferous (gold-bearing)	
DEAURARE	dorar	(to) gild, "to sugarcoat"	
	dorado (p.p.)	golden (color; also fig.), gilding	
	dorada (n.)	gilthead seabream (fish)	[biol. *Sparus **aurata***]
	El Dorado	El Dorado	

The Vulgar Latin form AURINA arose from an association with the color "gold" (AURUM). In Roman times, the verb URINARI had referred to a human-fluid interaction of an altogether different nature from that represented by its Romance successors: it meant "to plunge into water" or "to dive", and a URINATOR was a "diver", suggesting that the original meaning of URINA was probably "water" or "puddle". Only at a relatively late stage—the time of Caesar—did URINA come to be used as a "polite" or technical term for what had theretofore been known as LOTIUM (lit. "lotion"[31]), very likely due to the influence of the Greek word *ouron* for "urine" (cf. *urethra* and *diuretic*).

The two most common verbs among the Romans for the act of micturition were MINGERE and MEIERE (or MEIARE), both cognates of English (Germanic)

---

[31] Due to its efficacy as a cleaning agent for laundry.

mist and *mistletoe*.[32] The second verb was the more "popular" form, no doubt explaining why it has left a much greater mark on the Romance languages, including Spanish. Its direct descendant is the "colloquial" verb *mear*, used in a number of equally colloquial expressions, notably *mear(se) de risa*:

Cada vez que pienso en ello *me meo de risa.*	Every time I think of it I die of laughter.

MEIARE	mear	(to) pee	
	meada	pee, urine stain	
MICTUS	micción	*micturition*	(p.p. of MINGERE)

Private Parts

Not surprisingly, a wide variety of euphemisms has been applied to this area of the body, including

> las partes pudendas, las partes vergonzosas, las vergüenzas
> las partes naturales
> las partes nobles
> las partes íntimas

The first three all mean "the shameful parts" and have a parallel in English *pudenda* ("the human external genitalia, esp. of a woman"), from the Latin verb PUDERE ("to cause shame"), whose literal meaning is "those things of which one ought to be ashamed".

PUDOR	pudor	modesty, decency, *pudency*
	pudoroso ~ púdico	modest, bashful
	impudor ~ impudicia	impudicity (immodesty, shamelessness)
	impúdico	immodest, shameless
	impudente [rare]	shameless, impudent
VERECUNDIA	vergüenza	shame, modesty, disgrace, embarrassment
	vergonzoso	shameful, bashful
	avergonzar	(to) shame, (to) be ashamed
	desvergonzado	shameless, impudent
	desvergüenza	shamelessness, impudence

---

[32] *Mistletoe* owes its name to the fact that its seeds are propagated via the *droppings* (German *Mist*) of birds, notably the *missel* thrush, which consume its fruit.

sinvergüenza   shameless, brazen, scoundrel (m./f.)

Es un verdadero *sinvergüenza* capaz de hacer cualquier cosa por dinero.

He is a real *scoundrel* capable of doing anything for money.

VERECUNDIA comes from the verb VERERI, "to fear respectfully", whose compounded form REVERERI is the source of English *revere:*

REVERENTIA	reverencia	reverence, curtsy, bow	
	reverendo	Reverend (title), worthy of reverence	
	reverente	reverent	
	reverenciar	(to) revere or venerate	
	reverencial	reverential (reverent; inspiring reverence)	
IRREVERENTIA	irreverencia	irreverence	
	irreverente	irreverent	
PENIS	pene	penis	
PENICILLUS	pincel	(artist's) paintbrush	[*pencil*]
	[lápiz]	pencil	
	pincelada	brushstroke	
	penicilina	penicillin	
	———	penicillate (having a tuft of fine hairs)	
CODA (VL COLA)	cola (1)	tail	[*queue*]
	colilla	stub, butt (of cigarette)	
	coda	coda (music)	
	caudal (1)	caudal (pertaining to the tail or fin)	
(via Catalan)	cohete	fireworks, rocket	
(< CAPITALIS)	caudal (2)	flow (river), wealth or fortune	
(Gk. *kolla*)	cola (2)	glue (~ *pegamento*)	
	colágeno	collagen	
	collage	collage	(< Fr.)
(glued 1st page)	proto*colo*	proto*col* (code of conduct, various types of documents)	
(West African)	cola (3)	cola *or* kola (plant, nut)	
RAPUM ("turnip")	rabo	tail, stem (flower, leaf, fruit)	[*rapeseed*]
	taparrabo(s)	loincloth	(lit. "tail cover")

con el *rabo* entre las piernas)	with the *tail* between the legs (dejected, humiliated)

Latin PENIS had at an early stage in the history of the language meant "tail" of an animal. By the time of Cicero—who labeled the word as "obscene"—the meaning had definitively shifted to its "modern" sense. Such use of *tail* as a humorous metaphor (or euphemism) for the male sexual organ is not rare—other examples include Classical Greek, French, German, and *Spanish*.[33] Before its identity change, PENIS spawned a diminutive, PENICILLUS, to refer to a "brush" or "sponge" made from, or resembling, the curly hairs of an animal's tail. This is the source of Spanish and Old French *pincel,* as well as English *pencil* (originally an artist's paintbrush). *Penicillin* (genus *Penicillium*) owes its name to the resemblance, under a microscope, of the penicillin cells to small brushes.

CODA (or CAUDA), which replaced PENIS as "tail", is the source of Spanish *cola* (COLA presumably being a dialectal variant[34]), the musical *coda* ("tail" part of a piece), and the English *queue* in which one waits in line. *Rabo* comes from the Latin for "turnip", which has a "tail-like" appendage: it is used only for terrestrial animals, not for fish or birds.

TESTICULUS	testículo	testicle

TESTIS (from TRI-STIS, then TER-STIS) was Latin for "witness", -STIS coming from the root found in the verb STARE, so that the literal meaning would have been "*standing* as a *third* party" in a dispute. By metaphor, TESTIS (and its diminutive, TESTICULUS) came to refer to the *testicles,* witnesses to a man's virility. This metaphor also has parallels in Classical Greek and Old French. TESTIS is the origin of a large number of words relating to the act of being a witness, "to declare as a witness" (*protest*), "to execrate while calling God to witness" (*detest*), "to take or call to witness" (*contest*), etc.

TESTIFICARI	atestiguar ~ testificar	(to) testify, (to) attest
	testigo	witness, baton (relay)
TESTIMONIUM	testimonio	testimony

---

[33] French *queue*—from CODA—has various meanings, including "tail", "line of people", and *membre viril;* German *Schwanz* likewise means both "tail" and "male sexual organ". In Spanish, both *cola* and *rabo* are "vulgar" synonyms of *pene.*

[34] Another theory is that the *l* is due to the influence of the "related" word *culo* (Section 4.6 appendix, no. 3).

	testimonial	testimonial (serving as evidence)
	testimoniar	(to) attest, (to) testify
TESTAMENTUM	testamento	testament, will
PROTESTARI	protestar	(to) protest
	protesta	protest, protestation
	protestante	Protestant, protestant
	protestantismo	Protestantism
DETESTARI	detestar	(to) detest
	detestable	detestable
ATTESTARI	atestar	(to) attest
	atestación	attestation
CONTESTARI	contestar	(to) answer, (to) reply
	contestador (automático)	answering machine
	[concurso]	contest
	contestación	answer, reply (~ *respuesta*)
	contestatario	antiestablishment (& such person)
	incontestable	incontestable
INTESTATUS	intestado	intestate (with no legal will)
TESTARI	testar (1)	(to) make a will
TESTUM	test (< Eng.)	test
	testar (2)	(to) test

While a *contest* is frequently a *test* of wills, etymologically the two have nothing in common: *test* comes from Latin TESTUM, an "earthenware pot". It was taken into English with the meaning of *cupel*, i.e., a porous cup in which precious metals were heated in order to separate out base elements (such as lead). The same porous cup could also be used for *testing* the quality of the metals, and from this arose the more general sense of *test*. The feminine form, TESTA ("earthenware", "shard" [piece of broken pottery]), took on the meanings of "container used for drinking" and, with a humorous twist, "skull"—in French and Italian, this became the primary word for "head" (*tête, testa*), while in Spanish it is generally used only informally or jocularly.[35]

TESTUM	tiesto	flowerpot (~ *maceta*), potsherd
TESTA	testa	head (lit. and fig., e.g., "head for business")
	testarudo	stubborn, pigheaded
	testarudez	stubbornness, pigheadedness

---

[35] German *kopf* ("head")—hence English *dummkopf*—has an analogous origin: Latin CUPPA (= English *cup*).

VAGINA	vagina	vagina
	vaginal	vaginal
	invaginación	invagination
	vaina	sheath, scabbard, pod
	envainar	(to) sheathe
	desenvainar	(to) unsheathe
VAGINELLA	vainilla	vanilla

Many will be surprised to learn that etymologically *vanilla* means "little vagina". When in the late sixteenth century it became necessary to find a medical term for a heretofore unnamed part of the female anatomy, a certain "classical" sense of humor seems to have prevailed, and *vagina* was chosen.[36] VAGINA had been the *sheath* of a Roman sword and had no connection to the female anatomy. To refer to the region in question, the Romans employed a range of terms, including SINUS MULIEBRIS ("woman's curve or cavity")—as we have seen above, in Spanish SINUS has come to mean both "breast" and "womb" (*seno*). Ironically, while one "off-color" reference has survived concerning the suitability of the VAGINA as a parking place for a soldier's MACHAERA ("sword"), the reference was actually to a part of the male, rather than female, anatomy.

A diminutive form, VAGINULA, was applied in Roman times to the husk or pod of plants because of their sheath-like appearance, and it was with this sense that Spanish *vainilla* is first recorded in the mid-sixteenth century—the "small pod of a legume"—before its more long-lasting application the following century to "an aromatic American plant having a pod similar to that of a kidney bean".

Appendix

"State of *Mind*" Adverbs

Many adverbs of manner are constructed from the corresponding adjective by adding -*mente* to the *feminine* singular.

CLASS I ADJECTIVES: *DISTINCT MASCULINE AND FEMININE*

devoto, devota	devotamente	*devotedly, devoutly*	
lento, lenta	lentamente	slowly	[*lentitude*]

---

[36] The person generally given credit for this is the Italian anatomist Gabriello Fallopio (1523–1562), for whom *fallopian* tubes were named. Among his other vocabulary contributions is *placenta,* which in Classical Latin (and in the Vulgate as well) had been "(flat) cake".

| lógico, lógica | lógicamente | *logically* |
| rápido, rápida | rápidamente | *rapidly* |

CLASS II ADJECTIVES: *UNISEX*

constante	constantemente	*constantly*
feliz	felizmente	happily, *felicitously*
hábil	hábilmente	*ably*, adroitly
igual	igualmente	*equally*

MENTE was the ablative case form of the Latin noun MENS ("mind"), the initial idea being that the action was carried out in a certain "state of mind":

DEVOTA MENTE → devotamente   in a devout state of mind

Over time, this formulation was extended to include adjectives having less direct connection to the "mind":

RAPIDA MENTE → rápidamente   in a rapid manner

Since MENS was a feminine noun, the accompanying adjective was as well. This origin explains two additional characteristics of Spanish -*mente* adverbs:
a) Although written as one word, the adjective and -*mente* are pronounced as though independent, each with its own stress:

ló·gi·ca·men·te

b) Since -*mente* initially had an independent existence (and a person has only one mind!), it is capable of applying to more than one adjective at a time. Hence in a sequence of such adverbs only the last one uses *mente*:

habla *claramente*	he speaks *clearly*
habla *clara* y *enfática*mente	he speaks *clearly* and *emphatically*
contesta *humildemente*	he answers *humbly*
contesta *humilde* y *cortés*mente	he answers *humbly* and *courteously*

This usage parallels English with respect to adverbs using *manner*:

he speaks in a clear and emphatic *manner*

The -*mente* construction is possible with most but not all adjectives. Unfortunately, a Spanish-Spanish dictionary will often not be of much assistance, since -*mente* adverbs tend to be excluded, on the basis that their formation is so obvious.[37] Many Spanish-English dictionaries also follow suit. This, of course, makes very little sense: In En-

---

[37] The RAE's *Diccionario* is a partial exception. A substantially more complete coverage of -*mente* adverbs is found in Moliner's *Diccionario de uso del español*.

glish, how could one possibly confirm that the correct adverbial form is *contentedly* and not **contently* if dictionaries excluded all *-ly* adverbs? In Spanish, both *contento* and *feliz* mean "happy", but while one can say *felizmente* ("happily"), one cannot say **contentamente.*

One can use *-mente* to say "firstly"—*primeramente*—but not "secondly", "thirdly", etc.

en segundo lugar	secondly, in the second place
en tercer lugar	thirdly, in the third place

Similarly, *-mente* adverbs do not exist for the common adjectives *otro, tal,* and *ninguno:* [38]

de otra manera	de otro modo	in another manner
de tal manera	de tal modo	in such a way
de ninguna manera	de ningún modo	in no way, nowise

---

[38] *Otramente* and *talmente*—as well as *segundamente* and *terceramente*—technically exist (they are found in *DRAE*), but are rarely used.

Romance (Languages) and Politics

The standard family tree of Indo-European languages shows English to be far more closely related to, say, Swedish or Icelandic than it is to any of the Romance languages, including Spanish:

PROTO-INDO-EUROPEAN (PIE)				
↙			↘	
Germanic			**Italic**	
				Osco-
N. Germanic	**W. Germanic**	**E. Germanic**	**Latin**	**Umbrian**
Icelandic	English	Gothic (extinct)	Portuguese	[extinct]
Faeroese	Frisian		Spanish	
Norwegian	Dutch		Catalan	
Swedish	German		Occitan[1]	
Danish	Yiddish		French	
			Italian	
			Rhaeto-	
			Romance[2]	
			Romanian	

English is in the Germanic family, its closest "living" relative being the West Germanic Frisian language, spoken in coastal parts of Netherlands and Denmark. Nonetheless, one can easily argue that Latin (and its Romance descendants) share at least equal paternity. Their influence on English extends far beyond the typical back-and-forth borrowing that characterizes the development of many languages:

1. For several centuries following the Norman invasion of England in 1066, French was the "legal" language of England, spoken by the nobility as

---

[1] *Occitan* is the "modern" name for the *langue d'oc* of southern France, as opposed to the *langue d'oïl* of central and northern France—the two names arose from the contrasting manner in which the word "yes" was spoken. *Oïl* subsequently evolved into Modern French *oui*. *Occitan* is frequently known (especially outside of France) as *Provençal*.

[2] The term *Rhaeto-Romance* refers to a group of dialects spoken in southern Switzerland and northern Italy, of which one—*Romansh*—is an "official" language of Switzerland (along with German, French, and Italian).

their native language and used (along with Latin) for legal, religious, and commercial purposes. English continued to be spoken by the "common" people, however, and during (and immediately following) this period, the contribution of French to English vocabulary was enormous, adding to the existing vocabulary and in very many cases replacing previous words of Old English origin. In addition, definitions and uses of many *native* English words were influenced by those of their French counterparts.

2. When English eventually supplanted Latin as the language of scholarship, it took directly from Latin (or its Romance descendants) the overwhelming majority of its academic, scientific, and technical vocabulary. Indeed, it is not easy to find words in these fields that are "native" English ones.

3. In the legal system, despite several earlier attempts (in the fourteenth and seventeenth centuries), it was not until *1731* that it was finally decreed that all court proceedings and statutes "shall be in the English tongue and language only, and not in Latin or French". This has left its mark not only on quaint courtroom customs—*"Oyez, oyez, oyez!* The court is now in session!"—but on the overwhelming majority of legal vocabulary. Moreover, apart from the obvious legal words (*appeal, assault, battery, judge, jury, plaintiff, plea,* etc.), many everyday English words have their origins in "law French":[3]

asset, attach, cheat, entail, fee, gauge, hodgepodge, mere, misnomer, oust, puny, remainder, seize, several, size, suit, surmise, treasure trove, try, etc.

If further convincing is required, one need only compare two versions of the Preamble to the U.S. Constitution, the first from a Romance language (Spanish), the second from a Germanic one (German).

I. Nosotros, el pueblo de los Estados Unidos, a fin de formar una unión más perfecta, establecer la justicia, asegurar la tranquilidad interior, proveer la defensa común, promover el bienestar general y asegurar para nosotros y para nuestra posteridad los beneficios de la libertad, sancionamos y establecemos esta Constitución para los Estados Unidos de América.

II. Wir, das Volk der Vereinigten Staaten, von der Absicht geleitet, unseren Bund zu vervollkommnen, die Gerechtigkeit zu verwirklichen, die Ruhe im

---

[3] "Law French" refers to a specific form of *Anglo-French* (or *Anglo-Norman*) used in England in judicial proceedings, pleadings, and lawbooks until at least the late seventeenth century. For a modern guide, see J. H. Baker, *Manual of Law French,* 2nd ed. (Aldershot, UK: Scholar Press, 1990).

Innern zu sichern, für die Landesverteidigung zu sorgen, das allgemeine
Wohl zu fördern und das Glück der Freiheit uns selbst und unseren
Nachkommen zu bewahren, setzen und begründen diese Verfassung
für die Vereinigten Staaten von Amerika.

According to the normal classification of languages, a monolingual English
speaker will find the second version far easier to understand than the first.
Does this seem likely to you?

Let us look now at the English text, where words with Latin-Romance origin
are highlighted in bold.[4]

We the **people** of the **united states,** in **order** to **form** a more **perfect
union, establish justice, insure domestic tranquility, provide** for the
common defense, promote the **general** welfare, and **secure** the bless-
ings of **liberty** to ourselves and our **posterity,** do **ordain** and **establish**
this **Constitution** for the **United States** of *America.*[5]

A very clear pattern emerges: the large majority of articles, pronouns, prepositions, and conjunctions—what linguists would call *grammatical* words—are
Germanic, while the vast majority of the verbs, nouns, and adjectives—*lexical*
words—have Latin or Romance origin.[6] Although one could easily find examples with a less pronounced Latin/Romance influence, the general conclusion
remains unaltered:

Although the "highways" of English (i.e., grammatical words) have remained (almost entirely) Germanic, the "merchandise" transported on
these highways is predominantly of Latin and Romance origin.

Without perhaps consciously being aware of it, English speakers thus have a
natural foundation on which to build a deeper knowledge of Latin and the Romance languages.

In the remainder of this section, we will look at some of the highlights (and
lowlights) of the U.S. Constitution, followed by Lincoln's "Gettysburg Address".

---

[4] In the selections from the Constitution, spelling ("choose" for "chuse") and capitalization
have been modernized (in the original text, common nouns were uniformly capitalized, as is still
the case in German).

[5] *America* is of mixed origin: it comes from the name of the Italian explorer *Amerigo* Vespucci,
in its Latinized form *Americus. Amerigo* itself is of Germanic origin—from the Ostrogothic form
of "Henry".

[6] Most adverbs, of which the present example has none, are lexical.

Our final text will be a brief selection from the post-Franco Spanish Constitution of 1978 and will help to answer two important questions: (1) What is the official language of Spain? and (2) What percentage of the Spanish flag is red?

La Constitución de los Estados Unidos[7]

ARTÍCULO UNO

Primera Sección

Todos los poderes legislativos *otorgados* en la presente Constitución corresponderán a un Congreso de los Estados Unidos, que se *compondrá* de un Senado y una *Cámara* de Representantes.

a)	otorgar	(to) grant, (to) award
	otorgado (p.p.)	granted
	El que calla, otorga.	He who keeps silent, consents. ("Silence gives consent.")

The verb *otorgar* comes from Classical Latin AUCTORARE (via Vulgar Latin AUCTORICARE). The original meaning was "to guarantee" or "to rent or sell one's services"; the second sense was often used in connection with gladiators. AUCTORARE was formed from the noun AUCTOR—"creator", "promoter", "guarantor"—literally "one who *augments* confidence". This in turn came from the verb AUGERE (past participle AUCTUS), "to augment", "to increase". The earliest English forms of AUCTOR were *autor* and *auctor;* the *h* was introduced as a spelling variant in the sixteenth century, presumably from a mistaken belief that the word was of Greek origin.[8]

AUCTOR	autor (m.), autora (f.)	author
	autoridad	authority
	autorizar	(to) authorize
	autorización	authorization
	autoritario	authoritarian
AUCTIO(N)	[subasta]	auction
	[subastar]	(to) auction

---

[7] The Spanish translation comes (with minor adaptations) from the "Political Database of the Americas", Georgetown University (available online).

[8] In an example of what is known as *spelling pronunciation,* the pronunciation of *author, authority,* etc., eventually came to reflect the spelling.

	[asta]	flagpole, antler or horn, shaft	
	[a media asta]	at half-mast	[*hastate*]
AUGMENTARE	aumentar	(to) augment, (to) increase	
	aumento	augmentation, increase	

AUCTIO(N) took its name from the fact that with each bid the price *augmented*. A Roman auction was also known as a sale SUB HASTA ("under the spear"), from the tradition of planting a spear (HASTA) on property to be auctioned to pay its owner's debts to the state. The derived verb SUBHASTARE became popular in Medieval Latin and gave rise to Spanish *subastar* and *subasta*.

Also derived from AUGERE was the noun AUGUR, a member of a college of priests charged with making predictions of the future (AUGURIUM) based on celestial signals (thunder and lightning), the flight pattern of birds, etc.

AUGURIUM	agüero	augury, (ill) omen, sign (of bad luck)
	agorero (adj. & n.)	of ill omen, prophet (of doom), *augur*
	augurio	augury, omen
	augurar	(to) augur, (to) predict

The first two are "popular" (or evolved) forms; the latter two, "learned". The popular forms are more commonly associated with predictions based on superstition and coincidences—and tend in the vast majority of cases to be negative—whereas the more learned forms are simple predictions of the future, for better or for worse.

ave (pájaro) de *mal agüero*	bird of *ill omen*
No es un *buen augurio.*	It doesn't *bode well.*

The adjective AUGUSTUS referred to an object worthy of veneration because it had been blessed by the gods with favorable omens. It was the title accorded by the Roman Senate in 27 BC to Gaius Julius Caesar Octavianus (Julius Caesar's adopted son), and subsequently the month SEXTILIS was changed to AUGUSTUS in his honor.[9]

AUGUSTUS	agosto	August (eighth month)
	augusto	august (venerable)

---

[9] It was called SEXTILIS because August had been the *sixth* month in the ancient Roman calendar, in which the year began in March. Similarly, before being renamed for Julius Caesar, July had been called QUINTILIS.

Before installing someone in high office, suitable auguries had to be observed, following which the INAUGURATIO(N) could take place:

INAUGURATIO(N)	inauguración	inauguration
	inaugurar	(to) inaugurate

AUXILIUM was literally "reinforcement", i.e., an *augmentation* of forces.

AUXILIUM	auxilio	help (also: Help!!!)
	—primeros auxilios	—first aid
	auxiliar (adj. & n.)	auxiliary, assistant
	auxiliar (vb.)	(to) help, (to) aid

b)
componer	(to) put together, (to) *compose*	[*compound*]
componente	component	
descomponer	(to) *decompose,* (to) put out of order	
poner	(to) put, (to) place, (to) lay (eggs, the table)	
poner al día	(to) update	
ponente (m./f.)	speaker (at conference)	
ponencia	report or paper (presented by a *ponente*)	
deponer	(to) *depose,* (to) *depone*	
disponer	(to) *dispose* (incl. "arrange")	
disponible	disposable (free for use), available	
[desechable]	disposable (to be used once and thrown away)	
disponibilidad	availability	
exponer	(to) *expose,* (to) exhibit, (to) *expound*	
exponencial	exponential	
exponente	exponent (person, mathematical power)	
imponer	(to) *impose*	[*impound*]
imponente	imposing	
interponer	(to) *interpose*	
indisponer	(to) set one person against another, (to) *indispose*	
oponer	(to) *oppose,* (to) offer (resistance)	
oponente	opponent	
posponer	(to) postpone (delay; place after)	
presuponer	(to) *presuppose,* (to) budget	

proponer	(to) *propose*, (to) *propound*
proponente	proponent
reponer	(to) *reposit* (put back, replace)
sobreponer	(to) *superpose*, (to) superimpose
~ superponer	
suponer	(to) *suppose*
transponer /	(to) *transpose*
transponer	
yuxtaponer	(to) *juxtapose*

The *-poner* verbs correspond to English *-pose* verbs (apart from *posponer*— post*pone*[10]) and have associated nouns ending in *-posición*, e.g., *composición*, *imposición*. Their irregular past participles are of the form *-puesto;* a number of these were presented in Section 3.3, no. 5.

c)	*cámara*	*chamber*, camera
	música de cámara	chamber music

Latin CAMERA (or CAMARA) meant "vault" or "arch" and was taken by the Romans from Greek (where it had three A's). In Spanish, the word means "chamber" in the formal sense of a house of Congress or the *Chamber of Commerce* (*la Camára de Comercio*) and also refers to the principal room of a house ("parlor"), but this latter usage is primarily formal.

antecámara	antechamber
camarero	waiter
camarera	waitress, *chambermaid*
camarote	cabin, stateroom (on ship)
recámara	dressing room, bedroom (Amer.)
camarada (m./f.)	*comrade*
camaradería	camaraderie
chambelán	chamberlain

---

[10] At an early stage in the Romance languages, the verb PONERE ("to put"), whose past participle stem was POS-, became mixed up with POSARE (formerly PAUSARE), which initially meant "to stop or *pause*"—presumably because when one *reposed* (i.e., "repaused"), one put something (or oneself) down. In French (and hence English), the compond verbs from -PONERE all shifted to *-pose(r)* without changing their meanings. English *postpone* and *depone* were taken directly from Latin, while the English *-pound* verbs come from the Old French forms of the -PONERE verbs, before they had become "corrupted" by pose(r).

Camarada initially referred to "soldiers eating and sleeping in the same *cámara* (room)". It passed into English via French, its Spanish origin revealed by the middle *a* of *camaraderie*. *Chamberlain* is another early forerunner of globalization: It was based on a Greek word adopted by Latin; taken into Germanic and given the suffix *-ling;* then passed into French, where the initial *ca* was palatized to *ch;* and from there was incorporated into English and Spanish.

bicameral   bicameral
unicameral   unicameral

Now we can try our hand at a reverse translation of Article I, Section 1, from Spanish into English:

> All the legislative powers granted in the present Constitution will correspond [belong] to a Congress of the United States, which will be composed of a Senate and a House of Representatives.

Not as elegant or concise as the original:

> All legislative powers herein granted shall be vested in a Congress of the United States, which shall consist of a Senate and House of Representatives.

but nevertheless a serviceable translation.

Segunda Sección

1. La Cámara de Representantes estará formada por miembros *elegidos* cada dos años por los *habitantes* de los diversos Estados, y los electores *deberán* poseer en cada Estado las condiciones *requeridas* para los electores de la *rama* más numerosa de la legislatura local.

Section 2 (original text[11])

1. The House of Representatives shall be composed of members chosen every second year by the people of the several States, and the electors in each State shall have the qualifications requisite for electors of the most numerous branch of the State legislature.

a)   elegir   (to) elect, (to) choose   (Lat. ELIGERE)
        elegido (p.p.)   elected
        elegible   eligible
        elegibilidad   eligibility

---

[11] Where not specifically identified as "Literal", English versions are "original".

The past participle of ELIGERE was ELECTUS, from which English has constructed the verb *elect*. In Spanish, ELECTUS became *electo;* initially the past participle for the verb *elegir, electo* has been supplanted in this role by the regular form *elegido* and remains only as an adjective.

elección	election, choice	
electo	elected, elect (adj.)	(old p.p.)
—presidente electo	—president-elect	
electorado	electorate	
electoral	electoral	
elector	elector, voter	
electivo	elective	

b)   *habitante*   inhabitant

The origin of *habitante—inhabitant* is ultimately Latin HABERE ("to have"), through its *frequentative* form HABITARE ("to have something repeatedly", i.e., to *inhabit*). HABITUS, the past participle of HABERE, came to mean "manner of being, exterior aspect, clothes"; other derived forms were the adjective HABILIS, "easily managed, *able*", and the noun HABILITAS, *"ability"*.

HABERE	haber	(to) have	[*habeas* corpus]
	haber (n.)	credit (asset)	
	haberes (pl.)	assets, property	
HABITARE	habitar	(to) inhabit	
	habitación	habitation, room, dwelling	
	hábitat	habitat[12]	
	hábito	habit (custom, religious clothing, addiction)	
	habitual	habitual, customary	
	habituar	(to) habituate, (to) get used to	
COHABITARE	cohabitar	(to) cohabit	
	cohabitación	cohabitation	
HABILIS	hábil	*able,* skillful	
HABILITAS	habilidad	*ability,* skill	
REHABILITARE	rehabilitar	(to) rehabilitate, (to) rehab	
	rehabilitación	rehabilitation	

---

[12] *Habitat* comes directly from the third person singular verb form (HABITAT) and thus literally means "it inhabits".

c)   *deber*   (to) owe, should, must   [en*deavor*]

    deber (noun)   *duty,* obligation, *debt,*
                        devoir

    deberes (pl.)   homework, obligations

DEBERE was a contraction of DE and HABERE, literally to "have *from* someone", i.e., *to owe.* Its neuter past participle was DEBITUM (*plural* DEBITA).

DEBITA	deuda	*debt*	
	deudo	relative (esp. bereaved one)	
DEBITOR	deudor	*debtor*	
DEBITUM	débito	*debt, debit* (charge)	
	debido (p.p.)	*due,* fitting, proper	
	indebido	improper, unlawful, *undue*	
	debe	*debit* (side of accounts)	(lit. "he owes")
	debidamente	du*ly*	[*due* + -ly]
	adeudar	(to) owe (money)	
	adeudo	debt, customs *duty*	
	endeudar(se)	(to) fall into *debt*	
	endeudado (p.p.)	*indebted* (owing money)	

d)   requ**e**rir   (to) require, (to) request
                        officially (hence,
                        to require)

    requerido (p.p.) required, *requisite*

    requerimiento   requirement, request
                        (formal), summons (legal)

Requerir comes from REQUIRERE, "to search for or inquire after", "to be in need of"—RE + QUAERERE ("search", "seek", "desire"), the root of Spanish *querer.* Another form of seeking an answer was INQUIRERE, whose related noun INQUISITIO(N) acquired a certain notoriety in Spanish history.

	[solicitud]	request, application
	[solicitar]	(to) request, (to) apply for,
		(to) *solicit*
	[solícito]	obliging, *solicitous*
REQUISITUS	requisito	requisite, requirement
	—requisito	—prerequisite
	previo	
	requisar	(to) requisition,
		(to) confiscate

	requisición	requisition	
INQUIRERE	inquirir	(to) inquire into, (to) investigate	
	inquisición	inquisition, Inquisition	
	encuesta	opinion poll, survey	[*inquest*]
ACQUIRERE (ADQ-)	adquirir	(to) acquire	
	adquisición	acquisition	
PERQUISITA	pesquisa	inquiry, investigation	[*perquisite, perk*]
QUAERERE	querer	(to) want, (to) love	[*query*]
	querido (p.p.)	dear, beloved, lover (m./f.)	
	siquiera (adv. & conj.)	at least, although, even though	(si + quiera[13])
	ni siquiera	not even	
	dondequiera	anywhere, wherever	
	adondequiera	[to] anywhere, [to] wherever, whithersoever	
	cualquiera	whatever, whichever, any, anyone	
	quienquiera	who(m)ever	
QUAESTIO(N)	cuestión	question (issue, matter)[14]	
	cuestionable	questionable, debatable	
	incuestionable	unquestionable	
	cuestionar	(to) [call into] question	
	cuestionario	questionnaire	
CONQUISTARE	conquistar	(to) conquer,	
	conquista	(to) win over conquest	
	conquistador	conqueror, conquistador	
e)	*rama*	branch (of a tree, organization, etc.)	
	ramo	branch, bouquet (of flowers)	[*ramus*]

Latin RAMUS has been taken directly into English (ramus) with very specific meanings in anatomy and biology, including "a bony process extending like a

---

[13] Third person singular present subjunctive.
[14] For example: "It's a *question* for the mayor to decide". A question one asks is normally a *pregunta*, although in an exam or a poll it can be a *cuestión*.

branch from a larger bone". Spanish *ramo* and *rama* are an example of a couplet in which the feminine *rama* is the "superior" concept (see appendix to Annex A), with *ramo* being defined as:

> Rama de segundo orden o que sale de la rama madre.

> Second-order branch or that projects from the mother branch.

They share the definition:

> Cada una de las partes en que se considera dividida una ciencia, arte, industria, etc.

> Each of the parts in which a science, art, industry, etc., is considered to be divided.

RAMOSUS	ramoso	ramose (having many branches)
RAMIFICARE	ramificar(se)	(to) branch out, (to) *ramify*
	ramificación	ramification
	ramera	prostitute, whore, harlot

Ramera is a "popular" form of *prostituta*. Initially it referred to those plying their trade clandestinely and signaling their availability by placing a small branch on their door, analogous to the English *red light* (district).[15]

DE + RAMUS	derramar	(to) spill, (to) shed, (to) scatter
	derrame	spillage, bleeding
	derrame cerebral	cerebral hemorrhage

Initially meaning "to divide into branches", the notion of "spilling" arose from the similarity in shape between a spilled liquid (on a flat surface) and the branches of a tree.

> 2. No será representante ninguna persona que no haya *cumplido* 25 años de edad y que no haya sido *ciudadana* de los Estados Unidos durante siete años, y que no sea habitante del Estado en el cual se le designe, al tiempo de la elección.

> 2. No person shall be a Representative who shall not have attained to the age of twenty-five years, and been seven years a citizen of the United States, and

---

[15] A not very politically correct way to refer to the zone of such activities, at least in Spain, is *el barrio chino*.

who shall not, when elected, be an inhabitant of that State in which he shall be chosen.

a)	cumplir	(to) *accomplish,* (to) fulfill
	—cumplir con	—(to) *comply* with
	cumplido (p.p.)	complete (consummate), courteous, courtesy (act), *compliment*
	—misión cumplida	—mission accomplished
	incumplir	(to) fail to fulfill or *comply*

Cumplir comes from COMPLERE ("to fill up", "to *complete*"), whose past participle was COMPLETUS ("filled up", "*complete*", "*completed*"). While English *complete* normally means "to finish", it has also maintained the original Latin sense in the secondary definition "to make whole, with all necessary elements or parts".

English *complement* and *compliment,* not infrequently confused, both come from COMPLEMENTUM ("that which completes", in the sense of "filling up"). *Complement* comes straight from Latin and at one time in English also meant "ceremonies of civility or politeness" before being displaced in this role in the late seventeenth century by *compliment,* which took the more circular path of Latin → Spanish (*cumplimiento*) → Italian → French → English. Spanish *cumplimiento* had the meanings of both "compliment" and "accomplishment", though it was only the former that was exported to Italian (and hence to English). Since that time, *cumplimiento* has largely given up the meaning of "compliment", having been replaced in this sense by *cumplido.* Whether expressed by *cumplido* or *cumplimiento,* the "acts of courtesy" are generally acts of graciousness or thoughtfulness rather than mere words.

[acabar, terminar]	(to) complete (i.e., to finish)
cumplidamente	completely (fulfilling an obligation)
cumplimiento	fulfillment, *accomplishment, compliance*
incumplimiento	*noncompliance,* breach (of contract, promise)
cumplimentar	(to) pay one's respects (or *compliments*) to, (to) complete (task, form)
cumplidor	reliable, dependable
cumpleaños	birthday

Complimentary can be expressed in various manners, depending on whether the meaning is "free" (*gratuito, gratis, de regalo*) or "laudatory" (*elogioso, lisonjero*).

Spanish also has "learned" forms derived from COMPLERE that are distinguished by their vowels: (*o, e*) rather than (*u, i*).

completar	(to) complete, (to) complement
completo	complete (finished, entire, consummate)
completamente	completely
complemento	complement (incl. grammatical)
complementar	(to) complement
complementario	complementary, additional

b)　　*ciudadano*　　citizen

CIVITAS, a collection of "citizens" (CIVIS), initially was an abstract concept, with URBS representing the physical entity of a city, but over time, the two words became largely synonymous. Two adjectives referring to a citizen or group of citizens were CIVICUS and CIVILIS, while CIVILITAS represented the quality of a citizen, notably sociability and courtesy (*civility*).

CIVITAS	ciudad	*city*
	ciudadanía	*citizenship*
	ciudadela	*citadel*
CIVILIS	civil	civil, civilian (m./f.)
CIVICUS	cívico	civic
	civismo	civic-mindedness
CIVILITAS	civilidad	civility
	civilización	civilization
	civilizar	(to) civilize
URBS	urbe (f.)	(big) city
	suburbio	suburb (often "slum")
URBANUS	urbano	urban, urbane
URBANITAS	urbanidad	urbanity (refinement and elegance of manner)
	urbanización	urbanization
	urbanizar	(to) urbanize, (to) develop

In the following section, the text in brackets is no longer operative, having been modified by the Fourteenth and Sixteenth Amendments.

> 3. [Los representantes y los *impuestos* directos se prorratearán entre los distintos Estados que formen parte de esta Unión, de acuerdo con su *población* respectiva, la cual se determinará *sumando* al número total de personas *libres*,

inclusive las *obligadas* a prestar servicios durante cierto *término* de años y, excluyendo a los indios no sujetos al pago de *contribuciones,* las tres quintas partes de todas las personas restantes.] El *recuento* deberá hacerse efectiva- mente dentro de los tres años siguientes a la primera sesión del Congreso de los Estados Unidos y en lo sucesivo cada 10 años, en la forma que dicho cuerpo dis- ponga por medio de una *ley*. El número de representantes no excederá de uno por cada 30 mil habitantes con tal que cada Estado cuente con un representante *cuando menos;* y hasta que se efectúe dicho recuento, el Estado de Nueva Hamp- shire tendrá derecho a elegir tres; Massachusetts, ocho; Rhode Island y las Plantaciones de Providence, uno; Connecticut, cinco; Nueva York, seis; Nueva Jersey, cuatro; Pennsylvania, ocho; Delaware, uno; Maryland, seis; Virginia, diez; Carolina del Norte, cinco; Carolina del Sur, cinco y Georgia, tres.

3. [Representatives and direct taxes shall be apportioned among the several States which may be included within this Union, according to their respective numbers, which shall be determined by adding to the whole number of free persons, including those bound to service for a term of years, and excluding Indians not taxed, three-fifths of all other persons.] The actual enumeration shall be made within three years after the first meeting of the Congress of the United States, and within every subsequent term of ten years, in such manner as they shall by law direct. The number of Representatives shall not exceed one for every thirty thousand, but each State shall have at least one Representative; and until such enumeration shall be made, the State of New Hampshire shall be entitled to choose three; Massachusetts, eight; Rhode Island and Providence Plantations, one; Connecticut, five; New York, six; New Jersey, four; Pennsyl- vania, eight; Delaware, one; Maryland, six; Virginia, ten; North Carolina, five; South Carolina, five; and Georgia, three.

a)   *impuesto* (p.p. of *imponer*)   tax

From Latin IMPONERE, to *impose;* a tax is thus an *imposition.* Also commonly expressed as

contribuciones (pl.)	taxes
contribución	contribution, tax
contribuir	(to) contribute,
	(to) pay as a tax
contribuyente	taxpayer

b)   *población*   population, town

During the long period of the Roman Republic (up to the time of Caesar), the POPULUS and the SENATUS were the two essential elements of the Roman state. It was only during the period of Imperial Rome that POPULUS extended its scope to include the PLEBS ("common people"). Corresponding adjectives were PUBLICUS, "concerning the people (or state)", and POPULARIS, "from (or for) the people", "liked by the people". Matters of the people (public affairs) were referred to as RES PUBLICA—RES meaning "thing", "matter"—one of whose grammatical forms (ablative) was RE PUBLICA.

POPULUS	**pue**blo	village, small town, populace, *people*	[*pueblo*]
POPULARIS	popular	popular (incl. "of the people")	
	popularidad	popularity	
	poblar	(to) populate (incl. "inhabit"), (to) *people*	
	poblado (p.p.)	town, settlement	
	poblador	settler, inhabitant	
	populoso	populous	
	despoblar	depopulate	
	despoblación	depopulation	
PUBLICUS	público	public	
PUBLICARE	publicar	(to) publish, (to) make public	
	publicación	publication	
	[editorial (f.), editor]	publisher (firm, individual)	
	publicidad	publicity, advertising	
	publicitar	(to) publicize, (to) advertise	
RE PUBLICA	república	republic	
	republicano	republican	
PLEBS	plebe (f.)	*plebs* (common people, populace)	[*plebe*]
	plebeyo	plebeian	
	plebiscito	plebiscite	

The original meaning of PUBLICARE was "to make (property) public", while PUBLICATIO(N) referred to "confiscation or expropriation for the benefit of the state".

c)	*sumar*	(to) add, (to) *sum* up
	sumando (pres. part.)	adding; addend

d)   *libre*   free (but not gratis!), vacant
     librar   (to) free, (to) wage, (to) issue (judgment, etc.)
     —*líbra*nos del mal . . .   —*deliver* us from evil . . . (Matthew 6:13)
     liberar   (to) *liberate,* (to) free
     liberación   liberation
     liberal   liberal (incl. "tolerant")
     liberalizar   (to) liberalize
     libertad   liberty
     libertador (adj. & n.)   liberating, liberator
     libertar   (to) free or liberate (a person)
     libertario   anarchist(ic), libertarian
     libertino   libertine
     deliberar   (to) deliberate
     deliberado (p.p.)   deliberate
     deliberadamente   deliberately

e)   obligar   (to) oblige, (to) obligate
     obligado (p.p.)   obligated
     obligación   obligation, bond, debenture
     obligatorio   obligatory

f)   *término*   *term, terminus* (end), boundary, limit
     terminal (adj.)   terminal (final)
     terminal (n.f.)   terminal (bus, airport, port)
     terminal (n.m.)   terminal (computer, electrical)
     terminación   termination, ending
     terminar   (to) terminate (finish; bring to an end)
     terminante   definitive, final, categorical
     terminología   terminology

Término is a useful word for illustrating the importance of mastering the correct placement of stress (and written) accent in Spanish:

término   **tér**•mi•no   [as above]
termino   ter•**mi**•no   "I finish"
terminó   ter•mi•**nó**   "he/she/it finished"
[stressed syllable highlighted in bold]

g)   *recuento*   count, recount

h)   *ley* (f.)   law

Ley is from Latin LEX (acc. LEGEM). Related adjectives were LEGALIS, "relative to the laws", and LEGITIMUS, "established by law". LATUS was the (highly irregular) past participle of FERRE ("to bear", "to carry"), hence LEGIS LATOR ("bearer of law").

LEGALIS	legal	legal, lawful
	ilegal	illegal, unlawful
	legalidad	legality, lawfulness
	ilegalidad	illegality, unlawfulness
	legalizar	(to) legalize, (to) certify (document)
LEGITIMUS	legítimo	legitimate
	legitimidad	legitimacy
	ilegítimo	illegitimate
	ilegitimidad	illegitimacy
LEGITIMARE	legitimar	(to) legitimate, (to) legitimize
LEGIS LATOR	legislador	legislator
	legislatura	legislature, session of legislature
	legislativo	legislative
	legislación	legislation
	legislar	(to) legislate

i)   *cuando menos*   at (the) least ($\sim$ *al menos*)
      cuando   when
      —cuando menos lo esperes   —when you least expect it

4. Cuando ocurran vacantes en la representación de cualquier Estado, la autoridad ejecutiva del mismo *expedirá* un *decreto* en que se convocará a elecciones con el objeto de *llenarlas*.

Literal Translation: When vacancies occur in the representation of any State, the executive authority of the same [State] will issue a decree in which elections will be convoked with the object of filling them [the vacancies].

Actual Text: When vacancies happen in the representation from any State, the executive authority thereof shall issue writs of election to fill such vacancies.

a)   *expedir*   (to) send, (to) issue (decree, document)   [*expedite*]

Additional words related to *expedir* are presented in the discussion of *impeachment* in Clause 5.

b) *decreto*   decree

  decretar   (to) decree

c) llenar   (to) fill

  llenarlas   (to) fill them   (infinitive + direct object *las*)

Latin PLENUS, "full", was derived from PLERE, a rarely used verb found almost exclusively in compounds (notably COMPLERE, discussed above). Other related words were PLENITUDO, PLENIPOTENS ("all-powerful"), and PLENITAS ("fullness").

PLENUS	pleno (adj. & n.)	full, *plenum,* plenary session
	lleno	full
PLENITUDO	plenitud	plenitude, fullness
PLENITAS	———	*plenty*
	plenario	plenary
	plenipotenciario	plenipotentiary (invested with full power)
	luna llena	full moon
	~ plenilunio	
	rellenar	(to) fill (out), (to) refill (*replenish*), (to) stuff
	relleno (adj. & n.)	filled, stuffed, stuffing, filler
	repleto	*replete,* full, jam-packed

5. La Cámara de Representantes elegirá su presidente y demás funcionarios y será la única *facultada* para *declarar que hay lugar a proceder en los casos de responsabilidades oficiales.*

Literal Translation: The House of Representatives will elect its president and other officials and will be uniquely empowered to *decide whether there are grounds for proceeding [judicially] in cases of official responsibilities.*

Actual Text: The House of Representatives shall choose their Speaker and other officers; and shall have the sole power of *impeachment.*

a) facultar   (to) empower, (to) authorize

  facultado   empowered, authorized

  facultad   faculty (various definitions)

  facultativo (adj. & n.) optional, *facultative,* medical, physician

  facilidad   facility (ease)

fácil	easy, facile
facilitar	(to) facilitate, (to) supply or furnish
difícil	difficult, hard
dificultad	difficulty
dificultoso	difficult
dificultar	(to) make difficult, (to) impede

Facultad comes from Latin FACULTAS, which was essentially the same word as FACILITAS (source of *facility* and *facilidad*) by virtue of a phonetic "law" in Latin that dictated that *LT* be preceded by *U* and *LI* by *I*. The common root was the verb FACERE ("to do", Spanish *hacer*), and the two nouns came to specialize in the respective meanings of *capacity of doing* and *ease of doing,* which are essentially their Spanish and English definitions. The two languages also share the more specialized academic meaning for the former, e.g., *la Facultad de Leyes—the Faculty of Law.* The optional nature of *facultativo—facultative* comes from having the *faculty* to do something but not the obligation. A *difficulty* is literally a *dis-faculty.*

b) Despite *impeachment*'s Latin pedigree, it is apparent from the awkward translation that it does not have a direct Spanish equivalent. *Impeach* and *impeachment* come from French *empêcher* (initially "to impede", later "to prevent") and *empêchement* ("obstacle", "snag"), which were derived in turn from Latin IMPEDICARE, "to entangle", literally "to shackle the feet (PES/PEDEM) with a PEDICA (*fetter*)". IMPEDICARE was a later, more colorful form of the basic verb IMPEDIRE (IN + PEDE-), which simply meant "to restrict the feet" (hence, "to impede"), without specifying the nature of the IMPEDIMENTUM. The related verb INTERPEDIRE came to specialize in the entanglement of one's own feet, i.e., "to trip or stumble"; a Vulgar Latin form (INTERPEDIARE) later gave rise to Old Spanish *entropezar* and Modern Spanish *tropezar.*

French *empêcher* and *empêchement* arrived in English with their original meanings intact. At an early stage, however, they were apparently thought to have been derived from the (unrelated) Latin verb IMPETERE. They were therefore used to translate the Medieval Latin legal terms IMPETERE and IMPETITIO(N), which referred to the act of bringing a charge or accusation against someone— this remains the basic definition of *impeach:*

> **impeach**   **1a:** to bring an accusation against   **b:** to charge with a crime or misdemeanor; *specifically:* to charge (a public official) before a competent tribunal with misconduct in office . . . (*Merriam-Webster's Collegiate Dictionary*)

IMPETERE—in Classical Latin "to attack or assail"—was itself related to IMPETUS ("attack or assault", "violent impulse"), the source of English *impetus* and *impetuous*. The medieval legal use was a natural extension, literally "to attack in justice".

In the late fourteenth century, *empêcher* arrived to Spanish via Occitan (the so-called langue d'oc spoken in the south of France) in the form of *empachar*. While sharing the common "classical" definition with the learned *impedir, empachar* and its associated noun *empacho* have come to specialize in a very specific impediment, namely "indigestion".

IMPEDIMENTA, the neuter plural of IMPEDIMENTUM, had been used in Caesar's time in the sense of vehicles and baggage that *impede* the movement of an army. Around 1600, English "borrowed" *impedimenta,* with the rather more general meaning of "objects, such as provisions, that impede or encumber"; Spanish *impedimenta* has preserved the military connotation. In the nineteenth century, *impedance* was coined in English as a measure of the overall opposition to electric current, and the term then spread to a number of other languages, including Spanish.

If IMPEDIRE meant to restrict the feet, what did one say for the opposite situation, i.e., removing one's feet from the obstruction? The Latin answer was EXPEDIRE, source of a number of English (and Spanish) words, including *expedite* and *expedition.* The French answer was *dépêcher,* formed by replacing the *em-* of *empêcher* with *dé-.* This then became Spanish *despachar,* which is very likely the source of English *dispatch.*

IMPEDIRE	impedir	(to) impede, (to) hinder
IMPEDICARE	empachar	(to) *impede,* (to) give indigestion
	empacho	*impediment,* indigestion, surfeit
	—ningún empacho	—no qualms (uneasy feeling that *impedes*)
	[???]	(to) impeach
IMPEDIMENTUM	impedimento	impediment, hindrance
	impedimenta	impedimenta (esp. military)
	impedancia	impedance (electrical)
IMPETUS	ímpetu	impetus, momentum
	impetuoso	impetuous
INTERPEDIARE	tropezar	(to) stumble, (to) trip
	tropiezo	stumbling block, stumble (fig.)
	tropezón	stumble
	—a tropezones	—in fits and starts

EXPEDIRE	expedir	(to) expedite (issue officially, dispatch)
	expedición	expedition, shipment
	expedidor	shipper, sender
	expediente	dossier, file or record, court proceedings
	expedito	free from encumbrance, *expeditious* (manner)
	expeditivo	expeditious (person)
	despachar	(to) dispatch (send off, transact, put to death)
	despacho	office, dispatch

Spanish words derived from EXPEDIRE are typically used more in the sense of "to send" or "to dispatch" than in English, where the primary meaning is "to speed up the progress of, to facilitate". English *expedite,* however, still preserves the definition "to issue officially, to send out". A Spanish office is a *despacho* because it is where business is *dispatched.*

Sexta Sección

1. Los *senadores* y representantes recibirán por sus servicios una remuneración que será fijada por la ley y pagada por el tesoro de los *EE.UU.* En todos los casos, exceptuando los de traición, *delito* grave y perturbación del orden público, gozarán del privilegio de no ser arrestados durante el tiempo que asistan a las sesiones de sus respectivas Cámaras, así como al ir a ellas o regresar de las mismas, y no podrán ser objeto en ningún otro sitio de inquisición alguna con motivo de cualquier discusión o debate en una de las Cámaras.

Section 6

1. The Senators and Representatives shall receive a compensation for their services, to be ascertained by law, and paid out of the Treasury of the United States. They shall in all cases, except treason, felony and breach of the peace, be privileged from arrest during their attendance at the session of their respective Houses, and in going to and returning from the same; and for any speech or debate in either House, they shall not be questioned in any other place.

a)	*senador*	senator	
	senado	senate	
b)	*EE.UU.*	"Estados Unidos"	U.S.A

According to the RAE, the rule for abbreviations of plurals is as follows:

En abreviaturas formadas por una sola letra, el plural se expresa duplicando esta: *ss.* por *siguientes, EE. UU.* por *Estados Unidos.*[16]

In abbreviations formed by a single letter, the plural is expressed by duplicating this (letter): *ss.* for *siguientes, EE. UU.* for *Estados Unidos.*

Theoretically, there is a space between *EE.* and *UU.,* though in practice this is usually omitted; the periods are also frequently omitted. Other common examples are: *CC.OO. (Comisiones Obreras), FF.AA. (Fuerzas Armadas), JJ.OO. (Juegos Olímpicos), CC.AA. (Comunidades Autónomas).*

c)	*delito*	crime, offense, *delict*	(Lat. DELICTUM)
	flagrante delito	*flagrante delicto* (red-handed, in the very act)	(*or* delito flagrante)
	cuerpo del delito	*corpus delicti*	
	delictivo	criminal (adj.)	
	delincuente	delinquent	
	delincuencia	delinquency	
	delinquir	(to) break the law (commit a *delito*)	
	reliquia	relic	
	relicario	reliquary (shrine), locket	

LINQUERE was "to leave", and RELINQUERE (p.p. RELICTUS) was "to leave behind", hence *relinquish*—leaving behind a *relic* or *reliquia*—while DELINQUERE was to "leave" one's obligations, to be *delinquent*. The neuter past participle DELICTUM ("crime") is the source of Spanish *delito* as well as the English legal expression *in flagrante delicto* ("[caught] while the crime is blazing"). A Spanish "delight" (*deleite*) has nothing to do with a *delito,* coming instead (like the English) from DELECTARE, "to allure".

deleite	*delight,* pleasure
deleitar	(to) *delight,* (to) please
delicioso	delicious, delightful
delicia	delight

---

[16] RAE, *Diccionario panhispánico de dudas,* 9.

ARTÍCULO DOS

Primera Sección

1. Se deposita el poder ejecutivo en un Presidente de los Estados Unidos. *Desempeñará* su encargo durante un término de cuatro años y, juntamente con el *Vicepresidente* designado para el mismo período, será elegido como sigue:

ARTICLE II

Section 1

1. The executive power shall be vested in a President of the United States of America. He shall hold his office during the term of four years, and, together with the Vice President, chosen for the same term, be elected as follows:

a) *desempeñar*   (to) carry out (role, function),
                        (to) redeem or free from debt
    empeñar   (to) pledge, (to) pawn,   [rare *impignorate*]
                        (to) insist (on)
    empeño   pledge, insistence, determination
    —casa de empeño(s) —pawnshop
    empeñado (p.p.)   determined, resolved
    prenda   security, pledge, pawn,   (< PIGNORA)
                        article of clothing

Latin PIGNUS was "a pledge or guarantee", and the associated verb was PIGNORARE. English *pignorate* ("to give or take as a pledge") and *impignorate* ("to pawn") can be found in unabridged dictionaries, but are rarely if ever used in modern times. Spanish *desempeñar* has extended its original meaning of "to acquit oneself of a debt" to that of "discharging a duty". In addition to "pawn or pledge", *empeñar* means "to compel", "to insist"; the noun *empeño* means both "pledge" and "insistence or determination".

> *Se empeñó* en comprar un piso en el centro de Madrid.

> He *insisted* on ("was bent on") buying an apartment in the center of Madrid.

The plural of PIGNUS was PIGNORA, and this evolved (via *péñora*) to *prenda* ("pledge" or "pawn"); the sense of "clothing" presumably developed from expressions similar to English "I'd give (*pledge*) the shirt off my back [for something]".

b) *vicepresidente*   vice president
    viceversa   vice versa

vicisitud	vicissitude	
vicario	*vicar*	[*vicarious*]
virrey, virreina	*viceroy, vicereine*	
vez (pl. veces)	time, turn, occasion	
—a veces	—at times, occasionally	
~ algunas veces		
—dos veces	—twice	
—a la vez	—at the same time, simultaneously	
—cada vez	—each time, every time	
—cada vez más (menos)	—more and more (less and less)	
—de una vez	—in one go, once and for all	
—de vez en cuando	—from time to time	
—en vez de	—instead of	
—otra vez	—again, once more	
—rara vez	—rarely	
—tal vez	—perhaps, maybe	
—una vez más	—once again (~ *de nuevo, otra vez*)	

Latin VICIS was "change", "turn", and this developed into Spanish *vez*. Initially applied to all earthly representatives of God, English *vicar* came to specialize as a name for a person acting as a cleric in place of a parson or rector. These words are to be distinguished from a different type of *vice,* from an altogether different root (VITIUM):

vicio	vice, bad habit
vicioso	vicious, given to vice
viciar	(to) *vitiate,* (to) debase

El *Discurso* de Gettysburg (19 de noviembre de 1863)

Hace 87 años nuestros padres fundaron en este continente una nueva nación, concebida en la libertad y dedicada al *principio* de que todos los hombres son creados iguales.

Ahora nos *hallamos* empeñados en una gran guerra civil, que está poniendo a *prueba* si esta nación, o cualquier nación igualmente concebida y consagrada, puede perdurar. Estamos reunidos en un gran *campo* de batalla de esa guerra. Hemos venido a dedicar parte de ese campo como lugar de eterno *reposo* para aquellos que aquí dieron sus vidas para que esa nación pudiera *vivir.* Es perfectamente justo y apropiado que así lo hagamos.

Pero en un sentido más grande, no podemos dedicar—no podemos consagrar—no podemos santificar—esta tierra. Los valientes que aquí combatieron, los que murieron y los que sobrevivieron, lo han consagrado mucho más allá de la capacidad de nuestras pobres fuerzas para sumar o restar algo a su obra.

El *mundo advertirá* poco y no recordará mucho lo que aquí digamos nosotros, pero nunca podrá olvidar lo que ellos hicieron aquí. A nosotros que aún vivimos nos toca más bien dedicarnos ahora a la obra inacabada que aquellos que lucharon aquí, tan noblemente han *adelantado.*

Nos toca más bien dedicarnos a la gran tarea que nos queda por delante: que, por deber con estos gloriosos muertos, nos consagremos con mayor devoción a la causa por la cual dieron la última prueba de su devoción—que aquí resolvamos que su sacrificio no ha sido en vano—que esta nación, por la gracia de Dios, tendrá un nuevo nacimiento de libertad—y que el gobierno del pueblo, por el pueblo, y para el pueblo no desaparecerá de la faz de la tierra.

The Gettysburg Address (November 19, 1863)

Four score and seven years ago our fathers brought forth on this continent a new nation, conceived in liberty and dedicated to the proposition that all men are created equal.

Now we are engaged in a great civil war, testing whether that nation, or any nation so conceived and so dedicated, can long endure. We are met on a great battlefield of that war. We have come to dedicate a portion of that field as a final resting place for those who here gave their lives that that nation might live. It is altogether fitting and proper that we should do this.

But in a larger sense, we cannot dedicate—we cannot consecrate—we cannot hallow—this ground. The brave men, living and dead, who struggled here have consecrated it far above our poor power to add or detract.

The world will little note nor long remember what we say here, but it can never forget what they did here. It is for us the living rather to be dedicated here to the unfinished work which they who fought here have thus far so nobly advanced.

It is rather for us to be here dedicated to the great task remaining before us—that from these honored dead we take increased devotion to that cause for which they gave the last full measure of devotion—that we here highly resolve that these dead shall not have died in vain—that this nation, under God, shall have a new birth of freedom—and that government of the people, by the people, for the people shall not perish from the earth.

a)   *discurso*   speech, *discourse*, address

b)   *principio*   beginning, origin, *principle*
        principal   principal
        príncipe   prince
        princesa   princess
        principado   principality, princedom
        principiar   (to) begin (~ *empezar, comenzar*)
        principiante   beginner

The principal distinction between English *principle* and *principal* corresponds, at least in principle, to that between Spanish *principio* and *principal,* the roots in each case being Latin PRINCIPIUM and PRINCIPALIS. These in turn came from PRINCEPS (acc. PRINCIPEM), "the one who occupies the first place", i.e, the *prince* or *príncipe*. The associated noun and adjective were respectively PRINCIPIUM—"beginning, origin, foundation"—and PRINCIPALIS—"first, original, chief, *princely*". PRINCIPALIS, and its descendants in Spanish and English, also came to function as a noun, thereby leading to significant overlapping with PRINCIPIUM (and its descendants).

The English use of *principle*[17] to specifically mean "beginning" is now obsolete, but in Spanish *principio,* it remains the principal but not the only meaning. *Al principio* or *a principios de* means "in the beginning (of)"—*al principio del año, a principios de junio*—while *en principio* means "in principle". The verb *principiar* means unambiguously "to start", e.g.,

La Biblia *principia* con las palabras: "En el *principio* creó Dios los cielos y la tierra."

The Bible *begins* with the words: "In the *beginning* God created the heaven and the earth."

c)   *hallar*   (to) find, (to) discover
        hallazgo   discovery, find
        fallar (1)   (to) render judgment,   (to "find" judicially)
                           (to) pass sentence
        fallo (1)   decision, judgment, verdict   (judicial "finding")

---

[17] English *principle* comes from French *principe* (< PRINCIPIUM); when it entered English in the late fourteenth century, the ending was changed to the more familiar English *-le*. At the time, this caused no conflict with *principal* (imported the previous century), as the more "careful" pronunciation in those days distinguished the two words.

fallar (2)	(to) *fail*, (to) be deficient or wanting
falla	defect, flaw, *fault* (in material, geological, etc.)
fallo (2)	mistake, error, *failure* (software, etc.)
falaz	deceptive, *fallacious*
falacia	deception, deceitfulness, *fallacy*
falible	fallible
infalible	infallible
fallecer	(to) die, (to) pass away [*fail*]
desfallecer	(to) weaken, (to) debilitate
fallecimiento	death
fallido	unsuccessful, ineffectual
falta	*fault*, mistake, lack, foul (sports)
faltar	(to) be lacking or wanting, (to) *fail*
—Nos falta tiempo.	—We don't have (the) time.
falso	*false*, counterfeit
falsear	(to) counterfeit, (to) *falsify*, (to) weaken (~ *flaquear*)
falsedad	falseness, *falsity*, falsehood
falsete	falsetto
falsificación	falsification, forgery
falsificar	(to) falsify, (to) counterfeit, (to) forge

Hallar comes from Latin ADFLARE, "to blow or breathe on", literally "to pick up the scent". Applied to the judicial system—in the sense of "finding the facts"—it has produced *fallar,* "to render judgment". By an unfortunate phonetic accident, Latin FALLERE (root of *false* and *fallible*) came to the same result, so that Spanish *fallar* also means "to fail".

d)	probar	(to) *prove*, (to) sample, (to) try, (to) taste [*probe*]
	prueba	*proof,* test, trial, sample, ordeal
	probeta	test tube
	probidad	*probity*
	probación	trial, test (~ *prueba*), probation (within a religious order)
	probador	tester, fitting room
	probable	probable, *provable*
	improbable	improbable, *unprovable*
	aprobar	(to) *approve*, (to) pass (law, exam)
	aprobado (p.p.)	passing (mark)

aprobación	*approval,* approbation
comprobar	(to) verify, (to) check
comprobante	receipt, written proof (of something)
desaprobar	(to) *disapprove*
—desaprobación	—*disapproval*
reprobar	(to) *reprove,* (to) *reprobate* (disapprove of, condemn)
réprobo (adj. & n.)	*reprobate* (morally corrupt; preordained to damnation)

Latin PROBARE was "to test something as to its goodness", literally "to establish its *probity*". It is in this sense of a "trial" that the seemingly anomalous English expression *the exception proves the rule* can be understood, i.e., if a rule is sufficiently strong that it can survive the test of the (occasional) exception, then it isn't such a bad rule after all.

e) *campo*	field, country(side), *camp* (enemy, military, etc.)	
campamento	encampment, camp (~ *camping* < Eng.)	
campesino (adj. & n.)	rural, campesino (farmer, farm worker)	
campestre	*campestral* (relating to fields or open country), rural	
camposanto	cemetery (also *campo santo*)	
campus (< Eng.)	campus (university)	(Lat. CAMPUS)
campeón	*champion*	
campeonato	championship (title; competition)	
campaña	flat countryside, *campaign* (military, political, etc.)	
champán / champaña (m.)	*champagne*	
campana[18]	bell, bell-shaped object	
campanilla	small bell, hand bell, uvula, bellflower (genus *Campanula*)	
campanada	peal or ring (of a bell)	

---

[18] From *Campania,* a region in Italy known for its bronze (originally, *vasa campana,* "bronze vase").

—dar la campanada	—(to) cause a stir or scandal	
campanario	belfry, bell tower, *campanile*	
f) *reposo*	*repose,* rest	
reposar	(to) repose, (to) rest	
posar (1)	(to) *pose* (for camera, painter, etc.)	(< Fr. *poser*)
pose	pose	
postura	posture	
posar (2)	(to) place (hand, etc.), (to) alight (bird, insect)	(Lat. PAUSARE)
posada	inn, lodge	[*posada*]
g) *vivir*	(to) live	
vivido (p.p.)	personally experienced, firsthand	
vívido	*vivid*	
vivo	alive, living, *vivid,* intense	
viviente	living	
vivienda	dwelling, housing	
vivificar	(to) *vivify* (animate, enliven)	
vivaz	*vivacious,* lively, perennial (plant) (~ *perenne*)	
vivacidad	vivacity, vivaciousness	
viveza	liveliness, vivacity	
víveres (pl.)	food, provisions, *victuals* (*vittles*)	
vivero	tree nursery, fish hatchery	[*vivarium*]
convivir	(to) live together	[*convivial*]
convivencia	living together, coexistence	
revivir	(to) *revive* (come back to life), (to) relive (memories, etc.)	
reavivar	(to) *revive* (bring back to life)	
avivar	(to) enliven, (to) intensify	
sobrevivir	(to) *survive,* (to) outlive	(*supervivir* is rare)
sobreviviente	surviving, survivor (m./f.)	(also *superviviente*)
supervivencia	survival	
h) *mundo*	*world*	
—todo el mundo	—everybody	

—Tercer Mundo	—Third World, developing countries	
mundano	*mundane*, worldly	
mundial	world (adj.), worldwide	
mondo	clean, neat, bald	
mondar	(to) clean, (to) peel, (to) pare, (to) prune	
mondadientes	toothpick(s)	
inmundo	filthy, impure	[rare *immund*]
inmundicia	filth, filthiness (incl. moral)	

Latin MUNDUS as an adjective meant "clean" or "elegant". As a noun it had two very different senses: (a) a woman's "toiletries" (including chamber pot) or "finery"; and (b) "world" or "universe". The second definition arose from a conscious imitation of Greek *cosmos,* which itself had the dual meanings of: (a) "adornment", "decoration", or "embellishment" (hence *cosmetics* and *cosmetology*); and (b) "order", "world", or "universe" (*cosmos, cosmology*).

i)	*advertir*	(to) notice, (to) warn	[*advert*]
	inadvertido	unnoticed, unseen	[*inadvertent*]
	inadvertidamente	inadvertently	
	advertencia	admonition, warning, advice	

j)	adelante	ahead, forward	(a + delante)
	adelantar	(to) advance, (to) move forward, (to) overtake	
	adelantado (p.p.)	advanced, precocious, fast (clock)	
	—por adelantado	—in advance (payment)	
	adelanto	advance, progress	
	ante (prep.)	before, in the presence of	
	antes (adv.)	before, in the past	
	delante (de)	in front (of), ahead (of), in the presence (of)	(OldSp. *denante*[19])
	delantero (adj. & n.)	front, forward (basketball, soccer, hockey)	
	delantal	apron	

---

[19] Ultimately from Latin DE + IN + ANTE.

La Constitución Española de 1978 [20]

ARTÍCULO 3

1. *El castellano es la lengua española oficial del Estado.* Todos los españoles tienen el deber de conocerla y el derecho a usarla.

2. Las demás lenguas españolas serán también oficiales en las respectivas Comunidades Autónomas de acuerdo con sus Estatutos.

3. La riqueza de las distintas modalidades lingüísticas de España es un patrimonio cultural que será objeto de especial respeto y protección.

ARTÍCULO 4

1. La bandera de España está formada por tres *franjas* horizontales, roja, *amarilla* y roja, siendo la amarilla de doble anchura que cada una de las rojas.

2. Los estatutos podrán reconocer banderas y enseñas propias de las Comunidades Autónomas. Estas se utilizarán junto a la bandera de España en sus edificios públicos y en sus actos oficiales.

ARTÍCULO 5

La capital del Estado es la villa de Madrid.

The Spanish Constitution of 1978

ARTICLE 3

1. *Castilian is the official Spanish language of the State.* All Spaniards have the duty to know it and the right to use it.

2. The other Spanish languages shall also be official in the respective Self-governing Communities in accordance with their Statutes.

3. The richness of the different linguistic modalities of Spain is a cultural heritage that shall be specially respected and protected.

---

[20] From the Spanish Constitution's "official" website: www.constitucion.es; italics added.

ARTICLE 4

1. The flag of Spain consists of three horizontal stripes: red, yellow, and red, the yellow stripe being twice as wide as each red stripe.

2. The Statutes may recognize flags and ensigns of the Self-governing Communities. These shall be used together with the flag of Spain on their public buildings and in their official ceremonies.

ARTICLE 5

The capital of the State is the city of Madrid.

a)	*franja*	stripe, strip (of land), *fringe*
b)	*amarillo*	yellow
	amarillento	yellowish
	amargo	bitter
	amargar	(to) taste bitter, (to) embitter (flavor or feelings)
	amargura	bitterness, sorrow

The color *yellow* is "naturally" associated with *bitterness:* it is the color of both *bile*—one of the four "humors" traditionally thought to determine an individual's temperament—and *jaundice,* a disease essentially caused by an excess of bile. The English colors *yellow* (Old English *geolu*) and *gold* come from the same Indo-European root (meaning "to shine") found in *gall* (another name for "bile"); *jaundice* comes from French *jaune* ("yellow"). Spanish *amarillo* likewise arose from an association with "bitterness", most likely as a descriptive term for those suffering from jaundice.

The issue of whether the national language of Spain is *español* or *castellano* has historically been controversial, though more so in Spain than in Spanish- (or Castilian-) speaking America. If *Spanish* is the national language of Spain, then that might be interpreted to mean that the regional languages (principally Basque and Catalan) are secondary in nature, whereas calling it *castellano* puts them on a more equal footing. In the Americas, after independence many countries chose to call their language *castellano* to emphasize their break with Spain, but over time *español* has become increasingly common, and those who continue to refer to *castellano* seem to do so more from habit than due to any political sensibilities.[21]

---

[21] Beginning with the fifteenth edition (1925), the title of the RAE's dictionary changed from *Diccionario de la lengua castellana* to *Diccionario de la lengua española.*

ADDITIONAL WORDS

In the annexes that follow, some words presented earlier in the text are repeated, but generally only to the extent that these are elements of larger groups, whose other members are "new".

For convenience, the basic rule governing the explict marking of noun gender (masculine/feminine) is repeated below:

Simplified Gender Rule

1. **Nouns having one of the following endings are assumed to be feminine:**

   a) *-a*
   b) *-ión*
   c) *-d*
   d) *-umbre*
   e) *-ie*
   f) *-ez*
   g) *-triz*
   h) *-sis / -tis* (Greek words)

2. **Nouns ending in *-ista* are assumed to be *both* masculine and feminine.**

3. **All other nouns are assumed to be masculine.**

ONLY NOUNS WHOSE GENDER IS "UNPREDICTABLE" WILL BE EXPLICITLY MARKED.

Principal Exceptions to the "Simplified Gender Rule"

Spanish nouns essentially fall into three groups of almost equal size, according to whether they end in: *-a, -o,* or "something else". Dividing this last group into (1) those with one of the seven "feminine" endings other than *-a* in the "Simplified General Rule", and (2) *all others,* the gender structure of Spanish nouns can be summarized as follows:[1]

	Masculine (%)	Feminine (%)
-a	1–4	96–99
-o	99.8	0.2
"Something Else"		
(1) *-ión, -d, -umbre, -ie, -ez, -triz, -sis / -tis*	6	94
(2) *All Others*	94	6

The lower limit for nouns ending in *-a* (96%) is the overall "gross" figure. However, if one excludes nouns of Greek origin (see Section 2.2) and those found essentially only in dictionaries, the "true" percentage of feminines with this ending is at least 99 percent.

I. Nouns That "Should Be" FEMININE but Are Actually MASCULINE

a. *-a*

The principal exceptions are *el día* and *most* "Greek" nouns ending in *-a.*

el día	day
—el mediodía	—noon, south

"Greek" nouns ending in *-a:*
1. -ema or -oma (see Section 2.2, no. 4)
2. *-eta*

el cometa	*comet*
—**la** cometa	—kite
el delta	*delta* (river)
—**la** delta	—*delta* (Greek letter)

---

[1] Excluding "bisexual" *-ista* nouns.

el planeta	*planet*
el poeta / *la* poeta	*poet*
el atleta / *la* atleta	*athlete*

3. *ama*

el drama	*drama*
el panorama	*panorama*

-grama

el diagrama	*diagram*
el programa	*program*

4. Other

el clima	*climate, clime*
el cólera	*cholera* (disease)
—**la** cólera	—anger, rage, *choler*
el enigma	*enigma*
el mapa	*map*
el margarita	*margarita* (cocktail)
—**la** margarita	—daisy, *marguerite*
el papa	*Pope*
el pap**á**	*papa, poppa,* dad
el policía	*police*man
—**la** policía	—*police* (force), *police*woman
el trauma	*trauma*

Latin MAPPA ("tablecloth", origin of English *napkin* and *apron*) was *not* a Greek word but was perhaps mistaken for one in the combination MAPPA MUNDI ("tablecloth of the world"), hence *el mapa* ("map"). *El papa* ("pope") and *el papá* come from Greek (*pappas*, "father", shortened in Church Latin to PAPA) and French, respectively. *El sofá* and *el Canadá* are also exceptions, the stressed final *-a* betraying their non-Latin origin.

b. *-ión*

The most common exceptions are probably:

el anfitrión	host	(< Gk.)
—la anfitriona	—hostess	
el avión	airplane	(< Fr.)
—el hidroavión	—seaplane, hydroplane	
el camión	truck, *camion*	(< Fr.)

el embrión	*embryo*	(< Gk.)
el escorpión	*scorpion*	(< Gk.)
el guion, el guión	notes (for speech), script, hyphen	[*guide*]

Other exceptions include:

el aluvión	*alluvium* (sediment), *alluvion* (flood)	
el bastión	*bastion*	(< Germ.)
el centurión	*centurion*	
el colodión	*collodion*	(< Gk.)
el envión	push, shove	(< *enviar*, "to send")
el esturión	*sturgeon*	(< Germ.)
el gorrión	sparrow	
el histrión	theatrical actor	[*histrionics*]
el ion, el ión	*ion*	(< Gk.)
—el anión	—*anion* (negative)	
—el catión	—*cation* (positive)	
el limpión	light cleaning	[*limpid*]
el notición	sensational news	[*notice*]
el prion, el prión	*prion*	
el sarampión	measles	
el talión	*talion, retaliation*	
el turbión	squall, heavy shower	[*turbulent*]

c. -*d*

Principal exceptions are:

el abad	*abbot*	(< Gk.)
el alud	avalanche	(pre-Roman)
el ardid	stratagem, trick	(< Germ., related to *hardy*)
el áspid	*asp*	(< Gk.)
el ataúd	coffin	(< Arabic)
el césped	lawn, grass	[*cespitose*]
el huésped	guest	[*host*]
el laúd	*lute*	(< Arabic)
el quid	gist, crux	[*quid pro quo*]
el talud	slope	[*talus*]

In addition, a number of *English* words ending in -*d* have become Spanish masculine nouns, including:

el apartheid	*apartheid*	(< Afrikaans)
el lord	*lord* (used with respect to English lords only)	
el raid	*raid*	

el récord	*record* (athletic)	
el round	*round* (sports competition)	
el stand	*stand* (for sale or exhibition of products)	
el weekend	*weekend*	(not in *DRAE*)

d. *-umbre*

The only exception of any practical importance is

| el alumbre | *alum* |

e. *-ie*

The only (real) exception is

| el pie | foot |

Also (foreign imports):

| el walkie-talkie | walkie-talkie |
| el curie | curie (unit of radiation) |

f. *-ez* [2]

The principal exceptions are:

el ajedrez	chess	
el diez	ten (number)	
el doblez	fold, crease	[*double*]
el jerez	*sherry*	
el juez	*judge*	
el pez	fish	[*Pisces*]

g. *-triz*

No exceptions!

h. *-sis / -tis* (Greek words)

There are seven common exceptions from Greek *-sis* words—see Section 2.2, no. 3—plus the non-Greek *-sis / -tis* words listed below:

---

[2] The large majority of *-ez* nouns are feminine "abstracts" with the sense of "-ness" that have been formed from adjectives: *estúpido—estupidez* ("stupidity"), *líquido—liquidez* ("liquidity"), etc.

el chasis	*chassis*	
el cutis	skin	[*cuticle*]
el frontis	*frontispiece* (arch. only), facade	
el frotis	smear (medical)	(vb. *frotar*)
el mutis	(theatrical) exit (of an actor)	[*mutate*]

as well as the differently stressed

el mentís	flat denial	(vb. *mentir*)

II. Nouns That "Should Be" MASCULINE but Are Actually FEMININE

1. *-o*

la mano	hand	[*manual*]
la libido	*libido*	
la foto	*photo*	
la loto[3]	*lottery*	
la moto	*motorcycle*	
la polio	*polio*	
la radio[4]	*radio*	

Apart from *mano* and *libido*—which were feminine in Latin—the other principal exceptions are shortened forms of longer feminine nouns: *fotografía, lotería, motocicleta, poliomielitis, radiodifusión*.

2. *"All Other" Endings*

While "all other" endings are overwhelmingly masculine, there are nonetheless a significant number of common feminines with no easy rule (or "trick") for distinguishing these from the masculines. This is particularly the case for nouns ending in -*e*:

el aire	vs.	**la** torre	*air*	*tower*
el vinagre	vs.	**la** sangre	*vinegar*	*blood*
el monte	vs.	**la** fuente	*mountain*	*fountain*
el porte	vs.	**la** parte	de*port*ment	*part*
el frente	vs.	**la** frente	*front*, battle*front*	*forehead*
el hospital	vs.	**la** diagonal	*hospital*	*diagonal*
el corazón	vs.	**la** razón	heart	*reason*
el barniz	vs.	**la** raíz	*varnish*	root

---

[3] *El loto* is the *lotus* plant.
[4] *El radio* is "radium" and "radius".

Three endings are almost exclusively masculine:

(a) *-aje*

These correspond to English *-age* nouns (see Section 3.5, no. 14). There is only one exception, reflecting a different (Greek) origin:

la paralaje   *parallax*

(b) *-ón* ("bare")

That is, *-ón* words not ending in *-ión* (feminine) or *-zón* (60% masculine). **There are no exceptions.**[5]

(c) *-r*

Among the relatively few exceptions are:

la coliflor	*cauliflower*	
la flor	*flower*	
la labor	*labor*	
la mujer	woman, wife	
la sor	sister (religious: *Sor* María)	[*sorority*]
la bajamar	low tide	
la pleamar / la plenamar	high tide	

Appendix
Gender and Size

For a number of objects, Spanish has developed a distinction based on gender where the feminine noun is either larger than the masculine one and/or represents a "collection" of objects. Common examples include:

Masculine	Feminine	Masculine	Feminine
banco	banca	bank	banking system
batidor	batidora	whisk	electric mixer
bolso	bolsa	purse	stock exchange
brazo	braza	arm	fathom (~ 6 feet)
caldero	caldera	kettle	cauldron, boiler
canasto	canasta	basket	large round basket
charco	charca	puddle	pond
cubo	cuba	bucket	cask, barrel
cuenco	cuenca	earthen bowl	river basin

---

[5] *Maratón* ("marathon") can be either masculine or feminine, although in a number of dictionaries it is shown as masculine (only).

farol	farola	lantern, streetlamp	large streetlamp
hoyo	hoya	hole, pit	pit, valley
huerto	huerta	orchard, vegetable garden	large vegetable garden, irrigated region
huevo	hueva	egg	roe (fish eggs)
jarro	jarra	jar	jar, jug
leño	leña	log	firewood
mazo	maza	mallet	hammer of pile driver
río	ría	river	estuary, firth
secador	secadora	dryer	(larger) dryer
velo	vela	veil	sail

This distinction initially arose due to a peculiarity in Latin: neuter nouns that ended in -*um* had plurals ending in -*a* (e.g., DATUM → DATA), which happened also to be the most common ending of *feminine singular* nouns (e.g., ROSA). When the neuter was subsequently eliminated, the singular forms ending in -*um* became *masculine* Spanish nouns ending in -*o,* while the corresponding neuter *plurals* frequently became *feminine singular* nouns ending in -*a* (often with a collective sense). This *o/a* distinction was subsequently extended to various other nouns that were not "old" Latin neuters—e.g., the "naturally" feminine *cuba* was given a "little brother" *cubo.*

Among the exceptions to the "rule" are:

Masculine	Feminine	Masculine	Feminine
barco	barca	ship, boat	boat, small boat
cesto	cesta	hamper	basket
escuadrón	escuadra	squadron	squad, squadron (see Section 3.1)

ANNEX B
700 Not-So-Easy Words

There is nothing inherently difficult about the words presented in this section. However, in contrast to the large majority of other words presented in the text (and in Annexes C and D), they are not easily associated with English words having similar, or at least related, meanings.

The words generally fall into one of the following categories:
(a) Words of pre-Latin origin—Iberian, Celtic, or Basque, e.g., *izquierda*
(b) Words of Latin origin that
   (1) did not make it to English, e.g., *calle* (Latin CALLIS);
   (2) made it to English, but have since died out or are only very rarely used, e.g., *dirempt, indagate, propine* (Spanish *dirimir, indagar, propina*);
   (3) made it to English and are still in common use, but whose form and/or meaning (in English and/or Spanish) has been transformed in such a way that the relationship is no longer obvious, e.g., *acera—facade, arrojar—roll, pozo—pit, andar—amble*.

abanico	*fan*, range (of possibilities—i.e., "fan" of choices)	
—abanicar	—(to) *fan*	
abrigo	overcoat, shelter, protection	(Fr. *abri*)
—abrigar	—(to) shelter or protect, (to) harbor (idea, fear)	[† *apricate*]
acaparar	(to) hoard, (to) monopolize	
acera	sidewalk, side of a street	[*facade* (F → h → ø)]
acero	steel	(Fr. *acier*)
—acero inoxidable	—stainless steel	
acosar	(to) harass	[*coarse*]
—acoso	—harassment	
acudir	(to) go or come to, (to) go to the aid of	[*rescue*]
afán	zeal, eagerness, effort	[*fanatic* ?]
—afanar	—(to) strive, (to) toil	
agachar	(to) lower, (to) bend down	[*cache* ?]
alabar	(to) praise	
—alabanza	—praise	
alambre	wire	[*aeneus*]
—alambrada	—(barbed) wire fence	
—inalámbrico	—wireless (phone, etc.)	
alboroto	disturbance, uproar	
—alborotar	—(to) arouse, (to) agitate	

alcance	reach, scope, importance	
—de largo (corto) alcance	—long-range (short-range)	
—alcanzar	—(to) reach, (to) catch up to, (to) attain	[*caulk, calque*]
aliento	breath, encouragement	(† *anhelation*)
—alentar	—(to) encourage	("to blow on")
—alentador	—encouraging	
—desalentar	—(to) discourage, (to) dishearten	
—desaliento	—discouragement	
—anhelar[1]	—(to) long or yearn (for)	("pant for")
alrededor (adv.)	around, about (on all sides)	(< al derredor)
—alrededores (pl.)	—surrounding area, environs, outskirts	
—derredor	—circle (area around something)	[DE-RETRO, *derrière*]
amparar	(to) protect	[pre*pare*]
—amparo	—protection, shelter	
—desamparo	—abandonment, lack of protection	
—desamparar	—(to) abandon, (to) leave helpless or unprotected	
andar	(to) walk, (to) move, (to) work (machine)	[*amble*]
—andamio	—scaffold	
—andamiaje	—scaffolding	
—andante	—andante (music: moderately slow tempo)	
—andanza	—adventure, esp. during voyage (gen. pl. *andanzas*)	
—desandar	—(to) retrace (one's steps)	
andén	station platform (railway, metro)	
anuencia	consent, approbation	[*nutation*]
—anuente	—consenting	[ANNUIT COEPTIS[2]]
—renuente	—reluctant, unwilling	[*innuendo*]
—renuencia	—reluctance, unwillingness	
anzuelo	fishhook, trap (fig.)	[*hamulus*]
añorar	(to) pine for (absent person or thing)	[*ignore*: without news]
—añoranza	—pining, nostalgia	[*ignorance*]
apodo	nickname	[*putative*]
—apodar	—(to) nickname	[im*pute*]
apoyo	support, backing	[*podium, pew*]
—apoyar	—(to) support, (to) lean (something on), (to) back	

---

[1] *Anhelar* comes directly from Latin ANHELARE ("to exhale", "to pant"). In the "popular" language, the *n* and *l* were reversed, giving rise to *alentar* and related forms.

[2] The Latin expression on the back of the U.S. one-dollar bill, above the eye that forms the upper part of the pyramid. The literal meaning is "He nods (or has nodded) assent to things just started"; presumably, "God has favored our undertakings".

arrancar	(to) uproot, (to) pull out (an object; "to start moving" [e.g., bus])	
—arranque	—start, outburst, starter (motor)	
arrojar	(to) throw, (to) fling	[*roll*]
—arrojo	—daring, courage	
arrullo	coo, cooing, lullaby	
—arrullar	—(to) coo, (to) lull or sing to sleep	
asar	(to) roast	[† *assation*]
—asado (p.p.)	—roast	[*ardent*]
asco	repugnance, disgust	
—asqueroso	—filthy, revolting, disgusting	[*scar*]
aseo	restroom, cleanliness	[*assiduous*]
—asear	—(to) clean, (to) tidy up	[*assess*]
asequible	accessible, attainable, affordable	[*ensue*]
asestar	(to) deal (a blow to)	[*assess, siege*]
asomo	sign, inkling	[*sum, summit*]
—ni por asomo	—by no means, not by a long shot	
—asomar	—(to) [begin to] appear, (to) show [oneself]	
astilla	splinter, chip (of wood)	
—"de tal palo,	—from such a stick, such a chip	
—tal astilla"	—("chip off the old block")	
—astillar	—(to) splinter, (to) chip	
—astillero	—shipyard, dockyard	[*atelier*]
—**est**allar	—(to) explode, (to) burst (out)	(< **ast**ellar)
—estallido	—explosion, report (firearm), outbreak	
atar	(to) tie, (to) fasten, (to) bind	[*apt*]
—atadura	—tying, rope, bond or knot (often restrictive)	
—desatar	—(to) untie, (to) unleash	
—reata	—rope to tie animals, *riata* (or *reata*), *lariat* (< la reata)	
atasco	traffic jam, obstruction, blockage	
—atascar	—(to) clog, (to) obstruct	
—tasca	—tavern, bar-restaurant	
atisbar	(to) observe, (to) distinguish or make out (image, solution)	
—atisbo	—sign (e.g., of improvement), inkling	
atizar	(to) stoke or stir up (fire, passions)	[*entice*]
—tizón	—partially burned piece of wood	
—tizne (m./f.)	—soot	
—tiznar	—(to) blacken (with soot), (to) tarnish (a reputation)	
atracar	(to) hold up (rob), (to) moor	

—atraco	—holdup, robbery	
atrever(se)	(to) dare, (to) venture	[*attribute*]
—atrevido (p.p.)	—daring (adj.), bold, risqué	
—atrevimiento	—daring (n.), audacity, impudence	
aturdir	(to) stun, (to) bewilder	[*sturdy*³]
—aturdimiento	—bewilderment, giddiness	
aula	classroom, lecture hall	(AULA, "courtyard")
aval	guarantee (commercial), endorsement	[rare *aval*]
—avalar	—(to) guarantee (a transaction), (to) endorse	(a + valer ?)
baraja	pack or deck of cards	(see Appendix A)
—barajar	—(to) shuffle (cards)	
barato	inexpensive, cheap	[*barratry*]
—abaratar	—(to) reduce the price of (~ *rebajar*)	[*barter*]
—desbaratar	—(to) ruin, (to) wreck	
barro	mud, clay (pottery)	
basura	rubbish, trash, garbage	
—basurero	—garbage collector, garbage dump	
—barrer	—(to) sweep	
baúl	trunk	
beca	grant, scholarship	
—becar	—(to) award a grant or scholarship	
—becario	—grant or scholarship holder	
beso	kiss	(Fr. *baise*)
—besar	—(to) kiss	
bisagra	hinge	
bostezo	yawn	[**b**oca + *oscillate*]
—bostezar	—(to) yawn	
bóveda	*vault* (arched roof)	
—bóveda celeste	—vault of heaven, firmament	
brujo	sorcerer, wizard	
—bruja	—witch, sorceress	
—brujería	—witchcraft, sorcery	
—embrujar	—(to) bewitch	
—embrujo	—spell, charm	
brújula⁴	compass	[*box*]
bufanda	scarf, muffler	[*bouffant, buffoon*⁵]
bulto	bulk, lump, package, shadowy object	

---

³ *Sturdy* comes from the French verb *étourdir* ("to stun", "to daze") and can still be used as a synonym for *gid*: "A disease of herbivores, especially sheep . . . resulting in a staggering gait."

⁴ From Italian *bussola,* literally meaning "little *box*". It is possible that the *-r* in the Spanish word is due to the influence of *bruja* (a compass being a sort of "magic" box).

⁵ All these words originate from the idea of "swelling" or "puffing up".

—abultar	—(to) enlarge, (to) be bulky, (to) exaggerate	
buscar	(to) search for, (to) seek	[*busk*]
—busca	—search	
—buscador	—(gold) prospector, Internet search engine	
—búsqueda	—search (gen. more specific than *busca*)	
—rebuscar	—(to) search thoroughly, (to) glean (the fields)	
—rebuscado (p.p.)	—stilted, recherché (manner of speaking, etc.)	
butaca	armchair, orchestra seat (theater)	(< Amer.)
buzo	diver, overalls (regionally: jersey)	
—bucear	—(to) dive, (to) swim underwater	
—buceador	—diver (~ *buzo*)	
—buceo	—diving, dive	
—bocina	—horn, megaphone	[*bugle*]
buzón	letterbox, mailbox	
callar	(to) be silent, (to) become silent	[*calando*]
—callado (p.p.)	—quiet, silent	
—acallar	—(to) silence	
—calar	—(to) soak, (to) penetrate, (to) size up	
calle (f.)	street, road	
—callejero	—street (adj.), street directory or plan	
—callejón	—lane, alley	
—callejón sin salida	—blind alley, cul-de-sac, dead end	
—pasacalle	—lively march (music), *passacaglia*	(pasar + calle)
cama	bed	
cambiar	(to) *change,* (to) exchange	[*cambium*]
—cambio	—change (alteration; money), exchange	
—caja de cambios	—transmission (auto)	
—intercambiar	—(to) exchange, (to) swap, (to) *interchange*	
—intercambio	—exchange, interchange	
—recambio	—spare part, replacement (part)	
—canjear (< It.)	—(to) exchange (prisoners, diplomatic notes)	
—canje	—exchange	
caminar	(to) walk, (to) travel	
—camino	—path, way, course, journey	(Fr. *chemin*)
—caminata	—hike, long walk	
—caminante (m./f.)	—walker	
—encaminar	—(to) guide, (to) show the way, (to) direct	
cansar	(to) tire, (to) fatigue, (to) weary	
—cansado (p.p.)	—tired, tiring or tiresome	

—cansancio	—tiredness, weariness, fatigue	
—descansar	—(to) rest	
—Descanse en paz.	—Rest in peace.	
—descanso	—rest, break	
—incansable	—tireless, indefatigable	
cántaro	pitcher, jug	[*chanterelle*]
—llover a cántaros	—(to) rain cats and dogs	
caucho	rubber, *caoutchouc*	
cazar	(to) hunt	[*chase, catch*]
—caza	—hunting, hunt, game (animals), fighter plane	
—caza de brujas	—witch hunt	
—cacería	—hunt, animals killed in a hunt	
—cazador	—hunter, *chasseur* (hunter, light cavalry)	
—rechazar (< Fr.)	—(to) reject, (to) repulse (drive back)	[† *rechase*]
—rechazo	—rejection, rebuff	
cencerro	cowbell	
cepo	trap, pillory, stocks, (wheel) clamp	[rare *cippus*]
—cepa	—stump (underground), vine, stock (lineage)	[*cèpe*]
—de pura cepa	—of pure stock (genuine, authentic)	
—cepillo	—brush, carpenter's plane	
—cepillo de dientes	—toothbrush	
—cepillar	—(to) brush, (to) plane (make smooth or level)	
chabola	shack, shanty	[*cage, jail*]
chaleco	vest	(Fr. *gilet*)
—chaleco antibalas	—bulletproof vest	
—chaleco salvavidas	—life jacket	
charco	puddle	
—charca	—pond	
chico	boy, lad, kid (also as adjective: small)	
—chica	—girl	
—chiquito	—very small, tiny	[*Chiquita*®]
—chiquillo	—youngster, kid	
chillar	(to) shout, (to) scream, (to) shriek	[*fester, fistula*]
—chillido	—scream, shriek, squeal	
—chillón (-ona)	—loud, shrill, garish or gaudy (color)	
chirriar	(to) squeak, (to) creak, (to) screech	
—chirrido	—shrill sound	
chisme[6]	gossip (rumor), knickknack, "thing"	
—chinche (f.)	—bedbug, nuisance or pest (person)	[genus *Cimex*]

---

[6] There are two competing theories concerning the origin of *chisme*: (a) from SCHISMA (Spanish *cisma*), since gossip tends to cause friction and division; and (b) from CIMEX, "bedbug" or "stinkbug" (Spanish *chinche*), perhaps from the disagreeable odor it makes when crushed.

—chincheta	—thumbtack	
chispa	spark, small particle or amount, wit	
—chispeante	—sparkling, witty	
chiste	joke	
—chiste verde	—dirty joke	
—chistoso	—funny, humorous	
—chistar ~ rechistar	—(to) speak up, (to) start to say something	
—sin chistar ~sin rechistar	—without protest(ing)	
choza	hut, shack	
chupar	(to) suck, (to) soak up	(onom.)
—chupete	—pacifier (for babies)	
cieno	mud, silt	
—ciénaga	—muddy place, marsh	
cima	peak or summit, *cyme* (bot.)	[*cyma*—arch.]
—encima	—over, above	
coartada	alibi	
—coartar	—(to) restrict, (to) limit	[*coarctate*]
codicia	*cupidity,* greed	
—codiciar	—(to) *covet*	
—codicioso	—*covetous,* greedy	
coger[7]	(to) take, (to) seize, (to) catch	[*cull, coil, collect*]
—cogida	—goring (by a bull)	
—acoger	—(to) receive, (to) take in, (to) shelter	
—acogedor	—welcoming, hospitable, cozy	
—acogida	—reception, welcome	
—encoger	—(to) shrink, (to) contract, (to) draw in (e.g., legs)	
—escoger	—(to) choose, (to) *select*	
—recoger	—(to) pick up, (to) gather, (to) harvest	[*recollect*]
—recogida	—collection or pickup (garbage, mail, etc.)	
—cosecha[8]	—harvest, crop	[*collect*]

Caution When Using *Coger!*

Coger is an absolutely normal and very common word in the majority of Spanish-speaking countries for such mundane expressions as "to catch the bus" (*coger el auto-*

---

[7] *Coger* comes from Latin COLLIGERE ("to gather together"), whose past tense COLLECTUS gave rise to English *collect.*

[8] Formerly *cogecha* (a form, along with *collecha,* still found in some areas of Spain).

bús). In some countries, however, it is extremely vulgar, essentially being the equivalent of the English *f*-word. The overall situation can be summarized as follows:

En el sentido sexual *coger* es ya antiguo y fué (*sic*) corriente aun en España . . . ; pero en América, donde esta acepción se ha afirmado más, ello ha sido causa, por razones de pudor, de la decadencia de *coger* en las demás acepciones, hasta el extremo de que en el Río de la Plata (también en otras zonas, como en Méjico, pero menos intensamente . . .) se evita el uso de *coger* de manera sistemática, reemplazándolo por *agarrar* o *tomar*, y ocasionalmente *levantar, alzar* y *atrapar*; esta decadencia o desaparición total afecta asimismo a los derivados *acoger, recoger, escoger, encoger*, y aun al adjectivo independiente *cojo*.[9]

The use of *coger* in a sexual sense is very old and was (previously) common even in Spain . . . However in the Americas, where this meaning has become more pronounced, it has been the cause, for reasons of decency, of the decadence of the other meanings of *coger*, to such an extent that in the Río de la Plata region [Argentina and Uruguay] (and to a lesser extent in other areas, notably Mexico . . .) the use of *coger* is systematically avoided, being replaced by *agarrar* or *tomar*, and occasionally *levantar, alzar*, and *atrapar*; this decadence or total disappearance affects in an equal manner the derived verbs *acoger, recoger, escoger, encoger*, and even the unrelated adjective *cojo* ["lame"].

cojo (1)	lame, wobbly (e.g., table), lame person (m./f.)	
—cojear	—(to) limp, (to) hobble, (to) wobble	
—cojo (2)	—1st person singular present of verb *coger*	
colmo	topping, height (esp. epitome), limit	[*cumulus: m ↔ l*]
—colmar	—(to) fill to overflowing, (to) fulfill	[*cumulate*]
comprar	(to) buy, (to) purchase	
—compra	—purchase, shopping (goods purchased)	
—comprador	—buyer, purchaser	[*comprador*]
cosquillas (pl.)	tickling, ticklishness	
—cosquilleo	—tickling sensation	
cremallera	zipper	[*cremaster* muscle]
crujir	(to) creak, (to) crackle, (to) gnash (teeth)	[*crush*]
—crujido (p.p.)	—creak, crackle, gnashing	
cuna	cradle, crib	
—acunar	—(to) rock, (to) cradle	
—incunable	—*incunable*—book printed before 1501	
curtir	(to) tan (leather), (to) suntan, (to) inure	
delatar	(to) denounce, (to) inform against	[rare *delate*]
—delator	—denouncer, informer	[rare *delator*]
derretir	(to) melt, (to) squander (fortune)	

---

[9] Corominas and Pascual, 2:120–121.

deslizar	(to) slide, (to) skid, (to) slip in (or away)	
—desliz	—slip (mistake, indiscretion), false step	
—deslizamiento	—sliding, skidding	
despejar	(to) clear, (to) clear up	[*dispatch*]
—despejado (p.p.)	—clear, cloudless, bright (clever)	
despertar	(to) wake (up), (to) rouse	[† *expergefaction*]
—desp**ie**rto	—awake, alert	(old p.p.)
—despertador	—alarm clock	
dibujo	drawing, pattern	[*de-* + *bush*]
—dibujos animados	—cartoons (animated)	
—dibujar	—(to) draw, (to) sketch, (to) depict	
—dibujante (m./f.)	—drawer, draftsman/woman	
dirimir	(to) dissolve (relationship), (to) settle (dispute)	[† *dirempt*]
disfraz	disguise, costume	
—disfrazar	—(to) disguise	
dote (f.)	*dowry,* talent or gift (gen. pl.)	
—dotar	—(to) provide with, (to) *endow*	
—dotación	—resources, *endowment,* personnel (ship, military unit)	
embudo	funnel	[*imbue*]
embuste	lie, falsehood	
—embustero	—liar, deceiver	[*impostor* ?]
enagua	petticoat (gen. pl.)	(< Amer.)
enano (adj. & n.)	dwarf(ish), midget	[*nano*second]
enchufe	electric plug, socket, connection (personal)	
—enchufar	—(to) plug in, (to) connect	
engañar	(to) deceive, (to) mislead, (to) cheat	(It. *ingannare*)
—engaño	—deception, fraud, mistake	
—desengaño	—disappointment, disillusion(ment)	
—regañar	—(to) scold, (to) tell off, (to) quarrel	
—regaño	—scolding, rebuke	
—a regañadientes	—reluctantly, grudgingly	(regaña + dientes)
engranaje	gear (machine), gearing	[*ingrain, engrain*]
engreído	conceited	(en + creído)
esbozo	sketch, outline, rough draft	
—esbozar	—(to) sketch, (to) outline	[*emboss*]
—boceto	—sketch (painting), rough model (sculpture)	[*boss* "knob"]
escaño	seat (parliamentary or legislative)	[*shambles*]

From *Bench* to *General Disorder*

The pair *escaño—shambles* provides a good example of how words having a common origin can wind up with meanings that seem totally unrelated. *Escaño* comes directly from Latin SCAMNUM ("stool", "bench"), and its evolution to "parliamentary seat" is easily understandable. The diminutive of SCAMNUM was SCAMELLUM ("little bench"), and this was taken directly from Latin to become *Old* English *scamol*, which was used to refer both to (a) a footstool and (b) a bench or table on which merchandise was displayed or money counted. The subsequent sense development of the word can be traced as follows (with the date of first recorded use in parentheses):

1. a table on which *meat* was displayed (1305)
2. used in the plural, a *place* where meat was sold (1410)—by this point, the [sc] sound of Old English (*scamol*) had become [sh] (cf. *scip* → *sh*ip, *fisc* → *fish*)
3. a *slaughterhouse* (1548)—by this point, the *b* had been added, yielding the modern form *shambles*
4. a place of carnage or wholesale slaughter (1593)
5. a scene or condition of complete disorder or ruin; a total mess (1926)

escombros (pl.)	rubble, debris	[*encumbrance*]
—escombrera	—dump	
escueto	plain, unadorned, concise	[*Scots ?*]
esmero	(great) care	
—esmerar	—(to) polish, (to) take (great) care	
—mero (1) [10]	—pure, *mere* (of little importance)	
—mero (2)	—grouper (fish), jewfish	(unrelated)
esparadrapo	adhesive tape or bandage	[*drape*, † *sparadrap*]
estafa	swindle, fraud	[*staff, step*]
—estafar	—(to) swindle, (to) defraud	
—estafador	—swindler, con man/woman	
estrenar	(to) premiere, (to) use for the first time	
—estreno	—premiere, first use	
estrépito	din, racket	
—estrepitoso	—noisy, deafening, spectacular (failure)	[*obstreperous*]
estribo	stirrup, step or running board (vehicle), buttress (arch.)	
—estribar	—(to) be based on, (to) rest on, (to) lie in	
—estribillo	—refrain, chorus (the refrain serves as a "base")	
estribor [11]	*starboard*	

---

[10] Latin MERUS meant "undiluted" or "pure", particularly with respect to wine. At one stage, English *mere* was used similarly (e.g., "Our wine is here mingled with water and with myrrhe, there it is *mere* and unmixt"), but this sense is now obsolete.

[11] *Starboard* and its cognate *estribor* have nothing to do with the stars. Rather, they both ultimately come from *steer-board* (Old English *steorbord*): early Germanic boats were *steered* by a rudder or steering paddle on the *right* side of the ship. The left side of the ship—to which the helmsman had his *back*—was known as the *back-board*, hence Old English *bæcbord* (replaced by *larboard*, then by *port*) and Spanish *babor*.

—babor	—port (left side), larboard	[*backboard*]
estropear	(to) damage, (to) ruin	
estuche	case (glasses, pencils), *étui*	[*tweezers*]
etapa	stage, phase, field ration (mil.)	[*staple*]
fracaso	failure	[*fracas*]
—fracasar	—(to) fail, (to) come to nought	
frotar	(to) rub	[*frottage*]
gancho	hook, hanger or hairpin (Amer.)	
—enganchar	—(to) hook	
gemir	(to) moan, (to) groan	
—gemido (p.p.)	—moan, groan	
gordo	fat, thick, fatso (affectionate)	
—gordura	—fatness	
—engordar	—(to) put on weight, (to) get fat, (to) fatten	
gorro ~ gorra	cap, (baby) bonnet	
gremio	guild, profession (members collectively)	[*gregarious*]
grieta	crack, *crevice*, cleft, chap (skin)	[de*crepit*, *crepitate*]
—agrietar	—(to) crack, (to) chap	
grúa[12]	crane (construction), tow truck	[pedi*gree*]
—grulla	—crane (bird)	
guapo[13]	handsome, well-dressed, valiant (Amer.)	[*vapid*]
guata	(cotton) padding, *wad* (padding material)	
—bata	—white coat (doctor's), dressing gown	
guijarro	(rounded) pebble	
hiedra	ivy	[bot. **Hedera** *helix*]
hocico	snout (~ *morro*)	
hollar	(to) tread on, (to) step on	[to *full* (cloth)]
—huella	—footprint, track, trace	
—huella digital	—fingerprint (~ *huella dactilar*)	
hueco (adj. & n.)	hollow, spongy, hole, free time, empty space	[† *occation*]
—ahuecar	—(to) hollow out, (to) deepen (voice), to plump up (pillow)	
—oquedad	—cavity, hollow	

---

[12] English *pedigree* comes from Old French *pié de grue*, literally "crane's foot", the idea being that the branching lines in a genealogical tree resemble the three splayed-out toes of a crane.

[13] *Guapo* comes from Latin VAPPA ("flat, *vapid* wine") and underwent the following semantic development: insipid drink → useless person → rascal → scoundrel → ruffian → handsome/bold/dandy. At the "ruffian" stage, it was exported to the regions of Italy under Spanish control, and as Italian *guappo* it acquired the meaning of "thug" or "(Neapolitan) mafioso"; *guappo* is the source of the English vulgarism *wop*, a disparaging term for a person of Italian birth or descent. Spanish *guapo* in some regions can mean "bully".

huso	spindle	[*fuse, fusee, fuselage*]
—huso horario	—time zone	
idóneo	apt, fit, suitable	[† *idoneous*]
—idoneidad	—fitness, suitability, aptitude	[† *idoneity*]
ileso	unhurt, unscathed	["no *lesion*"]
indagar	(to) investigate	[† *indagate*]
—indagación	—investigation	
índole (f.)	innate quality or character	[† *indoles*]
indumentaria	clothing, clothes (~ *ropa, vestido*)	[rare *indumentum*]
izquierda (n.)	left, left hand	
—a la izquierda	—on the left	
—izquierdo (adj.)	—left, left-hand	
—zurdo	—left-handed	
jactar(se)	(to) brag, (to) boast	[*jactitation*]
—jactancia	—boasting, bragging	
jaula (< Fr.)	*cage*	[*jail / gaol*]
lacra	scar, blemish, defect or vice	[*lack* ?]
lata	(tin) can	[*lath*]
—hojalata	—tinplate, tin	
látigo	whip	
—latigazo	—(whip)lash, crack of a whip	
latir	(to) beat (heart), (to) throb	
—latido (p.p.)	—beat (heart, artery)	
lejía	bleach, lye	[*lixiviate*]
lienzo	canvas (painting), painting, *linen* cloth	[*lint*]
—lencería	—*lingerie, linens*	
—lona	—canvas (fabric)	(unrelated)
liso	smooth, even, plain (unadorned)	
—lisa y llanamente	—purely and simply	
lisonja	flattery	[*laudatory*]
—lisonjear	—(to) flatter	
—lisonjero	—flattering, complimentary	
lodo	mud	[*luting, pollute*]
—lodazal	—muddy place, bog	
losa	flagstone, gravestone	
—baldosa	—floor tile	(unrelated)
loza	china, porcelain, crockery	[*lavish* ?]
—lozano	—luxuriant, vigorous, full of life	
malvado (adj. & n.)	evil, wicked, wicked person	(Fr. *mauvais*)
mancha	stain, spot	[*macula*]
—manchar	—(to) stain, (to) *maculate*	
—manchado (p.p.)	—stained, soiled, spotted (animal)	

—inmaculado	—*immaculate*	
maraña	tangle, dense growth, complexity	
—enmarañar	—(to) entangle, (to) confuse	
—desenmarañar	—(to) disentangle, (to) unravel	
marchitar	(to) wither, (to) wilt, (to) fade	[† *marcor*]
—marchito	—withered, wilted, faded, shriveled	
—marcescente	—*marcescent* ("withering but not falling off, as a blossom")	
martillo	hammer, malleus (bone in ear)	[Charles Martel[14]]
—martillar ~ martillear	—(to) hammer	
—martillazo	—hammer blow	
—martilleo	—hammering	
matiz	shade (color, meaning), nuance	
—matizar	—(to) blend, (to) harmonize, (to) nuance	
mecenas (m./f.)	patron (of art or literature)	[*Maecenas*]
meta[15]	goal, finish line, objective, aim	[*metes* and bounds]
—guardameta	—goalkeeper, goalie (~ *portero, arquero*)	
metralleta	machine gun	
~ametralladora		
—metralla	—grapeshot, shrapnel	[rare *mitraille*]
mientras	while, meanwhile	[*interim*]
miga	crumb, soft part of bread	[*mica*]
mimar	(to) pet, (to) fondle, (to) spoil, (to) pamper	
—mimo (1)	—caress, pampering, extreme care	
—mimo (2)	—*mime* (actor, play)	(unrelated)
—mímica	—*mimicry*	
—mimetismo	—*mimicry* (biol.), *mimesis*	
—pantomima	—*pantomime*	
mismo	same, self	(Fr. *même*)
—el mismo rey	—the same king	
—el rey mismo	—the king himself	
—ellas mismas	—they (f.) themselves	
—asimismo	—likewise, also (~ *así mismo*)	
mochila	knapsack, backpack (~ *morral*)	
moho	mold, mildew, rust	

---

[14] Charles Martel (c. 688–741), or Charles the Hammer, was the ruler of the Franks who halted the Muslim invasion of Europe at Poitiers (France) in 732. In modern French the word has evolved to *marteau*.

[15] Spanish *meta* comes from Latin META ("cone" or "pyramid" used, among other things, for marking the two turning points on race courses such as the CIRCUS MAXIMUS) and bears no relation to the Greek *meta* ("with", "after") found in numerous English words (*metaphor, metamorphosis,* etc.). English *mete* (n.) means "boundary or limit".

—enmohecer	—(to) make or become moldy	
morcilla	blood sausage (blood pudding)	
morro	snout, nose (auto, airplane), knoll (serving as landmark from sea)	
—morral	—nosebag (feedbag), backpack, knapsack	
mozo (adj. & n.)	young (person), unmarried, waiter, *mozo*	
—mocedad	—youth (time of life), "wild oats"	
muchacho	boy, young person	
—muchacha	—girl	
mugre (f.)	filth, greasy dirt (e.g., kitchen)	[genus *Mucor*]
—mugriento	—filthy, greasy (dirty)	
—moco	—*mucus,* (melted) candle wax	
mustio	withered or faded (plant), sad, dejected	[*musty* ?]
navaja	pocketknife, (barber's) razor	[*novaculite*]
palanca	lever (device, "pull")	[*phalanx*]
—falange (f.)	—phalanx, phalange (bone of finger or toe)	
—falangista	—Falangist (member of political ruling party under Franco)	
pantalla	screen (TV, cinema, smoke, etc.), lampshade	
—salvapantalla	—screen saver	
pantano	swamp, marsh, reservoir ($\sim$ *embalse*)	
—pantanoso	—marshy, swampy, full of obstacles	
paulatino	slow, gradual	[*Paul*]
—paulatinamente	—slowly, gradually	
pavor	terror, dread	[med. *pavor nocturnus*]
—pavoroso	—dreadful, awful	
—impávido	—fearless, unafraid	[*pavid*]
—despavorido	—terrified	
—espantar	—(to) scare, (to) frighten away	(EX-PAVENTARE)
—espanto	—terror, fright	
—espantoso	—frightful, dreadful	
—espantapájaros	—scarecrow	
pegar[16]	(to) stick, (to) glue, (to) beat (hit)	[*pitch, pay*]
—pegamento	—glue ($\sim$ *cola*)	
—pegatina	—sticker ($\sim$ *adhesivo, autoadhesivo*)	
—pegadizo	—sticky, contagious, catchy (e.g., tune)	
—pegajoso	—sticky, contagious, clingy (person)	
—apegar(se)	—(to) become attached or devoted (to)	
—apego	—attachment, affection ($\sim$ *cariño*)	
—desapego	—lack of affection, indifference	

---

[16] *Pegar* comes from Latin PIX (acc. PICEM), the source of English *pitch* (sticky substance) and *pay* ("to coat or cover with waterproof material") and of Spanish *pez* ("pitch").

—despegar	—(to) unglue, (to) detach, (to) take off (airplane)	
—despegue	—takeoff (airplane, economy, etc.)	
peine	comb	[*pecten*]
—peinar	—(to) comb	
—peinado (p.p.)	—hairdo, coiffure	
—despeinar	—(to) dishevel, (to) ruffle (the hair)	
—piñón (1)	—*pinion* (small cogwheel)	
—piñón (2)	—*pine* nut	[*piñon/pinyon*]
peldaño	step (of stairs, of ladder)	[*pedal* ?]
pendencia	quarrel, brawl	[*penitence*]
—pendenciero (adj. & n.)	—quarrelsome, wrangler, brawler	
percance	mishap, unfortunate accident	[*purchase*]
pereza	laziness, sloth	[† *pigritia*]
—perezoso (adj. & n.)	—lazy, sloth (animal)	
pesebre	manger, crèche (Nativity scene)	[*Praesepe*— constellation]
pinacoteca	art gallery	[rare *pinacotheca*]
pinchar	(to) prick, (to) puncture	[*pinch* ?]
—pinchazo	—prick, puncture (e.g., flat tire)	
—pincho	—prickle, thorn, skewer, skewered meat (kebab)	
—pinza	—clothespin, tongs, tweezers (pl.), *pincers* (pl.)	
pito	whistle	(onom.)
—pitar	—(to) whistle	
—pitido	—whistle (sound)	
pizarra	blackboard, slate (mineral)	[Francisco *Pizarro*]
plazo	term, period of time	[at your *pleasure*]
—a corto plazo	—short-term (adj.)	
—a largo plazo	—long-term (adj.)	
—aplazar	—(to) postpone, (to) adjourn	[*plead*]
—aplazamiento	—postponement, adjournment, deferment	
—inaplazable	—urgent (can't be delayed or postponed)	
—emplazar[17]	—(to) summon (to appear at a specified time)	
porra	truncheon, bludgeon	(< puerro, "leek" ?)
—porrazo	—truncheon blow, blow or thump (general)	

---

[17] An unrelated *emplazar* means "to emplace" (see Annex D).

pozo	well, shaft, *pit*	(< PUTEUS)
—pozo sin fondo	—bottomless *pit*	
—pozo ciego, pozo negro	—cess*pit*, cesspool	
preconizar	(to) recommend publicly	[rare *preconize*]
—pregonar	—(to) proclaim, (to) announce, (to) hawk (merchandise)	
—pregón	—proclamation, opening address or speech	
—pregonero	—town crier, one who gives the *pregón*	
pregunta	question	[rare *percontation*]
—preguntar	—(to) ask, (to) inquire	
propina	tip (e.g., 10%), gratuity	[rare *propine*]
—propinar	—(to) give something disagreeable (medicine, blow)	
racimo	bunch or cluster (grapes, flowers), *raceme*	[*raisin*]
ráfaga	gust (wind), burst (gunfire), flash (light)	
ranura	slot (e.g., for coins), groove	[*runcinate*]
rasgar	(to) tear up, (to) rip	[*resect*]
—rasgo	—stroke (of pen), trait, features (pl.)	
reacio	reluctant, unwilling	[*reactionary* ?]
recio	sturdy, stout, strong	[*rigid* ?]
—arreciar	—(to) strengthen, (to) intensify (storm, anger)	
red	net, network	[*rete, reseau*]
—redada	—casting of a net, dragnet (for criminal suspects)	
—reticular	—*reticular* (net-like)	
—enredar	—(to) net, (to) entangle	
—enredadera	—climbing plant or vine, creeper	
regatear	(to) haggle, (to) bargain	
—regateo	—haggling, bargaining	
reja (1)	iron bars (in window or door), grating	[*royal* gate]
—entre rejas	—"behind bars" (in prison)	
reja (2)	plowshare (ploughshare)	[*rail, ruler*]
remo	oar, paddle, rowing (sport)	[*remex*]
—remar	—(to) *row*,[18] (to) paddle	
—remero	—rower, paddler	
—birreme	—*bireme* (ancient galley with two banks of oars)	
remolque	trailer, towing (n.), tow rope	
—remolcar	—(to) tow	

[18] *Remar* and *row* have a common Indo-European root, also found in *rudder*.

—remolcador (adj. & n.)	—towing (adj.), tugboat	
reñir	(to) quarrel, (to) fight, (to) scold	[*rictus*]
—riña	—quarrel, scolding	
reo	culprit	
resarcir	(to) compensate, (to) indemnify	
—resarcimiento	—compensation, indemnification	
—**zur**cir	—(to) darn, (to) mend	[*sartorial*]
resbalar	(to) slip, (to) slide	
—resbalón	—slip (fall), slip-up	
—resbaladizo	—slippery	
respingo	start (startled reaction or movement), wince	
reto	challenge (~ *desafío*)	[*reputation*]
—retar	—(to) challenge	
reventar	(to) burst (out), (to) explode, (to) ruin	
rocío	dew	[*rosemary*]
—rociar	—(to) sprinkle, (to) spray, (to) dew	
rozar	(to) touch lightly, (to) graze, (to) rub	[*rupture*]
—roce	—rubbing, friction, light touch	
ruido	noise	[animal *rut*]
—ruidoso	—noisy	
—rugir	—(to) roar	[*bruit*]
—rugido (p.p.)	—roar	
sacudir	(to) shake, (to) shake off (dust, dirt)	[*succussion*]
—sacudida	—shake, jolt, jerk	
saldo	account balance, sale (discount), liquidation	[*solid*]
—saldar	—(to) settle (account), (to) liquidate	[cons*olid*ate]
sastre	tailor	[*sartorial*]
—sastrería	—tailor's shop	
sendero ~ senda	path, footpath	
—senderismo	—hiking	
sesgo	slant, bias	
—sesgado	—slanted, biased	
sollozo	sob	[med. *singultus*]
—sollozar	—(to) sob	
soltar	(to) unfasten, (to) loosen, (to) let go (of)	[*solution*]
—soltura	—agility, fluency	
—**suel**to (adj. & n.)	—loose (free), loose-fitting, loose change (coins)	
sos**iego**	calm, quiet, tranquillity	[*sedative*]
—sosegar	—(to) calm, (to) soothe	
soslayar	(to) elude, (to) evade, (to) place at an angle	[*lax*]
—de soslayo	—obliquely, sideways, in passing	
súbdito	subject (of lord, king, state), citizen	[† *subdit*]

subir[19]	(to) go up, (to) climb, (to) raise	(= sub + ir)
—subida	—ascent, rise, climb	
—súbito	—*sudden*	[*subito*—music]
—súbitamente	—*suddenly*	
sumir	(to) sink or plunge (transitive)	[con*sume*]
su**r**co	furrow, groove, rut, wrinkle	[*sulcus*]
—surcar	—(to) furrow, (to) plow (incl. "cut through water")	
surtir	(to) supply, (to) spurt or spring (water)	[*surge*]
—surtir efecto	—(to) take effect, (to) have the desired effect	
—surtido (p.p.)	—*assorted, assortment*	
—surtidor	—jet (of water), gas pump	
susto	fright, scare	
—asustar	—(to) frighten, (to) scare	
susurro	whisper, murmur, *susurrus*	
—susurrar	—(to) whisper, (to) murmur, (to) rustle (leaves)	
tacaño (adj. & n.)	stingy, miserly, miser, scrooge	
tacha	flaw, defect	[*token, tetchy*]
—tachar	—(to) cross out, (to) find fault with	
—tachismo	—*tachisme* (style of abstract painting)	
—intachable	—faultless, irreproachable	
taco	plug, wad, *taco,* spike or cleat, billiard cue, swear word	
—tacón	—heel (of a shoe)	
taladro	*drill,* drill hole	
—taladrar	—(to) drill	
tallo	stem, stalk, shoot, sprout	[*thallus*]
tarro	jar, can	(< tierra ?)
tebeo[20]	(children's) comics, comic book	
tecla	key (piano, typewriter)	
—teclado	—keyboard (for typing or music)	
—teclear	—(to) type	
tela	cloth, fabric, membrane, canvas (art), *toile*	[*toilet*]
—telar	—loom	
—telón	—(theater) curtain	
—telón de acero	—"Iron Curtain" (lit. "*Steel* Curtain")	

[19] Before coming to specialize in "under", Latin SUB referred to an upward motion, from bottom to top; the converse motion was provided by DE. Hence SUBIRE (Spanish *subir*) meant "to approach from underneath", i.e., *to climb,* while the past participle SUBITUS (Spanish *súbito*) meant something that had *arisen* without notice, i.e., *sudden* (the English word comes, via French, from the related adjective SUBITANEUS).

[20] From the name of the children's comic magazine *TBO,* which began publication in Barcelona in 1917.

—telón de fondo	—backdrop	
—en tela de juicio²¹	—(to) be in doubt (with *estar*), (to) put in doubt (with *poner*)	
terco	stubborn, obstinate	
—terquedad	—stubbornness, obstinacy	
tergiversar	(to) distort, (to) misrepresent	[*tergiversate*]
—tergiversación	—twisting, distortion, misrepresentation	
—postergar	—(to) delay, (to) pass over (promotion, etc.)	[*post + tergum*]
tertulia	(literary or social) gathering	[*Tertullian*]
tez	complexion (~ *cutis*)	[*apt*]
—[complexión]	—constitution, temperament	[*complexion = obs. def.*]
tijeras (pl.), tijera	scissors, shears	[*tonsure*]
timón	rudder, helm	[rare *timoneer*]
tino	aim (marksmanship), good sense, tact	
—atinar	—(to) find (e.g., street), (to) hit the mark	[*destine*]
—atinado (p.p.)	—sensible, appropriate	
—desatino	—lack of "*tino*": blunder, error, nonsense	
tirar²²	(to) throw, (to) pull, (to) shoot, (to) draw	
—tirante (adj. & n.)	—tight, taut, tense, suspenders (pl.)	
—tiro	—shot, throw, chimney draft	
—tiro al blanco	—target shooting, target practice	
—tiro con arco	—*archery*	
—animales de tiro	—draft animals	
—tirón	—pull, tug, yank	
—tira	—strip (of fabric, paper, comics, etc.)	[*tier*]
—tirachinas	—slingshot	
—tirada	—throw (dice, ball, etc.), print run	[*tirade*]
—tirador	—shooter, marksman, knob (furniture), bell pull	
—tiroteo	—shooting (series of shots)	
—tirita	—Band-Aid	
—tiritar (unrelated)	—(to) shiver	
—estirar	—(to) stretch (out), (to) smooth out	
títere	puppet	
tiza	chalk (for blackboard, pool cue)	(< Amer.)
tonto (adj. & n.)	foolish, silly, stupid, fool, idiot, dolt	
—tontería	—silliness, foolishness, nonsense	
—atontar	—(to) stun, (to) bewilder, (to) make "*tonto*"	

---

²¹The *tela* in *tela de juicio* has nothing to do with *tela* (fabric), coming instead from Latin TELUM ("spear", "javelin").

²² *Tirar* corresponds to *-tire* in English *attire* and *retire*; the latter corresponds to Spanish *retirar* (Annex D).

traba	hindrance, fetter	[*trave, architrave*]
—sin trabas	—without restriction(s), in an unimpeded manner	
—poner trabas	—(to) make difficult, (to) impede	
—trabalenguas	—tongue twister	
—trabar	—(to) bind or join together, (to) thicken (food)	
—trabar amistad	—(to) strike up a friendship	
trago [23]	gulp, swallow	[*dragon*]
—unos tragos	—a few (alcoholic) drinks	
—tragar	—(to) swallow, (to) devour	[*rankle*]
—tragaluz	—skylight (~ *claraboya*)	
—(máquina) tragaperras	—slot machine (~ *tragamonedas*)	
—atragantar(se)	—(to) choke (on something)	
trama	weft, *tram* (used in weft), structure, plot (novel, criminal)	
—tramar	—(to) weave, (to) plot or scheme	
—entramado	—framework (lit. & fig.)	
trámite	(administrative) step or procedure	
—tramitar	—(to) process (administratively)	
trasto	old item (furniture, etc.), piece of junk	[*transom*]
—trastos (pl.)	—tools of the trade (e.g., fishing tackle)	
—trastero	—storage room, junk room	
—trastear	—(to) move things around	
—traste	—fret (guitar)	[*trestle*]
trenza	braid, plait	[*tress* = archaic def.]
trepar	(to) climb (person, or plant)	[*trip*]
—trepador	—climbing (plant)	
trillar	(to) thresh	[*tribulation*]
—trilla	—threshing, thrashing	
—trilladora	—threshing machine	
truco	trick, stratagem	(Fr. *truc*)
umbral	threshold	[*limen*]
vara	rod, stick, *vara* (in Castile: 83.6 cm ~ 33 in.)	
—varilla	—thin metal rod (e.g., umbrella rib)	
—varita mágica	—magic wand	
vástago	shoot (plant), offspring, piston rod	[*baton*]
vereda	path, trail, sidewalk (Amer.)	[*palfrey*]
viga	beam, joist, girder	
vínculo	link, tie, bond, *vinculum*	

[23] For the change of initial *dr-* to *-tr,* see the note under *trapo* in Annex D.

—vincular	—(to) bind, (to) link or connect	
—**br**inco[24]	—hop, skip, jump	(doublet of *vínculo*)
—brincar	—(to) hop, (to) skip, (to) jump	
volcar	(to) tip or knock over	[*vault*]
—vuelco	—overturning, upset, turnaround	[re*volve*]
yunque	anvil, *incus* (anvil-shaped bone in ear)	[*incuse*]
zambullir(se)	(to) dive or plunge (into water or an activity)	[*sepulchre*]
—zambullida	—dive, plunge	
zapato	shoe	[*sabot, sabotage*]
—zapata	—brake shoe (auto)	
—zapatero	—shoemaker, cobbler	
—zapatería	—shoe shop, cobbler's shop, shoemaker's trade	
—zapatilla	—slipper, light (tennis) shoe	
—zapatista	—follower of Emiliano Zapata (Mexican revolutionary)	
—zapateado	—*zapateado* (dance with rhythmic tapping of heels)	
zarza	blackberry (shrub), bramble	
—zarzal	—blackberry patch, brambles	
—zarzamora	—blackberry (shrub or fruit)	
—zarzaparrilla	—*sarsaparilla* (< Sp.)	(zarza + parrilla)
—parra	—(large) grapevine (~ *vid*)	
—parrilla (dim.)	—grill (utensil, place for eating), gridiron	

Appendix A
Spanish Playing Cards

An individual playing card is a *naipe* (or *carta*), a word of disputed origin. There are two types of card decks in Spain: the "native" variety (*la baraja española*), which has forty-eight cards (+ two jokers), and the "English" deck of fifty-two cards (+ jokers), which is generally known as *la baraja francesa*. In both sets of cards there are four suits (*palos*), but the names differ:

Baraja española		Baraja francesa	
oros	"(gold) coins"	diamantes	"*diamonds*"
copas	"*cups*"	corazones	"hearts"

---

[24] VINCULUM → *vinclo* → *blinco* → *brinco*. *Brinco* and *vínculo* are thus doublets.

| espadas | "swords" | picas | "*pikes*" |
| bastos | "*batons*" | tréboles | "*trefoils*", "clovers" |

When the "English" playing deck was imported from France, the symbols for the four suits were left unchanged. The English names, however, represent a mixture of French and Spanish/Italian ones: *diamonds* and *hearts* from the French, *spades* and *clubs* corresponding to Spanish *espadas* and *bastos*. The fact that an English *spade* bears at least a superficial resemblance to a *pike* (a weapon with a long wooden shaft and a pointed head of iron or steel) may have played a role as well.[25]

In the Spanish deck, all the cards are numbered, as compared to the English deck, where the three "face" cards (jack, queen, king) have no numbers. There are twelve cards in each suit (there is no queen), and numbers ten through twelve go by the following names:

10   sota
11   caballo
12   rey

Sota comes from Latin SUBTUS ("under") and refers to an underling of the king. The picture is of a *paje* ("page"), equivalent to the English *jack* (or *knave*). The *caballo* has a picture of a *horse* along with a *horseman* (or *knight*). Jokers in a Spanish deck are known as *comodines* (sing.: *comodín*) because they are "handy" cards (providing a certain *commodity*). In the French (English) deck, the jokers are called simply *jokers* (sing.: *joker*).

Appendix B
"Old" Trees

A number of Spanish tree names are recognizable only with difficulty, frequently having undergone a "popular" evolution. These include:

abedul	birch (tree and wood)	[genus *Betula*]
abeto	fir (tree and wood)	[genus *Abies*]
arce	maple (tree)	[genus *Acer*]
caoba	mahogany (tree, wood, color)	(< Amer.)
chopo (1)[26]	(black) *poplar*	(POPULUS)
—chopera	—poplar grove	
—chopo (2) (< It.)	—gun, musket	(unrelated)

---

[25] The English *digging* instrument and the Spanish *sword* are in fact related, although it is unlikely that this played any role: *spade* comes from the same Indo-European root (meaning "long, flat piece of wood") as Greek *spathe,* the latter being the ultimate source (via Latin SPATHA) of Spanish *espada.*

[26] The evolution seems to have been: POPULUS → PLOPPUS → *chopo,* with the initial *ch-* betraying likely Portuguese influence or origin.

—escopeta	—shotgun	
—escopetazo	—gunshot, gunshot wound, (unpleasant) surprise	
encina	evergreen oak, holm oak	[bot. *Quercus **ilex***]
fresno	ash (tree)	[genus *Fraxinus, Fresno*]
haya	beech (tree and wood)	[bot. ***Fagus** sylvatica*]
sauce	willow, *sallow*[27] (tree)	[genus *Salix*]
—sauce llorón	—weeping willow	
—salicina	—salicin	
—ácido acetil**salic**ílico	—acetyl**salic**yclic acid, aspirin	

---

[27] *Sallow* comes from the Germanic equivalent of Latin SALIX. The name of the tree comes from its *sallow* color (the original root of *sallow* meaning "dirty" or "gray").

ANNEX C
Verbs Ending in *-cer* and Related Words

In Spanish there is a large class of verbs that end in *-cer*. A number of these are descendants of Latin "inceptive" verbs,[1] in which the ending -SCERE was added to "normal" verbs to indicate the beginning of an action or process, e.g.,

FLORERE   (to) bloom or flower
FLORESCERE   (to) begin to bloom or flower

Over time, many such verbs were created referring to the process itself, not necessarily only to its beginning. Eventually, they were created from adjectives and nouns as well (e.g., *noble* → *ennoblecer*).

In the other Romance languages, the inceptive class of verbs also experienced exponential growth, and a large number of existing verbs were replaced by inceptive ones. This process was so widespread that it became, via Old French, the basis for the *-ish* endings of *English* verbs, e.g.,

abolish, accomplish, blemish, brandish, cherish, demolish, embellish, establish, finish, flourish (from FLORESCERE), furbish, furnish, garnish, impoverish, languish, nourish, perish, polish, ravish, relinquish, replenish, tarnish, vanish, etc.

The *-ish* ending in English became so popular that it was applied to a number of verbs that had not been inceptive in either Latin or French, e.g., *admonish, diminish, distinguish, famish, publish, vanquish*.

Spanish *-cer* verbs are generally part of a "family" of related words, and this section will introduce a number of such families.

abastecer	(to) supply, (to) provide
—bastante	—enough, sufficient
—bastar	—(to) suffice, (to) be enough
aborrecer	(to) *abhor*
—aborrecible	—*abhorrent*, detestable
—aburrir	—(to) bore, (to) be bored
—*Es* aburrido.	—He is boring (tiresome).
—*Está* aburrido.	—He is bored.
—aburrimiento	—boredom, tedium

---

[1] Their more formal name is *inchoative* verbs.

acontecer	(to) happen, (to) occur	[*contact*]
—acontecimiento	—event, happening, occurrence	[*contingency*]
adolecer	(to) be ill, (to) suffer from	
—dolor	—pain, ache, sorrow, *dolor*	
—doler	—(to) ache, (to) hurt	
—dolorido	—painful (feeling pain), aching, sore	
—doloroso	—painful (causing pain), distressing, *dolorous*	
—Dolores	—*Dolores* (from María de los *Dolores*)	
—duelo (1)	—grief, sorrow, mourning	
—duelo (2)	—*duel*	(unrelated)
—condolencia	—*condolence*	
—condoler(se)	—(to) sympathize with, (to) feel sorry for	[*condole*]
adormecer	(to) make sleepy, (to) lull, (to) fall asleep	
—adormecimiento	—drowsiness, sleepiness, numbness (e.g., leg)	
—dormir	—(to) sleep	
—dormilón	—sleepyhead	
—dormitar	—(to) nap, (to) doze	
—dormitorio	—bedroom, *dormitory*	
agradecer[2]	(to) be *grate*ful for	
—desagradecer	—(to) be un*grate*ful for	
—agradecimiento	—*grat*itude, thankfulness	
—agradecido (p.p.)	—*grate*ful, thankful	
—desagradecido (p.p.)	—un*grate*ful	
—de buen grado	—willingly, with pleasure	
—de mal grado	—unwillingly	
—agrado	—liking, pleasure, amiableness	
—agradable	—*agreeable*, pleasant	
—agradar	—(to) please, (to) be agreeable to	
—desagradable	—*disagreeable*, unpleasant	
—desagradar	—(to) displease, (to) be unpleasant to	
—grato	—pleasant, agreeable (~ *agradable*)	
—ingrato (adj. & n.)	—thankless, ungrateful, *ingrate* (ungrateful person)	
—persona non grata	—persona non grata (= *persona no grata*)	
amanecer	(to) dawn, (to) begin to get light	
—amanecer (n.)	—dawn, daybreak	
—mañana (adv. & n.)	—tomorrow, morning (f.), morrow (m.), *mañana*[3]	

---

[2] The basic root is Latin GRATUS ("pleasing", "grateful"), the root as well of *gracia* ("grace"), *gracias* ("thanks"), *desgracia* ("misfortune"), *desgraciadamente* ("unfortunately"), etc. An unrelated *grado* refers to "degree", "*grade*", "rank"—see Annex D.

[3] Apart from "tomorrow", English *mañana* has the definition of "an indefinite time in the future".

anochecer	(to) grow dark, (to) arrive at nightfall	
—anochecer (n.)	—nightfall	
—noche (f.)	—night	[*nocturnal*]
aparecer	(to) *appear* (become visible)	
—parecer	—(to) *appear* (seem or look to be)	
—comparecer	—(to) appear (in court, etc.)	
—desaparecer	—(to) *disappear*	
—reaparecer	—(to) *reappear*	
—apariencia	—appearance (aspect)	
—aparición	—appearance (act), *apparition*	
—aparente	—apparent, seeming, suitable	
—aparentemente	—apparently, seemingly	
—aparentar	—(to) appear (gen. falsely): feign indifference, look a certain age, etc.	
—desaparición	—disappearance	
apetecer	(to) desire, (to) have an *appetite* for	
—apetencia	—desire, appetite, *appetence*	
—apetito	—*appetite*, hunger	
—apetitoso	—*appetizing* (tasty)	
—apetecible	—*appetizing* (tempting, inviting), desirable	
atardecer	(to) grow dark	
—tarde (adv. & n.f.)	—late, afternoon (until nightfall)	
—tardar	—(to) be slow, long, or late	
—tardanza	—delay, *tardiness*	
—tardío	—*tardy,* late	
—tardo	—slow, sluggish	
—retardar	—(to) *retard,* (to) delay	
carecer	(to) lack	[*caret*[4]]
—carencia	—lack, deficiency	
—cariño	—affection, fondness, tenderness	
—cariñoso	—affectionate, loving	
—encariñar(se)	—(to) grow fond of, (to) become attached to	
conocer	(to) know, (to) be *acquainted* with	
—desconocer	—(to) not know, (to) fail to re*cognize,* (to) disown	
—reconocer	—(to) *recognize,* (to) *reconnoiter* or examine, (to) acknowledge	
—conocimiento	—knowledge, understanding, *cognizance, cognition*	
—reconocimiento	—*recognition,* gratitude, inspection, *reconnaissance*	
—conocido (p.p.)	—well-known, ac*quaint*aince (m./f.)	

---

[4] The *caret* (^) is a proofreading symbol used to indicate where something is to be inserted; CARET is the third person singular of the Latin verb CARERE ("to be without", "to lack") and hence means literally "it lacks".

—desconocido (p.p.)	—unknown, unre*cognizable* (changed), stranger (m./f.)
—reconocible	—recognizable
—irreconocible	—unrecognizable
convalecer	(to) *convalesce*
—convalecencia	—convalescence
—convaleciente	—convalescent
convencer	(to) *convince*
—convencimiento	—conviction (*not* legal): belief, certainty
—convicto	—convicted, convict (old p.p.)
—convicción	—conviction (*not* legal), convictions (pl.)
—convincente	—convincing
crecer	(to) grow, (to) in*crease*
—crecimiento	—growth, in*crease*
—creciente	—growing, in*creasing*, *crescent* (moon)
—crescendo	—crescendo (< It.)
—acrecentar	—(to) in*crease* [*accrue*]
decrecer	(to) *decrease*
—decrecimiento	—*decrease*
—decreciente	—*decreasing*
embellecer	(to) *embellish*, (to) *beautify*
—belleza	—*beauty*
—bello	—*beautiful*
emblanquecer	(to) whiten, (to) bleach, (to) *blanch*
—blanco (adj. & n.)	—white, target
—en blanco	—*blank* (page, check, document, mind, etc.)
—blanquear	(to) whiten, (to) bleach, (to) whitewash
—blanqueo de dinero	—money laundering (~ *blanqueo de capitales*)
—blancura	—whiteness
embrutecer	(to) make *brutish* or dull
—bruto (adj. & n.)	—*brutish*, rough, gross (w/out deduction), *brute*
—diamante en bruto	—uncut diamond
—brutal	—brutal
—brutalidad	—brutality, brutishness
empequeñecer	(to) make smaller, (to) diminish, (to) belittle
—pequeño	—small, little
empobrecer	(to) *impoverish*
—pobre (adj. & n.m./f.)	—*poor*, *pauper*
—pobreza	—*poverty*
—empobrecimiento	—*impoverishment*
enaltecer	(to) *exalt* (raise in status; praise) [*enhance*]
—alto (1)	—high, tall [*alto*]

—contralto	—contralto, alto
—altura	—height, elevation
—altitud	—altitude
—altímetro	—altimeter
—altiplanicie ~ altiplano	—high plateau, high *plains, altiplano*
—Alteza	—Highness
—Su Alteza Real el Príncipe	—His Royal Highness the Prince
—altivo	—*haughty*
—alzar	—(to) raise, (to) lift, (to) erect
—alzamiento	—uprising
—exaltar	—(to) *exalt,* (to) get excited
—ensalzar	—(to) *exalt* (~ *enaltecer, exaltar*)
—realzar	—(to) heighten, (to) *enhance,* (to) highlight
—realce	—embossment, *enhancement*
—alto (2)	—**h**alt, stop (both interjection and noun) (unrelated)
enardecer	(to) inflame
—arder	—(to) burn, (to) blaze
—ardiente	—*ardent,* burning
—ardor	—*ardor,* heat
encallecer	(to) make or become *calloused*
—callo	—*callus,* corn (on toe), tripe (pl.)
encanecer	(to) become white- or gray-haired [canescent]
—cano ~ canoso	—white- or gray-haired (also beard, mustache), hoary
—cana	—white or gray hair (gen. pl.)
encarecer	(to) raise the price of, (to) praise highly
—caro	—dear (expensive, *cherished*)
—caricia	—*caress*
—acariciar	—(to) *caress,* (to) fondle, (to) *cherish* (hopes, etc.)
—caridad	—*charity, charitableness*
—caritativo	—*charitable*
endurecer	(to) harden, (to) *indurate*
—duro	—hard, solid, *durum* wheat [dour]
—dureza	—hardness, harshness [duress]
—durar[5]	—(to) last, (to) endure (continue)

---

[5] In Latin, the verbs corresponding to "harden" and "endure" by chance had identical form (DURARE), while derived words (notably the compound verb INDURARE "to make hard") tended to become intermingled, a process aided by the fact that something that was "hard" was also likely to "endure". This "mixing" continued in English, where *endure* (from INDURARE) initially meant both "to harden" (i.e., to *indurate*) and "to last" before coming to specialize in the second sense.

—durabilidad	—*durability*	
—duradero ~ durable	—durable	
—duración	—duration	
—durante	—*during*	
—perdurar	—(to) *perdure* (last or endure for a long time)	
enflaquecer	(to) make thin or lean, (to) weaken	
—flaco	—skinny, lean	
—flácido / fláccido	—*flaccid,* flabby	
—flacidez / flaccidez	—flaccidity, flabbiness	
—flaqueza	—thinness, leanness, frailty	
—flaquear	—(to) weaken, (to) give way	
enfurecer	(to) enrage, (to) *infuriate*	
—furioso	—*furious*	[*furioso*— music]
—furibundo	—furious, enraged	
—furia	—fury	
—furor	—furor, fury	
engrandecer	(to) enlarge, (to) *aggrandize,* (to) exalt	
—grande (adj. & n.)	—big, large, great, *grand, grandee* (nobleman)	
—grandeza	—grandeur, greatness, *grandees* (as a group)	
—grandioso	—grandiose	
—grandilocuente	—highly eloquent, grandiloquent	
—agrandar	—(to) enlarge, (to) *aggrandize*	
ennegrecer	(to) blacken, (to) darken	
—negro	—black	[*Negro* < Sp.]
—denigrar	—(to) *denigrate*	
ennoblecer	(to) *ennoble*	
—noble	—noble, nobleman, noblewoman	
—nobleza	—nobility	
—**inn**oble	—ignoble	
enrarecer	(to) deteriorate (air, climate), (to) *rarefy,* (to) make *rare*	
—raro	—rare (scarce, uncommon, exceptional, odd)	
—rareza	—rarity, rareness	
ensombrecer	(to) darken, (to) cloud, (to) overshadow	
—sombra	—shade, shadow, *umbra*	[*sub* + *umbra*]
—sombrío	—*somber* (dark, gloomy, dismal)	
—sombrear	—(to) shade (esp. picture, text)	
—sombrero	—hat, sombrero	

—sombrilla	—(sun) *umbrella* [in some countries: rain umbrella]
—asombrar	—(to) amaze, (to) astonish
—asombro	—amazement, astonishment
—asombroso	—amazing, astonishing
—penumbra	—penumbra
ensordecer	(to) make deaf
—sordo	—deaf, silent, muffled (sound), *surd* (linguistics)
—sordera	—deafness
—sordomudo	—deaf and dumb, deaf-mute
—absurdo[6] (adj. & n.)	—*absurd,* absurdity (~ *absurdidad*)
entorpecer	(to) dull or blunt (mind, muscles), (to) obstruct
—torpe	—awkward, clumsy, slow (in thinking) [*turpitude*]
—torpeza	—awkwardness, clumsiness, stupidity, blunder
entristecer	(to) sadden, (to) make sad
—triste	—sad, *triste, tristful*
—tristeza	—sadness
entumecer	(to) make numb, (to) swell (river, sea) [*intumesce*]
—tumor	—*tumor*
envanecer	(to) make (or become) *vain* or conceited
—desvanecer	—(to) dissipate, (to) *evanesce,* (to) *vanish*
—evanescente	—*evanescent, vanishing,* fleeting
—vano	—*vain* (empty, useless, conceited)
—en vano	—in vain
—vanidoso	—vain, conceited
—vanidad	—vanity, conceit
—vanagloria	—vainglory (unwarranted pride, vain display)
—vanagloriar(se)	—(to) boast, (to) be vainglorious
—devaneo	—delirium, idle pursuit, flirtation
—desván[7]	—attic, loft, garret
envilecer	(to) *vilify,* (to) debase, (to) degrade
—vil	—*vile* (despicable, second-rate)
—en vilo	—"up in the air", "in suspense", "on tenterhooks"
—vileza	—vileness, vile act
esclarecer	(to) *clear* up, (to) *clarify* (elucidate)

---

[6] *Absurd* comes from AB + SURDUS and meant something that was insufferable to the ear, i.e., "ill-sounding", "incongruous", or "*absurd*".

[7] *Desván* literally means "empty space between the roof and top floor".

—claro (adj. & n.)	—*clear,* bright, *clearing*
—clara	—white (of an egg)
—aclarar	—(to) clear, (to) clear up, (to) *clarify,* (to) rinse
—claridad	—*clarity,* clearness, brightness
—clarificar	—(to) *clarify* (a point or a liquid)
—clarificación	—clarification
favorecer	(to) *favor*
—desfavorecer	—(to) disfavor
—favor	—favor
—por favor	—please, if you please
—favorable	—favorable
—favorito	—favorite
—favoritismo	—favoritism
—desfavorable	—unfavorable
florecer	(to) *flower,* (to) bloom, (to) *flourish*
—flor (f.)	—*flower*
—flora	—flora
—floral	—floral
—florear	—(to) decorate with flowers
—florero	—flower pot or vase
—florista	—florist
—floristería	—flower shop
—floresta	—pleasant woods or grove, *forest*[8]
—florido	—flowery, florid [*Florida*]
—aflorar	—(to) come to the surface, (to) emerge
—desflorar	—(to) deflower
humedecer	(to) humidify, (to) moisten
—húmedo	—*humid,* moist, damp, wet
—humedad	—humidity, moisture, dampness
languidecer	(to) *languish*
—lánguido	—languid (weak, listless, slow)
—languidez	—languidness, languor
merecer	(to) *merit,* (to) deserve
—desmerecer	—(to) be unworthy of, (to) be inferior to
—inmerecido	—unmerited, undeserved
—mérito	—merit
—meritorio	—meritorious
nacer	(to) be born
—renacer	—(to) be reborn, (to) spring up anew

---

[8] *Floresta* comes from Old French *forest* ("forest"), with the *l* due to the influence of *flor.*

—nacimiento	—*nascence,* birth, source or origin (e.g., river)	
—naciente	—*nascent,* incipient, rising (sun)	
—renacimiento	—rebirth, *renascence, renaissance*	
—renacentista	—Renaissance (adj.), scholar of the Renaissance	
—natal	—*natal,* native	[*Noël*]
—natalidad	—natality (birthrate)	
—natalicio (adj. & n.)	—birthday	
—nato (old p.p.)	—born (adj.), natural (e.g., leader)	[*née*]
—innato	—innate, inborn	
—nativo	—native	
—naíf, naif	—*naive* or *naif* (esp. style of art)	(< NATIVUS)
obedecer	(to) *obey*	
—desobedecer	—(to) *disobey*	
—obediente	—obedient	
—obediencia	—obedience	
—desobediente	—disobedient	
—desobediencia	—disobedience	
ofrecer	(to) *offer*	
—oferta	—*offer,* bid, supply (economics)	
—oferta y demanda	—supply and demand	
oscurecer / obscurecer	(to) darken, (to) *obscure*	
—oscuro / obscuro	—dark, *obscure,* uncertain	
—oscuridad / obscuridad	—darkness, *obscurity*	
padecer	(to) suffer	[*patience*]
—compadecer	—(to) pity, (to) feel *compassion* for	
—padecimiento	—suffering	[*passion*]
palidecer	(to) *pale*	
—pálido	—*pallid, pale*	
—palidez	—paleness, *pallor*	
perecer	(to) *perish,* (to) die	
—perecedero	—perishable, not lasting	
—imperecedero	—imperishable, undying	
permanecer	(to) stay, (to) *remain*	
—permanente	—*permanent* (adj.), *permanent* (hair wave—f.)	
—permanencia	—permanence, stay, sojourn	
pertenecer	(to) belong, (to) *pertain*	
—pertinente	—pertinent, relevant	
—pertinencia	—pertinence, relevance	
placer	(to) *please* (oneself)	
—placer (n.)	—*pleasure*	

—complacer	—(to) please (oneself, or another)
—complacencia	—*pleasure, complacency, complaisance*
—complaciente	—*complaisant* (cheerfully obliging), *complacent*
prevalecer	(to) *prevail*, (to) take root
—valer	—(to) cost (be *valued* at), (to) be worth, (to) be *valid*
—vale (1)	—voucher, promissory note
—vale (2) (interjection)	—okay, agreed (~ *de acuerdo*)
—valiente	—*valiant*, brave, courageous
—valentía	—bravery, courage, *valiance*
—valencia	—valence (chem.)
—Valencia	—Valencia (Sp. city & region)
—valenciano	—Valencian (resident of Valencia, dialect of Catalan)
—valeroso	—valorous, brave, courageous (~ *valiente*)
—válido	—valid
—valido (p.p.)	—court favorite, prime minister (of king or ruler)
—validar	—(to) validate
—validez	—validity
—inválido (adj. & n.)	—invalid (void; disabled), invalid (person)
—invalidar	—(to) invalidate
—invalidez	—invalidity, disability (physical)
—valía	—value or worth (of a person)
—valor	—value or worth (of an item), *valor*, courage
—valorar	—(to) appraise, (to) *value*
—valoración	—valuation, evaluation
—valioso	—valuable
—plusvalía	—capital gain, appreciation (in value), surplus value
—minusvalía	—physical or mental incapacity, capital loss
—minusválido	—handicapped, handicapped person
—devaluar ~ desvalorizar	—(to) devalue
—devaluación ~ desvalorización	—devaluation
—evaluar	—(to) evaluate, (to) assess
—evaluación	—evaluation
—polivalente	—multipurpose, all-purpose, *polyvalent* (chem.)
reblandecer	(to) soften [*blandish*]
—reblandecimiento	—softening
—blando	—soft [*bland*]

—blandura	—softness, mildness	
—ablandar	—(to) soften, (to) mollify	
recrudecer	(to) *recrudesce,* (to) worsen	
—recrudecimiento	—*recrudescence,* worsening	
—crudo	—raw, uncooked, harsh, *ecru* (color), *crude*	
—crudeza	—harshness, severity	
—cruel	—cruel	
—crueldad	—cruelty	
resplandecer	(to) shine brightly, (to) be *resplendent*	
—resplandor	—resplendence, radiance	
—esplendor	—splendor	
—espléndido	—splendid, generous	
reverdecer	(to) turn green again, (to) renew	
—verde	—green, *verdant,* unripe, off-color	[*vert*]
—verdor	—greenness, *verdancy*	
—verdura	—greens, vegetable, *verdure*	
—vergel	—flower and fruit garden	
—verdugo [9]	—executioner	
robustecer	(to) strengthen ("make *robust*")	
—robusto	—robust	
—robustez	—robustness	
—roble	—oak (tree and wood), *roble* (Californian oak)	

All of the -*cer* verbs presented above have the characteristic that their first person singular ends in -*zco* rather than the "expected" -*co* (*conozco, florezco, ofrezco, prevalezco*). A far smaller number of -*cer* verbs are not inceptive in origin and therefore do not have the -*zco* ending: [10]

cocer	(to) *cook*
—recocer	—(to) *recook,* (to) overcook
—escocer	—(to) smart, (to) cause a burning sensation
—escozor	—burning pain or sensation, irritation
—cocido (p.p.)	—"Spanish" stew (boiled meat and vegetables)
coercer	(to) *coerce*
—coerción	—coercion
—coercitivo	—coercive

---

[9] Initially a *verdugo* was a rod (branch cut while still *green*) used as a whip, then the person wielding the whip, and finally an executioner.

[10] The first person singular of these verbs in fact ends in -*zo*—a "regular" *orthographic change* to preserve the pronunciation of the "soft" *c* when followed by an -*a, -o,* or -*u* (see Section 3.5, no. 14).

ejercer	(to) *exercise* (apart from physical training)	
—ejercicio	—*exercise*, practice, drill	
—ejercitar	—(to) *exercise* (all senses), (to) train	
—ejército	—army	
mecer	(to) rock, (to) swing	[*mix*]
—mecedora	—rocking chair	
torcer	(to) twist	[*torsion*]
—destorcer	—(to) untwist	
—retorcer	—(to) twist, (to) dis*tort* (words)	[*retort*]
vencer	(to) *vanquish,* (to) defeat, (to) expire	
—vencedor	—*victor,* winner, *vanquisher*	
—vencimiento	—expiration, maturity	
—fecha de vencimiento	—expiration date, due date, maturity date	
—invencible	—*invincible*	

4,500 Relatively Easy Words

The large majority of these words—either collectively or as members of a group—have easily remembered etymological correspondences in English. (Such correspondences are italicized only in cases where they might not be immediately obvious or to call attention to the relationship).

abandonar	(to) abandon	
—abandono	—abandon, abandonment	
abatir	(to) bring down (sails, enemy aircraft, spirits)	[*abate*]
—abatido (p.p.)	—dejected, downcast	
abominable	abominable	
—abominar	—(to) abominate	
—abominación	—abomination	
aborto	abortion, miscarriage	
—abortar	—(to) abort, (to) miscarry	
—abortivo	—abortive	
abrupto	steep, craggy, *abrupt*	
absceso	abscess	
absoluto	absolute	
—en absoluto	—absolutely not	
—absolutamente	—absolutely (negative sense also possible)	
absorbente	absorbent	
—absorber	—(to) absorb	
—absorto	—absorbed or engrossed (in)	(old p.p.)
—sorber	—(to) suck, (to) sip, (to) soak up	
—sorbo	—sip, gulp	
—sorbete	—*sherbet*	(< Arabic)
abundancia	abundance	
—abundante	—abundant, plentiful	
—abundar	—(to) *abound*	
abuso	abuse	
—abusar	—(to) abuse	
—abusivo	—abusive, excessive (price)	
académico (adj. & n.)	academic, academician	
—academia	—academy, private school	
ácido (adj. & n.)	acidic, sour, acid	
—acidez	—acidity, sourness	

acrimonia	acrimony, bitterness	
—acre (1)	—*acrid,* tart, acrimonious	[*eager*]
—acritud	acridity, acrimony	[† *acritude*]
—acerbo	*acerbic* (sour or bitter tasting; biting)	
—exacerbar	—(to) *exacerbate*	(ex + acerb-)
—agrio	—sour, *acid,* citrus fruits (pl.)	
—agriar	—(to) sour, (to) embitter	
—acre (2) (< Eng.)	—*acre*	
acróbata (m./f.)	acrobat	
—acrobacia	—acrobatics	
—acrobático	—acrobatic	
actual	present, current, *actual*	
—actualidad	—present (time), current situation	[*actuality*]
—actualizar	—(to) update (~ *poner al día*)	[*actualize*]
—actualización	—updating	[*actualization*]
adecuado (p.p.)	appropriate, suitable	[*adequate*]
—adecuar	—(to) adapt, (to) make suitable	
—inadecuado	—unsuitable, *inadequate*	
aderezar	(to) season (cooking), (to) *dress* (salad, appearance)	
—aderezo	—seasoning, (salad) *dressing*	
—enderezar	—(to) straighten, (to) straighten out	[*direct, dress*]
adornar	(to) adorn	
—adorno	—adornment	
—ornamento	—ornament	
adverso	adverse	
—adversidad	—adversity	
—adversario	—adversary	
adyacente	adjacent	("lying near")
—yacer	—(to) lie (at rest)	
—yacimiento	—(mineral) deposit, (fossil) bed	[*joist, gite*]
afable	affable	
afecto (adj.)	affected (with illness), attached (partial to)	
—afecto (n.)	—affection, fondness, *affect* (feeling or emotion)	
—afectuoso	—affectionate	
—afectivo	—affective (emotional)	
—afectar (1)[1]	—(to) affect (influence, act on the emotions)	
—afectar (2)	—(to) affect (simulate, take the nature of)	
—afectado (1)	—affected (acted upon, emotionally stirred, afflicted)	

---

[1] In English, *affect* is generally considered to be two distinct verbs, reflecting their derivations from separate (albeit related) Latin verbs. By contrast, Spanish *afectar* is generally considered to be a single verb.

—afectado (2)	—affected (feigned or simulated)	
—afectación	—affectation	
—afección	—affection ("disease"; less freq. "fondness", "emotion")	
—afición	—fondness, inclination, hobby, enthusiasts or fans	
—aficionado	—aficionado, amateur	
afinidad	affinity (incl. "relationship by marriage")	
—afín	—kindred, related, *affined*	
—afinar	—(to) *refine* (argument, mineral), (to) tune	
aflicción	affliction, grief, sorrow	
—afligir	—(to) *afflict,* (to) distress, (to) grieve	
afluente	affluent (stream or river that flows into a larger one), tributary	
—afluencia	—in*flux,* affluence (great quantity, abundance)	
África	Africa	
—africano	—African	
agilidad	agility	
—ágil	—agile	
agitación	agitation, turmoil	
—agitar	—(to) agitate, (to) shake	
—agitador	—agitator (person or apparatus)	
agrario	agrarian	
—agro	—(cultivated) land, agricultural sector	[*acre* 2]
—agronomía	—agronomy	
—agrónomo	—agronomist	
agravación	aggravation	
—agravar	—(to) aggravate	
—agravante (adj. & n.)	—aggravating, aggravating factor or circumstance	
—agraviar	—(to) offend, (to) insult	[*aggrieve*]
—agravio	—offense, insult, injury (legal)	[*grievance*]
—agravio comparativo	—injustice, (unfair) discrimination	
agregar	(to) add, (to) attach (person to an office)	[*aggregate*]
—agregado (p.p.)	—*aggregate,* attaché (military, etc.)	
—agregación	—aggregation	
agricultura	agriculture, farming	
—agricultor	—agricultur(al)ist, farmer	
—agrícola	—agricultural	
ajustar	(to) *adjust,* (to) fit (transitive)	

---

2 Latin AGER (source of Spanish *agro*) and Germanic *acre* come from the same Indo-European root.

—ajustado (p.p.)	—*just* (fair), tight, close-fitting	
—ajuste	—adjustment, fit, agreement	
—ajuste de cuentas	—settling of *accounts,* vengeance	
álamo	poplar tree, *alamo*	
—alameda	—poplar grove, *alameda* (tree-shaded promenade)	
albino	albino	
—albo ("poetic")	—white	
—alba	—dawn, *alb* (ecclesiastical vestment)	
—alborada	—dawn, reveille, *aubade*	
—alborear	—(to) dawn (∼ *amanecer*)	
albores (pl.)	dawn (fig.), beginning	
álbum	album	
aleatorio	aleatory (dependent on chance or luck)	(Lat. ALEA, "a die")
alergia	allergy	
—alérgico	—allergic	
alerta	alert, on the alert (adv.)	
—alertar	—(to) alert	
alfabeto	alphabet	
—alfabetizar	—(to) alphabetize, (to) teach literacy	
—analfabeto	—illiterate, analphabetic	
—analfabetismo	—illiteracy	
alga, algas (pl.)	alga, algae, seaweed	
alianza	alliance, wedding ring	
—aliar	—(to) *ally,* (to) become allied	
—aliado (p.p.)	—ally	
aliviar	(to) *alleviate,* (to) lighten (burden)	
—alivio	—alleviation, relief	
almendra	*almond*	
alternancia	alternation	
—alternar	—(to) alternate, (to) mix (socially)	
—alternativo (adj.)	—alternative, alternate	
—alternativa (n.)	—alternative	
—alterno	—alternating, alternate	
—corriente alterna (CA)	—alternating current (AC)	
—alternador	—alternator	
altruismo	altruism	
—altruista (adj. & n.)	—altruistic, altruist	
alucinar	(to) *hallucinate,* (to) delude	
—alucinación	—*hallucination*	
alumno	pupil, student	[*alumnus*]

—alumnado	—student body	
amable	*amiable,* kind	
—amabilidad	—*amiability,* kindness	
—amistad	—friendship, *amity*	
—amistoso	—friendly, *amicable*	
—amor	—love	[par*amour*]
—amoroso	—*amorous,* loving	
—amar	—(to) love	
—amante	—loving, lover (m./f.)	
—enamorar	—(to) enamor	
—enamorado, enamorada	—in love, *enamored,* lover, *inamorato, inamorata*	
amarrar	(to) *moor,* (to) tie, (to) fasten	
—amarra	—*mooring* (rope, cable), "connections" (gen. pl.)	
—desamarrar	—(to) untie, (to) *unmoor*	
ambiente (adj. & n.)	*ambient, ambiance,* environment or surroundings	
—el medio ambiente	—environment (nature)	
—ámbito	—ambit (external boundary, scope)	
ambiguo	ambiguous	
—ambigüedad	—ambiguity	
ambulancia	ambulance	
—ambulante	—itinerant, traveling (e.g., circus, salesman)	[*ambulant*]
—ambulatorio (adj. & n.)	—ambulatory, outpatient, outpatient department	
amenaza	*menace,* threat	
—amenazar	—(to) menace, (to) threaten	
—conminar	—(to) warn or order (in a *menacing* manner)	[*commination*]
ameno	pleasant, agreeable	
—amenidad	—*amenity,* pleasantness	
—amenizar	—(to) make pleasant, (to) add a pleasant touch	
América	America	
—americano	—American (of or relating to the Americas)	
—centroamericano	—Central American	
—norteamericano	—North American (freq. ~ *estadounidense*)	
—sudamericano	—South American (~ *suramericano*)	
amnistía	amnesty (general pardon)	
—amnistiar	—(to) amnesty	
ampolla	blister, flask, *ampoule* (for injections)	
análisis (m.)	analysis	
—analista (1)	—analyst	
—analista (2)	—annalist (writer of *anales* = annals), chronicler	
—analizar	—(to) analyze	
—analítico	—analytic, analytical	

anarquía	anarchy	
—anarquismo	—anarchism	
—anarquista (adj. & n)	—anarchistic, anarchist	
anatomía	anatomy, dissection	
—anatómico	—anatomical	
anca	*haunch*	
—ancas de rana	—frogs' legs	
anciano (adj. & n.)	aged, old (persons, not things), old man or woman	
—ancianidad	—old age	[*ancient*]
anécdota	anecdote	
—anecdótico	—anecdotal	
angina	angina	
anguila	eel	[*Anguilla*³]
angustia	*anguish* (~ *ansiedad*)	
—angustiar	—(to) anguish, (to) distress	
—angosto⁴	—narrow	
—angostura	—narrowness, narrow passage	
—congoja⁵	—*anguish*	
—acongojar	—(to) distress, (to) *anguish*	
aniquilar	(to) *annihilate*	
—aniquilación	—annihilation	
ansiedad	*anxiety* (~ *angustia*)	
—ansioso	—*anxious* (incl. "eagerly or earnestly desirous"⁶)	
—ansia	—anxiety (incl. "eager desire")	
—ansiar	—(to) be anxious for (desire eagerly), (to) hanker after	
antena	antenna, aerial	
anterior	preceding, former, *anterior*	
—con anterioridad	—previously, beforehand	
anticipación	anticipation	

---

³The Caribbean island of Anguilla, sighted by Columbus in 1493, presumably owes its name to its eel-like shape; *anguilla* was the "old" form of *anguila* and is still current in Honduras, and perhaps elsewhere.

⁴Latin ANGUSTUS meant "narrow", "constricted", and ANGUSTIA, "narrow or constricted place", before the latter came to be applied to the particular constriction felt in one's chest when one is *anguished* or *anxious*.

⁵*Congoja* comes from Catalan *congoixa*, where it had been formed from CON-GUSTIA, a contraction of CO-ANGUSTIA. English *anguish* comes from French *angoisse* (< ANGUSTIA).

⁶The usage of *anxious* in the sense of "eager " is generally frowned upon by language purists. Such anxiety seems a bit misplaced, however, since this meaning is found not only in Spanish *ansioso* (dating back, as for English *anxious,* at least to the eighteenth century) but also in French *anxieux*, Italian *ansioso*, and Portuguese *ansioso*.

—con anticipación	—in advance, beforehand (~ *con antelación*)
—anticipar	—(to) *anticipate* (incl. "cause to happen earlier"; "prepay a debt")
—anticipo	—advance payment
antiguo	ancient, old (things; people—old friends, old hands, etc.)
—antigüedad	—antiquity, seniority, antiques (pl.)
—anticuario	—antiquarian, antique dealer or collector
—anticuado	—antiquated, outdated, obsolete
antorcha	*torch*
anular (1)	(to) *annul,* (to) *nullify*
—anulación	—annulment, nullification
—nulo	—*null* and void, null, incompetent
anular (2)	annular (ring-shaped), ring finger
—anillo	—ring
anunciar	(to) announce, (to) advertise
—anuncio	—announcement, notice, advertisement
—nuncio	—nuncio (papal ambassador or representative)
aparato	apparatus
—aparatoso	—ostentatious, showy, spectacular (accident)
apelar	(to) *appeal* (primarily in legal sense)
—apelativo	—appellative (gram.), name or descriptive epithet
—apellido	—family name, surname, last name
aplacar	(to) *placate,* (to) calm down
apogeo	apogee
apreciación	*appraisal,* appreciation (of a currency)
—apreciar	—(to) appreciate (various senses), (to) *appraise*
—apreciable	—appreciable, estimable (worthy of appreciation)
—inapreciable	—inappreciable (negative!), inestimable (positive!), *priceless*
—aprecio	—appreciation (apart from "rise in value")
—depreciar	—(to) depreciate
—depreciación	—depreciation
aprehender	(to) apprehend, (to) seize (contraband)
—aprehensión	—apprehension (arrest, understanding), seizure
—aprensión	—apprehension (esp. fear or dread— of infection, etc.)
—aprensivo	—apprehensive (fearful)
—aprender	—(to) learn [*apprise*]
—aprendiz	—*apprentice*
—aprendizaje	—apprenticeship
aproximación	approximation
—aproximar	—(to) bring near, (to) *approach,* (to) *approximate*

—aproximado (p.p.)	—approximate
—aproximadamente	—approximately
arable	arable
—arar	—(to) plow
—arado (p.p.)	—plow, plowing
arca	*ark,* chest, strongbox, coffers (pl.)
—arca de Noé	—Noah's Ark
—arcano (adj. & n.)	—arcane (mysterious, obscure), arcanum, arcana (pl.)
—arco	—*arch, arc,*[7] bow
—arco iris	—rainbow
—arquero	—*archer,* goalkeeper (~ *portero*)
—arcada	—arcade (series of arches), retching (freq. pl.)[8]
—arcángel	—archangel
—arquidiócesis, archi-	—archdiocese
—archiduque	—archduke
—archipiélago	—archipelago
—arquitecto	—architect
—arquitectura	—architecture
—arquetipo	—archetype
—arzobispo	—archbishop
archivo	archives, files, file (~ *fichero*)
—archivador	—filing cabinet (~ *fichero*), letter file (~ *carpeta*)
—archivar	—(to) file, (to) *archive*
—archivero	—archivist
arcilla	clay, *argil*
arduo	arduous
argumento	argument (reason, reasoning, abstract or summary)
—argüir	—(to) argue (show by reasoning, indicate), (to) deduce
—argumentar	—(to) argue (one's case), (to) dispute
—argumentación	—argumentation (reasoning, presentation of *argumentos*)

---

[7] Latin ARCUS was used for both *arch* and *arc* (something shaped like an *arch,* notably a rainbow and an *archer's* bow, as well as a segment of a circle), which is why in Spanish both have the form *arco.* French separated the two concepts into different words (*arche* and *arc*), which is how they arrived in English. Latin ARCA was a completely separate word meaning "chest" or "coffer", which came into English directly from Latin as *ark,* with final *k* to distinguish it orthographically from *arc.* (In French, just to confuse matters: English *ark* is *arche,* the *arch* of a bridge is an *arche,* but a *triumphal arch* is an *arc*). The *arch-* and *archi-* in *archangel, archbishop,* and *architect* have yet another origin: Greek *arkhi-,* meaning "chief".

[8] Because the retching person (involuntarily) assumes the shape of an arch.

árido	arid, dry	
—aridez	—aridity, dryness	
armonía	*harmony*	
—armonioso	—harmonious	
—armónica	—harmonica	
—armonizar	—(to) harmonize	
arrogante	arrogant	
—arrogancia	—arrogance	
arroyo	brook, stream, *arroyo*	
arruga	wrinkle (fabric or skin)	[*ruga*]
—arrugar	—(to) wrinkle, (to) crumple, (to) rumple	
—rugoso	—wrinkled, *rugose*	[*corrugated*]
—verruga	—*wart, verruca*	(unrelated)
arte (m. or f.) [9]	art, arts (pl.)	
—artista	—artist, artiste (performing artist)	
—artístico	—artistic	
—artesano (adj. & n.)	—artisanal, artisan, craftsman	
—artesanal	—artisanal	
—artesanía	—handicraft, craftsmanship	
artificial	artificial	
—artífice	—*artificer* (craftsman; architect [creator])	
—artificio	—device, contrivance, *artifice*	
—fuegos de artificio	—fireworks (~ *fuegos artificiales*)	
—artificiero	—specialist in munitions or fireworks	
—artefacto	—device (gen. large or explosive)	[*artifact*]
as	*ace* (card, die; talented performer)	
asalto	*assault,* round (boxing)	
—asaltar	—(to) *assault,* (to) *assail*	
—asaltante (m./f.)	—assailant	
asamblea	assembly	
asentir	(to) assent, (to) agree	
—asentimiento	—assent, consent	
Asia	Asia	
—asiático	—Asian, Asiatic	
asignar	(to) assign	
—asignación	—assignation (but not romantic!), allotment (money)	
—asignatura	—academic subject	
asilo	*asylum,* refuge	
aspereza	*asperity,* roughness	

---

[9] Normally masculine in the singular, feminine in the plural.

—áspero	—rough, harsh, gruff
aspirina	aspirin
astuto	astute, cunning, sly
—astucia	—astuteness, cunning, trick
ataque	attack
—atacar	—(to) attack
atención	attention
—atento	—attentive (observant, courteous, polite)
—ser atento	—(to) be attentive (courteous, polite)
—estar atento	—(to) be attentive (observant, watchful)
—desatento	—inattentive, discourteous
atenuar	(to) attenuate, (to) extenuate
—atenuante (adj. & n.f.)	—extenuating, extenuating circumstance
—extenuado	—debilitated, exhausted [*extenuated*]
atlas	atlas
atómico	atomic
—átomo	—atom
atraer	(to) *attract*
—atracción	—attraction
—atractivo	—attractive
—contraer	—(to) *contract*
—contracción	—contraction
—detraer	—(to) *detract* (take away; archaic "speak ill of")
—distraer	—(to) *distract,* (to) amuse
—distraído (p.p.)	—distracted, absent-minded
—distracción	—distraction, amusement
—extraer	—(to) *extract*
—extracto	—extract, abstract (summary)
—extracción	—extraction
—retraer	—(to) *retract* (draw back or in), (to) dissuade, (to) *retreat*
—retracción	—retraction (act of drawing in, e.g., of landing gear)
—retractar	—(to) retract (disavow)
—retractación	—retraction (disavowal)
—sustraer / substraer	—(to) *subtract,* (to) steal
—sustracción / subs-	—subtraction, theft
atributo	attribute
—atribuir	—(to) attribute (incl. obs. "grant or assign" [authority, prize])
—atribución	—attribution, authority or power ("attributed" to someone)

atrocidad	atrocity, atrociousness
—atroz	—atrocious
audiencia	audience, judicial hearing, tribunal, court (building)
—audible	—audible
—audición	—audition (incl. "sense of hearing"), concert, recital
—auditivo	—auditive (relating to hearing)
—auditoría	—audit, court of auditors
—auditor	—auditor
—auditorio	—auditorium, audience
aullar	(to) *howl*
—aullido	—howl
—ulular	—(to) *ululate,* (to) screech (owl)
austeridad	austerity
—austero	—austere
Australia	Australia
—australiano	—Australian
autonomía	autonomy
—autónomo	—autonomous
avalancha	avalanche (~ *alud*)
avance	advance
—avanzar	—(to) advance
avaricia	avarice
—avaricioso	—avaricious
—avaro (adj. & n.)	—avaricious, miser
aventajar	(to) surpass or be in the lead (take the *advantage*)
—ventaja	—*advantage*
—ventajoso	—*advantageous*
—desventaja	—*disadvantage*
—desventajoso	—*disadvantageous*
aventura	*adventure* (incl. "enterprise of a hazardous nature")
—aventurar	—(to) *venture,* (to) *adventure*
—aventurero (adj. & n.)	—adventurous, adventurer
—ventura	—happiness, luck or fortune (good or bad)
—buenaventura	—good luck, fortune (as told by fortune-teller)
—venturoso	—happy, fortunate (bringing *buenaventura*)
—desventura	—misfortune
ávido	avid
—avidez	—*avidity*
avisar	(to) *advise,* (to) warn, (to) inform
—aviso	—notice, warning, admonishment

ayuda	*aid,* assistance, help	
—ayudar	—(to) *aid,* (to) help	
—ayudante (m./f.)	—*aid* (assistant or helper), *aide, adjutant*	
bachiller	high school graduate	[*bachelor*]
—bachillerato	—high school diploma, high school studies	[*baccalaureate*]
bacteria	bacteria	
bagatela	bagatelle (trifle)	
bahía	*bay*	
balada	ballad	
balance	balance (but not scale), balance sheet	
—balanceo	—rocking, rolling (motion)	
—balancear	—(to) balance (incl. "sway or waver"), (to) rock	
—balanza	—balance (weighing device), scale	
—balanza comercial	—balance of trade	
—abalanzar(se)	—(to) throw or fling oneself at (on, into)	
balbucir	(to) babble, (to) stammer	
~ balbucear		
—balbuceo	—babbling, stammering	
balcón	balcony	
—palco[10]	—box (theater, stadium)	
balística	ballistics	
—ballesta	—*arbalest* (crossbow), suspension spring (auto)	
—ballestero	—crossbowman	
ballet	ballet	
—baile	—dance, *ball*	
—bailar	—(to) dance, (to) spin (e.g., a top)	
—bailarín (-ina)	—dancer, ballet dancer, *ballerina*	
—bailador	—dancer (esp. of Andalusian dances)	
balón	*ball* (gen. large, inflated)	[*balloon*]
—baloncesto	—basketball	
—balonmano	—team handball	
—béisbol	—*baseball*	
—bala	—bullet, *bale*	
—embalar	—(to) pack, (to) *bale*	
—embalaje	—packing, packaging	
balsa (1)	*balsa* (raft, tree, wood)	(< Sp.)
balsa (2)	pond, pool	
—embalse	—reservoir, artificial lake	
bálsamo	*balsam, balm*	
bambú	*bamboo*	

[10] *Balcón* and *palco* come from Italian, where *balco* and *palco* were dialectical variants of a Germanic word for "wooden beam". English *balk* (one of whose definitions is "a wooden beam or rafter") comes from the same Germanic root.

banal	banal	
—banalidad	banality	
barbacoa	*barbecue* (< Sp.)	
barbarie	barbarism, barbarousness, barbarity	
—bárbaro (adj. & n.)	—barbaric, barbarous, barbarian	[*Barbara*]
—barbarismo	—barbarism (barbaric act; impurity of language)	
barra	*bar*, rod	
—barrera	—*barrier*	
—bar (1) (< Eng.)	—bar (establishment)	
—bar (2)	—bar (unit of atmospheric pressure)	(unrelated)
barraca	cabin, hut, storage shed (Amer.)	[*barrack*]
barricada	barricade	
—barrica	—*barrel*, cask	
—barri**ga**	—belly	
barril	*barrel*, cask	
barroco	baroque	
báscula	scale (for weighing), *bascule* (drawbridge)	
base (f.)	base, basis	
—basa	—base (of column or statue)	
—básico	—basic	
—basar	—(to) base, (to) be based	
—rebasar	—(to) exceed, (to) go beyond	(< balsa (2), i.e., overflow)
—rebosar	—(to) overflow, (to) abound	(< reverso: $v \rightarrow b$, $rs \rightarrow s$)
basílica	basilica	
bastardo (adj. & n.)	bastard (illegitimate, spurious)	
—bastardear	—(to) bastardize (debase, adulterate)	
bastón	cane, walking stick, *baton*, rod (part of retina)	
batalla	*battle*	
—batallar	—(to) battle	
—batallón	—battalion	
—batir	—(to) *batter*, (to) beat (eggs, wings, the bushes, record, opponent, metal)	
—batido (p.p.)	—whipped (cream, etc.); *batter*, shake (milk or fruit)	
—batida	—search ("beat the bushes"), *battue*	
—batidor	—whisk (wire kitchen utensil for beating)	
—batidora	—electric mixer	
—bate (< Eng.)	—baseball *bat*	
—bateador	—*batter* (baseball)	
—batuta	—baton (music)	("baton" is unrelated)
—rebatir	—(to) rebut (refute; drive or beat back)	[*rebate*]

bayoneta	bayonet	
beatificar	(to) beatify	
—beatitud	—beatitude, blessedness	
—beato (adj. & n.)	—devout, sanctimonious, Blessed (beatified)	
beligerante (adj. & n.m./f.)	belligerent (engaged in war or of war-like disposition)	
—bélico	—of war, war-like	
—belicoso	—bellicose	
beneficiario	beneficiary	
—beneficiar	—(to) *benefit*	
—beneficencia	—beneficence, (public) charity	
—beneficio	—benefit, advantage, profit, *benefice* (eccl.)	
—beneficioso	—beneficial	
—benéfico	—beneficent, charitable	
—benefactor	—benefactor	
benigno	benign, benignant	
bicicleta	bicycle	
billete	ticket, *bill,* banknote	[*billet*-doux]
—billetero (-ra)	—billfold, wallet	
bizarro	brave, gallant	[*bizarre*]
bloque	*block, bloc* (coalition)	
—bloc	—writing pad or tablet	
—bloquear	—(to) block, (to) blockade	
—bloqueo	—blockade, blockage	
blusa	*blouse*	
bobo (adj. & n.)	silly, foolish, fool, *booby* (< Sp.), *boob*	
—bobada	—nonsense, foolishness, idiocy	
bofetada ~ bofetón	slap in the face, *buffet* (blow or cuff)	[*rebuff*]
boicot (< Eng.)	*boycott*	
—boicotear	—(to) boycott	
bola	ball, marble	[*bola* < Sp.]
—bolo	—*bowl*ing pin, bowling (pl.)	
—bolera	—bowling alley	
—bolero	—bolero (music or dance, short jacket open in the front), liar	
—bolígrafo	—ballpoint pen	
bomba (1)	pump	
—bombero	—fireman	
—bombear	—(to) pump	
bomba (2)	bomb, bombshell (sensational news)	
—bombardear	—(to) bombard, (to) bomb	
—bombardeo	—bombardment, bombing	
—bombardero	—bomber (airplane)	
—bombazo	—(bomb) explosion, bomb damage	

—bombilla[11]	—light bulb	
—bombo	—bass drum, revolving lottery box, ballyhoo	
—a bombo y platillo	—with much fanfare	
bonete	biretta (square cap worn by clerics)	[*bonnet*]
—boina	—beret	
bordar	(to) *broider*, (to) *embroider*	(OldSp. *brordar*)
—bordado (p.p.)	—embroidery (act, piece)	
—bordadura	—embroidery (piece)	
borde	*border*, edge, rim, brink	
—bordear	—(to) border, (to) go around, (to) skirt	
—bordo	—*board* (side of a ship)	
—a bordo	—on board, aboard	
—abordar	—(to) board (ship, plane, train), (to) tackle (a problem)	
—abordaje	—boarding of a ship (e.g., by pirates)	
—desbordar	—(to) overflow	
boreal	boreal, northern	
—aurora boreal	—aurora borealis, northern lights	
—borrasca	—storm, squall	
bosque	forest, woods	[*bush, boscage*]
—boscoso	—wooded, forested, *bosky*	
—bosquete	—grove, *bosquet*	[*bouquet*]
—bosquejo	—sketch, outline	
—bosquejar	—(to) sketch, (to) outline	
—emboscada	—*ambush, ambuscade*	
—emboscar	—(to) *ambush*	
bota (1)	wineskin, *butt* (cask, liquid measure)	
—botella	—*bottle*	
—embutir	—(to) stuff (animal intestine, suitcase, etc.)	
—embutido (p.p.)	—sausage	
bota (2)	*boot*	
—botín (1)	—ankle *boot*	
—botín (2)	—*booty*, plunder	(unrelated)
botar	(to) fling, (to) bounce, (to) launch a boat	[*butt* vb.]
—bote (1)	—bounce, jump, bound	
—rebotar	—(to) rebound, (to) ricochet	[*rebut*]
—rebote	—rebound, bounce (of a ball), ricochet	
bote (2)	*pot*, jar, can	(< pote)
—pote	—*pot*, jar	

---

[11] Literally a "small bomb", a description that made more sense in the early days when bombs were spherical.

—potaje	—pottage, soup, hodge-podge	
bote (3) (< Eng.)	(row) *boat*	
—bote salvavidas	—life boat	
botón	*button,* bud, knob	
—botones (sing.)	—bellboy, bellhop	
—abotonar	—(to) button (~ *abrochar*)	
botulismo	botulism	
boxeo	boxing	
—boxear	—(to) box	
—boxeador	—boxer	
—bóxer (< Eng.)	—boxer (dog)	
boya	*buoy*	
—boyante	—*buoyant*	
braga	panties, knickers (usually pl.)	[*breeches, britches*]
—bragueta	—fly (of trousers)	[*bracket*]
brasero	*brazier* (*brasier*)	
—brasa	—red-hot coal, ember	
—abrasar	—(to) scorch, (to) burn	[*braise*]
brecha	*breach* (esp. in fortress wall), head injury	
brevedad	brevity	
—breve	—*brief,* short	
—breviario	—breviary	
bricolaje	*bricolage,* do-it-yourself, DIY	
brida	*bridle,* clamp	
brigada	brigade, staff sergeant (m.)	
—general de brigada	—brigadier general	
brillante	brilliant, shining	
—brillar	—(to) shine, (to) glitter	
—brillo	—brilliance, shine, luster	[*Brillo*®]
brío	brio (vigor, verve, vivacity)	
brisa	*breeze* (prob. < Sp.)	
—parabrisas	—windshield	(parar + brisa)
brocha	(stubby) *brush* (painting, shaving)	
broche	*brooch,* clasp	
—abrochar	—(to) button (up) (~ *abotonar*)	
—desabrochar	—(to) unbutton, (to) unfasten	
bruma	brume (mist, fog)	
bruñir	(to) *burnish,* (to) polish (metal, stone)	[*brown*]
brusco	brusque, abrupt	
bucólico	bucolic	
bufé	buffet (meal)	
—bufete	—lawyer's office, desk	
bulevar	boulevard	

—baluarte	—*bulwark*, bastion, defense	
burdel	*bordello*, brothel	
burguesía	*bourgeoisie*, middle class	[*burg, borough*]
—burgués (-esa)	—*bourgeois*, middle class (person), *burgher*	[*burgess*]
—burgomaestre	—burgomaster (mayor)	
burla	mockery, joke, trick	
—burlar	—(to) mock, (to) deceive	
—burlesco	—comical, *burlesque*	
—burlón (-ona)	—mocking, mocker, joker	
buró	desk, *bureau* (writing desk)	
—burocracia	—bureaucracy	
—burócrata	—bureaucrat	
—burocrático	—bureaucratic	
cable	cable	
cactus, cacto	cactus	
cal (f.)	lime	[*calx, chalk*]
—cal viva	—quicklime	
—a cal y canto	—completely (referring to a shut door, or figuratively)	
—(piedra) caliza	—limestone	
—calcio	—*calcium*	
—calcificar	—(to) calcify	
—calcinar	—(to) burn, (to) reduce to ashes, (to) *calcine*	
—calzada	—*causeway*, paved part of road	
calabozo	dungeon, jail cell, *calaboose* (< Sp.)	
cálculo (1)	calculation, computation, calculus	
—cálculo[12] (2)	—stone (e.g., kidney), *calculus* (med.)	
—calcular	—(to) calculate	
—calculación	—calculation	
—calculador	—calculating	
—calculadora	—calculator (machine)	
—incalculable	—incalculable	
cáliz	*chalice*, calyx ("flower cup")	
—cauce	—riverbed, channel	(doublet of *cáliz*)
—encauzar	—(to) channel, (to) guide	
calma	calm, calmness, composure	
—calmar	—(to) calm, (to) calm down	
—calmante	—calmative or sedative (e.g., herbal tea), analgesic	

---

[12] Latin CALCULUS was a "small stone". The mathematical sense arose from the use of stones in counting and in making calculations (as with an abacus).

calzar[13]	(to) put on shoes, (to) wear or take (a certain size)	[*Chaucer*]
—calzado (p.p.)	—shod, footwear	[*calceolate*]
—calzón	—pants, trousers	[*calzone*]
—calzo	—chock, wedge	
—calzoncillo	—underpants, drawers	
—calcetín (~ media)	—sock, stocking	
—calcáneo	—*calcaneus* (heel bone)	
—calcar	—(to) trace, (to) copy	[*caulk, calk*]
—calco	—exact copy, *calque* (loan translation)	
—recalcar	—(to) stress (by speaking clearly or slowly, or by repeating)	
—descalzar	—(to) take off (shoes, socks), (to) remove chocks	
—descalzo	—barefoot, shoeless, *discalced*	
—recalcitrante	—stubborn, recalcitrant	
camión (m.)	truck, *camion*	
—camionero	—truck driver	
—camioneta	—small truck or bus	
camisa	shirt, *chemise*	[*camise*]
—camiseta	—T-shirt, undershirt, *camisole*	
—camisón	—nightshirt, nightgown, nightie	
camuflaje	*camouflage*	
—camuflar	—(to) camouflage	
canal	canal, *channel* (physical or broadcast), duct	
—canalizar	—(to) canalize, (to) channel	
canapé	sofa, *canapé* (cracker or bread + spread)	[*canopy*]
canasta	large round basket, basketball hoop, *canasta* (card game)	
—canasto	—basket (with narrow mouth)	
cancelar	(to) cancel	
—cancela[14]	—grating, grille, iron gate	[*chancel*]
—canciller	—*chancellor*	
—cancillería	—chancellery	

---

[13] These words come from Latin CALX (genit. CALCIS) meaning "heel" and gradually came to apply to footwear in general, and eventually to trousers. A Middle English *chaucer* was a maker of leather breeches, boots, etc. CALCARE was to trace something with the heel, hence Spanish *calcar* and, taking the idea of squeezing something together, English *caulk*. To *inculcate* arose from the notion of stamping in with the heel, while *recalcitrant* was literally "to dig in one's heels". CALX had an unrelated homonym that meant "limestone" or "pebble", and this is the source of the words listed under *cal* and *calculus* (a little stone).

[14] Latin CANCELLUS was a grating or lattice. If one wished to cross out or *cancel* something written, one did so by drawing lines across it in the form of a lattice, hence the verb CANCELLARE ("to cancel"). A *chancellor* (Latin CANCELLARIUS) was essentially the doorkeeper who guarded the grating separating the public from the judges.

candidato[15]	candidate	
—candidatura	—candidacy, candidature	
—cándido	—(snow) white, candid	
—candor	—candor, sincerity, (pure) whiteness	
—candela	—candle (~ *vela*), fire, *candela* (unit of luminous intensity)	
—incandescente	—incandescent	
caníbal	cannibal (< Sp.)	
—canibalismo	—cannibalism	
canoa	canoe	
canon	canon (ecclesiastical or secular law; precept)	
—canónico	—canonical	
—canonizar	—(to) canonize	
—canónigo	—canon (person)	
cantar	(to) sing	[*chant*]
—canción	—song, *chanson*	
—canto (1)	—singing, *chant*, song, *canto* (poem)	
—cantor	—singer	[*cantor, chanter*]
—cantante	—singing, singer (m./f.)	
—cantata	—cantata	
—chantaje (< Fr.)	—blackmail	
—chantajear	—(to) blackmail	(to make s.o. sing)
—chantajista	—blackmailer	
—encantar	—(to) *enchant*, (to) charm	
—encanto	—enchantment	
—encantador (adj. & n.)	—enchanting, charming, charmer, enchanter	
—encantadora	—enchantress	
cantidad[16]	quantity	
—cuantitativo	—quantitative	
—cuanto	—as much as, as many as	
—¿cuánto? ¿cuántos?	—how much? how many?	
—en cuanto	—as soon as	
—en cuanto a	—as for, regarding	
—cuanto antes	—as soon as possible	
—unos cuantos	—a few	

---

[15] The root *cand-* meant "shining", hence "white". A Roman CANDIDATUS was so-called because he wore a *white* toga (TOGA CANDIDA).

[16] The form *cuantidad* is also possible but far rarer.

—cuanto (n.)	—quantum (physics)	
cantina	mess hall, *canteen* (eating place)	
—cantimplora[17]	—canteen (water bottle)	
canto (2)	corner (table, building), edge	[*cant*]
—cantón	—canton, region, corner	
—acantonar	—(to) quarter (troops)	
—acantilado	—cliff, bluff	[*canted*]
—decantar	—(to) decant, (to) lean toward or choose ("tilt the balance")	
canto (3)	(rounded) stone	
—canto rodado	—boulder	
—cantera	—quarry	
—cantero	—stonecutter	
capacidad	capacity, ability	
—capaz	—capable, able, *capacious* (spacious or roomy)	
—capacitar	—(to) train, (to) *capacitate*	
—incapacidad	—incapacity	
—incapaz	—incapable, unable	
—incapacitar	—(to) incapacitate	
caravana	caravan, motor home	
carbono	carbon	
—carbón	—coal	
—papel carbón	—carbon paper	
—carbón vegetal	—charcoal (~ *carbón de leña*)	
—carbonato	—carbonate	
—carboncillo	—charcoal pencil	
—carbónico	—carbonic	
—carburador	—carburetor	
—carburante	—fuel	
caricatura	caricature, cartoon	
—caricaturista	—caricaturist, cartoonist	
—caricaturizar	—(to) caricature	
carpa (1)	carp (fish)	
carpeta	letter file, folder, writing-table cover or pad	[*carpet*]
—carpa (2)	—(circus) tent	(< carpeta ?)
carpintero	carpenter	
—carpintería	—carpentry, carpenter's shop	
carro	*car* (Amer.), *cart*, wagon, *chariot*	
—carrera	—run, race, *career* (incl. "path or course")	

---

[17] *Cantimplora* has no relation to *cantina* but instead comes, via Catalan, from *canta i plora* ("sings and cries"), the verb *plorar* being the Catalan equivalent to Spanish *llorar*. Explanation: "por el ruido que hace la cantimplora al gotear" (Corominas and Pascual, 1:816): "for the noise that the *cantimplora* makes when [its contents] drip out".

—carreta	—long, low *cart* drawn by animals (e.g., oxcart)
—carrete	—spool, reel, roll (of film)
—carretera	—road, highway
—carretero	—cart driver (*carter*), cart maker
—carretilla	—wheelbarrow, handcart
—carrocería	—body (of a car or train)
—carruaje	—*carriage*
—carril	—lane (of a road), rail (~ *raíl*, *riel*) for trains
—ferrocarril	—railroad
—acarrear	—(to) *carry*, (to) *cart*, (to) entail (*carry* [negative] consequence)
carta	letter, *charter, chart,* map, playing *card,* restaurant menu
—carta blanca	—*carte blanche* (unconditional authority)
—carta de crédito	—letter of credit (≠ credit card!)
—carta magna	—constitution of a country, *Magna Carta* (cap.)
—cartel (1)	—poster, placard
—cartel (2), cártel	—cartel
—cartera	—wallet, briefcase, purse (Amer.)
—cartero	—postman, mailman
—cartón	—cardboard, *carton, cartoon* (preparatory drawing for fresco, etc.)
—cartucho	—*cartridge* [*cartouche*]
—pancarta	—placard
casco	helmet, *casque,* bottle, fragment, hull, segment (fruit), *cask,* hoof
—casco azul	—United Nations soldier ("blue helmet")
—casco urbano	—city center or urban agglomeration
—cascos (pl.)	—headphones (~ *auriculares*)
—cáscara	—rind, peel, shell, husk [*cascara*]
—cascarón	—eggshell (esp. one from which chick has emerged)
—cascar	—(to) crack or break (egg, voice, etc.)
—cascanueces	—nutcracker
casi	almost, nearly, *quasi*
—cuasi	—*quasi*
caso	*case,* event
—acaso	—perhaps, maybe
—por si acaso	—just in case (e.g., bring the umbrella, just in case it rains)
castidad	*chastity*
—casto	—*chaste,* pure
—castizo	—typical of region (language, customs), authentic

castigar	(to) *castigate,* (to) *chastise,* (to) *chasten*	
—castigo	—*chastisement, castigation,* punishment	
casual	casual (in sense of "occurring by chance")	
—casualidad	—*chance,* hazard, *coincidence*	[*casualty*[18]]
catapulta	catapult	
—catapultar	—(to) catapult	
catarata	cataract (waterfall, eye disorder)	
catarro	common cold, *catarrh*	
categoría	category, rank, class	
—categórico	—categorical	
causa	cause, lawsuit, legal case	
—a causa de	—*because* of, on account of	
—causal	—causal	
—causalidad	—causality	
—causar	—(to) cause, (to) give rise to	
cautivo	*captive*	[*caitiff*]
—cautivar	—(to) captivate (incl. archaic "take prisoner")	
—cautividad ~ cautiverio	—captivity	
—cautivador	—captivating	
ceder	(to) cede, (to) yield, (to) slacken	
—cesión	—cession (of rights, territory, etc.)	
—cesar	—(to) *cease,* (to) stop	
—cese	—cessation, stoppage	
—incesante	—incessant, unceasing	
cedro	cedar (tree and wood)	
cédula	certificate, permit, document	[*schedule*]
—cédula de identidad	—identity card	
celo	zeal, ardor, heat (animals)	
—celos (pl.)	—jealousy	
—celoso	—zealous, jealous	
—celador	—monitor, guard, watchman	
—recelar	—(to) distrust, (to) suspect	(unrelated)
—recelo	—suspicion, distrust	
—receloso	—distrustful, mistrustful	
célula	*cell* (biological or small group)	
—celular	—cellular	
—celulitis	—cellulitis	
—celuloide	—celluloid	

[18] English *casualty* originally meant "chance", "accident". Thus, Samuel Johnson could write (in 1779) with reference to Alexander Pope: "Those performances, which strike with wonder, are combinations of skilful genius with happy *casualty*."

—celulosa	—cellulose	
—cel**d**a	—cell (jail, convent, of a beehive, of a statistical table, etc.)	
—celdilla	—cell (beehive)	
censura	censorship, censure, criticism	
—censor	—censor	
—censurar	—(to) censor, (to) censure	
centinela (m./f.)	*sentinel, sentry*	
cera	wax, *cere* (waxy bird membrane)	[*cerated, cere*cloth]
—cerumen	—cerumen (earwax)	
—cerilla	—(wax) taper, match, earwax	
—cirio	—long, thick candle (as in churches)	[*cereus* cactus]
—encerar	—(to) wax	[vb. *cere*]
—ciruela[19]	—plum	
—ciruela pasa	—prune	("raisin"-like plum)
—ciruelo	—plum tree	
cerámico	ceramic (adj.)	
—cerámica	—ceramics	
ceremonial	ceremonial	
—ceremonia	—ceremony, formality	
cesta	basket (freq. low and wide)	[*chest*]
—cesto	—basket (*DRAE:* "large *cesta,* higher than it is wide")	
chal	*shawl*	
champú	*shampoo*	
chaqueta	*jacket*	
—chaquetón	—coat	
charlatán (-ana)	chattering, chatterbox, gossip, *charlatan*	
—charlar	—(to) chatter, (to) chat	
—charla	—chat, informal talk (lecture)	
chimenea	*chimney,* smokestack, fireplace	
chófer, chofer (Amer.)	*chauffeur*	
cho**que**	*shock,* collision, clash	
—chocar	—(to) collide, (to) clash, (to) *shock* (surprise)	
—chocante	—surprising, strange, *shocking*	
cicatriz	scar, *cicatrix*	
—cicatrizar	—(to) *cicatrize,* (to) heal (wound)	
—cicatrización	—cicatrization (formation of a scar)	

[19] From CEREOLA PRUNA, "wax-colored plum (or prune)".

cigarro	cigar, cigarette	
—cigarrillo	—cigarette	
—cigarra	—*cicada*	(unrelated)
ciprés	cypress (tree and wood)	
circunferencia	circumference	
—circundar	—(to) surround, (to) encircle	
—circundante	—surrounding	
circunscribir	(to) circumscribe (encircle, limit, restrict)	
—circunscripción	—circumscription, (electoral) district, territory	
cisterna	cistern, water tank	
citar	(to) make an appointment with, (to) *cite* (quote, summon)	
—cita	—appointment, rendezvous, *citation* (quotation)	
—citación	—*citation* (legal), summons	
clandestino	clandestine	
—clandestinidad	—secrecy, clandestinity	
clarividencia	*clairvoyance*	
—clarividente	—clairvoyant	
cláusula	*clause* (legal or linguistic)	
claxon	klaxon, auto horn	
clemencia	clemency, mercy	
—clemente	—clement, merciful	
—inclemente	—inclement (attitude, weather)	
cliente (m./f.)	client, customer	(also *clienta*-f.)
—clientela	—clientele, customers	
clima (m.)	climate, *clime*	
—climático	—climatic	
—climatológico	—climatological	
—climatización	—air conditioning, heating of swimming pool, etc.	
clímax	climax	
clínica	clinic	
—clínico	—clinical	
cloaca	sewer (~ *alcantarilla*), *cloaca*	
coalición	coalition	
cobarde (adj. & n.)	*cowardly*, coward	
—cobardía	—cowardice	
cocina	*kitchen*, kitchen stove, *cuisine*	
—cocinero	—*cook*	
—cocinar	—(to) *cook*	
—cocer	—(to) *cook*, (to) boil	
—culinario	—culinary	
coche	car (auto or railway), *coach*	[*Kocs*, Hungary]

—cochera	—garage	
código	*code*	
—código penal	—criminal law, penal code	
—código civil	—civil law, civil code	
—código postal	—postal code	
—código de barras	—bar code	
—codificar	—(to) codify, (to) encode	
—descodificar, decodificar	—(to) decode	
—códice	—codex (old manuscript)	[Eng. pl. = *codices*]
cofre	*coffer*, trunk	[*coffin*]
coincidir	(to) coincide, (to) meet by chance	
—coincidencia	—coincidence	
colapso	collapse	
—colapsar	—(to) bring to a standstill, (to) collapse (e.g., business)	
colcha	bedspread, *quilt*	
—colchón	—mattress	
—colchoneta	—light mattress, exercise or gymastics mat	
—colchonería	—mattress store	
cólera (1) (m.)	*cholera* (disease)	
cólera (2)	anger, rage, *choler*	
—colérico	—choleric (angry, hot-tempered)	
—encolerizar	—(to) become enraged	
colon (1)	colon (intenstine)	
—cólico	—colic	
colon (2)	colon (~ *dos puntos*) *or* semicolon (~ *punto y coma*)	
colón	colón (currency of Costa Rica & El Salvador)	
—Cristóbal Colón	—Christopher *Columbus*	
coloquial	colloquial	
—coloquio	—colloquy, conversation, colloquium	
color	color	
—colorado	—*colored,* red or reddish (esp. face)	[*Colorado*]
—poner(se) colorado	—(to) blush, (to) redden	
—colorear	—(to) color, (to) dye, (to) become red (e.g., tomatoes, sun)	
—colorante	—coloring (agent), colorant	
—colorete	—rouge (cosmetic)	
—colorido	—coloring or coloration (clothes, painting, etc.)	
—descolorido	—pale, faded, *decolorized*	
—incoloro	—colorless	

colosal	colossal	
columna	column (numerous senses)	
—columna vertebral	—spine, spinal column	
—columnista	—columnist	
—colmillo	—fang, canine tooth, tusk	[*columella*]
combate	combat, battle	
—combatir	—(to) combat, (to) fight, (to) oppose	
—combatiente	—combatant	
—combativo	—combative	
combustión	combustion	
—combustible	—combustible (adj. & n.), fuel	
comenzar	(to) commence	
—comienzo	—commencement, beginning, start	
comercial	commercial (adj.)	
—comercio	—commerce, trade	
—comerciante (m./f.)	—merchant	
—comercializar	—(to) commercialize, (to) market	
—comercialización	—commercialization, marketing	
—comerciar	—(to) trade, (to) do business	
cometer	(to) *commit*	
—cometido (p.p.)	—*commission,* charge, duty	
—acometer	—(to) attack, (to) undertake	
—acometida	—attack, connection or intake (electricity, gas, etc.)	
cómic	comic (book, magazine) (~ *tebeo*)	
—cómico (adj. & n.)	—comic, comical, comedian	
—comedia	—theatrical play, comedy, farce	
—comediante (m./f.)	—actor, actress, comedian (-enne)	(also comedianta—f.)
cómodo	comfortable, convenient	[*commodious*]
—cómoda	—commode (chest of drawers; ≠ toilet or chamber pot!)	
—comodidad	—comfort, convenience	[*commodity*]
—comodín	—joker or wildcard	
—incómodo	—incommodious (inconvenient, uncomfortable)	
—incomodidad	—inconvenience, discomfort	
—incomodar	—(to) incommode (inconvenience, disturb)	
compacto	compact	
comparable	comparable	
—comparativo	—comparative	
—comparación	—comparison	
—comparar	—(to) compare	

—incomparable	—incomparable
compás	*compass* (geom., maritime), beat/measure/bar (music)
compatible	compatible
—compatibilidad	—compatibility
compendio	compendium (summary, abstract)
competente	competent
—competer	—(to) be incumbent on, (to) behoove
competición	competition
—competidor (adj. & n.)	—competing, competitor
—competitivo	—competitive
—competitividad	—competitiveness
—competir	—(to) compete, (to) vie
—competencia [20]	—*competition, competence* (ability, legal)
compilar	(to) compile
—compilación	—compilation
—recopilar [w/out *m*]	—(to) compile, (to) gather together
—recopilación	—compilation, compendium
cómplice (m./f.)	*accomplice*
—complicidad	—complicity
complot	*plot,* conspiracy, intrigue, *complot* (archaic—Shakespeare)
comportar	(to) entail or involve, (to) *comport* (oneself)
—comportamiento	—behavior, demeanor, *comportment*
compromiso	commitment, engagement, difficult situation [*compromise*]
—sin compromiso	—without obligation
—comprometer	—(to) *compromise* (jeopardize; obs. "bind by mutual agreement")
concernir	(to) concern, (to) be pertinent to (used only in 3rd person)
—en lo que concierne a	—concerning, as regards
conciso	concise
concreto (1)	concrete (opposed to *abstract*), real
—concretar	—(to) specify, (to) limit, (to) express *concretely*
—concreto (2) (Amer.)	—concrete (for construction ~ *hormigón*) (< Eng.)
concubina	concubine

---

[20] *Competir* and *competer* were originally the same verb, and *competencia* retains meanings from both.

condenación	*condemnation, damnation*
—condenar	—(to) condemn, (to) sentence, (to) damn
—condena	—sentence (e.g., ten years), condemnation (censure)
condición	condition
—condicional	—conditional
—condicionar	—(to) condition (make conditional)
—acondicionar	—(to) condition (render fit for work or use), (to) air-condition
—acondicionador	—conditioner (hair, etc.)
—acondicionador de aire	—air conditioner
—aire acondicionado	—air conditioning
conducta	conduct, behavior
—conducto	—*conduit, duct*
—conductor	—conductor, driver (~ *chófer*)
—conducir	—(to) conduct, (to) drive (vehicle), (to) *conduce*
conexión	connection
—conectar	—(to) connect, (to) plug in
—desconectar	—(to) disconnect, (to) unplug
—nexo	—*nexus,* link
confinar	(to) confine
—confín	—limit, boundary, *confine*
—confinamiento	—confinement
conflicto	conflict
conformidad	*conformity,* agreement
—conformar	—(to) adapt, (to) conform, (to) content oneself (with)
—conforme (adj.)	—in agreement or *conformity,* resigned (accepting)
—conforme a	—in accordance with, in conformity with
—conformista	—conformist
—inconforme ~ disconforme	—not in agreement, dissatisfied
—inconformista	—nonconformist
confortable	comfortable
—confort	—comfort (~ *comodidad*)
—confortar	—(to) comfort
confusión	confusion
—confundir	—(to) mix up, (to) *confuse,* (to) *confound*
—confuso	—confused, confusing, confounded (old p.p.)
congestión	congestion
—congestionar	—(to) congest

—descongestionar	—(to) decongest (nose, traffic)	
congratular(se) [21]	(to) be gratified or pleased	[*congratulate*]
congreso	congress, assembly	
—congresista	—congressman or -woman	
cónico	conical, conic	
—cono	—cone	
conjetura	conjecture, guess	
—conjeturar	—(to) conjecture, (to) guess	
conjunción	conjunction	
—conjunto (adj. & n.)	—*conjoint,* whole, ensemble (music, clothing, etc.)	
—coyuntura	—situation, opportunity, *joint* (articulation)	[*conjuncture*]
conjurar	(to) ward off, (to) *conjure,* (to) conspire	
—conjuración ~ conjura	—plot, conspiracy	[*conjuration* = archaic def.]
—conjuro	—conjuration (magical spell or incantation)	
conmoción	commotion, disturbance, shock	
—conmoción cerebral	—concussion	
—conmover	—(to) shake, (to) *move* (stir the emotions)	
—conmovedor	—moving, touching	
consignar	(to) state (in writing), (to) *consign*	
—consigna	—luggage room (station), orders or instructions, slogan	
consonante	consonant (adj.), rhyming, consonant (f.)	
consternación	consternation, dismay	
—consternar	—(to) consternate, (to) dismay	
cónsul	consul	
—consulado	—consulate	
consultar	(to) consult (incl. "look up", e.g., in dictionary)	
—consulta	—consultation, doctor's office	
—consultorio	—doctor's office, clinic, advice column (newspaper)	
consumir	(to) consume (incl. "destroy"; "waste")	
—consumidor	—consumer	
—consunción	—consumption (illness)	
—consumo	—consumption (act of consuming)	
—bienes de consumo	—consumer goods	
—consumición	—food and drink consumed (e.g., in a bar), consumption	

---

[21] While *congratulaciones* ("congratulations") exists, far more common are *felicitaciones* and *enhorabuena.*

—consumar	—(to) consummate, (to) finish
—consumado (p.p.)	—consummate, accomplished
—hecho consumado	—*fait* accompli
—consumación	—consummation (incl. "ultimate end, finish")
—consumación de los siglos	—end of the world (biblical)
—consomé (< Fr.)	—consommé
contacto	contact
—contactar	—(to) contact, (to) get in touch with
contagioso	contagious
—contagio	—contagion (spreading of disease; contagious disease)
—contagiar	—(to) infect with, (to) communicate (disease, ideas)
contener	(to) *contain*
—contenido (p.p.)	—content, contents
contento	contented, happy, pleased, content, contentment
—contentar	—(to) content, (to) please, (to) satisfy
—descontento	—discontented, displeased, discontent, discontentment
—descontentar	—(to) discontent, (to) displease
contexto	context
continente	continent (adj. & n.)
—continental	—continental
—incontinencia	—incontinence (medical and moral)
—incontinente	—incontinent
continuo	continuous, continual
—continuar	—(to) continue
—continuación	—continuation
—continuidad	—continuity
—sin solución de continuidad	—without break in continuity, uninterrupted
contrario (adj. & n.)	contrary, opponent
—al contrario	—on the contrary (~ *por el contrario*)
—contrariedad	—contrariety, vexation, setback
—contrariar	—(to) oppose, (to) vex, (to) annoy
—contra	—against, opposite, contra, con
—contra-	—*counter-* (counterattack, counteroffensive, etc.)
—contradanza [22]	—*country-dance, contra dance, contredanse*

---

[22] It all began with English *country-dance,* which was exported in the seventeenth century to France, initially as *contrée* ("*country*") *danse,* then becoming *contre-danse* ("*counter* dance"). This was then reexported to become Spanish *contradanza* and English *contredanse* (as well as *contra dance* and *contredance*). While these different forms arose by "mistake", they are nonetheless etymologically related: a *country* is literally the region lying *counter* (opposite) to one's position.

control	control, checkpoint	
—controlar	—(to) control, (to) check, (to) monitor	
conveniente	convenient, suitable	
—conveniencia	—convenience, suitability	
—inconveniente (adj. & n.)	—inconvenient, unsuitable, inconvenience (drawback)	
—inconveniencia	—inconvenience (trouble, discomfort), unsuitability	
—convenir	—(to) agree, (to) be *convenient* or suitable	[*convene*]
—convención	—convention, agreement	
—convencional	—conventional	
—convenio	—*covenant*, agreement, pact	
—convento	—convent	[*Covent* Garden]
—venir	—(to) come	
—venida	—coming (n.), coming back	[*venue*]
—venidero	—coming (adj.), "to come" (e.g., the world *to come*)	
—avenida	—*avenue*	
—bienvenida (n.)	—welcome	
—bienvenido (adj.)	—welcome	
—sobrevenir	—(to) *supervene* (occur unexpectedly; ensue)	
convergencia	convergence (objects, opinions)	
—convergente	—convergent, converging	
—converger, convergir	—(to) converge	
convocar	(to) *convoke*, (to) summon, (to) convene	
—convocatoria	—summons, letter of *convocation*	
copia	copy	
—copiar	—(to) copy	
—copioso	—copious, abundant	(lit. "having many *copies*")
—acopiar	—(to) gather, (to) store, (to) stock	
—acopio	—stock, supply	
copla	short poem for singing, verse, *couplet*	
—cópula	—copulation, copula	[*couple*]
—copular	—(to) copulate	
—acoplar	—(to) couple, (to) connect	
—acoplamiento	—coupling, connection	
coqueto, coqueta	vain, *coquettish*, flirt (m./f.), *coquette* (f.)	["little *cock*"]
—coquetería	—coquetry, flirtatiousness	
—coquetear	—(to) flirt, (to) *coquet*	
corona	*crown*, corona, *krone* (currency)	
—coronar	—(to) *crown*	
—coronación	—coronation	

—coronario	—coronary	
corral	farmyard, barnyard, *corral* (< Sp.)	
—acorralar	—(to) *corral,* (to) corner (thief, opponent)	
correcto	correct (incl. "proper", e.g., behavior)	(old p.p.)
—incorrecto	—incorrect, improper (conduct, act, etc.)	
—corrector	—corrector, proofreader	
—correctivo (adj. & n.)	—corrective, correction (punishment)	
—corrección	—correction (rectification), correctness	
—incorrección	—incorrectness, mistake, discourtesy	
—corregir	—(to) correct	
—corregible	—corrigible	
—incorregible	—incorrigible	
—corregidor	—Spanish royal magistrate (of town or region)	[*Corregidor*]
correspondiente	corresponding	
—corresponder	—(to) correspond, (to) belong, (to) reciprocate	
—correspondencia	—correspondence, connection (air, rail)	
—corresponsal	—*correspondent* (journalist)	
cortesía	*courtesy,* politeness	[*curtsey*]
—cortés	—*courteous,* polite	
—corte (f.)	—*court* (royal, law)	
—Las Cortes	—Spanish Parliament	
—descortés	—*discourteous,* impolite	
—descortesía	—*discourtesy*	
cosmopolita (adj. & n.m./f.)	cosmopolitan, cosmopolite	
cota (1)	*coat* of arms, *coat* of mail	
cota (2)	height above sea level	[*quota*]
—acotar (1)	—(to) mark elevations on a map, (to) annotate (text)	
—acotación	—marginal note, stage direction, elevation mark (on map)	
—cotejar	—(to) compare (e.g., fingerprints)	
—cotizar (< Fr.)	—(to) pay or collect dues, (to) *quote* (a price)	
—cotización	—dues, membership fees, *quotation* (price)	
—cuota	—fees, dues, share (e.g., of market)	[*quota*]
coto	reserve (e.g., hunting), preserve, boundary	[*caution*]
—acotar (2)	—(to) delimit, (to) set limits on	
cráter	crater	
creación	creation	
—crear	—(to) create	
—creador	—creator, Creator (cap.)	
—creativo	—creative	
—creatividad	—creativity	

—criar	—(to) raise, (to) rear, (to) breed
—criado (p.p.)	—servant, valet
—criada	—maid, female servant
—cría	—animal rearing, newborn animal, litter, brood
—criadero	—breeding place, nursery
—criador	—breeder, raiser, *Creator* (cap.), winegrower
—crianza	—breeding, raising, upbringing, aging (wine)
—criatura	—*creature* (being created by God), baby, infant
—criollo	—*Creole* (person), creole (language)
—procrear	—(to) procreate
—procreación	—procreation
crédito	credit (moral, financial, etc.)
—descrédito	—discredit
—desacreditar	—(to) discredit
—acreditar	—(to) *accredit*, (to) bring fame or credit
crepúsculo	crepuscule (twilight)
cresta	*crest*, comb (of a bird)
criminal	criminal
—crimen	—*crime*, felony
—criminalidad	—criminality
—incriminar	—(to) incriminate
criterio	criterion, point of view, discernment
criticar	(to) criticize, (to) critique
—crítico	—critical (multiple senses), critic (m.)
—crítica	—critique, criticism, critic (f.)
—criticismo	—[philosophical system, esp. of Kant ≠ Eng. *criticism* !]
croata	Croatian, Croat, Croatian language (m.)
—corbata[23]	—*cravat*, tie
Cuba	Cuba
—cubalibre[24] ~ cubata	—popular drink (mixture of cola and rum with lemon)
culpable (adj. & n.)	guilty, culpable, culprit
—culpa	—guilt, blame, fault
—mea culpa	—mea culpa (lit. "through my fault", i.e., the fault is mine)

---

[23] *Croatian* mercenaries in the employ of Louis XIII of France in the early seventeenth century were known for the linen scarves they wore—decorated with lace and wrapped twice around the neck. At that stage, the French word for "Croat" was *cravate*. The modern *cravat* (tie) emerged gradually, taking its current form only in the early twentieth century.

[24] The origin of *cubalibre* ("Free Cuba") goes back to the time of the Cuban War of Independence (1895–1898). There are various, perhaps somewhat romanticized, legends about how the mixture arose. Somewhat less romantically, the first English-language reference (*Harper's Weekly*, August 1898) refers to a concoction of "water and brown sugar".

—culpar	—(to) blame, (to) accuse
—culpabilidad	—culpability
—disculpa	—apology, excuse
—disculpar	—(to) excuse, (to) apologize
—exculpar	—(to) exculpate, (to) exonerate
—inculpar	—(to) accuse, (to) charge (with crime), (to) *inculpate*
cultivar	(to) cultivate
—cultivable	—cultivable
—cultivo	—cultivation, farming, culture (biol.)
cultural	cultural
—cultura	—culture
—culto (adj. & n.)	—cultured, learned, cult, worship, cultus
cupón	*coupon*
—cupo	—quota (e.g., import) (unrelated: < *caber*[25])
curiosidad	curiosity (desire to know; object of curiosity)
—curioso	—curious (having curiosity; on the rare side)
—curiosear	—(to) snoop, (to) pry, (to) browse (in a shop)
curso	*course* (school, river, of events)
—cursillo	—short course
—cursor	—cursor
—(letra) cursiva	—italics (~ *itálica*)
curva (n.)	curve, bend
—curvo (adj.)	—curved
—curvatura	—curvature
—curvar	—(to) curve, (to) bend
—encorvar	—(to) bend, (to) curve
custodia	custody, safekeeping
—custodiar	—(to) watch over, (to) guard
daga	*dagger*
danzar	(to) dance (~ *bailar*)
—danza	—dancing, dance
dar	(to) give
—dar a conocer	—(to) make known
—dado (p.p.)	—*die* (one of two *dice*)
—dato	—*datum*, fact, *data* (pl.)
—posdata (P.D.)	—postscript (PS) (also *postdata*)

---

[25] *Cupo* is the past tense (third person singular). The notion of "quota" arose from a now archaic definition of *caber*—"to be received as one's lot or share"; from its use in expressions like *lo que* **cupo** *a cada uno* ("that which *is received* by each one"), *cupo* transformed itself into a noun with the sense of "quota".

—datar	—(to) *date,* (to) date from	
—dativo	—dative (indirect object)	
—dá**d**iva	—gift, grant	
—dadivoso	—generous	
debate	debate	
—debatir	—(to) debate, (to) discuss, (to) struggle	
debilidad	debility, weakness	
—débil	—weak, feeble	
—debilitar	—(to) debilitate, (to) weaken	
—endeble	—feeble, frail	
decano, decana	*dean, doyen, doyenne* (f.)	(DECANUS = chief of ten)
decencia	decency	
—decente	—decent	
—indecencia	—indecency	
—indecente	—indecent	
decepción	disappointment, disillusionment, *deception*	
—decepcionar	—(to) disappoint, (to) disillusion	
decisivo	decisive	
—indeciso	—indecisive, undecided	
decomisar	(to) confiscate, (to) seize	[*decommission*]
—decomiso	—confiscation, seizure (~ *comiso*)	
decoración	decoration, decor	
—decorar	—(to) decorate, (to) adorn	
—decorativo	—decorative	
—decorador	—(interior) decorator	
—decoro	—*decorum, dignity*	
—decoroso	—decorous, dignified	
—indecoroso	—indecorous, unbecoming, undignified	
deducción	deduction (logical; subtraction)	
—deducir	—(to) *deduce,* (to) infer, (to) *deduct*	
—deducible	—deducible, deductible	
—deductivo	—deductive	
defecto	defect	
—defectuoso	—defective	
—defectivo	—defective (rare, apart from *defective* verb)	
—defección	—defection	
deferencia	deference, courtesy	
deficiencia	deficiency	
—deficiente	—deficient	
—déficit	—deficit, shortage	
—deficitario	—with a deficit, in deficit	
delirio	delirium	

—delirios de grandeza[26]	—delusions of grandeur	
—delirar	—(to) be delirious, (to) rave	
denotar	(to) denote, (to) indicate	
denunciar	(to) denounce (incl. "inform against, accuse")	
—denuncia	—denunciation, formal complaint	
depender	(to) depend	
—dependencia	—dependency, dependence	
—dependiente	—dependent, salesclerk (m./f.)	(also *dependienta*—f.)
—independiente	—independent	
—independencia	—independence	
deportar	(to) deport (~ *desterrar*)	
—deporte	—*sport*	(sport < disport)
—deportista	—sportsman, sportswoman	
—deportivo	—sporting, sport (adj.), sportive	
—(coche) deportivo	—sports car	
depósito	deposit, warehouse, tank (water, gasoline, etc.)	
—depósito de cadáveres	—morgue (~ *morgue*)	
—depositar	—(to) deposit	
depredación	depredation, plundering	
—depredar	—(to) *depredate* (plunder)	
—depredador (adj. & n.)	—*predatory, predator*	
derivación[27]	derivation, bypass (electrical, medical), shunt	
—derivar	—(to) derive, (to) shunt or divert (waters, boat, conversation)	
—deriva	—drift, drifting (of a boat)	
—(ir) a la deriva	—(to) drift (boats or people), (to) be adrift	
—deriva continental	—continental drift	
—derivativo	—derivative (rare: gen. only linguistics)	
—derivada	—derivative (math.)	
—derivado (p.p.)	—derivative (esp. chem., financial)	
desastre	disaster	
—desastroso	—disastrous	
descartar	(to) *discard* (reject; remove playing *card*), (to) rule out	

---

[26] According to both *DRAE* and Moliner, it is *delirio de grandezas* (lit. "delusion of grandeurs"), but this is rarely found.

[27] Latin DERIVARE was formed from DE ("from") and RIVUS ("small stream") and initially meant "to draw off or divert water".

descripción	description
—describir	—(to) describe (incl. "describe a circle with a compass")
—descriptivo	—descriptive
descender	(to) descend
—descendente	—descendent (*or* descendant), descending
—descendiente (m./f.)	—descendant (offspring)
—descendencia	—descendants, lineage
—descenso	—descent, fall (temperature, prices)
—ascender	—(to) ascend, (to) rise, (to) promote
—ascendente	—ascending, ascendant (adj.), ascendant (astrology)
—ascendiente	—ascending, ancestor (m./f.), ascendancy (m.)
—ascendencia	—ancestry, origin, *ascendancy*
—ascenso	—ascent, rise, promotion
—ascensión	—ascent, ascension, Ascension (cap.), accession (to throne, power)
—ascensor	—elevator
—condescender	—(to) accede or yield (out of kindness) [*condescend*]
—condescendiente	—agreeable, obliging [*condescending*]
desequilibrio	disequilibrium, imbalance
—desequilibrar	—(to) disequilibrate, (to) throw off balance
desesperación	*desperation, despair,* hopelessness
—desesperar	—(to) *despair,* (to) exasperate
—desesperado (p.p.)	—*desperate,* hopeless, desperate person (m./f.) [*desperado*]
—desesperanza	—*despair*
—esperar	—(to) hope, (to) hope for, (to) expect, (to) wait for
—inesperado	—unexpected
—esperanza	—hope, hopefulness
—espera	—wait, waiting
—lista de espera	—waiting list
—sala de espera	—waiting room
—esperanto	—Esperanto
desmayar	(to) faint, (to) lose heart, (to) *dismay*
—desmayo	—fainting, fainting spell, discouragement, *dismay*
desodorante	deodorant
—inodoro (adj. & n.)	—*inodorous,* odorless, toilet (!)
—olor[28]	—*odor*

---

[28] *L* was a dialectical variant for Latin *D*, so that in Roman times both ODOR and OLOR existed.

—oloroso	—*odorous,* fragrant	
—olfato	—sense of smell	
—olfatorio	—olfactory	
—olfatear	—(to) smell, (to) sniff, (to) scent	
despilfarrar	(to) squander, (to) waste	[*pilfer*]
—despilfarro	—waste, squandering	
desplazar	(to) *displace*	
—desplazamiento	—*displacement*	
despreciar	(to) *disprize* (archaic: disdain, scorn)	[*depreciate*]
—desprecio	—disdain, contempt	
—menospreciar	—(to) underestimate, (to) underrate, (to) scorn	[*minus + praise*]
—menosprecio	—undervaluation, scorn, contempt	
destacar	(to) emphasize, (to) stand out, (to) *detach* (mil.)	
—destacado (p.p.)	—outstanding, distinguished	
—destacamento	—*detachment* (mil.)	
destilar	(to) *distill* (incl. "drip")	
destino	destiny, destination (esp. place)	
—destinación	—destination (esp. purpose for which something is destined)	
—destinar	—(to) destine (incl. "assign for a specific use or purpose")	
—destinatario	—addressee, consignee	
destrucción	destruction	
—destruir	—(to) *destroy*	
—destructivo	—destructive	
—destructor	—destructive, destroyer (m./f.), naval destroyer (m.)	
—indestructible	—indestructible	
—destrozar [29]	—(to) destroy, (to) shatter	
—destrozo	—destruction, havoc	
—trozo	—piece, chunk, fragment	
desviación	deviation, detour (~ *desvío*)	(des + vía)
—desviar	—(to) deviate, (to) divert	
—extraviar	—(to) lead astray, (to) mislay	(extra + vía)
—extraviado (p.p.)	—lost, missing, out-of-the-way	(lit. "beyond the road")
—extravío	—going astray, loss (passport, etc.)	
detalle	*detail,* detailed account, gesture (courtesy)	

---

[29] The origins of *destrozar* and *trozo* are disputed: according to one theory, *destrozar* is another form of *destruir,* in which case *trozo* would be what was left afterward; according to another, *trozo* is an independent word (coming from Catalan), and *destrozar* was formed to represent the action of "breaking into *trozos* (pieces)".

—al detalle	—in detail (~ *en detalle*), retail (~ *al por menor*)	
—detallar	—(to) detail	
—detallista	—"specialist in details" (painter, etc.), retailer	
detener	(to) *detain,* (to) stop, (to) arrest	
—detención	—detention, arrest, thoroughness	
—detenimiento	—care, thoroughness	
—detenido (p.p.)	—careful, minute, *detainee* (prisoner)	
detergente (adj. & n.)	detergent	[*detersive*]
—terso	—smooth, clear, *terse* (style)	(lit. "cleansed")
deteriorar	(to) deteriorate	
—deterioro	—deterioration	
detrimento	detriment	
diagonal (adj. & n.f.)	diagonal	
diamante [30]	diamond	[*adamant*]
—diamantino ~ adamantino	—adamantine, diamond-like or -hard	
—imán (1)	—magnet, lodestone	
—imán (2)	—imam	(unrelated)
dialecto	dialect	
diatriba	diatribe	
dictador	dictator	
—dictadura	—dictatorship	
—dictatorial	—dictatorial	
—dictar	—(to) dictate (various senses)	
—dictamen	—ruling, (expert's) report, *dictum*	
diferencia	difference	
—diferenciar	—(to) differentiate, (to) distinguish between	
—diferente	—different	
—diferencial (adj. & n.)	—differential	
—diferir	—(to) *defer* (put off, postpone), (to) *differ*	
dignidad	dignity (worthy of respect; high office or rank)	
—dignatario	—dignitary	
—digno	—worthy, deserving, dignified	
—dignar(se)	—(to) *deign,* (to) condescend	
dilapidar	(to) squander	[*dilapidate* = obs. def.]

---

[30] *Diamond* and *adamant* (a hard stone, hence "stubbornness") were initially identical, as both come from Latin ADAMANTEM ("the hardest metal"), itself from Greek. In medieval times this was "rearranged" as DIAMANTEM, probably due to influence from the Greek prefix *dia-* of *diaphanous* and *diadem.* DIAMANTEM gave rise to both *diamante* and *diamond;* the "original" ADAMANTEM became English *adamant* and French *aimant,* the latter in turn the source of Spanish *imán* (1). *Imán* (2) comes from Arabic; the spelling *imam* can also be used, with no difference in pronunciation.

—dilapidación	—squandering	[*dilapidation* = obs. def.]
dilatar (1)	(to) *dilate*, (to) expand, (to) prolong	
—dilatado (p.p.)	—extensive, vast	
—dilatación	—dilatation, dilation	
dilatar (2)	(to) delay, (to) *defer* [31]	
—dilatorio	—*dilatory*, delaying	
—dilación	—delay	
—sin dilación	—without delay, immediately	
diligente	diligent	
—diligencia	—diligence (efficiency, stagecoach), administrative task/procedure	
diluir	(to) *dilute*, (to) dissolve	
—diluvio	—*deluge* (heavy downpour, flood)	
—antediluviano	—antediluvian (occurring before the Flood, old and antiquated)	
dinámico (adj.)	dynamic	
—dinámica (n.)	—dynamics	
—dinamismo	—dynamism	
dinamita	dynamite	
—dinamitar	—(to) dynamite	
dinero	money, currency	[*dinar, denier*]
—adinerado	—wealthy	
—denario	—denarius (Roman coin)	
dinosaurio	dinosaur	
diputado	*deputy*, representative, delegate	
—diputación	—deputation, provincial assembly	
dique (< Dutch)	*dike*	
—dique (seco)	—dry dock	
dirección	direction, address, management	
—director	—director, manager, conductor (music)	
—directriz	—directive, guidelines (pl.), *directrix* (geom.)	
—directiva	—directive, board of directors	
—directivo	—directive (adj.), director (member of board—m./f.)	
—directo	—direct, straight (~ *derecho*)	
—dirigir	—(to) direct, (to) manage	
—dirigente (m./f.)	—leader	
—dirigible	—dirigible	
discernir	(to) *discern*, (to) distinguish	

[31] *Defer* (in the sense of "postpone") comes from Latin DIFFERRE, whose irregular past participle DILATUS produced Spanish *dilatar* (2) and English *dilatory*. *Dilatar* (1) and English *dilate* are related to *latitude* (originally "width").

disco	*disk* (incl. phonograph record), *discus*
—disco compacto	—compact disk
—disco duro	—hard disk (computer)
—discoteca	—*discotheque,* record holder (furniture), record collection
discreción	discretion (being discreet), prudence
—a (su) discreción	—at (one's) discretion
—discrecional	—discretionary
—discreto	—*discreet, discrete*
—indiscreción	—indiscretion
—indiscreto	—indiscreet
discrepancia	discrepancy
—discrepar	—(to) differ, (to) disagree
—discrepante	—discrepant
disertar	(to) dissertate (discourse formally), (to) expound (upon)
—disertación	—exposition, discourse, *dissertation*
disimular	(to) hide, (to) *dissimulate,* (to) *dissemble*
—disimulo	—dissimulation, slyness
—simulacro	—simulation (fire drill, mock battle, etc.), *simulacrum*
disolver	(to) dissolve
—disolución	—dissolution, solution (in solvent)
—disoluto	—dissolute
—disolvente	—dissolvent, solvent
disparar[32]	(to) shoot, (to) fire, (to) discharge
—disparo	—shot
disparidad	disparity
—dispar	—unlike, unequal, disparate (i.e., not of a *pair*)
—disparatado	—absurd, preposterous (not directly related)
—disparate	—absurdity, nonsense, blunder
dispensar	(to) dispense (incl. "exempt")
—dispensa	—dispensation
—dispensario	—dispensary, clinic
—dispendio	—waste, wasteful expenditure
—indispensable	—indispensable
disputar	(to) dispute (incl. "contend or compete for")
—disputa	—dispute
—disputado (p.p.)	—hard-fought, close (decided by narrow margin)
disturbio	disturbance

---

[32] In the old days, users of crossbows and other such devices first had to "charge" (*preparar*) their weapons—a rather long process—before they were able to "discharge" (*disparar*) them.

—disturbar	(to) disturb
—estorbar	(to) hinder, (to) obstruct
—estorbo	hindrance, nuisance
divergir	(to) diverge (objects, opinions)
—divergente	—divergent
—divergencia	—divergence
dividendo	dividend
doctor	doctor (academic or medical)
—doctorar	—(to) confer (or obtain) doctorate
—doctorado (p.p.)	—doctorate
—doctoral	—doctoral
—[adulterar, amañar]	—(to) doctor (falsify)
—docto	—learned, well-educated
—docente (adj. & n.m./f.)	—educational, teaching, educator
doctrina	doctrine
dólar	dollar
domicilio	domicile (home, legal residence)
—domicilio social	—head office, corporate headquarters
—domiciliar	—(to) domicile, (to) take up residence, (to) pay by direct debit
dossier	dossier, file (< Fr.)
dramatización	dramatization
—dramatizar	—(to) dramatize
—dramaturgo	—dramaturge (playwright), dramatist
droga	*drug*
—drogar	—(to) drug
—drogadicción	—drug addiction
—drogadicto	—drug addict
—droguería	—drug store, pharmacy
duda	*doubt*
—poner en duda	—(to) put in doubt, (to) question
—sin duda	—no doubt *or* doubtless: "probably"
—sin duda alguna, sin ninguna duda	—no doubt *or* doubtless: "unquestionably"
—dudar	—(to) doubt
—dudoso	—*dubious,* doubtful
—indudable	—indubitable, undoubted
—indudablemente	—indubitably, undoubtedly
duna	dune
duque	duke
—duquesa	—duchess

—ducado	—duchy, dukedom, ducat
ébano	*ebony* (tree, wood)
—ebanista	—cabinetmaker
eclipse	eclipse
—eclipsar	—(to) eclipse
economía	economy, economics, savings (pl.)
—económico	—economic, economical, cheap, thrifty
—economista	—economist
—economizar	—(to) economize, (to) save
—econometría	—econometrics
ecuador, Ecuador	*equator*, Ecuador
—ecuatorial	—equatorial
editor	publisher, editor (esp. computer program)
—editar	—(to) publish, (to) edit (esp. on computer)
—editorial	—publishing house (f.), editorial (m.)
—edición	—publication, edition
edredón	duvet, *eiderdown*
efecto	effect
—efectivo	—effective, cash, effectives (troops—pl.)
—efectuar	—(to) effect, (to) effectuate
eficiente	efficient
—eficiencia	—efficiency
—eficacia	—efficacy, effectiveness
—eficaz	—efficacious, effective
efigie	effigy
ego	ego
—egocéntrico	—egocentric
—egoísta (adj. & n.)	—selfish, egoistic, egoist
—egoísmo	—egoism, selfishness
elaborar	(to) *elaborate* (incl. "create or produce")
—elaborado (p.p.)	—*elaborate,* manufactured
—elaboración	—*elaboration,* preparation, manufacture
electricidad	electricity
—eléctrico	—electric, electrical
—electrificar	—(to) electrify (provide with electric power)
—electrizar	—(to) electrify (charge with electricity; excite or enthuse)
—electrizante	—electrifying
—electricista	—electrician
—electrocardio-grama (m.)	—electrocardiogram
—electrocutar	—(to) electrocute
—electrodo	—electrode
—electrón	—electron

—electrónica (n.)	—electronics
—electrónico (adj.)	—electronic
elegante	elegant
—elegancia	—elegance
elegía	*elegy* (melancholic/sorrowful poem or music)
—elogio	—praise, *eulogy*[33] [rare *eloge*]
—elogiar	—(to) praise, (to) *eulogize*
elemento	element, component, rudiments of a subject (pl.)
—elemental	—elemental, elementary
elipse (f.)	ellipse
—elíptico	—elliptic or elliptical (of an ellipse, manner of speaking)
—elipsis	—ellipsis (omission of words, " ... ")
elocuente	eloquent
—elocuencia	—eloquence
eludir	(to) avoid, (to) evade, (to) *elude*
—ineludible	—unavoidable, inescapable
emanar	(to) emanate
—manar	—(to) spring or flow (from)
—manantial	—spring, source
embarcación	boat, ship, vessel, *embarkation*, voyage
—embarcar	—(to) embark (on boat, train, plane, venture), (to) load
—embarcadero	—pier, wharf (~ *muelle*), *embarcadero*
—embarque ~ embarco	—embarkation, loading
—desembarcar	—(to) disembark, (to) unload, (to) *debark*
—desembarque ~ -barco	—disembarkation, unloading, *debarkation*
—barco	—boat, ship, vessel [*bark (barque)*]
—barca	—small boat, launch [*barge*]
embargo	embargo (< Sp.), seizure, attachment (legal)
—embargar	—(to) seize or block (goods, movement, activity)
—sin embargo	—nevertheless (~ *no obstante*)
embrollo	*imbroglio,* muddle
—embrollar	—(to) muddle, (to) confuse, (to) *embroil*
emergencia	*emergence, emergency*
—emerger	—(to) emerge
—emergente	—emergent, emerging

[33] Latin ELOGIUM ("inscription on a tombstone") was formed in Roman times as a mixture of Greek *elegeia* ("elegy") with the Latin verb ELOQUI ("to speak out", as in *eloquent*). In post-Roman times, ELOGIUM seems to have become confused with Greek *eulogia* ("praise", lit. "fine words"): ELOGIUM and EULOGIUM were both used in the sense of "praise for the dead", i.e., *eulogy*. Spanish *elogio* (and English *eloge*) comes from ELOGIUM, English *eulogy* from EULOGIUM.

eminente	eminent	
—eminencia	—eminence	
—Su Eminencia	—His/Your Eminence (title & form of address for cardinal)	
emoción	emotion	
—emocional	—emotional (esp. "of the emotions"—e.g., *estado emocional*)	
—emotivo	—emotional, emotive	
—emocionante	—moving, touching, thrilling	
—emocionar	—(to) move, (to) touch, (to) thrill	
empírico	empirical	
emplasto	*plaster* (med.), poultice, unsatisfactory solution	
—aplastar [34]	—(to) flatten, (to) crush	
—aplastante	—crushing, overwhelming (e.g., victory)	
emplazar [35]	(to) *emplace,* (to) locate	
—emplazamiento	—emplacement, location	
emplear	(to) *employ*	
—empleado (p.p.)	—employee	
—empleo	—employ, employment	
—desempleado	—unemployed	
—desempleo	—unemployment	
empresa	company, *enterprise*	[*emprise*]
—emprender	—(to) undertake, (to) embark on	
—**empresario**	—*entrepreneur, impresario*	
emular	(to) emulate	
enclave	enclave	
—enclavar [36]	—(to) locate or site (lit. "to become an *enclave*")	
—clavar	—(to) nail, (to) drive in, (to) rivet or fix (eyes, etc.)	
—clavado (p.p.)	—stuck fast, "on the dot", "spitting image"	
—clavo [37]	—nail, *clove* (spice)	
—dar en el clavo	—(to) hit the nail on the head	
—clavel	—carnation	
—clave (f.)	—key (to puzzle, decisive element), *clef*	

---

[34] Of uncertain origin; possibly it arose in an analogous manner to the informal sense of English *plaster:* "to inflict heavy damage or injury on".

[35] An unrelated *emplazar* means "to summon" (see Annex B).

[36] Latin CLAVIS ("key") and CLAVUS ("nail") shared a common root—both referring to a way to make something secure. In derived words, there are often elements of both, i.e., an *enclave* can be something that is either "locked away" or "nailed down".

[37] Spanish *clavo* and English *clove* owe their names to the nail- or spike-like form of the flower from which they are extracted. Spanish *clavel* takes its name from its *clove*-like smell. The identical process has occurred in German, where *Nelke* (cognate with English *nail*) means both "clove" and "carnation".

—llave (f.)	—key (for door), faucet	
enfermo (adj. & n.)	sick, ill, sick person	[*infirm*]
—enfermedad	—illness, disease, sickness	[*infirmity*]
—enfermería	—*infirmary,* sickbay	
—enfermero	—nurse	
—enfermar	—(to) fall ill, (to) make ill	
—enfermizo	—sickly, unhealthy, *infirm*	
engendrar	(to) engender, (to) beget	
—engendro	—deformed offspring, freak, monstrosity	
enorme	enormous, huge	
—enormemente	—enormously	
—enormidad	—enormity	
ensayo	*essay* (composition; attempt or trial), *assay* (of metals)	
—ensayo general	—dress rehearsal	
—ensayar	—(to) rehearse, (to) *essay,* (to) *assay*	
—ensayista	—essayist	
entretener	(to) *entertain,* (to) amuse	
—entretenido (p.p.)	—entertaining, amusing	
—entretenimiento	—entertainment, pastime, amusement	
enviar	(to) send, (to) ship	(*en + vía*)
—enviado (p.p.)	—*envoy*	
—envío	—shipment, consignment	
envidia	*envy*	
—envidiar	—(to) envy	
—envidioso	—envious	[*invidious*]
épico (adj.)	epic	
—épica (n.)	—epic poetry	
—epopeya	—epic poem, epic poetry, epic (n.), *epopee*	
epidemia	epidemic (n.)	
—epidémico	—epidemic (adj.)	
—pandemia	—pandemic (epidemic over wide area)	
—pandémico	—pandemic (adj.)	
episodio	episode	
—episódico	—episodic	
equidistante	equidistant	
equilibrio	equilibrium	
—equilibrar	—(to) equilibrate, (to) balance	
equinoccio	*equinox*	
equipar	(to) *equip*	[*skipper*]
—equipaje	—baggage, luggage	[*equipage*]
—equipo	—team, *equipment*	[*ship*]
equiparar	(to) *compare,* (to) put on the same level	[*equal + -pare*]
equivalente (adj. & n.)	equivalent	

—equivalencia	—equivalency	
—equivaler	—(to) be equivalent (to)	
equívoco (adj. & n.)	*equivocal, equivocation, equivoque*	
—equivocar	—(to) mistake or confuse (e.g., date, route—often by inattention)	
—equivocación	—error, mistake	
erecto	erect	
—erección	—erection	
—eri**g**ir	—(to) *erect* (build; establish; obs. "elevate in status")	
—erguir	—(to) *erect* (raise to an upright position)	
esconder	(to) conceal, (to) hide	[*abscond*]
—a escondidas	—secretly	
—escondite	—hiding place (~ *escondrijo*), hide-and-seek	
—recóndito	—hidden, remote, *recondite*	
esmeralda	*emerald*	
esotérico	esoteric	
espasmo	spasm	
—espasmódico	—spasmodic	
—pasmo	—chill, astonishment, lockjaw (tetanus)	
—pasmado	—astonished, dumbfounded	
estima	*esteem*, respect, dead reckoning (by sea)	
—estimar	—(to) *esteem*, (to) *estimate*	
—estimación	—estimation (opinion or judgment, favorable regard)	
—inestimable	—inestimable, invaluable	
estuario	estuary	
—estero	—tideland, swamp or marsh (Amer.)	
etcétera, etc.	et cetera, etc.	
etiqueta	label, *etiquette*	[*ticket*]
Europa	Europe	
—europeo	—European	
evento	event	
—eventual	—temporary (contract, employee), *eventual*	
—eventualidad	—eventuality, contingency	
exacto	exact	
—inexacto	—inexact	
examinar	(to) examine	
—examinador	—examiner	
—examen	—examination, exam	
excavación	excavation	
—excavar	—(to) excavate	
—excavadora	—excavator (machine), bulldozer	
—cavar	—(to) dig, (to) excavate	

—caverna	—cavern, cave
—cavernoso	—cavernous
—cavernícola	—*cavernicolous,* cave-dwelling, cave dweller, caveman (m./f.)
—cavidad	—cavity (within body; dental cavity is *caries*)
—socavar	—(to) dig under, (to) undermine (SO = < SUB)
exceder	(to) *exceed,* (to) surpass
—exceso	—excess, surplus
—excesivo	—excessive
excelente	excellent
—excelencia	—excellence, Excellency (title)
—por excelencia	—*par excellence*
excitar	(to) excite
—excitante	—exciting, excitant (adj. & n.)
—excitación	—excitation, excitement
excremento	excrement
excusar	(to) excuse, (to) excuse from (exempt)
—excusa	—excuse
—excusado (1)	—excused
—excusado (2), escusado[38]	—restroom, toilet [*absconded*]
—inexcusable	—inexcusable
exhaustivo	exhaustive, thorough
—exhausto	—exhausted
exigente (adj. & n.)	exigent, *exacting,* demanding (person)
—exigencia	—demand, requirement, *exigencies* (pl.)
—exigir	—(to) demand, (to) *exact*
—exiguo	—exiguous (scanty, meager)
exilio	exile
—exiliar / exilar	—(to) exile, (to) go into exile
—exiliado / exilado (p.p.)	—exile (person)
éxito	success, successful *issue* (final result) [*exit*]
—exitoso	—successful
exonerar[39]	(to) exonerate (free from obligation or responsibility)

---

[38] The etymologically "correct", though far rarer, form is *escusado.* The ultimate origin is Latin ABSCONDERE ("to hide"), which also produced Spanish *esconder* and English *abscond.* A *cuarto escusado* was thus a room "hidden away" where one did things *a escondidas* ("secretly").

[39] *Exonerate* literally means to remove a weight ("ex" + "onerous"), so that the initial sense in both English and Spanish was "to free from a burden". In English, the burden has become increasingly specialized in "blame"; this sense is not found, at least officially, in Spanish *exonerar.* Through "contamination" with the unrelated *honor,* in some areas (notably Chile), *exonerar* has developed the somewhat conflicting definition of "to dismiss or remove from office" (i.e., "ex" + "*honor*").

—exoneración	—exoneration (lifting of burden)	
expensas (pl.)	expenses, costs	
—a expensas de	—at the expense of	
experiencia	experience, experiment	
experimento	experiment	
—experimental	—experimental	
—experimentar	—(to) experiment, (to) test, (to) experience	
—experimentación	—experimentation	
explanada	*esplanade*	
experto (adj. & n.)	expert	
—inexperto	—inexperienced, inexpert	
—perito (adj. & n.)	—*expert,* technical school graduate (electrician, agronomist, etc.)	
—pericia	—skill, *expertise, expertness*	
exquisito	exquisite	
exterior (adj. & n.)	exterior	
—Asuntos Exteriores	—Foreign Affairs	
—externo (adj. & n.)	—external, *extern* (day pupil)	
extra	extra (additional, superior), film extra (m./f.)	
—horas extras	—overtime (~ *horas extraordinaria*s)	
extraordinario	extraordinary	
fabricar	(to) manufacture, (to) *fabricate*	[*forge*]
—fábrica	—factory	
—fabricación	—manufacture, *fabrication*	
—fabricante (m./f.)	—manufacturer	
fachada	*facade*	
factoría	factory (incl. "trading station in foreign country")	
—factor	—factor	
—factible	—*feasible*	
—factura	—invoice, *facture* (workmanship)	[*feature*]
—facturar	—(to) invoice, (to) bill	
—facturación	—invoicing, billing	
famoso	famous, renowned	
—fama	—fame, renown, reputation	
—infame	—infamous, infamous person (m./f.)	
—infamia	—infamy	
fango	mud, mire (~ *barro, lodo*)	[*fen,* Fenway Park]
farsa	*farce*	
—farsante (m./f.)	—*farceur,* faker, impostor	
fatiga	fatigue	
—fatigar	—(to) fatigue, (to) tire, (to) weary	
—infatigable	—indefatigable, tireless	

fauna	fauna	
fecundo	fecund (~ *fértil*)	
—fecundar	—(to) fecundate, (to) fertilize (egg)	
—infecundo	—infertile, barren	
feliz	happy, fortunate, *felicitous*	[*Felix*]
—infeliz	—unhappy, unfortunate, *infelicitous*	
—felicidad	—*felicity*, happiness, good fortune	
feria	*fair*, market, *feria* (eccl.)	
—día feriado	—holiday	
fértil	fertile	
—fertilidad	—fertility	
—fertilizar	—(to) fertilize (soil)	
—fertilizante	—fertilizer	
—feraz	—fertile (~ *fértil*)	[rare *feracious*]
fetiche	*fetish*	
ficha	chip (cards), token, index card	[micro*fiche*]
—ficha técnica	—technical specs/details (also for movie, TV programs)	
—fichero	—file (incl. computer), filing cabinet	
—afiche (Amer.)	—poster, placard (~ *cartel*)	
fieltro	*felt*	
fila	*file* (line of people or objects), row	
—fila india	—single file, *Indian file*	
—filamento	—filament	
—filo	—(sharp) edge (e.g., knife), dividing line	
—afilar	—(to) sharpen	
—afilado (p.p.)	—sharp	
—desfilar	—(to) *defile*[40] (march in file), (to) parade (military)	
—desfile	—parade, *defile* (marching past of troops, in files)	
—desfiladero	—*defile* (narrow mountain pass or gorge)	
filtro (1)	filter	(< Germ.)
—filtrar	—(to) filter, (to) filtrate, (to) leak (information)	
—filtración	—filtration, leak (information)	
—infiltrar	—(to) infiltrate (liquid, enemy)	
—infiltración	—infiltration	
filtro (2)	*philter* (love potion)	(< Gk. *philo-*)
final (adj. & n.)	final, end, finale, finals (competition—f.)	
—fin	—end, *finish*	
—al fin	—at last, finally	
—por fin	—finally, at last	
—a fin de que	—in order that, so that	
—al fin y al cabo	—when all is said and done	

—a fines de	—at the end of (month, century, etc.)	
—sinfín	—endless number, no end (of)	(sin + fin)
—finalista	—finalist	
—finalizar	—(to) end, (to) finish, (to) conclude	[*finalize*]
—[ultimar]	—(to) finalize, (to) finish off	
—semifinal (f.)	—semifinal(s)	
—fenecer	—(to) come to an end (life, term of office, etc.)	[*finish*]
financiar	(to) finance	
—financiación	—financing	
—financiero (adj. & n.)	—financial, financier	
—finanzas (pl.)	—finances, finance	
finito	finite	
—infinito (adj. & n.)	—infinite, infinity (math.)	
—infinidad	—infinity	
—infinitud	—infinitude	
—infinitesimal	—infinitesimal	
—infinitivo	—infinitive	
fino (adj. & n.)	*fine* (thin, acute, delicate, refined), *fino* (sherry)	
—finura ~ fineza	—*fineness*, politeness, *finesse*	
firma	*firm* (n.), company, signature	[*farm*]
—firmar	—(to) sign	
—firmante (m./f.)	—signer, signatory	
—firme	—firm (adj.)	
—firmeza	—firmness	
—firmamento	—firmament (sky or heavens)	
flamenco (1)	*Flemish*, flamenco (dance), *Fleming* (native of *Flanders*)	
flamenco (2)	*flamingo*	[< *flame* ?]
flanco	*flank*, side	
flauta	*flute*	
—flautista	—flautist, flutist	
flecha	arrow	[*fletcher*, *fléchette*, *flèche*]
—flechazo	—arrow shot (or wound), love at first sight	
flexible	flexible	
—flexibilidad	—flexibility	
—flexión	—flexion, bending, *inflection* (gram.)	
flotar	(to) *float*	

---

[40] English *defile* ("to pollute") is unrelated.

—flotador	—float	
—flota	—*fleet* (boats, airplanes, trucks, etc.)	
—flotilla	—flotilla (small fleet)	(< Sp.)
—flotante	—floating	
—a flote	—afloat (esp. "free or out of difficulty")	
fluir	(to) flow	(unrelated)
—fluido (p.p.)	—fluid (adj. & n.), fluent	
—fluido eléctrico	—electric current, power	
—fluidez	—fluidity, fluency	
—fluvial	—fluvial (of or pertaining to a river)	
—confluir	—(to) flow together, (to) converge	
—confluencia	—confluence	
flúor	fluorine, fluoride (~ *fluoruro*)	
folclore, folclor, folklor(e)	folklore	(Sp. < Eng.)
—folclórico, folk-	—folkloric	
fomentar	(to) promote, (to) foster, (to) *foment*	
—fomento	—promotion, development, *fomentation* (poultice)	
—Ministerio de Fomento	Ministry of Development, Ministry of Public Works	
forestal	forestal (pert. to forests), forestry (adj.)	
—deforestación / des-	—deforestation	
—reforestación	—reforestation	
formal	formal, serious-minded, reliable	
—formalidad	—formality, seriousness, reliability	
—formalizar	—(to) formalize	
—informal	—informal, unreliable	
—informalidad	—informality, lack of seriousness, unreliability	
formato	format	
—formatear	—(to) format	
formidable	formidable	
fórmula	formula (incl. "recipe", esp. of medicine)	
—formular	—(to) formulate	
—formulario	—form (to be filled out), formulary (book)	
forro	lining (clothes), protective cover (book)	[*fur*]
—forrar	—(to) line, (to) cover, (to) get rich [41]	[*foray*]
fortuna	fortune (luck, good luck, fate, wealth)	
—afortunado	—lucky, fortunate, happy	
—afortunadamente	—fortunately, luckily	
—desafortunado	—unlucky, unfortunate	

---

[41] Cf. English "to line (one's) pockets".

—desafortuna- damente[42]	—unfortunately (~ *desgraciadamente*)	
fósil	fossil	
—fosilizar(se)	—(to) fossilize	
—fosa	—grave, pit, cavity, fossa	
—fosa nasal	—nostril	
—fosa séptica	—septic tank	
—foso	—pit (for musicians, long jumpers, car mechanics), moat, *fosse*	
frac	full dress, tails	[*frock*]
fractura	fracture	
—fracturar	—(to) fracture	
—fragmento	—fragment	
—fragmentario	—fragmentary	
—fragmentar	—(to) fragment	
fragata	*frigate*	
frecuente	*frequent*	
—frecuentemente	—frequently	
—frecuencia	—frequency	
frugal	frugal	
—frugalidad	—frugality	
fulgurante	*fulgurant* (flashing, dazzling)	
—fulgor	—brilliance, glow, *effulgence*	
—refulgente	—refulgent, fulgent, effulgent	
fundir	(to) *fuse* (melt, coalesce), (to) *found* (cast metal)	
—fundición	—*founding* (melting, casting), *foundry, font* (printing)[43]	
—refundir	—(to) recast (metal, ideas), (to) revise or adapt	[*refund*]
funeral	funeral (n.)	
—funerario (adj.)	—funerary (pert. to a funeral or burial)	
—funeraria (n.)	—funeral parlor	
—funesto	—baneful, fatal, lamentable	[rare *funest*]
—fúnebre	—funeral (adj.), funereal	
—pompas fúnebres (pl.)	—funeral, funeral parlor	

---

[42] Despite being in widespread use, the adverb *desafortunadamente* is absent from the vast majority of dictionaries and is apparently considered to be an *anglicismo*. Why it should be more of an *anglicismo* than *afortunadamente* (which was officially "consecrated" by the RAE in 1884) is a mystery, however.

[43] In practice, in the sense of "printing *font*", *fuente* is found far more commonly than *fundición*. This apparently represents a mistranslation of English *font*, of which there are two types, with different origins—*font* (basin, e.g., for baptisms) from FONS/FONTEM and corresponding to Spanish *fuente*, and *font* (printing type) from the verb FUNDERE, corresponding to Spanish *fundir* and *fundición*.

—pompa (1)	—*pomp*	
—pomposo	—*pompous*	
—pompa (2)	—(air) bubble	(< bomba [2])
—pompa de jabón	—*soap* bubble	
—burbuja	—bubble	[*burble*]
funicular	funicular (cable railway)	
furgón	van, boxcar, freight car, fourgon	
—furgón de cola	—caboose	
—furgoneta	—van, station wagon	
fusible	fuse (electric)	
fusil	rifle, gun, *fusil*	
—fusilero	—*fusilier*	
—fusilar	—(to) execute by shooting	[*fusillade*]
fútbol	soccer, *football* (UK)	
—fútbol americano	—football	
—futbolista	—soccer player	
fútil	*futile* (esp. "trifling and frivolous")	
—futilidad	—futility (esp. "triviality")	
gafas (pl.)	spectacles, glasses	[*gaff, gaffe*]
gala	full dress, *gala* (festive occasion)	
—galán	—*gallant* (fashionable young man), leading man (actor)	
—galante	—gallant (attentive to women)	
—galantería	—gallantry (marked courtesy, esp. to a woman)	
galaxia	galaxy	
—galáctico	—galactic	
galería	gallery	
—galera	—*galley* (boat, printing)	
—galeón	—galleon (three- or four-masted sailing ship with square rig)	
galimatías	*galimatias* (nonsense, gibberish)	
galope	*gallop*	
—galopar	—(to) gallop	
—galopante	—galloping	
garrote	club, cudgel, *garrote* (method of execution)	
gas	gas	
—gaseoso (adj.)	—gaseous, gassy	
—gaseosa (n.)	—carbonated drink, soft drink	
—gasolina	—gasoline, petrol (UK)	
—gasolinera	—gas station	
gástrico	gastric	
—gastritis	—gastritis	
—gastronómico	—gastronomic	
—gastronomía	—gastronomy	

—gastrónomo	—gastronome, gourmet	
gemelo	twin (sibling), calf muscle, cuff link, binoculars (pl.)	
—torres gemelas	—twin towers	
—Géminis	—Gemini (constellation)	
—mellizo	—twin (esp. fraternal)	(*gemel-* w/out *ge-*)
general	general (adj.), general (mil.)	
—en general, por lo general	—in general, generally	
—generalidad	—generality (incl. "the greater portion or number")	
—generalidades (pl.)	—essential elements (general principles) of a subject	
—generalizar	—(to) generalize, (to) spread (i.e., become general)	
—género	—sort, kind, *genre, genus, gender* (gram.)	
—genérico	—generic	
generoso	generous	
—generosidad	—generosity	
genético	genetic	
—código genético	—genetic code	
—genética	—genetics	
—gen / gene	—gene	
genio	temperament, disposition, *genius, genie*	
—genial	—*genial* (incl. rare "displaying or marked by genius")	
genocidio	genocide	
genuino	genuine, authentic	
gerundio	(mixture of Eng. pres. part. & *gerund*, e.g., *amando*)	
gestación	gestation	
—gestar	—(to) gestate	
—gestión	—effort or step (toward a goal), management	
—gestionar	—(to) arrange or deal with (administrative matter, etc.)	
gesto	*gesture*, expression	
—gesticular	—(to) gesticulate	
—gesta	—geste (heroic exploits, frequently told in verse)	[*jest*]
gigante	*gigantic, giant*	
glaciar	glacier	
—glacial	—glacial	
global	global	

—globo	—globe (incl. sphere, planet, glass lampshade), balloon
—glóbulo	—globule, corpuscle, blood cell (red, white)
—englobar	—(to) include, (to) lump together
gloria	glory, eternal bliss, delight
—glorioso	—glorious
—glorieta	—traffic circle (freq. with small plaza in middle)
—glorificar	—(to) *glorify*
glosario	glossary
—desglosar	—(to) decompose (separate into key elements)
golf (< Eng.)	golf
—minigolf	—miniature golf
—golfista	—golfer
golfo (1)	*gulf*
—Golfo de México	—Gulf of Mexico
golfo (2), golfa	loafer, vagabond, ragamuffin, prostitute (f.) [< *dolphin* !]
gracia	grace, witticism, thanks (pl.)
—gracias a . . .	—thanks to . . .
—dar (las) gracias	—(to) thank, (to) give thanks
—desgracia	—misfortune, mishap, *disgrace*
—desgraciado (adj. & n.)	—unfortunate, unlucky, wretched person
—desgraciadamente	—unfortunately (~ *por desgracia*)
—gracioso	—funny, *gracious, graceful, gracioso* ("buffoon"—m./f.)
grada (1)	harrow [*grate* (bars)]
grado[44]	*degree* (temperature, geometric), *grade*, rank
—gradual	—gradual
—graduación	—graduation, rank (military), strength (alcohol, in %)
—graduar	—(to) regulate, (to) graduate (incl. "arrange in gradations")
—gradación	—gradation
—grada (2)	—step (of stairs), *gradin*, bleachers (pl.)
gratis	gratis (free)
—gratuito	—gratuitous (free; unwarranted)
—gratitud	—gratitude
grava	*gravel* (prob. Celtic)
grave	grave (serious, low-pitched, accent mark)
—gravedad	—gravity
—gravitación	—gravitation

---

[44] There is also a completely separate *grado* referring to "willingness" (see Annex C under *agradecer*).

—gravitar	—(to) gravitate, (to) hang over (menace, threat)	
—ingravidez	—weightlessness	
—gravar	—(to) tax	
—gravamen	—tax, burden	[*gravamen*]
gregario	gregarious, following servilely ("herd instinct")	
—grey (f.)	—flock (animals or people, esp. religious)	[biol. *grex*]
grifo[45]	faucet, *griffin*	[*hippogriff*]
grotesco	grotesque	
—gruta	—*grotto* (cave or cavern)	[*crypt*]
gruñir	(to) grunt, (to) grumble, (to) growl	(onom.)
—gruñido (p.p.)	—grunt, grumble, growl	
—gruñón	—grumpy, grouchy	
grupo	group	
—agrupar	—(to) group	
—reagrupar	—(to) regroup	
gueto / ghetto	*ghetto*	(< It.)
guitarra	guitar	
—guitarrista	—guitarist	
gusto	taste, liking, pleasure	[*gusto*]
—con (mucho) gusto	—with (great) pleasure	
—gustar	—(to) taste, (to) please	
—Me gusta tu idea.	—I like your idea.	
—degustar	—(to) sample, (to) taste, (to) *degust*	
—degustación	—sampling, tasting, *degustation*	
—disgustar	—(to) displease, (to) annoy	[*disgust*]
—disgusto	—displeasure, annoyance	
gutural	guttural	
hamaca	*hammock* (< Sp.)	
harén, harem	*harem*	
helicóptero	helicopter	
—hélice (f.)	—propeller, *helix*	
hereditario	hereditary	
—heredero, heredera	—heir, heiress, inheritor	
—heredar	—(to) *inherit*	
—herencia[46]	—inheritance, heritage, heredity	
héroe	hero	

---

[45] *Griffins* and *hippogriffs* are fabulous creatures with the head and wings of an eagle, and the body of a lion or horse, respectively. The sense of *faucet* arose from the custom of adorning fountains with the heads of such fantastic animals, through the mouths of which water emerged.

[46] *Herencia* literally means "*adhering* things"—it belongs to the family of *adherencia* and *adhesivo*—and acquired its "modern" meaning through "contamination" with the *hered-ity* words.

—heroína (1)	—heroine
—heroína (2)	—heroin [47]
—heroico	—heroic
—heroísmo	—heroism
hilaridad	hilarity
—hilarante	—hilarious
himno	hymn
—himno nacional	—national anthem
hipertensión	hypertension (high blood pressure)
—hipotensión	—hypotension (low blood pressure)
hipócrita	hypocritical, hypocrite
(adj. & n.m./f.)	
—hipocresía	—hypocrisy
historia	*history, story*
—histórico	—historical (relating to history), historic (of great import)
—historiador	—historian
—historial	—case history, record
—historieta	—comic strip, anecdote
homogéneo	homogeneous
honor	honor (integrity, high respect, glory, credit)
—palabra de honor	—word of honor
—honra	—honor (self-respect, reputation, good name)
—honras fúnebres	—funeral
—honrar	—(to) honor
—honrado (p.p.)	—honest, upright, honorable (characterized by integrity)
—ser honrado	—(to) be honest (or honorable)
—estar honrado	—(to) be honored
—honradez	—honesty, integrity
—honroso	—honorable (consistent with honor or good name), decent
—honorable	—honorable (worthy of honor), reputable
—honorario	—honorary, honorarium (professional fee—gen. pl.)
—honorífico	—honorific, honorary
—mención honorífica	—honorable mention
—pundonor	—honor, dignity, self-respect [*point* of *honor*]

---

[47] *Heroin* was the registered trademark of a potent drug launched by Bayer in Germany in 1898. German sources seem unanimous that the name was created from Greek *heros* to reflect the "heroic" nature of the drug, though some English etymological dictionaries do not accept this explanation.

—honesto	—decent, honest (esp. "upright")
—honestidad	—decency, honesty (esp. "integrity")
—deshonor	—dishonor, disgrace
—deshonra	—dishonor, disgrace, shame (esp. with respect to a woman)
—deshonrar [48]	—(to) dishonor, (to) disgrace
—deshonroso	—dishonorable, disgraceful
—deshonesto	—improper, dishonest
—deshonestidad	—dishonesty
—denostar	—(to) insult, (to) revile [† *dehonestate*]
horizontal (adj. & n.f.)	horizontal
—horizonte	—horizon
horror	horror
—horrorizar	—(to) horrify
—horroroso	—horrifying, horrid
—horrible	—horrible
—horrendo	—horrendous
humano	humane, human (adj. & n.)
—ser humano	—human being
—humanitario	—humanitarian
—humanidad	—humanity, mankind, humaneness, humanities (pl.)
—humanizar	—(to) humanize
—inhumano	—inhuman, inhumane
—inhumanidad	—inhumanity
humor	humor (mood or disposition; funniness)
—humorístico	—humorous, humoristic
—humorista	—humorist
huracán	*hurricane* (< Sp.)
idea	idea
—ideal	—ideal
—idealismo	—idealismo
—idealista (adj. & n.)	—idealistic, idealist
—idear	—(to) think up, (to) invent, (to) ideate
idiota (adj. & n.m./f.)	idiotic, idiot
—idiotez	—idiocy
ignominia	ignominy
—ignominioso	—ignominious
ignorante (adj. & n.m./f.)	ignorant, ignoramus
—ignorancia	—ignorance

---

[48] *Deshonorar* also exists but is extremely rare.

—ignorar	—(to) be ignorant of, (to) ignore
imbécil	imbecilic, imbecile
(adj. & n.m./f.)	
—imbecilidad	—imbecility
imbuir	(to) *imbue*
imitación	imitation
—imitar	—(to) imitate
—remedar	—(to) *imitate,* (to) mimic, (to) ape (< re + imitar)
—remedo	—imitation, (poor) copy
impacto	impact
—impactar	—(to) impact (strike forcefully; have an impact on[49])
imparcial	impartial, unbiased
—imparcialidad	—impartiality
impartir	(to) give (lesson, course), (to) impart
imperial	imperial
—imperialismo	—imperialism
—imperialista	—imperialist
—imperio	—*empire*
—imperioso	—imperious (incl. "urgent, pressing")
—imperar	—(to) reign, (to) hold sway
—imperativo	—imperative
—emperador	—emperor
—emper**atriz**	—empress
impermeable	impermeable, waterproof, raincoat
(adj. & n.)	
—permeable	—permeable
implacable	implacable
importante	important
—importancia	—importance
impunidad	impunity
—impune	—*unpunished*
inanición	inanition (exhaustion, gen. from starvation)
—inane	—inane
incentivo	incentive
—incentivar	—(to) incentivize (offer incentives, motivate)
incidente	incident
—incidental	—incidental
—incidencia	—incidence, incident

---

[49] This use of *impact* is frowned upon by language mavens (84% of the "Usage Panel" for the *AHCD*); nonetheless, it is common with Spanish *impactar.* Ironically, *impactar* is a relatively new word in Spanish (only since 1984 in the *DRAE*), and it is very likely that the word—along with the "incorrect" definition—was imported from English.

—incidir	—(to) fall upon (light), (to) fall into (error), (to) influence	
incinerador, -ora	incinerator	
—incinerar	—(to) incinerate, (to) cremate	
—incineración	—incineration, cremation	
—ceniza	—ash, ashes (of a fire, or mortal remains—pl.)	[*cinereous*]
—cenicero	—ashtray	
incipiente	incipient	
incremento	increment, increase	
—incrementar	—(to) increase	
inculcar	(to) inculcate	
incumbencia	incumbency (duty or obligation, *but not political*)	
—incumbir	—(to) be incumbent upon, (to) be the duty of	
indiferente	indifferent	
—indiferencia	—indifference	
indígena (adj. & n.m./f.)	indigenous, indigen	
indigente (adj. & n.m./f.)	indigent, needy	
—indigencia	—indigence	
individual	individual (adj.), single (room, bed)	
—individuo	—individual (n.)	
—individualidad	—individuality	
—individualista (adj. & n.)	—individualistic, individualist	
indolente	indolent	
indomable	untamable, *indomitable*	
—indómito	—untamed, *indomitable*	
—domar	—(to) tame, (to) subdue	[*daunt*]
—domador	—tamer (lion, horse, etc.)	
inducir	(to) induce	
—inductor	—inducer, instigator, inductor (electrical)	
—inductivo	—inductive	
—inducción	—induction	
indulgencia	indulgence	
—indulgente	—indulgent	
—indulto	—judicial pardon	[*indult*]
—indultar	—(to) pardon (judicially)	
inevitable	inevitable, unavoidable	
—evitar	—(to) avoid	[† *evite*]
inexorable	inexorable	
ínfimo	lowest or least (quantity, quality, importance)	[*inferior*]
influencia	influence	

—influir   —(to) influence, (to) exert influence on
  ~ influenciar
—influyente   —influential
—influenza ~ gripe   —influenza, *flu, grippe*
información   information
—informar   —(to) inform
—informante (m./f.)   —informant
—informativo   —informative, news program
  (adj. & n.)
—informática   —computer science, data processing,
                               informatics
—informatizar   —(to) computerize
—informe (1)   —report (generally written)   (*in-* = "into")
—informe (2)   —shapeless, *formless, unformed*   (*in-* = "not")
infringir   (to) infringe, (to) violate
—infracción   —infraction, infringement
—infractor   —transgressor, infractor
ingenio   *ingenuity* (incl. "ingenious device   [*engine*]
                               or contrivance")
—ingenio azucarero   —sugar mill (~ *ingenio de azúcar*)
—ingenioso   —ingenious
—ingeniero   —*engineer*
ingenuo, ingenua   ingenuous, naïve, ingenuous person, *ingenue*
—ingenuidad   —ingenuousness, naiveté   [*ingenuity* =
                                                                     obs. def.]

ingrediente   ingredient
—ingreso   —ingress (entrance, entry), revenue
—ingresos (pl.)   —income, revenues, receipts
—ingresar   —(to) enter, (to) pay in (deposit),
                               (to) take in (money)
inherente   inherent
injuria   insult or offense, *injury* (legal, not physical)
—injuriar   —(to) offend or insult, (to) *injure*
                               ("do an *injustice* to")
—injurioso   —insulting, offensive, *injurious*
                               (abusive, defamatory)
inocente   innocent
  (adj. & n.m./f.)
—inocentada   —practical joke
—el día de los   —"Day of the Innocents" (Dec. 28)
  Inocentes   (~ April Fools' Day)
—inocencia   —innocence
insaciable   insatiable
inscripción   inscription, registration, enrollment

—inscribir	—(to) inscribe, (to) register, (to) enroll
instrumento	instrument (music or other)
—instrumental	—instrumental
—instrumentista	—instrumentalist
insuflar	(to) *insufflate* (blow or breathe in) [*soufflé*]
—**sop**lar	—(to) blow, (to) blow out (a flame)
—soplo	—blow, breath, instant, murmur (heart)
—soplido	—breath, puff
—soplete	—blowpipe, (blow)torch
insulto	insult
—insultar	—(to) insult
intacto	intact
intelectual	intellectual
—intelectualidad	—intellectuals (group), intelligentsia, intellectuality
—intelecto	—intellect
inteligente	intelligent
—inteligencia	—intelligence
—inteligible	—intelligible
intensivo	intensive
—intenso	—intense
—intensidad	—intensity
—intensificar	—(to) intensify
intercalar	(to) *intercalate* (insert or interpose)
interceptar	(to) intercept (incl. obs. "obstruct, hinder")
—interceptación, -cepción	—interception
interior	interior (adj. & n.)
Internet (f.)	Internet
interno (adj. & n.)	internal, intern
—internar	—(to) intern (confine), (to) hospitalize
—internado (p.p.)	—boarding school, internship, internee
—internista	—internist (med.)
interpolación	interpolation
—interpolar	—(to) interpolate
—tripular[50]	—(to) man or crew (ship, aircraft)
—tripulación	—crew (ship, aircraft)
—tripulante (m./f.)	—crew member
—no tripulado	—unmanned (aircraft, spaceship) (~ *sin tripulación*)

---

[50] The evolution was INTERPOLARE → *intrepolar* → *entripular* → *tripular*. The application to crews arose from the recruiting and placement (*interpolation*) of new seamen among the old hands (veterans).

interviú (f.) (< Eng.)	interview (journalistic)	
—entrevista	—*interview* (journalistic or job), meeting	
—entrevistar	—(to) interview, (to) have a meeting (with determined agenda)	
—entrever	—(to) glimpse, (to) catch sight of, (to) surmise	
intimar	(to) intimate, (to) become intimate	
—íntimo	—intimate	
—íntimamente	—intimately	
—intimidad	—intimacy, private life	[† *intimity*]
intransigente	intransigent, uncompromising	
—transigir	—(to) compromise, (to) make concessions	[*transact*]
intrépido	intrepid	
—intrepidez	—*intrepidity* (fearlessness, courage)	
intriga	*intrigue,* plot (real or theatrical), intense curiosity	
—intrigar	—(to) intrigue (plot or scheme; arouse curiosity)	
—intrigante (adj. & n.m./f.)	—intriguing, intriguer	
intrín**se**co	*intrinsic*	
—extrín**se**co	—*extrinsic*	
introvertido	introverted, introvert (m./f.)	
—extrovertido, extr**a**-[51]	—extroverted, extrovert (m./f.)	
inventor	inventor	
—invento ~ invención	—invention	
—inventar	—(to) invent	
—inventivo (adj.)	—inventive	
—inventiva (n.)	—inventiveness, creativity	
—invent**a**rio	—*inventory*	
investir	(to) *invest* (with authority), (to) *vest*	
—investidura	—investiture (ceremonial installation in office)	
—embestir	—(to) assail, (to) attack, (to) charge	[*invest* = besiege]
ira	ire	
—iracundo ~ irascible	—irascible	
ironía	irony, sarcasm	
—irónico	—ironic, ironical, sarcastic	
—ironizar	—(to) ironize (use irony)	
irrigar	(to) irrigate (incl. medical)	

[51] In both Spanish and English, the original *extr**a**-* has largely been replaced by *extr**o**-* due to the influence of *intr**o**vertido—intr**o**vert.*

—irrigación	—irrigation (land, colon)	
—regar	—(to) water (plants), (to) hose down, (to) *irrigate*	
—riego	—watering, *irrigation*	
—regadío (adj. & n.)	—irrigable (land), irrigation	
—regadera	—watering can, shower (Amer.)	
irrupción	irruption (bursting in, invasion)	
—irrumpir	—(to) *irrupt* (burst or break in)	
itinerario	itinerary (route)	
—itinerante (adj.)	—itinerant	
jerarquía	*hierarchy*	
—jerárquico	—hierarchical	
—jerarca (m./f.)	—hierarch	
jerga	*jargon,* slang	
jersey (< Eng.)	jersey, sweater	
jubilación	retirement, pension	[*jubilation*!]
—jubilar	—(to) retire, (to) pension off	
—jubilado (p.p.)	—retired, retiree, pensioner	
—júbilo	—jubilation, joy	
jubileo	jubilee	
judicial	judicial	
—judicatura	—judicature, judiciary	
—juez, jueza	—*judge*	
—juzgar	—(to) *judge*	
—juzgado (p.p.)	—court, tribunal, *jurisdiction* (territory)	[*hoosegow*[52]]
—juicio	—trial (legal), judgment (good sense)	
—juicio de Dios	—trial by ordeal	
—juicioso	—*judicious*	
—enjuiciar	—(to) judge, (to) institute legal proceedings against	
junta (n.)	meeting, assembly, *joint,* seam	
—junta directiva	—board of directors	
—junta militar	—(military) *junta*	
—juntar	—(to) *join,* (to) unite	
—junto (adj.)	—joined, close, together (i.e., *jointly*)	(old p.p.)
—juntura	—*juncture, junction,* joint	
—ayuntamiento	—municipal government, city hall, intercourse	
jurar	(to) swear (a legal oath or profanely)	
—jurado (p.p.)	—*jury, juror*	
—jura (de bandera)	—oath (of allegiance)	
—juramento	—oath, swearword	
—bajo juramento	—under oath	

---

[52] U.S. *hoosegow* ("jail") comes from the local Spanish pronunciation of *juzgado* as **juzgao* (see Section 3.4 on the disappearance of interior *d* in many regions).

—jurisdicción	—jurisdiction
—jurisprudencia	—jurisprudence, case law
—jurídico	—juridical
—persona jurídica	—*juridical person,* legal person (corporation, etc.)
justo	just, fair
—justicia	—justice
—justificar	—(to) justify
—justificante (adj. & n.)	—justifying, written proof (receipt, etc.)
—justificable	—justifiable
—justificación	—justification
—injusto	—unjust, unfair
—injusticia	—injustice
—injustificable	—unjustifiable
labor (f.)	labor, needlework (gen. pl.)
—laborioso	—laborious (requiring much labor; hard-working)
—laboratorio	—laboratory
—laborable	—working (day), arable
—laboral	—labor (adj.), work (adj.)
—laborar	—(to) work, (to) *labor*
—labrar	—(to) work (land, wood, stone)
—labrador	—farmer, peasant, *Labrador* (retriever)
—labranza	—tillage, farming
lacayo	*lackey* (footman, servile follower)
laminar	laminar (adj); (to) laminate
—lámina	—lamina (sheet, thin plate, layer), print (engraving)
lámpara	*lamp*
—relámpago	—lightning (flash)
lamprea	lamprey
lanzar	(to) hurl, (to) throw, (to) *launch*
—lanza	—*lance,* spear
—lanzamiento	—throwing (e.g., discus), *launch, launching*
—lancha[53]	—*launch* (small boat)
lapidar	(to) stone (~ *apedrear*) [† *lapidate*]
—lápida	—gravestone, memorial stone
—lapidario	—lapidary (engraved in stone, concise)
—lápiz	—pencil
—lapislázuli	—lapis lazuli (blue gemstone) (lápiz + azul)

---

[53] *Lancha—launch* are unrelated to *lanzar—launch.* The latter are from Latin, the former apparently from Malayan (→ Portuguese → Spanish → English).

lapso	*lapse* (period of time; careless error)	
—un lapso de tres años	—a lapse (period) of three years	
—lapsus	—lapse (careless error)	
lastre	*ballast,* dead weight, hindrance	[ballast = bare (?) + *last*]
—lastrar	—(to) *ballast,* (to) weigh down or burden	
latente	latent	
lateral	lateral, side (adj.)	
—la**d**o	—side (n.)	(Lat. LATUS)
—al lado (de)	—next to, beside	
—ladear	—(to) tilt or incline, (to) turn sideways	
—ladera	—hillside, slope	
laurel	laurel (tree), laurels (honor—pl.)	
—laurear	—(to) laurel (crown with laurel, honor)	
—laureado (p.p.)	—*laureate*	
lava	lava	
lavatorio	wash, washing, *lotion, lavatory* (sink; restroom—Amer.)	
—lavabo	—lavabo (sink), restroom	
—lavar	—(to) wash, (to) *lave*	
—lavable	—washable	
—lavadero	—washing place (often communal)	
—lavadora	—washing machine	
—lavamanos	—sink (esp. in Amer.)	
—lavandería	—*laundry* (establishment)	
—lavanda[54]	—lavender	
—lavaplatos	—dishwasher (machine, person)	
—lavavajillas	—dishwasher (machine), washing-up liquid	
—le**t**rina	—latrine	(Lat. LA[VA]TRINA)
lazo	bow, knot, bond, *lasso*	
—enlazar	—(to) tie, (to) *lace,* (to) link, (to) *lasso*	
—enlace	—link, liaison, wedding ("tying the knot"), hyperlink	
—enlace químico	—chemical bond	
—desenlazar	—(to) untie, (to) unravel (plot of novel, film, play)	
—desenlace	—outcome, denouement	
—entrelazar	—(to) *interlace,* (to) interweave	
lección	*lesson*	
—lectura	—reading	[*lecture*]

[54] *Lavanda* literally means "that which serves for washing", referring to lavender's use to perfume the water in which clothes (or people) were washed.

—lector	—reader, *lector*
legua	league (unit of measure ~ 3 miles)
—*Veinte mil leguas de viaje submarino*	—*Twenty Thousand Leagues Under the Sea*
leotardo	leotard
lepra	leprosy
—leproso (adj. & n.)	—leprous, leper
lesión	injury, wound, *lesion*
—lesionar	—(to) injure, (to) wound, (to) damage
letal	*lethal*
letargo	*lethargy*
letra	*letter*
—letrero	—poster, sign
—letrado (adj. & n.)	—*lettered* (highly educated), lawyer
—iletrado	—*illiterate, unlettered,* uneducated
levitación	levitation
—levitar	—(to) levitate
—levedad	—lightness, *levity* (lightness, inconstancy)
—leve	—light (~ *ligero*), slight, of little importance

—levar	—(to) weigh anchor, (to) set sail	[*levy*]
—llevar	—(to) carry, (to) wear, (to) take	[*lever*]
—conllevar	—(to) entail or lead to	("bring with", as consequence)
—sobrellevar	—(to) put up with, (to) endure	
—levantar	—(to) raise, (to) lift, (to) get up (from bed, etc.)	
—levantamiento	—raising, lifting, uprising	
—levante	—East, *levanter* (east wind), Mediterranean Spain, Levant	
—levantino	—*Levantine* (of the East—esp.Valencia and Murcia in Spain)	
—levadura	—yeast, *leaven, leavening*	
—sublevar	—(to) incite (to rebellion or anger), (to) rise up (in revolt)	
—sublevación	—revolt, uprising	
—liviano	—light, slight, frivolous	[*levity*]
—ligero (< Fr.)	—light (incl. "nimble")	[*legerdemain*]
—a la ligera	—lightly (without sufficient care or consideration)	
—ligereza	—lightness, *levity* (inconstancy, frivolity)	[*legerity*]
—aligerar	—(to) lighten, (to) *alleviate,* (to) hasten	
leyenda[55]	legend	
libro	book	

---

[55] From the verb *leer* (Latin LEGERE), the literal meaning is "things to be read".

—librería	—bookstore	[*library*]
—librero	—bookseller, bookshelf (Amer.)	
—libreta	—small book or notebook (address book, bank book)	
—libreto	—libretto (opera text)	
—libelo	—libel	("little book")
licencia	license (permission, permit)	
—licenciar	—(to) discharge or dismiss, (to) confer (or obtain) a degree	
—licenciado (p.p.)	—*licentiate* (degree holder; *licensed* to practice professionally)	
—licenciatura	—university degree (generally bachelor's, but varies)	
—licencioso	—licentious	
líder (< Eng.)	leader	
—liderazgo ~ liderato	—leadership	
límite	limit, boundary, border	
—limitación	—limitation	
—limitar	—(to) limit, (to) border with or be bounded on (north, etc.)	
—ilimitado	—unlimited, boundless	
—delimitar	—(to) delimit (establish the limits of)	
—**linde** (m./f.)	—*limit* (boundary)	(Lat. LIMITEM)
—lindar	—(to) border, (to) adjoin	
—colindar	—(to) be adjacent, (to) adjoin	
—colindante	—adjacent, adjoining	
—deslindar	—(to) fix the boundaries or limits (~ *delimitar*)	
—deslinde	—fixing of limits, *delimitation* (~ *delimitación*)	
lindo[56]	pretty, nice, fine, lovely	[*Linda*]
—de lo lindo	—greatly, a great deal (~ *mucho*)	
—lindeza	—prettiness, loveliness, insults (pl.)	
línea	*line* (multiple senses)	
—linaje	—lineage	
—lineal	—linear	[*lineal*]
—alinear	—(to) *align*, (to) *line* up (select members of a team)	
—alineamiento	—*alignment*	
—alineación	—alignment, *lineup* (sports)	
—aliñar	—(to) season (meal), (to) tidy or pretty up (appearance)	

---

[56] *Lindo* comes via a tortuous path from Latin LEGITIMUS → leídemo → lídemo → lidmo → limdo → lindo. Its meaning has likewise evolved from *legitimate* → *authentic* → *pure* → *good* → *pretty*. There are alternative explanations for the origin of the English name *Linda* (perhaps a shortening of *Belinda*?), but the Spanish deriviation is as likely as any.

—desaliñado	—untidy, unkempt, slovenly	[*dis* + *aligned*]
lingote	*ingot* (of gold, etc.)	
linterna[57]	*lantern,* flashlight	
lista	*list,* stripe[58]	
—pasar lista	—(to) call the roll	
—lista negra	—blacklist	
—listar	—(to) list	
—listado (p.p.)	—striped, listing, printout	
—ardilla listada	—chipmunk	("striped squirrel")
—alistar	—(to) *list* (enter on a list), (to) en*list,* (to) enroll	
—alistamiento	—en*listment*	
—listo	—ready (with *estar*), clever (with *ser*)	(unrelated)
litera	bunk bed, berth (train or boat), *litter* (vehicle)	[wagon-*lit*]
literal	literal	
literatura	literature	
—literario	—literary	
—literato	—writer	[*literati*]
litigar	(to) litigate	
—litigio	—lawsuit, litigation	
—litigante (adj. & n.m./f.)	—litigant, litigator	
litoral (adj. & n.)	coastal, *littoral,* seaboard, coast	[*Lido*]
locomotora (n.)	locomotive (engine)	
—locomotor (adj.)	—locomotive (f. = *locomotora* or *locomotriz*)	
—locomoción	—locomotion	
locuaz	*loquacious,* talkative	
—locución	—locution, phrase	
—locutor	—TV/radio announcer	
—interlocutor	—interlocutor	
logia	*lodge* (e.g., Masonic), *loggia*	
—alojar	—(to) *lodge*	
—alojamiento	—*lodging, lodgings*	
lubricante[59]	lubricant	
—lubricar	—(to) lubricate, (to) oil, (to) grease	
—lubricación	—lubrication	
lúcido	*lucid,* brilliant (intelligent)	
—lucidez	—lucidity	

---

[57] From *lanterna* (which still exists, although rare), influenced by (*luz*) *interna*.

[58] English *list* also includes the definition "a stripe or band of color"—this is generally treated as an altogether different word, although the ultimate etymological origin is the same.

[59] The words in this group have the alternate (much rarer) forms *lubrificante, lubrificar,* and *lubrificación.*

—luz (f.)	—light	[*lux*]
—dar a luz	—(to) give birth (~ *alumbrar, parir*)	("give to light")
—lucir	—(to) shine, (to) display, (to) plaster (walls)	
—lucido (p.p.)	—brilliant (splendid, magnificent)	
—lucero	—bright star, star (white spot on animal forehead)	
—lucero de la mañana	—morning star, Venus (also called *lucero del alba*)	
—lucero de la tarde	—evening star, Venus	
—luciérnaga	—glowworm, firefly	
—Lucifer	—Lucifer (archangel, planet Venus)	("light bringer")
—dilucidar	—(to) *elucidate*	
—relucir	—(to) shine or reflect	
—reluciente	—*relucent* (reflecting light; shining)	
—traslucir / trans-	—(to) reveal, (to) show, (to) make *translucent*	
—translúcido / tras-	—*translucent*	
lúgubre	lugubrious	
—luto	—mourning	(< LUCTUS)
lumbago	lumbago (backache)	
—lumbar	—lumbar	
—lomo	—back (of animal), *loin* (meat), spine (book)	
—loma	—small hill, slope	
—lonja (1) ~ loncha	—slice (meat, cheese)	
—solomillo	—*sirloin*[60]	
—lonja (2)[61]	—exchange, market	[*lodge*]
mágico	magic (adj.), magical	
—magia	—magic (n.)	
—mago	—wizard, *magician, magus*	
—los Reyes Magos	—the Three Wise Men, *Magi*	
—*El mago de Oz*	—*The Wizard of Oz*	
magistrado	magistrate, judge	
—magistratura	—magistracy, magistrature	
—magistral	—magistral, *magisterial, masterful*	
—magisterio	—teaching (profession; something taught)	[*magisterium*]
magnífico	magnificent	
—magnificencia	—magnificence	
magno	great	[*magnum* opus]
—Alejandro Magno	—Alexander the Great	

[60] Spanish *solomillo* (< *solomo*) means "*under* the loin", *so* being Old Spanish for "under" (< Latin SUB). English *sirloin* comes from French *surloigne* (Modern French *surlonge*), where *sur* (< Latin SUPER) means "over", so that the meaning is "*over* the loin". Sirloin was thus initially *surloyn*. Said to have been knighted (by Henry VIII, James I, Charles II, and perhaps others), *surloyn* subsequently became "Sir Loin", hence *sirloin*.

[61] *Lonja* (2) is of Germanic origin and unrelated to *lonja* (1).

mal (adv.)	badly	
—mal (n.)	—evil, harm	[*mal* de mer]
—malo (adj.)	—bad, wicked, evil	
—de mala fe	—*mala fide* (in bad faith)	
—maligno	—malign, malignant	
—malignidad	—malignancy, malignity	
—malicia	—malice, cunning	
—malicioso	—malicious, evil-minded	
—maléfico	—malefic, maleficent	
—maleficio	—evil spell or curse	[rare *malefice*]
—malévolo	—malevolent	
—maleza	—undergrowth, weeds	[*malice*]
—malaria	—malaria ($\sim$ *paludismo*)	("bad air")
mala[62]	*mail*, mailbag	
—maleta	—suitcase	
—maletín	—valise	
—maletero	—porter, trunk (auto), storage room (house)	
manía	mania (mental disorder, craze), aversion	
—maníaco, maniaco (adj. & n.)	—manic, maniacal, maniac (suffering from a mania)	
—maniático (adj. & n.)	—maniacal, maniac (excessive enthusiasm, frantic)	
—manicomio	—mental hospital, madhouse (place of great disorder)	
maniquí	mannequin (dummy; model—m./f.)	
mantener	(to) *maintain,* (to) keep	
—mantenimiento	—maintenance, sustenance	
manto	*mantle* (cloak, cover, geol., biol.), *mantel*	
—manta	—blanket	
—mantel	—tablecloth	
—mantelería	—table linen	
—mantilla	—mantilla, infant's frock	
—mantillo	—humus ($\sim$ *humus*), manure	
—mantón	—shawl ($\sim$ *chal*)	
—desmantelar	—(to) *dismantle*	
—salvamanteles	—coaster (placed under drinks, bowls, etc., to "*save*" tablecloth)	
maqueta	maquette (small model)	
máquina	*machine*	
—maquinaria	—*machinery, mechanism* (e.g., watch)	

[62] *Mala* comes from French *malle* ("valise", "trunk"), the source of English *mail; mala* is used only (and then only rarely) in reference to England or France, e.g., La *Mala* Real Inglesa (the Royal English Mail). The normal word for mail is *correo.*

—maquinar	—(to) *machinate* (scheme), (to) *machine* (metal)	
—maquinación	—*machination* (plot, scheme)	
—maquinista	—*machinist*, engineer (train)	
mar (m./f.[63])	sea	
—**la** mar de	—a lot of, no end of, "a sea of"	
—mar gruesa	—rough or heavy seas	
—alta mar	—high seas	
—bajamar (f.)	—low tide (~ *marea baja*)	
—pleamar (f.)	—high tide (~ *marea alta*)	(< plenamar [f.])
—Almirante de **la** Mar Océana	—"Admiral of the Ocean Sea" (title accorded to Columbus)	
—marea	—tide (sea; of people or things)	
—mareo	—mal de *mer* (seasickness), nausea, dizziness, annoyance	
—marear	—(to) navigate, (to) become nauseated or seasick, (to) annoy	
—marítimo	—maritime	
—marina	—navy, *marine* (fleet, seascape)	[*marina*]
—marino (adj. & n.)	—marine (of the sea), sailor	
—marinero (adj. & n.)	—of the sea, seaworthy, seaman, *mariner*	[*marinara*]
—marinar	—(to) *marinate*	
—submarino	—underwater, submarine (adj. & n.)	
maravilla	*marvel*, wonder	
—maravilloso	—marvelous, wonderful, wondrous	
—maravillar	—(to) astonish, (to) *marvel*	
marginal	marginal	
—margen (m./f.)	—(river)bank (gen. f.), *margin* (various senses—m.)	
marrón	brown	[*marron*]
—marrón rojizo	—*maroon*	
masa	*mass* (n.), dough	
—masivo	—massive, mass (adj.)	
—macizo (adj. & n.)	—*massive* (solid), *massif* (mountain *mass*), flower bed	
—oro macizo	—solid gold	
masacre (f.)	massacre	
—masacrar	—(to) massacre	
masaje	massage	

[63] Though *mar* is normally masculine, in various expressions (of both sailors and literati) and in some regions it is feminine (< Latin MARE, which was neuter).

—masajista	—masseur, masseuse	
máscara	*mask,* disguise, masquerader (m./f.)	[*mascara*]
—mascarada	—masquerade	
—[rímel]	—mascara	[*Rimmel London*]
masculino	*másculine*	(Lat. MASCULINUS)
—masculinidad	—masculinity	
—macho	—*male* (animal, plant, "male" plug), *macho*	(Lat. MASCULUS)
—machismo	—machismo	
—machista (adj. & n.)	—macho, male chauvinist	
masoquismo	masochism	
—masoquista (adj. & n.)	—masochistic, masochist	
mástil[64]	*mast* (boat, TV station, etc.), neck (guitar)	
mata[65]	shrub, bush	[*mat*]
—mata de pelo	—mop (or head) of hair	
—matorral	—scrubland, thicket, brush, bush (area, plant)	
mausoleo	mausoleum	
mayor	bigger, older, biggest, oldest, *major*	[*mayor*]
—mayor de edad	—of (legal) age	
—mayoral	—foreman, head shepherd	
—mayorazgo	—primogeniture, (entailed) family estate	
—mayoría	—majority	
—mayorista	—wholesaler	
—mayúsculo (adj.)	—larger than normal, capital or uppercase (letter)	
—mayúscula (n.)	—capital or uppercase letter	
maza	*mace* (staff, club), hammer of a pile driver	
—mazo	—maul, mallet, gavel, bundle or bunch (banknotes, flowers)	
—machacar	—(to) crush, (to) pound, (to) mash	
—machete	—machete (< Sp.)	
—maceta	—flowerpot, hammer (for breaking stone or brick)	
—macetero	—flowerpot stand	
—remachar	—(to) rivet, (to) hammer home (insist)	
—remache	—rivet, act of riveting	
mecha	wick, fuse, *match* ("easily ignited cord or wick")	
—mechero	—(bunsen) burner, cigarette lighter	
medalla	medal	
—medallón	—medallion, locket	
mediocre	mediocre	

---

[64] From Germanic *mast* (via French), with influence of *árbol* ("tree").

[65] The semantic development seems to have been *mat* (i.e., *cover*) *of trees or bushes* → *bush*.

—mediocridad	—mediocrity	
melodía	melody	
—melódico	—melodic	
—melodioso	—melodious	
melodrama	melodrama	
menaje	household goods	[*ménage à trois*]
meningitis	meningitis	
menopausia	menopause	
mercado	*market, mart*	
—supermercado	—supermarket	
—hipermercado	—hypermarket (supermarket + dept. store)	
—mercader[66] (n.)	—merchant	
—*El mercader de Venecia*	—*The Merchant of Venice*	
—mercadería	—merchandise	
—mercancía	—merchandise	
—mercante (adj.)	—merchant (ship, fleet)	
—mercantil	—mercantile, commercial	
—derecho mercantil	—commercial law	
—mercantilismo	—mercantilism	
—mercenario	—mercenary	
—mercería	—notions store[67] (U.S.), haberdashery (UK)	[*mercer*]
—merced	—grace, *mercy,* favor	(see Section 4.9)
—vuestra merced (→ usted)	—"your lord" (→ you [formal])	
merodear	(to) *maraud,* (to) prowl	
—merodeador	—marauder, prowler	
metabolismo	metabolism	
metal	metal, brass (music)	
—metálico	—metallic	
—en metálico	—in cash (~ *en efectivo*)	
—metalurgia	—metallurgy	
meteorito[68]	meteorite, meteoroid	
—meteoro	—atmospheric phenomenon, *meteor* ("shooting star")	

---

[66] *Mercader* and *mercadería* tend to be used more in a historical (often literary) sense, *comerciante* and *mercancía* in a more "modern" one.

[67] That is, a store selling fabrics, threads, needles, buttons, etc. An American haberdashery specializes in men's clothing and accessories.

[68] Contrary to what many (if not most) English speakers might think, a *meteor* is **not** a solid body moving through space that becomes a *meteorite* when it impacts the earth: this is in fact the definition of a *meteoroid*. An English *meteor,* exactly like its Spanish counterpart, is the "shooting star" that one sees as the *meteoroid* flashes through the sky. Spanish does not distinguish between *meteoroid* and *meteorite,* using *meteorito* for both. Technically, both *meteor* and *meteoro* apply to *all* atmospheric phenomena—wind, rain, thunder, rainbows, etc.—but this broad sense is rarely encountered in either language.

—meteorología	—meteorology	(study of "meteors")
—meteorólogo	—meteorologist	
—meteorismo	—meteorism (flatulence)	
microbio	microbe	
microscopio	microscope	
—microscópico	—microscopic	
militar (1) (adj. & n.)	military, soldier	
—militar (2)	—(to) serve in the army or in a political party, (to) *militate*	
—militante (adj. & n.m./f.)	—militant, activist	
—militarista (adj. & n.)	—militaristic, militarist	
—milicia	—militia (incl. obs. "arts of war")	
milla (náutica)	(nautical) *mile*	(Lat. MILLE: 1,000 paces)
mina	mine (extractive, explosive), lead (pencil)	
—minar	—(to) mine, (to) undermine	
—mineral	—mineral	
—minería	—mining (n.), mining industry	
—minero	—mining (adj.), miner	
ministro	minister	
—ministerio	—ministry (governmental)	
—ministerial	—ministerial	
—menester	—need, chore, occupation	[*métier*]
—ser menester	—(to) be necessary	
—menestra (< It.)	—vegetable stew	[*minestrone*]
—suministrar	—(to) supply	[† *subminister*]
—suministro	—supply, provision	
mitin (< Eng.)	(political) *meeting*, rally	
mixtura	mixture	
—mixto	—mixed	
—miscelánea	—miscellany, miscellanea	
—misceláneo	—miscellaneous	
—mezclar	—(to) *mix*	
—mezcla	—mixture, *mix*, mixing	[*melee*]
—mezcolanza	—*medley* (mixture, hodgepodge)	
—entremezclar	—(to) *intermix*, (to) intermingle	
—mestizo	—*métis, mestizo* (person of mixed racial ancestry)	
—inmiscuir(se)	—(to) *meddle*, (to) interfere	
—promiscuo	—promiscuous (incl. "composed of all sorts")	
—promiscuidad	—promiscuity (incl. "unruly mixture or mixing")	
modelo (adj. & n.)	model	

—modelar	—(to) model, (to) *mold* or fashion	
—modalidad	—modality, *mode* (method, form), category (e.g., "men's singles")	
—modal	—modal, manners (good, bad—pl.)	
modo	*mode* (manner, way), *mood* (gram.)	
—de todos modos	—anyhow, at any rate	
—de ningún modo	—by no means, under no circumstances	
—de otro modo	—otherwise	
—módico	—*moderate*, reasonable (esp. price)	[*modicum*]
modular (1)	modular (adj.)	
—modular (2)	—(to) modulate	
—módulo	—module, modulus	(Lat. MODULUS)
molde	*mold,* cast	(Lat. MODULUS)
—moldear	—(to) mold, (to) cast	
—amoldar	—(to) mold, (to) fashion, (to) adapt oneself	
molestar	(to) bother, (to) disturb, (to) *molest*	
—molestia	—bother, nuisance, discomfort	[*molestation*]
—molesto	—annoying, uncomfortable, annoyed	[*molested*]
momia	*mummy*	
—momificar	—(to) mummify	
monopolio	monopoly	
—monopolizar	—(to) monopolize	
—monopolista	—monopolist	
—monopolístico	—monopolistic	
monte	*mount, mountain,* woodland, *monte* (card game)	
—monte alto	—(high) forest, woodland (with tall trees)	
—monte bajo	—lower part of mountain (= scrubland, thicket, maquis)	
—montaña	—*mountain*, mountains (collectively, as singular)	[*Montana*]
—montaña rusa	—roller coaster	[*Russian mountain*]
—montañero	—mountaineer, mountain climber (~ *alpinista*)	
—montañés (-esa)	—highland (adj.), mountain (adj.), highlander	
—montañismo	—mountaineering, alpinism (~ *alpinismo, andinismo*)	
—montañoso	—mountainous	
—montar	—(to) *mount*, (to) assemble, (to) edit (film)	
—desmontar	—(to) *dismount*, (to) *demount* (disassemble)	
—monto	—*amount*, sum, total	
—montaje	—assembly or *mounting*, film editing, *montage*	
—montículo	—mound, hillock	[*monticule*]
—montón	—mountain ("large heap", "huge quantity")	
—montura	—*mount* (animal, jewel), saddle, frame (glasses)	
moratoria	moratorium (esp. of debt payments)	

—morar	—(to) dwell, (to) reside	
—morada	—dwelling, abode	
—mora[69]	—delay (esp. in payment), *mora* (poetry)	
—demorar	—(to) delay, (to) linger	[*demur*]
—demora	—delay	[*demurrage*]
—moroso[70]	—slow, tardy, delinquent (in payment)	
—morosidad	—slowness, tardiness, delinquency or arrears (payment)	
—rémora	—remora (suckerfish; hindrance, drag)	
morboso	*morbid* (diseased, gloomy, gruesome)	
—morbo	—disease, morbid interest or taste	(cholera *morbus*)
—mórbido	—*morbid* (med.)	
mortero	mortar (for pounding, artillery)	
mosaico	mosaic	
motín	*mutiny*, riot, uprising	
—amotinar	—(to) incite to mutiny, (to) mutiny	
—amotinado (p.p.)	—mutinous, mutineer	
motivación	motivation	
—motivar	—(to) motivate, (to) justify	
—motivación	—motivation	
—motivo	—motive, reason, *motif*	
motor (n.)	motor, engine	
—motor (adj.)	—motor (f. = *motora* or *motriz*)	
—fuerza motriz (motora)	—driving or *motive* force, *motive* power	
—motorista	—motorcyclist, motorist (very rare)	
—motocicleta, moto (f.)	—motorcycle	
—automovilista	—motorist, *automobilist*	
mover	(to) move	
—movible	—*movable*	
—movimiento	—movement	
—cantidad de movimiento	—momentum (physics) (~ *ímpetu*, *momento*)	
—móvil	—*mobile*, *motive*, mobile phone	
—movilidad	—*mobility*	
—movilizar	—(to) mobilize	
—movilización	—mobilization	
—inmóvil	—immobile, *motionless*	
—inmovilidad	—immobility	

---

[69] An unrelated *mora* means "mulberry" (see Section 1.6).

[70] English *morose* comes from a completely different root (that of *moral* and *morale*).

—inmovilizar	—(to) immobilize	
—inmovilización	—immobilization	
multa	fine, penalty, traffic ticket, *mulct*	
—multar	—(to) fine or penalize, (to) *mulct*	
municipal	municipal, city policeman	
(adj. & n.m./f.)		
—municipio	—municipality (town or city; town or city council)	
mural	mural	
—muralista	—muralist (painter of murals)	
—muro	—wall (esp. exterior)	[*immure*]
—intramuros	—intramural (within walls [limits] of city or institution)	
—extramuros	—extramural (occurring or situated outside walls or limits)	
—muralla	—rampart, wall	
—amurallar	—(to) wall (defend with walls, surround with ramparts)	
—muladar[71]	—trash heap, garbage dump	
museo	museum	
—musa	—Muse, muse (inspiration)	
música	music	
—músico	—musician	
—musical	—musical (adj. & n.)	
mutuo ~ mutual	mutual, reciprocal	
—mutualidad	—mutuality, mutual insurance company, friendly society (UK)	
natural	natural, *native* (e.g., of New York)	
—naturaleza ~ natura	—nature (*natura* tends to refer more to "Nature")	
—por naturaleza	—by nature, naturally	
—naturaleza humana	—human nature	
—naturaleza muerta	—still life (painting)	
—contra natura	—against nature, unnatural	
—naturalizar	—(to) naturalize (~ *nacionalizar*)	
—naturalista (adj. & n.)	—naturalistic, naturalist	
—naturista	—naturist (nudist)	
—sobrenatural	—supernatural	
naval	naval	
—nave (f.)	—ship, vessel, *nave* (of a church)	

---

[71] This was initially *muradal* (which still exists), with the not-uncharacteristic inversion of *r* and *l* (see Section 3.5, no. 8)—a trash dump was often located near the external walls of the city.

—nave espacial	—spaceship	
—quemar las naves	—"to burn one's boats" = "to burn one's bridges"	
—naufragio	—shipwreck (incl. "total loss or ruin")	[lit. *naval fracture*]
—náufrago	—shipwrecked, castaway	
necesario	necessary	
—necesidad	—necessity	
—necesitar	—(to) necessitate, (to) need	
—**in**necesario	—unnecessary	
negligente	negligent	
—negligencia	—negligence	
negociación	negotiation (incl. obs. "business transaction")	
—negociar	—(to) negotiate (incl. obs. "do business, engage in commerce")	
—negociable	—negotiable (open to discussion; transferable)	
—negociador	—negotiator	
—negocio[72]	—business (trade, affair, deal, commercial enterprise)	
—negociante (m./f.)	—trader, broker, merchant, businessman (-woman)	[*negotiant*]
—ocio	—leisure, idleness	(Lat. OTIUM)
—ocioso	—idle, pointless, *otiose*	
—ociosidad	—idleness, *otiosity*	
neumonía	*pneumonia*	
neutral	neutral (not taking sides)	
—neutro	—neutral (other senses), *neuter* (gram. & biol.)	
—neutralidad	—neutrality	
—neutralizar	—(to) neutralize	
—neutralización	—neutralization	
—neutrón	—neutron	
nevado (adj.)	snowy, snow-covered, snow-capped	[Sierra *Nevada*]
—nevada (n.)	—snowfall	
—nevado (n.)	—mountain covered with perpetual snow (Amer.)	
—nevera	—icebox, refrigerator	
—nevar	—(to) snow	
—**nie**ve (f.)	—snow	[*névé, nival*]
—níveo	—snow-white (poetic), *niveous*	[*Nivea*®]
nicho	*niche*	
nicotina	nicotine	

---

[72] There is an interesting parallel between *negocio* and *business: negocio* comes from Latin NEGOTIUM ("business"), formed from NEG- ("not", as in **neg**ate) + OTIUM ("leisure"), so that the literal meaning was "lack of leisure" or *busy-ness*. (In Roman times, business was not a highly valued activity, as those of independent means preferred not to give up their "leisure".)

níquel	*nickel*	
nítido	clear, sharp (esp. photo)	[*net, neat*]
—nitidez	—clarity, sharpness	
—neto	—*net* (weight, income, etc.)	
—beneficio neto	—*net* profit, *net benefit*	
nocivo	*noxious,* harmful	
nocturno (adj. & n.)	nocturnal, night (adj.), nocturne (music)	
—noctámbulo	—night owl	[night *ambler*]
—[sonámbulo]	—noctambulist, somnambulist, sleepwalker	
—pernoctar	—(to) pass the night (in a hotel, tent, etc.)	[rare *pernoctate*]
nómada (adj. & n.m./f.)	nomadic, nomad	
nostalgia	nostalgia	
—nostálgico	—nostalgic	
nota	note (various senses), grade, mark	
—notable	—notable, noteworthy, exam grade (higher than *aprobado,* lower than *sobresaliente*)	
—notación	—notation	
—notar	—(to) note, (to) notice	
—notario	—notary	
—notaría	—notary's office	
—noticia	—news, information	
—las noticias	—news (radio, TV)	
notificación	notification (esp. official letter or *notice*)	
—notificar	—(to) notify (incl. "make known, announce")	
notorio	well-known, notorious (w/out negative connotation)	
—notoriedad	—fame, renown, notoriety (objective, not negative)	
núbil	nubile	
—nupcias (pl.)	—nuptials (wedding ceremony)	
—nupcial	—nuptial	
—nube (f.) [73]	—cloud	
—nublar	—(to) cloud, (to) darken or dim	
—nublado (p.p.)	—cloudy, overcast, storm cloud	
—nuboso	—cloudy, overcast	[rare *nubilous*]
—nubosidad	—cloudiness, clouds	
nudismo	nudism	

---

[73] The Latin verb "to marry" (for a woman) was NUBERE. This literally meant "to cover" or "to veil", and seems to have been derived from NUBES (cloud). The most important element of the marriage ceremony was the woman's taking of the veil, "which symbolized the loss of liberty for the wife and (her) *reclusion* [imprisonment?] within the residence of the husband" (Ernout and Meillet, 449).

—nudista	—nudist
—desnudar	—(to) undress, (to) strip, (to) *denude*
—desnudo	—nude, naked
—desnudez	—nudity, nakedness
nudo	knot (numerous senses[74]), *node* (bot.), *nodus*
—nodo	—*node* (astron., physics)
—nódulo	—nodule
—nudillo	—knuckle
—anudar	—(to) knot, (to) unite
—desanudar	—(to) untie, (to) unknot, (to) disentangle [*denouement*]
—reanudar	—(to) renew, (to) resume
obelisco	obelisk
obeso	obese
—obesidad	—obesity
oblicuo	oblique
oboe	oboe
obsceno	obscene
—obscenidad	—obscenity
obsoleto	obsolete
obtener	(to) *obtain*
obtuso	obtuse
obvio	obvious
—obviar	—(to) obviate, (to) disregard (~ *pasar por alto*)
océano	ocean
—oceanografía	—oceanography
—oceanográfico	—oceanographic
—oceanógrafo	—oceanographer
oclusión	occlusion
—ocluir	—(to) occlude
—oclusivo	—occlusive
odio	odium, hate, hatred
—odiar	—(to) hate, (to) loathe
—odioso	—odious, hateful
—enojo	—*annoyance,* anger [*in-* + *odium*]
—enojar	—(to) *annoy,* (to) anger
—enojado (p.p.)	—*annoyed,* angry
ofender	(to) offend, (to) take offense
—ofensivo (adj.)	—offensive
—ofensiva (n.)	—offensive

---

[74] The knot that one ties, a unifying bond, a hard place or lump (esp. on a tree), a complex problem, a division of a log line used to measure the speed of a ship, a measure of nautical speed, etc. *Nudo,* which comes from Latin NODUS, has nothing to do with the words relating to nudity.

—ofensor (adj. & n.)	—offending, offender
oficial (adj. & n.m./f.)	official, officer
—oficiar	—(to) celebrate or *officiate* (eccl.), (to) inform officially
—oficio	—office (profession, role [eccl.]), official letter
—oficioso	—officious (unofficial; meddling; obs. "obliging")
—oficina	—office (workplace)
—oficinista	—office clerk
ogro	ogre
omnisciente	omniscient, all-knowing
opaco	*opaque* (not transparent)
—opacidad	—opacity
opinión	opinion
—opinar	—(to) *opine*, (to) be of the *opinion* that
opio	opium
oportunidad	opportunity, opportuneness
—oportuno	—opportune, timely
—inoportuno	—inopportune, untimely, inconvenient
—oportunista (adj. & n.)	—opportunistic, opportunist
optimismo	optimism
—optimista (adj. & n.)	—optimistic, optimist
—óptimo	—optimal, optimum (~ *buenísimo*)
—optimizar	—(to) optimize
opulencia	opulence
—opulento	—opulent
órbita	orbit (incl. "eye socket")
—orbital	—orbital
—orbe	—orb
—desorbitado	—"out of *orbit*" (excessive, extreme) [*deorbited*]
—precio desorbitado	—"sky high" or *exorbitant* price
—con los ojos desorbitados	—wide-eyed, pop-eyed (astonished)
—exorbitante	—exorbitant [*ex + orbit*]
orificio	*orifice*, opening
origen	origin
—original	—original
—originalidad	—originality
—originar	—(to) originate, (arise from; give rise to)
—originario	—original (initial), originating, native
—aborigen (adj. & n.m./f.)	—*aboriginal*, Aboriginal, *aborigine*, Aborigine (in Australia)
orquídea	orchid

ósmosis, osmosis	osmosis
ostentación	ostentation
—ostentoso	—ostentatious
—ostentar	—(to) flaunt, (to) display, (to) occupy (office or position)
—ostensible	—ostensible (incl. obs. "conspicuous")
ostracismo	ostracism
oxígeno	oxygen
—óxido	—oxide
ozono	ozone
—capa de ozono	—ozone layer
pabellón	*pavilion* (ornate tent, structure, obs. "flag or ensign")
paciente	patient (adj & n.m./f.)
—paciencia	—patience
—impaciente	—impatient
—impaciencia	—impatience
—impacientar	—to make (s.o.) lose patience
pacífico	pacific, *peaceful*
—(océano) Pacífico	—Pacific Ocean
—pacificar	—(to) *pacify*
—pacificación	—pacification
—pacificador	—pacifier (person), *peacemaker*
—pacifismo	—pacifism
—pacifista	—pacifist
pacto	pact
—pactar	—(to) agree to, (to) make a pact
—empate[75] (< It.)	—tie (game or vote), draw [*in-* + *pact*]
—empatar	—(to) tie, (to) draw
—desempate	—play-off, tiebreaker
—desempatar	—(to) break a tie (sports or vote)
—pauta[76]	—guideline or rule (line on paper or model to be followed)
—pautar	—(to) rule (paper), (to) gives rules or guidelines
—papel pautado	—ruled paper, music paper
pala	shovel, spade, blade (propeller, etc.), baker's *peel*
—paleta	—*palette,* trowel, paddle
palacio	palace
—palaciego	—pertaining to the royal *palace*

[75] The initial idea was "to make a *pact*", "to make *peace*".
[76] *Pauta* (from Latin PACTA, "pacts") has undergone a "semi-learned" phonetic evolution analogous to that of *auto* ("judicial *act*"); see Section 1.2.

palestra	arena, *palestra*	
paliativo	palliative (adj. & n.)	
—paliar	—(to) *palliate*	
palo	*pale*, stick, blow with a stick, suit (cards)	[beyond the *pale*]
—apalear	—(to) beat, (to) cane, (to) thrash	
—palillo	—small stick, toothpick, drumstick, chopsticks (pl.)	
—paliza	—beating, drubbing	
—empalar	—(to) *impale*	
—Vlad el Empalador	—Vlad the *Impaler* (Wallachian prince, 1431–1476; model for Dracula)	
—empalizada	—*palisade*, stockade	
pampa	pampa (treeless grassland area, esp. in Argentina)	
panacea	panacea	
panel	panel, noticeboard	
—paño	—cloth (material, piece)	[*pane*]
—paño de cocina	—dishcloth	
—en paños menores	—dressed only in underwear	
—paño de lágrimas	—one who sympathizes and consoles	
—pañuelo	—handkerchief, shawl	
—pañal	—diaper	
—empañar	—(to) diaper, (to) blur or fog up, (to) tarnish	
panfleto	*pamphlet*, leaflet	
pánico	panic	
panorama (m.)	panorama	
—panorámico	—panoramic	
pantalón *or*	*pants*, trousers, *pantaloons*	
pantalones (pl.)		
—pantalón corto	—short pants (also: *pantalones cortos*)	
—pantorrilla	—calf (of the leg)	(unrelated)
paquete	*package, pack, packet*	
—paquebote	—*packet* (boat), steamer	
—empaquetar	—(to) package, (to) pack	
—desempaquetar	—(to) unpack	
—empacar	—(to) pack, (to) package	
—empaque	—packing, packaging (also fig.—presence, bearing)	
—desempacar	—(to) unpack	
parada	*parade* (mil.), stop (bus), pause, *parry*	
—parar	—(to) stop, (to) *parry* (e.g., fencing)	
—parado (p.p.)	—unemployed	
—salir bien (mal) parado	—(to) come out well (poorly)	
—paro	—(work) stoppage, strike, unemployment	
—parador	—inn ("stop off"), *parador* (govt.-run hotel in Spain)	

—paradero	—whereabouts, stopping place	
—paraje	—place, spot	
—deparar	—(to) offer or furnish (opportunity, surprise, etc.)	
paradigma (m.)	paradigm	
páramo	barren land, *paramo* (treeless alpine plateau in S. Amer.)	
para*n*gón	comparison, parallel	[*paragon*]
—sin parangón	—matchless, incomparable	
paranoia	paranoia	
—paranoico (adj. & n.)	—paranoic (paranoiac), paranoid	
parcela	parcel (plot of land, tiny portion)	
parche	patch (band-aid, repair, software), drumhead	(unrelated)
—parchear ~ parchar	—(to) patch	
pared	wall, *paries* (wall of a body part)	
—parietal	—parietal (bone)	
—emparedar	—(to) wall in, (to) immure (in + mure = Sp. *muro*)	
—emparedado (p.p.)	—sandwich	("walled in")
parlamento	parliament, *parley,* long speech (actor)	
—parlamentario (adj. & n.)	—parliamentary, parliamentarian (member of a parliament)	
—parlamentar	—(to) *parley* (confer, discuss terms)	
parque	*park*	
—parque industrial	—industrial park	
—parque de atracciones	—amusement park	
—parque zoológico	—zoo	
—parque automovilístico	—total of cars (in a city, or country)	
—parque móvil	—aggregate of vehicles belonging to a public entity	
—aparcar	—(to) park (incl. "put aside for a while")	
—aparcamiento	—parking, parking lot	
párrafo / parágrafo	*paragraph*	
parte (1) (f.)	*part, party* ("concerned *parties*")	
—en todas partes	—everywhere ("in all *parts*")	
—por todas partes	—everywhere ("on all sides")	
—en ninguna parte	—nowhere ("in no *part*")	
—parte (2)	—dispatch, report (weather, medical)	
—parcial (adj. & n.)	—*partial* (incomplete, biased), midterm (exam)	
—partir	—(to) divide or separate into *parts,* (to) de*part*	
—partido (p.p.)	—*party* (political), game or match (soccer, tennis)	
—partida	—*departure,* consignment, game or match (chess), *party* (hunting, of bandits), certificate	

—partida de nacimiento	—birth certificate	
—partidario	—partisan, supporter, follower	
—partición	—partition (division)	
—repartición	—*repartition* (division, apportionment)	
—repartir	—(to) distribute, (to) divide up	
—reparto	—distribution, sharing out, cast (of a play)	[*repartee*]
—compartir	—(to) divide up, (to) share, (to) *part*ake of (< *part*-take)	
—compartimento, -miento	—compartment	
—aparte (adv., adj., n.)	—*apart*, aside, separately; separate, *apart*; aside (comment)	
—un mundo aparte	—"a world apart"	
—apartar	—(to) move or set *apart*, (to) separate	
—apartado (p.p.)	—distant, remote, PO Box, paragraph or section (law, contract)	
—apartamento	—apartment	
—departamento	—department, apartment (Amer.)	
particular (adj.)	particular (incl. obs. "peculiar, private [property, lesson]")	
—particular (n.)	—private individual, *particular* (item, detail)	
—clases particulares	—private lessons	
—particularidad	—particularity, peculiarity (distinctive feature)	
pasar	(to) pass	
—pasado (p.p.)	—past (time gone by; *past* tense)	
—la semana pasada	—last week ("the *past* week")	
—paso	—step, *pace, pass*	[El *Paso*]
—pasa[77]	—raisin	
—pasarela	—gangway, footbridge, catwalk	
—pasatiempo	—*pastime*, hobby	
—paseo	—walk, stroll, promenade	
—pasear	—(to) go for a walk (or ride), (to) *pace*	
—pasillo	—*passage*way, corridor, aisle	
—pasaporte	—passport	
—marcapasos	—pacemaker (med.)	[*pace marker*]
—repasar	—(to) review, (to) look over, (to) mend	
—sobrepasar	—(to) *surpass*	
—traspasar	—(to) *pass* over (or through or beyond)	[*trespass*]
—traspaso	—transfer, sale	

---

[77] From *uva pasa,* literally "spread-out grape", since raisins were made by spreading grapes out for drying in the sun: Latin PASSUS served both as the past participle of the verb PANDERE ("to spread out", "to *expand*") and as a separate (related) noun meaning "step", "*pace*".

—antepasado	—ancestor	[*ante- passed*]
pasivo	passive, liability or liabilities (financial)	
—pasividad	—passivity, passiveness	
—impasible	—impassive, impassible	
—impasibilidad	—impassiveness, impassibility	
patente (adj. & n.f.)	patent (obvious), patent (invention, license)	
—patentar	—(to) patent	
patio	patio, courtyard, orchestra section (theater)	
patrulla	*patrol*	
—patrullar	—(to) patrol	
paz (f.)	*peace*	[*Pax* Romana]
—hacer las paces	—(to) make peace, (to) reconcile	
—apacible	—*peaceable, peaceful,* gentle	
—apaciguar	—(to) *pacify,* (to) *appease,* (to) calm	
peculiar	particular (proper or characteristic of a person or thing)[78]	
—peculiaridad	—*peculiarity* (a distinguishing characteristic)	
pecuniario	pecuniary	
pelota	ball (~ balón), ball game	[*pellet*]
—pelota vasca	—jai alai, *pelota*	
—pelotón	—*platoon* (mil.), pack (e.g., racers)	
—bellota (< Arab.)	—acorn	
pena	*penalty, punishment, pain* (mental suffering, exertions)	
—pena de muerte	—death penalty (~ *pena capital*)	
—a duras penas	—(just) barely, with great difficulty	
—apenas	—hardly, scarcely, as soon as	[at *pains*]
—valer (merecer) la pena	—(to) be worthwhile, (to) be worth the trouble	
—penar	—(to) *punish,* (to) suffer *pain,* (to) *pine* for	
—penado (p.p.)	—convict	
—penoso	—*painful* (situation, effort), distressing	
—penal (adj. & n.)	—penal, prison, penalty shot (Amer.)	
—penalidad	—*penalty* (legal), hardship	
—penalti / penalty	—penalty shot (soccer)	
—penalizar	—(to) penalize	
—apenar	—(to) *pain,* (to) sadden	
pendiente (adj.)	*pending, pendent* (hanging), attentive (e.g., "hanging on her every word")	

---

[78] This is also a definition of English *peculiar,* though not the principal one ("strange or odd"), which in fact is peculiar to Modern English (cf. the nineteenth-century euphemism for "slavery" used by its defenders—the "*peculiar* institution", i.e., one that was *particular* to the South). Unlike English, Spanish *peculiar* and *particular* remain common synonyms.

—pendiente (m.)	—earring, *pendant*
—pendiente (f.)	—slope, incline, gradient, pitch (roof)
péndulo	pendulum
percha	hanger, hat or clothes rack, *perch* (for birds)
—perchero	—stand for hats, clothes, umbrellas
—pértiga	—pole (for vaulting)
—perca	—*perch* (fish) (unrelated)
perdición	perdition
—perder	—(to) lose
—perdido (p.p.)	—lost, stray, dissolute person ("lost soul"—m./f.) [*perdu*]
—pérdida	—loss, leakage, waste
—desperdiciar	—(to) waste, (to) squander
—desperdicio	—waste
perentorio	urgent, pressing, *peremptory* (legal sense) [79]
perfil	*profile*
—perfilar	—(to) profile (outline), (to) take shape
perfume	perfume
período, periodo	period (time, geological, menstrual)
—periódico (adj. & n.)	—periodic, periodical, newspaper ($\sim$ *diario*)
—periodista	—journalist
periscopio	periscope
perjurio	perjury
—perjurar	—(to) commit perjury
—perjuro	—perjurer
permiso	*permission, permit*
—permitir	—(to) *permit*, (to) allow
—permisible	—permissible
—permisivo	—permissive
pernicioso	pernicious
perpendicular (adj. & n.f.)	perpendicular
perseverar	(to) persevere
—perseverante	—persevering
—perseverancia	—perseverance
persiana	window blind, Venetian blind [*Persian*]
persona	person, people (pl.)
—personal (adj. & n.)	—personal, personnel, personal foul (f.)
—impersonal	—impersonal
—personalidad	—personality

---

[79] A time period or date absolutely fixed, without possibility of delay—e.g., for payment of a fine or for a court hearing.

—personaje	—personage (character in a literary work, celebrity)	
perspectiva	perspective, outlook or prospects (freq. pl.)	
—perspicaz	—*perspicacious*, sharp	
—perspicacia	—perspicacity	
pesimismo	pessimism	
—pesimista (adj. & n.)	—pessimistic, pessimist	
—pésimo	—extremely bad (~ *malísimo*)	
peste (f.)	pest (deadly epidemic, nuisance), stench	
—peste bubónica	—bubonic plague	
—pestilente	—foul (smelling), *pestilent*	
—pestilencia	—stench, *pestilence*	
—pesticida (m.)	—pesticide	
—apestar	—(to) infect (with the plague), (to) stink	
pétalo	petal	
petardo	*petard*, firecracker	(< Fr.)
—pedo	—"wind from the anus"[80]	
petróleo	petroleum	
—petrolero	—petroleum (adj.), oil (adj.), oil tanker	
—petroquímico	—petrochemical	
peyorativo	*pejorative*	
—peor	—worse (comparative of *malo*)	
—empeorar	—(to) worsen	[*impair*]
—empeoramiento	—worsening	
piano	piano	
—pianista	—*pianist*	
pieza	*piece*, part (e.g, spare), room (of a house)	
—empezar[81]	—(to) begin, (to) start, (to) commence	
—pedazo	—piece, fragment, bit	(unrelated)
—despedazar	—(to) tear to pieces	
pijama (m.)	pajama, pajamas	(< Eng.)
pila (1)	sink	[*pile* driver]
—pila bautismal	—baptismal font	
—nombre de pila	—first name	
pilar	*pillar*	
—pila (2)	—*pile*, stack, battery (flashlight)	
píldora	*pill*	
piloto	pilot, pilot light	
—pilotar	—(to) pilot	
pintar	(to) *paint*	

---

[80] *VOX New College Spanish and English Dictionary*. A more concise, albeit less elegant, English translation may occur to some readers.

[81] Literally "to start by cutting off a little *piece*".

—pintor	—*painter*
—pintura	—*paint,* painting
—pintoresco	—*picturesque*
—pictórico	—pictorial
pipa (1)	*pipe* (for smoking)
—pipeta	—*pipette*
pipa (2)	pip (~ *pepita*), seed (melon, sunflower, etc.)
piragua	pirogue (*or* piragua)
pirata	pirated, pirate (m./f.)
—piratería	—piracy
—piratear	—(to) pirate
pirueta	pirouette
pistola	pistol, spray gun
—pistolero	—gunman, gangster (armed with pistol)
pistón[82]	piston
—pista	—trail (path, trace or scent), track, *piste*
—pista de aterrizaje	—runway
—pista de tenis	—tennis court
—pista de hielo / de patinaje	—ice-skating rink / skating rink
—pisto	—ratatouille [*pesto*]
—autopista	—autoroute, turnpike
—despistar	—(to) mislead, (to) sidetrack, (to) go off track
—despiste	—a "going off track" (mind, cyclist, airplane)
—pisar	—(to) step on, (to) tread on
—pisada	—stepping on the foot, footprint, footstep
—pisapapeles	—paperweight
—pisotear	—(to) trample (tread harshly; treat harshly)
—pisotón	—(heavy) stepping on the foot
—piso	—apartment, floor (surface, story or level)
placa	*plaque,* panel (e.g., solar), badge, plate (geol., license)
—plaqueta	—(blood) platelet
plácido	placid
—placidez	—placidity
plagiario	plagiarist, kidnapper (Amer.)[83]

---

[82] English *piston, piste,* and *pesto* ultimately come from Latin PISTUS, the past participle of PINSERE ("to pound or beat"). The original idea of *pista—piste* was thus a path *beaten* out in the wilderness, analogous to the English expression *beaten path* (and to *route,* from VIA RUPTA, literally "a road *broken* open by force"). Spanish *pisar* comes from the related verb PINSARE (NS → n, Section 3.5, no. 6).

[83] Somewhat surprisingly, this definition is a natural extension of the *original* Latin definition of PLAGIARIUS—one who steals the slaves of another or sells into slavery a free person. While the application to literary works is first recorded in the first century AD, the "original" sense seems to have predominated throughout the Middle Ages, presumably reflecting the greater abundance of slaves compared to books.

—plagiar	—(to) plagiarize, (to) kidnap (Amer.)	
—plagio	—plagiarism, kidnapping (Amer.)	
plan	plan	
—planear (1)	—(to) plan	
—planear (2)	—(to) *plane* (soar or glide)	
—planeador	—glider	
—planificar	—(to) plan	
—planificación	—planning (~ *planeamiento*)	
—planificación familiar	—family planning	
plancha	sheet (metal), iron, ironing, gang*plank*	
—a la plancha	—grilled (food)	
—planchar	—(to) iron, (to) press	
—planchado (p.p.)	—ironing, pressing	
planeta (m.)	planet	
—planetario (adj. & n.)	—planetary, planetarium	
plat**a**forma	platform (stage, political)	
—plataforma continental	—continental shelf	
—plataforma de lanzamiento	—launch pad	
playa	beach, *plage* (< Fr.)	[*playa, plagio-*]
—playero	—beach (adj.)	
—explayar(se)	—(to) speak at length; (to) unburden oneself	
plaza	*plaza, place* (space; job or post), market*place*	
—plaza de toros	—bullring	
pleito	litigation, lawsuit, dispute	[*plea*]
—pleitear	—(to) litigate, (to) take to court	[*plead* = obs. def.]
poema (m.)	poem	
—poeta (m./f.), poetisa	—poet, poetess	
—poesía	—poetry, poem	
—poético	—poetic	
polar	polar	
—polo (1)	—pole	
—Polo Norte	—North Pole	
—Polo Sur	—South Pole	
—polea	—*pulley*	
—polo (2) (< Eng.)	—polo (game), polo shirt	(unrelated)
polémica (n.)	polemic, controversy, polemics	
—polémico (adj.)	—polemical, controversial	
político (adj. & n.)	political, politic, politician, *politico*	

—padre político	—father-in-law (see Section 4.8)	
—política	—politics, *policy*	
—politizar	—(to) politicize	
póliza	(insurance) *policy*, tax stamp	
polución	pollution[84]	
pomada	ointment, *pomade*	
—pomo	—*pommel* (sword), knob, *pome* (bot.)	
—pómulo	—cheekbone	("little apple")
ponche (< Eng.)	*punch* (drink)	
poncho	poncho	
ponzoña	*poison*, venom	
—ponzoñoso	—poisonous, venomous	
—emponzoñar	—(to) poison, (to) envenom, (to) *empoison*	
portar	(to) carry, (to) com*port* (oneself)	
—portaviones / portaaviones	—aircraft carrier	
—portador	—bearer, carrier	[*porter*]
—portaequipajes	—trunk (auto), luggage rack	
—portafolio, -folios	—portfolio (briefcase)	
—portátil	—*portable*	
—porte	—*portage* (transport; charges), bearing or appearance	
póstumo[85]	*posthumous*	
potable	potable (fit to drink)	
práctico (adj. & n.)	practical, harbor pilot	
—práctica	—practice, training (with skilled supervision—gen. pl.)	
—practicar	—(to) practice	
—practicante (adj. & n.)	—practicing, practitioner, medical assistant	
pradera	*prairie*, meadow, meadowland	
—prado	—meadow	
—Museo del Prado	—(in Madrid, one of the great art museums of the world)	
precaución	precaution	
—caución	—security or pledge (legal)	

[84] Both Spanish *polución* and English *pollution* initially meant "efusión del semen"; as late as 1970 this was the only definition to be found in the RAE's *Diccionario*. *Polución* is now often used in the (modern) English sense, though *contaminación* is far more common.

[85] Spanish *póstumo* is a direct continuation of Latin POSTUMUS, literally meaning "the last" or "coming after" (son or daughter). POSTHUMUS—from which the English derives—was a later "innovation", reflecting a presumed (but false) etymological connection with the words HUMUS ("soil", "*humus*") and HUMARE ("in*hume*"), so that POSTHUMUS would literally mean "post-burial".

—cautela	—caution	
—cauto ~ cauteloso	—cautious, wary	(Lat. CAUTUS)
—incauto	—incautious, unwary	
—precaver[86]	—(to) take *precautions* (against)	(PRAE-CAVERE)
—precavido (p.p.)	—*cautious*, prudent	[*caveat*]
preceder	(to) precede	
—precedente (adj. & n.)	—preceding, precedent	
—precedencia	—precedence	
—precesión	—precession (e.g., of the equinoxes)	
precepto	precept	
—preceptor	—preceptor, tutor (private teacher)	
precio	*price*	[*prize, praise*[87]]
—precioso	—*precious*, beautiful, lovely	
—preciosidad	—preciousness, beauty	
—preciar(se)	—(to) boast of or take pride in (lit. "to *praise* oneself for")	
—preciado (p.p.)	—*precious, prized*	
precoz	*precocious*	
—precocidad	—precocity	
predecesor	predecessor (incl. archaic "ancestor")	
—antecesor	—predecessor, *ancestor* (freq. pl.)	
—ancestral	—ancestral	
—anteceder	—(to) antecede (= precede)	
—antecedente	—antecedent	
preferencia	preference	
—preferir	—(to) prefer	
—preferente	—preferential	
—preferible	—preferable	
prejuicio	*prejudice* (bias, *prejudgment*)	
—prejuzgar	—(to) *prejudge*	
—prejudicial	—*pre-judicial* (to be decided before the case)	[≠ *prejudicial* !]
—**per**juicio	—*prejudice* (injury or damage)	
—**per**judicar	—(to) *prejudice* (cause injury or damage)	
—**per**judicial	—*prejudicial* (injurious, damaging)	
—**per**judicial para la salud	—*prejudicial* to health	
preliminar	preliminary	
premio	prize, reward, *premium*	

---

[86] The past participle of the Latin verb CAVERE ("to beware") was CAUTUS.

[87] *Price, prize,* and *praise* all come from Latin PRETIUM ("price", "value", "reward"). *Price* and *prize* were initially alternate spellings of the same English word before becoming specialized in sense.

—premiar	—(to) reward, (to) give an award to
—apremiar	—(to) *press,* (to) compel
—apremiante	—urgent, *pressing*
premisa	*premise*
premonición	premonition
prender	(to) set or catch on fire, (to) turn on [*apprehend*]
—desprender	—(to) detach, (to) give off
—desprendimiento	—detachment (separation, indifference), landslide
—desprendimiento de retina	—detached retina
preponderante	preponderant, predominant
—preponderancia	—preponderance
—ponderar	—(to) *ponder,* (to) give weight to, (to) (over)praise
—imponderable	—imponderable, inestimable
pre**rr**ogativa	prerogative (incl. "privilege")
presagio	presage, omen
—presagiar	—(to) presage, (to) portend
prescripción	prescription
—prescribir	—(to) prescribe (incl. "become invalid or unenforceable")
prestigio	prestige, renown
—prestigioso	—prestigious, renowned
—prestigiar	—(to) lend prestige to
—desprestigio	—discredit, loss of prestige
—desprestigiar	—(to) discredit, (to) disparage, (to) lose prestige
pretexto	pretext
prevenir[88]	(to) warn, (to) *prevent* (incl. obs. "provide beforehand", "anticipate or counter in advance", "prejudice")
—prevención	—prevention (esp. anticipatory measures; also obs. "bias, prejudice")
—preventivo	—preventive
—prevenido (p.p.)	—prepared, forewarned, prudent
—desprevenido	—unprepared, off-guard
previsión	prevision (foresight, forecast)
—previsible	—foreseeable, predictable
—prever	—(to) foresee, (to) anticipate, (to) *previse* [*preview*]
—imprevisible	—unforeseeable, unpredictable
—imprevisto	—unforeseen, unexpected

---

[88] Frequently considered "falsos amigos", *prevenir* and *prevent* share a range of common definitions; the Spanish meanings tend to focus on the notion of anticipating or acting beforehand, the English ones on that of impeding or frustrating. Elements of both notions are found in the shared expression "más vale *prevenir* que curar" / "*prevention* is better than cure".

primitivo	primitive	
primordial	primordial, essential, fundamental	
prior, priora	prior (n.), prioress	
—a priori	—a priori	
—prioridad	—priority	
—prioritario	—priority (adjectival—e.g., "*priority* project")	
—priorizar	—(to) give priority to	
prisa	haste, urgency	[*press*]
—tener prisa	—(to) be in a hurry, (to) be *pressed* for time	
—deprisa ~ aprisa	—rapidly (also: *de prisa, a prisa*)	[*press*ing]
prisión	*prison*	
—prisionero	—prisoner (of war, kidnappers, etc.)	
—preso	—prisoner (in jail)	
—aprisionar	—(to) imprison	
prisma (m.)	prism	
—prismáticos (pl.)	—binoculars (~ *gemelos*)	
privilegio	privilege	
—privilegiar	—(to) privilege, (to) favor	
proa	*prow* (bow of a ship)	
proceder	(to) proceed	
—proceder (n.)	—behavior, conduct	
—procedente	—proceeding (from), appropriate, admissible (e.g., evidence)	
—improcedente	—inappropriate, inadmissible	
—procedencia	—origin, source	
—procedimiento	—procedure, proceedings (legal)	
—proceso	—process (incl. legal: summons, writs, trial, etc.)	
—procesión	—procession	
—procesar	—(to) process (incl. "prosecute")	
proclividad	proclivity (~ *propensión*)	
—proclive	—prone (to), inclined	[† *proclive*]
—declive	—*declivity* (downward slope or inclination)	[† *declive*]
procurar	(to) procure (incl. obs. "endeavor ")	
—procurador	—attorney, *procurator*	[*proctor*]
prodigioso	prodigious (enormous, marvelous)	
—prodigio	—prodigy (marvel, person of exceptional talents)	
pródigo	*prodigal*	
—hijo pródigo	—prodigal son	
—prodigar	—(to) lavish, (to) waste, (to) appear in public	
profundo	deep, *profound*	
—profundidad	—depth, profundity	
—profundizar	—(to) deepen, (to) study in depth	
progenie	*progeny* (offspring; obs. "lineage")	
—progenitor	—progenitor (esp. father/mother)	

programa (m.)	program	
—programar	—(to) program	
—programador	—programmer	
—programación	—programming (computer, TV/radio), planning (economic)	
proletariado	proletariat	
—proletario	—proletarian	
—prole (f.)	—offspring, progeny	[*prole*]
promesa	*promise*	
—prometer	—(to) *promise*	
—prometedor	—promising	
—prometido (p.p.)	—betrothed, fiancé	
—prometida	—betrothed, fiancée	
pronosticar	(to) prognosticate, (to) forecast	
—pronóstico	—forecast, *prognosis*	
pronunciación	pronunciation	
—pronunciar	—(to) pronounce	
—pronunciamiento	—pronouncement (judicial), (military) rebellion	[pronuncia-miento < Sp.]
—impronunciable	—unpronounceable	
propender	(to) tend, (to) have a *propensity* for	
—propenso	—inclined or prone (to)	[† *propense*]
—propensión	—*propensity*, tendency	
propicio	*propitious*	
—propiciar	—(to) favor (facilitate), (to) *propitiate*	
prosa	prose	
prospecto	prospectus, (information) leaflet	
—prospección	—prospecting, market survey/research	
prosperidad	prosperity	
—prosperar	—(to) prosper	
—próspero	—prosperous	
protagonista	protagonist (main character)	
—protagonizar	—(to) play the lead in, (to) star in	
protección	protection	
—protector (adj. & n.)	—protective, protector	
—proteccionismo	—protectionism	
—proteccionista	—protectionist	
—protectorado	—protectorate	
—proteger	—(to) protect	
—protegido, -ida	—protected, *protégé, protégée*	
protón	proton	
provenir	(to) come or originate (from)	[*provenance*]
—proveniente	—coming or originating (from)	

provincia	province	
—provincial	—provincial (relating to a province)	
—provinciano (adj. & n.)	—provincial (resident of a province; lacking urban "refinement")	
proximidad	proximity	
—próximo	—proximate (near in time or space; next)	
pueril	puerile (juvenile, childish)	
—puericultura	—*puericulture* (science of child-rearing)	
pulcritud	neatness, tidiness	[*pulchritude*]
—pulcro	—neat, tidy, meticulous	
púlpito	pulpit	
punitivo	punitive	
puro (adj. & n.)	*pure,* cigar	
—pureza	—purity	
—puré	—purée	
—purificar	—(to) purify	
—purificación	—purification	
—purificador	—purifier (air, household water)	
—purista	—purist	
—puritano (adj. & n.)	—puritanical, puritan, Puritan	
—puritanismo	—puritanism, Puritanism	
—apuro	—tight spot, predicament, hardship	
—apurar	—(to) finish off (drink, etc.), (to) press (urge on)	
—depurar	—(to) *depurate* (cleanse or purify), (to) *purge* (organization)	
—depuración	—depuration (cleansing or purification), purge	
—depuradora	—water treatment plant, *depurator*	
—impuro	—impure	
—impureza	—impurity	
querella	complaint (legal or other), *quarrel,* lament	
quieto	quiet (still, calm)	
—quietud	—quietude, quiet, stillness	
—quedo (adj.)	—*quiet* (silent, hushed)	
—quedo (adv.)	—quietly, in a hushed voice	
—quedar	—(to) remain (stay, be left)	
—quedar(se) con	—(to) keep (to) retain	
—inquieto	—uneasy, worried, restless	
—inquietud	—inquietude (uneasiness, restlessness), disquiet	
—inquietar	—(to) disquiet (disturb, alarm)	
—inquietante	—disquieting	
—réquiem	—requiem	
quiosco, kiosco	*kiosk* (stand, booth, pavilion)	
quitar	(to) remove	[*quit, quiet*]
—quitamanchas	—spot remover	

—quitanieves	—snowplow	
—quitasol	—parasol, sunshade	
—desquitar	—(to) *requite* (repay, get even with)	
—desquite	—*requital* (return or recompense, revenge)	
racial	racial	
—racismo	—racism	
—raza	—race	
radiación	radiation	
—radiactivo	—radioactive	
—radiactividad	—radioactivity	
—radiar	—(to) radiate, (to) broadcast	
—radiante	—radiant	
—radiador	—radiator	
radial	radial	
radián	radian	
radio (1) (f.)	radio	
—radio (2)	—radius (geom., bone), spoke (wheel)	
—radio (3)	—radium (element)	
—radiografía	—X-ray, radiography	
—radar (< Eng.)	—radar	(**ra**dio **d**etecting **a**nd **r**anging)
raíl (< Eng.)	rail (for trains)	
—riel	—rail (for trains, curtains, etc.)	
rampa	ramp	
rancho	ranch, communal meal (e.g., for soldiers), rancho	
raqueta	*racquet*, paddle (table tennis), snowshoe	
raso (adj.)	flat, level, cloudless	["*razor* smooth"]
—soldado raso	—common soldier (private)	[*rascal*]
—al raso	—(out) in the open, "under the stars"	
—raso (n.)	—satin	
—arrasar	—(to) *raze* (demolish), (to) make level	
—arrastrar	—(to) drag	
—arrastre	—dragging, trawling	
—rascar	—(to) scratch, (to) scrape	[*rash*—n.]
—rascacielos	—skyscraper	(rasca + cielos)
—rastrillo	—rake	
—rastro	—trace, trail (~ *huella, pista*)	[*raster*]
—rastrear	—(to) track, (to) trail, (to) comb (search systematically)	
—rastreo	—tracking (person, package)	
raspar	(to) scrape, (to) *rasp*	
raya (1)	*ray* (fish)	

rayo	*ray,* beam, lightning (bolt), spoke	(Lat. RADIUS)
—raya (2)	—thin line, stripe, dash (—), boundary, part (hair), crease (trousers)	
—rayar	—(to) draw lines on, (to) scratch (e.g., disk)	
—subrayar	—(to) underline (draw a line under; stress)	
real (1)	real	(Lat. REALIS)
—realidad	—reality	
—realismo (1)	—realism	
—realista (1)	—realistic, realist	
—realización	—realization (act of carrying out)	
—realizar	—(to) realize (carry out), (to) direct (film)	
—realizador	—(film) director, (TV) producer	
—[dar(se) cuenta de]	—(to) realize (become aware)	
—irreal	—unreal	
—irrealidad	—unreality	
real (2)	*royal*	(Lat. REGALIS)
—realeza	—*royalty*	
—realismo (2)	—*royalism*	
—realista (2)	—*royalist*	
rebelión	rebellion (organized resistance)	
—rebelde (adj. & n.)	—rebellious, stubborn, rebel	
—rebeldía	—rebelliousness, rebellion (act or show of defiance)	
—rebelar(se)	—(to) rebel, (to) revolt	
recesión	recession	
recíproco	reciprocal	
—reciprocidad	—reciprocity	
reclamación	complaint, *claim* (demand), *reclamation*	
—reclamar	—(to) complain, (to) demand, (to) protest	[*reclaim*]
reclusión	seclusion, confinement, imprisonment, *reclusion*	
—recluir	—(to) confine, (to) imprison, (to) *seclude*	
—recluso	—prisoner, inmate (~ *preso*)	(old p.p.)
redactar	(to) redact (put in writing; edit)	
—redactor	—redactor, writer, editor	
—redacción	—redaction, wording, editorial staff	
redundante	redundant	
—redundancia	—redundancy	
—redundar	—(to) *redound* (have an effect, for good or ill)	
reemplazar	(to) *replace*	
—reemplazo	—*replacement*	
referencia	reference	
—referir	—(to) *refer,* (to) *relate*	
—referente	—*referent,* reference (standard of comparison)	

—referente a | —referring to, relating to
—referendo / referéndum | —referendum
—refrendar | —(to) ratify, (to) confirm | (< referendar)
refinería | refinery
—refinar | —(to) refine
reflexión | act of *reflection* (light, mental, in words)
—reflexionar | —(to) reflect (mental), (to) ponder
—reflejar | —(to) reflect (physical; make apparent or show)
—reflexivo | —reflective (reflecting; thoughtful), reflexive (gram.)
—reflejo (adj.) | —reflected, reflex, reflexive
—reflejo (n.) | —reflex, reflection (image)
—reflector | —reflector, spotlight, searchlight
reformar | (to) reform, (to) modify
—reforma, Reforma | —reform, modification, Reformation
—reformista | —reformist
—reformatorio | —reformatory
refugio | *refuge,* shelter
—refugiar | —(to) give refuge, (to) take refuge
refrán | proverb, saying | [*refrain*]
regata | regatta (boat race)
regimiento | regiment
—régimen (pl. regímenes) | —regime, regimen
región | *region*
—regional | —regional
registro | *register,* search, *registry* (office)
—registrar | —(to) register, (to) search
—registrador (adj. & n.) | —registering, register (device), registrar (esp. of property)
—caja registradora | —*cash register*
regresión | regression, retrogression
—regresar | —(to) return | [*regress* = obs. def.]
—regreso | —return, coming back
regular (adj.) | regular, ordinary
—por lo regular | —as a *rule,* ordinarily
—regular (vb.) | —(to) regulate
—regulación | —regulation (incl. control, as in *temperature regulation*)
—regulador (adj. & n.) | —regulatory, regulator (e.g., knob, throttle)
—regularidad | —regularity

—irregular	—irregular	
—irregularidad	—irregularity	
—regla	—*rule, regulation, ruler* (straightedge), (menstrual) period	(Lat. REGULA)
—reglamentación	—*rule*(s), *regulation*(s)	
—reglamento	—collection of rules, regulations	
—reglamentar	—(to) set rules or regulations for	
—renglón	—line (written or printed)	
—a renglón seguido	—immediately afterward	("on the next line")
—arreglar	—(to) arrange, (to) adjust, (to) fix	
—arreglo	—arrangement, repair	
relación	relation (incl. "account"), relationship	
—relacionar	—(to) relate (connect)	
—relato	—account, narrative, story	
—relatar	—(to) relate (narrate or tell)	
relativo	relative	
—relatividad	—relativity	
relevante	prominent, outstanding, *relevant* (important)	
—[pertinente]	—relevant (pertinent)	
—irrelevante	—unimportant, *irrelevant*	
relevar	(to) *relieve* (of duty, position, burden)	
—relevo	—*relief* (replacement), relay	
—relieve	—*relief* (prominence; geol.; art), *relievo*	
—poner de relieve	—(to) emphasize ("put in *relief*")	
—alto relieve, bajo relieve	—alto-relievo, basso-relievo (bas-relief)	
remanente	*remnant, remainder* (merchandise)	
remedio	remedy	
—remediar	—(to) remedy	
remisión	remission (debt, sin, disease), sending	
—remiso	—reluctant, *remiss*	
—remitir	—(to) *remit* (incl. "postpone"; "abate"), (to) send	
—remitente (m./f.)	—sender	
—remesa	—*remittance*, shipment	
remoto	remote	
rencor	*rancor*, grudge, animosity	
—rencoroso	—*rancorous*, spiteful	
rendir	(to) *surrender*, (to) force to *surrender*, (to) *render*	
—rendición	—*rendition* ("*surrender*")	
—rendimiento	—yield, output, performance	[*rent*]
—renta	—*rent*, income	
—renta vitalicia	—(life) annuity	
—rentable	—income-generating, profitable	[*rentable*]

—rentabilidad	—profitability, cost-effectiveness
—arrendar	—(to) *rent* (from or to)
—arrendamiento	—renting, rent (payment)
renunciar	(to) *renounce* (resign, give up)
—renuncia	—resignation (act or letter), renunciation
—renunciación ~ renunciamiento	—renunciation
repertorio	repertoire, repertory
replicar	(to) *reply,* (to) retort
—réplica	—*reply,* retort, rejoinder, *replica*
reporte	report (esp. news)
—reportaje	—(press) report, reportage
—reportero	—reporter
—reportar	—(to) bring (benefit, profit), (to) *report* (Amer.)
reprender	(to) *reprehend,* (to) scold
—reprensión	—*reprehension,* scolding
—reprensible	—*reprehensible*
represalia	*reprisal*
reproche	*reproach*
—reprochar	—(to) reproach
—irreprochable	—irreproachable
repudiar	(to) repudiate
—repudio	—repudiation
rescindir	(to) rescind
—escindir	—(to) divide, (to) split
—escisión	—*scission* (division, split)
—prescindir	—(to) do without, (to) dispense with [*prescind*]
—imprescindible	—indispensable, essential
reserva	reserve, reservation (hotel, doubt, tract of land)
—reservación (Amer.)	—reservation (hotel, theater, etc.)
—reservar	—(to) reserve (incl. "hold in *reserve*")
—reservado (p.p.)	—reserved (timid), confidential, private compartment (m.)
respecto	respect (feature or detail)
—al respecto	—in this respect, in this regard
—(con) respecto a	—with respect to, with regard to
—respectivo	—respective
—respectivamente	—respectively
—respeto	—respect (esteem)
—respetar	—(to) respect
—respetable (adj. & n.)	—respectable (incl. "considerable")
—respetuoso	—respectful

—irrespetuoso	—disrespectful	
—despectivo	—disparaging, pejorative	
responder	(to) respond, (to) reply	
—respuesta	—*response,* reply	[*riposte*]
responsable	responsible, liable	
—responsabilidad	—responsibility, liability	
—irresponsable	—irresponsible	
—irresponsabilidad	—irresponsibility	
restaurante	restaurant	
—restaurar	—(to) *restore*	
—restauración	—restoration	
—instaurar	—(to) establish or found	[† *instore*]
—instauración	—instauration (founding, establishment)	
resultado (p.p.)	result, outcome	
—resultar	—(to) result (from), (to) turn out to be	
—resultante	—resulting, resultant (adj. & n.f.)	
resumen	*résumé* (summary)	
—resumir	—(to) summarize, (to) sum up	[*resume*]
—reasumir	—(to) *resume,* (to) *reassume* (control, power)	
retener	(to) *retain,* (to) withhold	
—retención	—retention, withholding	
retirar	(to) *retire,* (to) withdraw, (to) remove	
—retiro	—retirement, retreat (place), pension	
—retirado (p.p.)	—remote, secluded, *retiree*	
—retirada	—retreat (mil.), withdrawal	
retorno	*return* (~ *vuelta*)	
—retornar	—(to) *return*	
—tornar	—(to) *return,* (to) *turn* into (become)	
—tornasol	—sunflower (~ *girasol*), litmus	
—torneo	—*tourney,* tournament	
—torno	—lathe	[*turner*]
—en torno a	—around, about	
—entorno	—environment, surroundings	[*entourage*]
—torniquete	—tourniquet, turnstile	
—tornillo	—screw	
—atornillar	—(to) screw (in)	
—destornillar	—(to) unscrew (~ *desatornillar*)	
—destornillador	—screwdriver (~ *atornillador, desatornillador*)	
—contorno	—*contour,* outline, surroundings (gen. pl.)	
—trastorno	—upset, disturbance, derangement	
—trastornar	—(to) "*turn* upside down", (to) derange	
retroceder	(to) retrocede (go backwards, *recede*)	
—retroceso	—*receding* (e.g., of glaciers), relapse, recoil (of weapon)	

reunión	meeting, *reunion*	
—reunir	—(to) meet, (to) gather, (to) *reunite*	
revelación	revelation	
—revelar	—(to) *reveal*, (to) develop (photo)	
—revelado (p.p.)	—photo developing	
—revelador (adj. & n.)	—revealing, developer (liquid, for photos)	
reverso	reverse	
—reversible	—reversible	
—reversibilidad	—reversibility	
—revertir	—(to) revert	
—revés	—other side, *reverse*, backhand	(Lat. REVERSUS)
—al revés	—backwards, inside out	
revisión	checkup, *review, revision*	
—revisar	—(to) check, (to) *review*, (to) *revise*	
—revista	—*review*, magazine, *revue*	
rienda	*rein*	
—dar rienda suelta	—(to) give free *rein*	
riesgo	*risk*	
—arriesgar	—(to) *risk*	
—arriesgado (p.p.)	—*risky*, daring	
rigor	rigor, severity	
—riguroso	—rigorous, severe	
rival	rival	
—rivalidad	—rivalry	
—rivalizar	—(to) rival, (to) compete	
—río[89]	—river	[*Rio* Grande]
—ría	—estuary, firth, *ria*[90]	
roca	*rock*	
—derrocar	—(to) demolish, (to) overthrow	("throw from a *rock*")
—derrochar (< Fr.)	—(to) waste, (to) squander	
—derroche	—waste, squandering	
—rococó	—rococo	
rollo	*roll* (something rolled up)	
—rol	—*role* (~ *papel*), *roll* (list of names)	
—enrollar	—(to) enroll (roll or wrap up)	
—enrolar	—(to) enroll (register), (to) enlist	

---

[89] From Latin RIVUS ("stream"), RIVALIS referred to those using the same stream, hence *rivals*. English *river* is unrelated.

[90] "Funnel-shaped estuary that occurs at a river mouth and is formed by the submergence of the lower portion of the river valley" (*Encyclopaedia Britannica*).

—arrollar	—(to) *roll* up, (to) *roll* over (run over; win easily)
—desarrollar	—(to) develop, (to) *unroll*
—desarrollo	—development
—ruleta	—roulette
ronco[91]	hoarse, *raucous* (voice, sound)
—ronquera	—hoarseness
—roncar	—(to) snore [*rhonchus*]
—ronquido	—snore, snoring
rosa	rose
—rosado	—pink, *rose* (color), *rosy, rosé* (wine)
rubí	*ruby*
—rubio, rubia	—blond, blonde, fair-haired (Lat. RUBEUS, "reddish")
—rubor	—blush (from embarrassment or shame)
—ruborizar(se)	—(to) blush, (to) turn red
—rubeola, rubéola	—*rubella* (German measles)
—[sarampión (m.)]	—*rubeola* (measles)
rúbrica	signature (flourish), *rubric*
—rubricar	—(to) sign (and seal), (to) initial (approve)
rudo	rude (rough, crude, coarse, etc.)
—rudeza	—rudeness (incl. "roughness")
—rudimento	—rudiment (freq. pl.)
—rudimentario	—rudimentary
ruina	ruin
—ruin	—vile, stingy
—ruinoso	—ruinous (falling to ruin; apt to cause ruin)
—arruinar	—(to) ruin
rumor	rumor, rumbling noise, murmur (e.g., ocean)
sabana	*savanna* (treeless plain)
—sábana[92]	—(bed) sheet
saciar	(to) *satiate*, (to) *sate*, (to) *satis*fy (hunger, etc.)
—saciedad	—satiety, satiation
—insaciable	—insatiable
saco	*sack* (bag), jacket (Amer.)
—saco de dormir	—sleeping bag
—saco amniótico	—amniotic *sac*
—sacar	—(to) remove, (to) obtain, (to) bring out (record), (to) serve (tennis)
—sacar la lengua	—(to) stick out the tongue

[91] *Ronco* was initially *roco* (the "natural" result from Latin RAUCUS) and subsequently took its *n* from the unrelated *roncar*.

[92] These two words are unrelated and pronounced differently: *sabana* (sa•**ba**•na) has a Caribbean origin, while *sábana* (**sá**•ba•na) comes from Greek (via Latin).

—sacacorchos	—corkscrew	
—saque	—kickoff, serve (tennis, volleyball, etc.)	
—saque de esquina	—corner kick (~ *córner*)	
—saqueo	—*sack* (pillage, looting), sacking	
—saquear	—(to) *sack* (plunder, loot)	
—saqueador	—looter	
—resaca	—undertow, hangover	
sadismo	sadism	
—sádico (adj. & n.)	—sadistic, sadist	
sagaz	*sagacious* (astute)	
—sagacidad	—*sagacity*	
saliente	outgoing (retiring), *salient* (adj. & n.m./f.)	
—presidente saliente	—outgoing president	
—salida	—exit (way out, departure)	[*sally*]
—salida del sol	—sunrise	
—salir	—(to) go out, (to) leave, (to) *sally* (forth)	
—sobresalir	—(to) project, (to) stand out, (to) excel	[*somersault*]
—sobresaliente	—standing out, outstanding, highest exam grade	[*super* + *salient*]
salto	jump, leap	
—salto de agua	—*sault,* waterfall	[*Sault* Sainte Marie]
—salto mortal	—somer*sault*	
—saltar	—(to) jump, (to) leap	[rare *saltate*]
—saltamontes	—grasshopper	("mountain jumper")
—saltador (adj. & n.)	—jumping, leaping, jumper, leaper	
—saltear	—(to) *sauté,* (to) *assault* ("highway robbery")	
—salteado (p.p.)	—*sautéed*	
—resaltar	—(to) jut out, (to) stand out, (to) highlight	[*result*]
salubre	salubrious, healthful	
—insalubre	—insalubrious, unhealthy	
sandalia	*sandal*	
sándwich (< Eng.)	sandwich	
sano	healthy, wholesome, sound	[*sane*]
—sano y *salvo*	—*safe* and sound	
—[cuerdo]	—sane, sensible (or such a person)	
—sanidad	—(public) health (system)	[*sanity*]
—sanatorio	—sanatorium, hospital	
—sanitario (adj.)	—sanitary (relating to health), health (adj.)	
—sanitarios (pl.)	—bathroom fixtures (toilet, sink, etc.)	
—sanar	—(to) heal, (to) recover (from sickness)	
—sanear	—(to) clean up, (to) drain (lands), (to) reorganize (business)	

—saneamiento	—cleaning up, improvement (e.g., land), sanitation	
—subsanar	—(to) remedy, (to) rectify	
sarcasmo	sarcasm	
—sarcástico	—sarcastic	
sargento	sergeant	
satélite	satellite	
sátira	satire	
—satírico	—satiric	
—satirizar	—(to) satirize	
—sátiro	—*satyr*	(unrelated)
sauna	sauna	
secesión	secession	
—secesionista	—secessionist	
secreto	secret, secrecy	
—secretar	—(to) secrete (give off a secretion)	
—secreción	—secretion	
—secretario	—secretary	
—secretaría	—job of secretary, secretariat	
secuestrar	(to) kidnap, (to) hijack, (to) *sequester* (confiscate)	
—secuestro	—kidnapping, highjacking, *sequestration* (seizure of property)	
—secuestrador	—kidnapper, highjacker	
seducción	seduction	
—seducir	—(to) seduce	
—seductor (adj. & n.)	—seductive, seducer	
seísmo, sismo (Amer.)	earthquake, *seism*	
—sísmico	—*seismic*	
selva	forest, jungle, *selva*	(Lat. SILVA)
—selva amazónica	—Amazon Rain Forest	
—selvático	—forest (adj.), *sylvan,* wild, *sylvatic*	(Lat. SILVATICUS)
—salvaje	—wild, *savage* (adj. & n.m./f.)	(Lat. SILVATICUS)
—silvestre	—wild, uncultivated	[*Sylvester, Silvester*]
—Pensilvania	—Pennsylvania	[*Penn's* forest]
sensible	sensible (perceptible by the senses), sensitive	
—sensibilidad	—sensibility (ability to feel or perceive), feeling, sensitivity	
—sensato	—sensible, judicious, wise	[*sensate*]
—sensatez	—good sense, wisdom	
—insensato	—senseless, *insensate* (foolish)	
—insensatez	—senselessness, foolishness, folly	

—sensual	—sensual, sensuous
sentencia	sentence (judgment), proverb or maxim[93]
—sentenciar	—(to) sentence, (to) pass judgment on
sepultura	*sepulture* (burial, tomb), grave
—sepultar	—(to) bury, (to) entomb
—sepulturero	—gravedigger
—sepulcro	—*sepulchre* (burial vault, receptacle for sacred relics)
—sepulcral	—sepulchral
—sepelio	—burial, interment
sereno (1)	serene (calm, cloudless)
—serenidad	—serenity
—sereno (2)	—night watchman, night dew
—serenata	—serenade, serenata
serie	series
—serial	—serial (adj. & n.)
serio	serious
—seriamente	—seriously (to a serious extent; in a serious manner)
—en serio	—seriously (in a serious manner)
—seriedad	—seriousness (situation; manner)
servir	(to) serve
—sirviente, sirvienta	—*servant*
—siervo	—*serf,* slave, *servant* (e.g., "of God", "humble")
severo	severe
—severidad	—severity
—aseverar	—(to) *asseverate* (affirm solemnly, assert emphatically)
—aseveración	—asseveration, assertion
sexo	sex
—sexual	—sexual
—sexy, sexi	—sexy
—sexista	—sexist
sibilante (adj. & n.f.)	sibilant (hissing sound)
—silbar[94]	—(to) whistle, (to) hiss (a performance) [*sibilate*]
—silbato	—whistle (device)
—silbido	—whistle (sound), whistling

---

[93] This is an "archaic" definition of English *sentence* as well: "Who fears a *sentence* or an old man's saw, Shall by a painted cloth be kept in awe" (Shakespeare, *The Rape of Lucrece*).

[94] Via the following transformations: SIBILARE → siblar → silbar. In *chiflar,* the *f* preserves a dialectical variant going back to Latin times, while the inital consonant was changed to *ch* to make it more "expressive".

—chiflar	—(to) whistle, (to) be crazy for (someone or something)	
—chiflado (p.p.)	—round the bend (~ *loco*), "nutty" or "nuts", smitten	
—rechifla	—hissing, derision	
SIDA (m.)	AIDS (**sí**ndrome de **i**nmuno**d**eficiencia **a**dquirida)	
significar	(to) signify	
—significado (p.p.)	—significance (meaning)	
—significación	—signification, significance (importance)	
—significativo	—significative, significant (important)	
—significante	—signifiant (linguistics)	
silencio	silence	
—silencioso	—silent	
—silenciar	—(to) silence, (to) keep silent about	
—silenciador	—silencer, muffler (auto)	
silo	silo (< Sp.)	
silueta	*silhouette*	(< Monsieur de *Silhouette*)
simple	simple, single (e.g., room)	
—simplicidad	—simplicity	
—simplificar	—(to) simplify	
—simplificación	—simplification	
—simplemente	—simply	
—simpleza	—simplicity (foolishness, naiveté), simplemindedness	
simultáneo	simultaneous	
—simultáneamente	—simultaneously (~ *al mismo tiempo*)	
—simultaneidad	—simultaneity	
sincero	sincere	
—sinceridad	—sincerity	
singular	singular	
—singularidad	—singularity	
—sencillo	—simple, plain, *single* (record—esp. 45 rpm)	(Lat. SINGELLUS)
—sencillez	—simplicity, plainness	
—sencillamente	—simply	
sin**ie**stro (adj.)	*sinister* (left [adj.], evil, baneful)	
—siniestro (n.)	—disaster (fire, shipwreck, etc.)	
—siniestra (n.)	—left hand	
sirena	siren (device, sea nymph), mermaid	
sitio (1)	*site*, place, location	
—sito	—*situated* (e.g., "a house *situated* at no. 5 Main Street")	
—situación	—situation	

—situar	—(to) *situate* (place, locate), (to) *site*
—sitiar [95]	—(to) besiege, (to) surround
—sitio (2)	—siege (~ *asedio*)
social	social
—sociable	—sociable
—socialismo	—socialism
—socialista	—socialist
—socializar	—(to) socialize (nationalize, carry out social policy, make sociable)
—socialización	—nationalization, socialization (integration into society)
—sociedad	—society
—sociedad anónima	—limited-liability company, corporation
—socio	—partner, member, *associate*
sofisticación	sophistication
—sofisticado	—sophisticated
solemne	solemn
—solemnidad	—solemnity
solo	*sole* (lone, one, only, alone), *solo* (adj. & n.)
—solamente ~ sólo	—only (adv.), *solo* (adv.), *solely*
—soledad	—*solitude,* loneliness [*Soledad,* CA]
—solitario (adj. & n.)	—solitary, *solitaire*
—soltero (adj. & n.m./f.)	—unmarried, bachelor (doublet of *solitario*)
solución	solution (to a mystery, and as a liquid)
—solucionar	—(to) solve (~ *resolver*)
solvente (adj. & n.)	solvent (financially; chemistry)
—solventar	—(to) pay a debt, (to) *resolve* a problem
—solvencia	—solvency, reliability
—insolvente	—insolvent
—insolvencia	—insolvency
sonata	sonata
sondear ~ sondar	(to) *sound* (measure or probe)
—sonda	—*sounding* line, probe, *sound* (med.), catheter
—sonda espacial	—space probe
—sondeo	—*sounding,* fathoming, probing, poll
soneto	sonnet
sonido	*sound*
—son	—*sound* (pleasant, esp. music)
—sonoro	—*sonorous,* voiced (consonant—linguistics)
—sonar (1)	—(to) *sound,* (to) strike or ring (clock), (to) blow (nose)

---

[95] *Sitiar* seems to represent a mixing of the verbs *situar* and *asediar* ("to besiege").

—sonar (2) (< Eng.)	—sonar (naval) [96]	
—resonar	—(to) *resound,* (to) *resonate,* (to) echo	
—resonancia	—resonance, echo	
soporífero	soporific (sleep-inducing; sleeping pill)	
—sopor	—drowsiness, sopor	
—somnífero	—somniferous, soporific (adj. & n.)	
sórdido	sordid	
—sordidez	—sordidness	
sorpresa	*surprise*	
—sorprender	—(to) surprise	
—sorprendente	—surprising	
sostener	(to) *sustain*	
—sostenimiento	—sustenance, support	
—sostenido (p.p.)	—sharp (music)	
—fa sostenido	—F sharp	
—sostenible	—*sustainable*	
—sostén	—support, brassiere	
—sustentar	—(to) *sustain*	
—sustento	—sustenance, support	
—sustentación	—sustentation, (aerodynamic) lift	
—sustentable	—sustainable	
suave	soft, smooth, mild, gentle	[*suave*]
—suavidad	—softness, smoothness, mildness	
—suavizante (adj. & n.)	—softening, fabric softener	
—suavizar	—(to) soften, (to) make smooth	[*assuage*]
subordinación	subordination	
—subordinar	—(to) subordinate	
—subordinado (p.p.)	—subordinate (adj. & n.)	
—insubordinación	—insubordination	
subterfugio	subterfuge	
sucumbir	(to) succumb (yield, give up, die)	
suficiente	sufficient	
—suficiencia	—sufficiency (esp. archaic "ability or competence")	
—insuficiente	—insufficient	
—insuficiencia	—insufficiency (esp. medical)	
sufragio	suffrage (incl. obs. "help, assistance")	
—sufragar	—(to) defray (costs), (to) vote (Amer.)	
sufrir	(to) suffer (incl. "bear, undergo")	
—sufrimiento	—suffering, sufferance	

---

[96] The coincidence between sonar (1) and sonar (2) is largely coincidental: English *sonar* is an acronym for **so**und **na**vigation and **r**anging, and was patterned after *radar* (**ra**dio **d**etecting **and r**anging).

—insufrible	—insufferable
suicidio	suicide
—suicida	—suicidal, suicide (person)
(adj. & n.m./f.)	
—suicidar(se)	—(to) commit suicide
sumergir	(to) *submerge,* (to) *immerse*
superior	superior, upper
—inferior	—inferior, lower
—posterior	—posterior ("after", in time or order), rear or back (adj.)
—ulterior	—ulterior (esp. "further", "subsequent")
—ulteriormente	—subsequently
superlativo	superlative
suplemento	supplement
—suplementario	—supplementary, supplemental (~ *suplemental*)
—suplir	—(to) *supplement,* (to) substitute [*supply*]
—suplente	—substitute
(adj. & n.m./f.)	
—supletorio	—additional, *supple*mentary (esp. telephone)
suplicante	*supplicant, suppliant,* humble petitioner
(adj. & n.m./f.)	
—suplicar	—(to) supplicate (ask for humbly, beseech)
—suplicio	—torture, torment [*supple*]
surgir	(to) arise, (to) spring forth, (to) *surge*
—resurgir	—(to) resurge, (to) revive
—resurgimiento	—resurgence
—insurgente	—insurgent
suscripción[97]	subscription
—suscribir	—(to) subscribe
—suscriptor	—subscriber
sutil	*subtle* (incl. obs. "thin, fine")
—sutileza	—subtlety
tabaco	*tobacco*
tabla	*table* (list, math.), board
—tabla de planchar	—ironing board
—tablero	—board (chess, checkers, drawing), panel
—tableta	—tablet (pill), chocolate bar
—entablar	—(to) board (up), (to) start (conversation, negotiation, etc.)
tabú	*taboo*
taburete	stool, *taboret* (or *tabouret*)
taciturno	taciturn
tacto	*tact* (incl. archaic "sense of touch"), touch

---

[97] *Suscripción* and the following words can also be written *subs-*.

—táctil	—tactile (perceptible to the touch, relating to sense of touch)	
talento	talent	
—talentoso	—talented	
tallar	(to) cut, (to) carve	[*tailor*]
—talla	—carving, height, stature, size (clothes)	[*intaglio*]
—talle	—waist, clothes measurement	[*tally*]
—tajar	—(to) cut or slice (e.g., melon)	[*tagliatelle*]
—tajante	—sharp, categorical (i.e., other possibilities lit. "cut off")	
—tajada	—cut, slice	
—sacar tajada (de)	—(to) benefit from ("get a *slice* of the pie", "take one's *cut*")	
—tajo	—cut, incision	
—atajar	—(to) put a stop to ("cut off"), (to) take a short cut	
—atajo	—shortcut	
—destajo	—piecework (paid by output rather than time)	[*detail*]
taller	workshop, studio, *atelier*	
tambor	drum, eardrum, *tambour*	
—tamboril ~ tamborín	—*tabor* (small drum), *tambourin*	
—[pandereta]	—*tambourine*	[*pandore*]
tangible	tangible	
—tangente (adj. & n.f.)	—tangent	
—tañer	—(to) play a musical instrument (~ *tocar*)	
—atañer	—(to) concern (lit. "touch")	[*attain*]
—por lo que atañe a	—as far as [something] is concerned (~ *en cuanto a*)	
tapiz	*tapestry*	
—tapizar	—(to) hang tapestries, (to) upholster	
—tapicería	—tapestry (art), upholstery, upholstery shop	
tapón	stopper, plug, cork	[*tap, tampion*]
—taponar	—(to) plug, (to) stop up, (to) *tampon*	
—tapa	—lid, cover, cap, top, *tapa* (appetizer)	
—tapadera	—lid, cover	
—tapar	—(to) cover, (to) plug, (to) stop up	
—taparrabo(s)	—loincloth ("tail cover")	(*tapa* + *rabo* = "tail")
—tampón	—tampon, stamp (ink) pad	
—destapar	—(to) uncover, (to) remove the lid from	
—destape	—uncovering, nudity (cinema, theater)	
tarjeta	card	[*target*]
—tarjeta de crédito	—credit card	

—tarjeta de identidad	—identity card
—tarjeta de embarque	—boarding card (plane or ship)
—tarjeta postal	—postcard (~ *postal*—f.)
tatuaje	tatoo, tatooing
—tatuar	—(to) tatoo
tedioso	tedious, boring
—tedio	—tedium, boredom
telescopio	telescope
—telescópico	—telescopic
temeridad	temerity, rashness
—temerario	—temerarious ("rashly or presumptuously daring")
temperamento	temperament
—temperamental	—temperamental
temperatura	temperature
tenacidad	tenacity
—tenaz	—*tenacious*
—tenaza	—pincers, tongs (sing. or pl.) [*tenaculum*]
—atenazar	—(to) hold with tongs, (to) grip tightly (esp. with fear)
—pertinaz	—*pertinacious* ($e \rightarrow i$: Section 1.3)
—pertinacia	—pertinacity
tenis	tennis
—tenista	—tennis player
tenor	tenor (general sense; musical voice or singer)
—a tenor de	—in accordance with
—tener	—(to) have
—abstener	—(to) *abstain,* (to) refrain
—atener(se)	—(to) abide by, (to) conform to (rule, norm) (see also: con-, de-, entre-, man-, ob-, re-, sos- *plus* tener)
—tenencia	—possession (control or occupancy) [*tenancy*]
—teniente (m./f.)	—lieu*t*enant (mil.), deputy (e.g., mayor)
—lugarteniente	—deputy, substitute, *lieutenant*
tentar	(to) *tempt*
—tentación	—*temptation*
—tentador (-ora)	—tempting, tempter (temptress)
—tentativo (adj.)	—tentative
—tentativa (n.)	—*attempt*
—atentar	—(to) *attempt* or commit (a crime)
—atentado (p.p.)	—*attempt* (attack or assault)

—intento	—*intent, attempt* (effort or try)	
—intentar	—(to) *attempt* (make an effort)	
—intención	—intention	
—intencional	—intentional, deliberate (~ *intencionado*)	
—bien intencionado	—well-intentioned	
tenue	*tenuous* (long and thin, weak), faint (light, etc.)	
terror	terror	
—aterrorizar	—(to) terrorize	
—terrible	—terrible	
—terrorífico	—terrifying, terrific ("causing terror or great fear")	
—terrorismo	—terrorism	
—terrorista	—terrorist	
tifus	*typhus, typhoid*	(Gk. *tuphos,* "smoke")
—fiebre tifoidea	—*typhoid fever*	
—tufo	—fume, disagreeable smell (lit. and fig.)	
timbre	(door) bell, (tax) stamp or seal, *timbre*	
—tímpano	—*tympanum* (ear drum, arch.), drum	
típico	*typical*	
—tipo	—*type* (kind, sort, printing), person ("guy")	
—tipo de interés	—*interest* rate	
—tipo de cambio	—*exchange* rate	
—prototipo	—prototype	
—arquetipo	—archetype	
—tipográfico	—typographical	
toalla	*towel*	
—toallero	—towel rack	
toca	*toque* (hat), wimple (nun's)	
—tocado (1)	—headdress, hairstyle, coiffure	
tocar	(to) *touch,* (to) play (an instrument)	
—tocado (2) (p.p.)	—*touched* (unbalanced), bruised (fruit, athlete or team)	
—toque	—*touch* (tap or "personal"), taps (musical signal)	
—toque de queda	—curfew	[*touch* of *quiet*]
—tocador	—dressing table (with mirror), player (of musical instrument)	
—tocadiscos	—record player	
—tocata	—toccata (keyboard composition)	
—retocar	—(to) *retouch,* (to) put the final *touches* on	
tolerante	tolerant	
—tolerancia	—tolerance, toleration	
—tolerar	—(to) tolerate	
—tolerable	—tolerable	
—intolerante	—intolerant	

—intolerancia	—intolerance	
—intolerable	—intolerable	
tono	tono	
—sin *ton* ni son [98]	—"without rhyme or reason"	[without *tone* or *sound*]
—tonada	—*tune*, song	
—tonalidad	—tonality	
—tónico (adj. & n.)	—tonic	
—entonar	—(to) sing (*in tune*), (to) *intone*, (to) *tone* up	
—**e**ntonación	—intonation	
tópico	*topical* or local (med.), platitude, *topic* (esp. Amer.) [99]	
tornado	tornado	
torpedo	torpedo	
torrente	torrent (incl. "flood"—of people, words, etc.)	
—torrente sanguíneo	—bloodstream (~ *torrente circulatorio*)	
—torrencial	—torrential	
tórrido	torrid	
tos (f.)	cough, *tussis*	
—tos ferina	—*pertussis* (whooping cough)	[*ferine* = "untamed"]
—toser	—(to) cough	
tóxico (adj. & n.)	toxic, toxic substance	
—toxicomanía	—drug addiction	
—toxicómano	—drug addict	
—toxina	—toxin	
—intoxicar	—(to) poison, (to) intoxicate	
—intoxicación	—intoxication (poisoning by drug or toxic substance)	
—desintoxicación	—detoxification, detox	
tractor	tractor	
—tracción	—traction	
—traer	—(to) bring, (to) wear	
—traje	—dress, suit, costume	[*train* of a gown]
—traje de baño	—swimsuit, bathing suit	
traducir	(to) translate (into)	[*transduce*]
—traducción	—translation (of a text or speech)	
—traductor	—translator	
tráfico	traffic (vehicles, merchandise)	

---

[98] The shortened form *ton* of *tono* is found only in this expression.

[99] According to the RAE, this sense "should be avoided", as it is a *calco inaceptable* ("unacceptable loan translation") of English *topic*.

—traficar	—(to) traffic (esp. carry on trade in illegal goods)	
—traficante (adj. & n.m./f.)	—trafficker (trader, dealer)	
—narcotráfico	—(large-scale) drug traffic	
—narcotraficante (m./f.)	—drug dealer	
tragedia	tragedy	
—trágico	—tragic	
traidor ~ traicionero	*traitorous*, treacherous, *traitor*	
—traición	—*treason*	[*tradition*]
—traicionar	—(to) *betray*	
tra**m**pa	*trap*, trapdoor, deceit (act)	
—hacer trampa(s)	—(to) cheat	
—tramposo (adj. & n.)	—deceitful, cheating, trickster, cheater	
—entrampar	—(to) *entrap*, (to) trap	
—atrapar (< Fr.)	—(to) catch (person, ball), (to) *trap*	
trampolín	*trampoline*, springboard	
tranquilo	tranquil	
—tranquilidad	—tranquillity	
—tranquilizar	—(to) tranquilize (calm, relax)	
—tranquilizante (adj. & n.)	—tranquilizing (sedative), tranquilizer	
—tranquilizador	—tranquilizing (reassuring)	
transeúnte	*transient* (person), passerby	
—trance	—critical moment or juncture, *trance*	[< Fr.]
—en trance de	—at the point of (death, extinction, etc.)	
transferir	(to) transfer	
—transferencia	—transfer (of position, bank transfer, etc.), transference	
—trasladar[100]	—(to) *transfer*, (to) *translate* (esp. math.)	
—traslado	—*transfer* (esp. of employee or residence)	
—traslación / trans-	—uniform movement (e.g., Earth around Sun), *transfer*, *translation*	
transistor	transistor	
transparente / tras-	transparent	
—transparencia / tras-	—transparency	
transportar / tras-	(to) transport, (to) transpose (music)	
—transporte / tras-	—transport, transportation	

---

[100] In Latin, the past participle of the verb FERRE ("to carry") was LATUS; hence the English pairs *refer—relate* and *transfer—translate*. Spanish *trasladar* and *traslación* can refer to language *translation*, but this is far more commonly expressed by *traducir* and *traducción*.

—transportador /	—transporting, transporter, protractor	
tras-	(instrument)	
trapo[101]	rag	[drape]
—a todo trapo	—"at full sail", "at full (or high) speed"	
—trapos sucios	—"dirty linen/laundry" (secrets)	
trascender / trans-	(to) transcend, (to) become known	
—trascendental /	—far-reaching, transcendent, transcendental	
trans-	(~ *trascendente*)	
tratar	(to) *treat,* (to) deal with	
—¿De qué se trata?	—What's it about? What does it have to do with?	
—Se trata de . . .	—It's about . . . It concerns . . .	
—trato	—*treat*ment (manner), dealings	[trait]
—trata	—(slave) trade	
—tratable	—*treatable, tractable*	
—tratado (p.p.)	—*treaty, treatise*	
—tratamiento	—*treatment,* form of address (*tú, usted, excelencia,* etc.)	
—tratante (m./f.)	—trader, dealer	
—contratar	—(to) *contract* for, (to) hire	
—contrato	—contract, agreement	
—maltratar	—(to) *maltreat,* (to) mistreat	
—maltrato	—maltreatment, mistreatment	
—retratar	—(to) por*tray*	[retrace]
—retrato	—por*trait*	
—retrete	—toilet, rest room	[retreat]
trazo	line (drawn), stroke (pen, pencil)	[trace]
—trazar	—(to) *trace* (draw, sketch, delineate)	
—trazado (p.p.)	—*trace* or (proposed) route (highway, rail, etc.)	
—traza	—design, appearance, *trace* (mark or vestige; geom.)	
tremendo	tremendous (incl. "terrible")	
tren	*train* (railroad, linked mechanical parts)	
—tren de aterrizaje	—landing gear (aircraft)	
—tren de vida	—way of life, life-style	
—entrenar	—(to) *train,* (to) coach	
—entrenador	—trainer, coach	
—entrenamiento	—training, coaching	
—trajín	—bustle, activity	
—trineo	—sled, sleigh	[rare *traineau*]
tribulación	tribulation	

---

[101] *Trapo* comes from Latin DRAPPUS ("piece of cloth"). The initial *tr* is probably due to the fact that in Spanish initial *dr* is very rare: there are nearly twenty times as many words beginning with *tr* compared to *dr,* and most of the latter are either "learned" (*drama*) or imported (*droga*).

tribunal	tribunal
—Tribunal Supremo	—Supreme Court
—tribuna	—tribune (raised platform or dais), grandstand
—tribuno	—tribune (Roman official)
—tribu (f.)	—tribe
tributo	tribute (monetary or respect)
—tributario	—tributary (paying tribute or tax; river joining larger one)
—tributar	—(to) pay tribute (tax, respect)
trinchera	*trench*
—atrincherar	—(to) *entrench* (oneself), (to) dig in
tripa	intestine, belly, *tripe*, innards (pl.)
triturar	(to) triturate (crush, grind, pulverize)
—trituración	—trituration (crushing, grinding)
triu**n**fo	*triumph, trump* (card)
—triunfar	—(to) triumph
—triunfal	—triumphal
—triunfante	—triumphant
tro**m**peta	*trumpet*
—trompetista	—trumpeter
—trompa	—horn, trunk (elephant), proboscis (insect), tube
—trompa de Falopio	—Fallopian tube
tro**p**a	*troop, troops*
—tropel	—mob, disorderly heap (of things) [*troupe*]
—atropellar	—(to) run over, (to) ride roughshod over
—atropello	—running over (of person or animal), outrage, abuse
trotar	(to) *trot* (incl. "proceed briskly")
—trote	—trot
trovador	*troubadour, trouvère*
—trova	—verse, (love) song
truhan, truhán	rogue, rascal (also as adjective) [*truant*]
tubo	*tube*, pipe
—tubo de ensayo	—test tube
—tubo de escape	—exhaust pipe
—tubería	—pipes, piping
—tubular	—tubular
tulipán	*tulip*
tu**m**ba	*tomb*
—túmulo	—tumulus (burial mound), tomb
—tumbo[102]	—jolt, stagger, tumble
—tumbar	—(to) knock down, (to) lie down

---

[102] *Tumbo, tumbar,* and *retumbar* are unrelated to *tumba.*

—retumbar	—(to) resound, (to) echo, (to) rumble	
tumulto	tumult	
—tumultuoso	—tumultuous	
túnica	tunic	
turba (1)	*turf* (peat)	[*turbary*]
turba (2)	mob, crowd	
—turbar	—(to) *disturb*	
—turbación	—*disturbance, perturbation*	
—turbio	—*turbid*	
—turbulento	—turbulent	
—turbulencia	—turbulence	
—torbellino	—whirlwind (~ *remolino*)	
turbante	turban	
turbina	turbine	
turismo	tourism	
—turista	—tourist	
turno[103] (< Fr.)	*turn,* shift	
—de turno	—on duty, (designated to be) open (e.g., *farmacia de turno*)	
—turnar	—(to) take *turns*	
tutor	tutor, guardian (legal)	
—tutela ~ tutoría	—tutelage	
ubicuidad	ubiquity	
—ubicuo	—ubiquitous	
—ubicar	—(to) situate (place), (to) be situated (located)	
—ubicación	—location, position	
úlcera	ulcer	
ultimátum	ultimatum	
—último	—last, final, ultimate	
—ultimar	—(to) finalize (negotiations, etc.), (to) kill (Amer.)	
—últimamente	—lately, recently	
—penúltimo	—penultimate (next to last)	
ultra-	ultra-	
—ultramar	—land beyond the seas (overseas)	[*ultramarine*]
—ultraje[104]	—*outrage* (freq. criminal ones)	
—ultrajante	—*outrageous,* offensive	
—ultrajar	—(to) *outrage*	
—a ultranza	—"to the death", resolute(ly), "at all costs"	
unción	unction, *anointing*	

---

[103] See also the numerous related "native" Spanish words listed under *retorno.*

[104] *Outrage* thus has nothing to do with either *out* or *rage*—it is simply the typical French *-age* ending added to *outre* (< ULTRA, "beyond"). The literal sense is thus something that is "out of bounds" or "beyond the pale".

—untuoso	—*unctuous* (greasy, oily), sticky	
—ungir	—(to) an*oint*	
—ungüento	—*oint*ment	
—untar	—(to) spread, (to) smear, (to) bribe	
único	*unique*, sole	
—únicamente	—only, solely, *uniquely*	
uniforme (adj. & n.)	uniform	
—uniformidad	—uniformity	
—uniformar	—(to) uniform (make uniform; provide with uniforms)	
urgente	urgent	
—urgentemente	—urgently	
—urgencia	—urgency, emergency	
—urgir	—(to) be urgent, (to) urge	
urna	urn (incl. for voting), ballot box	
uso	use, usage	
—usar	—(to) use	
—usado (p.p.)	—used (second-hand)	
—usuario	—user	
—usual	—usual	
—**in**usual	—unusual	
—inusitado	—unusual	[† *inusitate*]
—desuso	—disuse	
usura	*usury*	
—usurero	—usurer	
utensilio	utensil	
utopía	utopia	
—utópico	—utopian (adj.)	
—utopista	—utopian (n.)	
vacío (adj. & n.)	empty, *vacant*, *void* (empty space), *vacuum*	
—vaciar	—(to) empty, (to) hollow out, (to) cast (form in a mold)	
—vaciado (p.p.)	—cast (mold), excavation	
—vacuo	—*vacuous* (empty, devoid of substance)	(Lat. VACUUS)
—vacante (adj. & n.f.)	—vacant, vacancy	
—vacaciones (pl.)	—vacation, holidays	
—va**g**o (1)	—lazy (~ *holgazán, perezoso*)	(Lat. VACUUS)
—va**g**uear (1) ~ va**g**ar (1)	—(to) be idle, (to) lie around	
vadem**é**cum	*vade mecum* (handbook, manual)	("go with me")
—vadear	—(to) *wade*, (to) ford	
—vado	—ford, modified curb for vehicle entry	[*wade*]
—vaivén[105]	—to-and-fro motion, ups and downs (pl.)	

---

[105] Literally meaning "goes and comes", *vaivén* probably comes from Catalan (the "native" Castilian form would be **va y viene*).

vago (2)	*vague*	(Lat. VAGUS)
—vagar (2) ~ vaguear (2)	—(to) wander aimlessly, (to) roam	[*vagary*]
—vaguedad	—vagueness	
—vagabundo (adj. & n.)	—*vagabond*, vagrant	
—vagabundear	—(to) vagabond (wander, roam about)	
—divagar	—(to) divagate (ramble, digress)	
—extravagante	—odd, outlandish	[*extravagant* = obs. def.[106]]
—extravagancia	—oddness, outlandishness	[*extravagance*]
vagón	railroad car or *wagon*	
—vagoneta	—small wagon, open railroad wagon	
valija	*valise*, mailbag	
—valija diplomática	—diplomatic pouch	
—desvalijar	—(to) rob, (to) burgle	[*dis* + *valise*]
vals	*waltz*	
valva	valve (biol., bot.)	
—válvula	—valve (mechanical, electrical, anatomical)	
—válvula de escape	—escape valve (physical, emotional)	
vampiro	vampire, vampire bat	
variación	variation	
—variable (adj. & n.f.)	—variable	
—vario	—varied, several (pl.), various (pl.)	
—variedad	—variety, variety show (pl.)	
—variar	—(to) *vary,* (to) change	
—variado (p.p.)	—varied (diverse; of different colors)	
—variante (adj. & n.f.)	—variant, bypass (road)	
—variable (adj. & n.f.)	—variable	
—invariable	—invariable	
—desvarío	—delirium, raving, nonsense	
—desvariar	—(to) talk nonsense, (to) rave	
varicela	*varicella* (chicken pox)	
—viruela	—*variola* (smallpox)	
vasallo	*vassal*	
—vasallaje	—vassalage	
vaticinar	(to) vaticinate (predict, prophesy)	
—vaticinio	—vaticination (prediction, prophecy)	
vatio, kilovatio	*watt, kilowatt*	

---

[106] Literally "wandering beyond or outside (the limits)".

—voltio	—*volt*	
—voltaje	—*voltage*	
vehículo	vehicle	(Lat. VEHERE, "carry")
—vector	—vector (carrier; math.)	(VECTUS p.p.)
—invectiva	—invective, diatribe	
vela (1)	*vigil,* candle	(Lat. VIGILIA)
—en vela	—awake, sleepless	
—velar (1)	—(to) keep *vigil* (watch), (to) hold a wake over	
—velada	—social evening, soiree	
—velatorio	—wake, *vigil* over the deceased	
—desvelar (1)	—(to) keep awake, (to) lose sleep	
—desvelo	—sleeplessness, watchfulness or care	
velo	*veil*	(Lat. VELUM)
—velo del paladar	—*velum* or soft *palate* (roof of mouth)	
—velar (2) (adj. & n.f.)	—velar, velar consonant (e.g., *k*)	
—velar (3)	—(to) *veil,* (to) fog or blur (photo)	
—vela (2)	—sail	(Lat. VELA)
—velero	—sailing ship, sailboat	
—veleta	—weathervane, weathercock (incl. "fickle person")	
—develar	—(to) un*veil,* (to) re*veal*	
—desvelar (2)	—(to) re*veal*	
velocidad	velocity, speed	
—veloz	—fast, swift	
vender	(to) sell, (to) *vend*	
—vendedor	—*vendor,* seller	
—venta	—sale, selling	
—en venta	—for sale	
—servicio posventa / post-	—after-sales service	
—revender	—(to) resell, (to) retail	
—revendedor	—retailer, reseller	
venganza	*vengeance,* re*venge*	
—vengar	—(to) avenge, (to) revenge	
—vengador (adj. & n.)	—avenging, avenger	
—vengativo	—vengeful, *vindictive*	
—vendetta	—vendetta	[< It.]
—revancha (< Fr.)	—*revenge*	
—devengar	—(to) earn (wages), (to) accrue (interest)	
verbo	verb	
—verbal	verbal	
—verborrea	—*verbal diarrhea* (extreme verbosity)	

—adverbio	—adverb
—proverbio	—proverb
verga	yard or spar (nautical), *verge* (rod, penis)
—envergadura	—wingspan, breadth, scope
vernáculo	vernacular
verosimilitud	verisimilitude (appearance of being true or real)
—verosímil	—verisimilar (appearing to be true or real) [*very similar*]
—inverosimilitud	—lack of verisimilitude (unlikelihood)
—inverosímil	—not verisimilar (unlikely, implausible)
versátil	*versatile* (incl. "variable, changeable")
—versatilidad	—*versatility* (incl. "changeability, inconstancy")
verso	verse
—versar (sobre)	—(to) be about, (to) deal with
—malversar	—(to) embezzle (public funds)
—malversación	—embezzlement, *malversation*
vertical (adj. & n.f.)	vertical
vértice	*vertex*
—verter	—(to) pour, (to) spill [di*vert*]
—vertiente (f.)	—slope (mountain, roof), side or aspect (of an issue)
—vertedero	—(garbage or rubbish) dump
vértigo	vertigo (dizziness)
—vertiginoso	—vertiginous
vestíbulo	vestibule, hall, lobby
vestir	(to) clothe, (to) dress [*vest*]
—vestido (p.p.)	—dress, clothes, clothing [*vested*]
—vestidura ∼ vestimenta	—clothing, *vesture*, *vestment* (gen. pl.)
—vestuario	—wardrobe, dressing room, locker room, *vestry*
—desvestir	—(to) undress, (to) *divest* (of clothes)
—revestir	—(to) cover or coat (e.g., wall) [*revet, revest*]
—revestimiento	—(protective or decorative) covering or coating [*revetment*]
—travesti, travestí (m./f.)	—*transvestite* (m./f.) [*travesty*]
veterinario (adj. & n.)	veterinary, veterinarian
—veterinaria (n.)	—veterinary medicine
vía (n.)	*way*,[107] road, track
—vías respiratorias	—respiratory tract
—vía(s) de comunicación	—means of communication
—vía (prep.)	—via
—vía satélite	—via satellite

---

[107] Germanic *way* and Latin VIA come from the same Indo-European root.

—viaducto	—viaduct	
—tranvía (m.)	—tramway, streetcar	(< Eng.)
—viaje	—*voyage,* journey, trip	
—viajero (adj. & n.)	—traveling, *voyager,* traveler, passenger	
—viajar	—(to) travel, (to) *voyage*	
—viajante	—traveling salesman (-woman)	
—*Muerte de un viajante*	—*Death of a Salesman* (by Arthur Miller)	
—trivio	—junction of three roads, *trivium*	
—trivial	—trivial	
—trivialidad	—triviality	
viable	viable	(< Lat. VITA, "life")
—viabilidad	—viability	
—inviable	—nonviable, inviable	
victoria	victory	
—victorioso	—victorious	
vigilancia	vigilance, sur*veillance*	
—vigilante (adj. & n.m./f.)	—vigilant, watchman, guard	[*vigilante*]
—vigilar	—(to) watch (over), (to) *surveil*	
—vigilia	—vigil (watch; eve of religious festival)	(doublet of *vela* [1])
vigor	vigor (incl. "legal effectiveness or validity")	
—entrar en vigor	—(to) go into effect	
—vigoroso	—vigorous, strong	
—vigorizar	—(to) invigorate, (to) strengthen	
—vigente	—in force or in effect (law, custom, etc.)	
—vigencia	—state of being in force (law, etc.), validity	
villa	*villa* (country house)	
—villano (adj. & n.)	—*villainous* (incl. archaic "boorish"), *villain* (incl. archaic " boor"), *villein*	
—villancico	—Christmas carol	
vindicar	(to) *avenge,* (to) *vindicate*	(doublet of *vengar*)
—reivindicar	—(to) assert or claim a right, (to) claim responsibility for	[rare *revendicate*]
—reivindicación	—claim, demand	
violación	violation, rape, desecration	
—violar	—(to) violate, (to) rape, (to) desecrate	
violento	violent	
—violencia	—violence	
violeta	violet (color—adj. & n.m.), violet (flower—f.)	
violín	violin	

—violinista	—violinist
—violón	—double bass
—violonchelo, -celo, chelo	—violoncello, cello
—viola	—viola
virar	(to) *veer*, (to) tone (photo—"*veer*" the colors)
—viraje	—turn (*veering*), toning (photo)
virgen (adj. & n.)	virgin
—virginal	—virginal
—virginidad	—virginity
viril	virile
—virilidad	—virility
virtual	virtual
—realidad virtual	—virtual reality
virus	virus
—virulento	—virulent
—virulencia	—virulence
visado, visa (Amer.)	*visa*
visión	vision
—visible	—visible
—visibilidad	—visibility
—invisible	—invisible
—invisibilidad	—invisibility
—visionario	—visionary
—vista	—sight (eyesight, *view*), *vista*
—punto de vista	—*point of view*, stand*point*
—vistazo	—glance, look
—vistoso	—eye-catching, colorful
—visera	—*visor*
—divisar[108]	—(to) make out (in the distance), (to) espy
—divisa	—foreign currency or exchange , emblem or motto
visita	visit
—visitar	—(to) visit
—visitante (adj. & n.m./f.)	—visiting, visitor
visual	visual, line of sight
—visualizar	—(to) visualize (form a mental image; make visible)

[108] *Divisar* and *divisa* are etymologically unrelated to *visión,* as they are instead cognates of *divide—division.* In the case of *divisar,* the notion was to "discern things in the distance", i.e., to *divide* them from the "rest", while a *divisa* (initially a medieval badge or emblem) was a *device* allowing one to *divide* the "home team" from the others.

—visualización	—visualization
vocabulario	vocabulary
—vocablo	—*vocable* (word as letters, w/out regard to meaning)
vocal (adj. & n.f.)	vocal, *vowel*
—vocal (m./f.)	—board or committee member (having a "*voice*")
—vocalista	—vocalist
—vocalizar	—(to) vocalize
volcán	volcano
—volcánico	—volcanic
voluntario (adj. & n.)	voluntary, volunteer
—involuntario	—involuntary
vómito	vomit
—vomitar	—(to) vomit
—vomitivo	—vomitive, emetic (vomit inducing)
—vomitorio	—*vomitory* (stadium passageway leading to seats)
voraz	*voracious* (also applied to destructive fires)
—voracidad	—voracity, voraciousness
—devorar	—(to) *devour*
—vorágine (f.)	—whirlpool, vortex
voz (f.)	*voice*
—altavoz	—loudspeaker
—portavoz	—spokesperson
vulnerable	vulnerable
—vulnerabilidad	—vulnerability
—invulnerable	—invulnerable
—vulnerar	—(to) infringe or violate (law), (to) damage or harm
whisky, whiskey, güisqui	whiskey
yate (< Eng.)	*yacht*
yodo / iodo	*iodine*
yoga (m.)	yoga
yugo	*yoke*
—yugular (adj. & n.f.)	—*jugular*
—sojuzgar	—(to) *subjugate*	(z from *juzgar*)
—subyugar	—(to) *subjugate*	("learned" form)
zafiro	*sapphire*
zodíaco, zodiaco	zodiac
zona	zone
—zona(s) verde(s)	—"green zone" (part of city reserved for parks & gardens)

Selected References

Spanish Dictionaries

Enciclopedia Universal Multimedia. 2006. Madrid: Micronet. Apart from the encyclopedia, there is a Spanish-Spanish dictionary with English correspondences for most words.

Moliner, María. 1998. *Diccionario de uso del español*. Madrid: Editorial Gredos. Also available on CD-ROM.

Ramondino, Salvatore, ed. 1996. *The New World Spanish/English English/Spanish Dictionary*. New York: Signet.

Real Academia Española. 2001. *Diccionario de la lengua española*. Madrid: Espasa Calpe. Also available at: www.rae.es

———. 2005. *Diccionario panhispánico de dudas*. Madrid: Santillana. Also available at: www.rae.es

VOX Diccionario avanzado: Lengua española. 1997. Barcelona: Bibliograf.

VOX Diccionario para la enseñanza de la lengua española: Español para extranjeros. 2000. Barcelona: Bibliograf.

VOX New College Spanish and English Dictionary. 1994. Lincolnwood: NTC Publishing Group.

English Dictionaries

The American Heritage College Dictionary. 2004. Boston: Houghton Mifflin.

The New Shorter Oxford English Dictionary. 1993. Oxford: Oxford University Press.

Oxford English Dictionary. 2002. CD-Rom version. Oxford: Oxford University Press.

Webster's Third New International Dictionary, Unabridged. 2002. CD-Rom version. Springfield, Mass.: Merriam-Webster.

Etymological Dictionaries

Barnhart, Robert K., ed. 1988. *Chambers Dictionary of Etymology*. Edinburgh: Chambers.

Bénaben, Michel. 2000. *Dictionnaire étymologique de l'espagnol*. Paris: Ellipses.

Buck, Carl Darling. 1988. *A Dictionary of Selected Synonyms in the Principal Indo-European Languages*. Chicago: University of Chicago Press.

Celdrán, Pancracio. 2003. *Diccionario de topónimos españoles y sus gentilicios*. Madrid: Espasa Calpe.

Corominas, Joan. 1973. *Breve diccionario etimológico de la lengua castellana*. Madrid: Editorial Gredos.

Corominas, Joan, and José A. Pascual. 1980–1991 (6 volumes). *Diccionario crítico etimológico castellano e hispánico*. Madrid: Editorial Gredos.

Cortelazzo, Manlio, and Paolo Zolli. 1999. *Il nuovo etimologico: DELI—Dizionario Etimologico della Lingua Italiana*. Bologna: Zanichelli.

Ernout, Alfred, and Alfred Meillet. 2001. *Dictionnaire étymologique de la langue latine*. Paris: Klincksieck.

Faure Sabater, Roberto. 2004. *Diccionario de nombres geográficos y étnicos del mundo*. Madrid: Espasa Calpe.

———. 2002. *Diccionario de nombres propios*. Madrid: Espasa Calpe.

Hoad, T. F. 1996. *The Concise Oxford Dictionary of English Etymology*. Oxford: Oxford University Press.

Martin, F. 1976. *Les mots latins, groupés par familles étymologiques*. Paris: Hachette.

Partridge, Eric. 1983. *Origins: A Short Etymological Dictionary of Modern English*. New York: Greenwich House.

Pfeifer, Wolfgang (under the direction of). 1993. *Etymologisches Wörterbuch des Deutschen*. Munich: Deutscher Taschenbuch Verlag.

Rey, Alain (under the direction of). 1998. *Dictionnaire historique de la langue française*. Paris: Dictionnaires Le Robert.

Roberts, Edward A., and Bárbara Pastor. 2001. *Diccionario etimológico indoeuropeo de la lengua española*. Madrid: Alianza Editorial.

Watkins, Calvert, ed. 2000. *The American Heritage Dictionary of Indo-European Roots*. Boston: Houghton Mifflin.

Other References

Bonnassie, Pierre, Pierre Guichard, and Marie-Claude Gerbet. 2001. *Las Españas medievales*. Barcelona: Editorial Crítica. Translated from original French.

Boyd-Bowman, Peter. 1980. *From Latin to Romance in Sound Charts*. Washington: Georgetown University Press.

Brodsky, David. 2005. *Spanish Verbs Made Simple(r)*. Austin: University of Texas Press.

Cano Aguilar, Rafael. 1999. *El español a través de los tiempos*. Madrid: Arco/Libros.

Encyclopaedia Britannica 2006. Ultimate Reference Suite DVD.

Entwistle, William J. 1962. *The Spanish Language, Together with Portuguese, Catalan and Basque*. London: Faber & Faber. Also available in Spanish translation.

Fradejas Rueda, José Manuel. 2000. *Fonología histórica del español*. Madrid: Visor Libros.

Lapesa, Rafael. 1997. *Historia de la lengua española*. Madrid: Editorial Gredos.

Lathrop, Thomas A. 2003. *The Evolution of Spanish*. University of Delaware: Juan de la Cuesta. Also available in Spanish translation.

Menéndez Pidal, Ramón. 1940. *Manual de gramática histórica española*. Madrid: Espasa Calpe.

———. 1956. *Orígenes del español: Estado lingüístico de la península ibérica hasta el siglo XI.* Madrid: Espasa Calpe.

Penny, Ralph. 2002. *A History of the Spanish Language.* Cambridge: Cambridge University Press. Also available in Spanish translation.

Rohlfs, Gerhard. 1979. *Estudios sobre el léxico románico.* Madrid: Editorial Gredos.

Turner, Howard R. 1995. *Science in Medieval Islam.* Austin: University of Texas Press.

Williams, Mark. 2000. *The Story of Spain.* Málaga, Spain: Santana Books.

Lightning Source UK Ltd.
Milton Keynes UK
UKOW03f0955090114

224257UK00001B/6/P